PRAISE FOR
RICHARD WHITTLE AND *THE DREAM MACHINE*

"[A] book that takes off like a novel and flies like a well-sourced histori-cal investigation."

—Gretel C. Kovach, *The San Diego Union-Tribune*

"Whittle skillfully depicts the evolution of the aircraft from drawing board to reality. A military version of Tracy Kidder's *The Soul of a New Machine*."

—*Kirkus Reviews*

"It's a great yarn for those in love with military gee-whiz technology and aviation."

—Mark Thompson, *Washington Monthly*

"By recounting the story of the Marine Corps'... devotion to the Osprey through years of catastrophic mishaps, budgetary obstacles, and political hoops—not to mention lost lives—Whittle has told the most instructive tale of the way things are done in Washington in some time. Anybody interested in modern government, modern politics, and modern mili-tary policy—and would like to find the three in one fascinating pack-age—will read *The Dream Machine* with pleasure and profit."

—Philip Terzian, *The Weekly Standard*

"What makes *The Dream Machine* interesting is the light it sheds on Washington's 'permanent government,' the lobbyists and consultants and bureaucrats and contractors... One of the lessons of Whittle's book is that no one misses a chance to swim in the giant pool of money and power that is the nation's capital, where the defense industry is the big-gest fish of all."

—Matthew Continetti, *The Washington Post Book World*

"Tom Wolfe would probably have forgiven... Whittle if he had called this aviation history *The Rotor Stuff*, since its narrative style is as read-able as Wolfe's chronicle of the jet pilots who crossed the frontiers of 'mach shock' to enter the vacuum of space. Read this book. It is more than a valuable aviation history; it is a reminder of the human toll the technological revolution exacts while simultaneously promising future compensation in the very same currency."

—Col. David H. Gurney, USMC (Ret.), *Proceedings*

"Richard Whittle's chronicle of the development and acquisition of this storied aircraft is destined to become a classic . . . It may be almost impossible to find a finer work."

—Col. Will Holahan, USMCR (Ret.), *The Officer*

"Whittle says his goal in writing about the Osprey was 'simply to tell its story, good and bad, and let the facts speak for themselves.' He has succeeded."

—Steve Weinberg, *Dallas Morning News*

"Drawing on more than 200 interviews, Whittle reconstructs the Pentagon strategy sessions and covert Capitol Hill meetings that kept the Osprey going despite crashes, production delays, and billion-dollar cost overruns. . . . a fine book."

—Dale Eisman, *The Virginian-Pilot*

"Whittle takes the reader behind the closed doors of the military-industrial complex and into the cockpits of the Ospreys that went down, telling a story as gripping as it is important."

—*Aviation Maintenance*

Whittle "pulls no punches, but takes no cheap shots either. The result is a truly readable book that spins a fascinating yarn of science, politics, and intrigue."

—Military.com's "Line of Departure"

"Meticulously researched . . . an inside look at the mind-bogglingly complex Pentagon procurement system."

—Nathan Hodge, *Wired*'s "Danger Room"

"An engineering saga and a guide to the technical intricacies of Pentagon politics."

—Ben Steelman, *Star-News* (Wilmington, NC)

"That the Osprey was able to survive as a program is one of those true stories that one simply could not make up . . . Whittle brings us to the back rooms and briefing spaces where the debate and infighting actually took place. He sheds light on the myriad little known facts that constitute the Osprey's story and does not shy away from the controversies."

—Col. Bill Powers, USMC (Ret.), *Marine Corps Gazette*

"*The Dream Machine* is a wonderful combination of personal drama, technological detective story, military history, and vivid explanation of major issues affecting America's military and economic future. This is a valuable and engrossing book that will be read for many years to come."

—James Fallows, *Atlantic Monthly*, and author of *National Defense*

"A fascinating, inside history of the most controversial airplane in the past quarter century. Whittle presents an even-handed description of the promise and dangers in the new, new military flying machine that may shape the future of commercial aviation."

—Bing West, *New York Times* bestselling author of
The Village and *The Strongest Tribe*

"In this compelling and important book a real reporter's reporter asks all the hard questions and refuses to settle for any of the easy answers. Whittle has solved the real-life mystery of the raging, twenty-five year battle the Marines waged to get the V-22 Osprey. You owe it to yourself as a reader and as a citizen to read *The Dream Machine*."

—Mark Shields, syndicated columnist and PBS *Newshour* political analyst

"*The Dream Machine* is the gripping story of the quest for the Osprey, an ideal flying machine that transfixed the aviation world and eventually cost billions of dollars and dozens of lives. Like the helicopter-airplane that tantalized generals, engineers, and pilots for decades, *The Dream Machine* is also an irresistible hybrid—a cross between *The Soul of a New Machine* and *Black Hawk Down*."

—Brad Matsen, former aviator and *New York Times* bestselling author of
Titanic's Last Secrets and *Jacques Cousteau: The Sea King*

"Meticulously researched and tautly written, Richard Whittle's *The Dream Machine* expertly weaves telling technical details with heart-stopping human drama into a riveting, fast-paced history of one of the military's most controversial war machines, the V-22 Osprey."

—Eric Schmitt, terrorism correspondent, *The New York Times*

THE DREAM MACHINE

The Untold History of the Notorious V-22 Osprey

RICHARD WHITTLE

Simon & Schuster Paperbacks

NEW YORK LONDON TORONTO SYDNEY

Simon & Schuster Paperbacks
A Division of Simon & Schuster, Inc.
1230 Avenue of the Americas
New York, NY 10020

First Simon & Schuster trade paperback edition May 2011

SIMON & SCHUSTER PAPERBACKS and colophon are
registered trademarks of Simon & Schuster, Inc.

For information about special discounts for bulk purchases,
please contact Simon & Schuster Special Sales at
1-866-506-1949 or business@simonandschuster.com.

The Simon & Schuster Speakers Bureau can bring authors
to your live event. For more information or to book an event,
contact the Simon & Schuster Speakers Bureau at
1-866-248-3049 or visit our website at www.simonspeakers.com.

Text designed by Paul Dippolito

Manufactured in the United States of America

1   3   5   7   9   10   8   6   4   2

The Library of Congress has cataloged the hardcover edition as follows:
Whittle, Rick.
The dream machine : the untold history of the notorious V-22 Osprey /
Rick Whittle.
p. cm.
Includes bibliographical references.
1. V-22 Osprey (Transport plane)—Design and construction—History.
2. V-22 Osprey (Transport plane)—Testing—History. 3. Convertiplanes—United
States—History. 4. United States. Marine Corps—Procurement. I. Title.
TL685.W46 2010
623.74'65—dc22   2009026071
ISBN 978-1-4165-6295-5
ISBN 978-1-4165-6296-2 (pbk)
ISBN 978-1-4165-6319-8 (ebook)

This book is dedicated to the civilians and Marines
who lost their lives developing the V-22 Osprey,
and to their loved ones and friends.

JULY 20, 1992, QUANTICO, VIRGINIA

Gerald W. Mayan
Robert L. Rayburn
Anthony J. Stecyk, Jr.
Patrick J. Sullivan
Major Brian J. James
Master Gunnery Sergeant Gary Leader
Gunnery Sergeant Sean P. Joyce

APRIL 8, 2000, MARANA, ARIZONA

Aircrew
Lieutenant Colonel John A. Brow
(posthumously promoted)
Major Brooks S. Gruber
Staff Sergeant William B. Nelson
Corporal Kelly S. Keith

Infantry
3rd Battalion/5th Marines:
Second Lieutenant Clayton J. Kennedy
Sergeant Jose Alvarez, Jr.
Corporal Adam C. Neely

Corporal Can Soler
Lance Corporal Jason T. Duke
Lance Corporal Jesus Gonzales-Sanchez
Lance Corporal Seth G. Jones
Lance Corporal Jorge A. Morin
Lance Corporal Kenneth O. Paddio
Private First Class Gabriel C. Clevenger
Private First Class Alfred Corona
Private First Class George P. Santos
Private First Class Keoki P. Santos
Private Adam L. Tatro

Marine Wing Communication
Squadron 38
Corporal Eric J. Martinez

DECEMBER 11, 2000, NEW RIVER,
NORTH CAROLINA

Lieutenant Colonel Keith M. Sweaney
Lieutenant Colonel Michael L. Murphy
(posthumously promoted)
Staff Sergeant Avely W. Runnels
Sergeant Jason A. Buyck

CONTENTS

CONTENTS

PROLOGUE

"A salesman is got to dream, boy. It comes with the territory."
—*DEATH OF A SALESMAN,* BY ARTHUR MILLER, 1949

Where he was and what he was doing when he first heard the news is seared into Dick Spivey's memory. The disaster took place in the desert near Marana, Arizona, at two minutes before eight o'clock in the evening, local time, on April 8, 2000. Spivey's brain stores that data alongside November 22, 1963, and September 11, 2001, in the lobe reserved for devastating events. "For me, that's the same kind of thing," Spivey explains in a native Georgia drawl seasoned with an acquired Texas twang.

When it happened, Spivey was 5,300 miles and seven time zones away from Marana, lying in bed in his room at the Thistle Hotel Victoria in central London as the sun rose. Barely awake, he was listening to, but not watching, a morning television news broadcast. The Thistle Victoria, a somewhat timeworn but convenient pile of stone and faux marble attached to the city's throbbing Victoria Station rail terminal, is mostly an affordable place to flop for tourists. Spivey, a fifty-nine-year-old aeronautical engineer-turned-marketer for Bell Helicopter of Fort Worth, Texas, was there because the hotel was the site of an aviation conference that Monday. He and a U.S. Marine Corps general were to speak there about a peculiar aircraft Spivey had helped sell the Marines on two decades earlier. It had been the service's top priority ever since.

The aircraft was the V-22 Osprey "tiltrotor," called that because it tilts two giant rotors on its wingtips upward to take off and land and swivels them forward to fly fast. The tiltrotor was Bell's solution to an engineering challenge that had tantalized inventors and engineers and industrialists and the military since the 1920s: how to build a vehicle able to take off, land, and hover with the agility of a helicopter yet fly as fast and far as an airplane. Spivey had had a hand in designing the tiltrotor in his engineering days. Since becoming a marketer in the 1970s, he had promoted it to anyone who would listen. But Dick Spivey was not just a salesman with a product, he was a salesman with a dream. Spivey expected the tiltrotor to change the way people fly as much as the jet engine had—and the jet engine had *changed the world*. That's what Dick Spivey told people all the time, and that was what Dick Spivey believed.

By the spring of 2000, the Osprey was nine years behind schedule and billions of dollars over budget. Its developers had been whipsawed between technological hurdles and political interference. They had struggled with manufacturing problems. They had been undermined by business rivalries and their own overly ambitious promises. They had been emotionally scarred and financially stung by an epic political battle in Washington over whether to build the Osprey at all. After they had won that fight, the Marine Corps had pressed relentlessly to get the Osprey into service. Now, at last, everything seemed to be on track. The Marines were practicing mock missions with the Osprey as a prelude to fielding it as a troop transport in 2001. The general with Spivey would tell the conference about that. Spivey planned to talk about an even more audacious tiltrotor he and others at Bell had been working on—a tiltrotor bigger than the military's bulky C-130 Hercules cargo plane. The designers were calling it the Quad TiltRotor because instead of the Osprey's two rotors it would have four, mounted on two wings instead of one. The theoretical behemoth would dwarf the V-22, carrying four times the troops and cargo that could fit in an Osprey. Spivey was going to tell the conference all the great things a bird like that could do for the military. If anybody asked, he would also gladly explain how the tiltrotor was not just going to change but *revolutionize* civilian air travel, too, solving the airport congestion problem by making it possible to fly without runways. In the future, he had no doubt, tiltrotors would carry civilian passengers from, say, the heart of London to the heart of Paris in less time than it took to get from Victoria Station to London Heathrow Airport by train or taxi. Spivey sometimes got so worked up at the prospects he found it hard to sleep at night.

That morning in London, though, as he lay there drowsily listening to the TV in his hotel room, Spivey heard a news item that jolted him awake. "They were talking about this jet that had crashed in the U.S. and killed nineteen people—a Marine Corps jet," Spivey recalled.

"I had this rush throughout my body thing, but then they called it a jet. I thought, 'What Marine Corps jet do they have that will carry nineteen people?' That made me feel better for a few minutes. But then this chill ran through me and I called the general."

The general called headquarters in Washington, then rang Spivey back with awful news. The plane that had gone down near Marana a few hours earlier, killing its crew of four and fifteen Marine infantry riding in back, hadn't been a jet. It had been an Osprey.

★ ★ ★

Paul J. Rock Jr., a square-jawed, red-haired, tightly wound Marine Corps pilot—radio call sign "Rocket"—was another who would never forget Marana. The "mishap aircraft," in the dry terminology of military accident investigation reports, was one of four Ospreys taking part in a mock embassy evacuation—the very mission for which Spivey and other believers had long touted the tiltrotor as ideal. Rock, a young major at the time, was copiloting one of two Ospreys trailing two others as they flew to a tiny airfield near Marana, a desert town about twenty-five miles northwest of Tucson. A group of role players were waiting there to be "rescued."

After the first two aircraft approached the airfield and tilted their rotors upward to land, a nightmare began. Without warning, the second Osprey snapped into a right roll and plowed into the ground with its belly up. It exploded in a fireball that lit the evening sky for miles. Rock saw the orange flames in his rearview mirror as his Osprey circled five miles away. Four of Rock's squadron mates and fifteen other Marines riding in the back of the Osprey that went down were killed instantly.

Investigators attributed the crash to "human factors" and the Marines went ahead with their plans for the Osprey. Eight months later, though, Rock lost another four squadron mates when yet another Osprey went down in a boggy forest near their coastal North Carolina home base, New River Marine Corps Air Station. Pentagon officials, who had been expected to approve plans to build 360 Ospreys in all for the Marines, grounded the few already built.

Four days after the New River crash, Secretary of Defense William Cohen formed a commission to examine whether the tiltrotor—despite decades and billions spent developing it—might in fact be fatally flawed.

The panel had barely started its work when a national scandal over the Osprey erupted. The commander of the Osprey training squadron at New River was accused of telling his mechanics to lie about how frequently the aircraft couldn't fly because of mechanical problems. The Defense Department opened a criminal investigation.

The crashes, the grounding, and the maintenance scandal disheartened the Osprey pilots at New River. All pilots love to fly. Most pilots *live* to fly. For the next two years, though, Marine pilots were forbidden to take an Osprey off the ground—or even sit in one and crank the engines. Headquarters Marine Corps was afraid something new might go wrong.

Reduced to reviewing and revising maintenance manuals, Rock and other Osprey pilots began to fear they might never fly the tiltrotor again—might even be tainted by having flown it at all. Critics were calling the Osprey a boondoggle and a death trap, a "widow-maker." They said the Marines were foolhardy at best and delusional at worst for wasting so many taxpayer dollars and so many promising lives on such a Rube Goldberg contraption. The Osprey's foes urged the Pentagon and Congress to destroy the beast before it killed again.

Rock was a U.S. Naval Academy graduate who planned to make the military his life's work. He had joined the Osprey program in 1997 full of zest, certain he was at the cutting edge of Marine Corps aviation. He had been proud to fly the most prized aircraft in the Marine Corps stable, an innovative piece of technology expected to revolutionize the way his service fought wars. Yet, after the crashes and the grounding, after attending the funerals of friends and being interrogated about the maintenance scandal by Defense Department investigators, after watching nearly every other pilot in the Osprey squadron transfer out, Rock was demoralized. He thought of asking for a transfer, maybe even resigning his commission.

In 2001, like the Ospreys in the Arizona desert and the North Carolina woods, Paul Rock's career and Dick Spivey's dreams lay in ashes.

★ ★ ★

In October 2007, Lieutenant Colonel Paul Rock led the first squadron of V-22 Ospreys ever to fly actual military operations into Iraq, where a U.S.-led invasion four years earlier had ignited ethnic and religious blood feuds and an insurgency that had taken thousands of lives. By then, the bitter debate over how the war had begun was largely over. It was hard to remember why the war's sponsors had thought it would be so easy, and so cheap in dollars and lives, to change the world.

The war in Iraq was a fitting stage for the Osprey's combat debut—a project sold for a mission once deemed existential, a venture begun under the influence of a dream that soon became a nightmare. The Osprey and its first war had much in common.

CHAPTER ONE

THE DREAM

The contract bid consisted of thousands of pages of text and graphs and charts, along with engineering drawings, illustrations, and mathematical equations bristling with Greek letters. These were the days before you could put such a thing on computer disks, and it was printed on about a thousand pounds of paper, organized in dozens of beautiful, shiny white binders. The shiny white binders filled about thirty cardboard boxes. Not too bulky for a plan to create an aeronautical dream machine, perhaps, but a heck of a load for one man. Even so, Dick Spivey decided to deliver it to Washington, D.C., himself.

Delivering contract bids wasn't Spivey's job at Bell Helicopter, where he had worked since his freshman year in college, in 1959. Skinny but athletic back then, in this winter of 1983 Spivey was bald and a touch overweight. He had turned forty-two the previous December 6, just two weeks after getting remarried. Only a few years earlier, to the great relief of friends and co-workers, he'd finally given up the shaggy red wigs, gold chains, and pastel leisure suits he'd worn during his disco days. Spivey's appearance and dress now were more in keeping, some felt, with what he was: an accomplished aeronautical engineer, owner of a patent on a special type of helicopter rotor blade he'd designed during his first twenty-four years with Bell. These days, however, Spivey was primarily a marketer and salesman, and he had been marketing and selling this proposal for years now. If Bell and its partner on the project won the contract, it had the potential to gain them a whole new market beyond helicopters—a market potentially worth billions of dollars. That could secure Bell's future for decades. Spivey, though, wanted to take the proposal to Washington himself because this project promised to make a dream that had become his obsession a reality. Those binders held a plan to build the U.S. military an aircraft like no other, a machine whose ability to swivel two wingtip rotors upward or forward gave it an astounding characteristic. Spivey often described it in sales pitches by holding his arms at his sides and pointing his index fingers skyward while explaining that this tiltrotor, as the aircraft was called, "takes off like a helicopter." Then he would rotate his arms and fingers forward and add: "Flies like an airplane." The tiltrotor was a hybrid, designed to combine the vertical agility of a helicopter with the speed of an airplane. Unlike helicopters, whose top speed—and thus range—is severely limited by the aerodynamics of their fixed rotors, the tiltrotor would transform itself in flight, using its rotors as propellers to fly nearly as fast and far as a conventional turboprop airplane. Unlike airplanes, however, the tiltrotor would need no runways or big-deck aircraft carriers to take off and land.

Under government contracts, Bell had built and experimented with two small tiltrotors for three decades, working out most of the basic engineering problems. Spivey had chipped in on the design of the second one. The tiltrotor Bell and the Boeing Vertol Company were proposing to the military in those shiny white binders, however, would be far larger than those experimental models, which had carried only a pilot and copilot. This tiltrotor was going to be big enough to carry two dozen troops four times as far at twice the speed and twice the altitude of a standard troop transport helicopter. With no troops or cargo to carry, it was going to be able to fly more than two thousand miles on a tank of gas or nearly unlimited distances with aerial refueling. Building it would be one of the most daunting engineering challenges Bell had ever faced. Even Boeing Vertol, a division of the aerospace giant Boeing Company, would find its part of the project demanding. If the military proved the technology valid on such a scale, though, Spivey had no doubt that a new age in aviation would dawn, one in which civilians would demand to fly in such dream machines, too. The vexing problem of airport congestion would be history. Travelers would flit from city to city without wasting the time and enduring the annoyance of slogging their way to and from and through airports, except to make long-distance trips by jet. Small towns in remote areas would enjoy regular air service without building runways. Tiltrotors would pick up passengers from heliports, riverside piers, maybe even shopping center parking lots and comfortably whisk them most any place they needed to go. And Dick Spivey would have helped make that dream a reality.

Spivey was far from the first to be seized with such visions. An aircraft

with the tiltrotor's advertised abilities had been one of the great technological dreams of aviation since the earliest days of powered flight. The
dream was potent. It had inspired individuals and energized institutions
for decades. A long line of inventors, engineers, entrepreneurs, industrialists, and military strategists had theorized, discussed, designed, and
tried to build similar aircraft for generations without ever quite pulling
it off. Some had run through their personal fortunes pursuing the idea.
Scores of designs had been floated; dozens had been built, then abandoned for one reason or the other. The quest had been aviation's equivalent of the search for the Northwest Passage.

It began as a search for perfection. After the Wright brothers inaugurated the era of powered flight at Kitty Hawk, North Carolina, in December 1903, aviation became the new frontier. The sky was enticing virgin
territory for men and women infected with a passion for discovery but
born too late to help fulfill the nation's Manifest Destiny. These aviation pioneers were out to do more than just fly; they intended to conquer the air every bit as much as their pioneer forebears had conquered
the West. For the most idealistic, that meant fixed-wing airplanes were
just a start. Dr. Alexander Klemin, the highly respected chairman of
the Daniel Guggenheim School of Aeronautics at New York University,
described the challenge in testimony to the U.S. House Committee on
Military Affairs in April 1938: "The conquest of the air in its broadest
sense will only come when we can do in the air substantially everything
that a bird can do in the air. The airplane with all its marvelous achievements cannot possibly give us such complete mastery of the air."

Doing "substantially everything a bird can do" meant being able
to take off and land just about anywhere, plus—ideally—being able
to hover. While the airplane had become commonplace by the time
Klemin gave that testimony in 1938, no one in the United States had
yet managed to build a useful helicopter, meaning one that could rise
more than a few feet off the ground, hover stably, and fly under control.
Indeed, many in aviation viewed the various inventors working on helicopters as hopeless romantics. Only two years earlier, no less an authority than Orville Wright had dismissed such efforts as futile, judging that
"the helicopter type of aeroplane offers several seemingly insurmountable difficulties." Yet the most ambitious dreamers were already trying to
design aircraft that would fly like an airplane *and* a helicopter *combined*.
Such a machine would rise vertically, convert in midair to horizontal

flight, then convert back to land, so in time, they came to call these dream machines "convertiplanes."

Convertiplanes would do away with the airplane's need for long runways or aircraft carriers with catapults and arresting gear, the dreamers promised, because they would fly instead from downtown rooftops, the decks of small ships, maybe even a good-sized backyard. The most utopian enthusiasts envisioned a convertiplane in every garage. They urged convertiplane designers to add "road-ability" to their concepts. "A vehicle that can take you from your home to your office, to your country club, to your bank or to your friend's house, by air or by road, whichever is most convenient, will have a vast usefulness," test pilot James G. Ray told a Philadelphia aviation conference in October 1938. "It will become a competitor of the automobile. Such a machine can and will be built."

One dreamer who shared that vision was Gerardus Post Herrick, known as Gerard, whose obituary in the September 10, 1955, *New York Times* noted that he was the "generally acknowledged father of convertiplanes." In a 1943 article for the magazine *Mechanix Illustrated*, Herrick shared his notion of how convertiplanes were about to change the world: "Little Jimmie Jr. looks up from his 1950 Model tricycle toward a tiny speck just above the horizon. He watches intently as it streaks nearer at more than 6 miles a minute, then he calls, 'Hey, Dad! Better get the lawn mower out of the way—Ma's coming in for a landing!' "

A bald, bespectacled, bow-tie-wearing lawyer and engineer who had graduated from Princeton University in 1895 at age twenty-two and New York Law School two years later, Herrick was bitten by the aviation bug not long after the Wright brothers flew. While serving as a captain in the Army Air Service during World War I, his interest "crystallized into a desire to see if I could not use my own special training and experiences and resources to assist in perfecting flight," he later recalled. After studying the matter to see where "improvement was most needed," Herrick decided to concentrate on safety. He reasoned that "for a large proportion of the public to take up flying they would have eventually to be convinced of its safety and reliability." His first thought was to try designing a helicopter, but then he concluded he could get "perhaps 90 percent" of the still-theoretical helicopter's safety and convenience by simply adding a rotor to a fixed-wing airplane.

Airplane wings and rotor blades are both airfoils—material forms with a curved top and a relatively flat bottom that create lift or thrust when air flows over them. A conventional airplane's wings generate lift as the craft's propellers or, since the 1940s, jet engines pull or push the wings forward into the air. To keep its wings lifting, though, an airplane has to maintain a minimum speed in flight; otherwise it can stall or spin out of control. Here rotors offer an advantage: their blades travel in a circle, creating thrust, and therefore lift, whether the rotor is moving forward or not. Thus the helicopter's ability to hover. A rotor has its limitations, too, of course. A rotor that descends fast enough to start ingesting its own turbulent downwash can stop producing enough thrust to provide lift. A rotor, however, also can generate lift even if no engine is powering it, if it keeps turning and descends with sufficient speed. The force of the air flowing up through the rotor will cause the blades to turn and create lift on their own.

Spanish engineer and inventor Juan de la Cierva was one of the first to decide that adding a rotor to an ordinary airplane could make it safer, a goal he set for himself in 1919 after a trimotor plane he had designed stalled and crashed. Four years later, Cierva flew and patented his "Autogiro." The machine had a small fixed wing under the fuselage, or in some later models no fixed wing at all, and a propeller on its nose for forward thrust. What made it an Autogiro was an unpowered, freewheeling rotor over the pilot's head to provide most or all of the lift. This "rotating wing," as rotors are often called, worked like the sail of a windmill, turning as it was hit by the relative wind created when the aircraft moved forward. (*Relative wind* is an aeronautics term for the air that flows over an airfoil or aircraft in motion.) Its rotating wing's lift allowed Cierva's Autogiro to take off within 200 to 300 feet, depending on the actual wind, and to land in a space the size of a tennis court. In theory, that made the Autogiro far safer than the airplane. Even if the engine failed, relative wind and inertia would keep the rotor whirling, providing enough lift to feather the Autogiro to earth, much as a spinning maple seed falls. This method of landing is called autorotation.

The Autogiro's rotating wing, though, also added greatly to the aircraft's drag, or wind resistance, making it far slower than an airplane and causing it to burn more fuel. Nor was it able to hover, since its rotor was unpowered. American convertiplane inventor Gerard Herrick's initial idea, which he once said came to him before he was familiar with Cierva's Autogiro, was that a powered rotor would lift his machine into the air like a helicopter. Then a special mechanism would stop the rotating wing in mid-flight, converting the rotor into a fixed wing and the aircraft into a biplane. To land or to fly at speeds so slow as to nearly hover, the pilot would release the rotor so it could spin again. After studying the matter in depth in the 1920s, however, Herrick concluded that building a plane that could take off and land like a helicopter required too much "radical development." He decided instead to focus on devising a hybrid craft with an unpowered rotor that either could be locked in place or released to spin freely in the wind. Herrick saw this as the way to combine the airplane's speed with the Autogiro's slow landing ability. This "convertible" would take off and fly like a biplane but release its rotating wing in midair to fly slowly or land. The inventor initially called his design the "Vertaplane," or sometimes "Vertoplane." It quickly became his dream machine, a project that absorbed his energies and finances until his death thirty years later.

Herrick worked on his concept for a year with help from Alexander Klemin and others at the Guggenheim School of Aeronautics, then in 1930 formed the Vertoplane Development Corporation of New York. With his own money, he had a Chicago company build him a full-sized monoplane with a 24-foot, mast-mounted wooden rotor on top. On November 6, 1931, he and pilot Merrill Lambert took the new HV-1 Vertaplane to a field near Nile, Michigan, about twenty-five miles east of Lake Michigan, to test it.

With the upper wing locked in the biplane position, Lambert taxied a bit just to make sure the rudder pedals worked, then took off and flew at low level for three or four minutes to check the other controls. He landed, then took off again, and flew another fifteen minutes at a few hundred feet. So far, so good: he could control the plane, it was stable, and he could maneuver it well. He and Herrick agreed to continue. Using a special starter, Lambert set the rotary wing spinning and taxied down the field about 300 feet, resisting the plane's urge to take off. Then he let it hop into the air a few times, just ten to thirty feet, but cut the engine and let the Vertaplane feather down in a short, steep landing. It worked just fine. Lambert took off and flew down the field one more time at about ten feet to make sure he had enough control with the rotor spinning. He did. Next he tested the upper wing release mechanism in a few taxi runs to make sure the rotor would start turning when the wind hit it. It did. Now Herrick and Lambert decided to see if the Vertaplane would live up to its name.

With the upper wing locked in biplane position, Lambert took off and climbed to 4,000 feet. He wanted enough altitude to bail out if something went wrong. It did. When he released the rotor, it turned a few times, then teetered violently, clipping the propeller in front and the tail fin in back. The Vertaplane went out of control. As it plunged toward the ground, Lambert managed to scramble out, but his parachute didn't open. Merrill Lambert became the first man to die trying to make a convertiplane work.

With the tunnel vision that so often accompanies obsession, Herrick treated Lambert's death not as a tragedy casting a shadow over his quest but as an inconvenience in figuring out how his invention had malfunctioned. "Unfortunately the pilot's parachute failed to open, although he succeeded in getting clear of the ship, and our analysis of the cause of the accident had to be made solely upon the basis of an examination of the plane," Herrick wrote in 1933 to the National Advisory Committee for Aeronautics. "This was rendered comparatively easy, because of the fact that the machine was practically intact," he reassured the panel. A year earlier, only two months after the crash and no doubt shaken by what Lambert's death might do to his invention's image, Herrick had been downright duplicitous about what happened that day at Nile. In an article for *Aviation Engineering* magazine describing the flights and the crash, Herrick noted that the final flight was at 4,000 feet so that if "something should go wrong, the pilot could take to his parachute." Herrick omitted any mention, however, of what happened when Lambert did, leaving the reader to assume the pilot had bailed out safely.

The National Advisory Committee for Aeronautics, or NACA, created in 1915, was the forerunner of the National Aeronautics and Space Administration, NASA. Herrick was asking the agency to let him use a full-size wind tunnel—one able to hold an entire aircraft—to test a new Vertaplane he had built since Lambert's demise. He explained in his application that "I have expended between forty and fifty thousand dollars and between five and six years on this work and find myself obliged to at least slow down if not temporarily stop the work, due to the fact that I have no more available present resources, partly due to the present financial situation, for going ahead without some outside assistance."

The "present financial situation" was the Great Depression, which was holding back other aviation dreamers as well, and leading many to seek government contracts, often without success.

★ ★ ★

When Dick Spivey flew to Washington in 1983 to deliver the Bell-Boeing tiltrotor proposal to the Naval Air Systems Command, he was treading what by then was a well-worn path. Since World War II, the military's special needs, massive budgets, and lack of a profit motive have made it a driving force behind new technology—especially in aviation. "You can't make a business case to develop a risky plane from scratch just for the commercial world," Spivey once explained to me. "It takes a long time to develop an airplane, and in the commercial world, you don't get any money until you sell the first airplane. In the military, you get progress payments. They create the leading-edge technologies because it's too risky for commercial ventures. The military has been a source of what we call 'patient capital.' They were willing to put money into a program in order to advance technology that might be an advantage on the battlefield."

Since World War II, the military's "patient capital" has led to innumerable, often stunning advances in technology. It also spawned and sustains what President Dwight D. Eisenhower called the "military-industrial complex." Eisenhower was referring to the web of political and personal relationships between industry representatives and military officials that germinates when they do business or collaborate on projects. As institutions, defense companies and the government are often at odds over the costs and capabilities of weapons and other equipment; there is plenty of friction in the relationship. On a personal level, though, friendships and alliances spring up between individuals on either side of the divide, whether as a work by-product or by calculated cultivation. In the end, those who work for the contractors and those who manage their programs for the military share a compelling interest in making the project succeed. That tie can blur the line between the best interests of a company and the best interests of "The Customer," as defense contractors call the government. Sometimes it can blur the line between the best interests of industry and the nation. Eisenhower, who as a five-star general had led the Allies in defeating Nazi Germany, warned of this larger danger in a farewell address as he left the White House in 1961. "We must guard against the acquisition of unwarranted influence, whether sought or unsought, by the military-industrial complex," Eisenhower declared. He also noted that the "conjunction of an immense military establishment and a large arms industry is new in the American experience."

During the Great Depression, the U.S. military wasn't immense and the aircraft industry was tiny. Both would grow rapidly with the approach of World War II, but for most of the decade preceding that conflict, America's armed forces numbered around 250,000 active-duty personnel, compared to roughly 1.4 million today, and the entire military budget was under $1 billion—less than one five-hundredth of its size in recent years, without adjusting for inflation. The Pentagon didn't exist and there was no unified Department of Defense. The Army was overseen by the War Department, the Navy and the Marine Corps by the separate Navy Department. Many aircraft companies whose names are now famous—Boeing, Douglas, Lockheed, McDonnell, Northrop, Grumman—already were in business or getting started, but commercial aircraft accounted for most of their work in the 1930s.

Even so, from its earliest days the U.S. aircraft industry relied on military contracts. The first recorded sale of an airplane for profit in the United States came when Orville and Wilbur Wright were paid $25,000 to provide the Army Signal Corps one airplane and pilot training in 1908. (This first military aircraft crashed, less than a month after the Army bought it, because of a defective propeller, severely injuring Orville and killing a young lieutenant he had been training to fly.) Until the late 1930s, however, the Army and Navy were conservative in their airplane purchases and shied away from most experimental aircraft. The military didn't make progress payments of the sort Dick Spivey would one day cite as key to developing leading-edge technologies. The armed services paid for airplanes when delivered and didn't reimburse companies for development costs. Moreover, observed Donald M. Pattillo in his detailed history, *Pushing the Envelope: The American Aircraft Industry*, "there was no cohesive structure for dealings between the industry and the government. Contracting and procurement were largely on an adversarial and ad hoc basis."

This was a problem for Harold Pitcairn.

The youngest son of a Pittsburgh Plate Glass Company co-founder, Harold F. Pitcairn was a pilot and entrepreneur who in the late 1920s owned various aviation businesses, including airmail routes, based near Philadelphia. During a trip to Europe, Pitcairn saw Cierva's Autogiro. Certain it was going to replace the airplane as the preferred means of flight, Pitcairn bought the U.S. rights to the invention and sold off his other aviation businesses in July 1929. His timing was bad. Three months later, the stock market crashed, starting the Great Depression.

Pitcairn nevertheless got off to a good start with his Autogiro venture. He used test flights of the first Autogiro his company built not only to get government approval for this new type of aircraft but also to generate publicity. He took deposits on Autogiros his own company would build and licensed two other companies to build Autogiros as well. The National Aeronautic Association awarded Pitcairn's team the Collier Trophy for 1930, aviation's equivalent of the "Best Picture" Oscar, for demonstrating the Autogiro as a form of "safe aerial transport." President Herbert Hoover presented Pitcairn the trophy on April 22, 1931, at the White House. During the event, test pilot James G. Ray—the same James G. Ray who later envisioned a convertiplane in every garage—landed an Autogiro on the White House lawn and took off in it again. For a while, Pitcairn's and his licensees' Autogiros looked like they might take off financially, too. To gin up congressional support for military purchases, Pitcairn arranged for Jim Ray to set an Autogiro down one day on the parking lot that existed in those days on the East Front of the U.S. Capitol. Ray picked up Senator Hiram Bingham, a Connecticut Republican and former Army aviator, and whisked him off to the exclusive Burning Tree Club in the Maryland suburb of Bethesda for a round of golf. The Army later bought a few Autogiros to test as artillery spotters and observation aircraft. Celebrity aviators including Amelia Earhart tried Autogiros in those years. A couple of newspapers bought them as photo planes. An Autogiro was used to haul mail from Camden, New Jersey, to Philadelphia, where the aircraft landed and took off from the roof of the city's main post office. An Autogiro even made a cameo appearance in the 1934 Clark Gable movie *It Happened One Night*. That same year, however, the Depression reached full force and the demand for Autogiros dried up. By 1938, Pitcairn was desperate for business and having trouble persuading the Army to buy more Autogiros from him and his licensees. Pitcairn turned for help to his congressman, Representative Frank Dorsey, a second-term Democrat from Philadelphia.

Dorsey didn't need much persuading. He had been interested in safer aircraft ever since a hair-raising flight over Ohio a few years earlier in a plane that had barely skirted a tornado. "After dropping about two thousand feet, and then about twelve hundred in a pocket, and not knowing whether I was going to land safely or not, and looking down and seeing nothing but trees below me, I thought there surely must be some kind of an aircraft can keep you in the air, or let you down on top of a tree somewhere without cracking everybody up," Dorsey later recalled. In 1938, Dorsey also was up for reelection, and Pitcairn was an important constituent. His business provided jobs in Dorsey's district, and jobs were scarce. Pitcairn was delighted when Dorsey introduced a bill to provide $2 million to the War Department to buy Autogiros for Army research and testing. That was a lot of cash back then—about a third as much as the Army's entire research budget.

Despite Dorsey's lack of seniority in the House, the atmosphere for such a move must have seemed ripe. War with Nazi Germany was looming. Hitler had absorbed a largely willing Austria into the Third Reich in March and was threatening to take over Czechoslovakia's Sudetenland by force. Congress was beefing up the military budget. When the House Committee on Military Affairs held hearings on Dorsey's bill that April, though, the lawmaker and his constituents got an unwelcome surprise.

Dorsey tried to inspire his colleagues to vote for his bill by wowing them with the promise of the Autogiro. Appearing as a witness before the 26-member panel, he conjured up a vision remarkably similar—in fact, nearly identical—to the one that would enthrall Dick Spivey and other tiltrotor advocates decades later. "Contemplate the military and civilian advantages of a giro able to transport, say, twenty passengers or the equivalent in weight and with a cruising range of over a thousand miles," Dorsey urged. "A giro with this cruising range and pay load, able to rise or descend vertically, would revolutionize aviation both military and commercial."

The military already had tried the Autogiro, though, and was unimpressed. Assistant Secretary of the Navy Charles Edison—the son of inventor Thomas Edison, who had unsuccessfully tried to invent a helicopter in the 1880s—testified that the Navy Department was "really not interested in this bill" because of the Autogiro's limited speed and endurance. The head of research and development for the War Department, Army Major E. N. Harmon, had two objections to Dorsey's bill. First, his department disliked Congress earmarking money for special projects (a habit House and Senate members would never break). Secondly, the Army had bought three Autogiros already and "the results have been unfortunate," Harmon reported. All three "cracked up in a very short time." Of course, he added, "With any new type of aircraft like that, there is always the danger that one of them is going to have an accident and crack up."

To make matters worse for Pitcairn, revered aeronautical engineer Alexander Klemin counseled the committee to fund not just Autogiros but "any machine having a rotating wing." That meant the helicopter, which unlike the Autogiro would have a powered rotor that could lift the machine into the air as well as set it down gently. In Germany, a helicopter with two rotors side by side, the Focke-Wulf 61, or Fw 61, had just been demonstrated, Klemin noted, suggesting that this form of aircraft likely would be the next stage in the conquest of the air. "If you will read imaginative works you will see conceptions emerging of craft which would be capable of leaving a roof top and landing in a back yard," Klemin advised. "Besides my scientific knowledge of the subject, I have the subconscious feeling that that will be the next step."

Klemin turned out to be right—partly due to Pitcairn's scheme to get the Army to buy more of his Autogiros. By the end of two days of hearings on Dorsey's bill, the promise of the helicopter was outshining that of the Autogiro, and Dorsey was in full retreat. When the legislation became law that June as the Dorsey-Logan Act, it authorized the War Department to spend $2 million, but not just for Autogiros. The money was to go for research, development, purchase and testing of "rotary-wing and other aircraft."

★ ★ ★

Suddenly a pot of real gold beckoned at the end of the rotary-wing rainbow. Excited by the prospect, visionaries from the competing rotary wing tribes—Autogiro, helicopter, and convertiplane—gathered to debate how it should be spent. They met at the Franklin Institute, a renowned engineering school and museum in the heart of Philadelphia, the de facto capital of rotary wing experimentation. The Autogiro companies were in Philadelphia. Key figures in what would become the helicopter industry lived and worked in or near the city. It was Congressman Dorsey's hometown. Registration for the "Rotating Wing Aircraft Meeting" of October 28–29, 1938, was held in the institute's Hall of Aviation—an apt choice of rooms, given the unanticipated result of Pitcairn's attempt to get Congress to shoehorn his Autogiros into the armed forces. Hanging from the ceiling was the first Autogiro built in the United States, already a museum piece.

One of Vertaplane inventor Gerard Herrick's kindred souls, E. Burke Wilford, organized the meeting, which would prove a seminal event for what became the rotary wing aircraft industry. An engineer and manufacturer by profession, and a wealthy man, Wilford was another free-thinker and aviation entrepreneur who bubbled with enthusiasm for the idea of rotary wing aircraft. He had been drawn to aviation by a contest to develop safer aircraft in 1927, the year Charles Lindbergh became the first to fly across the Atlantic solo in his *Spirit of St. Louis*. Since then, Wilford had built a gyroplane, a machine similar to an Autogiro, based on a design he had bought during a visit to Germany in the 1920s.

Now Germany's Fw 61 helicopter was causing a sensation among the rotary wing crowd. The Fw 61 bore a strong resemblance to the future tiltrotor. It had the fuselage and tail of an airplane, but instead of wings, the craft had two big vertical rotors held out to the sides by outrigger pylons. The Nazis were using it for propaganda. Earlier in 1938, their famous female test pilot, Hanna Reitsch, had flown the revolutionary machine—indoors—for six minutes each evening during the big annual auto show at Berlin's new Deutschlandhalle arena. This was the helicopter Klemin had told the House committee about, and it was much on the minds of others at the Philadelphia conference.

Wilford gaveled the meeting into session in the Franklin Institute's Lecture Hall, an auditorium in neoclassical style with theater seating in sharply rising rows. "As this is probably the first rotary wing aircraft conference occurring in the world, we hope to make a little history here, and the only way that we can do that is for everyone to say what he thinks," Wilford told the nearly full auditorium. He was looking up at 242 engineers, inventors, aviation industry executives, and military officers. Looking down on them from niches on the wall to their right were murals of Newton, Galileo, and Copernicus—reminders of what scientists with iconoclastic vision can achieve. There was also another mural, this one depicting an alchemist and the ill-destined medieval quest to turn base metals into gold—a reminder that not all iconoclastic scientific theories pan out. Seated in the audience was nearly everyone who already was somebody or someday would *be* somebody in this avant-garde cohort of aviation. "Don't be afraid of hurting anybody's feelings, or departing from the conventional procedure," Wilford counseled.

"That's what this meeting is for, and we hope that it will be the start of a real boom in the rotary wing aircraft industry."

Shortly into the first day's meeting, rotary wing guru Klemin took the chair. He was in a buoyant mood. The previous evening, Klemin had spoken to a special meeting at the Franklin Institute to kick off today's conference. His remarks had made the front page of this morning's *Philadelphia Inquirer* under the headline "Rotary Wings Touted For Fool-Proof Plane." The second speaker Klemin called on was Vertaplane inventor Herrick, who frequently had sought Klemin's advice, and whose quirky personality and ideas clearly amused the professor. Klemin seemed to view Herrick as a sort of alchemist of aviation. He introduced him as "a man who is captain of his own soul." When Herrick finished speaking, Klemin called his ideas "refreshing," then added, drawing a laugh from the audience, "The only thing I don't approve of are his mathematics. I think his mathematics are of the type of which the college professor, in marking down a paper, says, 'I think I shall give him a C, minus.'"

Seven years after the crash of his first Vertaplane, Herrick was now calling his dream machine the "Convertaplane." Klemin teased Herrick as the inventor began his talk. "I would like to know whether it is 'Convertoplane' or 'Convertaplane,'" Klemin demanded.

Herrick walked to a blackboard, picked up some chalk, and wrote: CONVERT ible Air PLANE. "I represent a hybrid, an occupant of the aviation stables that more closely resembles, perhaps, the mule than anything else," the amiable inventor began. "We are all interested to find out whether or not it is the start of a new and important breed." Then he told a joke. Then he read a poem. Then he recalled how he had once explained to "a Southerner" how he had spent ten years working on his invention, to which Herrick said the man replied: "It is a pity that you could not have bred an airplane to a helicopter and let nature take its course; it takes less than a year to foal a mule."

Finally, Herrick described his Convertaplane in some detail, at times sounding a bit self-conscious. At one point he mused that, "Every very radical research needs an eccentric person who, by a certain amount of freedom from convention is not too afraid to go far afield for solutions."

One man in the audience who probably agreed was Arthur Middleton Young, a fellow Princeton alumnus thirty-two years Herrick's junior. Young had grown up on his financially comfortable family's estate in the

Philadelphia suburb of Radnor, amusing himself by making models and mechanical toys and tinkering with radios. While studying mathematics at Princeton, Young decided to become a philosopher. He wanted to found his own new philosophy, but after trying for a while at school, he decided he knew too little as yet about how the real world worked. To fill that void, he set out after graduating in 1927 to invent a helicopter—not because he wanted to fly but "to determine if I was learning how nature works," he explained after succeeding and moving on to found the Institute for the Study of Consciousness in Berkeley, California.

Art Young was a genial young genius with brown hair, a widow's peak, and a fit build. He loved to Indian wrestle. After finishing at Princeton, he had spent more than a year traveling to public libraries in major cities to read up on helicopter theory. Then he set about his task like any respectable mad scientist might: he turned a corner of the stable on his family's estate into a workshop. There he spent nine years obsessively designing and building and redesigning and rebuilding a remote-controlled model helicopter with a rotor about six feet in diameter. His materials were wood and scrap metal foraged for him from junkyards by boys in the neighborhood. His engines, at first, were rubber bands and electric motors. He designed and built gauges to measure lift and calculate stress on metal parts. He tested and retested rotors of various shapes. By 1938, Young was working on a large new model with a 20-horsepower engine. He hadn't yet succeeded in making it even stay in one piece once the rotor started spinning, much less fly, but he felt he was making progress. So he used his modest inheritance to buy a farm at Paoli, Pennsylvania, where he rebuilt an old barn into a big workshop to construct and test his models. Then he went to the Rotating Wing Aircraft Meeting in Philadelphia.

Two things Young heard there inspired him. One was in a paper on helicopters delivered by Haviland H. Platt, a mechanical engineer, inventor of the first automatic transmission for cars, and yet another pioneer out to conquer the air. Young was struck by Platt's theoretical solution to the confounding question of how to keep rotor blades stable in flight. Young thought Platt wrong, but the paper got him thinking. When Young returned to his workshop, Platt's argument stirred him to come up with a device called a "stabilizer bar" that solved the problem. Young's other eureka moment at the conference came when he saw a film there in which aircraft designer Igor Sikorsky proposed a solution to another gnawing dilemma: the fact that the torque, or twisting force, of the main rotor makes a helicopter's fuselage want to rotate in the other direction. Sikorsky suggested adding a tail rotor, today standard on most single-rotor helicopters.

Young knew he had to take what Sikorsky said to heart. Igor Ivanovich Sikorsky was no starry-eyed dreamer but an aviation practitioner of the first order. Some aviation historians put him on a par with the Wright brothers. He is known as the father of the helicopter.

A Ukraine-born émigré from imperial Russia, where he had made a name for himself as a pilot and airplane designer, Sikorsky in 1938 headed a subsidiary of the aviation conglomerate United Aircraft in Stratford, Connecticut. His Sikorsky Aircraft division had specialized for years in building "flying boats," which took off and landed on water. Flying boats had been popular as airliners for a time but now they were fading from the scene. Earlier in 1938, Sikorsky had learned that United planned to shut his division down. He persuaded top executives to let him put his team of engineers to work on a helicopter instead. Sikorsky had attempted a helicopter years ago in Russia but given up. Engines back then didn't produce enough power per pound to lift themselves, a pilot, and an aircraft straight up into the air. Over the years, though, engines had improved and Sikorsky had continued to ponder how to make a helicopter work. Once United gave the go-ahead, it didn't take him long to succeed.

Two weeks after Nazi Germany's September 1, 1939, invasion of Poland ignited World War II, Sikorsky flew the first successful helicopter in the United States at Stratford, his VS-300. Nine months later, the Army began using Dorsey-Logan Act money to buy prototype helicopters rather than Autogiros. The second helicopter contract went to Sikorsky Aircraft. The Autogiro soon would be largely forgotten. The helicopter's long and dubious gestation, however, was over. A new industry was being born. One of its fathers was Igor Sikorsky.

Another was Lawrence D. Bell, founder and namesake of the company Dick Spivey was representing when he took the Bell-Boeing tiltrotor bid to Washington in 1983. Larry Bell was a visionary, too, but he was neither inventor nor engineer. Bell was an airplane mechanic turned aviation executive who had a keen eye for the next big chance and a knack for public relations. Thickset and good-natured, Bell encouraged innovation at his company, which he had formed in 1935 in Buffalo,

New York, to build fighter planes. Bell Aircraft not only produced thousands of P-39 Airacobra fighter planes during World War II, it also built America's first jet fighter in those years, though the craft was experimental and never saw combat. After the war, Bell Aircraft built the X-1, the stubby-winged rocket plane that test pilot Chuck Yeager was flying on October 14, 1947, when he became the first human to break the sound barrier and live to tell about it.

Three months before Japan attacked Pearl Harbor on December 7, 1941, bringing the United States into World War II, Larry Bell played a hunch. In 1938, Bell had been one of a group of industrialists sent on a tour of Germany by President Franklin D. Roosevelt to report back on Hitler's capabilities. During the trip, Bell saw the Fw 61 helicopter with its side-by-side rotors. Now the U.S. Army was getting interested in helicopters and there was money to be made on them. When one of Bell's engineers heard about Art Young, who by then was able to fly his remote-controlled model helicopter in and out the door of his Paoli barn, they invited Young up to Bell's plant in Buffalo for a demonstration.

Young arrived, carrying his model helicopter in a suitcase, on September 3, 1941. He flew the model around inside a fighter plane hangar, impressing Bell's engineers with how he could control it completely in flight and make the little helicopter hover. Two months later, Young signed a deal with Bell Aircraft. The company agreed to spend as much as $250,000 to build two full-size helicopters according to Young's designs. In exchange, Young signed over to Bell various patents he had obtained over the years. Thanks to Larry Bell's willingness to gamble on the esoteric inventor, Bell Aircraft was one of four companies in the world that sold helicopters in any volume during the 1940s.

★ ★ ★

The helicopter caught on slowly. "The matter of the actual military value of the helicopter was widely debated after 1938," noted an Army Air Forces study written in 1946. "There was doubt in the minds of some AAF personnel as to whether this machine had any real combat value." The Army Air Forces spent $45 million on helicopters during World War II, buying 151 from Sikorsky Aircraft and another 201 of Sikorsky's design from another company. Helicopters flew in combat only nineteen times, however, being used only in the China-Burma-India Theater to rescue downed pilots or wounded soldiers. Still, the helicopter's advent made imaginations soar in the aviation world. After all, if the *helicopter* could be made to work, why, just about *anything* must be possible, because people had been trying to build helicopters *forever*. The first attempt is thought to have been made by Leonardo da Vinci in the late fifteenth century. Now, at long last, the stubborn problem of vertical flight had been solved. The arrival of the helicopter kindled new, wider, and far stronger interest in convertiplanes for another reason as well. It quickly became apparent that helicopters had an Achilles heel: the aerodynamics of rotors dictated that they would never be able to fly very fast.

A rotor works well in a hover but creates all kinds of aerodynamic problems in forward flight. One of the most important is the fact that when a helicopter flies forward, the speed of each rotor blade compared to the relative wind varies dramatically, depending on whether the blade is moving toward the front or rear of the aircraft. A blade moving forward and into the relative wind, an "advancing blade," creates far more lift than one moving backward and away from the relative wind, a "retreating blade." The helicopter became possible only because inventors and engineers developed mechanisms to compensate for this, in part by changing the angle, or "pitch," of the blades as they turn so that they meet the air at a higher angle during their retreating arc. The faster a helicopter goes, though, the higher the pitch on the retreating blade must be to produce as much lift as the advancing blade does. At a certain point, the task becomes impossible and the retreating blade stops producing lift. This "retreating blade stall" limits a helicopter's top speed, usually to well less than 200 miles per hour. By the end of World War II, with jets zooming through the sky at hundreds of miles an hour but helicopters barely breaking 100, the dream of the convertiplane began to entice more than just starry-eyed inventors such as Gerard Herrick.

"Engineers are devoting increasing attention to the convertaplane, an aircraft combining the hovering and slow-landing features of the helicopter with the high-speed characteristics of the conventional airplane," *Aviation Week* magazine reported in April 1948, borrowing Herrick's spelling. "Such a combination of features offers interesting and attractive possibilities not only as a means of increasing the utility and safety of the passenger plane but as a military weapon. . . ." The NACA's Aerodynamics Committee had studied the possibilities in 1947, the article noted, and "recommended, last November, further examination of the configuration." In a brief survey of the six main ideas proposed so far, *Aviation Week* cited Herrick's efforts. It noted that he was "continuing his work in New York."

Herrick, now seventy-five years old, was indeed continuing his work, obsessed as ever and still flexible on how to spell his invention's name. Among his papers when he died was a typewritten "RECORD OF INVENTION" that begins: "At 2 A.M. on May 8, 1949, I Gerard P. Herrick conceived the mechanical arrangement for stopping the rotor on a convertible aircraft. . . ."

Burke Wilford, the gyroplane developer who had organized the 1938 Rotating Wing Aircraft Meeting, was now committed to the quest for the convertiplane himself. On December 9, 1949, he organized another conference in Philadelphia, this time at the posh Warwick Hotel at Seventeenth and Locust streets. Somewhat pompously, Wilford called the event the "First Convertible Aircraft Congress." Co-sponsored by the Institute of the Aeronautical Sciences and the five-year-old American Helicopter Society, the gathering attracted 250 engineers and others eager to talk about convertiplanes. Herrick was among the speakers, of course. The organizers presented the old man with a plaque honoring him as the "father of convertible aircraft." In a foreword to the published proceedings of the conference—written before detailed histories of Nazi Germany lent the phrase he used the jarring ring it has today—Wilford gushed that the convertiplane would be "the final solution of useful flight for humanity."

The days when the quest for the dream machine would be led by such iconoclastic inventors and individual entrepreneurs as Herrick and Wilford, however, were ending. The newly emerging military-industrial complex was about to take it over.

CHAPTER TWO

THE SALESMAN

T he north Texas sky was clear that Thursday in early spring but the air was already muggy around 9 A.M. when a Greyhound bus stopped in front of a one-story industrial building in Hurst, a suburb thirteen miles northeast of Fort Worth on Highway 10. A young man with square shoulders, a muscular swimmer's neck, and short red hair stepped out into the dust wearing a new suit and shiny black leather shoes. As the bus pulled away, the youth walked through an open gate and knocked at the door of a small blockhouse. A guard stuck his head out. The visitor smiled and introduced himself politely in his Georgia drawl, then got some bad news. Yes, this was Bell Helicopter, but it wasn't the main plant, where the Engineering Department was. "You need to be down the road a piece," the guard told him. The main plant was a mile and a half away, over a big hill in the distance. And no, sorry, there wouldn't be another bus for a couple of hours. The young man grimaced, thanked the guard and started walking. *Great. First day on the job and I'm late already.*

The date was April 2, 1959. Richard F. Spivey was eighteen years old.

Spivey liked to say later in life that he became an aeronautical engineer because his parents didn't have enough money to pay his way through college, and that he ended up at Bell because he couldn't spell. Born in Chicopee, Georgia, and raised in Marietta, where his father worked for the phone company, Spivey had entered the Georgia Institute of Technology in Atlanta as a freshman the previous fall because he could pay his own way there. Georgia Tech let students earn tuition money and gain job experience by splitting their time between going to school and working for companies that were in its "co-op" program. Students would spend an academic quarter at school, then one at a company, alternating back and forth until their senior year. Georgia Tech didn't have a co-op program for physics, which was what he wanted to study, but Spivey could co-op in aerospace engineering, which involved a lot of physics. One co-op opportunity was with a company at Cape Canaveral working on the space program. That sounded really cool, so Spivey signed up for that. But on the final exam in his first term English theme-writing course he misspelled three words, enough to fail him for the quarter. He had to repeat the course. The F disqualified him from co-oping next term anyway, so he stayed at school that winter. By spring term, he had requalified for the co-op program, but by then the Cape Canaveral job was taken. The alternative was Bell Helicopter.

Spivey was late when he reached the low-slung, yellow-brick building that housed Bell's executives and engineers. To his relief, the engineering personnel director, Warren Jones, who met him in the lobby, seemed to take no notice of the new co-op's tardiness, the perspiration on his brow, or the gritty dust on what had started the day as his carefully shined black shoes. He welcomed Spivey with a smile and handshake and began showing him around.

Spivey immediately liked the place. Indoors, what interested him most was the helicopter assembly line, a long sort of warehouse behind the administrative building. There, workers in dungarees and short sleeves were assembling aircraft against a cacophony of whining power tools and metallic clunks and clanks. Outdoors, on the west side of the factory, beyond two cinder-block and aluminum hangars with massive blue doors, was a long, concrete flight line. Out there, Jones explained, test pilots ran hours of ground checks on every new helicopter, sitting in the cockpit with the aircraft tethered to the ground for safety. Then they flew each one at least three hours before turning it over to its purchaser. Bell's business was thriving, Spivey could see. Parked on the apron were various versions of those neat little piston-engine Model 47 helicopters, the kind with the glass bubble canopy featured in the current hit TV show *Whirlybirds* and the just-canceled *Highway Patrol*. A specially modified blue and white Model 47J had picked President Dwight D. Eisenhower up on the White House lawn in 1957 and taken him to Camp David, inaugurating the practice of presidents using helicopters for short trips. The same model helicopter would be featured years later in the opening credits of the TV show *M*A*S*H*. Spivey also saw a couple of HU-1As, a brand-new, turbine-engine helicopter that Bell was building for the Army, which had named it the "Iroquois." Soldiers would dub it the "Huey," a nickname that would stick even after the Army changed the aircraft's designation to UH-1.

Spivey especially liked how friendly and casual almost everyone at Bell seemed. It wasn't like Lockheed Aircraft's factory in Marietta, where he had worked the previous summer after graduating from high school. Sure, the few dozen engineers among the 3,200 employees here wore neckties with their short-sleeve white shirts and pocket protectors, but no one acted stiff. The relaxed atmosphere had minuses as well as pluses, though. Everywhere Jones took him that day—the administration building, the steamy back hangar where Spivey would work for Bell's flight test engineers that spring, the offices of Bell's cocky test pilots—the personnel director introduced him as "Dick." Spivey's mother always called him Richard. His friends called him Rick. Spivey always respected his elders, though, and he was easygoing by nature. He felt it would be rude to contradict Mr. Jones. So he just let the personnel director call him "Dick," and the nickname stuck. Spivey didn't mind. He was just happy to be here—so happy, he forgot he'd loosened his tie and unbuttoned his collar on his rush to the main gate. No one seemed to mind, though, not even when Jones took him to meet the intellectually formidable, if generally genial, Bart Kelley, vice president for engineering.

Tall, rail-thin, and cerebral, Bartram Kelley had a master's degree in physics from Harvard but had come to Bell in 1941 for ninety cents an hour as helicopter inventor Arthur Young's right-hand man. They had been childhood friends in Pennsylvania, though Young was four years older than Kelley. They started Bell Aircraft's helicopter operation in Gardenville, New York, near Buffalo, but in 1951 Larry Bell moved it to Fort Worth. Bell wanted to take advantage of the better flying weather, a friendlier tax climate, and the absence of strong labor unions. A violent strike by workers at his New York factory in 1949 had left Bell bitter. He also wanted to get the helicopter operation out from under the shadow of the company's far larger fixed-wing projects. The fixed-wing engineers and administrators were good at elbowing the helicopter types aside when it came time to divvy up resources. Besides, with the Cold War under way, the Pentagon was encouraging defense companies to move away from the east and west coasts to make them harder for the Soviet Union to attack. Bell's move was financed by a big contract to build a new antisubmarine warfare helicopter for the Navy. After the move, Bell Helicopter Corporation was formed as a wholly owned subsidiary of

Bell Aircraft Corporation. By then, Art Young had gone back to his farm in Paoli to continue his philosophical and metaphysical investigations, but Kelley moved with Bell Helicopter to Texas. Aside from becoming the company's top engineer there, he indulged his passion for playing oboe by helping found the Dallas Chamber Music Society.

Kelley scared the crap out of Spivey. The former prep school teacher wore wire-rimmed glasses and a dark mustache. He had a broad smile and he was generous with it, but he was also a stern taskmaster and a stickler for proper English. Kelley would mark grammatical or spelling errors in memos his engineers gave him with a red pencil and send them back for correction. Troy Gaffey, a Purdue University grad who retired in 2003 as senior vice president for engineering after thirty-eight years with Bell, never forgot how Kelley once brought a memo so marked up it looked like it was bleeding back to an Australian engineer the company had hired. He stood by the man's desk, said "I can't understand this," then dropped it in a trash can and walked away. In the 1960s, after Spivey had graduated from Georgia Tech and returned to Bell as an engineer, his inept spelling often got him into trouble with Kelley. If Spivey found Kelley intimidating, though, he also looked up to him. Spivey tried to emulate the older man's discipline of keeping a diary of his work in inch-thick, dusky brown "Computation Books" ordered from the Harvard/MIT Cooperative Society.

Another man Spivey would work for at Bell who scared him more than a little was yet another Pennsylvanian, Robert L. Lichten. A brainy, opinionated engineer with a dark complexion and often matching demeanor, Lichten was chief of flight technology. He was Bart Kelley's deputy and heir apparent as chief engineer. He was also—at Bell—the father of the tiltrotor.

Unlike Kelley, the Philadelphia-born Lichten was rough around the edges, Spivey found, and "if he didn't like something you did, he'd upbraid you pretty good." Nearly every Bell engineer who worked with Lichten seemed to have a story about a run-in or confrontation with him. Towering and handsome, Lichten was also domineering. He was never crude, but he was often dismissive of subordinates. If he didn't agree with what you were telling him, he might just turn on his heels and walk away without a word. If he really didn't like what you were telling him, he might belittle you on the spot. Lichten had earned his degree in aeronautical engineering from the Massachusetts Institute of Technology in 1943. He set great store by analysis and calculation, which wasn't the habit at Bell. Starting with Art Young and Bart Kelley, the culture among engineers there had been trial and error, or "cut and try." That also bothered Kenneth G. Wernicke, Lichten's deputy in those days. Wernicke liked Lichten. He thought he was "hard on people because he expected more of them than they were capable of." Lichten looked down on those who disappointed him, and a lot of people didn't like him.

Even so, Lichten oversaw the engineering of some of Bell's most successful helicopters over the years, including the Huey for the Army and Marines and the civilian JetRanger, a big seller. Outside work, he was a political liberal whose passion was civil rights, an understandable interest, perhaps, for a Jew who came to maturity during World War II. Lichten was a life member of the NAACP. He was a leader in the Dallas chapter of the American Jewish Committee, the Dallas United Nations Association, the Dallas chapter of the American Civil Liberties Union, and the Texas Civil Liberties Union. Like Kelley, he also belonged to the Dallas Chamber Music Society. Lichten's obsession, though, what drove him most throughout his career, was his dream machine: the tiltrotor.

Lichten spoke of the tiltrotor as an addiction. When he made Wernicke his chief tiltrotor engineer in 1965, Lichten warned his protégé not to make the concept the "only thing in your life," as Lichten said he had done. "I don't want you doing that," Lichten told Wernicke. "I want you to realize there are other things besides that in life.'"

The tiltrotor was Lichten's "baby," as Wernicke saw it, but in truth, Lichten was only the concept's adoptive father. The configuration's technological DNA can be traced to Germany and the Fw 61, the helicopter with side-by-side rotors that so impressed rotary wing guru Alexander Klemin and other Americans in the 1930s. Among those who saw Hanna Reitsch fly the Fw 61 in Berlin's Deutschlandhalle in 1938 was Larry Bell, one of the industrialists President Roosevelt sent to Germany that year to assess Nazi war-making capacity. Another who saw the Fw 61 in Berlin was W. Laurence LePage, a British-born engineer who had worked on Autogiros for Harold Pitcairn and for one of his licensees. LePage came back from Germany with a film of Reitsch flying the Fw 61. He showed it to the Army and to the 1938 Rotating Wing Aircraft Meeting in Philadelphia, which he helped organize. Shortly afterward, LePage and Haviland H. Platt set up a company in Eddystone, Pennsylvania, to build a similar helicopter. Among the engineers they hired was Bob Lichten.

Like the German machine, the Platt-LePage helicopter had two rotors placed laterally, where an airplane's wings would be, held away from the fuselage by winglike outriggers. The company also designed a similar machine with mechanisms to allow the rotors to tilt forward. Platt-LePage never built this tiltrotor, but Lichten fell in love with the concept. It was a fairly elegant solution to a central problem for convertiplane designers: how to equip an aircraft with two forms of lift and thrust—one each for vertical and horizontal flight—yet avoid loading it down with two sets of machinery that would add impossible amounts of weight and aerodynamic drag. After World War II, as the development of the helicopter kindled new interest in the convertiplane, Lichten and a couple of partners formed a new firm to develop a tiltrotor. Fittingly, given what the tiltrotor was meant to do, they called their firm the "Transcendental Aircraft Company."

Within two years, Lichten left for Bell, where helicopter inventor Art Young had been intrigued by the convertiplane idea for some time. At the First Convertible Aircraft Congress in Philadelphia in 1949, the year after he joined Bell, Lichten showed a film made in the early 1940s of Young flying a crude model convertiplane with a single tilting rotor on a wing. Young had established a project at Bell to pursue the technology, calling it the Model 50 Convert-O-Plane. In 1947, though, with Bell now producing helicopters based on his earlier work, Young left the company and returned to his farm in Pennsylvania. Young was more interested in philosophy.

When Lichten brought his ideas about the tiltrotor to Bell the next year, he was only one of many aircraft industry engineers embarking on such a project. By 1949, when the First Convertible Aircraft Congress proclaimed self-described eccentric Gerard Herrick the "Father of the Convertiplane," the center of gravity in the quest for the dream machine was rapidly shifting. It was passing from the realm of maverick inventors to a hungry aircraft industry and a military gearing up for new conflicts. That year, the communists took power in China by winning a civil war. The Soviet Union tested its first atomic bombs. The United States and its European allies formed NATO, the North Atlantic Treaty Organization, to protect Western Europe against a feared Soviet invasion. With an alarmed Congress providing money, the U.S. military soon would start rearming for the coming confrontation with communism.

At the moment, though, American aircraft companies were still

struggling to recover from the loss of their huge World War II contracts, and they were looking for new products. Bell Aircraft's revenues
had plummeted from $317 million in 1944 to $11.5 million in 1946, the
year after the war ended. Larry Bell and others in the new helicopter
industry were working hard in the late 1940s to gain public acceptance
for their odd-looking new aircraft, but the "egg-beaters," as wags dubbed
them, were catching on slowly. Even the military was hesitant about
them. The Army Air Forces and the Coast Guard had used some during
World War II, but those services still regarded the machine as a work in
progress. Helicopters were still too fragile and new for the military to
adopt wholesale. Even forward-looking tacticians and strategists were
largely unsure what the helicopter could really do and how best to use it.
Their frame of mind was illustrated by a cartoon in the July 1948 issue of
the two-and-a-half-year-old magazine *American Helicopter*. The drawing shows an Army officer slouched in a folding lawn chair, his uniform
cap on the ground, his jacket draped on the side of a small, round garden
table that holds a cocktail glass. Overhead, held in place by a rope tied to
a stake in the ground near the lounging officer, hovers a small helicopter
bearing the military's star-in-a-circle insignia. The officer cools himself
under the rotor downwash as two soldiers in the lower right-hand corner take in the spectacle. "I was wondering what that infantry colonel
was going to do with a helicopter," one says to the other.

When that cartoon appeared, the only service fully sold on the helicopter as a weapon of war was the Marine Corps. The Marines were
studying helicopters as a better way than landing craft to get troops
from ship to shore in amphibious operations. During the Korean War,
1950–53, the helicopter would come into its own, proving a great way
to evacuate wounded, carry supplies to troops, rescue pilots downed
behind enemy lines or at sea, and on occasion take soldiers and Marines
into battle. In 1948, though, the only thing most military officers knew
for sure about helicopters was that the things were frustratingly slow.
And this was the dawn of the jet age. The turbojet and the turboprop,
engines developed during World War II, were enabling aircraft designers to come up with machines of phenomenal speed. The power of such
engines was also leading more and more engineers and military officers
to take the old convertiplane dream seriously for the first time. With the
sound barrier broken and people talking about space travel, anything
seemed possible.

Against that backdrop, the U.S. military—like the militaries of the antagonistic Soviet Union and of America's richest allies, Britain, France, and West Germany—spent millions of dollars over the next two decades on experimental convertiplanes. John P. Campbell, a senior NASA aeronautical engineer, wrote a book on the subject in 1962. He concluded that, counting the helicopter, there were sixteen categories of what experts by then were no longer calling convertiplanes but instead "VTOLs," an acronym for Vertical Take Off and Landing, pronounced "VEE-talls." A VTOL aircraft's type depended on what method of propulsion was paired with what means of converting from vertical to horizontal flight. There were four basic methods of propulsion: rotors, propellers, turbojets, and ducted fans, the last meaning propellers or multibladed fans spinning inside enclosed cowlings. There were four basic methods of conversion: tilting the whole aircraft from vertical to horizontal, tilting only the thrust, deflecting the thrust downward for vertical and rearward for horizontal flight, or using two separate methods of thrust on the same aircraft—one vertical, one horizontal. By the time Campbell published his book, almost all sixteen forms had been tried, mostly with poor results.

Some of the designs the military and NASA paid for look downright zany in retrospect. As has always been the custom with aircraft, they were known by an alphabet soup of letters and numbers. The Navy financed the Convair XFY-1 and Lockheed XFV-1 "tail-sitters," also known as "Pogos." Both resembled conventional airplanes, except that they had two huge, counterrotating propellers on their noses and were designed to take off literally sitting on their tails and pointing straight up. This was hard on the pilot, who was expected to begin his flight lying on his back with his feet in the air and end it the same way, landing the monster on its tail while looking over his shoulder as if parallel parking. The Convair XFY-1 took off and landed this way several times and even converted from vertical to horizontal flight. The Lockheed Pogo flew as a conventional plane but never managed to take off or land vertically. The Navy abandoned both designs in the mid-1950s as impractical, especially with the introduction of jet fighter planes.

Equally bizarre-looking were a couple of "deflected slipstream" aircraft financed by the Army, the Ryan VZ-3 and the Fairchild VZ-5. They were essentially conventional airplanes with propellers on their wings and massive flaps that directed the propeller thrust downward so they could take off and land vertically or hover—at least in theory. Neither showed great promise, and one test pilot barely managed to eject before the VZ-3 went out of control and crashed as he tried to convert it. The U.S. and other militaries financed, and aircraft companies produced, dozens of other VTOL prototypes. Thousands more were designed but never built. In the 1990s, aerospace engineer and VTOL historian Michael J. Hirschberg refined a graphic of the various attempts that someone at the old McDonnell aircraft company had put together in the 1960s. The graphic, which can be found on the Internet, took the form of a "Wheel of Misfortune." The wheel represented only those VTOLs actually built. There were forty-five, not including three dozen exotic helicopters Hirschberg later wished he'd included.

When Hirschberg published his version of the wheel, only one of the VTOLs on it was still flying, and only two had ever gone into full production and service. One was the Soviet Yak-38 "Forger," withdrawn from service in 1992. The other was the Harrier, a "jump jet" designed in Britain in the 1960s for the Royal Air Force and bought by the U.S. Marine Corps in the 1970s and 1980s. This "vectored thrust" aircraft, which could point its jet exhaust downward to take off and land vertically or hover, was strictly a one-seat fighter plane. It was far removed from the passenger machines the true believers in the convertiplane had envisioned, and by the mid-1970s, engineers had concluded that building a VTOL passenger jet was impractical. For one thing, jet engines create thrust by accelerating a relatively small stream of air to high speeds, which requires burning fuel at high rates. A machine big enough to carry passengers would burn so much fuel lifting off vertically it would have little range. The convertiplane believers were after an aircraft without such limitations, one that would carry passengers and "do in the air substantially everything that a bird can do," in the words of 1930s aeronautics icon Alexander Klemin. They wanted to revolutionize not only military but also civilian aviation. They wanted a dream machine.

★　★　★

There was a reason the quest for the convertiplane was like searching for the Northwest Passage or seeking the Holy Grail. The engineering problems were devilish. One of the biggest hurdles was weight.

Aircraft designers judge helicopters and airplanes partly on their "empty weight" to "gross weight" ratio, meaning how much they weigh sitting on the tarmac unloaded and with no fuel in their tanks versus how much they weigh carrying their maximum load. An ideal but frequently elusive target is an empty weight to gross weight ratio of 50 percent. This makes it possible to carry some combination of passengers, cargo, and fuel equal to the weight of the machine itself. As Bell engineer Ken Wernicke saw it, that ratio was the problem that stumped most VTOL aircraft designers. "A lot of these things have been able to lift themselves off the ground but they were so heavy they couldn't carry very much fuel and they couldn't even carry any more payload," Wernicke explained. "That is the biggest issue: it's the weight, because in any case, you're either going to have to have a double lift system or you're going to have to have a double propulsion system to move you forward." Like his mentor Bob Lichten, Wernicke saw the tiltrotor as the best solution, though he tried others. Once he and a brilliant Italian engineer Bell had hired, Emilio Bianchi, spent months trying to design a worthwhile "compound helicopter," meaning a conventional helicopter with an added means of propulsion for forward flight, such as a propeller or jet. The extra form of propulsion yields a helicopter that can escape the speed limit retreating blade stall and other aerodynamic limitations usually impose on rotors, but the added weight means the aircraft can carry less fuel, which limits its range. One day Bianchi threw his pencil down on their drawing board in disgust and sputtered, "This is all monkey vomit!" Wernicke and Bianchi concluded that a compound helicopter just wouldn't work well enough to justify itself because its weight would limit its range to the point where its additional speed became irrelevant. "If you can't go very far, why go very fast?" Wernicke reasoned. "It doesn't take you long to get there anyway, because you're not going very far." Moreover, such a machine isn't aerodynamically efficient in forward flight "because now the crap you use to hover with, you've got to drag it along with you."

That was the advantage of a tiltrotor, the way Wernicke and others at Bell saw it. If you tilted the rotor over and used it as a propeller—presto, no extra "crap" creating drag, and no more weight penalty. Wernicke loved that.

With Bob Lichten in charge of the project, Bell Helicopter won a contract to build an experimental tiltrotor as part of a 1951 convertiplane competition run by the Air Force but financed by the Army and the National Advisory Committee on Aeronautics, NASA's predecessor.

Two other contracts went to McDonnell and to Sikorsky Aircraft Company, which by then was shaping up as Bell's chief rival in the helicopter market. McDonnell offered what amounted to a compound helicopter. Sikorsky designed but never built a jet with delta-shaped wings and a rotor atop its fuselage that was to fold away after lifting the craft into the air and unfold to set the aircraft down.

The military designated Bell's tiltrotor entry the XV-3 Convertiplane.

★　★　★

A single glimpse can give birth to infatuation. Infatuation can mature into passion, and passion is obsession's parent. Dick Spivey caught his first glimpse of the XV-3 the day he arrived at Bell in 1959. It was sitting on the flight line as Warren Jones showed him around. Spivey was infatuated right away.

This first Bell tiltrotor piqued Spivey's curiosity because it was such a "strange-looking beast, compared to everything else," he remembered years later. The XV-3 had been cobbled together with parts from existing aircraft, and it showed. It looked like a helicopter that had been rear-ended by an airplane. From the wing forward, the fuselage was boxy, like most helicopters in those days, with windows enclosing the cockpit and extending behind it. From the wing back, it was all airplane. Except that protruding from its wingtips were two small, teardrop-shaped swiveling pods called "pylons," each of which held a two-bladed rotor measuring twenty-three feet in diameter. The engine that drove the rotors was inside the fuselage, which was painted silver. The pylons were bright orange, as was the rudder. The craft's oversized tail was silver, too, except for a yellow triangle at its bottom that bore the label "NASA" in big black letters. (NASA had taken the place of the NACA the previous October.) The top of the tail was labeled "U.S. Army," also in black letters. A pair of skids served as landing gear. Spivey thought it was really cool.

The XV-3 Spivey saw was the surviving one of two Bell had built. The first had been destroyed two and a half years earlier during one of its first flight tests, leaving its pilot, Dick Stansbury, crippled for life. During initial flight tests in August 1955, when another pilot took the XV-3 up into a hover, the craft started shaking. Bell and NASA put it through wind tunnel tests for a few months to study the problem, then Stansbury climbed in on October 25, 1956, to test it again in a hover and see what it would do when the rotors were tilted forward. He got the XV-3 to hover, but when Stansbury moved the rotors forward 17 degrees, the craft started to shudder violently, shaking the cockpit so hard he blacked out from being slung around inside. The XV-3 went out of control and fell to the ground, breaking Stansbury's back. Afterward, Bell and NASA spent a couple of years figuring out the cause: a phenomenon called "dynamic instability," sometimes referred to as "air resonance," in which centrifugal force can start a propeller or a rotor and its mast wobbling at ever-increasing rates if the structure holding them isn't built just right. The first XV-3 had three-bladed rotors with hinges in them so they could flap up and down and lag independently, a standard feature on helicopter rotors of the sort. The hinges were meant to keep the rotor blades from bending their mast as the wind buffeted them up and down. Complex aerodynamic forces, however, caused the side-by-side rotors to get so far out of kilter with each other they were shaking the aircraft to the point it was uncontrollable. Bell and NASA engineers finally solved the problem, in part by substituting a two-bladed rotor, in part by putting a strut under each wing. Without computers to analyze such things, it was daunting, time-consuming work. After a long recovery, Dick Stansbury came back to Bell as a research and development engineer, hobbling around on aluminum braces that went up over his elbows, but still enthusiastic about the tiltrotor.

As a $1.78 an hour co-op student, Spivey wouldn't get to work on the XV-3 directly that first spring at Bell, but like many budding and fully grown engineers, he was fascinated by almost any new technology and open to new ideas. Spivey crawled all over the XV-3 anytime he could find a pilot or engineer working on the thing to show him something. Otherwise, the closest he got to the novelty was when he got assigned to do "data reduction" on some of its flight tests. That meant plotting the flight-induced strains on the XV-3's major wood and metal parts, which would be fitted with "strain gauges"—small electric wires—to measure stress. Strain gauges "look like a lightbulb filament," Spivey explained. "They glue them to the surface, and then if you put a load on it, the surface bends very slightly. That changes the resistance in the wires and you measure that to make sure the aircraft is not getting close to something failing." Today, the data from strain gauges is fed into computers. Back then, the gauges were hooked up to an oscillograph, a machine that recorded data in squiggly lines on a moving roll of graph paper, something like an electrocardiograph did before the digital age. Bell had just bought a new automatic oscillograph reader that spring whose purpose was to transfer that data to punch cards so it could be plotted by another machine. The new device intimidated some of the old-timers, so they put Spivey to work learning how to use the thing, much as a parent today might ask a teenager to get a new computer running. Mostly, though, the new co-op ran errands on a bicycle from one part of the sprawling facility to another. He got to know the place pretty well.

The XV-3 left Fort Worth that summer. Bell shipped it out to NASA's Ames Research Center in Mountain View, California, about forty miles southeast of San Francisco, for three months of flight-testing. But the tiltrotor stuck in young Spivey's mind. He saw it and examined it again from time to time during his co-op quarters at Bell, studying every aspect of it. When he took his first aerodynamics course at Georgia Tech during his junior year, Spivey gave the first of probably two thousand or more tiltrotor briefings he would deliver over the next forty years. This was a class assignment. Everyone had to come up with some sort of briefing to give the class, a way of honing one of the key skills an aerospace engineer needs: the ability to explain a design to others and argue for it. "The premise was that the class didn't want to build a tiltrotor, they wanted to build a regular helicopter, and I built a briefing to convince them to build a tiltrotor," Spivey recalled. "I don't know that I convinced anybody, but I came up with the reasons why it was a good idea. I compared the helicopter with the tiltrotor, and I think I got a pretty good grade."

★ ★ ★

Spivey became infatuated a second time that summer. Her name was Janis Lee Glanzer. She was a year younger than he—to the day—and a sophomore at Texas Christian University. They met at a lakeside picnic for college singles organized by a Sunday school class at the First United Methodist Church, which Spivey had started attending partly as a way to meet people his age. There weren't any at Bell. The church was just around the corner from a boardinghouse he'd moved into after a week or so at the YMCA. Things started clicking between Spivey and Jan almost as soon as he introduced himself at the picnic. Soon they were double-dating a lot with another couple, Spivey's friend from First United, Howard Schenck (who pronounced his name "Skenk"), and his girlfriend. The two couples went to restaurants in Fort Worth's touristy Stockyards area, they saw movies, they went dancing, and as often as Spivey and Schenck could talk the girls into it, they went to the lake.

Howard was a good mechanic. He had put a Corvette car engine into a 14-foot runabout boat he owned and he and Spivey both loved to water-ski behind it. Howard's boat was so fast it was a little scary— it would beat you half to death as it bounced over the water—but they loved to take it out on Eagle Mountain Lake, a big body of water north-west of Fort Worth. One year, Spivey brought back from Georgia a prim-itive hang glider he had built out of bamboo poles, a piece of rayon cloth for a sail, a wooden, trapeze-style seat, and a handlebar to shift your cen-ter of gravity. He based it on a NASA design for space capsule recovery he'd read about. He and Schenck tied the glider to Howard's boat with a ski rope and rode it all around Eagle Mountain Lake. The rider would get airborne by sitting on the seat and skiing behind the boat until the glider took off. Usually, whoever was flying just trailed along thirty or forty feet high behind the boat and came down for a gentle landing on his skis as the boat slowed, but one day Spivey had an idea. He had just finished a course at Georgia Tech that led him to believe he could really fly his glider, so he rigged it with a car seat belt buckle to release the ski rope. Howard gunned his boat down the lake and Spivey kicked off his skis as he got airborne. He let the glider soar far higher than usual—which he later thought was stupid—then released it from the boat. When he did, the glider nosed over and dove toward the water at a speed Spivey was sure would kill him when it hit. He desperately tried to shift his weight back to move the center of gravity and come out of the dive. He succeeded just in time, buzzing the boat at what must have been 55 or 60 miles an hour. Somehow he managed to land in the water, uninjured but scared to death. It was a stark reminder of something he was already learning at Bell: experimental aircraft can be dangerous.

Spivey and Jan Glanzer married on August 22, 1964, a couple of months after he graduated from Georgia Tech, at her parents' church in Hous-ton. They moved into an apartment in Atlanta near Emory University, where Jan had begun work on a master's degree in Christian education. Spivey began work on a master's in aerospace engineering at Georgia Tech a couple of weeks later. To pay the bills, he also took a night job at Lockheed's aircraft plant in Marietta. He'd worked full-time there that past summer, doing data reduction on a project that was secret then but was later seen in the John Wayne movie *The Green Berets*, the James Bond movie *Thunderball*, and a couple of TV shows. It was called the "Fulton Pickup System."

The Fulton Pickup System is a way for a fixed-wing plane to rescue a human being, such as a pilot downed behind enemy lines, without landing. It works this way: the plane doing the pickup drops the stranded pilot a kit containing a big balloon, a canister of helium, a flight suit with a special buckle on it, and 500 feet of nylon cord. The pilot dons the suit, attaches one end of the nylon cord to the special buckle and the other to the balloon, fills the balloon with helium, and lets it rise. The rescue aircraft, seeing the balloon, swoops down and snags the nylon cord with a sort of fork or set of "horns" attached to its nose. As the plane flies on, the pilot is whisked into the air, dangling from the cord, which the aircraft crew snares with a sturdy, J-shaped hook. The crew attaches the cord to a winch, which pulls the rescued pilot into the aircraft as it flies. Depending on the speed of the plane, the rescuee might pull as many as 10 G's—ten times the force of gravity—as the horns jerk him into the air, sometimes swinging him up higher than the airplane's tail before he settles into a steady position behind it. Someone who did it once told Spivey it was an "E Ticket ride," definitely not for the fainthearted.

The CIA had used such a system a couple of times in the early 1960s with a plane that cruised at about 175 mph. Now Lockheed was trying it in various climates at various altitudes with a special operations version of its bigger, faster C-130 cargo plane. Spivey was part of a team that flew in a C-130 out to Yuma, Arizona, and then to Edwards Air Force Base in California to test the system in the desert. His job was to handle two life-sized dummies equipped with instrumentation including an oscillograph. He was to turn on the oscillograph about ten seconds before the C-130's hook hit the nylon cord—then run. The C-130 had a cable from its nose to its wingtips to keep the nylon cord from getting tangled in its four propellers. Even so, one day the pilot missed the cord with his hook and it slid down the wing and got wrapped up in his number-three propeller. The dummy was jerked into the air, the cord broke, and the dummy plunged to earth. Spivey saw it happen. He later heard about another time the system failed. The Navy was testing the system at sea and picked up a volunteer from a raft. The winch hauled him up and he got his hands on the sides of a hatch in the belly of the plane, ready to pull himself in, but the winch kept turning. The cord snapped. The volunteer fell into the ocean. He was never seen again.

★ ★ ★

Spivey and Jan decided to move back to Fort Worth after just one semester in Atlanta. He was working all the time, earning next to nothing and doing poorly in grad school. She was homesick. Jan transferred to a master's program at Texas Christian. Bell was happy to hire Spivey full-time as an aerodynamicist in engineering. He went back to work there in January 1965.

Business was booming at Bell. Since 1956, the year Larry Bell died of a heart attack, the company had been selling the Army its Huey helicopters, first as medevac aircraft, then as troop transports. In 1962, a board of officers and civilian experts had endorsed a plan for the Army to establish "air cavalry" units equipped with helicopters. A few months after Spivey went back to work at Bell, the 1st Battalion/7th Cavalry of the Army's newly redesignated 1st Cavalry Division (Airmobile) used Hueys to launch the first large-scale helicopter-borne air assault in history into Vietnam's Ia Drang Valley. Soon the Army was buying Hueys and an armed gunship version called the HueyCobra by the thousands. Bell was pumping them out the two big doors of its assembly plant like a Krispy Kreme store making doughnuts. Its test pilots could barely run ground tests on them and fly each one the required three hours before the Army sent in flocks of pilots—twenty-five at a time, some days—to fly the helicopters away. At its Vietnam-era peak, Bell was producing 150 Hueys a month for the Army and about fifty other kinds of helicopters as well. Aside from Da Nang, the massive U.S. military airfield in Vietnam, Bell's was perhaps the busiest heliport in the world.

One of Spivey's first assignments as an aerodynamicist—an engineer who analyzes forces imposed on an aircraft by the air, such as drag—was to work on the HueyCobra gunship. Within his first three years back at Bell, Spivey came up with a rotor tip design for the HueyCobra so good he was able to patent it. He swept the tip of the blade into a shape that retarded the onset of "compressibility," an aerodynamic phenomenon that limits a helicopter's speed. Compressibility also causes the loud "whump, whump, whump" noise characteristic of some helicopters, such as early models of the Huey. Spivey's design was called the "Whisper Tip" because it reduced the rotor blade's noise.

Spivey was soon regarded as a rotor expert at Bell, though his calculations didn't always come out right, even on the Whisper Tip. Bart Kelley and others in management were keenly interested in equipping the HueyCobra with a quieter blade because the prototype was unbelievably loud—a bad characteristic for a combat aircraft. Early on, Spivey thought he had it figured out, so he had the shop fabricate a rotor based on his calculations and install it on the HueyCobra prototype. One day a test pilot took off in the machine and flew out toward the horizon. Pilots, engineers, and others gathered on the edge of the heliport in anticipation. Kelley even came out. Dorman Cannon, a longtime Bell test pilot, couldn't help laughing when he remembered how Spivey stood out on the ramp with his bosses nearby, waiting for his moment of triumph. The machine flew south out of eyesight and earshot, but when it turned to come back, you could hear it before you could see it. It was even louder than the standard blade. Kelley turned on his heels and went back to his office without a word. For years afterward, even after Spivey succeeded in designing a true Whisper Tip blade, the test pilots called him "Whisper Dick."

The test pilots liked to tease Spivey. He was always bugging them to test some new rotor design, which meant juggling their schedules. A lot of other people at Bell ribbed him a lot, too, because of the way he dressed. Spivey was the company flower child. Not that he was a hippie. He didn't smoke dope or anything like that. In 1968 and '72 he voted for Nixon. But as the Age of Aquarius dawned in the '60s, Spivey awoke to it. He started showing up at work in plaid bell bottoms, blindingly loud sport coats, and wide ties in the godawfulest patterns you ever saw. (He didn't let on that his mother was making some of the ties for him.) He drove a snazzy little red convertible Karmann Ghia, Volkswagen's version of a sports car, until he totaled it in front of the plant one day. He was only in his twenties, but his naturally red hair was thinning, and what was left, he wore long. As the disco era began, Spivey got into that, too. He started showing up to work in white shoes and leisure suits. One of his favorites was rose pink—pinker than his skin. But most people at Bell liked Spivey, even if he was a bit of a free spirit. He always had a smile on his face and a kind word on his lips. He was easy to get along with.

★ ★ ★

One day in 1971, Spivey's boss, Jack Buyers, called him into his office.

"Ted Hoffmann wants you to move over and work for him in marketing," Buyers said. Hoffmann was one of Bell's top military marketers. Spivey was startled. He was also intrigued. He didn't know a lot about how Bell sold its helicopters, but he'd worked with its marketers as they'd tried to interest the Army in a new helicopter he'd helped engineer. The marketers would go talk to Army officials, then come back and give the engineers ideas about what might sell. Spivey also had spent time with some of Bell's marketers at trade shows and the annual American Helicopter Society convention. He liked them. They seemed to have interesting jobs.

"What do you think I should do?" Spivey asked. Buyers told him the move might be good for his career. Management liked people to work in more than one department, to broaden their perspective. Marketing was being reorganized and needed somebody with the technical expertise to pursue research and development contracts. Spivey could work there a while, then move back to engineering with a better chance of getting a promotion in the future. "Marketing is strange, but you'll learn an awful lot about the business of the company," Buyers said.

The vice president for military marketing, Cliff Kalista, told Spivey he'd seen him deliver talks at American Helicopter Society conventions and liked his briefing style. Kalista also told him, only half jokingly, that he was especially impressed with how at conventions Spivey was "one of only two people who were still awake at one in the morning in the hospitality suite," where alcohol flowed freely. Spivey knew what Kalista was saying: "You're a party animal and therefore you fit into the Marketing Department."

Spivey decided to do it.

Soon he moved from the somewhat spartan, tile-floored offices in Engineering, where desks were crammed together so tightly engineers had to stand to let each other by, into the carpeted offices of Marketing. The decor was nicer in Marketing because military officers and corporate executives—potential customers—often came to call.

Spivey's new title was "Sales Engineer." Like other defense contractors, Bell avoided the term *salesman*. The military and NASA didn't like the idea they were being "sold" anything. Most companies even shied away from the term *marketer*, which to some people implied a greasy salesman telling lies. "NASA hates marketing guys; they like to deal with engineers," Spivey observed. Eventually, like other defense contractors, Bell dropped the term *marketer* altogether. Marketers were given titles such as "Director, Business Development" or "Manager, Military Applications."

Bell had three marketing divisions: International, Commercial, and Military. The military division's ten or twelve marketers had a team system. "Sales engineers" like Spivey, who could explain the technical aspects of Bell's aircraft, teamed with "applications engineers." The latter weren't necessarily trained engineers; they were former military officers, usually pilots, who knew the armed forces and their strategies and tactics. Most importantly, the applications engineers had contacts in the services, in the Pentagon, at military bases, and in the fleet. They could call up a guy they had served with, swap war stories, ask about the wife and kids, find out what the troops thought they needed and what the brass was thinking about buying. The applications engineer's job was to "kick down the door" so the sales engineer could pitch a product to The Customer, as defense contractors call the military. But that was just part of it.

Selling the military an aircraft or a major weapons system isn't like selling a car. It's more a courtship or a seduction than a sale. A defense company such as Bell won't build a military aircraft on speculation, the way Ford builds sedans. But it will spend its own money to develop a concept for a new aircraft or an improved model of an existing one, designed to suit some presumed future military need, and try to get the services interested in developing it. Company engineers will do a "predesign study" including drawings of the configuration—where the engines go, things like that—and compile charts of engineering data to show what, in theory, the craft would be able to do. Marketers will take the study and produce briefings showing how the theoretical aircraft would perform in specific military missions. Then they take it on the road. They show it to military officers and relevant Defense Department civilians. The marketers carefully note their reactions, pro and con. Some might think the aircraft should carry more troops or more fuel, be armed with more or different weapons, or fly higher or farther than the engineers were thinking. If the concept isn't just right—and it never is—the marketers go home and huddle with the engineers to tweak the design, trying to tailor the concept to what the military seems to want and Congress will buy. "They want this; can you do that?" the marketers might ask the engineers. The engineers modify the design, then the marketers take it back out and brief it again and come back with still more suggestions. This can go on for years.

"Marketing is the concept of exploring for needs and developing a response for that," offered Phil Norwine, a former Navy helicopter pilot who spent thirty-five years marketing for Bell and at one time was Dick Spivey's boss. "You have to find the needs or develop the needs or develop a response that they [the military] haven't thought about." Norwine liked to start with the lower ranks in the field and then work his way up through captains, majors, then lieutenant colonels in command of squadrons, asking them what they needed in a new aircraft or modifications to old ones. Then he would use that information. "You want to work at the lower level and find out what the troops really want, then you tell the general," Norwine explained. Ideally, he added, when you brief a colonel or a general, "you come in with an idea that you know he needs, an idea that would get him a promotion." Starting at the lower levels also has another advantage, Norwine said: "A guy that might be a major this year in a few years might be a general."

Along the way, the marketers brief members of Congress and their aides—especially the staffs of the committees that write the defense budget. The goal is to be able to tell that colonel or general, when the timing is right, that if he's interested in this new aircraft, there's support for it in Congress, which has to provide the money. By the time the Pentagon solicits bids for a contract to actually build the thing, the company hopes its concept is already the favorite. The job of the sales engineers and applications engineers was to scheme and plot and travel together to reach that goal.

The new job was a challenge, though Spivey felt he had the right personality for it. He made friends easily. He was a good talker. Better yet, he was a good listener. He already knew how to give an engineering briefing, and Ted Hoffman taught him a lot about how to boil things down so he could brief a busy military officer or bureaucrat in the least possible time. Never put more than three bullets on a chart. Keep the number of words on your Vu-Graph slides—PowerPoint didn't exist back then—to a minimum. No sentences, just a few phrases to remind you what you want to say. Use as many pictures as possible; they'll remember pictures, they won't remember words. Tell them what they're looking at in the pictures. Keep It Simple Stupid. And prepare an "elevator briefing," a pitch you can make between the first and third floors. If you see a guy you want to reach in a Pentagon hallway, know the one most important thing you're going to tell him before he gets away.

Spivey knew Bell's products and could explain them, but he had a lot to learn about The Customer. As a Georgia Tech student, he'd been in Air Force ROTC, but he hadn't served in the military. The Vietnam War was escalating when he graduated, but Bell got him a draft deferment as an essential defense industry employee. What he knew about the military he'd learned on the job. Now he spent a lot of time reading *Aviation Week, Sea Power, Army Times, Proceedings* and other military journals to learn what the services were buying, what aircraft and weapons they might want in the future, how military strategy and tactics were changing, what Congress was doing to the defense budget. He got the applications engineers—there was at least one for each arm of the military—to tutor him in how the services were organized, what weapons they had, and how they used them, especially aircraft. He turned his thoughts from gauging the air pressure distribution on airfoils to learning who was who in the intricate bureaucracy of the military "systems commands," which handled research and development contracts.

The biggest change in Spivey's life came in how much he traveled. His wife, Jan, wasn't thrilled with that. She was left at home with their two young sons. Brett was three when Spivey became a marketer, and Eric was born that same year. As an engineer, Spivey had made one or two trips a year to wind tunnels in California or on Long Island and maybe to a convention or two, but mostly he'd been home at night. Now he was on the road two or three times a month for several days, flying up to Washington, to Wright-Patterson Air Force Base in Dayton, Ohio, or to the Army aviation command in St. Louis. Applications engineers arranged to get him onto Army and Marine Corps bases to meet people and observe military exercises. They got him out on Navy aircraft carriers and amphibious assault ships used by the Marines. Spivey loved that stuff. He was fascinated by the technology, especially out on the ships, and seeing the military use it was a thrill.

Then there were the big aerospace trade fairs, the Paris Air Show in odd-numbered years and the Farnborough International Airshow near London in even-numbered ones. Those were a must for aircraft manufacturers and their marketers. The shows were a chance to show off products to a lot of top people in a week's time. Bell and other companies always put their aircraft on display, stationed marketers at indoor booths offering brochures and briefings, and set up temporary two-story "chalets" along the flight line with outside decks. They stocked their chalets with fine wines and first-class chefs. This allowed their guests—generals and admirals from nearly every military in the world, U.S. congressmen and senators, Arab kings and other potentates—to dine and drink in comfort while they watched the companies' aircraft perform eye-popping aerobatic displays.

One of Spivey's most memorable trips abroad, though, was to Iran when it was ruled by the pro-American dictator Shah Mohammed Reza Pahlavi. At the 1971 Paris Air Show, the Shah's deputy minister of war for armaments, Lieutenant General Hassan Toufanian, visited Bell's chalet and chatted up some of Bell's top executives about buying their helicopters for Iran's military. In August 1972, Spivey was among a team of forty engineers, marketers, test pilots, and executives who went to Iran to demonstrate the HueyCobra and another Huey-derivative called the 214 Super Huey. Spivey had worked for three years as a top engineer on the 214, which Bell hoped to sell the U.S. Army as it retired its older Hueys. But by the time the 214 was flying in 1971, the Army had decided to hold a competition for a new helicopter to replace the Huey.

The Bell team worked months to get ready for the trip. Toufanian had promised Bell's new president, Jim Atkins, that if his helicopters did well in Iran's hot climate, the Shah would buy a lot of them. For four weeks, the Bell team's test pilots and top Iranian officials flew the 214 and a Cobra in Iran's broiling deserts, the thin air of its mountains, and off Kharg Island in the Persian Gulf. One day an Iranian army two-star, Major General Manuchehr Khosrowdad, flew a 214 out in the desert and shot up a series of targets with the gunship. Spivey was there when Khosrowdad came back from his flight and swaggered into a bar in the hotel where the Bell team was staying. "He was so elated he took his gun out of his holster and threw it down the bar—a loaded gun—threw it down the bar and hollered, 'Bartender, I'm buying drinks for all these sons of bitches,'" Spivey recalled. "That fuckin' gun was rollin' down the bar. Scared the shit out of me, you know? And he was just like he was a fifth-grader."

When the Bell team got back to Texas in September, the Shah had ordered 287 Super Hueys and 202 Cobras—a deal Fort Worth's increasingly powerful congressman, Jim Wright, would announce in December—and Spivey had gone bald. "I went from a full head of hair to what I've got the year that I went to Iran," Spivey said, gently rubbing the pink skin on top of his head where red hair once grew. "I don't know how, but it happened in a year. Just, poof!" Not long after he got back to Fort Worth, he bought a cheap red wig, just as a lark, and wore it to the office one day. The hair was dark red and shaped like a pageboy haircut, the Prince Valiant look. Most of his colleagues smirked or even laughed at it. Bart Kelley, though, who was also bald, said, "Dick, if I were young again, I would do the same thing." Spivey revered Kelley. If the vice president for engineering thought the wig was okay, that made it cool. For years afterward, Spivey wore a red wig all the time. He bought a new one now and then as styles changed and because, like hats, the wigs made his head perspire. They got pretty sticky and stinky after a while. People got used to Spivey's wigs, but friends wished Dick would just learn to live with being bald.

On Thanksgiving Day after his return from Iran, while he and Jan and their boys were visiting her parents in Houston, Spivey got a call from Phil Norwine wanting to know how soon he could come back to Fort Worth. He was needed for an important new project, Norwine said. In 1968, Bell's second XV-3 tiltrotor had been destroyed when both wingtip pylons simply blew off during a wind tunnel test at NASA's Ames Research Center in California. The cause proved to be a fatigue crack and some loose rivets in the left wing. Since then, as Spivey knew, a tiny team of engineers under Ken Wernicke had been designing a new experimental tiltrotor. Spivey had helped design its fuselage and rotor before he left engineering. The previous year, tiltrotor guru Bob Lichten had been killed when his car went off the road while he drove home from a Texas Civil Liberties Union meeting in Austin. Troy Gaffey and others on Wernicke's team had feared Bell might drop its tiltrotor research after Lichten's death, but NASA's interest had actually increased in the past year. The agency had opened a tiltrotor project of its own and, in a joint program with the Army, was going to offer a contract to build two tiltrotors to the company that submitted the best design. Boeing Vertol, the helicopter division of Boeing Company, was the competition. Spivey was wanted to help write Bell's proposal. If Bell won the deal, Norwine added, Spivey would become Bell's chief tiltrotor marketer.

Spivey liked that idea. He liked it a lot. He thought about the tiltrotor all the time. He thought it was a dream machine. He thought it was Bell's future. Now it looked like it could be his, too.

★ ★ ★

Bell won NASA's tiltrotor design competition, beating out Boeing Vertol, which had built a tilt-wing aircraft once but never a tiltrotor. In 1973, NASA and the Army gave Bell a $26,415,000 contract to build two copies of the sleek little two-seat tiltrotor the company had designed, which except for its rotors looked a lot like an executive jet. NASA designated it the XV-15. Spivey and Bell's tiltrotor engineers were elated. Now Bell was going to build an aircraft that would prove the tiltrotor wasn't just a pipe dream, another convertiplane that looked good on paper but was bad in the air. Everyone knew, though, that this was just a small first step toward establishing the tiltrotor as a new way to fly, and thus as a lucrative new product for Bell. If the tiltrotor was going to catch on, Bell needed to sell one of some sort to the military, a customer willing to take risks on new technology, a source of "patient capital."

From now on, Spivey's job was to promote the tiltrotor concept and try to get Bell a production contract with the military. For quite a while, though, he and his marketing colleagues were slowed by the fact that they didn't have a real tiltrotor to show. It took Bell four years to get the XV-15 flying. Engineers had to wrestle through some tough manufacturing problems and conduct hundreds of hours of wind tunnel and other tests on models and parts before they could build the XV-15. In the meantime, Spivey and others on Bell's military marketing team tried to get the Air Force, Navy, and Marine Corps interested in tiltrotors, too.

Spivey flew to Washington two or three times a month in those years, sometimes with one of Bell's "applications engineers," to talk tiltrotor in the Pentagon, often in a trio with Bell's XV-15 program manager, Tommy H. Thomason, and Rodney Wernicke, who like his twin brother Ken was a tiltrotor engineer. Spivey and his traveling companions went to every military base and Navy ship they could get aboard. They went to Capitol Hill regularly to see congressional aides and members. They attended American Helicopter Society meetings to give tiltrotor briefings. They went to the annual Washington conventions of the major nonprofit groups that back the armed forces—the Association of the United States Army, the Air Force Association, the Navy League, and the Marine Corps Association. They gave hundreds of briefings and answered thousands of questions. The idea they tried to pound home most, though, was simple: a tiltrotor would take off and land like a helicopter but fly twice as fast and at least twice as far. Twice as fast and twice as far. *Twice as fast and twice as far.*

Until the XV-15 was in the air, all they could show people were artist conceptions of other tiltrotors Bell's engineers had conceived, or illustrations of how, in theory, tiltrotors might perform old or new military missions. The idea, consequently, was slow to gain traction in the Pentagon. Shortly after NASA and the Army gave Bell its XV-15 contract, the company offered the Navy two for the bargain price of $15 million as antisubmarine warfare planes. Even at that price, the admirals didn't bite. The Navy's pride were its big-deck aircraft carriers, symbols of American power that presidents had used for decades as intimidating diplomatic tools and potent weapons of war. The carrier faction wasn't much interested in small little aircraft that didn't need big decks to land and take off.

The Air Force wasn't much interested, either. Its priorities were its jet fighters and strategic bombers, though some in the Air Force showed strong interest in the idea of using tiltrotors to rescue pilots downed behind enemy lines or at sea. Marine Corps officers Spivey talked to often were intrigued, but their service had the smallest aviation budget of all. Nor was it clear what they would do with a tiltrotor as small as the XV-15, though Spivey offered the idea of a tiltrotor gunship that size.

Spivey quickly learned that selling a dream, no matter how much you believed in it, was a lot like being a missionary. You had to make one convert at a time, and you had to have a lot of faith. The more Spivey preached the tiltrotor gospel, the more faith and fervor he put into his mission, the more his own faith in the dream machine grew.

Virginia Copeland, who became his assistant twenty years later, joined Bell's marketing department in 1974. The XV-15 wouldn't fly for another three years, and hanging over Spivey's desk from a string attached to the ceiling was a model of it someone had hung to rib him. If you turned a floor fan on and aimed it up, you could make the little model sway in the air. Every now and then, Spivey would call out, "Come on, look at this! Someday that thing is going to fly! Someday you're going to see that in the air!" Spivey's enthusiasm wasn't limited to the XV-15. "If it tilted its rotor, he loved it," Copeland thought. Spivey really believed tiltrotors were going to change the world. "He couldn't

figure out why everybody else couldn't see this," she said, and he was
determined to make them. "He took the time to figure out who needed
to know, and then he went and sought them out and convinced them
that his dream was right," Copeland said, obviously exaggerating his
success. Before he went, "He would spend hours making a briefing zing.
He'd make it so it'd catch the eye, and put as much pizzazz as he could
into it."

Those were the days before e-mail or even faxes. If you wanted someone to see something, you had to go show it to them, so Spivey was on
the road a lot. All the time, or so it seemed to his wife, Jan. For a few
years, she endured Dick's absences, but they wore on their marriage.
More and more, she thought Dick was married to his job, and mainly in
love with the tiltrotor. She and Dick were less and less happy when they
were together. Spivey began to think about divorce, though he'd been
raised to regard it as wrong. Even thinking about it felt like going against
God. After a while, though, he had to admit to himself that his passion
for Jan had faded away. They separated in February 1978. Their divorce
became final in July.

Spivey's only passion now was the tiltrotor.

CHAPTER THREE

THE CUSTOMER

Each November 10, wherever two or more Marines are together, they buy, bake, or requisition a cake to enact a ritual instituted in 1921 by one of the Marine Corps' most revered commandants, John A. Lejeune. The rite is performed around the world at gala Marine Corps Birthday Balls, where officers and enlisted Marines wear elegant, dark blue dress uniforms. Marines clad in jungle or desert camouflage also carry it out more simply wherever they find themselves: aboard an amphibious assault ship off the African coast, behind sandbag and concrete walls at a forward operating base in Iraq, in a lonely observation post overlooking Korea's demilitarized zone. At its most formal, the ritual unfolds this way: The highest-ranking Marine present cuts a piece of the cake using a Mameluke sword, a ceremonial blade with cross hilt and ivory grip modeled on weapons used by Ottoman warriors. The sword is a remembrance of victories the Marines won in 1804 against the Barbary pirates on the north coast of Africa, commemorated in the famous line in the Marine Corps Hymn "to the shores of Tripoli." The first piece of cake cut with the sword goes to the guest of honor. The host then cuts a second piece and gives it to the oldest Marine present, often a retiree, whose name, age, and date of enlistment are read out by a narrator. There is no such thing as an "ex-Marine," they say: "Once a Marine, always a Marine." The oldest Marine, sometimes infirm and in a wheelchair, passes the cake to the youngest Marine present, usually a private just out of basic training. The youngest Marine's name, age, and date of enlistment are read out, eliciting howls from the old veterans in the crowd. The passing of the cake symbolizes the "passing of experience and knowledge from the old to the young of our Corps," explains the narrator in a standard cake-cutting script. Now a third piece is cut and given to the oldest Marine, "further emphasizing the fact that we care for our young Marines before we look to our own needs." The narrator pauses, then adds, "And so it must be."

The annual Marine Corps Birthday Ball in Washington is conducted with all the pomp of a royal wedding, hosted by the commandant and featuring the president of the United States as guest of honor some years. Bugles sound as the commandant and his guest lead a stately processional. The Marine Band plays "The Star-Spangled Banner" and "The Marines' Hymn" as four Marines ceremoniously roll in the birthday cake. All stand reverently as an adjutant reads General Lejeune's birthday message of 1921. Then the cake is cut.

An outside guest watching this ritual, usually conducted under subdued lighting and with all the reverence of Holy Communion, can feel like a jungle explorer who has stumbled onto natives performing a tribal rite. "The mystique of the Corps transcends individuals," wrote Victor H. Krulak in his book *First to Fight*. Krulak retired as a lieutenant general, a three-star. His son, Charles, became commandant. "The Corps is in a sense like a primitive tribe where each generation has its medicine men—keepers of the tribal mythology, protectors of the tribal customs, and guardians of the tribal standards," Victor Krulak wrote.

This cultivated tribal mentality—some prefer to call it "warrior culture"—stems from the Marine Corps' unique history. Today the Marine Corps is known as the toughest and most elite of America's armed services, the one that has fought and won many of the nation's bloodiest battles. For much of its first two hundred or so years, though, the other armed services treated the Corps like a bastard child. Created in 1775 to provide the Navy a landing force, keep order aboard ships, and fire down from the tops of masts onto enemy crews in sea battles, the Marine Corps has always been the smallest of America's armed forces. Today it numbers just over 200,000 officers and enlisted personnel. The Army has more than 530,000 active-duty members and the Navy and Air Force more than 300,000 each. Their budgets are also far larger. Yet from the Marine Corps' earliest days, Navy and Army leaders resented the Corps and coveted the money spent to maintain it. The Marines had to wrestle the other services politically every few years just to stay in existence. In 1830, President Andrew Jackson urged Congress to merge the Marine Corps into the Army. A similar proposal provoked hot debates in Congress during the Civil War. The Marines beat back such moves through a potent combination of glory in battle and crafty lobbying on Capitol Hill, and those victories entered their tribal mythology. The battles for survival also bred tribal unity—and a distinct Marine Corps paranoia.

Proposals to abolish the Marine Corps rose again with the advent of steel ships powered by steam around the turn of the twentieth century—no more firing down from masts on exposed enemy crews. The Marines decided they needed a new mission to justify their existence. They found it in amphibious warfare, which they made their specialty between World War I and World War II. They acquired landing craft known as "Higgins boats" and other amphibious warfare gear. They developed tactics that brought them glory in the Pacific during the island-hopping campaigns of World War II. Their reputation flourished. When five Marines and a Navy medical corpsman raised a U.S. flag on Mount Suribachi during the pitiless battle of Iwo Jima—in five weeks Marine casualties on the five-mile-long island totaled 25,581, including 738 Navy doctors and medics—Secretary of the Navy James V. Forrestal famously said that "the raising of that flag on Suribachi means a Marine Corps for the next five hundred years."

Barely eighteen months later, all that became ancient history. The U.S. military set off two atomic devices at Bikini Atoll in the Marshall Islands in July 1946 to gauge the new weapon's effects on ships and their equipment. Out of more than 90 surplus ships assembled for the test and anchored offshore, 16 were sunk and the rest were drenched in radioactive fallout. Commandant Alexander A. Vandegrift had sent Lieutenant General Roy S. Geiger to observe the Bikini tests. Geiger could see it would be suicide to mount a traditional amphibious assault in the age of the A-bomb "since our probable future enemy will be in possession of this weapon." He reported back that the Marines needed to do "a complete review and study of our concept of amphibious operations."

"The Marine Corps was in a quandary," remembered Thomas H. Miller, Jr., who retired as a lieutenant general in 1979 after four years running Marine Corps aviation. As a young captain, Tom Miller flew F4U-1 Corsair fighter planes in the Pacific during World War II with his best friend, John Glenn, the future astronaut and U.S. senator. In an amphibious landing World War II-style, ships carrying troops and their Higgins boats had to be brought near the beach, usually within a few thousand yards. "Well, if they get in that close to shore and you get enough ships assembled around there to protect them from submarines and air strikes, you've got a task force that can be wiped out by one atomic bomb," Miller observed.

This revelation came at an awkward time for the Marines, for in addition to the atomic bomb, in 1946 they were facing another new threat to their existence. His name was Harry S. Truman. He was president of the United States.

With Truman's backing, the War Department was proposing that Congress create a unified Department of Defense that would have little room for the Marine Corps. Until then, the Army had come under the War Department and the Navy and Marines under the separate Navy Department. The new Defense Department would oversee the Army, the Navy, and a newly independent Air Force, until then an arm of the Army. The Marines would be a mere element of the Navy, their commandant excluded from the Joint Chiefs of Staff. Alarmed at this prospect, Marine leaders were gearing up for battle on Capitol Hill when the Bikini tests vaporized one of their strongest arguments: their amphibious warfare prowess.

The Marines quickly formed a special board of three generals to consider the possibilities. Their answer was a new tactic called "vertical envelopment." No longer would Marines mount amphibious assaults primarily by splashing ashore in wave after wave of landing craft. Instead, they would stage from dispersed ships sailing over the horizon, twenty-five miles or more out to sea, leaping over enemy shore defenses in helicopters. In 1947, the Marines formed their first helicopter squadron, Marine Helicopter Experimental Squadron One, known as HMX-1, each letter and the numeral pronounced distinctly: "H-M-X-One." They bought two small Sikorsky helicopters big enough to carry a pilot and two combat-equipped troops. They started training pilots. They began rewriting their amphibious assault doctrine, the template for how to conduct such operations. They fell in love with the helicopter. "The Marine Corps just latched on to it and went hook, line, and sinker for it," Miller remembered.

The new doctrine, along with some fancy footwork on Capitol Hill, helped the Marines win their battle to remain a serious armed service. As Congress debated the National Security Act of 1947, which created the Defense Department, amendments drafted by Marine officers and slipped to friends in Congress found their way into the legislation. The new law specified that the Marines were to have their own air and ground forces "organized, trained and equipped" for "the seizure or defense of advanced naval bases and for the conduct of such land operations as may be essential to the prosecution of a naval campaign."

"Congress is, of course, what saved them," Miller said of the Marines. "They wrote into the law what's called Title 10. That has been our savior."

Truman later cemented the Marines' victory when Congress revisited the law in 1950. Irked by the Corps' lobbying, Democrat Truman wrote a scalding letter to one of his Republican congressional critics. "For your information, the Marine Corps is the Navy's police force and as long as I am President that is what it will remain," Truman wrote. "They have a propaganda machine that is almost equal to Stalin's."

His critic promptly put the letter into the Congressional Record. Marines were fighting and dying in Korea at the time and the letter ignited a political firestorm. The president ended up publicly apologizing to the Marine Corps.

★ ★ ★

The helicopter wasn't advanced enough by the Korean War for the Marines to truly use it for "vertical envelopment," though they tried some aerial assaults. It would take another decade or more, until the Vietnam War, for helicopters to become sturdy and reliable and numerous enough to carry serious numbers of troops into battle. Mainly they used helicopters to haul supplies, lay communications wires, and evacuate the wounded or pilots who had been shot down. But the Marines became the helicopter's biggest user among the U.S. armed services. When the conflict ended, the Corps had more helicopters and more trained pilots per capita than any other military service in the world.

By the end of that war, Tom Miller recalled, "The helicopter had now proved itself and the Marine Corps could see its way." The helicopter would allow the Marines to launch amphibious assaults from "ships widely separated and further off the shore than ten or fifteen miles," Miller explained. "That's why it was so important to the Marine Corps, because it enabled them to continue amphibious landings into a hostile shore. That's their reason for existence." The Korean experience, though, left the Marines hungry for more speed. In 1954, an Army pilot had set a new world helicopter speed record of 156 miles per hour. That wasn't enough for the Marines.

In January 1956, an article in the inaugural issue of the *Journal of the*

American Helicopter Society noted that the Marine Corps "has shown as much interest as other branches of the armed services in the possibilities of combining the advantages of rotary-wing and fixed-wing flight in some type of convertiplane. . . . A speed of better than 200 knots [230 mph] is considered a requisite for the Marine assault aircraft of the next decade."

By then, the military services had begun their experiments with such aircraft, but the convertiplane was still just a dream machine. In the 1960s, like the Army and Navy, the Marines bought more and more helicopters, especially during the Vietnam War. They bought small Huey utility birds and agile Cobra helicopter gunships from Bell. They bought tandem-rotor CH-46 Sea Knights from Boeing Vertol of Philadelphia to carry troops and do other "medium-lift" missions. They bought massive twin-engine CH-53 Sea Stallions from Sikorsky to haul heavy cargo and equipment. None could cruise at anywhere near 200 knots. But the idea of getting a rotary-wing aircraft that could didn't go away.

One Marine officer interested in convertiplanes was Keith McCutcheon, a pioneer in helicopter tactics. As a lieutenant colonel, McCutcheon commanded HMX-1 in its early days and led a helicopter squadron in the Korean War. As a two-star general in the late 1960s, he ran Marine Corps aviation. Tom Miller was a colonel on McCutcheon's staff and revered him. "McCutcheon used to say, 'Don't get enamored with helicopters, now. They're very limited in speed and range,'" Miller told me shortly before he passed away in 2007. "'It's an interim vehicle.' That used to be his word, 'It's an interim aircraft.' He kept saying, 'We've got to find something [faster]. We can't go into the twenty-first century with no better performance than a helicopter carrying our troops.'"

One of Miller's assignments was to study how the Marines should replace their CH-46 Sea Knight assault helicopters. The CH-46 was a tandem-rotor that cruised at about 125 miles an hour. Its main mission was to haul up to eighteen Marines at a time to the beach in amphibious assaults launched from fifty miles or less offshore and get back to the ship. That was roughly the limit of the CH-46's endurance with that kind of payload. Its official nickname was "Sea Knight," but because it made short hops to shore from the lily pad of an amphibious assault ship, Marines affectionately called the CH-46 the "Frog"—often spelled "Phrog," either to be cute or to distinguish it from nature's amphibian. During the Vietnam War, the Marines had bought 600 Sea Knights to carry troops and supplies into battle. As part of his study in the late 1960s, Miller wrote up requirements for a new helicopter, a list of what it would need to be able to do. Miller didn't know that much about helicopters—he was a fighter pilot by trade—so he decided the Marine Corps' next troop transport should cruise at 200 knots. He based that on his experience in Vietnam, where he'd seen small patrols of Marines get into firefights with bigger forces and have to wait hours for helicopters to bring reinforcements or evacuate them. Miller thought the Marines needed aircraft that could get troops to a fight within thirty minutes, the same time goal the Corps had for responding to calls from ground troops for fighter-bomber attacks on enemy forces. Helicopter company marketers he talked it over with told Miller he was dreaming. "I didn't know that they couldn't reach two hundred knots at the time, but they told me that I was out of my mind because they couldn't make a helicopter that would cruise at two hundred," Miller said.

By 1975, Miller was a lieutenant general and, like his mentor McCutcheon before him, deputy chief of staff for aviation, in charge of all Marine Corps aircraft matters. Nearly a decade after he'd started working on the problem, the Marines were still trying to figure out how to replace their Sea Knight troop transports, and now the issue was taking on more urgency. In Vietnam, the Marines hadn't relied on amphibious assault. They had fought much like the Army, though armed far more lightly. Their last major amphibious landing under fire had been in 1950 at Inchon, Korea. No one was openly advocating the abolition of the Marine Corps just yet, but with the Vietnam War over, the Soviet Union throwing its weight around, and the American public soured on the idea of U.S. military intervention in "small wars" overseas, some defense experts in Congress and think tanks were arguing that the Corps had to change. It should either be cut way down in size, they argued, or start spending its money on heavy weapons so it could fight the Soviet-led Warsaw Pact in Europe, if that day came. Once again, the Marines were searching for a way to preserve their status as the nation's "power projection" force, the one presidents would turn to first in a crisis—"First to Fight," as one of their slogans put it. Finding a way to get Marines into battle faster than a Phrog could carry them would help, Miller reasoned.

One day in 1978 one of his subordinates showed Miller a film of an experimental Canadian aircraft called the CL-84, a propeller plane that could take off vertically by tilting its whole wing upward. The film showed the tilt-wing CL-84 operating off an amphibious landing ship and doing almost 200 knots as it flew like an airplane. Miller and his staff were intrigued. Miller was already a believer in VTOL aircraft, as people were calling convertiplanes by now. Back in 1968, when he was still a colonel working for General McCutcheon, Miller had been the first Marine to fly a British-made jet fighter, the Harrier, that could take off and land vertically by swiveling exhaust nozzles under its wings downward. The Marines started buying Harriers in 1971, seeing the plane as a way to finally reach their goal of providing close air support to troops within thirty minutes of getting a call. The "jump jet" could take off from a road or even a clearing in the jungle, which meant it could be based just back of the front lines. Miller also had never forgotten his mentor McCutcheon's admonition that the helicopter was just an "interim aircraft." The Canadian tilt-wing he was seeing in the film didn't look just right, and it was incredibly noisy, but if the Marines only had a troop transport that could take off and land vertically, yet fly as fast as this tilt-wing could, getting reinforcements into battle within thirty minutes might be possible—and the debate about amphibious assault might be over.

"I asked my staff to check into what did we have in this country that was anywhere close," Miller recalled. "Well, the answer came back, 'The XV-15.'"

The little experimental tiltrotor Bell had built for NASA and the Army had just starting flying the previous year, but all those briefings and meetings Dick Spivey and Bell's other marketers had done in the past few years— *"Twice as fast and twice as far"*—were beginning to have their intended effect. Word of the tiltrotor was getting to the right places.

Before long, a wrenching event would provide a vivid new argument for their sales pitch and dramatically expand the ranks of the converts.

★ ★ ★

A military helicopter is a relatively slow and extremely noisy way to fly. At times, it can be a treacherous way to travel as well. Especially at low altitude in hostile territory. Especially at night without lights. Especially through desert dust and unfamiliar canyons. That was where Marine Major James H. Schaefer and fifteen other handpicked U.S. military pilots and copilots found themselves the night of Thursday, April 24,

1980. They were at the controls of eight RH-53D Sea Stallions, a Navy variant of the Sikorsky CH-53 built for minesweeping and equipped with extra fuel tanks. They were churning through a navigator's nightmare of darkness and dust above Islamic revolutionary Ayatollah Khomeini's Iran. They were also flying under radio silence, and at gut-wrenchingly low altitudes to avoid radar detection.

The Sea Stallions were a crucial element in Operation Eagle Claw, an audacious secret mission of Rubik's Cube complexity. The mission's goal was to rescue fifty-three Americans held hostage in Iran over the previous five and a half months, since Islamic radicals had seized the 27-acre U.S. Embassy compound in Tehran on November 4, 1979. Without helicopters, Eagle Claw's planners had decided, there was no good way to get the 118 Delta Force commandos and other troops chosen for the mission close enough to the Iranian capital to infiltrate the city of five million, rush the embassy, overpower the estimated 200 guards, and free the hostages. Without helicopters, there would be no good way to get the hostages and commandos out of Tehran. The choppers were to pick them up there and take them to Manzariyeh, thirty-five miles south. There, a detachment of U.S. Army Rangers was to descend upon an airfield and take it over so Air Force C-141 Starlifter cargo planes could swoop in and spirit everyone away to safety.

If the helicopters were essential, Delta Force's founder and commander, Army Colonel Charles Beckwith, also deemed them one of the riskiest elements of the plan. Beckwith didn't like helicopters. He thought they were all ugly. He'd been shot down in helicopters three times in Vietnam. He came out of that war believing that while choppers often saved lives, they could be undependable as well. A helicopter has thousands of moving parts, and when the engines are roaring and the rotors are whirling at several hundred miles an hour, those parts and the liquids that keep them working—oil, grease, and hydraulic fluid—vibrate constantly. In helicopters of that era, the shaking often caused tubes and hydraulic seals to spring leaks or led mechanical parts to malfunction. If helicopters were needed for a mission, prudent military planners often asked for extras in case of breakdowns. Operation Eagle Claw's intricate choreography demanded six Sea Stallions at minimum to succeed, which was why eight were in the air as the mission began. Yet even with that insurance, the helicopters would prove the operation's undoing.

The Sea Stallion is one of the most muscular choppers in the U.S. military inventory. It can carry thirty people with a maximum load of fuel and forty or fifty if its tanks aren't full. Its massive, six-bladed titanium and fiberglass rotors are more than 72 feet in diameter, about a fourth as long as a football field. They can lift tons of people and cargo. The Sea Stallions, however, would be unable to make the 900 miles from an aircraft carrier deck in the Gulf of Oman to Tehran without refueling. For this reason, the mission template for the first night called for Schaefer and his fellow pilots to fly to a rendezvous in the desert 265 miles southeast of Tehran. To do so, they would have to navigate through the darkness wearing eye-straining, first-generation night-vision goggles that distorted their depth perception. At the desert landing zone, they would meet six Air Force C-130 cargo planes carrying Delta Force, a company of U.S. Army Rangers, and giant rubber bladders of aviation fuel. The helicopters were to refuel from the bladders in the C-130s, then load the troops and fly them to a "hide site" sixty-five miles southeast of Tehran. The choppers would then take off again and fly another fifteen miles to hide themselves through the next day in the hills near Garmsar, a village sixty miles southeast of Tehran. On the second night of the mission, the assault force would drive into Tehran on trucks, bust into the embassy, and free the hostages. The troops would wear Levi's, dark blue Navy watch caps, and field jackets dyed black. They would uncover a taped-over U.S. flag patch on their sleeves when they reached the embassy.

When the troops had freed the hostages, the Sea Stallions—painted in Iranian army colors—would fly into the city. One or two would land near the embassy, if no obstructions prevented it, or on the field of a soccer stadium across the street. A third would set down near the Foreign Ministry building, where other hostages would be freed by a separate team of Army Special Forces troops. The helicopters would then transport everyone to the airfield at Manzariyeh, where all involved would board the C-141s and fly out of Iran. Operation Eagle Claw's planners dubbed the first night refueling site "Desert One."

Schaefer's helicopter was the first to land at Desert One, where Beckwith, his troops, and the crews of the Air Force cargo planes had arrived more than an hour earlier and were waiting impatiently. Everything depended on completing the mission's initial stage in what military planners call "one period of darkness," meaning after sunset one day and before dawn the next. They were already behind schedule.

When Schaefer climbed out of his Sea Stallion and walked around front to take a leak in the sand after his five-hour flight, Beckwith rushed over, expecting to find Marine Lieutenant Colonel Ed Seiffert, the commanding officer for the eight Sea Stallions. He was surprised to see Schaefer—and even more surprised at Schaefer's state of mind. Beckwith wrote three years later in his book *Delta Force* that he told Schaefer he was glad to see him. As Beckwith reported it, Schaefer just looked at him and replied, "It's been a hell of a trip." Then, according to Beckwith, Schaefer uttered "words to the effect that if we had any sense we would move the helos out into the desert and load everyone on the C-130s and go home." With that, Schaefer got back into his RH-53D.

Schaefer recalled the scene differently.

Beckwith greeted him by growling, "Where the hell is everybody?" Schaefer told me. "And I said, 'It's been a hell of a night.' I said, 'They're either going to be here or they're on the side of a mountain.' That's what I said."

The flight to Desert One from the nuclear aircraft carrier USS *Nimitz* had been wretched. Less than 200 miles into Iran, one of the eight Sea Stallions had broken down with a cracked rotor blade and been abandoned, the crew climbing aboard another that landed to help. Then the choppers had run into what Iranians call *haboobs*—clouds of powdery white sand suspended in the air for miles by shifts in the atmospheric pressure above the desert floor. The talcum-like dust from the *haboobs* had penetrated every nook and cranny of the aircraft, seeping into the engines, the cockpits, and the thousands of moving parts and raising the temperature inside the machines. In the murk of the *haboobs* and under orders to stay off the radio, the pilots had lost track of one another. Their formation had fallen apart and they had lost valuable time trying to get back together. After the loss of the first helicopter, the cockpit warning lights for various pieces of equipment in a second had lit up and its pilot had turned back to the *Nimitz* while the others struggled on. These pilots had been chosen for their moxie and coolness under fire, but by the time those remaining got to Desert One, after hours of flying nearly blind in the heat and the haze and the vertigo induced by the night-vision goggles, they were frazzled and exhausted. To make matters worse, as Schaefer made a rolling landing at Desert One, his front landing gear hit a rut in the sand and turned sideways, knocking the tires off their rims and deflating them. He could no longer taxi. Instead, he would need to move his Sea Stallion around the rendezvous site by using its rotor to lift the giant's nose gear off the ground.

The six choppers necessary to continue the mission had made it to the rendezvous point, but Beckwith would write that he found Schaefer and another of the pilots "pretty well shattered," and that shocked him.

Beckwith was so shocked because he knew Jim Schaefer was one of the best and ballsiest helicopter pilots in the Marine Corps. Born in Washington, D.C., and raised in the San Fernando Valley of California, Schaefer had joined the Corps in 1966, after graduating from St. Martin's College in Olympia, Washington. He wanted to fly jets, and he had the "right stuff," as test pilots called it. He got his wings in 1968 after finishing basic flight school in an uncommon seven and a half months instead of the usual eighteen. His flight school scores would have qualified him for jets easily if he'd been in the Navy, but the much smaller Marine Corps' quota for fixed-wing pilots was already filled that year, so Schaefer became a CH-53 pilot. He was soon sent to Vietnam, where he flew five hundred combat missions in fourteen months—cargo resupply, search and rescue, troop insertions and pickups. CH-53s were pretty new then and weren't supposed to fly into "hot" zones where they would take fire. Hueys and Cobras and CH-46 troop transports did that, but they were assault aircraft. The H-53, as pilots called it, was the Marine Corps' airborne tractor-trailer, a heavy lifter whose main job was to haul beans and bullets in big loads to troops in the countryside. Vietnam being what it was in those days, though, H-53s came under fire, too. Schaefer learned how to keep his cool with bullets flying around and even through his cockpit.

Schaefer's reputation as a "good stick" got him assigned as the first director of helicopter tactics and operations at a new aviation school the Marines opened in Yuma, Arizona, in June 1978. They called it Marine Air Weapons and Tactics Squadron One, abbreviated MAWTS-1 and pronounced "moughts one." MAWTS-1 was a pet project of the deputy chief of staff for aviation of the day, John Glenn's friend and World War II squadron mate Tom Miller, now a lieutenant general. Over the years, the Marine Corps' use of fighter jets and helicopters to support ground troops had gotten more and more complicated. Miller saw a need for better training to allow all the moving parts of what the Marines call the combined air-ground task force to work together. Schaefer was at MAWTS-1 in November 1979 when the organizers of the Iran hostage rescue attempt turned to him to help plan Operation Eagle Claw and train the mission's helicopter pilots.

Shortly after Schaefer's and the other helicopters arrived at Desert One that night in Iran, the crew of one discovered that a hydraulic pump on their aircraft had broken down. The chopper was out of action, at risk of its controls seizing up if the remaining hydraulic pump went. That left the mission with only five helicopters—one less than the minimum. After heated discussion on the scene and calls via secure radio up the chain of command to Washington, where President Jimmy Carter and top aides and advisers were monitoring the mission, Delta commander Beckwith declared Operation Eagle Claw an "abort." He ordered Delta and the Rangers to load up on the C-130s so they could fly out of Iran.

Schaefer's helicopter was sitting next to the C-130 he had refueled from when a ground controller came over to his cockpit and told him he needed to move the chopper so the plane could turn around and take off. The controller ran out into the night to guide Schaefer as he repositioned his helicopter. Desert One was a maelstrom of noise and dust. All the rotors and propellers of all the aircraft were whirling. Soldiers were piling aboard the C-130 as Schaefer lifted his Sea Stallion up into a hover of about fifteen feet. As he did, his rotors blasted so much sand into the air that all he could see was "just a signalman out there," Schaefer recalled. The controller moved back toward the C-130 to escape the sand. Schaefer was so focused on his own aircraft that he didn't notice the man had moved. "As you took off, all you could see was that lone dark figure, and that was the only reference we had for the ground," Schaefer said. "I guess we ended up drifting in the general direction of that particular guy and we ended up clipping the wing of that 130 that night. I wouldn't say clipped—we hit him pretty good, and I don't remember too much after that."

Schaefer's helicopter crashed into the cockpit of the C-130, igniting the fuel in both aircraft. The concussion from the explosion knocked him out for a moment. The soldiers scrambled out of the C-130 before the flames consumed it, but five members of the cargo plane's Air Force crew and three Marines in Schaefer's Sea Stallion died in the inferno. Schaefer barely got out alive. When he came to, the window next to his seat looked like the only way to get out. Schaefer opened it inward. Heat and flames gushed into the cockpit, scorching his face and choking him. Still groggy, he managed to eject the window back outward and dive out, tumbling to the sand. When he got up, he was surrounded by a wall of flames. He dove through. He got up and saw another C-130, already moving. Other survivors had piled into the remaining airplanes, which were getting ready to take off. Schaefer staggered toward the plane, unable to run, barely able to walk. He fell a couple of times. Then someone saw him. The C-130 stopped and a door opened. Someone helped him in and propped him up on one of the big fuel bladders. A bunch of other guys were sitting on the bladders, including Schaefer's copilot. The planes took off and flew to Egypt, leaving behind the dead, the burntout C-130, and the five helicopters that had made it to Desert One and were still intact. Left with too little time to set off incendiary explosives in the helicopters to render them useless, Beckwith radioed a request for an air strike to destroy the helicopters. When he arrived in Egypt, he was told the White House had vetoed the strike for fear of harming Iranians in the area.

The next day, a disheartened President Carter went on television and took full responsibility for the debacle. The disaster reinforced the post-Vietnam image of the U.S. military as a gang that couldn't shoot straight. It also contributed mightily to Carter's defeat a few months later by Ronald Reagan in the 1980 presidential election.

Desert One would haunt America's military for years and inspire profound changes. One was a restructuring Congress imposed on the armed services to foster "jointness"—cooperation among the Air Force, Army, Navy, and Marines—instead of the interservice rivalry and insularity that had characterized their relations forever. Another was a new emphasis on training troops and pilots for special operations. A third was new interest in the Pentagon and Congress in buying equipment for such missions: better night-vision goggles, special radios, new radars and other electronic gear to make it easier to operate in darkness, and new weapons and aircraft. What the U.S. military already had, it was now clear, wasn't adequate. For defense contractors like Bell Helicopter and military marketers like Dick Spivey, that added up to a sales opportunity.

Well before Desert One, Spivey had been one of many company reps who often showed up at MAWTS-1 in Yuma to talk about their products. MAWTS-1's job was to develop aviation tactics for all Marine aircraft, not just helicopters, and to work with defense contractors on new concepts. Spivey came to talk about Bell Helicopter's new experimental tiltrotor, the XV-15, which had started flying in 1977. He would tell Jim Schaefer and other pilots at MAWTS-1 about the latest test results on the XV-15 and ask them what a tiltrotor for the Marine Corps might need to be able to do. "We'd talk about what they'd want in an airplane like that," Spivey said. "We were basically asking their advice. 'Do you want this radio? Do you want that radar?' That gets them involved in the design. It also gets them interested."

Schaefer invited Spivey and other industry reps out a couple of times a year for what he called "Technology Week," and Spivey always looked forward to his trips to Yuma. He'd never been in the military and wasn't a pilot, but he and Schaefer had become friends. Schaefer was single then and liked to have a good time. So was Spivey. Most guys liked Schaefer. Girls liked him a lot. He was laid-back and had a sardonic sense of humor. He was fun to be around. To kick off Technology Week, Schaefer always threw a party at the Spanish-style stucco house he and another pilot shared in Yuma. Spivey and the other industry reps were invited, and the instructors and student pilots of MAWTS-1 would show up with their wives and girlfriends. They'd eat Mexican food and "do things we shouldn't do—jump in swimming pools and drink way too many beers and worry about it the next day," Schaefer remembered wryly.

When Spivey visited Yuma in November 1979, a couple of weeks after the Iran hostage crisis began, Schaefer and two other Marine pilots Spivey was used to seeing were absent. Nobody seemed to know where they were, but with TV broadcasters Walter Cronkite and Ted Koppel telling the nation every night how many days those American hostages had been held in Iran, it wasn't hard to guess. Schaefer and the other pilots were fifty miles away in the desert, practicing for their mission to Iran.

Schaefer always enjoyed talking to Spivey about the potential of the tiltrotor. "It was refreshing to see someone go beyond the box that helicopters live in," Schaefer said. "We were looking for airspeed. The least amount of time you're in there with the enemy, mixing it up, the more survivable you are. Get in, get out. Get the job done and get out of there. This was a refreshing way to consider it." Schaefer also was drawn to the tiltrotor because it held out the promise of lifting Marine Corps helicopter pilots out of what he and others felt was their second-class citizenship. As the smallest service, the Marine Corps also has the smallest military budget. There's never enough money to pay for everything its leaders want to do. In those days, the way Schaefer saw it, when it came time to write the aviation budget, the lion's share always seemed to go to the jet jockeys. Fighter pilots were seen, and saw themselves, as dashing, white-scarf, right-stuff guys. Helicopter pilots were treated like bus drivers. Fighter pilots and helo pilots kept apart. They had separate officers clubs and drank amongst themselves. Schaefer saw the tiltrotor as a machine that might lend a little glamour to the helo pilots likely to fly them. He liked that idea.

Two days after Desert One, a Saturday, Spivey and his oldest son, ten-year-old Brett, were watching TV at Spivey's house in Fort Worth when they saw a news report on the mission's aftermath. The story showed one of the injured being brought on a gurney into Brooke Army Medical Center in San Antonio, one of the military's premier burn units. Spivey sat bolt upright. He recognized the wounded man, though his face was partially bandaged. It was Jim Schaefer.

"I know him," Spivey told Brett.

Spivey and others at Bell talked about the mission at work all day that Monday, and that night, Spivey stayed up until 3 A.M. creating a new tiltrotor briefing. It showed how the hostages might have been rescued successfully if only the military had been able to use tiltrotors instead of helicopters. With tiltrotors, Spivey's briefing argued, the mission could have been done without Eagle Claw's complex choreography and risky timeline, which required the U.S. force to spend two nights and a day in Iran. With tiltrotors, there would have been no need for the deadly refueling rendezvous at Desert One. Delta Force, or whatever troops were chosen, might simply have climbed into tiltrotors aboard an aircraft carrier or on the territory of some friendly Middle Eastern country, flown directly to the vicinity of Tehran, infiltrated the city, taken down the guards, freed the hostages, met the tiltrotors outside the embassy or even on its grounds, loaded everybody aboard, and flown straight back to the ship. Time from incursion to extraction: no more than eight hours. One night. Or the classic "one period of darkness."

A month after Desert One, Spivey's marketing colleague Rod Wernicke went to Yuma and showed their new tiltrotor briefing to a major he knew there. "He liked it," Spivey noted in his work diary. A month after that, Spivey went to Yuma himself to try out the new briefing on other pilots at MAWTS-1, including Jim Schaefer. After weeks of painful treatment in San Antonio for burns on his face, hands, back, and legs, Schaefer was back on the job.

On his way to Yuma, Spivey picked up a copy of *Newsweek* in the airport and read it on the plane. The June 30, 1980, cover story was about the revolution in computer technology, which was "producing a new generation of 'smart' machines that magnify the power of man's brain and can be used even by untrained laymen," the magazine reported. What caught Spivey's eye was an article inside titled "New Light on the Rescue Mission." It was a detailed analysis of what had gone wrong at Desert One, including a discussion of Schaefer's helicopter hitting the C-130. "The chopper's pilot, Maj. James Shaefer [*sic*], was ordered to bank left and away from the C-130 and fly to a refueling position behind another of the transport planes," *Newsweek* reported. "Shaefer acknowledged the order and started to bank left. Then he apparently became disoriented. He reversed his course, banked right and crashed into the C-130. Both craft burst into flames." The article was accompanied by a photo of Schaefer on the gurney as he was wheeled into the San Antonio burn center two days after the failed mission.

Spivey had the magazine with him when he got to Schaefer's office at MAWTS-1. Schaefer had just come in from working out and was still in gym clothes. Spivey saw burn marks on his legs.

"Jim, have you seen this?" Spivey asked, handing him the *Newsweek*.

"No, I haven't," Schaefer said, frowning as he took the magazine. He'd written a harsh letter to *Newsweek* swearing never to read it again after its May 5 issue, whose cover story, "Fiasco in Iran," included an Associated Press photo showing the charred remains of Schaefer's helicopter and one of the Americans killed at Desert One. Schaefer recognized the corpse as his crew chief. He barely glanced at the article Spivey handed him with its photo of Schaefer being wheeled into the hospital.

"Well, you know what I think about that?" Schaefer sneered.

"No, what?"

In one fluid motion, Schaefer turned around, bent over, grabbed his gym shorts with both hands, and mooned Spivey.

They nearly busted a gut laughing.

Within a few weeks, Schaefer and other helicopter pilots were training up for a possible second try at rescuing the hostages. Operation Honey Badger, as this one was called, became moot on January 20, 1981, when Iran released the Americans precisely as Ronald Reagan took the oath of office as president. Reagan had won the election partly by portraying Carter as weak-kneed. Reagan promised to get tough with

America's foes, not only the Islamic revolutionaries in Iran but also the Soviet Union. Moscow had grown bold with America's demoralization after Vietnam and Watergate. The Soviets had invaded Afghanistan in 1979. They were aiding leftist revolutionaries in Central America. Reagan warned of a new Soviet threat to Europe. He pledged to rebuild America's military to counter it. Most generals and admirals were ecstatic to hear that, especially those in the business of buying weapons. The post-Vietnam years under Carter had been hell on procurement budgets. The Marines, for example, had been trying to get the Navy to put money into its long-term budget to replace their CH-46 troop transport helicopters. Carter's political appointees had blocked them. Under Reagan, getting money for things like that was going to be a lot easier for those in the Pentagon.

* * *

Most military officers dread working in the Pentagon—"The Building," as insiders call it. They'd rather be in the field or in the fleet, leading troops or sailors, or flying, if they're pilots. Infantry officers like to be in the open air, out on the firing range hearing the crack of rifles or on maneuvers, smelling gunpowder and diesel exhaust as they hone their own and their troops' combat skills. Pilots crave time in the cockpit putting a jet fighter or a helicopter through its paces, doing things they can tell stories about at the officers club. Working in The Building makes such officers feel like Jonah in the belly of the whale. They pray to get out.

The Pentagon is really five multistory buildings, constructed during World War II in a series of rings connected by ten long, spokelike corridors. The sprawling structure covers thirty-four acres, including an interior courtyard. It has 17.5 miles of hallways. The rings are lettered A through E and the corridors are numbered 1 through 10, but officers who go to work there for the first time can easily get lost—or lose focus, or grow cynical. Working in The Building saps the health and strains the home life of some. Aside from being cooped up in an office behind a desk, working in The Building means processing or creating paperwork by the pile. It means long hours on the job, often from well before sunup until well after sundown. It means sitting through interminable meetings day in and day out. It can mean taking guff from civilian bureaucrats and political appointees and congressional aides who fancy themselves astute military strategists, even if they've never worn a uniform or heard a shot fired in anger. "Action officers"—usually majors and lieutenant colonels or Navy lieutenant commanders and commanders—handle individual issues or programs. Depending on their personalities, that means they wield real power, for while action officers don't officially decide things, the colonels they work for usually rely on their advice, and the generals above them usually rely on the advice of their colonels. Being an action officer, though, also can mean slaving against tight deadlines to get a program or decision ready for action, only to see it torpedoed or mangled or postponed for political reasons after the general signs off on it. Some action officers come off their Pentagon tours wan and weary. Some lose their lust for military service. Yet for an officer who wants to make senior rank—colonel or general in the Army, Air Force, and Marines; captain or admiral in the Navy—and thus get a major command, working in The Building is essential. In modern times, hardly anyone has risen to senior rank without working as an action officer. Most officers who hope to one day wear stars on their shoulders simply endure it.

Robert Magnus thrived on it. Brown-haired, blue-eyed, and charming when he wanted to be, Magnus was a New Yorker by birth, the youngest child of a bookkeeper and his seamstress wife. After Bobby was born in 1947 they moved from Flatbush in Brooklyn to Levittown on Long Island, where Magnus grew up in what he called "a typical Jewish home." Unlike most other Jewish kids he knew, Magnus aspired to a career in the military. *Magnus* means "large" in Latin; Bobby Magnus wasn't. He was five foot five when fully grown, and like a lot of little guys, sometimes he acted as if he had something to prove. Most of his friends' parents wanted their sons to be doctors or lawyers or rabbis. Bobby grew up watching World War II movies and TV shows like *The Silent Service*, a 1950s series about submarine warfare. In his teens, he decided he wanted to be a naval gunnery officer, so he went to the University of Virginia on a Navy ROTC scholarship, majoring in European and Russian history. While he was there, he decided what he really wanted to be was a Marine infantry officer, like two of his most impressive ROTC instructors. When he graduated in 1969, Magnus was commissioned as a second lieutenant in the Marine Corps, then went to The Basic School at Quantico, Virginia, the first stop for new lieutenants. He intended to be an infantry officer, but a friend Magnus made there challenged him to apply for flight school instead. Bob Magnus couldn't resist a challenge. He applied and became a helicopter pilot.

Magnus served his required four years, then developed a new ambition: making money. He got out and went to work on Wall Street. A year later, he found he didn't much like it. He missed flying and he missed the Corps. He went back in, determined to make a career of it this time. He flew CH-46 Sea Knights at New River, North Carolina. He served in a staff job with a Marine air group. Then he went to MAWTS-1 and became a weapons and tactics instructor. At Yuma, squadron mates gave the Jewish kid from New York a radio call sign he liked, but which he stopped signing e-mails with years later because it bothered his wife. It was "Heeb."

From MAWTS-1, Magnus volunteered for a tour at Headquarters Marine Corps, figuring he'd never make senior rank without serving there. In July 1980, Major Magnus reported for duty as an action officer in the Marine Corps aviation branch. The aviation branch decides what kind of aircraft and other aviation equipment the Corps needs, writes requirements for programs to provide them, and figures out how to fit those programs into the Marine Corps' portion of the Navy Department budget.

If many action officers found the atmosphere at headquarters wilting, Magnus blossomed in it. At first, he got all the "SLJs"—shitty little jobs. He was the aircrew training devices officer. He was the nuclear, biological, and chemical defense gear officer. He was the coffee mess officer. He got all the assignments no one else wanted. He bit into them like a terrier, and his superiors loved him. Not long after Magnus arrived, Lieutenant Colonel Joe Moody, the action officer assigned to keep the Corps' CH-46 Sea Knights in shape and recommend an aircraft to replace the Vietnam-era helicopters, told Magnus he wanted his help. The new assignment gave Magnus a license to talk with all manner of people, and he made extravagant use of it. Headquarters Marine Corps was in the Navy Annex, a drab, World War II-vintage four-story brick office building on a hill overlooking Arlington National Cemetery and the Pentagon. Magnus wasn't there a lot. He was always in motion, it seemed, in the Pentagon, on Capitol Hill, or making trips to places where he could learn something or talk to someone who might help the Marines come up with a CH-46 replacement. He visited bureaucrats and officers in the Navy Department. He traveled to Marine bases to gather data on how long the CH-46 might last and talk to pilots about what the Corps' next troop transport ought to be able to do. He went to aircraft factories and talked to industry reps about possible replacements for the Phrog. He came back and gave briefings to generals and admirals on what he found out. One of Magnus's bosses toward the end of his first tour in the aviation branch was Colonel Robert Balch. "I wrote a fitness report for him that said, 'This major is the best colonel I've ever had working for me,'" Balch chuckled. "Magnus always thought at least two ranks ahead and acted two ranks ahead."

Through his research and travels, Magnus became intrigued by the XV-15 tiltrotor that Bell Helicopter had developed for NASA and the Army. Bell had built two XV-15s by 1980 and was doing flight tests with one in Fort Worth. NASA had the other at its Ames Research Center outside Palo Alto, California. Somewhere during that period, Magnus met Dick Spivey, who came by the aviation branch one day to introduce himself. They started talking on the phone regularly, and when Spivey was in Washington, he often went to see Magnus. He would update him on the XV-15 and talk about other possible tiltrotor designs and how they might fit into the Marine Corps. Spivey soon began to feel that in Magnus he had a potential ally. Magnus was just a major, but he was full of energy and ideas, and he wasn't shy about sharing them. What Spivey liked about him most, though, was that Magnus saw promise in the tiltrotor.

★ ★ ★

Magnus wasn't the only Marine officer getting interested in the tiltrotor. Spivey had been talking up the concept to officers in the aviation branch long before Magnus got there. One of them was Bob Balch, back then still a lieutenant colonel and an action officer himself. "Spivey and I talked a lot, and we talked about how to do some of the selling of the idea up front," Balch recalled. Balch told Spivey that if Bell hoped to sell tilt-rotors to the Marine Corps, it would have to come up with one far bigger than the two-seat XV-15 demonstrator. A tiltrotor for the Marines would need to carry at least twenty-four troops fully loaded for combat, he advised.

Balch also helped Bell keep the XV-15 flying in 1978, when NASA and the Army came close to shutting the project down. One day that year, one of Balch's counterparts in the Army, an action officer who worked on his service's aviation programs, dropped by the aviation branch and told Balch, "Hey, the Army's getting ready to do something

stupid." The inflation rate had hit double digits in the late 1970s, eroding the government's buying power just as the XV-15 program was at
its most expensive. NASA had put one of the two XV-15s into its wind
tunnel at Ames recently and the tests had left the aircraft unfit to fly.
Bell still had one XV-15 flying in Fort Worth, but to the chagrin of the
NASA and Army engineers working on the tiltrotor, neither NASA's nor
the Army's top leaders wanted to spend the money to get the XV-15 at
Ames back in the air. NASA's priority was its space program; the Army
was more interested in spending its rotary wing aircraft research money
on a new attack helicopter.

Balch took this nugget of information to Lieutenant General Tom
Miller, who was now a few months from retirement as deputy chief of
staff for aviation. Miller already knew about the XV-15, which his staff
had briefed him on after he'd seen the film of the Canadian tilt-wing
aircraft, and he was interested in the tiltrotor. Miller told Balch he'd see
if he couldn't get the Navy to come up with some money to keep the
XV-15 flying.

Miller called a Navy rear admiral he had known for years. They went
to see the assistant secretary of the Navy for research and development,
David E. Mann, and persuaded Mann to put enough money into the
XV-15 program to keep it going. Mann agreed that the Navy and the
Marines ought to see whether this tiltrotor technology had any potential
for them. The Naval Air Systems Command, known as Navair, put $4
million into the NASA/Army XV-15 program over the next three years,
starting in 1979.

After the Navy started investing in the XV-15, the agency's leaders
decided to send a pilot to Fort Worth to fly the one Bell had there and
write a report. In October 1979, an order to do that came to the director
of the Attack/Assault Branch of the Rotary Wing Aircraft Test Directorate at Patuxent River Naval Air Station in Maryland, where Navair's test
pilots work. Marine Major William S. Lawrence, the director, thought
the assignment looked interesting, so he gave it to himself. Test pilots
love to record "firsts," and up until then, only three other men had flown
the XV-15: Bell test pilots Ron Erhart and Dorman Cannon and NASA
pilot Dan Dugan, a former Army lieutenant colonel. Bill Lawrence liked
the idea of being the first Marine to fly the XV-15. Besides, Fort Worth
was Lawrence's hometown.

When he first saw the XV-15, Lawrence was surprised at how compact it was, and how sleek. It was only about 42 feet long, roughly the length of a Huey helicopter. Bell had designed the XV-15 small so it would fit into NASA's 40-foot-by-80-foot wind tunnel. The little tiltrotor's fuselage looked something like an executive jet; the rear cabin was large enough to hold eight or nine passengers but was crammed with instruments to monitor and record data picked up by strain gauges attached to nearly every part of the aircraft. The XV-15's wings were swept forward six and a half degrees on each side, giving it a rakish look. The angle was needed to keep its two big rotors—25 feet in diameter each—from flapping and scraping the wings when swiveling pods that held the craft's rotors on the wingtips swung them down so the XV-15 could fly like an airplane. The rotors were interesting, too. Unlike the predecessor XV-3 Convertiplane's flimsy-looking helicopter rotors, the XV-15's had three blades and a special twist to make them function more like propellers when tilted forward. Lawrence thought the XV-15 looked a lot like some of the little twin-engine turboprop airplanes he'd flown.

Dorman Cannon gave Lawrence two half-hour familiarization flights on May 19 and 20, 1980, at Bell's Flight Research Center at Arlington Municipal Airport, a few miles from Fort Worth. Lawrence returned June 5 and flew the XV-15 with Cannon two more times during the next four days. Twenty-seven years later, he still felt that of the 110 different aircraft he'd piloted in his career, the XV-15 was by far the easiest to fly. It was also the most fun, for it seemed to defy the ordinary laws of aerodynamics.

A pilot can slow a conventional fixed-wing airplane one of two ways: either by decreasing power or by increasing the "angle of attack," meaning the angle at which the wing hits the air. Decrease power to slow down without changing the angle of attack and the airplane will lose altitude; increase power to go faster without changing the angle of attack and the aircraft will climb. To counter those effects and maintain altitude while speeding up or slowing down, the pilot also has to change the plane's angle of attack.

Lawrence was amazed to find that the tiltrotor was immune to the customary relationship between angle of attack and airspeed. This was so because it got lift not just from its wings but also from its rotors. Flying in airplane mode, the pilot could reduce the XV-15's airspeed without losing altitude simply by pushing a thumb switch that tilted the rotors upward a few degrees. No need to change the angle of attack because the lift from the rotors would compensate for the loss of wing lift at a slower speed. No conventional airplane or helicopter could do that. "It was just unique in that regard," he said. Lawrence took a cassette tape recorder on his XV-15 flights to record his comments so he could listen to them while writing his report for Navair. On the tape of the first flight in which he took the controls, Lawrence can be heard gushing about the ease of flying the tiltrotor and the surprising things it could do. "This is just goin' slicker 'n grease," Lawrence says as he and Cannon prepare to put the craft into a practice stall. "It's smoother 'n silk," he says a few minutes later as they convert from airplane mode to helicopter flight. "It just floats along." As they climb with the nacelles tilted at 70 degrees, Lawrence marvels that "there's just no pilot workload." When they descend again in airplane mode, Lawrence tells Cannon, "Got to love it." Lawrence chuckles as he makes his first landing, slowing the aircraft to a hover, then setting it down gently on the runway. After they taxi back to the ramp and shut down the engines, the doors are heard opening. "Let's get out of this hotbox," Cannon tells Lawrence. As they climb out, Lawrence is heard again. "Woooo!" he whoops. "Well, Dorman, that is *all* right. I think you got yourself a machine."

Lawrence was still grinning when he got to the hangar and met with a bunch of Bell engineers and others. One was Dick Spivey, whose title since 1974 had been Manager, Military Tilt Rotor Business Development. Spivey struck Lawrence as a real schmoozer, but he liked him. Spivey had arranged for a photographer to snap pictures of Lawrence in the XV-15. After Lawrence left Fort Worth, Spivey also had someone on his staff get a certificate printed up for the pilot commemorating his flight and send it to him.

Before his XV-15 flights, Lawrence hadn't thought much about the tiltrotor; afterward, he was sold. Back at Patuxent River, he wrote a 44-page report that said the tiltrotor held "excellent potential for a variety of Navy/Marine Corps V/STOL missions." The report went to Navair, then began floating around Headquarters Marine Corps. Lawrence also went to the Navy Annex to brief the concept to the deputy chief of staff for aviation, Lieutenant General William J. White, who had replaced Tom Miller in June 1979. Spivey noted Lawrence's meeting with White in his work diary. He also had his staff look into buying plaques that Bell could give to future XV-15 "guest pilots." Spivey and others at Bell could see from Lawrence's reaction that the XV-15 wasn't just a successful experiment, it could also be powerful marketing tool. They started making plans to use it that way.

As 1980 ended, Spivey felt things were finally looking up. He and a handful of others at Bell had spent eight years now marketing the tiltrotor to the military without getting close to a sale. It was still hard to tell if one was coming soon, but now they had a powerful argument for the tiltrotor in the disaster at Desert One, they had a crackerjack marketing tool in the XV-15, and they had a growing list of Marine Corps allies. For years, Spivey and Bell had focused mainly on selling the tiltrotor to the Army, the Navy, or the Air Force, the services with the biggest budgets. Now Spivey was beginning to think the most likely customer might be the one with the least to spend but the greatest need—the one most anxious to replace a big part of its helicopter fleet, the one most eager to surpass the helicopter's limited speed, the one most paranoid about its future, the one most skilled at getting its way with Congress. The Marine Corps.

CHAPTER FOUR

THE SALE

Paris is seductive, especially in late spring. Artists, poets, songwriters, lovers have known it forever. For decades, so have the world's top aviation executives, which is why almost all of them show up for the biennial Paris Air Show. They gripe about the cost and bother of bringing their aircraft to Le Bourget, the historic airfield northeast of Paris where Lindbergh landed and the show is staged. They grumble about the expense of renting chalets on the flight line to wine and dine VIPs as they watch planes and helicopters fly. They grouse about rushing back into Paris each evening to attend lavish dinners and receptions for potential customers and the media at posh hotels and famed restaurants. Still, almost all of them go, for there is something about Paris in the spring that can seduce a customer just as it can a lover. Big deals are often consummated, or at least conceived, during the Paris Air Show.

James F. Atkins learned that even before he became president of Bell Helicopter in 1972. Some of Bell's best deals over the years had sprung from relaxed conversations with customers at the Paris Air Show. It was at Paris in 1971, when Atkins was a vice president and preparing to take over the company, that Iran's deputy minister of war for armaments told him the Shah was interested in Bell's helicopters. That chat led to Bell's biggest foreign sale ever—$500 million for nearly five hundred utility and attack helicopters. After the initial contract, Iran gave the company another multimillion-dollar deal to train 4,500 military pilots and 6,000 mechanics while providing all the support needed to keep Iran's choppers flying. By the late 1970s, Bell had set up a subsidiary to handle the work, whose value ran into the billions. Bell Helicopter International had 5,000 employees and 8,000 dependents living in Iran—so many, the Shah's government built an entire village to house them at Isfahan.

The Iran contracts helped Bell remain profitable during the 1970s, an otherwise disappointing decade for the company. First Bell lost an Army competition to build a new utility helicopter to replace the service's Bell Hueys. Sikorsky Aircraft Corporation, a subsidiary of United Technologies, won that multibillion-dollar contract with its new UH-60 Black Hawk. Then Bell lost a four-year competition to provide attack helicopters to replace the HueyCobras the Army had used in Vietnam. The Army bought AH-64 Apaches from Hughes Helicopters. The Iran deal eased Bell's pain at losing its best U.S. military customer. By 1980, though, the Shah was gone—deposed by Islamic revolutionaries and chased out of the country to die of cancer in Egypt—and so was Bell's business in Iran. Jim Atkins saw the end coming in September 1978, when he had his last of many meetings with the Shah. They were seated side by side on a love seat in the monarch's palace. Revolutionaries were marching in the capital nearly every day, sometimes rioting. "There is no problem in the streets," the Shah replied dismissively when Atkins asked how he planned to deal with the unrest. As Atkins rode to the airport, his car became engulfed in a street battle between protesters and the Shah's police. The driver had the American executive slump down in the backseat. Atkins got through unharmed but unnerved. When he returned to Fort Worth, he had Bell lease ten Boeing 747s from Pan Am and evacuate its employees' dependents from Iran. After the Shah fled in January 1979, Bell started evacuating its employees as well. The last got out in December, a month after students stormed the U.S. Embassy and took the Americans there hostage.

After that, Jim Atkins was eagerly searching for new military business, and as he surveyed the possibilities, the best shot he saw for Bell to establish a new market for one of its products wasn't a helicopter. For years, Atkins and other Bell executives had seen the tiltrotor largely as a science experiment. Now, with the market for military helicopters saturated, with the XV-15 proving you could build an aircraft that would fly both like a helicopter and an airplane, and with the failed Iran rescue mission of April 1980 inspiring the military to take a harder look at new technologies, the tiltrotor became a business proposition for Atkins. Naturally, his thoughts turned to Paris.

One day Bell test pilot Dorman Cannon was sitting in his office when the phone rang. Cannon, a former Marine Corps helicopter pilot, raised in Texas, nearly stood and snapped to attention when his caller identified himself. It wasn't every day the president of Bell Helicopter called you on your own little telephone.

"Dorman, I'm thinking of taking the XV-15 to the Paris Air Show," Atkins said. "What would you think of it?"

"Mr. Atkins, in my opinion, it's too green," Cannon told him. "We just haven't matured the flight envelope enough to go to the Paris Air Show."

"Well thank you, Dorman. I value your opinion," Atkins said, ringing off.

Bell's other XV-15 test pilot, Ron Erhart, soon got the same call. He gave Atkins the same answer.

Not long afterward, a hundred or so Bell managers gathered for an annual retreat at a lakeside tennis resort near Austin, in the verdant Texas hill country. Atkins stunned the group. "We've been flying the XV-15," he said. "We've had pretty good results. Let's consider taking it to Paris." Several of the engineers spoke up. Like the test pilots, they were opposed. Flying the XV-15 in Paris would be risky, they warned. What if it crashed? What if parts broke and they couldn't get it to fly some of its scheduled demonstrations? What if it flew and no one cared? Where would they be then? Besides, getting to Le Bourget would mean disassembling the XV-15 so it would fit into a cargo plane, putting it back together and flight-testing it once it arrived, flying it for ten days straight during the show, then taking it apart, hauling it back to Texas, and putting it back together again. The engineers would lose weeks of flight test time. It would cost a ton of money, too.

Dick Spivey was all for it. Sure it would be risky, but it might be worth it, Spivey thought. Spivey had proved the previous summer he wasn't afraid to take risks to sell the tiltrotor. Against Cannon's better judgment, Spivey had talked the test pilot into doing a vertical takeoff in the XV-15, putting it into a low hover and then accelerating to top speed while simultaneously tilting the rotors into airplane mode as fast as possible. The conversion would take twelve seconds. Spivey wanted to make a film of the maneuver to show potential buyers how fast the tiltrotor could exit a landing zone—a big selling point for a combat aircraft. Spivey stationed photographers at various points around the runway at Arlington Municipal Airport on July 30, 1979, to capture the "get out of Dodge" move Cannon was to perform. The cameras faithfully recorded what could have been a final flight for Cannon, fellow test pilot Erhart, and their XV-15. Cannon put the XV-15 into a low hover over a helicopter landing pad on the ramp, then headed south a few feet above a grass field parallel to the runway, using the thumb switch to swivel the rotors forward as fast as they'd go. The air was calm, and with no headwind to help boost relative speed, the XV-15 didn't accelerate fast enough. The rotors were already in full airplane mode, tilted straight ahead like propellers and describing a circle whose lower arc reached more than twelve feet below the wing, before the wing fully took over the job of providing lift. With the rotors no longer supplying any, the XV-15 lost a couple of feet of altitude, putting the lower arc of the rotors on a collision course with a barbed-wire fence and some hackberry trees at the end of the field. Neither Cannon nor Erhart noticed the looming disaster at first, but at the last second Cannon pulled back on the stick and pointed the XV-15's nose up. The aircraft cleared the fence but the pilots heard one rotor scrape the tops of the trees. Spivey and others watching from nearby heard it, too: "Pop-pop-pop-pop."

"Oh, shit!" Spivey muttered through clenched teeth as Cannon whipped the XV-15 into a tight turn so he could set it back down on the field in a hurry. Spivey and the others ran over as Cannon and Erhart climbed out. There was no major damage, but the strain gauges on the end of one rotor's blades had torn loose and the tips of the blades were stained green. Cannon figured higher-ups at Bell were going to be very unhappy about this near accident with the XV-15. When he, Erhart, Spivey, and the engineers convened in the hangar to talk about what had happened, Cannon let them know he wasn't going to take the blame alone. "Okay, I'm going to find out which one of you bastards is going to stick with me after this," Cannon told them. For a minute, it was so quiet he could hear himself breathe.

Spivey knew he'd just about instigated a disaster that could have cost Bell a wad of money and himself his job, maybe even injured or killed Cannon and Erhart. But he really wanted that get-out-of-Dodge film to show military customers, and when he looked at what the photographers had gotten, he thought it wasn't bad. Spivey waited a few months until everybody had cooled down, then started showing the film to people. When the XV-15 program manager, Tommy H. Thomason, heard about it, he was livid. "Tommy says he will get me fired if I use the tree chop movie any more," Spivey recorded in his work diary. He stopped showing it. Not that Thomason was surprised. Thomason felt Spivey was a loose cannon, always doing what he thought best to promote the tiltrotor, regardless of direction or orders from above. Spivey's favorite saying irked Thomason no end: "It's better to ask for forgiveness than permission."

Risky or not, taking the XV-15 to Paris sounded like a great idea to Spivey, no matter what the test pilots and engineers might think. By 1980, he'd been marketing the tiltrotor full-time for eight years with only nibbles. The salesman was hungry for a sale.

Jim Atkins was eager to sell the tiltrotor, too. Not the XV-15, which was built purely to prove a tiltrotor was feasible. The XV-15 was a technology demonstrator made from parts designed for other aircraft, not a production model built for real missions. Its engines guzzled fuel and its empty weight to gross weight ratio was lousy. It couldn't carry much more than two pilots, about a thousand pounds of instruments needed to record its every move, and enough fuel to fly 400 miles or so. The purpose of taking it to Paris wouldn't be to sell the XV-15; it would be to show the aviation world that tiltrotor technology was proven, mature, ready to be applied to new, bigger aircraft.

Atkins thought his engineers and pilots too cautious. Unlike a lot of aviation executives, he wasn't an engineer or a pilot himself. He'd joined Bell Aircraft in the 1940s as an accounts payable clerk and worked his way to the top. He was a finance expert, astute at deciding where to put the company's money. Bell's parent corporation, a Rhode Island conglomerate called Textron Inc., which had bought Bell Helicopter in 1960, let Atkins run it more or less independently, and he prided himself on being a hands-on manager. Atkins ignored the chain of command and dug down into the company, talking to people several ranks below to make sure he knew what was really going on. He was always a gentleman with them, as dignified as he looked and almost courtly in his manner, though he could be stern when he thought you'd done something wrong. He combed his full head of graying hair straight back from his forehead, which with his piercing eyes gave him the look of an eagle. The look reflected his attitude. Atkins had a keen eye for business and confidence in his own judgment. He had already talked to NASA about taking the XV-15 to Paris and the agency was amenable. NASA's mandate since its founding had been to keep the United States at the global forefront of aviation and space technology, and those in charge of its XV-15 program were as avid as Bell to promote the tiltrotor. At the

Austin retreat, Atkins let his managers air their views awhile, then said, "Well, we're going to go."

★ ★ ★

Cannon and Erhart flew a carefully choreographed routine with the XV-15 every day from June 4 to 14 at the 1981 Paris Air Show. They wowed their audiences. The XV-15 looked sharp. It was painted white, with a thick blue stripe along the length of its sides and red trim at the tops and bottoms of its H-shaped double tail. Its fuselage bore the names of its sponsors—NASA, the Army, and Bell—along with its assigned air show number, 53. Cannon and Erhart traded off each day as aircraft commander; NASA's Dan Dugan was always copilot. When the emcee announced the XV-15, they lifted it a dozen feet into the air over the ramp where they'd been waiting and slowly "air-taxied" out over the end of the runway with the rotors vertical, like a helicopter. They held the tiny tiltrotor there a few seconds to show how stable it was, then made a 360-degree turn while hovering in place. They flew it sideways a little in each direction, each time returning to their original spot over the runway. Next they aimed it down the runway, tilted the rotors aft, and flew backward at 25 or 30 miles per hour. Even as they did, they began swiveling the rotors forward again to 15 degrees, causing the XV-15 to pause in midair, then suddenly jump into forward flight. The effect was to make the tiltrotor look faster than it would have if it had started from a hover—a stunt to impress the audience.

As they flew over the runway at low level, they pushed the rotors fully forward, picking up speed as they did. By the time the rotors fully converted, the XV-15 was doing nearly 160 mph—faster than the cruising speed of most helicopters. Now they rolled into a hard left turn and then snapped the XV-15 back right 270 degrees, circling back in the direction they'd taken off from. They turned again at the end of the runway and made another low pass, then pulled up abruptly, converting back to helicopter mode as they did. They put the aircraft into a tight turn and a steep descent, then brought it to a hover over the spot on the runway where they'd started their routine. That was when Cannon and Erhart did a trick that really stole the show. They tilted the rotors 5 degrees aft while pushing the stick forward. When they did, instead of moving backward in the air, the XV-15 hovered in place and its nose dipped down. It looked as if the little thing was bowing to the crowd. No other rotorcraft could do that. Audiences just adored it. The *New York Times* wrote that "if ever there was a lovable plane, it is the Bell XV-15 . . . the hit of the show."

★ ★ ★

A great piece of artistry, whether executed by a painter, a musician, a dancer, or a pilot flying an aerobatic routine, can affect the emotions of even the toughest men. John Lehman was a tough man. That was one reason newly elected President Ronald Reagan had chosen him as his first secretary of the Navy, the civilian who oversees the Navy and Marine Corps and holds sway over what they buy. When Lehman saw the XV-15 at the 1981 Paris Air Show, his pulse quickened.

Lehman was a flyer himself, a bombardier-navigator in A-6 Intruder fighter-bombers as a Naval Reserve lieutenant commander. After he became Navy secretary, he also started learning to fly helicopters. Lehman arrived at Paris and saw the XV-15 on June 5. That same day, the secretary's military assistant, Marine Colonel Russ Porter, started making what turned into repeated visits to the Bell Helicopter chalet to deliver a message from his boss: Lehman wanted to fly in the XV-15. At the air show.

Now Dick Spivey's pulse quickened. You didn't get marketing opportunities like *this* every day. But after checking with colleagues, he had to turn Porter down. NASA said only test pilots Cannon, Erhart, and Dugan could fly the XV-15 at the air show. Porter left but came back a little later. Lehman wanted NASA to make an exception in his case. Discussions between Bell and NASA officials ensued, but the answer was the same. The XV-15 belonged to NASA, and NASA wasn't allowing guest flights at the air show. Besides, the XV-15 pilots didn't think the show's rules would permit them to fly a guest over Le Bourget, and they wouldn't want to fly one outside the show. Getting permission to depart the field and return would be hard, and they weren't familiar with the territory. Porter left again but was back a little later, this time acting a little steamed. Spivey was nearly as frustrated as Porter, who kept coming back, even though he always got the same answer. This went on for two days. Secretary Lehman didn't like being told no.

They called him "Young Winston," a moniker inspired by a 1972 movie of that name that recounted Winston Churchill's youth. John Francis Lehman, Jr., bore no physical resemblance to the British political legend. At five-foot-nine and 175 pounds, Lehman was wiry, with a bend in his nose suggesting his pugnacious nature and a forelock of thick brown hair that tended to tumble down boyishly across his forehead. But like Churchill before World War I, Lehman was brassy, and he took over his nation's Navy at a strikingly young age. Lehman was thirty-eight when he was sworn in as the nation's sixty-fifth secretary of the Navy—the youngest in history.

Like Churchill, Lehman also had famous relatives. Born into a well-to-do Philadelphia family, he was a cousin to Princess Grace of Monaco, the former American actress Grace Kelly. His grandmother and Grace Kelly's father were sister and brother. Lehman earned his undergraduate degree at St. Joseph's College in Philadelphia, then earned a master's in law and diplomacy from Cambridge University in England. He spent school vacations in Monaco with Princess Grace and her husband, Prince Rainier. After Cambridge, Lehman worked for Henry Kissinger at the National Security Council in President Richard Nixon's White House. During Democrat Jimmy Carter's presidency, Lehman was active in the Republican Party and wrote a book on aircraft carriers that argued for buying more big ones. He also had a defense consulting company based in Washington, the Abington Corporation, and was a defense adviser to Reagan's 1980 presidential campaign. All that and the backing of two powerful senators—Cold Warriors John Tower, a Texas Republican, and Henry M. Jackson of Washington, the leading hawk in the Democratic Party—helped Lehman land the Navy secretary job.

Like the real Young Winston, Lehman seethed with ambition and audacity. He set bold goals and went after them boldly, and he ran the Navy like no secretary in memory before or since, bossing around older admirals in ways many found hard to swallow. That endeared him to some top Marine Corps generals, at least those with a permanent chip on their shoulder toward the Navy. They liked Lehman's swashbuckling style. He was the Reagan administration's Errol Flynn, outfoxing rivals and sneering in the faces of his foes. His biggest goal was a 600-ship Navy by 1989, up from the 479 vessels in the fleet when he came to office. Once during his tenure, the deputy defense secretary, Paul Thayer, tried to slow the massive growth in the Navy budget that Lehman's pet project would require. Lehman got allies in the White House to include in a news release naming two new aircraft carriers a seemingly matter-of-fact statement by President Reagan declaring a 600-ship Navy his goal. Argument over.

Lehman was aware of the XV-15 before he got to the 1981 Paris Air Show, but as he watched it from a VIP box with Monaco's Prince Rainier and his son, Prince Albert, Lehman had an epiphany. "As opposed to a helicopter, this did not look like a loose confederacy of warring parts," Lehman recalled. "It looked like an airplane, like a bird. Your impression would be, 'Gee, yeah, that makes sense. That's going to work.'" He was intrigued by the tiltrotor's military possibilities. "I was very much taken with the technology," he said. "I've always been a believer, being a helicopter pilot myself, that helicopters are very vulnerable in battle. They're very vulnerable to ground fire and every other kind of fire." When he saw how fast the XV-15 could fly, Lehman thought the tiltrotor "offered the prospect of a 300-knot entry into the battle area and a rapid setdown and a rapid departure."

Lehman wasn't the only VIP smitten by the XV-15 at Paris. Another was silver-haired Senator Barry Goldwater, then seventy-two, a World War II pilot, organizer of the Arizona Air National Guard, and an Air Force Reserve major general. First elected to the Senate in 1953, Goldwater had been the cantankerous conservative Republican nominee for president in 1964. Now he was a power on the Senate Armed Services Committee. He showed up at the Bell chalet with the diminutive, sartorially vain Senator Tower of Texas, another conservative Republican. With their party's takeover of the Senate in the 1980 elections, Tower now chaired the Armed Services Committee. He was also a longtime backer of Bell, one of his home state's major employers.

Inside the chalet, there were round tables seating eight to ten people, not far from sliding glass doors that led to a balcony for watching the aerial displays. Other companies were serving French delicacies in their chalets; Bell offered Texas beef barbecue, Lone Star beer in longneck bottles, American wines. But Tower and Goldwater hadn't come for food and drink, they'd come to talk tiltrotor. They sat down at one of the tables and spent a long time with some Bell officials and Major Bill Lawrence, the Marine Corps pilot who'd flown the XV-15 for the Naval Air Systems Command a year earlier. It was heady stuff for Lawrence, who had wangled a trip to the air show by calling Spivey a few months earlier. Lawrence asked Spivey to put in a request to Headquarters Marine Corps for Lawrence to join Bell's contingent in Paris. "Done,"

Spivey replied. So here was Bill Lawrence, a thirty-nine-year-old major, answering questions from living legend Barry Goldwater and the powerful John Tower about his XV-15 flights and his opinion of the tiltrotor. They wanted to know how it flew, what military aircraft it might replace, what its future as a civilian aircraft might be, what was dangerous about it, what its best points were.

"Goldwater was just doing backflips" about the technology, Lawrence recalled. "He was a consummate pilot. He'd flown more airplanes than I have. Goldwater thought it was the greatest thing since sliced bread." Lawrence told the senators the military "could do anything with the tiltrotor, and we had already ginned up some scenarios."

One night toward the end of the air show, Bell threw a lavish dinner for a couple of hundred VIP guests in one of the elegant rental pavilions in the Bois de Boulogne, a vast, forested park on the west side of Paris. Atkins and other Bell executives were there to hobnob with members of Congress, U.S. and foreign military officers, government officials, and other important customers. No Texas barbecue that night; the party was served an elegant French dinner, preceded by canapés and champagne, accompanied by fine wines and orchestra music and eaten by candlelight. At the end, a parade of smartly dressed waiters came marching in to a jaunty tune, carrying plates of Baked Alaska decorated with lit sparklers—all except the waiter at the head of the line. His plate held a foot-long model of the XV-15, the toast of the 1981 Paris Air Show.

Dick Spivey felt especially proud of his company that night. This evening they'd done it up right, he thought, and the XV-15 had flown in Paris like a true dream machine. It felt like a tiltrotor sale to the military might be just around the corner.

★ ★ ★

Two weeks after the air show, General P. X. Kelley received his fourth star and took over two of the most powerful jobs in the Marine Corps: assistant commandant and chief of staff. Kelley, a red-haired, raspy-voiced Boston native, was an infantry officer, but during his first few weeks in his new post, the most pressing item on his agenda was an aviation matter: how to replace the Corps' aging CH-46 Sea Knight troop transport helicopters, the "Phrogs" the Marines had bought in the 1960s. The Navy Department had just done a study showing that at the rate the Phrogs were wearing out, within a few years the Corps would be unable to mount a standard amphibious landing—its defining mission. For Marine leaders, that was a horrible vision. If the Corps ever got to the point where it was unable to put troops on a hostile beach, who could say how long it would be before people started talking once again about folding them into the Army? To make sure that didn't happen, the Marines needed to start getting new troop transport aircraft by 1991 at the latest, the study said. As Kelley saw it, the future of the Marine Corps was riding on it.

The Marines had been trying for more than a decade to get money for a CH-46 replacement, but defense spending had declined after the Vietnam War and stayed tight under Carter. Every time action officers working on the issue came up with a plan, they lost in the annual budget battles. In 1980, though, as concern about the Soviet Union and the Middle East rose, the Navy had created an office to develop an aircraft for the Marines to replace the Phrog. When Kelley arrived at Headquarters Marine Corps that summer, the plan was to hold a "paper competition"—a comparison of designs—in 1982 and pick a new aircraft in 1983.

Kelley attended several meetings on the issue that summer. He heard the tiltrotor mentioned maybe once. The commandant, General Robert Barrow, and the deputy chief of staff for aviation, Lieutenant General William White, seemed to be leaning toward the Model 360, a new tandem-rotor helicopter proposed by the Phrog's maker, Boeing Vertol. Insiders called the 360 the "Plastic Phrog" because it was going to resemble the CH-46 but be made of a relatively new class of lightweight but strong materials called "composites," such as graphite epoxy. The Plastic Phrog was to carry eighteen to twenty-four troops, and Boeing said it would cruise at 180 knots, about 30 faster than the CH-46's top speed. Early estimates were that it would cost $1.3 billion to $2 billion to build a couple of Model 360 prototypes. Over the years, Dick Spivey and other Bell reps had gotten a number of lower-ranking officers interested in the tiltrotor, but as far as those wearing stars on their shoulders were concerned, it wasn't in the running to replace the CH-46.

Navy Secretary John Lehman was about to give the brass new instructions.

On September 24, Kelley was scheduled to attend a briefing on the CH-46 situation in Lehman's fourth-floor office on the E Ring of the Pentagon. White and other top Marine generals and the commander of

Navair, Vice Admiral Richard Seymour, were to be there. Kelley rushed to the Pentagon from Capitol Hill and arrived a touch late for the 1:30 P.M. session. Dick Seymour was in the anteroom, alone.

"Where is everybody?" Kelley asked him.

"The secretary's canceled the meeting." Seymour shrugged.

Lehman heard them talking and stuck his head out of his office door. "Come on in here, you two," he said. "I want to talk to you."

Kelley and Seymour sat down on a sofa opposite Lehman, who got right to the point. "I am not going to spend two billion dollars of non-recurring cost to evaluate a new helicopter," he told them. The United States was now competing with the Soviet Union not just militarily but also economically and for global leadership in aerospace. "I want to bring the Marine Corps into the twenty-first century on the leading edge of technology, and that leading edge is tiltrotor," Lehman said.

As far as Kelley was concerned, that was that. "I went back to Head-quarters Marine Corps and called the appropriate people into my office as assistant commandant and chief of staff," Kelley told me, "and I said, 'The decision has been made. It's not going to be another helicopter. It's going to be the tiltrotor concept.'"

Kelley was already a star in the Pentagon, viewed as the comman-dant's heir apparent. When the commandant sneezes, the Marine Corps catches pneumonia, and Kelley's word carried just as much weight. From then on, as far as the Marines were concerned, they were going to buy a tiltrotor.

★ ★ ★

Nothing is that simple in the brambly world of defense procurement, a thicket of regulations, bureaucracy, and politics where no path leads in a straight line. Ordinarily, the Marines might have found it next to impos-sible to get enough money into their budget to develop an expensive, complex, advanced technology aircraft such as the tiltrotor, even with Lehman's backing. Marine Corps aircraft are funded by the Navy bud-get, and the admirals who run the Navy have their own priorities. The admirals can't tell the Marines what to buy, but they have their hand on the spigot. The Marines had struggled for years to get in place the mod-est CH-46 replacement plan that Lehman had just told them to forget. But as Lehman, Kelley, and Seymour knew, a means was at hand to let the Marines defy the odds and get the tiltrotor they now wanted.

Ronald Reagan was elected partly on a promise to restore U.S. power and prestige abroad by rebuilding the "hollow" military. He set out to do that by spending vastly more on defense. In 1981, his administration's first defense budget asked Congress for $222.2 billion in fiscal year 1982—a whopping $26 billion more than President Jimmy Carter had proposed before he left office. In the Pentagon, happy days were here again. The armed services dusted off all kinds of proposals that had languished under Carter—far more, given what it would cost to complete them, than the Pentagon would be able to afford even if the defense budget kept soaring. Even the promilitary members of the defense committees in Congress soon started complaining that the armed services were trying to start too many new programs, especially helicopter and small aircraft projects.

The Marines wanted to replace the CH-46. The Army wanted a new plane to fly over enemy territory using secret electronic gear to intercept or jam communications. The Navy had been talking for years about replacing several types of helicopters and airplanes with a single type of "VSTOL" aircraft. (The acronym VSTOL, pronounced "VEE-stall," came into vogue with the Harrier jump jet as a more precise variation of VTOL. It means "vertical or short take off and landing.") The Navy and Air Force both wanted new combat search-and-rescue aircraft. The Air Force also wanted a new helicopter to carry special operations troops on low-level, nighttime missions like the failed hostage rescue attempt in Iran. Where was the money for all those programs going to come from, critics wanted to know?

Reagan's new undersecretary of defense for research and development, Richard D. DeLauer, wondered that, too. DeLauer was a former naval officer with a Ph.D. in aeronautics and mathematics who had been an executive with defense contractor TRW Inc. for the previous thirteen years. One member of the staff he inherited at the Pentagon was Marine Colonel William Scheuren, his "coordinator for rotary wing aircraft issues." A test pilot and a former commander of the Corps' first Harrier squadron, Scheuren also had been an action officer in the Marine Corps aviation branch. When he gave DeLauer a briefing on the issues in his area, he told him how the services wanted to buy six or seven new types of helicopters and airplanes. Scheuren suggested it would make more sense, and be cheaper, to get the armed forces to pool their money and develop one common VSTOL aircraft that each service could adapt to its own missions. A joint program like that might get a good reception on the Hill, Scheuren and DeLauer agreed. The Iran mission had revealed how clumsy the services were at working together. One way to make it easier, many defense experts were arguing, would be to make them buy more common equipment. DeLauer told Scheuren to see if he could get them to sign up to such a plan. "Okay, with that kind of guidance, the obvious choice is the tiltrotor or something similar," Scheuren remembered telling DeLauer.

Scheuren knew he'd just talked himself into a tall order. Coaxing four services into rewriting their budget plans and starting a joint program would be like turning four ocean liners at once. Joint programs had been in vogue among "defense intellectuals" at least since Robert McNamara, but the services generally didn't like them, and big ones rarely succeeded. In the 1960s, the Air Force's F-111 fighter-bomber had begun as a joint program with the Navy to buy a common aircraft, but the Navy dropped out and developed its F-14 Tomcat instead. After Vietnam, the Air Force developed the F-16 and the Navy its F-18 despite pressure from top civilian Pentagon officials to build and buy a common fighter plane. Preliminary meetings between the two services had literally turned into shouting matches. Even when joint programs got started, they were hard to manage to each service's satisfaction. They tended to bog down in interservice disputes over specifications, budget battles between and within the services, and cultural clashes between institutions with different needs, different priorities, different ways of doing things, and unique internal politics. If Scheuren was going to sell the services on a joint program, he was going to need help drafting memos, studying the services' needs, writing papers to show how their requirements could be met by one aircraft. He was going to need help briefing—in other words, persuading—the one-stars, two-stars, three-stars, four-stars, and senior civilian officials who would have to approve such a plan in the Army Department, the Air Force Department, the Navy Department, and the Office of the Secretary of Defense.

Scheuren had a couple of friends in the Army and Air Force he could ask to help, but for the heavy lifting he turned to his own tribe, the Marine Corps. Going back to his time in the Marine aviation branch, he was buddies with a cadre of Marine colonels and lieutenant colonels there, at Navair, and elsewhere who had worked on replacing the CH-46. Scheuren was sure they would see his new project as a golden opportunity to solve the Marine Corps' Phrog problem. One of those he turned to was Lieutenant Colonel Joe Moody, who had been working on the CH-46 issue for the aviation branch for a couple of years. Moody assigned his assistant, Major Bob Magnus, to work with Scheuren as well.

In August, Scheuren and Magnus wrote a memo making the argument for a joint VSTOL program for the Air Force, Navy, and Marines. It said their requirements "could best be met with a single, advanced but mature technology, rotary wing aircraft such as an operational derivative of the XV-15 tilt rotor." They left out the Army—the XV-15's first military sponsor—by design, correctly calculating that this would get its leadership's competitive juices flowing. With help from his "bit of a Marine Corps mafia," as he called it, Scheuren started circulating the document around the Pentagon. Before long, Army leaders weren't just demanding to be *part* of the new joint program, they were demanding to *lead* it. Magnus, meanwhile, got the memo to General Kelley, who in turn sent a memo to Lehman saying the proposed joint program could solve the CH-46 problem for the Marines. Kelley also said that, given the urgency of the problem, he was declaring it "Marine Aviation's Number One development priority."

Two weeks later was when Lehman called Kelley and Seymour into his office and told them to get the Marines a tiltrotor. Word of that quickly got back down to Magnus and the others in the Marine Corps mafia. Officially and publicly, the Marines were still just supporting an effort by DeLauer's office to get a joint program going that might end up buying the services of any kind of VSTOL aircraft. For many reasons, including defense procurement regulations and the danger of stirring up opposition, it would be impolitic for the Marines to advertise that they'd already decided—or Lehman had for them—that the joint program should produce a tiltrotor. Kelley didn't even mention the tiltrotor in a Memorandum for Record he wrote about the decisive September 24 conversation in Lehman's office. The joint program was the horse the Marines were going ride into the budget battles as they fought for their CH-46 replacement. In the beginning, it was a Trojan horse.

★ ★ ★

Before a big-ticket program gets started, the service that wants to buy the gear or weapon or machine in question has to write an Operational

Requirements Document setting out why the item is needed, how it fits into the service's warfighting doctrine, what it has to be able to do, and a host of other details. If more than one service wants it, the services have to write a Joint Operational Requirements Document. This JORD—pronounced the way it looks—then has to be approved by a long list of service and Pentagon officials. Separately, the new item has to win a place in long-term Pentagon spending plans, which two-star and three-star budget officers within each service and senior civilian officials of the Defense Department study, argue over, and revise each year. After a program passes that hurdle, it also has to survive periodic reviews by a top-level Pentagon committee that must approve major programs before they can pass various official "milestones" in their development. The bureaucratic maze doesn't end there. Once the civilian leadership in the Pentagon approves a program, it still has to go through much the same process each year to be included in the defense budget, which gets reviewed by the Office of Management and Budget, a White House agency. Then Congress takes its turn, starting with hearings throughout the spring and summer where members take testimony from top military and Pentagon officials and often debate the details of specific programs with them. By summer or fall, in a good year, members of the House and Senate have voted in committees and on the floor of each chamber on two major defense budget bills, one authorizing each program in the Pentagon's budget, another actually appropriating money for it in the coming fiscal year. A program can get cut, "plussed up," "zeroed out," or revised beyond recognition at any stage.

This is why defense contractors, like other special interests, pay lobbyists fat fees or salaries to track the budget process and try to influence it in their product's favor. Most lobbyists do this partly by trying to make sure the right Pentagon officials and military officers, members of Congress, and congressional aides get persuasive briefings about their products. First they have to get their attention, of course, which requires gaining access to them. To get access, almost all lobbyists make campaign contributions and get their clients to make them as well. Many also host fund-raising parties for members or solicit donations from others, then "bundle" them and pass them on so the congressman or senator knows where to direct his or her gratitude. Crooked lobbyists sometimes bribe or try to bribe lawmakers, though that's probably less common than popularly assumed. Usually, lobbyists cultivate influence in far subtler ways, most often just by trying to become friends with members or key aides, especially top committee aides.

However a lobbyist gets it, access is the key. The typical member's schedule is packed with committee meetings, floor votes, news conferences, and back-to-back meetings in the office, all sandwiched between evening fund-raisers and weekend trips home to see constituents or campaign for reelection. Getting a member's ear is the first step in getting a member's vote, so access becomes influence. That's why *who* a lobbyist knows is often far more important than *what* a lobbyist knows. For that reason, the ranks of Washington lobbyists teem with people who got into the influence game because they already had personal contacts on Capitol Hill. Many lobbyists are former members of Congress, former congressional aides, or veterans of the government's many legislative liaison offices.

Around the time Jim Atkins decided Bell should take the XV-15 to Paris, he also hired his company a new Washington lobbyist. George G. Troutman, a gregarious native of Albany, Georgia, with smiley eyes and a bulldog grin, was a former World War II bomber pilot who learned his way around Capitol Hill as an Air Force legislative liaison officer. After retiring from the Air Force with twenty-two years in uniform, Troutman lobbied for General Dynamics and then General Electric, whose products include aircraft engines.

"I hired George Troutman, and the reason he came with Bell was the tiltrotor; that's the only reason," Atkins remembered.

Troutman, who died of cancer in 2000, was smooth and wily. In a 1979 *Business Week* article on defense lobbyists, a California congressman called him "very likely the best in the business." *Business Week* said the "No. 1 rule" for good lobbyists was "no lying," but that there was a "corollary, sometimes known as 'Troutman's law.' As one Troutman confidant puts it, 'Never lie, but don't necessarily blab the truth.'"

"He was a jewel," Dick Spivey's former marketing boss, Phil Norwine, said of Troutman. "Very clever. I watched him write letters to himself, one for a congressman [to sign] and one for a general." At Christmas, Norwine remembered, Troutman would give the guards at the Pentagon parking lot little gift-wrapped bottles of champagne. In pre-9/11 days, security was more lax; the guards always let Troutman park close to the building. He just drove past them at the gate and waved.

Troutman knew everybody on Capitol Hill, it seemed, and was good friends with key members. He and House Majority Leader Jim Wright, a Fort Worth Democrat whose district included Bell Helicopter's plants, had been friends since Troutman was an Air Force legislative liaison officer. Troutman and Goldwater, a fellow World War II and Air Force veteran, were fishing buddies. It was Troutman who brought the senator to the Bell chalet at the 1981 Paris Air Show. After the air show, Leonard M. "Jack" Horner, a Bell vice president and former Marine pilot who was being groomed to succeed Atkins as president, started going to Washington nearly every week. Troutman took Horner to meet members of Congress and Pentagon officials to sell them on the tiltrotor. "He was fantastic," Horner said. "He had access to everybody and had a very innovative mind." Troutman explained that "in Washington, you don't have to worry about people saying 'yes,' you got to worry about people saying 'no,'" Horner said. "So we wanted to make sure we got everything through the system without somebody saying 'no.' They didn't have to say 'yes.' He helped me work that."

By the 1980s, the "military-industrial complex" had evolved into something even more complicated—a triple entente among the armed services, industry, and members of Congress who back defense procurement projects that create jobs in their districts or states. In a 1981 book on defense contracting, Gordon Adams of the Center on Budget and Policy Priorities, a Washington think tank focused on curbing defense spending, called this natural alliance of economic, bureaucratic, and political interests the "Iron Triangle." As word got back to Bell Helicopter that Lehman was sold on the tiltrotor and the Marines were trying to get a joint program started to buy one for themselves and the other services, Bell focused on getting the congressional leg of the Iron Triangle in place.

Troutman, Horner, Spivey, and others made the rounds on Capitol Hill constantly. They spread the word in the Texas delegation that the tiltrotor was ready for prime time and that a military contract to build one could bring billions of dollars and thousands of jobs to the Lone Star State. They briefed key members of the defense committees on how the tiltrotor could have avoided the disaster at Desert One, and how a contract to build one for the military would mean subcontracts that might create jobs in their states, too. Troutman told Horner it wasn't going to be enough, though, to win over the defense committees. To create a political base strong enough to get and keep a military tiltrotor program sold, Bell needed allies among members who took little interest in defense issues. When talking to them, Troutman said, they should stress that the tiltrotor was a technology that would revolutionize civil aviation. Aircraft able to take off and land vertically but fly as fast and far as a turboprop airplane would reduce airport congestion and bring air service to remote communities in states like Alaska. When the tiltrotor was proven by the military and adapted to civilian use, the United States would sell tiltrotors to the rest of the world and reap a huge economic harvest. Who wouldn't be for that? But the military would have to prove the technology first, for commercial aviation would never take the risk. "He was the one who came up with that great idea, the fact that the tiltrotor was good for America," Horner said of Troutman. "That was our whole theme: this was a technology that needed an opportunity."

★ ★ ★

Troutman was crafty, but the XV-15 remained Bell's best marketing tool. Even before Paris, Spivey had been urging his bosses to get NASA to let the company keep one of the two XV-15s in Texas so he could invite guest pilots to fly. NASA had been cool to the idea in the past, but after the air show, the agency's attitude changed. NASA's aeronautics arm was thrilled with the XV-15's performance in Paris and the resulting good publicity for its tiltrotor project. For years, the space program had gotten most of NASA's money and nearly all the publicity, casting a large shadow over those in the agency working on aircraft. The Paris Air Show was a first for NASA, which had never before allowed one of its experimental aircraft to fly at such an event. It had been a gamble, and officials at NASA's Ames Research Center thought the gamble had paid off handsomely. In October, NASA signed one of the two XV-15s over to Bell for flight tests, air show appearances, and to let guest pilots fly at company expense. NASA's official history of the XV-15 project explains that "with this arrangement, Bell would be able to demonstrate the capabilities of the tilt rotor aircraft to military and civilian aviation decision makers in an attempt to seek and develop potential markets."

Bell wasted no time putting its XV-15 to use. On October 30, Barry Goldwater was on his way home to Arizona for surgery to replace his left hip, his second such operation. The senator stopped in Fort Worth first to fly the XV-15. Goldwater's friend Troutman had made the arrangements, and Spivey and others at Bell were excited when the icon of the right wing arrived. Test pilot Ron Erhart felt sure Goldwater would get them a military contract of some kind once he flew the XV-15. Bell president Atkins met the senator and escorted him out to the aircraft. Stenciled on the fuselage under the XV-15's left cockpit window: SEN. BARRY M. GOLDWATER.

It was Dorman Cannon's day to fly, so he sat in the right seat. Goldwater's bad hip made it a struggle for him to get into the cockpit, but the senator was in a good mood; he didn't grumble. Cannon took them up into a hover, then headed south under gray, cloudy skies, tilting the XV-15's rotors forward into airplane mode and gaining altitude as they went. Once they were flying like a conventional turboprop airplane, Cannon looked over and said, "Mr. Goldwater, would you like to fly?"

"Yeah," Goldwater said cheerfully, taking command of the plane with his set of the dual controls. Then he turned to Cannon and asked, deadpan, "Anybody ever rolled this sonuvabitch?"

Cannon wasn't sure Goldwater was kidding. "No," the test pilot replied firmly, "and we're not going to do it now, either."

Goldwater looked through his horn-rimmed glasses and gave Cannon a sly grin.

Roy Hopkins, one of Bell's helicopter test pilots in those days, was sitting by the door to the Bell Flight Research Center offices when Cannon and Goldwater returned. As they came through the door, Goldwater declared to no one in particular, "Man, you guys got something there!" Then he hobbled into a tiny conference room packed with engineers, marketers, and managers. He told them about his flight and what a bright future he could see for the tiltrotor. When he left, Spivey had no doubt: the senator was sold.

By November, Scheuren, Magnus, and the others in the Marine Corps mafia were well on their way to getting the joint VSTOL program created. The services were now openly discussing the idea with each other and the defense companies that might bid on such a project. Magnus told me that as he worked on the studies needed to justify a joint program, "I started drinking the Kool-Aid" on the tiltrotor.

Bell officials—especially Horner, Troutman, and Spivey—were doing everything they could to get others to take a sip. Spivey started inviting every officer and official he thought might matter to Fort Worth to fly the XV-15. Troutman helped get them to come. From November 30 through December 12, Navair commander Seymour, Marine Corps aviation chief White, and six other Air Force, Army, and Marine generals flew the XV-15. Over three days from December 14 to 16, Bell brought in ten Marine Corps officers, including Magnus, Scheuren, and the rest of the Marine Corps mafia helping sell the joint program. Four flew the first day. Three more, including Magnus and Scheuren, flew the next. The third day, Colonels Bob Balch, Darwin Lundberg, and James Creech, the manager of the Navair office created to replace the CH-46, got their turn. Spivey made sure each guest pilot got a plaque signed by the Bell pilot they'd flown with and by Jim Atkins. Each plaque was inscribed: "Know all men by these presents that [name] did on this day fly the XV-15 tilt rotor, the world's most advanced and efficient high-speed rotorcraft, [date]."

When Balch, Lundberg, and Creech finished their flights, Atkins invited them to his office. "Now I want to hear it from you guys' mouths," the Bell president said. "If I make a large commitment to this thing, is it going to make it?"

They all said it would.

"I'd feel a hell of a lot more comfortable if you all didn't have exactly the same suit on," Atkins told the three Marines.

Atkins knew the other services weren't sold on the tiltrotor the way the Marines and Lehman were. By now, it appeared certain a joint VSTOL aircraft program would be created, but it was uncertain how long it might actually last. The Army had started the XV-15 with NASA a decade earlier, looking for a faster way to evacuate battlefield casualties, but had almost dropped out just a couple of years ago. Spivey and others at Bell were hearing that the top brass weren't sure the tiltrotor's speed would make all that much difference to the Army. Some Army generals were more interested in trying to build a new combination attack/scout helicopter with stealth technology to evade enemy radar. Navy admirals, meanwhile, were less enthusiastic than Lehman about investing a lot of money to buy a complex new aircraft largely for the Marine Corps while trying to build a 600-ship Navy, new fighter planes, and a lot of other things.

Two weeks after Atkins and the Marine colonels talked, DeLauer got Deputy Defense Secretary Frank Carlucci to sign an order directing the Army, the Navy, and the Air Force to chip in $1.5 million each to create a joint VSTOL program for themselves and the Marines, a step called "Milestone Zero." But that was just a start. The next steps would be to get the services to really commit to the program and Congress to fund it.

For the time being, the potential new aircraft would be called the JVX, for "Joint Services, Vertical Lift and Experimental." Reports in the trade press said that if it went forward, the project would be huge—$20 billion or more in all, though the real estimate was $41 billion. The Marines were to buy 552 of the new aircraft to replace their CH-46s and CH-53D Sea Stallion helicopters. The Navy would buy 50 for various missions. The Air Force wanted 200 for special operations and combat search and rescue. The Army was expected to buy 288 for electronic surveillance, to carry troops, and for medical evacuation. The JVX would be a bonanza for whatever company won a design competition to be held in 1983, after a new program office had done all the necessary studies and paperwork. The Army would be in charge, but the program manager would be Marine Colonel Jimmie Creech, who had run the Navair office searching for a CH-46 replacement and flown the XV-15 in December.

In January, the new program office organized a meeting at Quantico Marine Base of the four armed services to decide the minimum requirements the JVX would have to meet—speed, range, altitude, payload, etc. Each service sent a small group of experts. Magnus led the Marine Corps delegation. (Another participant grinned when he recalled how Magnus introduced himself as "Bob Magnus, Commandant Marine Corps." After all, he was *representing* the commandant.) The panel deliberated for a week and wrote a Joint Services Operational Requirement. Officially, the JVX might be a tiltrotor, a tilt-wing, a compound helicopter Sikorsky was working on called the Advancing Blade Concept, or some other VSTOL craft—all were theoretical candidates. The requirements committee, though, decided the JVX would need to cruise at 250 knots—close to 290 miles per hour—and fly as high as 30,000 feet to do what the Marines and the Army wanted. Only the tiltrotor had shown it could do that.

The JVX program office also assembled a 54-member team of experts to assess the various VSTOL technologies against the Joint Services Operational Requirements. Magnus was on that panel, too. The technology committee, which studied the options from February through April, decided only the tiltrotor could meet the requirements.

Spivey and others at Bell were excited by the way things were unfolding but still unsure they would win the deal. Nobody but Bell had ever built a tiltrotor, but in theory, another company could. Boeing Vertol had competed against Bell for the NASA/Army project that produced the XV-15. Spivey didn't know it at the time, but even before the JVX program was announced, the Boeing executive who'd been in charge of trying to sell the Marines the Plastic Phrog had written a memo to the company's president urging him to create a tiltrotor program of their own as soon as possible. Spivey also heard from Magnus that Sikorsky might design a tiltrotor of its own and bid it. By now, Magnus was on the phone fairly frequently with Spivey. "We were properly but pretty closely knit," Magnus said. But even Magnus wasn't sure Bell had the manufacturing ability to build a tiltrotor as big and capable as the Marines wanted.

As the JVX program got under way, Magnus and the rest of the Marine Corps mafia went into high gear to get it through the budget process—approved by the Navy Department, into the Pentagon's future defense spending plans, okayed by top civilian officials, and funded by Congress. Magnus was in the office by about five-thirty each morning and left after dark each evening. The admirals were resisting, throwing hurdles in the way of a program that was going to spend a big chunk of their future budgets on the Marine Corps. They used a standard tactic: requesting studies. Magnus worked on almost all of them. He also worked on studies Lehman and Kelley ordered up aimed at reassuring Marine aviation chief White and Commandant Barrow, who were antsy about the course Lehman had set for them.

With House Majority Leader Wright, Senator Tower, and the rest of the Texas delegation looking out for Bell Helicopter's interests, however, and with Bell lobbying others in Congress, momentum for the JVX was quickly growing. Magnus also was working on Congress to make sure the JVX got funded. Normally, the Marine Corps legislative liaison office would handle that kind of thing, but in January, Magnus started going to Capitol Hill on his own to brief House and Senate armed services committee aides on why the Marines wanted the JVX program and the tiltrotor. He was doing what Kelley wanted, but he was poaching on legislative liaison's turf, so sometimes he went to the Hill in civilian clothes to avoid notice.

"Magnus was the type of guy that just thought, 'Congressional liaison's fine but it takes too long to bring them up to speed,'" said Bob Balch, Magnus's onetime superior in the aviation branch. "He was a 'let's get it done in the next forty-five seconds' kind of guy. And of course, in his mind, it was the most important thing on Earth because 'It's my program.' He had his own back channels. He was a genius at that kind of stuff. He loved it, because he understood that was how Washington worked. It was information and who has it. It was understanding where the money was and who controlled it."

For a fitness report, Balch once had Magnus list what he had done to get the JVX program off the ground. In Magnus's small, neat handwriting—part print, part cursive—the list ran five pages and included nearly fifty items.

As word spread that the JVX surely would be a tiltrotor, guest pilots flocked to Texas to fly the XV-15. "People wanted to fly in that thing just as if you had a candy store," pilot Dorman Cannon chuckled. More generals flew, as did one of Senator Tower's top aides. To promote the tiltrotor's civil aviation potential, Spivey brought in two pilots from the Federal Aviation Administration to fly it as well. Then Lehman finally got his turn.

Lehman had been practicing his helicopter piloting skills at the Marine Corps Base in Quantico, Virginia, a forty-five-minute drive south of Washington, with HMX-1, the squadron that flies the president in "Marine One," as the big green and white choppers are known when the chief executive is inside. In late March, a team of Bell officials including test pilot Cannon and Spivey took the XV-15 there. They were met by Lehman—and by Magnus, who gave the secretary an update on where the JVX program stood. Spivey briefed Lehman on the XV-15's technology, showed him data, and talked about how tiltrotors could have avoided the humiliation of Desert One. Lehman didn't give either much time. He was there to fly. As Cannon gave him a preflight briefing on how to pilot the XV-15 and eject from it if necessary, Lehman literally kept licking his lips, whether out of nervousness or eagerness, Cannon wasn't sure. Soon Cannon and Lehman took off on the flight Young Winston had wanted since Paris. Lehman agreed to come back only when the fuel warning light went on.

A photo of him climbing out of the aircraft upon their return tells the rest of the tale. Wearing a flight suit and aviator sunglasses, Lehman has to stoop to exit the XV-15's narrow hatch, but his head is up, and he beams out at those awaiting him with that smile little kids wear when they get off a roller coaster for the first time, just before they beg, "Can I go again? *Puh-leeze?*"

Two days later, Lehman visited House Majority Leader Wright in his Capitol office. They talked about Lehman's XV-15 flight and about how to ensure the JVX program got funded in that year's defense bills. "I didn't take too much encouraging," Wright told me. If Bell could sell tiltrotors to the military, that would create jobs in Wright's Fort Worth district. If the military building it enabled the tiltrotor to succeed as a civilian aircraft, that would guarantee those jobs even if military spending declined. "It struck me as a win-win situation," Wright said. Democrat Wright and Republican Senator Tower, a fellow Texan and one of Lehman's mentors, often worked together to promote military projects in Texas. Soon they were coordinating their efforts to win allies in Congress for the JVX, too.

★ ★ ★

After the program was announced, Jim Atkins sought Lehman's advice on what Bell needed to do to win the contract. "I see the program being so large that you need a partner," Lehman told him. "That is up to you, it's your choice. Do what you want."

At that point, what Atkins wanted was whatever Lehman wanted. Atkins pondered the possibilities and approached Joseph P. Mallen, the president of Boeing Vertol, which had designed a tiltrotor once upon a time and built a tilt-wing. Boeing Vertol was experienced in building big helicopters with cabins large enough to hold twenty-four troops, which Atkins knew would be one of the JVX requirements, and Mallen and Lehman had a personal relationship. Lehman had been a consultant to Boeing Vertol before he became Navy secretary. For a lot of reasons, teaming with Boeing would be a better bet for Bell than competing with them for the JVX deal.

The two executives met poolside during an aviation trade fair in the Southwest that winter and continued their conversation in Atkins's suite. They took to each other immediately, and by the end of their talk, they'd shaken hands on a deal to form a 50–50 partnership to design a big, new military tiltrotor and bid it for the JVX.

The Bell-Boeing partnership was announced in June 1982. A month later, Horner, Troutman, and Spivey went to Philadelphia for a meeting with their Boeing counterparts. Spivey thought it was a natural fit. Boeing Vertol had always built big helicopters and Bell had always built small ones; they weren't direct competitors, the way Bell and Sikorsky were, so there was no bad blood between them. Boeing was also one of the aviation industry's best "systems integrators," a company skilled at incorporating high-tech gear into an aircraft. Bell's new partner also offered considerable political clout. Boeing Vertol's helicopter factory was just outside Philadelphia, Lehman's hometown, and Pennsylvania's delegation was one of the largest in Congress. Boeing Vertol's corporate parent, the aerospace giant Boeing Company, could muster political support in a lot of other states as well. Combined with Bell's backing from the large and powerful Texas delegation, which included the House majority leader, the Senate Armed Services Committee chairman, and other influential members, the Bell-Boeing team looked politically unstoppable.

When the partnership was announced, a lot of people following the JVX figured the competition was over. Spivey wasn't so sure. In July, he noted in his work diary that Sikorsky had gotten the Army to extend the expected deadline for the JVX competition by three months. "Worried about Syk. killing it," Spivey wrote, characteristically misspelling his abbreviation for Sikorsky.

A month later, the JVX program office invited representatives from twenty-five companies to a briefing where program officials told them the tiltrotor was the "favored technology," the only one able to meet the requirements of all four armed services. This ruled out Sikorsky's Advancing Blade Concept helicopter, but JVX program officials were still hoping to get Sikorsky to bid. If Bell-Boeing had no competition, it might be hard to get a good price out of them. There was also the chance that either Congress or the Reagan administration might cancel the program if there were no competition. On August 26, 1982, Spivey noted in his work diary that Sikorsky had "asked for XV-15 FLT," and a Sikorsky pilot in fact flew NASA's XV-15 in October.

By the fall, Spivey wasn't just worried about competition from Sikorsky, he feared the whole JVX program might implode. It was looking shaky. The three service secretaries had finally signed an agreement in June saying they would go ahead with the JVX, and the top leadership of the Marine Corps was clearly on the same page at last, partly because White had retired in June as well. He was replaced as deputy chief of staff for aviation by Lieutenant General William F. Fitch, a believer in VSTOL aircraft. Six weeks after he replaced White, Fitch went to Fort Worth and flew the XV-15. In the next year's budget hearings, Fitch would tell a

Senate committee that the tiltrotor was "a step comparable to the introduction of the jet engine for fighter aircraft."

The Army, though, which had started out demanding that it run
the JVX program because it was NASA's partner on the XV-15, soon
cooled to the project. During internal budget battles in 1982, pressure
from generals more interested in other ways of spending the Army's
money rose. The undersecretary of the Army, James Ambrose, started
arguing internally that a tiltrotor was going to be too expensive and
too visible to enemy radar for the Army's electronic warfare mission. In
October, Lehman met with him and Army Secretary John Marsh, and
while Ambrose didn't say the Army wanted to pull out altogether, he and
Marsh wanted to hand off the Army's role as executive agency. Under
the joint services agreement, the Navy was supposed to provide 50 percent of the money and buy most of the aircraft anyway. Lehman said the
Navy would be happy to take over, and Navair started running the JVX
program in December.

That same month, Navair solicited bids. The program office had sent
draft copies to about a hundred defense companies for comment during
the summer. Boeing Vertol had sent about fifty engineers to Bell in Fort
Worth, and the companies were nearly done putting their bid together.
Personal computers and compact disks were still mere visions in those
days, so the Bell-Boeing proposal was on about a thousand pounds of
paper. Spivey helped put it together, wondering all the while if Sikorsky
was going to snatch away the deal he'd been working toward all these
years. The latest rumor was that Sikorsky wasn't going to bid after all,
but you could never be sure. He decided to take the bid to Washington
himself.

By now, Dick Spivey was forty-two years old and a salesman with a
dream he'd been selling more than half his career. He'd lost his hair and
his first wife since he'd embarked on his quest. He'd traveled thousands
of miles and spent countless lonely nights in hotel rooms. He'd recently
remarried, but at the moment, he was captivated by the JVX bid. He and
his new bride, a nurse anesthetist named Terry, had wed in November
but delayed a honeymoon until June. Spivey thought his future might
be decided by whether Bell-Boeing won this contract. After a plunge in
civilian helicopter sales that year, Bell had just laid off more than 1,500
of 8,000 employees.

On February 22, 1983, Spivey took an American Airlines flight to

Washington National Airport. He was met in a rented van by a colleague
from Bell's Washington office, Gerald Gard. They stopped by the cargo
terminal to pick up the thirty or so cardboard boxes containing Bell-
Boeing's bid, then drove two and a half miles to an outcropping of speck-
led-granite high-rises known as Crystal City. They parked underneath
the Holiday Inn Crystal City, whose basement garage was connected to
an adjacent high-rise called Jefferson Plaza One, where Navair's offices
were. Spivey spent the night in the Holiday Inn. The next morning, he
and Gard borrowed a hand truck, loaded the cardboard boxes on it, and
wheeled them over to Navair. A guard directed them to an empty room,
where they stacked the boxes on the carpeted floor and got a receipt
from a bureaucrat.

"Do you have room for everybody's proposals?" Gard asked a receptionist, fishing to find out if Sikorsky was going to bid.

"You're the only ones who're going to be bringing in a proposal,"
she replied. So Sikorsky wasn't going to bid after all, Gard concluded.
He gave Spivey the news and headed back to his office. Spivey, though,
wasn't sure the receptionist knew what she was talking about, and he
couldn't bring himself to leave. He just had to see for himself.

He found a chair somewhere and sat down outside the room where
he and Gard had put the Bell-Boeing proposal. The receptionist wasn't
very chatty, so Spivey just sat there all day, reading newspapers and getting up now and then to pace the hall or get a drink of water. At times,
he found himself hoping the receptionist was right and no one else was
bidding, but then he feared what might happen if that were so. He could
imagine the Pentagon throwing out Bell-Boeing's proposal for lack of
competition and starting over. The virtue of free market competition
was a constant Reagan refrain. On the other hand, it wouldn't be Bell-
Boeing's fault if no one else chose to compete.

By the 4:30 P.M. bid deadline, no one else had shown up. Two months
later, on April 25, Navair announced it was giving Bell-Boeing a $68.7
million contract to design a tiltrotor for the JVX, build a prototype rotor
and other parts, and conduct wind tunnel tests. If all went well, this
first contract would lead later to multibillion-dollar deals to build prototype aircraft, test them, and produce the new tiltrotor by the hundreds.
Spivey braced himself for a protest by Sikorsky. When none came, he
was ecstatic.

Spivey felt proud. He hadn't sold the tiltrotor by himself, but he'd been selling it longer than just about anyone else, and with as much or more enthusiasm. The contacts he'd cultivated among mid-level officers in the Marine Corps had been vital to the sale, and so had Bell's use of the XV-15 as a marketing tool. Spivey's guest pilot program had been a major part of that. Everyone agreed the XV-15 had been the key. Horner teased Spivey about that. "We didn't need you," he'd say. "The airplane sold itself." Spivey didn't mind when Horner said that; he knew the boss was just ribbing him. Horner also liked to tell Spivey his business card really ought to say "tiltrotor pedlar," and one day Spivey called his bluff. He got some cards made up that said just that, and when he gave one to Horner, they had a good laugh. It rankled Spivey, though, when others at Bell started saying the tiltrotor had sold itself. He knew some engineers and others looked down on marketers. "We were supposed to be 'hucksters,'" Spivey said. "We were 'selling snake oil.'"

The XV-15 was far from snake oil, but what it represented—and what it had sold—was the dream, not a useful machine. The little tiltrotor stoked the imaginations of a widening circle of believers much as model planes fuel the fantasies of children. The XV-15 met the ultimate aviation challenge much the way venerated aeronautics professor Alexander Klemin had stated it in 1938. It could do "substantially everything that a bird can do in the air." But the XV-15 and the big, beefy tiltrotor that Bell-Boeing had just contracted to design—and promised to have ready for the battlefield in a mere eight years—were only superficially alike. They were the same genus but different species.

The XV-15 weighed about 10,000 pounds. It could carry two pilots, roughly 1,500 pounds of fuel, and a thousand pounds or so of test instruments. It was never flown in the rain or other bad weather because nearly every inch of its fuselage, wing, and rotors was covered with data-gathering gauges that could be damaged by precipitation.

The tiltrotor the services wanted—and that Bell-Boeing had promised—was to carry an aircrew of three and twenty-four Marines with packs and weapons from the deck of a ship to a shore a couple of hundred miles away, turn back to the ship, and do the same thing over again. It was to cruise at 250 knots, "dash" at up to 300, and fly nearly 2,400 miles without refueling. It was to use the latest computerized "fly-by-wire" flight controls instead of the XV-15's bell cranks and push-pull rods. It was to incorporate electronic gear allowing it to fly in any weather, day or night, in any climate. It was to be used for ten different missions by four armed services. It was going to be the superplane of military transports—a real dream machine.

Nearly a quarter century later, Bob Magnus, by then a white-haired four-star general and assistant commandant of the Marine Corps, told me that, compared with what he and the others who set the requirements for the JVX envisioned, "The XV-15 was a Tinker Toy."

"The XV-15 proved that there was nothing magic or fatal about tiltrotor technology," Magnus said. Then he added, "Now of course, you could always screw it up when you built one."

CHAPTER FIVE

THE MACHINE

When convertiplane visionary Gerard Herrick took the stage at the 1938 Rotating Wing Aircraft Meeting in Philadelphia, he quickly lived up to his introduction as "a man who is captain of his own soul." Herrick softened up his audience of engineers, inventors, and aviation executives with a poem whose author he identified only as Al F. Davis. It was called "One of Our Simple Problems."

> *"Design a plane" the head men say,*
> *It must be built in such a way,*
> *That the dumbest mug can fly hands off,*
> *Make the hardest landing still feel soft,*
> *Make up for brains that the pilot lacks,*
> *Make the seats lean forward and still lean back,*
> *Supply and demand will be the thing,*
> *Forget the span and chord of wing.*
> *The spar must be just six feet long,*
> *For scraps of spruce cost but a song.*
> *The fuselage can be tied with a string,*
> *Or by similar method hung to the wing,*
> *It must be safe and in the main,*
> *Be able to stand a hurricane,*
> *It must be fast and not land hot*
> *(What a helluva job the designer's got!)*
> *Fast and light and comfortable too,*
> *With a cruising range to Timbuctoo.*
> *Of course this is no common hack,*
> *For it must carry the load of a ten-ton Mack.*
> *It must climb straight up and land straight down,*

But the pilot must scarcely feel the ground.
Yes, flaps and brakes and retractable gear,
Hell's bells! They must think the millennium's here.
And one last word the head men say,
"It's gotta be finished by yesterday."
On second thought there's one thing more,
They'll have to sell at the ten-cent store!

Kenneth G. Wernicke was only six years old, a kid in Kansas City, when Gerard Herrick entertained the rotary wing pioneers with that aircraft designer's satirical lament. Forty-four years later, Wernicke was an aircraft designer himself, Bell's chief tiltrotor engineer. When the Bell-Boeing team got the specifications for the JVX and Wernicke saw what the military was demanding, he might have penned a sardonic rhyme himself—if he hadn't been so appalled.

Wernicke had no problem with the basic requirements: high speed, long range, a fuselage big enough for two squads of Marines or an F-18 fighter jet engine. That was all expected. But that was just the beginning. They also wanted the JVX to be tougher than any helicopter ever built, able to shrug off gunfire and keep flying, dodge or fool enemy missiles, carry its own guns to fire back. That was going to make it heavy. They wanted the latest and greatest electronic gear installed so it could fly anytime, anywhere, in any weather. That was going to make it heavier. Worst of all, they wanted it to operate from an amphibious assault ship. That meant it would need intricate mechanisms to fold its rotors and rotate its wing so it would fit on a ship's elevator and underneath the deck to be stowed or worked on. That was going to make it heavier still. But the kicker was this: operating from the ship also meant the rotors would have to be undersized, which would make it even harder for the aircraft to carry its required payload.

"Anything that anybody had ever wanted, they asked for," Wernicke told me. "It was going to be excessively heavy. They wanted too much and it could only be big enough to go down a carrier elevator. The whole thing was bad news."

Ken Wernicke's view was hardly insignificant. He was Bell Helicopter's premier tiltrotor engineer. Arguably, that made him the premier tiltrotor engineer in the world. No one but Bell had ever built a tiltrotor that worked.

Slender and serious, with short brown hair and handsome features, Wernicke had been tiltrotor pioneer Robert Lichten's protégé. Wernicke joined Bell in 1955, after earning a master's degree in aeronautical engineering from the University of Kansas. Aeronautical engineers, like artists, tend to understand and work in several aspects of their field but specialize in just one. Art has its great painters, architects, and sculptors, but only a rare genius such as Michelangelo masters multiple disciplines. Some aeronautical engineers are aerodynamicists, who predict air flows and their effects on aircraft. Others are dynamicists, who detect and find ways to reduce or eliminate stresses caused by the motion of an aircraft and its moving parts. Structural engineers focus on configuring aircraft to withstand the aerodynamic and dynamic forces they encounter in flight. Wernicke was a Michelangelo, brilliant in all disciplines. "He was good in everything. It didn't matter: aerodynamics, dynamics, structures," said Troy Gaffey, who worked for Wernicke as a dynamicist on the XV-15.

In the 1960s, Wernicke headed a team of eight or nine tiltrotor engineers who included his twin brother, Rodney. Back then, for a company that was churning out thousands of combat helicopters for the Army and Marines to fly in Vietnam, the tiltrotor was a sideshow, an indulgence, a long-shot bet on the future at best. Wernicke's team was largely left alone. They worked at desks and on drawing boards in a cramped little space on the second floor of Bell's engineering building, one of two yellow brick structures fronting on Highway 10 in the sparsely populated Fort Worth suburb of Hurst. Their little bullpen was separated from a larger herd of research and development engineers by a low wall topped with frosted glass framed in metal, but it was noisy in there. A secretary who sat near Wernicke was always clacking away on her electric typewriter. The engineers were constantly talking, either to each other, to someone on the phone, or to a colleague from another section of Bell's engineering department who'd dropped by to noodle through some problem.

"We'd have big arguments about various things," Gaffey recalled. "It was exciting. We were finding things out. It was the Age of Discovery. Unless we were dead asleep, we were thinking about the tiltrotor and how we were going to solve the problem. We had a great passion to get the tiltrotor up and running." Often, one of the tiltrotor engineers would get up and take an idea down the hall, sit on the edge of a colleague's desk, show him a sketch, and say, "What do you think of this?" or "Look at this!" As the engineers talked, they'd take turns drawing their ideas. Engineers find it easier to talk about their work with pen or pencil in hand and a piece of paper in front of them, even if it's just a napkin. They'll sketch a rotor blade or a tail fin, draw a graph or diagram, write out an equation to show what they mean. This is true even today, though computerized design software long ago replaced the drafting board and slide rule in the engineering workplace. In the 1960s, engineers still worked on paper.

They also played with it. Gaffey loved to tell how, one day around 5 P.M., the tiltrotor engineers held an impromptu contest. They made paper airplanes out of their time cards, engineered them for distance by attaching paper clips, then took turns standing on top of the office conference table and flinging the planes to see whose flew farthest. Wernicke had just climbed up on the table to launch his entry when Bell's dignified president, Jim Atkins, happened down the hall past the open door. "I can still remember Atkins looking at him like, 'What are you *doing?*'" Gaffey chuckled.

Atkins's office was in the administration building, another yellow brick rectangle facing Highway 10 and situated on the other side of a guard shack just inside the front gate. Bell's executives, lawyers, marketers and other nonengineers were in that building. Gaffey called it "the Far Side," after the zany comic strip by Gary Larson. Bell's engineers were often at odds with its management and marketers, though until Bell got its contract to build the XV-15 for NASA in 1972, the tiltrotor engineers were an exception. They were just a small band of brothers on a quest for aviation's Holy Grail, largely undistracted by considerations other than science. As Bell designed the XV-15, though, the number of tiltrotor engineers grew. They moved into a larger workspace and, in effect, into the real world. When Atkins decided the tiltrotor was ripe for harvest and Bell turned the XV-15 into a marketing tool, the tiltrotor engineers lost their splendid isolation.

A couple of years before the JVX came along, marketing asked Wernicke's team for a conceptual design of a tiltrotor big enough to carry twenty-four Marines. A lively debate ensued. The engineers already had a conceptual design for a tiltrotor about the size of the XV-15, just large enough to hold twelve troops. They wanted marketing to sell *that*. Dick Spivey told them the Marines didn't care what engineers wanted. The

Marines wanted an aircraft that could carry twenty-four troops. Given the limited number of amphibious assault ships in the fleet, the Marines felt they needed an aircraft that size to get enough troops ashore quickly enough in a standard assault. Besides, if they agreed to buy an aircraft that held only twelve troops, others in the Pentagon would surely force them to buy Sikorsky's UH-60 Black Hawk helicopter. The Black Hawk was just that size, already flown by the Army, and would be cheaper than a tiltrotor. After years of cultivating the Marines, Spivey also thought they were loath to buy the same helicopters as the Army because "the more they got like the Army, the more likely they were to be absorbed *into* the Army."

The big-versus-small tiltrotor debate at Bell came to a head in 1980, when some of the engineers tried to convince Atkins that Bell's first tilt-rotor product should be their twelve-passenger design. At a meeting on the issue, Spivey told them he couldn't sell a tiltrotor that size to the military. Marketing won the argument. Atkins had favored the bigger machine anyway. He wanted to sell the military a tiltrotor big enough to be adapted to a civilian version holding about forty-four passengers, a machine that might compete with jets for the regional air transport market.

Not long before the JVX program got started, marketing put together a brochure touting a big, sleek tiltrotor that would hold twenty-four Marines and operate from amphibious landing ships. Wernicke paid no attention. He was utterly absorbed by his own engineering work, nearly oblivious to what went on around him. He wouldn't even open his mail unless someone complained about getting no response. He just let it pile up in the in-basket on the corner of his desk until it leaned like the Tower of Pisa, then tipped it over into the wastebasket. Wernicke only focused on what the military wanted in the JVX when he read the draft specifications the companies got as they were gearing up to bid. When he saw them, he hit the ceiling.

"I went in and told the vice president of engineering, Bob Lynn, that I wasn't going to do it, that I thought it would be the downfall of the tilt-rotor," Wernicke told me.

Wernicke believed in the tiltrotor as much as anybody. He'd watched with pride as the XV-15 performed at the Paris Air Show in 1981, beamed when it did its little bow and the audience cheered. He knew he could design a tiltrotor the same size as the XV-15 for the Navy or Marines that would be just about perfect, or even a bigger one for the Air Force or the Army, who wouldn't want to fly theirs from ships. Long-range transport to and from rugged areas was the ideal tiltrotor mission, he thought, a task where its vertical takeoff and landing ability would be needed but speed and range would be its ace in the hole. As Wernicke saw it, the military was buying this tiltrotor for the wrong mission.

The JVX was to perform a long list of chores for all four armed services, but its main job would be to carry Marines from ship to shore over distances of no more than about 50 to 110 nautical miles—roughly 55 to 125 statute miles—while flying no higher than 3,500 feet. On such missions, the aircraft would have to take off and land vertically, hover at each end of its flight, and repeat the trip before it was refueled. Wernicke saw that as a helicopter mission, a job for an aircraft that could hover efficiently—that is, using minimal fuel—and needn't fly high. A tiltrotor could never hover as efficiently as a helicopter because its rotors had to serve as propellers, too. Their dual function was why Bell called them "proprotors." To work as propellers, proprotor blades have to be shorter than helicopter rotor blades and twisted more to provide efficient thrust in forward flight. The smaller diameter and greater twist of its blades meant a proprotor needed more power than a helicopter rotor to lift the same weight and hold it in the air. A proprotor also wasn't an ideal propeller—its blades were too long—but it wasn't a bad one, if configured the right way. That argued against the Marine Corps mission, too, Wernicke thought. A tiltrotor would give the Marines speed all right, but it would give them speed efficiently only at high altitude, where thinner air allows an aircraft to fly faster for less fuel. "A tiltrotor mission is one where you take advantage of the capability . . . to go at high speed and cruise over long distances," Wernicke said. The tiltrotor's ideal altitude for flying fast, he calculated, would be way up at 40,000 feet, where the density of the air is about 25 percent of what it is at sea level. No such mission was in the requirements.

The straw that promised to break this camel's back for Wernicke, though, was the requirement that the JVX be able to operate from a Tarawa-class amphibious assault ship, known as an LHA. An LHA isn't a small ship. It can carry a complete Marine battalion, their supplies and equipment, a couple of dozen helicopters to get them ashore, and six Harrier fighter jets as well. It has ten "deck spots" for vertical take-offs and landings, and space enough to park a number of aircraft topside while others fly to and from the vessel. But the specs said the JVX had to taxi past the ship's superstructure with its rotors turning. As it did, the tip of the closest rotor would have to clear the "island," as it's called, by no less than twelve feet, eight inches, and the landing gear tires would have to stay five feet from the outboard edge of the deck. Any closer would risk the aircraft rolling over the side. This narrow corridor meant each proprotor could be no more than thirty-eight feet in diameter— smaller than Wernicke knew was warranted for the aircraft's bulk.

Some on the four-service committee that wrote the basic require-ments envisioned a tiltrotor weighing about 20,000–25,000 pounds empty, maybe 4,000 pounds more than the CH-46 the JVX was to replace. But they had underestimated how much all the things they wanted in it were going to weigh. Moved by U.S. helicopter losses dur-ing the war in Vietnam, where more than 40 percent of those flown were lost, the panel had written requirements for "survivability" that far outstripped any ever required in a helicopter. "Flight-critical systems" must be either tough enough to withstand hits from 14.5-millime-ter armor-piercing incendiary projectiles—the size fired by the larg-est Soviet-made machine gun of the day—or installed in multiple sets, so that if one was disabled, the extras would keep the JVX flying. The exhaust from the JVX's turbine engines had to be cloaked from heat-seeking missiles by heavy devices called infrared suppressors. Depend-ing on the mission, the JVX also was to carry "automatic weapons for in-zone suppressive fire and missiles for air-to-air defense," the require-ments said, as well as a long list of special electronic gear. The Naval Air Systems Command engineers who had written the detailed specifica-tions were more realistic than the four-service committee that drafted the mission requirements. Navair set an upper limit of 31,886 pounds on the JVX's "weight empty," how much it would tip the scales without any fuel, pilots, passengers, or cargo aboard. Wernicke could see right off the bat, though, that with its big fuselage, with mechanisms to tilt its engines and rotors, with still more mechanisms to fold its rotors and stow its wings, plus all the other requirements, this bird proba-bly was going to weigh a lot more than that. Moreover, its normal fly-ing weight—what engineers call "design gross weight"—would surely be well north of 45,000 pounds. The military's great expectations were bordering on mission impossible.

All aircraft designs involve compromise. Size, speed, range, and so forth have to be traded off against one another and balanced to meet the requirements for the aircraft being created. A fundamental question for the designer, however, is how heavy the aircraft will be, for weight dictates how much power is needed to lift a machine into the air and carry a useful load. When a rotorcraft takes off straight up or hovers, it has to produce a pound of thrust for every pound it weighs, plus enough to compensate for whatever portion of its rotor downwash pushes down on the fuselage and other parts of the machine. How much horsepower is needed to produce that thrust determines a rotorcraft's "hover efficiency," meaning how much lifting power it actually gets out of the horsepower its engines generate. Hover efficiency affects fuel consumption and thus operating cost.

One way to determine how much horsepower will be needed in a rotorcraft is to calculate its "disk loading." The "disk" in question is the area of the circle described by a rotor's blades. The "loading" is how much thrust the disk must create to lift the required weight. A bigger rotor moves more air over a larger disk area than a smaller rotor, and thus requires less energy—less horsepower and fuel—to generate an equal amount of thrust. Disk loading is expressed in pounds per square foot and calculated by dividing the machine's normal flying weight—its design gross weight—by the area of the disk. The larger the disk area, the lower the disk loading. Other things help determine hover efficiency, but in general, the lower the disk loading, the less power required to lift the aircraft and keep it hovering.

Most helicopters have disk loading of four to ten pounds per square foot. Thanks to its small rotor diameter and heavy weight, the JVX's disk loading was going to be an uncommonly high twenty pounds per square foot or more. Such high disk loading raised a number of questions, some of which would spark hot debates years later. For now, though, what worried Wernicke most about the limit on rotor size was that it would necessitate *increasing* the JVX's weight. Smaller rotors and high disk loading meant the aircraft was going to need beefier engines than if its rotors could have been sized for its weight rather than to fit on the ship's deck. More powerful engines would be bigger; bigger engines would be heavier; bigger, heavier engines would need bigger, heavier transmissions. Nor did it stop there. As an aircraft gets heavier, it needs stronger internal structures, and stronger internal structures usually add more weight. A heavier aircraft also needs more fuel to fly; more fuel means more weight. Extra fuel may require extra fuel tanks, and extra fuel tanks mean extra weight. And so on. Pretty soon, things get to a point where the designer can't "close the design loop," as engineers put it. There's so much aircraft to lift that insufficient room is left for the payload the machine was being designed to haul. Wernicke thought the JVX was close to that point at conception.

"I thought from the git-go that it was going to be so heavy that there wouldn't be enough useful load for the price of the aircraft to make it cost-effective," he told me.

That was why, after he studied the specs, Ken Wernicke went to Bob Lynn, Bell's senior vice president for engineering, and told him he just wasn't going to do it, he wasn't going to design this JVX. It was going to be too complicated, too heavy, and too costly. It was probably going to discredit the tiltrotor forever.

Lynn talked Wernicke into it.

"He said there was no one else who could do it and I should do it and it was the only game in town," Wernicke recalled. "Of course, I knew it was the only game in town."

★ ★ ★

Lynn apparently wasn't shocked or dismayed by Wernicke's threat to boycott the project. Years later, he said he didn't remember it, though Lynn didn't doubt Wernicke's recollection. "He was like that," Lynn said. Everyone knew Ken Wernicke was irascible much of the time and impassioned about the tiltrotor always. It was his dream machine. Wernicke also had a "build it and they will come" notion of marketing, as Lynn saw it. Lynn and others at Bell and Boeing Vertol didn't underestimate the challenges the JVX posed, but they were more pragmatic. Unlike Ken Wernicke, his bosses had dealt with the Pentagon for years. Stanley Martin, Jr., a vice president under Lynn and Wernicke's supervisor in those days, was among them. "Some of us had learned that you do what your customer wants, you don't try to tell your customer what he wants," Martin told me.

Besides, the military often issued unrealistic requirements for big procurements, in part to spur industry on to greater heights, in part because the officers who wrote the requirements could be poor judges of what was possible, in part to justify starting a new program. After all, some reasoned, if what the military wants to build isn't going to be a lot better than what it already has, the Pentagon's civilian leaders and Congress might refuse to fund it. When it came to writing requirements, the services always asked for the sky and contractors always told them they could deliver it "by yesterday" and priced to "sell at the ten-cent store," in the words of the Al F. Davis poem. That was why stories on outrageous schedule delays and cost overruns were a staple for reporters on the Pentagon beat. Development schedules and cost estimates for major military hardware—especially aircraft—were almost always ridiculously optimistic. The incentive on both sides, for the military and for the contractors, was to shoot for the moon and worry later about how much they were going to miss it by.

After the JVX requirements were written but before Bell-Boeing got the initial contract, the companies weren't going to tell The Customer he was asking for too much. "You don't want to do anything that would take you away from your chance of getting a chance to do it," Lynn said. Besides, most at Bell or Boeing Vertol didn't think what the military was asking *couldn't* be done, they just knew it was going to be damned hard. Lynn put it this way: "I don't believe in doing something you *know* will not work, but if you don't *know* it will not work, then I'm sort of reluctant to say it *won't* work."

Emotion as well as reason figured into the equation. Lynn had been Bell's chief of research and development when the company built and flew the XV-3, its first tiltrotor. He'd shepherded the XV-15 along as well. The JVX looked to Lynn like "the last chance for the tiltrotor, and I'd been working on this system since the early fifties. I wanted to see it go because I thought, no matter what, that we'd come out and give them a capability that we didn't have now."

Anyway, there was an escape clause in the Joint Services Operational Requirement. "All capabilities and performance goals established herein shall be subjected to cost, weight, capability and performance sensitivity analyses," it said. In other words, the requirements could be eased if the companies could prove to Navair there was no choice. After Bell-Boeing won the contract in 1983, Lynn and others at the companies broached the idea of easing some of the requirements with Navair but got nowhere. The attitude among Navair officials seemed to be "Don't bother me with facts, my mind's made up," Lynn found. Arguments that the requirements were too ambitious fell on deaf ears in that phase of the program, when the JVX was still just a "paper airplane."

* * *

A paper airplane was all the JVX was for several years, but that was the normal course of things. A multibillion-dollar military aircraft procurement unfolds in long, complicated stages. Each can take years to complete and require one or several contracts and dozens of subcontracts. Bell-Boeing's initial JVX contract, in April 1983, was for preliminary design. What they had given Navair in their bid was just a concept, rudimentary drawings backed by performance and cost estimates. A team of engineers from both companies put the bid together in 1982, after Lynn talked Wernicke down from his high dudgeon. Boeing Vertol's director of engineering, William Peck, led about fifty of his engineers to Bell's main facility in Hurst from their plant in Ridley Park, Pennsylvania, a borough just south of Philadelphia. They rented apartments and stayed several months. About the time the Boeing engineers got used to seeing workers in cowboy hats and cowboy boots eating biscuits with gravy for breakfast in Bell's cafeteria, the bid was done and the Boeing Vertol engineers went home to Pennsylvania. Now, in 1983, the companies had to get down to actually designing this new tiltrotor, figuring out how its major components should be shaped aerodynamically, selecting and testing the materials they'd use to build it, and getting Navair to approve their plans and give them a contract to build some prototypes.

The broad outlines were clear from the start. In aircraft design, "form follows function" more intrinsically than in architecture, the source of that alliterative principle. An aircraft's purpose usually determines its form. Most fighter jets have a streamlined fuselage and short wings to make them fast and maneuverable. With notable exceptions, such as the Concorde SST and the bat-winged B-2 stealth bomber, long-range airliners or bombers usually have big, round fuselages to carry a lot and long, slender wings for fuel-efficient flight at high altitude. In the Western world, conventional helicopters usually come in one of two basic configurations: they either have a main rotor that turns horizontally for lift and thrust and a small tail rotor that turns vertically for directional control, or they have two large rotors, one behind the other. Only two successful tiltrotors, the XV-3 and the XV-15, had ever been built when Bell and Boeing Vertol started the JVX, but the configuration was clear. A tiltrotor was a helicopter-airplane hybrid, so it combined elements of both. Like an airplane, it had a fuselage with a wing and a tail; like a helicopter, it had rotors. The rotors were positioned on the wingtips and held in "nacelles"—pods—that swiveled to tilt them. That was a tiltrotor configuration. Its form followed its function.

The companies decided the broad division of labor early on. Bell had the most tiltrotor experience, so it would take charge of the wing, the proprotors, and the nacelles. Boeing Vertol specialized in big, tandem-rotor helicopters, so it would do the fuselage and landing gear. Boeing also would take primary responsibility for the electrical and hydraulic systems and the computerized electronic "fly-by-wire" flight controls, though Bell would have a lot to say about those items. Boeing also would take charge of the avionics—a contraction of "aviation electronics." The engines would be GFE—"government-furnished equipment"—bought by Navair from one of the big four aircraft engine makers under separate contract and provided to Bell for installation in the nacelles.

If you were Ken Wernicke of Bell or Thomas W. Griffith of Boeing Vertol, the chief JVX designers, your first step was to size the aircraft to meet the requirements. Okay, you might say to your design team, it has to fit on this amphibious assault ship, so its total width, rotor tip to rotor tip, can't be more than 84 feet, 7 inches. When it flies in airplane mode, we need clearance between the rotor tips and the fuselage, which has to be as big as a CH-46. If the rotor tips clear the fuselage by a foot, the wingspan including the nacelles needs to be 45 feet, 10 inches, rotor hub to rotor hub. That gives us a rotor diameter of 38 feet. Now, how long is this thing going to be? Besides holding twenty-four troops, the fuselage has to have a rear ramp for loading people and cargo, room up front for the cockpit, space for the forward landing gear and a refueling probe, and so on. It's going to be a little longer when we rotate the wing to stow it, but the requirement says it can't take up more than one-point-two times as much space as a CH-46. So the length can be 63 feet maximum. How are we going to fold the rotors and stow the wing? And where are we going to put all the fuel we need to get the range they want? The wing's the usual place, but we're going to need more fuel than the wing will hold, so where do we put extra tanks? The nacelles need to be big enough to hold the engines and gearboxes and transmissions, and we've got to put infrared suppressors at the bottom of them. How much is this thing going to weigh? How much of it has to be metal? How much can we make out of composites? . . . And so forth.

Hundreds of engineers were assigned to the project in Hurst and

Ridley Park, organized into "design" and "technology" groups at each location, the principal two divisions in engineering departments at most helicopter companies. Design engineers were figuring out how the various components and subsystems of the aircraft would be shaped and fit together. Technology engineers were analyzing the aerodynamics and dynamics and the materials to be used. Within each group were dozens of specialists in acoustics, vibration, and other arcane engineering disciplines. One of their main jobs was what's called "risk reduction."

In this context, "risk" doesn't mean whether the aircraft will be safe but whether it's going to perform as advertised. For example, in their bid the companies proposed using carbon fiber composites rather than aluminum to build the basic structure, the aircraft's skeleton and skin. This was near revolutionary. Composite structures begin as pliable, clothlike weaves or sticky, tapelike strips of special fibers that are laid down in layers to form a desired shape. The shape is then baked in an autoclave, a kind of pressurized kiln, to create a stiff, strong structure. Composites had been used in aircraft before, but never to the extent Bell-Boeing planned. "Frankly, we didn't know how to do it," said Allen Schoen, who was Boeing Vertol's technology director on the project.

Both companies had made composite rotor blades before, but there was a lot they didn't know about using composites in larger structures, and manufacturing methods for specific parts still had to be figured out. Using composites as much as possible was going to be vital to holding the JVX's empty weight down, but Navair required the companies to prove they could measure and predict how the materials would behave under the stresses and strains of flight. To assess the risk of the materials failing, the companies had to fabricate major parts of the aircraft in model size or full scale, then test them in various ways. During preliminary design, Bell built a 25-foot composite rotor with the twist it planned to use in the JVX's 38-foot rotors. Bell also fabricated the structure of a wing out of composites. Boeing Vertol used composites to build a 34-foot "test specimen" of the fuselage, but that was just a start. Boeing Vertol alone made more than 14,000 samples of composite parts to test, ranging from small joints for holding bits of the fuselage together to large panels of aircraft skin. Engineers usually tested such things in wind tunnels, on special machines that pulled and twisted the parts to gauge their resistance to stretching and tearing, or in portable "environmental chambers," where the materials could be broiled or frozen, soaked with simulated rain or drenched in salt water. So much of what they planned to do with composites was novel, though, that some parts would give them trouble for years. On these, the testing continued well after preliminary design was over, and the engineers were forced to get creative at times.

That's why Bell materials engineer Greg Marshall had a hard time explaining what that was in the back of his car when a Texas state trooper pulled him over as he drove from Fort Worth to San Antonio one summer evening in 1988. Nestled in the cargo area of Marshall's company car, an avocado green station wagon with wood paneling on the sides that had seen better days, was a large black object that looked mighty suspicious to that trooper. It was a composite part that had been giving Bell fits: a rotor grip formed by laying down layers of carbon fiber one over the other until the sides were as much as an inch and a half thick and the grip weighed forty pounds. The companies were two years into building their first prototype aircraft by now and Bell still wasn't certain this part was going to work. The young engineer was on his way to San Antonio to run a special test on the grip, which was roughly the size and shape of those elephant's foot umbrella stands big-game hunters used to bring back from Africa in colonial days. The grip was nearly square at the bottom and open at each end. The round end would hold one of the JVX's proprotor blades by its stem. The square end would fasten to the rotor yoke, a solid part with three arms for connecting the rotor blades to the rotor hub. Besides holding the blades onto the yoke, the grip would have to twist and turn constantly in flight to change their pitch. No one had ever built rotor grips out of composite before, and this was going to be one of the keys to reducing the JVX's weight. There would be six rotor grips on each aircraft, and they cost more than a quarter of a million dollars each to make. If the composite grips didn't work, the alternative would be steel, which would be three times heavier, so the technical risk was huge.

The key to figuring out how to make the rotor grips correctly was to find a way to inspect their insides when they came out of the autoclave to ensure there weren't wrinkles or voids in the layers of tape, which might make a grip fail as the rotor spun at hundreds of revolutions per minute. Ultrasound and X-rays, the usual methods, weren't yielding good enough evidence to satisfy Navair. Then an engineer at a company in San Antonio gave Bell a suggestion. Why not give the rotor grip a CAT scan?

Computerized axial tomography scans take hundreds of X-ray "slices" to generate a 3-D image of an opaque object, usually a human body. CAT scans were fairly new in those days, and scanners were a little rare, but there was a scanner at Bexar County Hospital in San Antonio, part of the University of Texas Health Science Center. Hospital officials readily agreed when Bell's contact requested an appointment for a rotor grip. That's where Marshall was headed when the trooper stopped him.

"You realize you got a headlight out?" the trooper asked Marshall. No, sir, the engineer replied in his native Texan drawl. This was a company car, he explained, and he hadn't realized the light was out. He'd get it fixed soon as he could. When the trooper heard "company car," he shined his flashlight around the outside of the old station wagon and frowned. "Where you from?" he asked leerily. "Where you going?" Then he swept his flashlight beam into the back of the station wagon and saw the big, black rotor grip. "What's that in the back of your car, son?" the trooper demanded. Marshall, dressed in jeans and a Windbreaker, was twenty-seven at the time. His thick black hair cascaded over the edges of his ears a bit, and he wore a mustache.

Marshall gave a straightforward answer. The black thing was part of a new tiltrotor aircraft his company was building for the military, he explained. "What's a tiltrotor?" the trooper replied. Marshall elaborated, but the trooper had a hard time with the concept. Part helicopter, part airplane? The more Marshall talked, the more skeptical the trooper looked. What's that thing made of? Is it dangerous? Can it blow up? Where you going with it? The trooper had a lot of questions. Marshall assured him the grip was perfectly safe, ominous as it might look. He was just taking it to UT Southwestern to get it scanned in a special X-ray machine. Oops. Now the trooper wanted to know if that thing was radioactive. It was supposed to be tagged if it was. Marshall was sure the trooper was going to give him a ticket of some kind, or at least take him and the rotor grip to the station. Finally, though, after Marshall pulled out his Bell ID badge and did a lot more talking, the trooper let him go.

The next morning, Marshall wheeled the rotor grip into the hospital on a dolley. He was told to put it on a gurney, same as any other patient. He wheeled the gurney into the CAT scan room, laid the grip on a table as instructed, and watched a bemused technician prop pillows under the faux elephant's foot to position it correctly, same as any other patient. When the scan was done, Marshall put the grip back on the gurney and wheeled it back out into the corridor. He couldn't restrain himself when he saw how a couple of elderly patients awaiting CAT scans gawked at what was on his gurney. "We cooked this one a little too long," he told them gravely.

The CAT scan showed voids in the rotor grip that ultrasound hadn't revealed, which allowed Bell's engineers to refine their manufacturing and inspection methods to Navair's satisfaction. "Right away, management wanted to CAT scan everything in the plant," Marshall chuckled. In the years that followed, they didn't scan everything, but as local hospitals started offering CAT scans, Bell's rotor grips were among their regular patients.

* * *

As is probably the case with any arranged marriage in which the couple know each other only slightly but have mutual respect, the Bell-Boeing partnership began smoothly enough. After the champagne was drunk and the honeymoon was over, though, the newlyweds started getting to know each other. They quickly saw it wasn't a match made in heaven.

Compared to Boeing Vertol and its parent, Boeing Company, Bell Helicopter and its parent, Textron, were small fry. This was why Bell president Jim Atkins had offered Boeing Vertol president Joe Mallen a 50–50 partnership when they first met, rather than the 60–40 split Atkins would have preferred, or at least 51–49 so Bell could be in control. Atkins came to rue the even-steven split, but at the time, he figured there was no way "big, bad Boeing" would take a minority position in such a venture. Mallen told me Atkins was right. As they and many others in their companies and in the government came to fully appreciate only too late, however, a 50–50 partnership has a fundamental weakness: no one is in charge. When tough issues arose, as they often did, there was no easy way to settle them. They became speed bumps.

Size wasn't the only thing that mattered. The companies' personalities—their corporate cultures—were as far apart as their locations, which were separated by 1,400 miles and, perhaps more significantly, the Mason-Dixon Line.

Bell's culture reflected its beginnings and surroundings as much as its status in the aviation business. The company had sprung from the savvy of entrepreneur Larry Bell and the genius of helicopter inventor Art Young. Bell's culture nurtured individuality. Engineers were allowed to pursue their own ideas. Workers were treated like artisans, not cogs in a machine. Two different assemblers might put together a part in slightly different ways; as long as it worked—okay! Bell's corporate parent, Textron, was a conglomerate that had pioneered diversification in the 1960s. Its other companies made watchbands, fountain pens, golf carts, snowmobiles, greeting cards. There was little if any overlap among its businesses, and the small corporate headquarters in Providence largely let Textron's subsidiaries have their heads, as long as they contributed to the bottom line. Contribute to the bottom line they must, though, and every year, if possible. Textron wasn't into losses, even short term.

Boeing Vertol also traced its corporate genealogy to one of the founding fathers of the helicopter industry, Frank Piasecki. But Piasecki's imprint had been erased in corporate makeovers that ended in 1960, when Boeing bought Vertol Aircraft Corporation, successor to Piasecki Helicopter Corporation. ("Vertol" was an acronym for "vertical take off and landing.") Seattle-based Boeing was an aerospace behemoth, the New York Yankees of the aviation game: rich, powerful, strong at all positions. Commercial and military aircraft manufacture, space technology, missiles, helicopters—you name it, if it was an aviation business, Boeing was a leader in it. There was a lot of cross-fertilization among Boeing's many subsidiaries, and Boeing wasn't afraid of long-term investment. That was part of building commercial aircraft. But the corporation was adamant about schedules, and Boeing's philosophy prized process over people. "It's process that gets things done, it's not people," a Boeing Vertol engineer once argued to one of his peers at Bell. Like Yankees owner George Steinbrenner, Boeing changed managers a lot. Executives were often reassigned, transferred, or simply removed. Top engineers were traded or loaned within the corporation like ballplayers within a league, though some stayed put. A few had been at Boeing Vertol for years, even worked for Frank Piasecki in a few cases. But they were governed by Seattle's rules and procedures.

Boeing Vertol employees were also Yankees geographically and temperamentally, born and raised in Philadelphia or its environs, for the most part. Bell employees were mostly from Texas, or at least the South or Southwest. The North-South differences were a source of good-natured ribbing, but they also made for a partnership that combined the two qualities John F. Kennedy famously saw in the city of Washington, D.C.: "Southern efficiency and Northern charm."

The Yankees from Boeing Vertol talked and worked at a big-city pace and had big-city manners. They had sharp elbows. The southerners at Bell went about life more placidly amid the noise and haste. Courtesy was important to them. To many at Bell, the Boeing Vertol people always seemed to be in a hurry. They were pushy, and sometimes downright rude. Lord, they'd even shout and curse at each other in meetings! ("We in Philadelphia have long enjoyed a culture of insult," acknowledged a longtime Ridley Park employee I asked about this.) Boeing Vertol's Yankees also talked a lot more than they listened, many at Bell thought, though that didn't matter that much, because you couldn't tell them anything anyway; they thought they knew it all already. Bell test pilot Ron Erhart remembered a meeting with a Textron executive who warned: "Those Yankees up there in Philadelphia will walk all over you if you let 'em."

Boeing Vertol engineers and executives found the atmosphere at Bell amazingly casual and disconcertingly lax in procedures. At Boeing, if you wanted to redesign a part, you first did engineering drawings and got them approved and released to the shop. Only then would a new part be made. At Bell, the first step was often to "cut and try." The drawings to document a change could be done after the fact. Some at Boeing Vertol thought that was no way to run an aircraft factory. But what did Bell know about building big aircraft anyway? Boeing Vertol built brawny, complex helicopters; Bell was just a little company that made little helicopters. "Bell, as far as we were concerned, only built these little puddle jumpers," one retired Boeing Vertol engineer told me. "They were not used to, or experienced in, building stuff that size." This engineer and others at Boeing Vertol knew Bell was going to *need* their help to build this big tiltrotor.

Troy Gaffey got acquainted with that attitude when he visited Ridley Park for the first time. His Boeing Vertol counterpart took him to meet the vice president for engineering, Kenneth Grina, a bearish man who ruled his engineers by intimidation. "When he said jump, all we said was, 'How high?'" remembered William Rumberger, an engineer who worked for him. Grina "would come out of his office and throw everything off your drawing board and you'd start all over again," Rumberger told me. "He was top dog." Joe Mallen, Boeing Vertol's president at the time, said Grina "was smart as hell and he didn't take any crap from anybody, including me." Grina had been the father of the Model 360, the mostly composite "Plastic Phrog" helicopter Boeing Vertol was trying to sell the Marines before the JVX came along. "That was his dream," Mallen said. Grina wasn't a fan of the tiltrotor. He thought it too complex, not as good as a helicopter and not as good as an airplane. He also didn't think much of Bell Helicopter, as Gaffey learned.

"Grina was another one of these great engineers, probably as good as they come, with a specialty in structures," Gaffey told me. When Gaffey went to meet him, the two companies were having an argument about how to make the JVX's composite skin. Grina was standing behind his desk with his hands on his hips when Gaffey came in. "He leaned forward and looked at me from behind his desk—didn't even hold his hand out to shake—and said, 'I want you to tell me why you don't believe Boeing's right,' or something like that—and I mean in a loud voice," Gaffey said. "I was dumbfounded by this guy. And he started yelling and ranting and raving and carrying on about the fact that Boeing knew more about helicopters than Bell Helicopter had ever even dreamed about."

Many at Bell weren't so sure they needed Boeing Vertol, either. The company had bid against Bell for the XV-15 back in 1972, and some Boeing engineers had been working on tiltrotor designs when they learned Joe Mallen had agreed to team with Bell for the JVX. Even so, Bell engineers regarded the tiltrotor as *their* technology. *They* were the tiltrotor experts; Boeing Vertol was just going to build "the box," the fuselage. Bell's engineers had poured three decades of hard work into developing the tiltrotor. Many weren't anxious to share what they'd learned with Boeing, which as far as they knew might use it to compete with them for some other contract in the future. Bell's managers sometimes had to order subordinates to share information about the tiltrotor with Boeing Vertol.

Grina's counterpart at Bell was Bob Lynn, who found working with Boeing "one of the hardest things I've ever done in my life." Delays in getting work done often arose because the companies couldn't agree on how to do something, or lower-level engineers would agree, only to have their solution vetoed by higher-ups—frequently Grina. "I would always let other people try to handle him," Lynn said. "He was impossible to work with. If he wanted to do something, by God he was going to do it."

The inherent friction in the partnership wasn't a huge problem at lower levels. Most engineers had limited contact with the other company, though Bell and Boeing Vertol each sent a few people to the other's facility to look over their partner's shoulder and help coordinate things. Face-to-face meetings occurred most regularly in a steering committee of senior executives who met every other month. They thought about setting up videoconferencing for the engineers, but that was cumbersome in those days and expensive. Instead, the separate engineering teams held a telephone conference call each Monday afternoon to review their progress and talk about the week ahead. Individual engineers could get on the phone with each other, and small groups often traveled from Hurst to Ridley Park, from Ridley Park to Hurst, or from both places to Navair's headquarters at Crystal City, just outside Washington. Designs were often faxed back and forth. But when they disagreed on a decision and it got kicked to higher levels, the culture clash between the companies and the 50–50 partnership often got in the way. "When decisions were made that one of the companies did not like, there was the tendency to either drag their feet or not do it at all," observed a 1989 master's thesis on the program written by a Naval Postgraduate School student.

★ ★ ★

All the challenges—making the JVX "shipboard compatible" while keeping its weight down, trying to use composites in ways never tried before, reaching decisions in a 50–50 partnership of companies so dissimilar—came together in a perfect storm when they set out to design the wing stow mechanism. This was the device needed to rotate the wing from crosswise to lengthwise along the fuselage so the aircraft could fit beneath an amphibious assault ship's deck. The wing stow mechanism was Boeing's responsibility, because it was part of the fuselage, but Bell's wing had to attach to it, so the companies had to agree on the design. For a couple of years, they couldn't.

The Navy and Marines had flown planes whose wings folded for aircraft carrier operation since World War II, but with its big nacelles and rotors, simply putting hinges in the wing wasn't an option for the JVX. The alternative was to install a pivot in the top of the fuselage so the wing would rotate. Sounds simple enough, but it was excruciatingly tricky.

The mechanism would need to lock the wing into position for flight, then unlock it and swing it 90 degrees for stowing, all the while bearing the huge weight of the wingtip nacelles, which would bow the wing in the middle. It also would have to move the wing without transmitting strains into the fuselage that could distort its shape. "You have a fuselage that looks like it's sturdy as heck, but yet it can bend and it can deflect, and you have a wing that can also bend and deflect," Ken Wernicke explained. "So if one of them bends and the other one doesn't, you're binding up the wing stow mechanism." The trick was to create a gizmo that would insulate the fuselage from the motions of the wing, not only when the wing was being stowed but also in flight.

There was more. The wing stow mechanism also had to hold and turn clusters of hydraulic and fuel lines, thousands of electrical, flight control, and other wires, plus a big driveshaft that needed to run through the area. The driveshaft's purpose was to connect the rotors so that a single engine could power both of them if the other engine failed. On top of all that, the requirements said the mechanism had to stow the wings while the aircraft sat on the deck of a ship that might be pitching up and down as much as 3 degrees fore and aft, rolling side to side as much as 15 degrees, and sailing in 50-mph winds. And it had to do its job in no more than ninety seconds.

It was a monster of an engineering problem.

Small groups of engineers at both companies girded themselves for battle and rode out to slay this dragon, but they couldn't agree on a plan of attack. For months, all they did was joust with each other over more than forty designs without ever agreeing to one. At that point, Boeing Vertol's director of engineering, Bill Peck, and its JVX design chief, Tom Griffith, looked around for a new champion, a white knight with a design breakthrough in his armory. They thought they might have one in Bill Rumberger, an old-timer at Boeing Vertol who'd cut his teeth in engineering a quarter century earlier.

Rumberger had grown up down the road from Ridley Park in Essington and gotten his engineering degree from what was then Drexel Institute in Philadelphia. He'd worked at Boeing Vertol since 1959, had several patents under his belt, and was known for thinking outside the box. He was also personable and diplomatic by nature. As he started working on the wing stow problem, Rumberger got along well with the Bell engineers, even the notoriously difficult Ken Wernicke. But he soon felt he'd entered Never-Never Land. "Bell would do their own thing and Boeing would do its own thing and then we'd come together and have a wing stow meeting," Rumberger said. "We'd walk away from each other agreeing to disagree on what we had each come up with. Each one had a veto power." The diplomatic solution, Rumberger decided, would be to try to combine the best features of some of the dozens of designs both companies had already proposed, and thus win hearts and minds.

What he came up with was a large central bearing for the wing to pivot around, something like a giant ballpoint pen tip three feet in diameter. Rumberger showed it to other engineers at Boeing Vertol and they liked it. Ken Grina didn't. He said it was too complex. Anyway, Grina wanted the wing stow mechanism to be made of composites. Rumberger went back to his drawing board.

Higher-ups at Boeing Vertol, meanwhile, brought in several engineers from "Big Boeing" in Seattle to solve the problem, a sort of SWAT team. By now, the matter was becoming urgent. Bell and Boeing Vertol needed to resolve their differences to get Navair to approve their design and give them a contract to start building prototypes. Over a period of weeks, the SWAT team came up with a new mechanism. Bell and Grina approved it, so the Seattle engineers went back home. The next day, Grina called Peck into his office and told him he wasn't going to accept the SWAT team's design after all. It was too complex, he'd decided. Grina didn't want "that junk on my airplane."

While the SWAT team was at Ridley Park, Rumberger had been off on his own, quietly working on a new idea. By the mid-1980s, many engineers were using computers to design things, but Rumberger wasn't among them. As he'd always done, he drafted his designs on paper, then constructed cardboard models to test his theories. Rumberger always kept cardboard and a bottle of Elmer's Carpenter's Glue at his desk for that purpose. He called his new concept the Composite Flex Ring because it rotated and was going to be supple enough to handle the wing's bending. It was especially designed to satisfy Grina's demands. Rumberger modeled it, Grina, Peck and Bell approved it, and Boeing Vertol had a subcontractor fabricate a prototype. They tested it for nearly a year. Then one day, to Rumberger's shock, senior managers at Big Boeing in Seattle rejected his Composite Flex Ring. Too novel and risky, they said. Rumberger thought Seattle's real problem with his idea was that it was simply too new.

Now Grina came up with his own design, a "bed frame" system using a stationary ring—made of stainless steel, not composites. Bell and Boeing ended up putting Grina's wing stow mechanism on their prototype aircraft, but it proved to be heavy, maintenance-intensive, and costly.

Rumberger, though, never gave up on his flex ring. He refined it, adding a sort of capstan—a rotating post—to hold cables that would turn the ring. To get a feel for how they needed to wrap and unwrap, he brought a ball of string in to work, cut strands to represent the cables, and made them wind and unwind around a cardboard capstan he'd fashioned. Years later, after Grina retired, Rumberger's stainless steel flex ring replaced Grina's "bed frame." The flex ring was 300 pounds lighter and cost $300,000 a copy less. When his design was accepted, Rumberger's buddies at the office gave him a nickname: "Lord of the Ring."

"It wasted a lot of time," Rumberger shrugged.

The partners had endless debates over every issue imaginable, from who was going to manufacture the avionics to whether the flight controls should work like a helicopter's or an airplane's to how the aircraft's tail should be shaped. Bell wanted the JVX to have an H-shaped tail, same as the XV-15. Boeing Vertol's engineers wanted a T-shaped tail, which they thought would be aerodynamically superior and sleeker. They tried to sweet-talk Bell into a T-shaped tail by labeling their design the "Texas T." The Bell engineers were amused, not seduced, by the ploy. Wind tunnel tests showed that either tail would work aerodynamically, but as with many issues, the requirement to operate aboard ships settled the argument. They'd had to make the rear fuselage higher than originally planned to allow room for the cargo ramp, which meant the Texas T was too tall to fit below the deck of a ship. The JVX would have a shorter H-tail.

Both companies argued bitterly with the Naval Air Systems Command, too, especially about materials. Shipboard operation was at the root of many of their disputes. One of the most stinging arguments with Navair—the kind that leads people never to speak to each other again—centered on something called honeycomb. Aircraft makers had been using honeycomb since the 1950s to cut weight in fuselages, wings, and other structures. Like the beehives in nature that inspired it, aerospace honeycomb is an arrangement of hexagonal shells—usually made of aluminum—that are hollow. The shells cut weight by substituting air for solid structure, but their shape makes them strong enough to reinforce the surprisingly thin skin of an aircraft, which is often no more than twelve-thousandths of an inch thick. Bell wanted to use aluminum honeycomb in the JVX's wing, and Boeing Vertol wanted to use honeycomb made of a composite called Nomex in the fuselage. The companies figured to save hundreds of pounds that way. But there was a problem with honeycomb: if water got inside its hexagonal shells—and it often did—the moisture would add weight and could rust the aluminum or freeze and make the honeycomb separate from the skin. This could create weaknesses that would make an aircraft unsafe to fly. Water can seep into honeycomb through scratches and dings in the "face sheets" of the skin or through seams between skin panels. As the Navy had learned, the problem was even worse at sea, where salt spray gets onto and into nearly everything. Navair's chief structures engineer, a snappish career bureaucrat named Mike Dubberly, was adamantly against using honeycomb in the JVX. Ken Grina, the snappish head of engineering at Boeing Vertol, was just as adamantly in favor of it.

Bell largely gave up debating the issue with Dubberly after he agreed they could use honeycomb in the JVX's rotors. Boeing Vertol's engineers, caught between Dubberly and Grina, tried repeatedly to change Dubberly's mind. "There's only one way we're going to get this airplane to the weight that Navair's looking for, and that's with honeycomb," Grina told his engineers. Every few weeks, during design review meetings at Navair's offices in Crystal City, Dubberly would veto Boeing Vertol's latest plans to use honeycomb, only to have them come back with new designs incorporating it again. "Honeycomb with you guys is like a fungus," Dubberly groused more than once. "Every time I turn my back, go away for a month and come back, another little hunk has popped up somewhere, so we have to come back and eradicate it again." Dubberly was often more profane than that—nasty enough that, after a while, Boeing Vertol's chief JVX design engineer, Tom Griffith, refused to meet or talk with him anymore.

One day Dubberly's boss came to him and said, "The secretary of the Navy is asking what did you do to these poor Vertol guys?" Someone at Boeing had complained about Dubberly by name to Navy Secretary John Lehman. Dubberly's boss seemed more amused than annoyed; Dubberly was more annoyed than amused. Going way over his head didn't alter his attitude. "They just pissed me off," Dubberly told me. "The problem was that these guys were not technically competent enough to know how to design a stiffened skin. Honeycomb is for lazy and not very clever designers, and that's what these guys were." Dubberly returned the favor by sharing his opinion of the Boeing Vertol engineers with a top Boeing Seattle executive.

The only concession Dubberly made to Grina's engineers was to allow them to use Nomex honeycomb in the doors and small removable panels of the JVX fuselage, items easily replaced. But he allowed that only years later, after Bell-Boeing had started building prototypes. During preliminary design, Dubberly vetoed honeycomb. The alternative was to make the skin out of solid composite, five to twelve layers thick, depending on how strong the skin needed to be at any given point. Boeing Vertol came up with a way to make the solid composite skin hold its shape by adding J-shaped "stiffeners" on the inside of the fuselage, but compared to honeycomb, the stiffened skin was heavy.

Dubberly also nixed a Boeing Vertol plan to use the famous composite Kevlar, the stuff used in bulletproof vests, in the underflooring of the fuselage. The Kevlar was supposed to help protect the occupants of the aircraft in a crash. Boeing Vertol engineer Derek Hart had been working on that when he heard some bad news from Boeing Seattle. Big Boeing had used Kevlar skins with honeycomb inside the flaps and ailerons of its Boeing 757 commercial airliners, which went into service in 1983. On flights from Los Angeles to Mexico City, the 757s often flew through extremes of hot and cold air, causing moisture to condense on the Kevlar skins. As it turned out, the skins weren't impermeable. Moisture was getting into the honeycomb, freezing, and popping the Kevlar skins. Hart was still pondering the problem when his phone rang one day. It was Dubberly.

"Get your ass down here, I want to talk to you about Kevlar," Dubberly ordered. Hart drove down to Navair's offices in Crystal City the next day. When he got to Dubberly's office, he got explicit instructions from The Customer. "I know you've got designs going on right now which have got Kevlar under the floor," Dubberly told Hart. "Get that shit out of my airplane."

* * *

The one simple problem they never could solve was weight. As preliminary design neared its end, the JVX was still going to be several thousand pounds over Navair's initial requirement of 31,886 pounds empty. It was even going to be over a 2,500-pound "weight contingency"—an overweight allowance—Navair had granted. That was going to make the aircraft pricier. In those days, the rule of thumb in aircraft design was that structure cost about $1,000 a pound. The blade fold and wing stow mechanisms alone weighed a couple of thousand pounds—in other words, cost a couple of million dollars. Not using honeycomb in the composite fuselage was going to add more. Using more powerful engines would cost weight, too. The list went on and on.

The engineers had always known weight was going to be a problem in a tiltrotor this big, but no one expected it to be this bad. Composites were supposed to make the JVX about 25 percent lighter than an aluminum aircraft the same size. "Fly-by-wire" flight controls were supposed to reduce weight, too. Instead, both ended up *adding* it.

The all-composite fuselage was going to be a lot heavier not only because they couldn't use honeycomb but also because of a surprise Boeing Vertol got when they did their risk reduction studies. It turned out that composite ribs for the fuselage—called "frames" or "formers," depending on their size—had to be thicker than expected to turn corners and hold their shape under the loads they would have to bear. There was also another problem with composite frames and formers. As Boeing Vertol workers hand-built samples to test, they found it almost impossible to make any two come out of the autoclave the same thickness and strength. It was a little like trying to make a bracket for a bookshelf by forming layers of electrician's tape in a right angle and baking them hard. The epoxy that held the fibers together would be a little too thick here, a little too thin there, creating wrinkles and voids, and thus weaknesses when it was baked. Three or four out of every ten frames and formers—items that took a laborious and expensive three to four weeks to make—had to be thrown away.

Fly-by-wire wasn't the weight saver Bell-Boeing had expected, either. Logically, electronic flight controls should be far lighter than mechanical ones; wires are lighter than steel rods. But not if you have to install them in triplicate so you can keep flying even if a bullet knocks out one system. These weren't thin little wires of the sort that run from your computer or TV to the wall, either. They were bulky cables, consisting of thousands of wires encased in rubber insulation and wrapped together into bundles, some as thick as the trunk of a sapling. The weight of the wires in the three fly-by-wire systems turned out to be heavier than a single mechanical control system would have been. But with the JVX's survivability requirements, a single mechanical system wasn't an option.

Weight also drove another decision that ended up causing a lot of headaches and heartaches once the JVX started flying. Rather than the typical hydraulic system used in helicopters and most airplanes in those days, the companies decided to use a special, lighter one. Hydraulics move heavy objects by forcing a liquid, usually oil, through tubes to a cylinder with a piston in the middle. When the trapped fluid is pumped through the cylinder, or "actuator," it pushes the piston, which pushes a metal rod, which moves the heavy object, such as a rotor blade or aileron. Helicopters and most airplanes in those days used hydraulic systems whose internal pressure was 3,000 pounds per square inch (psi). Fighter plane makers had begun using 5,000-psi hydraulic systems, which pushed far smaller amounts of fluid through far smaller tubes to move far smaller actuators, making the system much lighter. To save weight, Bell and Boeing Vertol decided to go with a 5,000-psi system and make the tubes of titanium rather than the usual stainless steel. Titanium was just as strong and about half as heavy as stainless steel, but it was also more brittle, which meant it could spring leaks more easily. Some JVX engineers figured the 5,000-psi system could end up being a maintenance problem, because its hydraulic tubes would have to turn corners and bend as the nacelles tilted, unlike the tubes in a fighter jet. They also figured they had no choice. It appeared there was no way to build a tiltrotor this size using a standard 3,000-psi hydraulic system, partly because of the size and weight of the actuators required, so the hydraulics were going to be 5,000-psi.

Even with weight-saving measures like that, the estimates kept showing that the JVX was going to tip the scales empty at maybe 34,000 or 35,000 pounds, well above Navair's required weight of 31,886 pounds. If the engines were powerful enough and the proprotors were aerodynamically adequate, they might still meet the payload requirements, but not by much.

By 1985, the preliminary design was finished and the companies began doing the thousands of detailed drawings needed to fabricate components to build prototype aircraft. Wernicke was still distressed by how this first real-world tiltrotor was likely to turn out. He kept telling his boss, Stan Martin, that Bell-Boeing just had to persuade Navair to cut some requirements. There was no other way to get the weight down to a reasonable level. "We should take the position of, 'Screw those guys, we're either going to build them a good airplane or not build it at all,'" Wernicke told Martin. "Well," Wernicke told me, "that's not how it works. We either take their money and build it or we don't have a program."

Wernicke had expressed his views on the requirements to The Customer as well, which got back to his bosses. Wernicke only went to Navair once or twice, though. He quickly decided it was a waste of his time. Eventually, he took things a step further and stopped going to management meetings at Bell, too. As the companies began building their prototypes, Bell moved Wernicke aside and gave his chief tiltrotor designer job to someone else. Wernicke got a new assignment. From now on, he would no longer supervise a large team of engineers. Instead he would spend all day every day trying to find ways to get the aircraft's weight down.

"He didn't want to continue on the [project] because he didn't believe in it and we were agreeable to that, because we didn't want anybody on it that couldn't embrace it with one hundred and ten percent of their enthusiasm," Wernicke's boss at the time, Stan Martin, told me.

The first prototype wouldn't fly for several years yet, but now they knew how it would look. Wernicke had made a lot of the decisions that helped dictate the aircraft's appearance, and he was sick at heart about it.

Over the two decades since Robert Lichten had taken him under his wing, Wernicke had become a true believer in the tiltrotor. He never forgot Lichten's admonition against letting the tiltrotor take over his life, but over time, it had captured his imagination. Wernicke had begun his career in the 1950s as one of those who genuinely expected to see a helicopter in every garage some day and hoped to help make it happen. By 1965, he knew it never would, and that frustrated him. Lichten and the tiltrotor had given him new inspiration—saved his career, he thought, by giving him something to work on that was really going to matter. Other engineers and inventors had been trying for a good thirty years before Wernicke came along to make an aircraft with commercial potential that could take off and land vertically yet fly as well as an airplane—a machine that could conquer the air. Wernicke was proud that he and Bob Lichten were two of the first to see that the tiltrotor was the only true way to make such a dream machine. Lichten had seen it first, of course, but as Wernicke led Bell's engineers in designing and building the XV-15, he became utterly convinced the tiltrotor was going to change the world. It just had to be, Wernicke thought. He was so sure of it, sometimes he'd look around and think, "Why build helicopters anymore? Why aren't they all building tiltrotors?" When the XV-15 stole the Paris Air Show in 1981—on the very airfield where Charles Lindbergh had changed aviation history, and the world, by completing the first nonstop transatlantic flight in 1927—Wernicke thought that was the turning point. Now, he was sure, Bell would get a chance to build a real production tiltrotor, a chance to prove to the world that the tiltrotor really was the dream machine. Then the military had come up with the JVX and its ridiculous requirements, a straitjacket of constraints that had forced him to design an aircraft that just might make people think the tiltrotor was an idea whose time hadn't come after all, and never would.

Wernicke had done the best he could supervising the JVX's design, but he was chagrined with the result. The XV-15, now that was a beauty. She had clean lines, a pretty face, a cute little tail, and nacelles just the right size. The JVX was going to be a beast by comparison. Bell-Boeing's conceptual drawings had shown an aerodynamically refined aircraft. The JVX had turned out differently. It had a nose like a porpoise and a body as chunky as a whale's. Bulging out to the sides from the fuselage's bottom were big protuberances called "sponsons," large compartments to house the rear landing gear and some of the avionics. The engineers had been forced to replace the sleek sponsons in the original Bell-Boeing concept with these blubbery-looking things because they needed a place to carry enough fuel to meet the JVX's range requirement. They resembled a failed dieter's spare tire, and at that point, the JVX was indeed a failed dieter. The only grace in its lines was the way its rear end tapered up to the H-shaped tail, but the tail itself was oversized. The afterbody was also swaybacked to allow room for a nacelle to swing over it when the wing was stowed. The wing, which hung over the new tiltrotor's back like a yoke over an ox's neck, was thick and stubby, and its tips swept slightly forward. On the wingtips hung the Osprey's most striking feature: two jarringly big nacelles that ballooned out like Popeye the Sailor's bulging forearms. Each nacelle was to hold a beefy turbine engine—the engines would have to be big to lift such a machine—and attached to each engine would be those undersized, yet immense-looking, three-bladed proprotors.

"It's a very chubby airplane," Wernicke told me. "I've always thought it was ugly." When he said it, he sounded sad.

CHAPTER SIX

YOUNG WINSTON'S OSPREY

O n the evening of Friday, November 9, 1984, Boeing Vertol president Joe Mallen was at the glitzy Washington Hilton Hotel, shuffling through the reception line at the annual Marine Corps Birthday Ball, when he came to John Lehman. The young, tuxedo-clad Navy secretary flashed a Cheshire cat grin, grabbed Mallen's hand, and pulled him aside.

"We're going to call it the 'Osprey,'" Lehman confided. "Have your people put together a couple of logos."

Like the proud parent he was, Lehman had picked the name for the JVX himself. Earlier that year, Lehman had told Bell Helicopter, Boeing Vertol, and the Naval Air Systems Command to hold internal contests to come up with suggestions. Some evoked the way the tiltrotor would fly; most were drawn from history, legend and mythology. Bell's suggestions were Centaur, Condor, Excalibur, Griffin, and Pegasus. Navair offered Bandit, Centurion, Comanche, Dragonfly, Javelin, or Stalker. Boeing Vertol came up with Hummingbird, Lancer, Olympian, Panther, and Osprey. "Osprey" suited Lehman's temperament. The osprey, *Pandion haliaetus,* is an aquatic bird of prey, a medium-sized, brown and white raptor found all over the world. Nature's osprey feeds almost exclusively on fish, which it hovers over before diving to snare them with its powerful talons. The bird then takes off vertically to haul its catch to shore and eat it. The JVX wasn't going to devour America's enemies itself, but it was being built to carry Marines who would pounce on them. Lehman liked the analogy. A Department of Defense directive determined the new tiltrotor's "Mission Design Series" letter and number: "V" for Vertical Take Off and Landing, "22" because that was its place on the historical list of "V" aircraft. In January 1985, the JVX officially became the V-22 Osprey.

Naming the Osprey himself was just one sign of Lehman's paternalistic attitude toward the project he sired when he told the Marines to buy a tiltrotor. Lehman also had steered Bell Helicopter and Boeing Vertol together to bid on the program by telling each of their presidents to find a partner. He had helped the Marines and the companies kindle support in Congress to get the program started. He had forced the Navy to take charge when the Army balked at running the program in December 1982. Until he left office in 1987, Lehman used his cunning and clout to ward off attacks on the Osprey, or at least blunt them.

Bell and Boeing were grateful for such a patron at first, for the Osprey was an endangered species from the day Lehman hatched it. Competing interests in the defense industry, within the armed services, and on Capitol Hill were jealously circling the fledgling from the start, hungrily eyeing the estimated billions of dollars the Pentagon was expected to spend on the new tiltrotor over the next couple of decades. If Lehman hadn't kept it under his wing, the Osprey's natural enemies likely would have swooped down and plucked it clean before the preliminary design was done. Dick Spivey and others at Bell and Boeing were happy to have Lehman act as if he owned the Osprey at first. By the time he left office, though, they were glad to see him go.

* * *

The Osprey's political troubles began when it was still just called the JVX. The troublemaker was the Army's second-ranking civilian, Undersecretary James R. Ambrose, a gray, thin-lipped workaholic who had joined the Reagan administration after thirty-six years as a defense industry executive. When he got to the Pentagon, Ambrose quickly became known for driving subordinates and others to distraction with insatiable demands for information. If he was dying to know the answer to a question, he didn't hesitate to call Army program managers at 2 or 3 A.M. Ambrose called his style "Management By Asking Questions," and after he had asked enough questions about the tiltrotor, he decided the Army had higher priorities.

First, in December 1982, Ambrose handed over management of the JVX to the Navy Department. Then, on May 13, 1983, barely two weeks after Navair gave Bell-Boeing their contract for the new tiltrotor,

Ambrose announced he was pulling the Army out of the program altogether. "Request you advise all appropriate offices and agencies that we are no longer participants," he said in a memo to the Army staff.

Ambrose's decision hit the Marines and Lehman like a sucker punch. They hadn't seen it coming, and without the Army, the whole JVX program might implode. The Army dropping out would undermine support in the Pentagon and Congress in several ways. For starters, the Army wouldn't be taking the 288 Ospreys it had planned to buy for electronic spying missions. That would make those bought by the Marines, the Navy, and the Air Force more expensive, for like most manufacturers, aircraft makers can offer cheaper prices when they sell in greater volume. The Air Force already had cut the number of Ospreys it planned to buy from 200 to 80. If the tiltrotor got more expensive, the Air Force might follow the Army's lead and quit the program entirely, too. Even if the Air Force stayed in, the Marines might have a harder time getting money for the JVX. Not only would the Army no longer be arguing *for* the tiltrotor, it would be trying to get money for *other* projects instead. Worst of all, without the Army, the JVX would no longer be a true "joint program," one of its chief selling points. People in the Office of the Secretary of Defense and Congress would have to wonder if the Marines, with the smallest of service budgets, could really afford this expensive new machine. Each Osprey already was expected to cost about $15 million, without even counting future inflation or the cost of developing the new tiltrotor.

The Marines decided to fight—to try to get Ambrose's decision reversed, or at least amended. The Navy Department quickly got the issue put on the fall agenda of the Defense Resources Board, a committee of top officials who divvied up the Pentagon budget in those days. When the DRB took up the issue, General P. X. Kelley, who became commandant of the Marine Corps that July, would "brief off" against General John Wickham, the chief of staff of the Army. Headquarters Marine Corps assigned Major Bob Magnus to prepare Kelley. Magnus canceled his summer leave and started working up a briefing.

On Capitol Hill, meanwhile, the Marines started trying to defuse the "too-costly" argument. Lieutenant General William Fitch, the deputy chief of staff for aviation, was at the Senate Defense Appropriations Subcommittee on July 28, 1983, to testify on the Marine Corps aviation budget. The chairman, Republican senator Ted Stevens of Alaska, had been an Army Air Corps transport pilot in World War II and was a friend of the military. When lobbyist George Troutman started working the Hill for Bell Helicopter two years earlier, Stevens was a prime target for his argument that the tiltrotor would be ideal not only for military but civilian aviation. Stevens agreed.

The July hearing was held in the neo-Roman pomp of room SD-192 in the Dirksen Senate Office Building, a high-ceilinged space whose walls were paneled in light teak and green Monte Verde marble wainscoting. Stevens and a couple of other senators sat behind the slightly raised, semicircular dais. Fitch sat at a long, wooden witness table. Behind him in leather chairs hovered several aides—"horse holders," in military slang—to back him up. One was Magnus, one of Fitch's favorites.

Stevens played devil's advocate, conducting a mock interrogation so Fitch could get the Marine Corps' arguments on the record, a way to try to shape opinion on the Hill before staffers and senators formed strong opinions about the consequences of the Army quitting the JVX. "I happen to be personally very much enthused by the JVX tiltrotor," Stevens told Fitch, "but under the circumstances of the budget . . . why should we proceed with the tiltrotor for the Marines alone?"

"We still have a joint program," Fitch stoutly insisted. Even if the Army and the Air Force were to drop out, though, "there is adequate justification to go it alone, if that is what it takes," he declared. "JVX is probably the highest aviation priority that we have in research and development."

Why not buy Black Hawk helicopters instead, Stevens wondered? The Navy, he noted, was already buying Black Hawks that Sikorsky Aircraft had "marinized"—modified to resist the corrosion of salt spray and other strains of shipboard use.

This was an argument the tiltrotor's advocates had started hearing only recently, and one they wanted to nip in the bud. It was being raised by one of the most powerful bureaucrats in the Pentagon, David S. C. Chu, director of the Office of Program Analysis and Evaluation, known as "P, A and E." Chu headed a staff of economists and mathematicians whose job was to analyze the cost-effectiveness of major defense programs—figure out how to get more bang for the buck, in the popular phrase. Chu's staff had done some back-of-the-envelope calculations. A cursory look suggested tiltrotors would be far more costly than Black Hawks, maybe five times as much per aircraft. Stevens was doing Fitch a favor by raising the issue, though, for Magnus had armed the general with a powerful reply.

If the Marines bought Black Hawks instead of tiltrotors "you would have to buy about six additional ships to carry those Black Hawk helicopters," Fitch warned. Magnus had extrapolated that from the fact that the Black Hawk carried only eleven troops while the JVX was going to carry twenty-four, and an amphibious assault ship deck can hold only so many aircraft. If roughly twice as many Black Hawks as JVX's would be needed to get an equal number of Marines ashore in the same amount of time, more ships would be needed to launch those Black Hawks, and ships cost a lot more than aircraft.

As the exchange went on, Stevens assumed a new role: the concerned parent obliged to try to talk a headstrong child out of a risky plan, but so proud of the kid's moxie that, well, shucks, how could you say no?

"You realize it is a forty-one billion dollar program you are embarking on?" Stevens asked, using an estimate of what the Osprey was going to cost over twenty years with inflation.

"Yes, sir, I fully understand that," Fitch assured him.

"All alone," Steven admonished. "And if the Congress does not give you the money, you will be without helicopters."

"We are not alone but with the Department of the Navy, sir," Fitch answered.

Fitch didn't need to add that the Department of the Navy was run by Lehman, and Lehman wanted to keep the Army in the JVX program. While the Marines were pleading their case on the Hill and preparing to fight Ambrose, Lehman came up with the winning strategy. He went over Ambrose's head.

On Army procurement decisions, Ambrose's word was usually final. Army Secretary John O. Marsh, Jr., was a former Virginia congressman who also had been assistant secretary of defense for legislative affairs. Marsh preferred to deal with policy and the Hill and let Ambrose handle technology and procurement issues. Marsh was also friendly with Lehman, however. The two met every few days over lunch or coffee, and one day that summer, Lehman offered Marsh a deal: if the Army would just agree to buy the JVX once it was built, Lehman wouldn't fight to make them help pay for developing the tiltrotor. "To me, that was the best of all worlds," Lehman told me, "because that would give us the cover of Army support without having them at the table to muck up the program." Their deal still had to be ratified, however, by the Defense Resources Board, where Army Chief of Staff Wickham and Marine Commandant Kelley were to conduct their "brief-off" on the issue.

The DRB met on September 19, 1983, in the secretary of defense's conference room, a space in the Pentagon's E-Ring dominated by a long table. After Lehman's talk with Marsh, the issue had been recast as whether the Army would buy the Marine Corps version of the JVX or drop out of the program altogether. Seventeen top officials, including Lehman, Chu, and Ambrose, were present, but they wouldn't get a vote. The DRB wasn't a democratic body, just a forum for debate. As usual, Deputy Defense Secretary Paul Thayer was presiding and would make the final decision.

Wickham began the discussion of the JVX, arguing that his service had no great need for the big, beefy tiltrotor the Marines wanted but was desperate for a light and versatile helicopter called the LHX, one of Ambrose's pet projects. Kelley went next, armed with a detailed fifteen-slide briefing that Magnus had created showing how great the tiltrotor would be for hauling troops and cargo and lots of other missions, too. One slide said the Army could use 231 of them to carry troops into battle or casualties out of it. Electronic spying, the Army's original mission for the JVX, would be done by other aircraft, the slide noted. As Kelley talked, Wickham started deriding the JVX and its huge rotors. "It's a behemoth!" he scoffed. Kelley strode silently over to where Wickham was seated. At five foot eight and 155 pounds, Wickham wasn't small, but he was slight. With the six-foot, 200-pound Kelley looming over him, Wickham looked downright puny. "John," Kelley rasped, "to you, *anything* would be large."

The room erupted in laughter. When it subsided, Thayer said: "Okay, let's go with both."

That ratified Lehman's deal with Marsh. The Army would spend no money to help develop the JVX but would agree—in principle—to buy 231 of the Marine Corps version when the tiltrotor was ready. The Navy Department and Air Force would pay all the development bills, but the tiltrotor's advocates could still tell Congress or anyone else who asked that the Army was in the program; it had a "requirement" for precisely 231. Colonel Glenn Yarborough, a military aide to the assistant secretary of the Army for research and development, had provided the number. "I plucked it out of the air," Yarborough told me. Yarborough was going to use a round figure at first but decided that 231 sounded more "analytical."

At the Senate hearing, Stevens had told Fitch: "If you want it that bad, we will do our best to get it for you, but you will have to hold on to your hat on that one, I think."

Stevens was right. The quest for their dream machine was going to take the Marines on a wild ride—the procurement equivalent of the Fulton Pickup System, the James Bond-style rescue scheme Dick Spivey had worked on in the 1960s. In the Fulton Pickup, a stranded pilot or spy was to be snatched off the ground when an airplane with a fork on its nose snagged a cable attaching the rescuee to a helium balloon. Momentum would fling him into the sky at up to ten times the force of gravity, then the airplane would haul him through the air behind it as a winch reeled him into its belly and safety.

For the Marines, the balloon had just gone up.

★ ★ ★

Four months after the DRB meeting, on a cold and soggy January afternoon, Spivey and Magnus were in Greenwich, England. The Bell Helicopter marketer and the Marine Corps action officer were in Britain on business, but this afternoon Spivey had talked Magnus into taking a few minutes to stop by the Royal Observatory, situated atop a grassy hill just southeast of London. Spivey wanted to straddle the Prime Meridian, the imaginary line that runs from the North Pole to the South Pole and divides the Eastern from the Western Hemisphere.

Spivey and Magnus had long been straddling the invisible and often imaginary line between the defense industry and the military. For nearly three years they had been promoting the tiltrotor as a team, a microcosm of the military-industrial complex in action. When Spivey was in Fort Worth and Magnus in Washington, they talked on the phone, trading rumors and information, discussing tactics and strategy, cooking up new ways to ensure the JVX program's success. Magnus might call to suggest that Bell invite this general or that government official to fly in the XV-15, or to share impressions he'd picked up while briefing someone on Capitol Hill or in a Pentagon meeting. Spivey would call Magnus with progress reports from the engineers, data Magnus could use in briefings, or to ask what was happening on the program in the Pentagon or at Navair. When Spivey was in Washington, he and Magnus often paired up to give briefings on the JVX to key officials. They also took their "dog and pony show," as Spivey called it, to aviation conferences around the country. Magnus would use elaborate slides to explain how the Marines planned to use the tiltrotor, how it was going to revive the Corps' eroding amphibious assault capability, make the Marines vastly more agile on the battlefield, and let them reach anywhere in the world in a hurry. Spivey, drawing on his background as an aeronautical engineer, would talk about the peculiarities of tiltrotor technology, how Bell and Boeing engineers were designing the JVX, what it would be able to do, and how this new way to fly was going to revolutionize aviation, military and civilian alike.

The day before their visit to Greenwich, Spivey and Magnus had put on their show for some military officers and defense industry officials at Whitehall, the main building of the British Ministry of Defence, in a visit John Lehman had arranged. Spivey wasn't optimistic about the chances of the British joining the program—they didn't—but he and other Bell and Boeing marketers, lobbyists, and executives knew they needed to broaden and strengthen the JVX's base of support.

In Washington, no program is ever truly sold, no issue ever truly settled; the annual budget cycle ensures that. This was why defense companies kept marketers like Spivey, lobbyists like George Troutman, and public relations teams on their payrolls. The marketers would have to keep explaining the JVX to new Pentagon action officers and uniformed military leaders, who rotate to new assignments every three or four years. The lobbyists would need to educate new members of Congress and their aides, new administration officials and others in government, and curry favor with them. The public relations people—"flacks," as reporters called them, an anglicization of the German abbreviation for air defense artillery, FLAK—would have to try to shape public opinion by periodically firing off encouraging reports of the JVX's progress in press releases and staying ready to shoot down any incoming attacks on the tiltrotor.

Troutman and Bell's PR staff often relied on Spivey to do briefings or media interviews. There was no one else at Bell or Boeing who knew the tiltrotor's history and technology as well as he did and also could talk about it in a way nonengineers could grasp. Spivey was a walking encyclopedia on the technology and where things stood with the JVX, partly because he went to engineering meetings every chance he got. Engineers often viewed marketers with something just short of contempt, Spivey knew, but Bell engineers accepted Spivey. He had been one of them once upon a time. Spivey was as much a hybrid as the tiltrotor: part engineer, part salesman. The engineer understood the technical details of the tiltrotor; the salesman could convert them into a sales pitch most anyone could understand. Spivey made sure of that by trying out new lines on his elderly mother in Georgia when he could before using them in his briefings.

There was also something else about Spivey that few at Bell and Boeing had, at least not to the same degree. Spivey was a salesman with a dream—a dream that moved him so much, he sometimes sounded more like a prophet with a vision than a marketer with a product. When Spivey went out to spread his gospel, he was a polite pastor, not a fire-breathing evangelist; there was no shouting or arm waving. Often, though, he would hold his elbows to his sides with his forearms and index fingers pointing up and explain that a tiltrotor "takes off like a helicopter," then rotate his arms forward and add, "flies like an airplane." When he did, Spivey would smile like a magician who's just performed a mind-boggling trick. Spivey thought the tiltrotor was amazing, and he was sure it was going to work magic on the world of aviation.

A couple of days after Ambrose dropped his bombshell about the Army's lack of interest in the JVX, Spivey assured reporter Joe Simnacher of the *Dallas Morning News* that by the mid-1990s—within a decade—a tiltrotor much like the one Bell and Boeing were developing for the military would be "the workhorse of offshore oil companies." Civilian versions would be flying forty passengers at a time from downtown Dallas or Fort Worth to the central business district of Houston, he predicted. In the meantime, the military tiltrotor project was going to create at least ten thousand jobs in the Fort Worth area alone. Spivey took the figure from a study done for Bell at Texas A&M University.

Visions like those were why Leonard M. "Jack" Horner, who succeeded Jim Atkins as Bell's president in 1983, called Spivey "one of the believers."

There were other believers. An important one was Hans Mark, the deputy administrator of NASA in 1983, who had been trying to help Bell perfect and promote the tiltrotor for years. The son of a renowned chemist who had fled Nazi Germany with his family in 1940, Mark was an MIT-educated nuclear physicist who had worked at top labs and taught at top schools before becoming director of NASA's Ames Research Center in 1969 at age forty. One of the first projects that caught Mark's eye at Ames was the tiltrotor. The idea of a flying machine that didn't need airports intrigued him. In 1973, when lower-level officials at Bell and NASA couldn't agree on a contract to build the XV-15, Mark flew to Fort Worth and made the deal himself with Bell president Jim Atkins. In 1979, Mark joined the Carter administration as undersecretary of the Air Force, then became secretary when his predecessor resigned. The next year, when Bell was looking for transportation to take the XV-15 to the Paris Air Show, Mark arranged for the Air Force to put two big cargo aircraft at the company's disposal. When Reagan became president in 1981, Mark went back to NASA as deputy administrator, but he was at the Paris Air Show that summer when Lehman saw the XV-15 fly for the first time. When they got back to Washington, Lehman asked Mark's view of the tiltrotor. Mark told him it held extraordinary promise.

Two years later, with the Ambrose crisis just resolved, Bell sought Mark's advice on how to shore up the JVX politically. "Dr. Mark said make it into a national program," Spivey recorded in his work diary. At a November 22, 1983, marketing meeting, Bell's JVX team decided on their strategy. They dubbed it "Keep the Program Sold." Horner would visit the editorial boards of the *Washington Post, New York Times, Los Angeles Times*, and other newspapers to talk up the tiltrotor. Bell would send the XV-15 out into the country to make flight demonstrations. Spivey also would rev up the XV-15 "guest pilot" program, which had flown nearly fifty government officials and military officers in 1981–82 but only nine in 1983. Bell would convene a symposium for potential Osprey subcontractors to school them on the tiltrotor and urge them to tell their members of Congress how important it could be to their company, their local economy, and the nation. Spivey would travel with Horner to visit larger potential suppliers—avionics contractors, engine makers, and the like—to "convince them that the program was real," as Spivey put it, so they would pitch in on the lobbying. Everywhere they went, Horner, Spivey, and others would emphasize that the tiltrotor wasn't just another aircraft but a "national asset." The goal, Spivey wrote in his notebook, was to brand that idea into the public and political consciousness within six to nine months: "national asset."

The next year, Bell sent its XV-15 on a 3,500-mile, fifty-five-flight "Eastern U.S. Tour." The tour concluded October 2 with the XV-15 picking Horner up at the New York Port Authority heliport near the World Trade Center and flying him to Bolling Air Force Base in Washington, D.C., to show off the tiltrotor's potential as an executive transport. The 200-mile trip took sixty-six minutes. The same year, thirty-nine guest pilots flew the XV-15. The engineers were still just designing the Osprey, but Spivey had no doubt it would make its first flight in 1987 as planned and be in production by 1989. On June 12, 1984, he wrote in his work diary: "Get DOT [the U.S. Department of Transportation] to borrow a few JVX from DoD [Department of Defense] in '89 to set up a city-center to city-center transportation pilot system."

★ ★ ★

One of Lehman's big ideas for the Osprey program was to use it as a test case for his belief that free market competition could cure the ills of military procurement. Four years into the Reagan administration, it was clear to everyone paying attention that the defense procurement system was riddled with waste, fraud, and abuse. Stories of $640 toilet seats and $7,622 coffee pots sold to the military, indictments of defense contractors for bilking the government out of millions, cost overruns in the billions were standard journalistic fare—one outrage after another topping the last. Lehman wasn't the only one who thought competition was the cure for this cancer. In 1985, Congress passed a range of defense procurement reforms largely aimed at injecting more competition into military contracting. More competition between defense companies, Lehman and the reformers in Congress were sure, would keep contractors honest, hold prices down, and stop cost overruns. This was why, after no one but the Bell-Boeing team bid on the JVX in 1983, Lehman decided to split the companies up after they had designed and built a dozen or so Ospreys and make them compete with each other for production contracts. This was a variation on what Lehman called his "leader-follower" policy, in which the winner of a design competition was forced to give enough information to the loser for the loser to produce the item according to the winner's design. The resulting dual sources would then duel for production contracts, with each guaranteed a share big enough to keep both interested. That way, Lehman reasoned, there would be competition every year on big contracts, rather than just at the start of a big program, which would give the Defense Department a tool to hold prices down. "You had no leverage with a contractor if you had no place to go," Lehman said. "If you don't have an annual competition, everybody gets lazy." Defense contractors despised the idea.

Bell-Boeing's teaming agreement, signed in May 1982, said the companies would remain partners on the JVX until at least five years after they delivered the first one to go into service. Lehman's decision to break them up sooner drove a wedge between the companies. Executives and engineers at both became wary of sharing all the information they should with a partner they would have to go head-to-head against in just a few years to win production contracts, which offer contractors their biggest profits.

Lehman presented Bell and Boeing with a bigger surprise in the fall of 1985. In those days, the second stage of major Pentagon procurements, following preliminary design, was called Full Scale Development, referred to as FSD, each letter pronounced individually. In FSD, the company or companies developing an aircraft or other big item would get ready for production by making and buying tools, purchasing parts and supplies, building prototypes and testing them, then redesigning and fixing things that hadn't worked as expected. FSD was where the government started spending serious money on a program, and where contractors often discovered problems in their design. Bell and Boeing Vertol started negotiating with Navair for an FSD contract in 1984, while their engineers were still designing the Osprey. In July 1985, the companies told Navair they could build six prototypes for flight-testing and four for ground tests for a minimum price of $1.6 billion and a maximum $1.8 billion. They requested the usual terms: "cost plus incentive fee," meaning the government would cover all costs as the companies built the prototypes, up to the ceiling price of $1.8 billion. If the companies spent less than the ceiling price, they would get a bonus—extra profit. If they ran over it, the government would have to cover the overrun, or else the contractors could quit work, just drop the project.

Navair agreed to their offer and Bell-Boeing signed a cost-plus contract. All that remained was for Lehman to approve it. Navair and Bell-Boeing figured that was a mere formality, so to keep to the schedule, which envisioned the Osprey making its first flight in 1987, the companies started doing FSD work on their own money. When Navair officials took the contract to Lehman on September 9, 1985, however, they got a shock. He was sick of cost overruns, Lehman told them. He wasn't going to have another one. Go back and make the Osprey contract "fixed price," Lehman told the Navair officials. Under a fixed-price contract, the companies would have to finish FSD at their own expense if they busted the ceiling price.

Lehman wanted something else as well: a "Not to Exceed" price— a cap—on how much Bell-Boeing could charge for each Osprey in the first couple of lots produced, which the companies would be allowed to build together.

"Sandbagged by SECNAV," Spivey wrote in his work diary the next day, using the Pentagon abbreviation for secretary of the Navy.

Bell president Horner nearly fell off his chair when he heard Lehman's demands. It would be a *huge* gamble, Horner knew, for the companies to agree to a fixed price for FSD on an aircraft as complex as the Osprey, a machine incorporating new forms of composites, incredibly complicated computerized flight controls, things the companies weren't entirely sure yet how to build. All kinds of unforeseeable problems might arise that would increase the cost, things engineers call "unknown unknowns" or "unk-unks." The companies would be *nuts* to agree to a fixed price for FSD, Horner thought. Others at Bell and Boeing agreed.

On October 10, 1985, Horner, Joe Mallen of Boeing Vertol, and two top executives from their parent companies—Beverly Dolan, chief executive officer of Bell corporate parent Textron Inc., and Lionel Alford, a senior vice president of Boeing—went to the Pentagon hoping to reason with Lehman. Harry Bendorf, a retired Air Force general who ran Boeing Vertol's office in Washington, took them to Lehman's office and waited in the anteroom. When they emerged a half hour later, Bendorf could tell it hadn't gone well. The executives stormed out, their faces red. When they stopped to talk in the hall, Textron executive Dolan was particularly irate. Dolan couldn't believe Lehman's arrogance. "I'm not sure we need to do this," he sputtered.

Horner later gave Spivey and others at Bell an account of what had happened. "John, we're playing with dynamite here," Horner remembered telling Lehman. The companies had given Navair a price they thought would cover all the costs of FSD, but it was just an estimate. "Who knows whether we're right or wrong within ten or fifteen percent—or more?" Horner pleaded. Fixed-price contracts would make sense once the Osprey went into production, but in FSD there were too many unk-unks.

"Look, I don't want you to lose money," Lehman answered. The government was partly to blame for cost overruns; he knew that, he said. Government program offices had a bad habit of changing requirements and making contractors add or upgrade gear as ships and aircraft were being developed. That added cost. This would be the beauty of a fixed-price contract, Lehman told the executives: Navair wouldn't be able to do that on the Osprey because the companies could just say no to changes that weren't reasonable, tell Navair they wouldn't do them without extra money. "Look, you're going to have to be our policeman on these requirements," Lehman said. "If you're ready to fixed-price it, then we can go forward." If not, the Osprey could stay in preliminary design until the companies were confident enough in their engineering to risk FSD at a fixed price. Look on the bright side, Lehman urged: "If this program is successful, this building will buy more of these airplanes than you can imagine!"

"Threat—then carrot," Spivey wrote in his notebook.

The companies convened a meeting of top executives to decide whether to agree to a fixed-price deal. Subordinates from the Bell and Boeing contract and finance departments presented an analysis showing that, even if all went perfectly, it would probably cost at least $100 million more than the $1.8 billion Bell-Boeing had offered Navair. They had made that offer, of course, when they were talking about a cost-plus contract, under which the government would have to pay for overruns. Now they were talking about their own money.

Boeing was used to such gambles. Investing money in a new aircraft was normal in the commercial airliner business. Alford, the Boeing senior vice president overseeing the Osprey program for his corporation, was ready to make the deal. "We should be able to perform this contract for one-point-eight billion," he declared. "If we can't do that, we shouldn't be in this business." Dan McCrary, Bell's director of government contracts at the time, thought his bosses, Textron CEO Bev Dolan and Bell president Horner, took Alford's bluster as a challenge to their manhood. Suddenly the issue seemed to be "who's got the biggest balls," McCrary remembered. Dolan and Horner seemed to be saying, "Well, we're big boys, too. Let's just go do it." They decided they would.

Navair and the companies finished renegotiating the contract on March 19, 1986. The new deal set a target price of $1.714 billion and a ceiling price $100 million higher, $1.810 billion, for six Osprey prototypes and other FSD work over the next seven years. If FSD cost more than the target price, the government would pay 60 percent of overruns up to the ceiling price. If FSD cost more than $1.810 billion, the companies would foot the rest of the bill—no matter how much more it was. As Lehman demanded, Bell and Boeing also agreed to give Navair an option to buy the first twelve production model Ospreys for no more than $1.2 billion. The price sounds exorbitant but wasn't, given what is known in industry as the "learning curve." Aircraft makers, like shoppers who buy build-it-yourself furniture from stores like Ikea, need a lot more time to build an item the first time they try it than they do after they get the hang of it. Over the life of the program, the average price of the Osprey was expected to be more like $30 million apiece, not the $100 million each contemplated for the first lot of twelve. Since an agency like Navair can never guarantee how many aircraft the government really will buy in the end, it normally pays the full production price from the start, taking savings as the learning curve comes down. Given how many design and engineering problems Bell and Boeing were facing, they couldn't be sure in 1985 that they actually could build the first twelve Ospreys for as *little* as $1.2 billion.

"One of these days, we're really going to regret this," Horner told Spivey when the decision was made. "When we get there, I'll take the blame for what I did."

★ ★ ★

Lehman soon threw the companies another curve. The Osprey was going to need engines designed to function smoothly when vertical, horizontal, and at all angles in between. Navair's plan was to hold a competition for a new, more advanced gas turbine engine than existing ones, then buy the engines and give them to Bell to install in the Osprey's nacelles. Three companies were in the running for the contract. Two—a Pratt & Whitney division in Florida and a General Electric division in Massachusetts—offered new engines they were developing under an Army program aimed at getting a lighter, cheaper, more fuel-efficient turbine for helicopters. The Pratt and GE engines weren't quite ready for prime time, but either promised to carry an aircraft much farther on less fuel than existing engines. They were also compact, as turbine engines go, which held down their weight. The third bidder, the Indiana-based Allison Gas Turbine Division of General Motors, offered a descendant of its T56, a venerable turboprop engine used in C-130 cargo planes and P-3 surveillance aircraft for decades. Allison's proposed T406 wouldn't be as fuel-efficient as the Pratt or GE entries, but it was proven technology, so the company could offer the Navy a great price. The Allison engine's design also left a lot of room to boost its horsepower if necessary.

Among those following the competition, the smart money was on GE. Its entry weighed about 850 pounds and promised great "specific fuel consumption," or SFC, the term engineers use to describe how many pounds of fuel an engine burns per hour to produce a given amount of horsepower. Bell's engineers figured the Osprey's engines would need the best SFC possible to meet its range requirements. With weight such a problem, lighter engines would be better, too. Bell didn't have enough engineers with the required expertise to design nacelles for all three engine candidates, so they had been focusing on designs for the GE engine. They had done some work on nacelles to hold Pratt's engine, too, but more or less written off Allison's. At 1,050 pounds, Allison's entry seemed far too heavy, and with its higher SFC far too "thirsty."

Navair evaluated the entries in the fall of 1985. Its experts largely agreed with Bell that the GE engine seemed the best choice, though some favored the Allison engine because of its extra potential power. Navair officials went to Lehman's office to brief him in December, expecting him to ratify their recommendation to go with the GE engine. Lehman listened, then said to give Allison the contract at a firm fixed price—the government wouldn't pay anything for overruns. The Allison engine would be cheaper because it was based on proven technology, Lehman said, and while its SFC wasn't as good as GE's and Pratt's, there was a silver lining in that. Allison's engine was thirstier partly because it burned fuel at lower temperatures than the other engines. That would make Allison's engine last longer, and if necessary, its power output could be increased by "turning up the wick." That would be a good feature, Lehman said, if the Osprey's weight increased in coming years, as aircraft weights always did. Navair gave Allison the contract for $76.4 million, far less than the prices GE and Pratt had offered.

Bell's engineers were stunned. Now they had to redesign the Osprey's engine mounts, redesign how its fuel lines would connect to the engines, alter the shape of the nacelles. Worst of all, the Allison engines would add 600 pounds to the Osprey, including design changes to accommodate it. What had gotten into Lehman, they wondered? Was he giving Allison the contract to keep it in the military aircraft engine business, to protect the "defense industrial base?" Had someone at General Motors influenced him? Had he decided it was better to tick off *both* GE and Pratt, two political powerhouses, rather than favor one over the other? Theories and rumors ran rampant.

"That's just fantasy," Lehman told me. "For political reasons, Allison would have been the dumbest choice. GM-Allison had virtually no clout on the Hill or with the White House, whereas GE and Pratt were very powerful, and every time I made a decision against one or the other I'd hear from the White House, I'd hear from OSD [the Office of the Secretary of Defense], because their lobbyists or their chairmen would raise hell about it."

Lehman sided with the Navair engineers who believed the Osprey was going to get heavier and would need more power in the future, he said. "Purely and simply, I agreed with them, and that's why I picked the Allison engine."

Whatever his reasons, Lehman's decision had just added to the Osprey's biggest problems: weight and schedule. The Osprey was still way too heavy, and what with all the design difficulties, what with Boeing's fight with Navair over what composites could be used in the fuselage, and now with the engine switch, the program was falling behind schedule. The first flight had been planned for 1987. Soon it was rescheduled for 1988.

★ ★ ★

One day in March 1985, Spivey wrote in his MIT notebook:

> Ask Not . . .
>   Can We Afford JVX (V-22)?
> But instead . . .
>   Can we afford <u>NOT</u> to field the V-22?

Soon, PA&E chief David Chu wasn't the only one asking the first question. In late 1985, House Armed Services Committee aide Douglas Necessary decided to do a study for members and staff on whether the Osprey was really the best buy for the Marine Corps. Necessary finished his study in early spring 1986 and circulated copies to other committee aides. He titled it "The V-22 Osprey: Is the Case for Tilt Rotor Tilted?" "We may be acquiring the wrong aircraft at the wrong time for the wrong reasons," Necessary wrote. "The question isn't, 'Can the tiltrotor be developed to do the job?' But can the helicopter do the job for significantly less money?" Necessary questioned whether the Marines really needed the Osprey's range for amphibious assaults, the reason they said they wanted it. The Osprey might be able to carry troops to an assault point 230 miles away, he noted, but the helicopters needed to carry artillery and other heavy equipment still would be limited to 150 miles. So would the Marines' helicopter gunships, which the Osprey might need as armed escorts, at least for the foreseeable future. Some Marine planners envisioned a day when the Osprey, a transport by now expected to be armed for self-defense with one gun at best, might be escorted by tiltrotor gunships, but no actual plan to build any existed. "The V-22-borne troops would be without firepower, or 'naked,' until the rest of the team arrives," Necessary wrote. In amphibious assaults launched within ranges helicopters could handle, he added, the Osprey's extra speed would be no advantage.

Someone gave the Marine Corps a copy of his study, and Necessary soon started hearing from fellow House staffers that the Marines didn't think much of the study, or of him. Action officers in the Marine Corps aviation branch were furious, in fact. They had spent hours explaining to Necessary that in an amphibious assault, the Marines in the first wave couldn't come ashore with artillery in any event. It had long been Marine Corps doctrine to rely on fighter-bombers, not artillery, to attack enemy formations in the early part of an assault. This was why they'd bought the Harrier jump jet. Necessary seemed to ignore that fact. He was unqualified, unprofessional, and didn't know what he was doing, those action officers were telling people on the Hill.

Clearly, Necessary thought, he'd struck a nerve. He was sure of it in early April, when Bell and Boeing Vertol sent defense reporters a thirty-one-page rebuttal to his twenty-one-page study. The rebuttal said Necessary's was "not a careful analysis" and was "based on old, incomplete data."

"Why are they responding in such a paranoid manner?" Necessary plaintively asked in an interview with *Defense News*, a newspaper focused on military affairs.

Part of the answer was timing. Necessary's report happened to start circulating about the same time that PA&E, the green-eyeshade office run by David Chu, was using a similar analysis to try to stop the Osprey program in its tracks. Before Full Scale Development could start, the Navy Department needed approval from a high-level Pentagon committee called the Defense Systems Acquisition Review Council. The DSARC—insiders called it "the DEE-sark"—made its decision on April 17. In that meeting, Chu cited studies done for the Marines by a federally funded research center called the Center for Naval Analyses. One concluded that while the Osprey would be more effective than helicopters at bringing troops ashore, the tiltrotor would cost far more. Based on that and PA&E's own analysis, Chu suggested the Marines buy Black Hawk helicopters to carry troops instead. Lehman and Commandant Kelley argued against him at the DSARC and FSD was approved. The Marines and Bell-Boeing were beginning to see, though, that they were going to have to fight to keep the Osprey alive, and the simple idea that the tiltrotor would get Marines to shore faster from farther at sea in an amphibious assault wasn't going to be enough ammunition.

The Osprey program's manager at Navair in those days, Marine Colonel Harry Blot, issued that warning in an interview with the journal *Amphibious Warfare Review* after the DSARC approved FSD. Blot said Necessary's study had asked "a legitimate question" about the Osprey. "We Marines, however, were caught unprepared for his challenge. In our own minds, we knew very well how we were going to employ the aircraft once ashore, however, all we justified and explained was how the aircraft was to be employed in the ship-to-shore movement during an amphibious operation." Blot said the Marines actually had a list of thirty missions the Osprey could do for them.

The Marines began expanding their arguments. That spring, the Corps asked the Center for Naval Analyses for a new study on "the best arguments to get the V-22 program approved." The center delivered the study in July. From then on, in Pentagon meetings, in congressional testimony, in articles for military journals, Marine officers described more and more things the tiltrotor would do for the Corps. The Osprey wasn't just going to let them launch amphibious assaults from "over the horizon," beyond the range of antiship missiles, it was also going to self-deploy—fly across oceans with aerial refueling. Helicopters can't fly across oceans; when they go to war, they have to be carried on ships or dismantled, put into big cargo planes two or three at a time and flown to a staging area, then reassembled and flight-tested before they go into battle. Getting helicopters overseas takes weeks. The Osprey was going to fly *itself* over the ocean. That was going to give the Corps a unique way to live up to one of its mottos: "First to Fight." If the Soviet Union invaded Western Europe—the worst military contingency imaginable in the 1980s—the Marines' tiltrotors would fly to Europe in a day or two at most, meet ground troops there, and carry them into the fray right away. Knowing the Marines could do this would help deter the Soviets, some officers argued, and if a war began in Europe or elsewhere, the Osprey would be a "force multiplier." It would give commanders a way to shuttle troops from one point to another before the enemy knew what had hit him, then shift them somewhere else to strike again. It would refuel other aircraft in-flight. It would rush casualties to medical treatment. It would keep frontline troops supplied with beans and bullets.

As the Marines expanded their arguments for the Osprey, the tiltrotor's value seemed to increase in their own minds. Slowly but surely—not in a sudden shudder of inspiration, but in a gradual, osmotic way—the idea took hold within the Corps that the tiltrotor was going to transform the Marines. Without the Osprey, they would have to buy new helicopters to replace their old ones, and from time to time fend off those who wanted to reduce their cult of warriors to shipboard sheriffs and embassy guards, maybe even merge them with the Army. *With* the Osprey, they were going to be a vital weapon for the commander in chief, truly indispensable. The Marines would be first to fight, and when they fought, the tiltrotor would dazzle and confuse their enemies. The Osprey promised to ensure the Marine Corps' future in a way that planting the flag on Mount Suribachi during the World War II battle of Iwo Jima hadn't.

In time, winning at Iwo Jima would seem simple compared to getting the Osprey.

★ ★ ★

Lehman handpicked Colonel Harry Blot to take over the Osprey program. In the fall of 1985, with FSD on the horizon, the Osprey was getting expensive enough to attract attention from those eager to cut defense spending. Soaring federal budget deficits had prompted Congress that year to pass the Gramm-Rudman-Hollings Act, a law requiring automatic spending cuts if deficit targets weren't met. Navair was going to need a strong hand on the reins to keep the Osprey on schedule and on budget. In Blot, Lehman thought he had his man.

Harold W. Blot grew up in the Bronx, graduated from Villanova University in 1962 with a mechanical engineering degree, then became a Marine Corps fighter pilot. He flew F-8 Crusader fighter-bombers in Vietnam, then became a test pilot and went into training to be an astronaut. When NASA's manned orbital laboratory program was canceled, Blot was transferred to Patuxent River Naval Air Station in coastal Maryland, where Navy and Marine Corps aircraft are tested. Blot was sent to England to evaluate the Harrier when the Marines got interested in the vertical takeoff jet around 1970, and he joined the first Harrier squadron the Corps formed the next year. Later in the '70s, he worked on the Harrier program at Navair, then came back a few years later to run it.

Lehman was impressed with how Blot had held McDonnell Douglas Corporation's feet to the fire to fix a string of mechanical and other problems on the AV-8B Harrier, a new version of the jump jet. Lehman inquired about him and was told Blot was near the end of his expected three-year tour managing the Harrier program. Blot was eager to get out of Navair's dull high-rise in Crystal City and back to flying. He was also hoping to get command of a Marine air group, which could lead to a promotion to brigadier general if he did the job well. Then a Navair admiral told him one day: "Harry, you're not going to like this, but I've got the feeling that you're going to be the next V-22 program manager."

"Oh, no," Blot said. Soon he got a call to report to the commandant's office.

Commandant Kelley told Blot he'd tried to talk Lehman out of putting Blot in charge of the Osprey program. "Hey, we're going to give him a group," Kelley had told Lehman. "This guy has general potential," meaning the rank.

"You mean if I put him in charge of the most important program in the Marine Corps that it will cause him not to make general?" Lehman replied. "If that's true, then you've had your last Marine Corps program manager."

After reciting that conversation, Kelley told Blot: "Harry, show up Monday." As Blot walked toward the door, Kelley called after him.

"Harry?"

"Yes, sir?"

"When you get there, *smile*."

★ ★ ★

By nature, Blot wasn't a big smiler. He was a poker-faced listener with iceberg eyes—cold and piercing. Nor did he find much to smile about when he saw where things stood with the Osprey. Lehman had told him the program wasn't coming together the way it should, and Blot agreed. Bell was paralyzed by the size and complexity of the program, afraid to make decisions, he found. "They just weren't used to that many zeroes in the numbers," Blot told me: "a million-dollar company with a billion-dollar program." Boeing Vertol seemed more comfortable with the size of the project, but things were going slowly because the companies weren't coordinating with each other. On paper, they had a Joint Program Office, but employees assigned to it worked in Fort Worth or Ridley Park, not together, and all decisions were made by higher-ups. Blot told Bell and Boeing to open a *real* joint office, locate it across the street from Navair in Crystal City, hire somebody savvy to run it, and give that person real authority. Under their teaming agreement, Bell had the right to name the Joint Program Office director, and Horner hired Clyde Skeen, a former top Boeing executive and a multimillionaire. Skeen was used to big numbers.

In April 1986, two weeks after the Defense Systems Acquisition Review Council approved FSD, Blot convened Bell and Boeing marketers and others in Crystal City to tell them what he wanted them to do to shore up the Osprey politically. According to Spivey's notes, Blot said the Osprey's problem was that "everyone is an enemy because of the costs." A program this large had to be sold to the public. The companies weren't doing enough advertising. They needed to talk the tiltrotor up in the press more—an "informed press is best," Blot said—and the Marine Corps shouldn't be the focus when they did. The point to emphasize was that the tiltrotor was a "new concept in aviation," a "national asset" with "commercial fallout." Blot also told them to stop thinking of the tiltrotor as a new kind of helicopter, a natural tendency for two helicopter companies. He said they needed a "fixed-wing mentality."

Blot showed them what he meant by that when he went to Fort Worth on May 21, 1986, to fly the XV-15. He took the controls of the little tiltrotor from Bell pilot Ron Erhart and flew in formation with a helicopter and a turboprop airplane, a tricky thing for someone flying the XV-15 for the first time. Erhart thought Blot handled the aircraft beautifully. Blot was dissatisfied. He could have done better, Blot told Erhart, if the XV-15's power control didn't work like a helicopter's.

Airplane and helicopter pilots have to manipulate three primary devices to control their aircraft: a center stick, foot pedals, and a power lever. In airplanes and helicopters both, direction is primarily controlled by the stick and pedals, which govern different mechanisms but move the same way in each type of aircraft. A helicopter's stick and pedals change the pitch of its rotor blades. An airplane's stick and pedals change the angles of its elevators, ailerons, and rudder. Osprey pilots wouldn't have to think about this, for three flight control computers would handle the tricky transition between helicopter and airplane flight. When the rotors were providing most of the lift, the computers would make the Osprey's stick and pedals control rotor blade pitch. When the Osprey gained enough forward speed for its wing to become its primary source of lift, the computers would gradually transfer the functions of the stick and pedals from changing the pitch of its rotor blades to operating its elevators, ailerons, and rudders. Designing the Osprey's power lever, however, required making a choice between airplane and helicopter methods.

In airplanes and helicopters both, the lever that controls power is to the left of the pilot, but there the resemblance ends. In airplanes, the power lever is called a throttle and is normally mounted perpendicular to the floor. Pushing the throttle forward adds power, and thus speed; pulling it back reduces power and slows the plane down. In a helicopter, the power lever is called a "collective" because it alters the pitch of the rotor blades equally, or collectively, which increases or decreases total thrust. Unlike a throttle, a collective angles up from the floor like the emergency brake in many cars. Pulling the collective up and back adds thrust, causing the helicopter to rise or speed up; pushing it forward and down reduces power, causing the helicopter to slow or descend. Bell built helicopters, so when it designed the XV-15, it gave the tiltrotor a collective. Boeing Vertol was a helicopter maker, too, and the companies were planning to give the Osprey a power lever that worked like a collective, same as the XV-15's. To Blot, that was just wrong. He was a fixed-wing guy with a fixed-wing mentality. He saw the Osprey as a fixed-wing aircraft that would take off and land vertically but fly mostly like an airplane, much like the Harrier. The Osprey should have a throttle, not a collective, Blot told the companies, a power lever the pilot moved forward for more thrust and back for less.

Erhart and fellow Bell pilot Dorman Cannon tried to persuade Blot he was wrong. The Osprey might spend less time flying like a helicopter than an airplane, they argued, but the time it spent as a helicopter would be the most critical. That was when you could smack into the ground and die. Osprey pilots were going to need helicopter skills to hover and handle vertical takeoffs and landings, and pilots trained in helicopters were going to be accustomed to a collective. Pilots tend to fall back on old habits in the last few seconds of a flight, especially if anything is going wrong. Those used to a collective might go the wrong way with the power lever if it worked like a throttle, with potentially disastrous results, the helicopter pilots warned.

Philip Dunford, Boeing Vertol's technology manager on the Osprey in those days, was assigned to brief Blot on why a collective was the way to go. Blot went to Ridley Park one day, listened to Dunford for half an hour, looked at his color slides, and never said a word. When Dunford was done, Blot said, "Well, Phil, I think that was a really good presentation, but it was a waste of time, because we're having a throttle."

The companies designed a hybrid control. Like a throttle, you pushed it forward for more power; like a collective, it moved at an angle. Officially, it was the Thrust Control Lever. Unofficially, everybody called it the "Blottle." Just not to Blot's face.

* * *

For a while after Blot took over, the Osprey program looked like it was picking up steam. In June 1986, Lehman announced that the Navy wouldn't buy just 80 for search-and-rescue missions but also another 300 to replace its S-3 Viking antisubmarine warfare planes, an idea Spivey had been trying to sell the Navy on for years. A month after Lehman's announcement, Bell began a $3.5 million expansion of its Flight Research Center at Arlington Municipal Airport, between Fort Worth and Dallas, adding 80,000 square feet to the 100,000-square-foot facility, to get ready for assembling Osprey prototypes. By November, Bell and Boeing had selected 131 of 201 major subcontractors. In December, Navair approved the Osprey's design.

Urged on by Blot, the companies were also making new headway toward selling the tiltrotor as a "national asset." Bell got the Federal Aviation Administration, the Defense Department, and NASA to do a study of how tiltrotors of all sizes might fit into the U.S. transportation system. The report was written by thirty-four engineers, financial experts, and marketers from Bell and Boeing, including Spivey, under the aegis of a nine-member government steering committee. It predicted that "tiltrotors could capture 1/3 to 2/3 of the high-density, short-haul air travel market." It also said tiltrotors would be a great way for corporate executives to fly, "clearly superior" as a way to take oil workers to and from offshore drilling platforms, and had potential as a commercial cargo carrier as well. The FAA and the U.S. Department of Transportation also commissioned another study in 1987, by the Port Authority of New York and New Jersey, on how tiltrotors could be used to carry passengers on regional flights around the New York–New Jersey–Pennsylvania area. In August, FAA administrator Allan McArtor flew the XV-15. Afterward, McArtor made it an FAA priority to "certificate" the tiltrotor as safe for use as a civilian passenger aircraft, a lengthy process. McArtor also established a Civilian Tiltrotor Office in the FAA that gave $1.9 million in grants to six states and Puerto Rico to start planning new landing sites for commercial passenger tiltrotors of the future. On November 18, two House subcommittees held a hearing on civilian uses for tiltrotors, taking testimony on the steps needed to modify the air traffic control and airport systems to accommodate them. Hans Mark testified that the tiltrotor was an "American success story."

It wasn't looking that way on the shop floors in Fort Worth and Ridley Park, where Bell and the newly renamed Boeing Helicopter Company were building the first Osprey prototype. The companies were finding it hard to make all the composite parts in the design, and the Osprey section of the shop floor at Ridley Park, where Boeing also built CH-47 Chinook helicopters, was in chaos. The CH-47 manager had grudgingly given the Osprey team about half the space they needed to build the fuselage. Boeing was having all sorts of trouble making fuselage frames and formers out of composites. Bell was struggling to make its composite rotor grip work. The Osprey was still far too heavy, too. Between them, the companies had twenty-eight engineers assigned full-time to do nothing else but look for ways to reduce the aircraft's weight. Blot and the Marine Corps were pressing Bell-Boeing to get a first prototype built and flying, though, because the political wind was blowing in the wrong direction.

In 1987, Pentagon leaders were looking for ways to cut the defense budget to comply with the Gramm-Rudman Act's mandatory deficit targets. At the same time, while the tiltrotor as a concept was gaining allies,

the Osprey was losing important ones. In April, Lehman resigned as
Navy secretary to go make money in the private sector. In June, Commandant Kelley retired. A few months later, the Army decided it had no
need for 231 Ospreys after all. It dropped out of the program altogether
in February 1988. The same month, the Air Force announced it was
reducing the number of Ospreys it would buy from 80 to 55. A month
after that, the Navy decided it wasn't going to need those 300 Ospreys
for antisubmarine warfare, which had never officially been added to the
program. The Navy was still on the books to take 50 as search-and-rescue aircraft, but within a single month, the number of Ospreys the services were planning to buy had plunged from a potential 1,213 to 657.
Those were now expected to cost $30 million each—more than double
the original estimated price. Blot, Bell, and Boeing could see that if the
Osprey was going to fly, it had better do it soon.

★ ★ ★

On January 26, 1988, a sunny day in Texas, a massive "Super Guppy"
cargo aircraft owned by NASA landed at Arlington Municipal Airport.
Within a few minutes, the nose of the cargo plane opened up like the
jaws of a great white shark and the Guppy began to disgorge something
big and white and shaped not a little like Moby Dick. The first Osprey
fuselage, built in Ridley Park by Boeing Helicopter, had arrived at Bell's
Flight Research Center to be mated with Bell's wing, nacelles, rotors,
and tail.

"Boeing Helicopter Company has completed the assembly of the
fuselage for the first V-22 Osprey Flight Test Aircraft," a Bell-Boeing
news release dated December 3, 1987, had said. "The first flight of this
revolutionary new tilt-rotor aircraft is scheduled for June 1988." The
fuselage wasn't really complete, though, and the Osprey wasn't going to
fly that soon. A lot of parts in the fuselage weren't fitting together properly because new computer programs the engineers used to design it
weren't accurate enough. Boeing had to use thousands of shims—extra
pieces of graphite epoxy or metal—to fill in gaps where sections of the
fuselage hadn't been made to just the right size. Major electrical and
mechanical systems had yet to be installed. So much work remained to
be done that Boeing sent about twenty-five engineers, mechanics, elec-
tricians, material handlers, and other "touch labor" workers to Arlington to finish the job. They moved into apartments and started working

twelve to fourteen hours a day, seven days a week, to get the fuselage ready to fly.

Most of the Boeing workers were rough-cut Yankees, steak-and-cheese kind of guys who called their hometown "Philly," loved the Philadelphia Eagles football team, hated the Dallas Cowboys, and had a hard time getting used to the slow-talking, slow-moving Texans at Bell. After they'd been in Arlington a few weeks, though, some started getting into the local cowboy culture. Jim Curren, a sheet metal worker, got a kick out of seeing other guys from Philly show up to go out for a beer at night wearing cowboy boots, Stetson hats, and belt buckles the size of satellite dishes. Even Tony Stecyk, a burly mechanic and flight test technician who favored the biker look—mustache, goatee, and a Harley-Davidson T-shirt—bought cowboy boots, a belt buckle, and a cowboy hat. One night Bell hosted a "hoedown" for its and Boeing's test teams. The venue was Billy Bob's, a famed cowboy nightclub in Fort Worth's touristy Stockyards district housed in a building big enough to hold a bull riding ring. There was a contest to judge which Boeing Yankees were wearing western clothing authentic enough to pass for Texans. Stecyk and his wife, Michelle, both in cowboy boots, cowboy hats, western shirts, and jeans, won it.

Cowboy culture didn't appeal to others in the crew from Philadelphia. Joe Lombardo, who supervised the test technicians Boeing had sent, was short, gruff, and foul-mouthed, a real South Philly kind of guy. He wasn't into the Wild West. That night at Billy Bob's, though, the other Boeing guys razzed Lombardo into going up against a quick-draw "gunslinger" who was part of the entertainment. Lombardo walked out onto the floor, strapped on a six-shooter loaded with blanks, then told the gunfighter: "Okay, let's do this on the count of three. One! Two!"—then drew and fired. The gunfighter fell, playing along. "That's the way we do it in South Philly," Lombardo sneered at the Bell contingent.

The Texans gave each other wry smiles. You really *couldn't* trust these Boeing guys, could you?

★ ★ ★

The Osprey was still months away from being ready to fly that spring, but the wing and fuselage had been mated, and the Marines were eager to show progress. Bell and Boeing were, too, so on May 23, they staged a "rollout" of Aircraft 1, a public unveiling. They hired Hollywood producers and New York set designers and scriptwriters to stage the event. They invited fifty generals and admirals, eight congressmen and senators from Texas and Pennsylvania, local and national reporters, and hundreds of other guests—more than two thousand in all.

The event began with receptions the night before at various locations in Fort Worth. The next day, everyone gathered at Bell's Plant 6 in Arlington inside a hangar whose interior was draped with black curtains. A baritone-voiced announcer introduced top Bell and Boeing executives and VIP guests, including House Speaker Jim Wright, who was also the local Fort Worth congressman, and General Alfred M. Gray, Jr., Kelley's successor as commandant. A military honor guard paraded the colors as a Marine band played "The Star-Spangled Banner." A video of the tiltrotor's history, *The Dream*, played on a big screen. "The V-22 Osprey represents the latest success in the persistent path toward achieving the full range of flight," a narrator read over clips of the XV-3, Boeing's early attempt at a tilt-wing aircraft, and the XV-15 flying. "But the potential is not yet fulfilled. Military and civil applications abound, both here in the United States and overseas. Future uses of the tiltrotor are limited only by our imagination." Speeches followed. Gray told the audience the Osprey was "urgently needed" by the Marines, who were eager to put it into service in the 1990s. "This program remains our number-one aviation priority," he added. When the speeches were done, the band played a fanfare and the announcer boomed: "Ladies and gentlemen, the Naval Air Systems Command, the United States Marine Corps, the Bell-Boeing tiltrotor team, its hundreds of suppliers, and Allison Gas Turbine Division of General Motors proudly present to you—and to the *world*— the aircraft that will take flight to a new dimension. The V-22 Osprey!" The lights grew dim, a new fanfare played, and the black curtains on the stage parted to reveal the Osprey, bathed in a dreamlike haze of dry-ice fog and lit by beams of red light. Oohs and aahs.

The Osprey looked ready for combat. It was painted in green and gray Marine Corps camouflage and its nacelles stood straight up, as if the big bird were flexing its muscles. Soon the crowd of several hundred filtered outside to wait as workers hitched a small tow tractor to the Osprey's front landing gear and pulled it out into the sunlight. Once on the tarmac, the Osprey's rear ramp slowly opened to the ground and VIPs were invited to walk up into the cabin. House Speaker Wright went forward into the cockpit, sat in the right-hand pilot's seat, stuck his head out the side window, flashed a toothy smile, and raised one hand in a V-for-victory sign. As Gray exited down the back ramp after his tour, someone asked what he thought. "Great aircraft," Gray grunted. "Super future."

After the crowd left, workers hosed off the camouflage paint, which was watercolor. Underneath was the white paint Navair required for prototypes. In the Texas heat and humidity, the camouflage had started peeling in places during the rollout. Bell and Boeing flacks were relieved that no one had seemed to notice that, or the fact that some gaps in the fuselage panels were covered with duct tape and painted over. Nor did anyone seem to notice that the Osprey's rear ramp only opened and closed because mechanic Marty LeCloux was in the back cabin, discreetly pulling levers on a portable hydraulic power unit to make it work. LeCloux felt like a puppeteer putting on a show.

"There was a lot of smoke and mirrors with the rollout," Jim Curren told me two decades later, when the former sheet metal worker had risen to a management job at Ridley Park. "We had to function the ramp and the lights and everything else to make it look like we were real close to that first flight. It wasn't ready."

★ ★ ★

Nine months after the rollout, on February 22, 1989, Phil Dunford and some other Boeing and Bell engineers left Navair's offices in the Washington suburb of Crystal City in a buoyant mood. The past year had been nerve-racking for those trying to get the Osprey flying. All sorts of problems, especially the difficulty of making trustworthy rotor grips out of composites, had busted the first-flight target date again and again. Program manager Blot, who in April had been promoted to brigadier general, had been putting a good face on things publicly. In a September 1988 interview with *Aviation Week*, he conceded that the Osprey was behind schedule but said, "So far, technically, this program's been a dream." Behind the scenes, though, the engineers had been suffering nightmares. Blot and their corporate bosses were putting intense pressure on them to get the Osprey airborne, and the corporate executives were more worried than even Blot knew. In 1988, Bell and Boeing could see they were going to overrun their $1.8 billion FSD contract badly, and under the fixed-price terms, there was no end to the red ink in sight. Lehman's theory that a fixed price would let the companies resist

Navair demands for changes in the design wasn't panning out. Navair kept insisting on changes and the companies felt they had to go along to stay on good terms with The Customer. "All these fine words of, 'Oh, you can be the policeman'—the contractor can't do that role," Webb Joiner, Bell's vice president for finance at the time and later its president, told me. "Can you really go to your customer and say, 'Hey, I know you're the guy who's going to make all the decisions, I know you're the guy who's going to decide whether to continue this program, but I'm going to tell you what you can and can't do'? The reality of the thing is, that'd be about like somebody working for a company going in to the president and telling him what he's going to do. You just can't do that."

As the year went on, the sums in monthly reports on the overruns kept growing. Textron's executives were angry about them. Boeing was causing most of the overruns, but under their 50–50 partnership, Textron subsidiary Bell was having to foot half the bill. Not long after the Osprey rollout in May, the companies held a meeting where Bell contracts director Dan McCrary and others reported that by the time FSD was over, Bell-Boeing's combined losses might reach $300 million. At monthly meetings, Textron's chief operating officer, William A. Anders, and Boeing executive Alford argued violently about who was to blame. Anders, a wiry 1955 U.S. Naval Academy graduate with the self-assurance of the former astronaut he was, would explode at Alford, a corpulent, old-school defense contractor who had begun his career as a test pilot. They would get red in the face, pound the table, shout at each other in ways that made others in the room cringe. Joiner liked to joke that the Anders-versus-Alford bouts were so regular and exciting, maybe Bell and Boeing could cover their cost overruns by selling tickets to their meetings.

As Dunford and the other engineers left their meeting at Navair in February 1989, though, they were blissfully ignorant of those corporate clashes. To the engineers, things were looking up. They had decided the Osprey was finally ready for its first flight, and Navair had agreed. To mark the milestone, the engineers went to Washington's trendy Georgetown neighborhood for dinner at an Italian restaurant called the Mondo Cucina. There, after a few drinks, they divided themselves into two factions, the "Wizards" and the "Turtles," and made a complicated wager. The losers would treat the winners to dinner at one of three restaurants on a sliding scale of elegance, depending on how close the Wizards came to predicting the power needed to hover the Osprey on its first flight. The next day, one of them drew up the terms in an elaborate document labeled "The Mondo Cucina Accords." To the engineers, the Osprey's future looked bright.

On March 19, a cloudy Sunday in Arlington, Texas, test pilots Dorman Cannon of Bell and Dick Balzer of Boeing climbed into the first Osprey prototype, painted white with red and blue markings and wired with strain gauges all over. The Osprey was loaded with monitoring instruments to detect vibration and stress throughout the aircraft and radio data to a telemetry room in a hangar so engineers there could warn the pilots if something bad was about to happen. The aircraft's total weight was 39,450 pounds, well above Navair's empty weight spec of 31,886, and that was with some nonessential parts left off. No media had been invited, only a couple of dozen Bell and Boeing employees. No reason to have a lot of people watching if the Osprey didn't end up flying, or worse.

Soon Cannon taxied the Osprey to the north end of the runway, its rotors thrumming in a distinctive, throaty roar. At 10:56 A.M. Central Standard Time, he pushed the Blottle forward and the Osprey lumbered two or three feet into the air. The downdraft from the rotors with their high disk loading started kicking up dirt and rocks and asphalt, pelting the fuselage and windshield. Cannon gave it more power to get up and out of the debris storm, but a little more than he'd intended. The Osprey hopped up to about 40 feet. Cannon kept it in a hover there. The controls were a little more sensitive than he had expected, but the Osprey handled just as it had in the computerized simulator he and Balzer had used to train for the flight. As they hovered, Cannon used the foot pedals to make some rudder turns, then gingerly tilted the rotors a bit forward to see if the thrust would go where he expected. It did. The Osprey started moving over the runway at about 20 knots. Cannon put the rotors back to 90 degrees and held the Osprey in a hover for ten or twelve minutes. He liked the way the big tiltrotor was responding to the computerized flight controls, but he was a little surprised by the force of the downdraft from its rotors. The turbulence was curling up the edges of the asphalt runway below and throwing up a lot of gravel. Cannon said to Balzer, "Hey, Dick, let's just land this thing and taxi it back." They did. They took it up briefly again later, but that was the Osprey's first flight.

To Cannon, after so many hours in the simulator, it seemed anticlimactic.

To engineer Phil Dunford and the other "Wizards," it was a happy but costly moment. They had underestimated how much power it would take to hover the Osprey. The four Wizards had to take the Turtles, the test pilots, and their wives to a chic French restaurant, where the bill for the steak, duck, and fine wines the winners ordered was steep.

To Spivey, watching the Osprey's first flight was like witnessing the birth of a baby. Like disillusioned tiltrotor engineer Ken Wernicke, Spivey thought the Osprey ugly, a clumsy-looking thing. When he saw it fly, though, his heart soared. He felt a warm glow, just like a new father.

CHAPTER SEVEN

ONE PERIOD OF
DARKNESS

O ne day on Capitol Hill, Democratic representative Charles Wilson arrived early for a meeting of the Texas delegation to Congress. Republican senator John Tower of Texas was already there, waiting for the session to start.

"Dang, John," drawled Wilson. "That's a beautiful suit. Where'd you get it?"

"Got this suit on Savile Row in London. Cost six hundred dollars," Tower sniffed.

"Gaw*dam*!" Wilson replied. "What would it cost in a *man's* size?!"

That story—probably apocryphal but possibly true—was a favorite among those who followed the Texas delegation to Congress in the 1980s. Charlie Wilson, well over six feet tall, was a caricaturist's conception of a Texan: big, brash, raw as a barrel of West Texas Intermediate crude, seductive to women, seduced by booze. Wilson was a cheeky rogue, apt to blurt out whatever outrageous observation came to mind. Tom Hanks portrayed him faithfully, if charitably, in the 2007 film *Charlie Wilson's War*. The movie, based on former CBS-TV producer George Crile's book by the same name, recounted Wilson's oxymoronically public 1980s crusade to make the CIA "covertly" funnel arms to Islamic rebels fighting the Soviet Union's occupation of Afghanistan.

John Goodwin Tower, who stood five foot five, was a Methodist minister's son born in Houston, but he looked as if he might have stepped out of a novel by British humorist P. G. Wodehouse or satirist Evelyn Waugh. A Navy enlisted man during World War II, Tower earned bachelor's and master's degrees at Southern Methodist University in Dallas after the war, then spent a year at the London School of Economics. The rest of his life, he affected the dress and style of an English gentleman between the world wars: tailored three-piece suits with handkerchief in left breast pocket; starched shirts with French cuffs; English-blend cigarettes plucked from a silver case and lit with a silver lighter. John Tower, who served in the Senate from 1961 to 1985, exuded self-importance the way Charlie Wilson oozed self-indulgence. Wilson and Tower, though, also shared at least a couple of attributes. Both were fond of pretty women and strong drink.

Tower's thirst was why Dick Spivey got home about two-thirty one morning shortly before Christmas 1988. Spivey had joined Bell Helicopter president Jack Horner and a couple of other colleagues that evening at a Fort Worth hotel to hear a speech by former senator Tower, now President-elect George H. W. Bush's rumored nominee for defense secretary. The idea of Tower running the Pentagon cheered those at Bell. Tower had seen the XV-15 fly at the 1981 Paris Air Show and had been a tiltrotor supporter ever since. As chairman of the Senate Armed Services Committee during his last term in Congress, Tower had helped get the Osprey program started. Since leaving the Senate, Tower had been a U.S. arms control negotiator and run a commission for President Reagan that investigated the Iran-Contra affair. Since May 1988, he had been a $10,000-a-month consultant to Bell Helicopter parent Textron on the Osprey program. The new Bush administration was going to have to cut defense spending to live up to the president-elect's famous campaign pledge of "no new taxes," that was clear. With Tower atop the Pentagon, however, the Osprey figured to be safe.

After Tower gave his speech that evening in Fort Worth, he wanted a drink, so Horner, Spivey, and the others from Bell joined him for cocktails in the lobby of the Hyatt Regency, formerly the Hotel Texas, where President John F. Kennedy had spent the last night of his life twenty-five years earlier. The group drank and talked until 2 A.M., mostly about the Osprey. Spivey told Tower about all the steps the engineers were taking to try to get the Osprey's weight down. When he left to go home, Spivey was feeling good, not just from the drinks, but about the Osprey's future once the Senate confirmed Tower as defense secretary.

The Senate didn't. Tower's confirmation hearings turned into a soap opera the day they began, on January 31, 1989. Paul Weyrich, a conservative activist scandalized by what he viewed as Tower's turpitude, told the Senate Armed Services Committee there was truth in rumors that the nominee was a womanizer and an alcohol abuser, allegations raised by Tower's second wife during a nasty 1987 divorce. Weyrich himself had seen Tower "in a condition—lack of sobriety—as well as with women to whom he was not married," Weyrich testified.

The FBI had investigated such allegations before Bush nominated Tower, and Tower denied he had a drinking problem. But some members of the Armed Services Committee said they needed to be sure the defense secretary would have "clarity of thought at all times," as Senator Sam Nunn, the Georgia Democrat who chaired the panel, put it. Other committee members questioned whether Tower was too cozy with the defense industry. Textron was only one of half a dozen defense contractors who had paid Tower a combined $763,777 in consulting fees since he had left the Senate. Tower promised to go on the wagon if confirmed and take no part in decisions affecting his former clients, but his sharp partisanship and proud manner had alienated too many colleagues over the years, it seemed, especially Democrats. On March 9, the Senate rejected his nomination 53–47, with one of its 45 Republicans and all but three of its 55 Democrats voting against him. Spivey and others at Bell were disappointed.

Four days later, President Bush named the second-ranking Republican leader in the House, Wyoming representative Dick Cheney, to replace Tower. After a cheery one-day hearing before a relieved Armed Services Committee, the Senate confirmed Cheney 92–0 on March 17, two days before the Osprey's first flight.

Cheney made two things clear at his confirmation hearing. First, as President Bush had promised when he sent his first budget to Congress in February, the new administration was going to increase defense spending just enough to keep up with inflation. Fighting the massive deficits left over from the Reagan years was issue number one in Washington in 1989. Under the Gramm-Rudman budget-balancing law, Congress and Bush were going to have to hold the deficit for the next fiscal year to $100 billion.

Cheney's second major point was that he believed in executive power, as he would prove beyond a doubt during his two terms as vice president from 2001 to 2009. Though he had served ten years in the House, Cheney had begun his political rise in the 1970s as Donald Rumsfeld's deputy when that future defense secretary was counselor in the Nixon White House. Cheney thought the balance of power in Washington had swung too far toward the legislative branch since President Richard Nixon's resignation in 1974 amid the Watergate scandals; the pendulum needed to swing back toward the executive branch, especially in defense and foreign policy. At his hearing, Cheney declared that "sometimes having a confrontation with the Congress is the right way to go."

Cheney quickly got a chance to test his theory. Bush had sent his first budget to Congress in February, and it was dead on arrival. With the Cold War thawing and the Soviet Union teetering on its foundations, the Democrats who controlled both houses of Congress wanted more cuts in defense spending than Bush proposed to meet the Gramm-Rudman deficit target. Bush sent his budget director to a "summit" with congressional leaders, and days after the Senate confirmed Cheney, a deal was struck. Bush agreed to take an additional $10 billion out of the $305.6 billion defense budget he'd proposed in February. He also pledged to cut Pentagon spending by more than $64 billion over the next five years. Figuring out what to cut was Cheney's first task.

★ ★ ★

When the budget deal was announced on April 14, Spivey was in Jacksonville, Florida, where he had been manning the Bell Helicopter display at a Naval Helicopter Association meeting and talking up the tiltrotor for three days. He was getting ready to go home when he got a call in his hotel room from Harry Bendorf, the former Air Force general who ran Boeing Helicopter's office in Washington. Spivey thought Bendorf sounded shaken. He'd just picked up some bad news from one of his contacts, Bendorf said. Cheney had decided to cut the defense budget by canceling some big programs. The Osprey was going to be one of them.

Spivey couldn't believe it. He told Bendorf his sources had to be wrong. *Cancel it? Just when we've finally gotten it to fly? After spending two billion dollars on it? Cancel the Marine Corps' top priority in aviation? Kill the next revolution in flight? Somebody must be pulling Bendorf's leg.* Bendorf assured Spivey it was true, though not yet official. Cheney's mind was made up, Bendorf was hearing.

Spivey's mind was racing when he got off the phone. *Was there some way to stop this? What was Cheney thinking? Weren't the Marines telling him how important the Osprey was to them? Had anyone explained to Cheney how important the tiltrotor was to civilian aviation? Didn't he understand that the tiltrotor was a national asset? Who in the world had talked Cheney into this?*

The answer was Pentagon bureaucrat David Chu, the tall, slender, cerebral economist who ran the Office of Program Analysis and Evaluation, PA&E, whose by-the-numbers, dollars-and-cents assessments could torpedo an expensive procurement. Chu had a lot of clout, partly because he had a lot of experience. Civilian leaders in the Pentagon are by and large political appointees who stay a couple of years. Chu had come to PA&E as its director from the Congressional Budget Office in May 1981, kept the job through the Reagan administration, seen his title elevated to Assistant Secretary of Defense for Program Analysis and Evaluation in 1988, and been asked to stay when President Bush took office in 1989. Chu liked it in the Pentagon, where everyone called him "Dr. Chu."

The son of a Chinese immigrant and his American-born wife, Chu had graduated magna cum laude from Yale University in 1964 with a degree in economics and mathematics. He began work on a doctorate in economics, but as an undergraduate he had joined the ROTC and owed the Army two years of service. He reported for duty in 1968. As a first lieutenant, he became an instructor in the dry art of getting supplies and equipment from one place to another, then went to Vietnam as a member of a logistics team. When he got out of the Army in 1970, he finished his Ph.D. and gravitated toward government service.

David S. C. Chu's middle initials stood for nothing in English. His parents had derived "S.C." from Chinese characters associated with an aphorism attributed to the ancient Chinese philosopher Confucius. "The superior man has nine things which are subjects with him of thoughtful consideration," Confucius said. "In regard to the use of his eyes, he is anxious to see clearly. In regard to the use of his ears, he is anxious to hear distinctly. In regard to his countenance, he is anxious that it should be benign. In regard to his speech, he is anxious that it should be sincere. In regard to his doing of business, he is anxious that it should be reverently careful. In regard to what he doubts about, he is anxious to question others. When he is angry, he thinks of the difficulties his anger may involve him in. When he sees gain to be got, he thinks of righteousness." Chu's parents got "S.C." by translating the Chinese for "thinking nine times," and their son lived up to his initials. In Pentagon meetings, where PA&E's decisions and Chu himself often were strongly attacked, his countenance remained benign, his speech sincere. He was careful with his words. With his short, black hair, a thin face that narrowed to a V, his sonorous bass voice, and his unemotional manner, Chu evoked the *Star Trek* character Spock, the half-Vulcan, half-human executive officer of the starship *Enterprise,* who saw every situation through the cold prism of logic. Chu tried to look at issues logically, by thinking nine times, so to speak.

Chu had thought at least nine times about the Osprey before Cheney took over the Pentagon. Chu's opinion hadn't changed since 1983, when he told the Marines they might be better off buying a mix of Sikorsky Aircraft's UH-60 Black Hawk and CH-53E Super Stallion helicopters rather than investing the time and money it would take to develop a tiltrotor to replace their CH-46 helicopters. John Lehman and the Marines had brushed Chu's argument aside. In 1986, when the Osprey needed Defense Systems Acquisition Review Council approval to go into Full Scale Development, Chu tried to stop it again. Lehman and the Marines won that debate, too. "Lehman made a command decision that he was intrigued by this technology, thought it was revolutionary in character," Chu told me. "The sincere difference of view is, we couldn't see the revolution. We, the analytic community, couldn't see what the payoff was to this investment." Chu didn't have anything against the tiltrotor, he just thought it too rich for the Marine Corps' blood. He also didn't buy the idea that the tiltrotor was going to revolutionize civilian aviation but had to be developed by the military first. Chu believed in the wisdom of the free market. If the tiltrotor was that desirable for civil aviation, why wasn't the private sector developing it already, he wondered? If the Defense Department needed to pay to develop the Osprey, that was a strong signal that the tiltrotor must not really be all that attractive economically. To Chu, this was simply logic.

When Cheney arrived at the Pentagon, he asked Chu for a list of programs he might scrap to squeeze $10 billion out of the budget. The Osprey was automatically on Chu's list, and it was one of nine major procurement programs Cheney decided to kill. The Army's AH-64 Apache attack helicopter, the Navy's F-14D Tomcat fighter jet, one of its SSN-688 attack submarines, and the Air Force's F-15 Eagle fighter were among the others. A lot of members of Congress were going to be unhappy, Cheney knew, but the president had told him to cut the defense budget, and the president was paid to lead. Sometimes having a confrontation with the Congress was the right way to go.

★ ★ ★

U.S. Representative Curt Weldon, whose 7th District of Pennsylvania included a slice of Boeing's sprawling helicopter plant at Ridley Park, relished confrontation. It got his adrenaline flowing. Unlike David Chu, Weldon believed logic didn't matter in a political battle. Votes did. To get votes, you had to rally people to your cause. At times, you had to form coalitions. Every chance you got, you had to attract attention to your issue. Confrontation, coalition building, and attracting attention were second nature to Weldon, who had grown up the youngest of nine kids in a textile worker's family. They lived in company housing, squeezed into a small brick row home like dozens around it, in Marcus Hook, Pennsylvania.

Weldon's congressional district was a swatch of gritty industrial suburbs just south of Philadelphia. Marcus Hook was one of the grittiest, a tiny borough dominated by a chemical plant and two oil refineries whose tank farms crowded the bank of the Delaware River. The population of Marcus Hook, like the rest of the 7th District, was mostly white, working class, solidly Republican, and patriotic. Each of Weldon's six brothers went into the military after high school, and his two sisters married military men. A good student, Curt won an appointment to the U.S. Air Force Academy as a high school senior but failed his eye exam. He went to nearby West Chester State College instead, returned home in 1969 with a degree in humanities, and became a schoolteacher. Like his father and all his brothers, Curt also became a volunteer firefighter. Fires were a constant hazard in an oil refinery town like Marcus Hook, and Weldon was passionate about fighting them. In his spare time, as he and his wife began raising the first of their five children, Weldon earned a degree in fire sciences technology from Delaware County College and began speaking at national firefighter conferences around the country. He also went into politics.

Curt Weldon got elected mayor of Marcus Hook in 1977, in part by promising to take on the Pagans Motorcycle Club, a biker gang that had been terrorizing the borough. Marcus Hook was the gang's national headquarters—Weldon had grown up with their president—and the bikers acted as if they owned the town. Weldon didn't look tough. He slicked down his longish brown hair and wore muttonchop sideburns that crept below his ears like moss on an oak root. The dark frames of his glasses looked heavy enough to break his nose. Weldon sizzled with energy, though, and he didn't mind a fight. As mayor, he had the town police put the Pagans under twenty-four-hour surveillance. That cramped the gang's style. State and federal investigations of drug deals and murders by members of the Pagans followed and the club left Marcus Hook. Weldon boosted his popularity by obtaining a $90,000 federal grant to install night lights at the town's ball fields, literally creating a bright spot for a community depressed by industrial decline and layoffs. He was reelected mayor two times, served a term on the Delaware County Council, then won his seat in Congress.

When Weldon heard Cheney was going to cancel the Osprey, possibly costing hundreds and maybe thousands of his constituents their jobs, there was no doubt in his mind what he was going to do. On April 18, 1989, three days after newspaper reports confirmed Cheney's plan, Weldon sent the defense secretary a letter declaring his "adamant opposition to the rumored elimination of the V-22 Osprey." Weldon vowed to "vehemently oppose" such a move.

But how? As a junior member of the minority party in a House whose 260 Democrats could steamroll its 175 Republicans any time, Weldon had no power. He knew how to build a coalition, though. Weldon had proved he could do that his first year in Congress, when he organized the Congressional Fire Services Caucus, an idea that came to him as he looked for a way to gain some influence. There were volunteer firefighters in every congressional district in the nation. By leading a caucus focused on issues dear to those firefighters' hearts as well as his own, Weldon would have a way to connect with every member of the House and Senate, and even influence some. Through Mason Lankford, a volunteer firefighter from Texas he met at a conference, Weldon even got House Speaker Jim Wright, Fort Worth's congressman and the most powerful member of the House, to join his caucus. A Democratic House Speaker had no reason to pay any mind to a freshman Republican like Weldon, but with Lankford's introduction, Wright not only joined Weldon's fire caucus but helped kick it off at a news conference. The first time they talked, Weldon pointed out to the Speaker that his district, like Wright's, was home to one of the plants that was building the Osprey. Great program, they agreed.

★ ★ ★

By the time Cheney decided to cancel the Osprey two years later, Jim Wright was no longer so powerful. Representative Newt Gingrich, a right-wing Republican firebrand from Georgia as audacious as he was ambitious, had been pursuing ethics charges against the Democratic Speaker of the House for months. On April 17, 1989, a couple of days after Cheney decided to take David Chu's advice on the Osprey, the House Ethics Committee's three Democrats and three Republicans unanimously concluded there was "reason to believe" Wright had committed sixty-nine violations of House rules in his personal finances. The Speaker—Bell Helicopter's congressman and one of the tiltrotor's most important supporters in Congress—was now going to be too busy trying to save himself to save the Osprey. Others would have to try to do that.

On April 19, Republican senator Ted Stevens of Alaska and Democrat John Glenn of Ohio fired a first shot across Cheney's bow. Glenn, best known as a former astronaut, was a former Marine pilot who had flown the XV-15 tiltrotor demonstrator in 1986. He and Stevens took the unusual step of offering a freestanding resolution in the Senate urging the Bush administration to fully fund the V-22. In a nearly empty chamber, the resolution was adopted by voice vote.

Six days later, Cheney came before the 52-member House Armed Services Committee for the first time to defend the new budget and his decision to kill nine major procurement programs. In those days, Cheney didn't suffer from the aloof, grim, even sinister public image he acquired after he got rich in the 1990s running Texas-based oil services giant Halliburton Company and in 2001 became vice president. Cheney had been a popular, if highly partisan, member of the House, rarely sunny but courteous, accessible, and often wry. At the House hearing that April 25, the Democratic chairman, Les Aspin of Wisconsin, greeted Cheney warmly. Other members praised him as they got their customary five minutes to ask questions. A surprising number also peppered Cheney with complaints about his decision to cancel the Osprey. Weldon was one of a half dozen members who took Cheney to task for the decision.

Cheney had known he would face resistance in Congress to the defense cuts he was proposing. "My former colleagues have been great," he said in an opening statement. "I have heard from a lot of them in the last couple of weeks, all of them interested in making certain that I don't close their base, or cut their weapons system, or cancel a program that they believe is absolutely essential to national defense." Cheney also knew the Marines and their allies were especially unhappy about the Osprey. He had heard a lot about that particular decision, Cheney said, "and I now know for certain that nobody ever leaves the Marine Corps." He stood his ground, if defensively. "I want to assure everybody that I have no designs upon the Marine Corps whatsoever," Cheney volunteered, answering an accusation no one had made. The tiltrotor was "an interesting concept" and "probably a good aircraft," but it was being built for a "very narrow mission"—amphibious assault—and helicopters were a good and cheaper way to do that. If the Army were still interested in the Osprey, Cheney volunteered, that might make it affordable, but the Army wasn't. "I would like to be able to preserve it," he said, but with orders to cut $10 billion in defense spending, "I don't know how we shoehorn it in."

When Cheney left, he and his aides were a little surprised by how many Osprey questions he'd gotten, but they didn't think they were in for a big battle on the issue. They were wrong.

★ ★ ★

Three days after Cheney testified, the Bell-Boeing Joint Program Office sent a letter to the Naval Air Systems Command declaring that "with great reluctance" the companies would stop work on the Osprey in one week. The letter didn't say so, but if the Defense Department wasn't going to produce the Osprey, as Cheney had decided, the companies didn't want to pour more money into developing it. Their cost overruns were mounting and profits on future production model Ospreys were their only hope of getting their money back. If there weren't going to *be* any production models, there would be no profits.

A week later, the companies withdrew the threat. A Washington law firm had studied the FSD contract for them and concluded it was airtight. If Bell and Boeing walked away from it, the government could make them pay back the money they'd already been paid for FSD. Besides, the Osprey's friends in Congress were telling them to hang on. Cheney or no Cheney, the Marines wanted the Osprey badly, and the Marines were good at getting their way in Congress. No service was better at that.

The Marines already had a strategy. They would do for the Osprey's friends in Congress what Charlie Wilson and the CIA had done for the Afghan rebels: arm them covertly, in this case with the weapons and ammunition of Washington policy battles—information and intelligence. It was a strategy all the armed services used from time to time, but over their history, the Marines had been forced to turn to it more often than the other services—at times to preserve their very existence. That was one reason they were so good at it. Another was the Marine Corps' popularity in Congress, most of whose members admired the elite service and not a few of whose members had served in it. "Once a Marine, always a Marine," the saying went, and in 1989, there were two dozen or so Marine Corps vets in Congress. Every month or so, Marine Corps liaison officers would organize a breakfast on the Hill where the commandant or another top general would meet with members of Congress and aides who had been Marines to talk about the Corps' needs. After Cheney's decision, the Osprey was often a major topic of those closed-door talks.

Marine Corps leaders would have to be careful, though. The secretary of defense sets policy for the Pentagon, and military leaders can't officially oppose him. Once the secretary declares a policy, top generals and admirals are expected to salute and support it, no matter how much it irks them. Cheney signaled his first week in office that he was going to demand that kind of loyalty. At his first news conference, he sent a shock wave through the Pentagon by openly rebuking the Air Force chief of staff, General Larry D. Welch, for trying to work out a deal with members of Congress on plans for basing nuclear missiles. Welch was "freelancing," Cheney said at his news conference, and what the general had done was "inappropriate." Cheney was going to see Welch in his office to personally express his displeasure with him, he announced. For a four-star general in charge of an entire armed service, it was an extraordinary humiliation.

Marine Corps leaders didn't want to risk the Welch treatment, but there were ways to avoid it. The Senate has to confirm top military officers in their assignments, and at confirmation hearings, generals and admirals are always required to promise under oath that, when asked, they will give Congress their personal views on military issues, even if they differ with their civilian bosses. This was why, when he was asked about the Osprey on May 4, 1989, in testimony to the Senate Armed Services Committee, General Alfred M. Gray, Jr., the commandant, responded in a manner reminiscent of the ancient Roman god Janus, the double-headed guardian who faced two ways at once.

First Gray called the Osprey "a national resource and a national requirement" with "enormous commercial potential" and "enormous potential" for the Marines. Then he said: "I support the president and the secretary of defense's decision" to cancel it. Then Gray said that "based on the information he was given," Cheney's had been "a good decision." Then he said: "I do not agree with the cost advice that he got, nor do I agree with the advice on military operations."

Sam Nunn, the committee chairman, tried to interpret: "You believe Secretary Cheney made the best decision he could make based on faulty information. Am I hearing you correct on that?"

Gray wouldn't go that far. "No," he said, "based on the information he was given by learned people who have their right to believe that they are correct."

"But you do not believe they were correct?" Nunn asked.

"No, I do not," Gray finally conceded. "But I had my day in court."

This was how a service chief could deftly dance the line between insurbordination and his desire to thwart a defense secretary's decision.

★ ★ ★

Cheney and his top aides couldn't complain about the commandant testifying as Gray had, but they didn't take kindly to it when they caught other Marine officers talking as if the Osprey were going to survive. A week after Gray's testimony, Brigadier General Harry Blot, the Osprey program manager, spoke at a conference on the civilian potential of the tiltrotor held by *Rotor & Wing International* magazine in Crystal City. On May 15, the *New York Times* published an article about the conference under the headline "Copter-Plane Called a Cure for Crowded Airports." Buried amid praise for the tiltrotor from officials of NASA and the Federal Aviation Administration was this paragraph: "A helicopter has only one-fourth the range and can be heard four times as far away as a tilt-rotor aircraft, said Brig. Gen. Harry Blot of the Marine Corps, who is managing the military's program to develop a tilt-rotor aircraft. He said he was optimistic about the $28 billion program to build 682 craft, labeled V-22 Ospreys, even though Defense Secretary Dick Cheney has said he will cancel it Oct. 1 to save money."

The article appeared on a Monday. A few days later, Blot was confronted by one of Cheney's aides, Air Force Brigadier General Buster Glosson, the deputy assistant secretary of defense for legislative affairs. Glosson scolded Blot for contradicting Cheney in public.

"What's your objective by trying to create a confrontation with the secretary of defense in the news media?" Glosson demanded. Blot should show some loyalty to the secretary, Glosson counseled.

Blot said he knew the meaning of loyalty, "But I cannot lie. I'm not going to lie." Years later, Blot also remembered Glosson telling him he'd better not comment publicly on the Osprey again. Glosson told me he never said that.

In any event, when they parted, Blot got on the phone to the deputy chief of staff for aviation, Lieutenant General Charles "Chuck" Pitman, and told him Cheney's people were trying to muzzle him. That afternoon, as Blot remembered it, he got a call from Cheney's office telling him the Senate Armed Services Committee staff wanted Blot and PA&E head David Chu to brief them on the Osprey the next Monday at 8 A.M. Blot later heard that someone at Headquarters Marine Corps instigated the invitation. What better way to get the Marine Corps view on the Osprey to the committee than for Blot, a combat pilot and a general, to debate Chu, a bureaucratic numbers cruncher?

Blot went home that evening and told his wife, "This is it. We're done. Come the end of Monday, my career is finished, because I'm going to say what I've said all along and they're going to say the opposite."

Two decades after the fact, and after dozens of such sessions with congressional aides over the years, Chu couldn't remember doing such a briefing with Blot. For Blot, the memory was vivid. "We got in there and it was brutal," he told me. "Instead of the normal seats, they had three hard-backed chairs sitting out there," one for Blot, one for Chu, one for another Pentagon official responsible for tactical aircraft. The committee staff questioned them for more than an hour. Blot remembered contradicting nearly everything Chu said.

Blot went back to his office in a psychological cringe, sure he would pay for the things he had said in the briefing. Cheney would hear about Blot's defense of the Osprey, he figured, and give him some version of the Welch treatment. Chuck Pitman, however, the three-star general running Marine aviation, had a plan to avoid that: out of sight, out of mind. Within days, Blot got orders to report to the Marine Corps air station at Cherry Point, North Carolina, for six weeks of refresher training in Harrier jump jets. When he returned to Washington that summer, Blot immediately got orders to spend another six weeks at Whiting Field Naval Air Station in Florida to hone his helicopter piloting skills. After that, in December 1989, Blot was ordered to California to serve as assistant commander of the 3rd Marine Aircraft Wing, based near San Diego. The Osprey program got a new manager: Colonel Jim Schaefer, who in 1980, as a major, had piloted the helicopter that caused the disaster at Desert One in Iran. Schaefer had been advocating the tiltrotor ever since.

* * *

Dick Spivey had been in the gallery of the U.S. House of Representatives before, but never for such a momentous event. On May 31, 1989, a Wednesday, Spivey sat there transfixed, with Bell lobbyist George Troutman and a couple of other colleagues, as they watched House Speaker Jim Wright—their company's most important ally in Congress, and one of Troutman's best friends for three decades—surrender to his enemies. Wright would resign as Speaker the next week, he announced, and by the end of June give up the House seat he had held for thirty-four years. Speaking from the well of the chamber for an hour, Wright was defiant at times, apologetic at others, sometimes nostalgic. He didn't cry, but he looked as if he wanted to, Spivey thought. Spivey and Troutman wanted to cry themselves. They felt for their friend. They also worried about what would happen to the Osprey with Wright out of the picture. Only weeks ago, even with his own career in its death throes, Wright had told Textron and Bell not to give up on the Osprey, that the Marines and their friends in Congress would keep it going.

Spivey had been in Washington a lot in the six weeks since he'd gotten word Cheney was going to kill the Osprey. At first, he was flying back and forth to strategize with Troutman and Textron's lobbyists. Later, Spivey became their go-to briefer, on call twenty-four hours a day to come to Washington and explain the Osprey and the tiltrotor's civilian potential to members of Congress and their aides. To his briefing's explanations of how helicopter speeds were limited by retreating blade stall and how tiltrotors could have avoided the disaster at Desert One, Spivey added a slide noting that Article I of the Constitution granted Congress—not the executive branch—the power to "raise and support Armies" and "provide and maintain a Navy." He wanted to remind the members of Congress he briefed that they had a constitutional right to overrule Cheney.

In those first weeks after Cheney's decision, some at Textron and Boeing were still murmuring about abandoning the Osprey. Spivey couldn't imagine that. If the Osprey died, the tiltrotor dream—his life's work—might die with it. Besides, Spivey was an optimist. He was sure this was just another bump in the road to get over, another hill the Marines would take. He sure wished he could get in to see Cheney, though. Spivey just knew he could sell Cheney on the dream if he briefed him, but no one from Bell or Boeing could get an appointment with the defense secretary to talk about the Osprey.

A week after Wright's resignation speech, Spivey and others in the usual Bell contingent flew to France for the 1989 Paris Air Show. Spivey took along his two sons from his first marriage, Brett, then twenty, and Eric, eighteen. While their father worked at Bell's chalet, the boys mostly wandered through the static displays of aircraft at historic Le Bourget field and marveled at the daily aerial displays flown by some of the world's best pilots in the world's hottest aircraft. They arrived in Paris too late to witness the crash on the show's first day of a Soviet MiG-29 fighter jet, whose pilot had parachuted to safety but whose wreckage still lay on a grassy part of the field. One day Spivey's sons came to the Bell chalet to watch him brief the media on the Osprey and the coming tiltrotor revolution. The boys had heard most of it before, during weekend visits with their dad as they grew up. Spivey loved to tell his sons about his visits to military bases and what the tiltrotor could do for the services. He often brought home models and showed the boys how "cool" the tiltrotor was. As he got older, Eric could see that selling the tiltrotor wasn't just his dad's job, it was his passion. His dad was a little bit crazy on the subject, Eric thought. When he saw him meet the press and take their questions at Paris, though, Eric was impressed. The old man really knew his stuff.

Bell president Horner talked to reporters in Paris that year, too, when the Bell-Boeing partnership announced that it had just signed agreements with three big aerospace companies—British Aerospace, Dornier of West Germany, and Aeritalia of Italy—to assess the military and civilian markets for tiltrotors in their countries. If the Defense Department canceled the Osprey, Horner said, Bell would look for tiltrotor support abroad. "We are not going to build an airplane just to put it in the Smithsonian Museum," Horner asserted. "I'm going to find a way to keep this program going."

★ ★ ★

Representative Curt Weldon had already found a way: form a coalition. Cheney's hit list of programs included the F-14D Tomcat, a swing-wing

Navy fighter jet made on Long Island. The New York congressional delegation and members from other states who had Navy bases in their
districts were eager to keep the Tomcat going, and like the Osprey's
advocates, they were short of votes. As the House Armed Services Committee prepared to vote on the defense authorization bill that year, the
Osprey and Tomcat camps made a deal: you vote for my program and
I'll vote for yours.

When the Armed Services Committee took up the defense bill that
June 22, Weldon and his allies stunned its Democratic chairman, Representative Les Aspin of Wisconsin. Aspin, saying Cheney deserved a
vote of confidence for trying to bring defense spending under control,
had vowed to block amendments to the Republican defense secretary's
proposed $10 billion in cuts. The chairman appeared confident he could
do that even after the committee voted 28–15 for an amendment offered
by Weldon and a Tomcat supporter that included $508 million for the
Osprey and $230 million to build new Tomcats. Aspin just grinned. He
was expecting to nullify that and all other amendments by waiting until
the end of the bill-writing session and then calling a vote on the original, unamended bill. If Aspin won that vote, all amendments would fall,
a tactic known as "King of the Hill." When Aspin offered the original
bill, though, it failed on a 26–26 tie—the narrowest possible margin. The
chairman was mortified.

"We beat his ass, it's as simple as that," Weldon declared nearly two
decades later, still savoring the victory.

Two days after the committee voted, the panel's senior Republican
announced that there would be no effort on the administration's behalf
to strip the Osprey and Tomcat money out of the defense bill when it
came to the House floor. "I don't think it can be reversed," explained
Representative Bill Dickinson of Alabama.

The Osprey camp had won their first, and most important, battle.
They had defied both Cheney and the House Armed Services Committee chairman and saved the Osprey from sudden death. What has
been called the dance of legislation, however, is a duet. A bill has to
go through the same process in the Senate as the House, and after the
chambers have passed their separate versions of a measure, a conference committee of senators and representatives has to resolve the inevi-
table differences. The Senate version of the bill included $255 million to
keep building and testing Osprey prototypes. Unlike the House, how-

ever, the Senate included no funding for "long lead items"—parts and tools Bell and Boeing would need to start building production models. That was a big problem for the companies, which had started setting up their production lines using money Congress had voted in 1988, the year before Cheney became defense secretary. That year, Navair had exercised its option to order the first twelve production model Ospreys for $1.2 billion. If the next defense budget included no production money, Spivey told *Aviation Week*, the Osprey would fall two years behind schedule.

In fact, the problem was much larger than that. With no production money, the Osprey was just a science project. With no production money, Bell and Boeing couldn't hope to recover their massive cost overruns under the fixed-price Full Scale Development contract. The companies were pouring more money into that contract every day, and there would be a limit to how long they could do that with no guarantee the Osprey would be produced. Cheney and his aides recognized Bell-Boeing's dilemma early on and adopted it as their strategy. If they couldn't kill the Osprey outright, they would try to strangle it to death by preventing it from going into production.

The House-Senate conference on the defense bill became Cheney's first victory on the issue. The Senate's position on the Osprey prevailed. The final bill omitted Osprey production money, and the conference committee's report said Congress should defer a decision on production until the Defense Department had an independent study done comparing the tiltrotor's cost and effectiveness to helicopters.

The Osprey camp was disappointed, but as long as the final decision rested with Congress, the Marines and their allies could be optimistic. The companies could keep preparing for production using the money Congress had provided pre-Cheney while Weldon and his coalition tried to get Osprey production money into the next year's defense bill. That was their plan as Congress adjourned for the year that November.

A week later, Cheney showed them he wasn't going to step aside and leave the Osprey's fate up to Congress. He had Navair cancel the contract Bell and Boeing had signed in March to build the first dozen production models. The Pentagon also took back $200 million of the production funds Congress had approved in 1988.

Weldon and other lawmakers were outraged. Cheney was trying to use executive power to preempt Congress in deciding the Osprey's future. The new defense secretary clearly wanted a fight. Weldon and his allies were going to give him one.

★ ★ ★

On September 13, 1989, Preston M. "Pete" Geren, Jr., a thirty-seven-year-old Fort Worth lawyer whose political experience consisted of three years as a Senate aide and an unsuccessful run for Congress, won former Speaker Jim Wright's seat in the U.S. House. Geren was a Democrat, and at the request of the Republican Party, Weldon had campaigned for his opponent. When Geren got to Washington that fall, though, he and Weldon fast became allies, and then fast friends. The Osprey brought them together.

Bell Helicopter was one of the biggest employers in Geren's district, and he went to Congress pledged to fight for the Osprey. As Geren quickly learned, Weldon was way ahead of him. Weldon already had organized an Osprey team which was meeting at least every other week to plot strategy, usually in Weldon's office. The regulars included interested House members or aides, lobbyists for Textron, Bell, and Boeing, and a lobbyist for the United Auto Workers, the union that represented workers at Boeing's and Bell's plants. A Marine Corps legislative liaison officer also would be there, though others were admonished to keep quiet about that.

Soon the Corps' maneuvering to thwart Cheney on the Osprey would be a secret as poorly kept as Charlie Wilson's crusade to arm the Afghan rebels "covertly," but the Marines didn't want to advertise how they were doing it. There was nothing unusual about liaison officers providing information to Congress. Plotting strategy with Cheney's foes wasn't illegal, either, but it was a political sin. For that reason, when Marine Colonel Parker Miller became a legislative liaison officer in the summer of 1990, he didn't share the details of what he was doing to help get the Osprey funded with the commandant or other generals, though he and other liaison officers reported to them regularly.

There were a lot of details Miller could have shared. In the fall of 1989, Weldon had drafted a "V-22 Action Plan" that included every tactic imaginable. Weldon and the company lobbyists would brief congressional delegations to make sure they knew how much the tiltrotor meant to their states in jobs and economic development. A Textron lobbyist would keep a list, updated weekly, of how individual members were likely to vote if Osprey funding came up. Bell and Boeing would invite as many lawmakers and their aides as possible to visit their factories in Texas and Pennsylvania to see how the Osprey was being built and watch prototypes fly. They would host Osprey luncheons in Washington for those who couldn't make such trips. The lobbyists and Marine liaison officers would draft questions for members of Congress to ask in hearings when the Osprey came up. Bell, Boeing, and engine maker Allison would send "political action packets" to their subcontractors, located in nearly every state. The packets would include pro-Osprey editorials that the subcontractors or their employees could submit to local newspapers, pro-Osprey form letters they could send to members of Congress and state legislators, phone numbers they could use to call lawmakers and urge them to vote for the Osprey. The liaison officers would send similar packets to Marine Corps Reserve associations. They also would arm Weldon with alternative proposals for funding the Osprey, analyses of just how much money the program needed for various purposes, and details on the Corps' aviation goals—ammunition for hearings and defense bill votes. Weldon assigned himself to get as many House and Senate committees as he could to hold hearings on the Osprey and the civilian potential of the tiltrotor. His group also would organize a "Tilt-Rotor Technology Coalition" of big-name business and union leaders, politicians, former top government officials, and prominent academics who would speak out in favor of the Osprey and promote the tiltrotor for civilian aviation.

Dick Cheney and David Chu might think they had logic on their side; Curt Weldon knew logic didn't count in politics. Votes did. To get votes, you had to rally people to your cause. Sometimes, you had to form coalitions. Every chance you got, you had to attract attention to your issue.

★ ★ ★

Weldon was a master at attracting attention. One day he was browsing in a hobby shop in his district and saw a one-twenty-fourth scale model of the Osprey. When he picked up the box, the first thing that caught his eye was "Made in South Korea." *Perfect!* He bought the model and took it to an Osprey strategy group meeting. A few months later, Bell delivered one to every congressional office, along with a color poster showing a stern-looking Marine in dress blues. Under the photo of retired

Marine major and public relations consultant Fred Lash was this cap-
tion: "The V-22 is a weapon my troops can't afford to lose." Below was a
280-word text touting the tiltrotor's virtues. With the model and poster
went a "Dear Colleague" letter signed by Weldon, Geren, and a congressman from Indiana, where the Osprey's engines were made. "Today
you received a V-22 model which was manufactured in South Korea,"
the letter said. "That's O.K.—as long as the real thing is made here in the
United States, where it was developed." The letter reported that Japan's
minister of trade, Hikaru Matsunaga, had commented during a summer
tour of Bell's tiltrotor factory: "If you build it, we will buy it. If you don't
build it, we will."

Pete Geren marveled at Weldon's showmanship. He was a regular P.
T. Barnum.

★ ★ ★

Capitol Hill often took on a circus atmosphere in those days. In spring,
good weather and the eye-catching backdrop of the Capitol dome
turned the Hill into a sprawling outdoor stage for demonstrations, news
conferences, and grassroots gatherings aimed at attracting attention to
issues before Congress. An asphalt parking lot, removed in later years,
stretched across the East Front of the Capitol, the side where presidential inaugurations were held until Ronald Reagan took his oath of office
on the West Front in 1981. In the 1980s and 1990s, the East Front parking lot often served as an impromptu midway for sideshows of democ-
racy. Gaggles of tourists and schoolchildren mingled with troupes of old
soldiers in Veterans of Foreign Wars caps and activists carrying signs
and wearing buttons promoting every imaginable cause. The tourists
might come across displays of air-bag-equipped cars, tractors fueled by
corn, or some other industrial novelty brought to the Hill by interest
groups seeking federal help or relief. More often than not, perched on
the East Front steps would be some solitary soul with rapturous eyes,
dressed as Jesus or Abraham Lincoln and clearly sure that he was. You
never knew what you might see outside the Capitol.

Just before noon on April 25, 1990, a mild and partly sunny day in
Washington, Pete Geren was walking down the East Front steps behind
some other House members when he heard one say, "Wonder what that
is?" Sitting on the parking lot was a peculiar aircraft about the size of an
executive jet, but with rotors on its two wingtips.

"Looks to me like a defense program in trouble," quipped Representative Barney Frank, a Massachusetts Democrat known for his wit. Everyone laughed. Geren knew Frank was right.

The XV-15 had been sitting on the parking lot since dawn, when Bell pilots Ron Erhart and Tom Warren had flown the little tiltrotor demonstrator in from an airfield in Manassas, Virginia. Bringing the XV-15 to the Capitol was the sort of idea Curt Weldon or P. T. Barnum might have come up with, but it had occurred to Bell lobbyist George Troutman the previous fall. Troutman had been working on it ever since, for it had taken months of string-pulling. The Federal Aviation Administration had balked. The airspace around the Capitol was tightly restricted. Landing any aircraft on the Capitol grounds was rare; landing an experimental hybrid like the XV-15 was extraordinary, a request beyond anything in living memory. When Troutman went to the FAA to seek permission, he was told there were only three reasons aircraft could land at the Capitol: for law enforcement, to transport government VIPs, or on "official government business." Troutman got his friend Representative James Oberstar, a Minnesota Democrat and tiltrotor believer who chaired the House Aviation Subcommittee, to ask House Speaker Thomas Foley to declare landing the XV-15 at the Capitol "official government business." Oberstar was planning a hearing on the tiltrotor's civil aviation potential; having the XV-15 at the Capitol would help members understand the issue. Foley, whose district in Washington state included a Boeing plant, obliged. At Foley's request, the FAA agreed the XV-15 could land at the Capitol, but the agency's bureaucrats wanted assurances the tiltrotor could get in and out of Washington without endangering the populace. Troutman sent for Dick Spivey and Bell pilot Erhart. After hours of discussion, they persuaded a roomful of officials from the FAA, the U.S. Park Police, the Architect of the Capitol office, the Secret Service, and other agencies that there would be no serious risk if the XV-15 entered the District of Columbia flying in helicopter mode over the Anacostia River, went north of the Capitol, then circled back and followed railroad tracks south over Union Station before landing on the East Front parking lot. The FAA also wanted the XV-15 to arrive and depart after dark to minimize the number of people on the streets below. The tiltrotor demonstrator had no lights and wasn't certified to fly at night, though, so in a compromise, the FAA agreed the XV-15 could arrive as soon after sunup as possible and leave at sunup the next morning. Things had grown complicated since the 1930s, when test pilot James G. Ray landed an Autogiro on the East Front parking lot in an attempt to get Congress to buy that early hybrid for the Army—an event long forgotten by 1990.

Erhart would have bet four months' salary he'd never be where he was about noon that day as he strapped into the cockpit of the XV-15, its fuselage painted white with red highlights and xv-15 TILTROTOR in blue along its sides. Several hundred congressmen, aides, reporters, and tourists were watching from the Capitol steps, along with Troutman and Spivey, as Erhart and Warren cranked up the engines.

They began their show by doing a few turns while taxiing around the parking lot, then tilting the nacelles backward a couple of degrees to show off how the XV-15 could back up. With the downwash from its rotors kicking up clouds of dust, Erhart then lifted the XV-15 into a hover and climbed vertically to about 100 feet, roughly a third as high as the Capitol dome. The crowd craned their necks as Erhart made the XV-15 perform a quick aerial ballet, flying sideways a little, then back, then pirouetting over the parking lot before coming to a hover over the south end. Now he tilted the nacelles forward 20 degrees. The little tilt-rotor zipped toward the Senate end of the Capitol, the wind from its rotors lashing the leafy branches of oaks and elms on the nearby lawns. Erhart had to bring the nacelles as far aft as he could in a hurry to keep from overshooting the north end of the lot. He hovered over a guard shack there, did a couple of more turns, then set the craft down in the middle of the parking lot. That was it. As the XV-15 taxied back to the south end of the lot, the spectators on the steps applauded.

"This is the most significant contribution to civilian aviation since the dawn of the jet age," Oberstar told reporters at a news conference afterward on a triangle of lawn next to the parking lot. He, Weldon, and other members declared it vital that Congress keep funding the Osprey. Weldon and Geren realized only later that a lot of their colleagues thought that was what they had just seen fly—the Osprey. So did others. The *Los Angeles Times* described how "a flashy red-white-and-blue warplane" had won "hearty applause" by landing at the Capitol. "The reception was typical of what has greeted the plane, a V-22 Osprey, since its inception," the *Times* mistakenly reported.

As assistant secretary of defense for legislative affairs, David Gribbin was Cheney's eyes and ears on Capitol Hill. His job was to help Cheney get his way with Congress. When Gribbin heard what the Osprey's supporters had pulled off that day, he thought: "These guys are good."

The effect was electric. There never had been any strong opposition in Congress to the Osprey as a machine, but there had been a lot of concern about how much it would cost amid pressure to cut the defense budget. Even General Gray, the commandant, had conceded in congressional testimony that the Osprey was "an expensive airplane, and this is a hell of a time to have an expensive program." On that point, Dick Cheney and David Chu still had logic on their side. Curt Weldon, though, could have told Cheney and Chu that logic didn't win political battles. Votes did. One way you got votes was by rallying people to your cause; one way you did that was by attracting attention to your issue and giving people a simple way to understand it. Pete Geren had spent a lot of time since he arrived in Congress the previous fall trying to explain the tiltrotor to busy colleagues and get them to join the Osprey coalition. After the XV-15 flew at the Capitol, it was easy to get to yes. Just as it had captured John Lehman's imagination at the 1981 Paris Air Show, the XV-15 had sold the tiltrotor on Capitol Hill. That, however, wasn't going to be enough.

* * *

David Chu was a mysterious character to many of those trying to defeat his logic on the Osprey. The Osprey camp often groused about him and speculated on his motives. One senior Marine general referred to Chu privately as a "Chinese Communist," adding an alliterative vulgar epithet. Others in the Osprey camp suggested Chu was in Sikorsky's pocket. Bell president Jack Horner knew Sikorsky too well to buy that. Horner's father had run Sikorsky's parent corporation, United Technologies Corporation. Jack Horner himself, after serving in the Marine Corps, had worked at Sikorsky for eighteen years before joining Bell. Besides, Horner had met Chu and even heard a version of the briefing Chu had given Cheney urging him to cancel the Osprey. Horner had to admit that, if he had been Cheney, he probably would have killed the Osprey, too, after hearing Chu's arguments. Horner still thought Chu was wrong, of course, but something he'd seen in the Pentagon parking lot also told him there was no hope of changing Chu's mind. "I saw his little sports car out there with his name on the bottom of it," Horner told me two decades later. "I said, 'He's got an ego. Nobody drives a car like that and parks it at the Pentagon.'" The car, usually parked right by the steps to the Pentagon's River Entrance, was a fancy red Porsche Carrera with a vanity license plate that read "DC PA&E." Marines had seen and commented on the Porsche, too, unaware that it actually belonged to PA&E analyst Deborah Christie. Chu always said "yes" when young officers asked him, "Is that your red car out there, sir?" For years, he puzzled over why they were so intrigued by his red Oldsmobile sedan.

Spivey just had to be there when he heard Chu was going to testify to the Senate Defense Appropriations Subcommittee in July 1990. This was Spivey's first chance to actually see the Osprey's chief antagonist, the man trying to kill his dream. Chu had been called to testify on the study Congress had ordered the Pentagon to do the previous year to help members decide whether to fund Osprey production. A few days earlier, Cheney had rejected the study's results. Spivey wanted to see Chu explain why.

In Washington, information is a weapon, and big studies are heavy artillery. The classified, 1,200-page study compared the Osprey's cost and effectiveness in military missions to the Black Hawk and various other kinds of helicopters. It had been done by the Institute for Defense Analyses, a federally funded think tank created to do independent research for the Pentagon. IDA, pronounced like the woman's name, had spent months on the effort, and its study was a potential turning point in the fight with Cheney over production money. If IDA agreed with Chu and PA&E that the tiltrotor was too expensive for what it would bring the Marines, that might explode any chance of getting the Senate to agree to fund production.

In theory, studies by think tanks such as IDA take a cold, hard look at facts and reach unbiased conclusions, but in the analytical world, there's an old saw: "Tell me the assumptions and I'll tell you what the study is going to conclude." Spivey and others in the Osprey camp had been nervous about what assumptions IDA would use, especially after they saw a memo to the study team by the project leader as it began. In his memo, IDA analyst L. Dean Simmons included a white paper "provided by Sikorsky Aircraft that identifies some of the issues that we will need to resolve." Sikorsky's paper laid out "major claims" for the Osprey and offered conclusions. "The true costs of the V-22 have been significantly understated," was one. A second was that the "V-22 is not more survivable"—no less vulnerable to enemy fire—than the Black Hawk. A final one said the Osprey "is perhaps useful technology. However, as a troubled full scale development program with near term production decisions to be made, and given the availability of proven alternatives, the V-22 is not very affordable."

When Bell and Boeing got wind of the Sikorsky memo, they commissioned a study of their own by the U.S. Energy Department's Lawrence Livermore National Laboratory, which agreed to do it on the condition that its study be published no matter the results. Spivey flew to Washington to observe a war game the lab ran. Role players in different rooms—experienced military officers—fought out a fictional assault on terrorists in Lebanon's Bekaa Valley, sending in imaginary Marines aboard imaginary Ospreys or helicopters. Computers calculated the results, and Spivey was happy with them. The Livermore study found that the tiltrotor's speed could make a critical difference in battle.

The Osprey camp was ecstatic when IDA's study reached similar conclusions. The institute found that while the Osprey would cost more than helicopters to buy, the costs would even out over twenty years because the Osprey was expected to be more reliable and cheaper to maintain than existing helicopters. The Osprey also would be much more effective than helicopters in most military missions because of its speed and range, IDA concluded, though only slightly better in an opposed amphibious assault. Ospreys would be harder to shoot down than helicopters, the IDA study said, but the tiltrotor's speed would be less of an advantage in an amphibious assault because heavy-lift helicopters would be needed to haul artillery and trucks to shore. This meant the entire force would have to start within helicopter range of the objective.

Chu told the subcommittee he questioned IDA's assumptions. IDA's estimate of how much the Osprey would cost was probably low, Chu said, and its assumption on how many CH-53E heavy-lift helicopters would be needed in an amphibious assault ignored a "promising" idea called the "dual-sling option." Chu said the Marines could use half as many CH-53Es in an amphibious assault if each of the behemoth helicopters carried two Humvees slung under its belly in cargo netting. That would make their air fleet cheaper. To make the dual-sling option work, though, the Humvees would have to be bolted together so they wouldn't swing in different directions and cause the helicopter carrying them to crash. Senator Arlen Specter, a Pennsylvania Republican, reminded Chu that in a recent House hearing, Commandant Gray had derided the idea of dual-slinging Humvees as "totally ridiculous." Chu said he "respectfully" disagreed with Gray.

Specter let Chu have it. The Defense Department was being "misleading, if not disingenuous," he told him. Specter said he didn't understand Chu's answers to various questions. He scolded him for interrupting when Chu hadn't, saying, "Excuse me, wait until I finish my question." Chu remained Spock-like: polite, unemotional, unyielding. The dual-sling option, he insisted, was logical.

When the three-hour hearing was over, Spivey and his colleagues were glowing. Specter had really raked Chu over the coals, they agreed. Bell and Boeing bought hundreds of copies of the hearing transcript from the Government Printing Office and sent them to subcontractors, members of the Tilt-Rotor Technology Coalition, members of Congress, reporters covering the Osprey battle—anyone they could think of.

Chu asked a Cheney aide who had accompanied him to the hearing how he'd done. He'd testified so little in his career, Chu had no feel for such things. "After that hearing, there'll be no more hearings," the aide told him. Chu, he said, had made a great case for Cheney's position that the Osprey was simply too expensive.

When the defense bills were done that year, though, they included $238 million to continue work on the six Osprey prototypes and another $165 million to start gearing up for production. Cheney was losing his confrontation with Congress, but the Marines and their allies on the Hill had no illusions. He wasn't giving up.

The Osprey's iffy future and curtailed budget were making things sticky for Bell-Boeing and Colonel Jim Schaefer's V-22 program office at Navair. By early 1990, the companies had built four of the six prototypes planned and the fifth and sixth were in their early stages. The companies were flight-testing the prototypes, too, though money for that was short and they were way behind schedule. Schaefer had instructions from Cheney's office: the program could do anything that fell within the rubric of Full Scale Development but nothing more. No money was to be spent on getting ready to make production model Ospreys or building facilities for them. There weren't going to be any, as far as Cheney was concerned.

Schaefer knew from personal experience that Cheney meant that. One day the defense secretary paid a visit to Anacostia Naval Station, a small facility on the Potomac River in Washington used by HMX-1, the Marine Corps squadron that flies the white-topped helicopters known as "Marine One" when the president is aboard. As Cheney toured a new hangar under construction there, the squadron commander proudly pointed out that it was designed to accommodate the Osprey, with its peculiar blade-folding and wing stow mechanisms, if the tiltrotor ever became the presidential aircraft. Unofficially, the Marines had been figuring on that before Cheney took over the Pentagon.

The next morning, Schaefer was summoned to Cheney's office. Cheney was sitting at his desk as Schaefer entered. Sean O'Keefe, the top Pentagon budget official at the time, was also in the room. As he came in, Schaefer looked out the window wistfully at the sunshine glinting off the Potomac. *I could be out there playing golf instead of getting my ass chewed off*, he thought as he stood before Cheney's big desk.

"I thought you were instructed not to spend military construction money on this program?" Cheney said sternly. "You're authorized a test program, that's it."

Schaefer assured Cheney the HMX-1 hangar hadn't been paid for out of the Osprey program's budget. It had been started "before you and I got here" and it was being built to accommodate helicopters, too, not just the Osprey, Schaefer explained.

Cheney said okay, but as Schaefer made ready to leave, the secretary added: "You understand my instructions?"

"Yes, sir," Schaefer said.

★ ★ ★

Since he was authorized a test program, Schaefer wanted to get as much done as possible to get ready for production, just in case Cheney lost his battle with Congress, as Schaefer hoped he would. Part of the flight test plan was to take the Osprey aboard an amphibious assault ship to prove it could do what it needed to do on such a vessel: land and take off from the deck safely, fold its rotor blades and stow its wing as the vessel sailed, be towed onto an aircraft elevator and put into a hangar deck below without problems, be worked on by mechanics above and below decks. That fall, ships were in short supply. Most were busy taking troops and equipment to Saudi Arabia, where U.S. forces were building up for a campaign to oust Iraqi dictator Saddam Hussein's army from Kuwait, which Iraq had invaded in August. By chance, Schaefer heard that the USS *Wasp*, the first of a new class of amphibious assault ships called LHDs, was scheduled to start sea trials in late 1990. The *Wasp*'s skipper was an old acquaintance from a stint Schaefer had done in the Navy Department.

On December 4, a Marine Corps test pilot from Navair and a Boeing pilot flew the fourth Osprey prototype, designated Aircraft 4, from Patuxent River Naval Air Station in coastal Maryland to the *Wasp* as it sailed fifty miles at sea, and landed on the deck like a helicopter. For the next three days, Aircraft 4 was used to test the blade fold/wing stow mechanisms and let the *Wasp*'s deck crews move the Osprey around the vessel. On December 7, Aircraft 3, flown by another Marine Corps test pilot and one from Bell, flew out from Patuxent River and did thirteen takeoffs and landings to see how the Osprey would handle in various positions. Bell and Boeing engineers in a 45-foot-long "telemetry van" parked on the deck monitored data transmitted from instruments aboard Aircraft 3 as it flew. The ocean was calm, but it was a cold, wet day. Schaefer watched from the bridge, sipping coffee with his friend the captain.

The tests went well. The deck crews were able to work under the Osprey despite the powerful downwash from its rotors with their high disk loading. Metal deflectors added to the bottoms of the nacelles prevented the red-hot exhaust roaring out of the Osprey's engines from damaging the ship's deck. Worries that the wingtip placement of the thirty-eight-foot rotors would cause big problems when one rotor was over the deck and the other was over the water far below proved exaggerated. The pilots had to compensate by banking the wing right a little to keep from rolling left, but they could handle that. The biggest problem, the pilots said in a 288-page report filed later, was holding the Osprey in a steady hover five feet or less over the deck. The aircraft wanted to roll right or left, and it took "excessive pilot compensation" to keep it over one spot without losing control. The electronic flight controls would need to be refined before more sea trials were flown, the pilots said. As it was, the test pilots' report said, "The excessive pilot compensation required . . . will not allow the combat assault pilot to make consistent, safe shipboard landings and will result in significant damage to aircraft and/or ship equipment and/or injury to flight deck personnel."

The next month, a series of color photographs of the Osprey operating on and over the *Wasp*'s deck made the cover of *Aviation Week*, which published a detailed article on the shipboard tests. "The favorable test results are expected to provide a boost to tiltrotor proponents seeking to save the V-22 production program from cancellation," the magazine reported.

Schaefer was summoned to Cheney's office again. As he walked in, Cheney held up the magazine. "What's this?" he demanded.

Schaefer was ready. Commandant Gray had called him in advance and warned that "Mr. Cheney's a little upset."

"It's a good picture, though, isn't it?" Schaefer had told Gray.

"Damn right it is," Gray said.

Schaefer assured Cheney he'd had nothing to do with the photo or the article. He had no control over what *Aviation Week* published. After he left Cheney's office, though, Schaefer decided it might be best if the Osprey program avoided publicity for a while.

Five months later, Schaefer was reminded that publicity isn't something you can always control.

★ ★ ★

Five seconds into the flight, by the time they were ten feet in the air, test pilot Grady Wilson knew he had a tiger by the tail. A minute and a half later, he was sure he and his copilot were about to meet their maker.

The maiden flight of the fifth Osprey prototype, Aircraft 5, began just after 6 P.M. on June 11, 1991, at Greater Wilmington Airport in Delaware, where Boeing Helicopter had its flight test center. Wilson, fifty at the time, had gone to work for Boeing just seven months earlier, but test pilots didn't come with much more experience. A crusty good ole boy from Mississippi, Wilson had learned his trade flying helicopters and airplanes in the Army for twenty-three years, fourteen of them as a test pilot. He spent five of those at NASA's Ames Research Center in California, where he flew the XV-15. Wilson's copilot in Aircraft 5 that day was Lynn Freisner, the fifty-four-year-old flight test director at Boeing Helicopter. Freisner had hired Wilson. Now it seemed they might die together.

They lifted off after an annoying couple of hours in the cockpit spent sweating up their flight suits as engineers fixed finicky monitoring instruments in the back cabin. The Osprey prototypes had lousy air-conditioning, and though it was only 70 degrees outside, sunshine streaming through the windshield was baking the pilots. The cockpit's four computerized Multi-Function Displays—cathode-ray tubes designed to take the place of the dials and gauges on older aircraft— were generating so much heat they were starting to fail. By the time the engineers climbed out, Wilson could think of several reasons he and Freisner should just go back to the hangar. Instead, they taxied out to an asphalt test pad to start flying.

Aircraft 5, painted in Marine Corps camouflage, had never flown before. This was just to be a brief hover, no more than thirty minutes at no more than thirty feet, a shakedown to check out some systems and check off a box so Boeing could get a step closer to turning Aircraft 5 over to the government and getting paid for it. Boeing and Bell had started the fifth prototype in 1988 but stopped for several months in 1989 after Cheney announced he was canceling the Osprey. The companies resumed work on Aircraft 5 later that year, after Congress voted more money, but finishing touches were still being put on the Osprey prototype in a hangar at Wilmington just days before Wilson and Freisner climbed aboard.

Workers at Wilmington showed signs of being rushed. Government inspectors had been complaining for months about sloppiness at the facility. The inspectors kept finding FOD—"foreign object debris"—in and around the Osprey prototypes there. FOD, which rhymes with *sod*, is anything that might damage an aircraft—a bit of wire, a coin, a mislaid tool, metal shavings, you name it. FOD sucked into a turbine engine can cause thousands of dollars worth of damage, even a crash. That's why runways at military bases and flight decks of aircraft carriers are regularly walked by lines of troops or sailors looking for FOD. Over the previous six months, government inspectors had found electric plugs, scissors, rags, a vacuum tool attachment, a six-inch drill bit, a flashlight, nuts, washers, all kinds of FOD in the Osprey prototypes at Wilmington, including Aircraft 5. Seven days before Wilson's and Freisner's flight, the government supervisor at Wilmington had suspended flight operations there and stopped payments to Boeing until the company took action to stop the problem. Boeing drew up an anti-FOD plan and the flight suspension was lifted the morning of June 11.

Freisner was copiloting that day only because the engineers had needed so much time to get Aircraft 5 ready. The scheduled copilot had a doctor's appointment he didn't want to miss, so Freisner offered to substitute. Like Wilson, Freisner knew something was wrong within seconds after they took off. Aircraft 5 heaved into the air unsteadily, wobbling from side to side like a patient standing up after months of being bedridden. Wilson couldn't make it do what he wanted. The stick felt sluggish, unresponsive. In nearly three decades of flying, he'd never had an aircraft behave this way. As he struggled with the stick, Freisner said, "Look, let's get on the ground now."

"Yeah, we've got to get it on the ground," Wilson muttered, clearly too busy to talk.

Jim Schaefer was in the flight test center tower, watching on closed-circuit video with some flight test engineers. "Aren't we paying our pilots enough, or are we not training them enough?" Schaefer cracked as they watched the Osprey weave.

Almost as soon as Schaefer spoke, he could see that Wilson had decided to land. Still teetering, the aircraft eased down gradually to about six feet, but then rose back up to about fifteen. It eased down again, this time getting to two or three feet off the ground, but then rose back up to ten feet or so. It started settling again, then went back up, then down, this time more slowly. Finally the wheels touched the ground. As they did, the Osprey started acting like a rodeo bull in the starting gate. First it shrugged left, then hard to the right. As it did, it bounced off its right tire and rolled left so violently the bottom of the nacelle on that side bashed into the asphalt, crushing its base like a beer can. Now the Osprey leapt into the air as if stung.

From his right side seat in the cockpit, Wilson hadn't seen what hit the ground, but he'd felt the impact. When he did, he added power to lift up and try to land again, as helicopter pilots often do when they aren't happy with a landing. But as the Osprey got back up to fifteen feet or so, it truly seemed to have a mind of its own. The more Wilson tried to control it by moving the stick, the more out of control the Osprey got. From the tower, Schaefer and the engineers watched dumbstruck as Aircraft 5 moved away from the camera toward a concrete runway in the distance, staggering through the air like a drunk trying to walk a line. Inside the cockpit, Wilson's brain was overloaded. He was wrestling with the stick, which by now was making the Osprey do the opposite of what Wilson was asking. When Wilson pushed the stick left, the Osprey rolled right; when he pushed the stick right, it rolled left. The wrestling match didn't last long. The Osprey's wing rolled wildly to the left, then wildly to the right, then back to the left so far that the left rotor dug into the concrete, spewing chunks of composite as its blades disintegrated. With the right rotor still intact and whirling, the Osprey performed a ghastly pirouette on its left nacelle, heeled over like a sinking ship, burrowed its nose into the runway, then plowed along with flames and black smoke pouring from underneath until it skidded to a stop.

Freisner's left-side copilot seat was flush with the ground when they came to rest. He looked back toward the cabin and saw a gap where the fuselage had cracked open just behind the cockpit on his side.

"Grady, there's a hole back here we can get out of!" Freisner shouted as he unbuckled his lap belt and shoulder harness. "Follow me!" Then Freisner scrambled out and ran.

Wilson was hanging nearly upside down. He heard Freisner yell to follow him, but Wilson's training kicked in. Instead of following Freisner, Wilson jettisoned the cockpit window on his side, struggling with a metal handle until the glass popped out, then unstrapped and climbed out onto the overturned nose of the Osprey. He jumped about ten feet to the ground and stumbled away from the wreck to where Freisner was standing, next to a yellow fire truck whose crew had responded within seconds and was spraying foam on the fire. A giant column of black smoke was billowing up into the sky from the Osprey's left side.

Wilson had some scrapes on his face, but his most severe injury was a badly bruised heel from jumping off the fallen Osprey. Freisner didn't have a scratch. The fire crew put out the blaze quickly, but the aircraft itself would have to be written off. It had flown less than two minutes.

The next day, Navair suspended all Osprey flights pending an investigation. TV stations and newspapers around the nation were reporting on the accident. This was just the kind of publicity the Osprey didn't need. Weldon tried to douse any sparks of doubt before they could ignite opposition. "The point of the prototypes is to work out any bugs or problems with the system," he told the *Delaware County Daily Times*. "I'd rather it happen now than with Marines on board."

CHAPTER EIGHT
SURVIVABILITY

B ell Helicopter test pilot Ron Erhart called Grady Wilson the day after the crash to see how he was. Except for a bad bruise on his heel, he was okay, Wilson said, but he was still trying to figure out why he'd nearly died in Aircraft 5. Something weird had been going on with the Osprey prototype's controls. That was what started the trouble. Wilson told Erhart he thought he might have gotten it down safely, though, if not for the Blottle, as a lot of people called the Osprey's power control. "I was going to plant it on the ground and I went the wrong way," Wilson told his friend.

Officially called the Thrust Control Lever, or TCL, the Blottle worked like an airplane throttle, as Brigadier General Harry Blot had insisted it must when he ran the Osprey program for Navair in the late 1980s: you pushed it forward for more power and pulled it back for less. Bell and Boeing had wanted the TCL to work like a helicopter collective, as the power lever in the XV-15 did: you pulled it up and back for more power and pushed it down and forward for less. Most pilots will revert to training and instinct in an emergency, especially near the ground, where there's often no time to think. When a veteran helicopter pilot gets into a situation like Wilson faced in Aircraft 5 and wants to land in a hurry, training and instinct say to "dump collective"—shove the power lever all the way forward. "This thing was ass-backwards to anything a helicopter guy had ever seen," Wilson told me years later. A lot of what had happened in the cockpit the day of the crash was a blur to Wilson even when he and Erhart talked, and always would be. Wilson could never shake the feeling, though, that he might have suffered an attack of what some Osprey pilots called "collective dyslexia." He would always suspect he had unconsciously tried to dump collective one of those times when he'd gotten Aircraft 5 close to the ground. That would explain why, to the surprise of those watching, the Osprey had hopped back up into the air. "I have no doubt that in my subconscious, and fighting it like that, I probably reverted to what I'd been trained to do," Wilson told me. "Consciously, I don't remember that."

The Navy Department's investigators didn't blame the Blottle, or even mention it in their report. Aircraft 5's strange behavior, they found, was caused by a device in the Osprey's "fly-by-wire" flight control system called a "vyro." A vyro is an electronic sensor, essentially a gyroscope, that measures an aircraft's roll rate, meaning how fast it is rotating around its longitudinal axis, an imaginary line from its nose to its tail. A vyro sends signals to a flight control computer, which makes tiny rapid-fire adjustments to help keep the aircraft stable in flight, much as an auto driver unconsciously moves the steering wheel back and forth constantly to steer a straight line. The purpose of the vyros was to refine the commands given by the pilot moving the stick, and thus keep the Osprey stable.

As part of its "survivability" requirement—the military's dictate that it be able to take enemy fire and keep flying—the Osprey had three sets of electronic flight controls, and those three sets of controls had one vyro each to measure the aircraft's roll rate. If the signals sent by one of the three vyros contradicted the other two, the majority would rule; the two vyros that agreed with each other would "vote" the first off line. The investigation found that two of the three roll rate vyros in Aircraft 5 had been wired in reverse. This turned the prototype into an aircraft out of Bizarro World, the cube-shaped planet in the *Superman* comic books where all the rules are the reverse of Earth's. When Wilson moved the stick left or right quickly, the aircraft rolled left or right slowly; when he moved the stick slowly, the aircraft rolled quickly. The two bad vyros were sensing Aircraft 5's roll rate in reverse—reading slow as fast and fast as slow—and voting the good vyro off line. The effect was gradual at first, but as Wilson moved the stick faster and farther, frantically trying to gain control, his aircraft started doing nearly the opposite of what he intended. The stick ultimately got almost 180 degrees "out of phase," as it's called, so far out of sync that trying to bring Aircraft 5 under control was actually making it less stable.

Aircraft crash for many reasons, often because mundane things like FOD set in motion a sinister chain of events. FOD didn't cause Aircraft 5 to crash, but inattention akin to what led to the FOD problem at Boeing's flight test center did. The vyros were connected to the Osprey's flight control computer by bulky bundles of wires—120 wires in each sapling-thick bundle. Errors were detected after the bundles were made in 1988 and rewiring was done as Boeing fabricated the cockpits of the prototypes. Work on Aircraft 5 was halted after its vyros were rewired, though, because Cheney had decided to cancel the Osprey. When that happened, whoever had rewired Aircraft 5's vyros failed to fill out paperwork showing the task had been completed. When work resumed after Congress kept the Osprey alive, workers found an open order to reverse wires 59 and 60 on two of the prototype's roll rate vyros. They did, undoing the correction made months earlier.

The mistakes didn't end there, investigators found. Five days before Aircraft 5's crash, Bell found one miswired vyro on the first Osprey prototype, Aircraft 1. The day before the crash, a Bell flight control engineer told a Boeing flight control engineer about the discovery. The next day—the day of the crash—another Bell engineer sent an e-mail to colleagues suggesting all vyros in the prototypes be checked. At 4 P.M., two hours before Wilson and Freisner lifted off, a third Bell engineer who had read the e-mail called a Boeing engineer to suggest checking the vyros in the Osprey prototypes at Wilmington, Aircraft 2, Aircraft 4, and Aircraft 5. "The engineers involved in the conversation did not believe that there was an 'immediate flight safety risk,'" the crash report said, and after the phone call, the Boeing engineer simply went home. "Basically it was the end of the day and he took no further action."

★ ★ ★

The loss of Aircraft 5 had no discernible effect in Congress. The idea that new aircraft sometimes crash in testing wasn't hard to grasp, and the investigation dispelled any suspicions that the accident was caused by some inherent aerodynamic defect in the tiltrotor. Besides, on the Osprey issue, the Marines already had taken the Hill. By 1991, Congress was firmly on the Corps' side.

The lobbying campaign Representative Curt Weldon had devised and his military-industrial complex allies had implemented was working well. Briefings and trips to the Bell and Boeing factories, organized by the companies and often escorted by Marine Corps legislative liaison officers, had educated many members of Congress and key aides on the issue. Campaign donations and payments of up to two thousand dollars for taking the time to drop by a factory or listen to a briefing—so-called "honorariums," then legal but since banned—helped get the attention of some. The XV-15's flight at the Capitol had given many in Congress a vivid idea of what a tiltrotor was and stirred imaginations. Even members of Congress uninterested in defense issues were now intrigued by the tiltrotor's civil potential. The Institute for Defense Analyses study, meanwhile, had blunted David Chu's argument that the Osprey wasn't worth the extra money for the Marines. All in all, the Osprey camp had defined the issue on its own terms: a technological revolution that would help the Marines win wars with fewer casualties, solve civilian aviation's biggest problems, and bring billions of dollars into the economy from overseas was going down the drain because Dick Cheney had listened to a Pentagon pencil pusher who saw the cost of everything and the value of nothing.

The Osprey camp's grassroots machinery was also in place and well oiled. The Osprey didn't usually face a floor vote in the House or Senate, but when it landed on a committee agenda, Capitol Hill phones would ring like church bells at a coronation and congressional mailbags would overflow with pleas and demands from union members, Bell-Boeing subcontractors, and retired Marines to fund the tiltrotor. At Weldon's urging, the United Auto Workers even put support for the Osprey on their congressional "scorecard," a device interest groups use to rate lawmakers. Most Democrats try to score 100 percent on labor union scorecards; most Republicans try to score 100 percent on the U.S. Chamber of Commerce scorecard. The first thing many members do when they walk onto the floor of the House or Senate to vote is to find out whether the issue is on the scorecard of an interest group whose endorsements and campaign contributions they want when they run for reelection. Any member who wanted a rating of 100 percent from the UAW in those days had to vote for the Osprey. Texas congressman Pete Geren thought that was one of Weldon's cleverest moves. Now even liberal Democrats who reflexively voted against defense spending were backing the Osprey to please Big Labor.

All those things helped. What was keeping the Osprey alive politically, though, was the Marine Corps' zeal for the tiltrotor and its clout in Congress. Commandant Al Gray had played nice when testifying to Congress in 1989, saying he supported Cheney's decision to kill the Osprey but the secretary had gotten bad advice. Two years later, now sure of the

Osprey's political support and headed toward retirement that summer, Gray told the Senate Armed Services Committee it would be "criminal" to delay any longer. The Marines "felt like the V-22 was the key to their continued relevance," Geren told me in 2007, when he was secretary of the Army. The tiltrotor was going to be a way to "take their conventional Marine mission and put it on steroids, allow them to stay relevant in a world of stand-off warfare and be able to self-deploy around the world." Geren remembered Gray saying once that the Marines wanted the Osprey "more than they want to go to heaven." Their alumni and friends in Congress were eager to help. Each year, Cheney would leave the Osprey out of his budget; each year, Marine Corps and Osprey allies on key congressional committees would put it back in.

Dick Cheney understood Congress. He'd served there ten years, been one of the top Republican leaders in the House, and he could see early on that he wasn't going to get his way on the Osprey by winning votes. After 1989, Cheney conceded that with so much money already spent, it made sense to finish Full Scale Development of the Osprey and see whether the aircraft worked. Adamant as the Marines were that they needed the Osprey, though, Cheney was just as adamant that the Pentagon couldn't afford it, and he was determined to make his decision stick. He would go along with the Osprey as a science project: prototypes could be tested, then put on the shelf. Where Cheney drew the line was at buying tools and parts to produce Ospreys for the military, and behind that line lay a strategy. If Cheney could keep the Osprey in FSD, at some point Bell and Boeing might be forced to give up just to keep from pouring more of their own money into the project under their fixed-price contract. If he could stall it long enough, the Marines might get desperate enough to replace their CH-46 Sea Knights with helicopters instead of waiting for the Osprey. In 1989, Cheney refused to spend $200 million Congress had provided to start Osprey production before he took over the Pentagon. In 1990, he refused to spend another $165 million Congress provided for the same purpose. Cheney's strategy was to starve the Osprey to death.

By 1991, the Marines were ravenous. A Navy study a decade earlier had said this was the year the Marines' fleet of CH-46s would be so degraded by age and losses they would have too few to mount a major amphibious assault. This was the year the Marines had counted on getting the Osprey when they'd embarked on the project in 1982 on Navy

Secretary John Lehman's orders. In the mid-1980s, with the Osprey hatched but taking longer to fly than expected, the Marines had spent enough on the CH-46 to keep it flying, but by 1991, wear and tear and crashes had pared the fleet to a mere 234. Just over a third of the "Phrogs" the Marines had bought were still flying, and for safety's sake, there were limits on them. In combat, the Sea Knight was supposed to carry eighteen troops and do evasive maneuvers; in training, the Marines no longer dared put more than nine troops inside, and extreme maneuvers were barred. Bowing to necessity after Cheney's decision to cancel the Osprey, the Marine Corps had created a new program to replace their CH-46s, opening the door to the possibility of accepting a modern troop transport helicopter if they couldn't get the tiltrotor. The Marines didn't *want* a new helicopter instead of the Osprey, but if they couldn't get *some* kind of new troop carrier by 1996, on paper they might be unable to launch a major amphibious assault anymore. Unthinkable. Within their cult of warriors, it was an article of faith that amphibious assault was the reason America *had* a Marine Corps. If they lost the ability to do that mission, they just might lose the Corps.

Inside The Building, and publicly, in 1991, the Marines were keeping their options open. On the Hill, and behind closed doors, they were getting more aggressive.

One day that autumn, Marine Colonel Parker Miller, a legislative liaison officer whose job was to monitor Marine Corps programs in the House, was in Curt Weldon's office with the congressman and Textron lobbyist Mary Howell. A purer example of the "Iron Triangle"—the inbred alliance of industrial, military, and political interests that undergirds defense procurement—would be hard to find. Miller and Howell were advising Weldon as he negotiated the final form of legislation aimed at forcing Cheney to give up.

Shortly after General Carl E. Mundy, Jr., succeeded Gray as commandant in July 1991, Mundy asked Colonel Jim Schaefer, the Osprey program manager, what it would take to get the tiltrotor ready for production and in service by 1996. A lot, Schaefer told him. The Osprey camp had been trying for two years to make Cheney spend money to start production. In February, after Cheney refused for the second year running, Dick Spivey told the *Fort Worth Star-Telegram* he wasn't sure how much longer Textron and Boeing stockholders would wait to start recovering the money the companies had put into the Osprey. "Clearly, we are ready for production," Spivey said. Schaefer knew the aircraft was far from it. Despite all the work over the past eight years, the design still wasn't right, and the prototypes couldn't meet the Osprey's performance requirements.

The wing stow mechanism—the stainless steel "bed frame" device designed by Boeing engineer Kenneth Grina—was too heavy, too costly, and too slow. The Osprey was supposed to fold its rotor blades and stow its wing along the fuselage, or unstow the wing and unfold the blades, in no more than ninety seconds. Aboard the USS *Wasp* that past December, those tasks had taken at least 107 seconds every time. The mechanism also tended to bind, stopping the wing midway through stowing at times. Lots of other things were wrong. Bell was still having trouble making composite rotor grips. The Allison engines burned too much fuel. Boeing's fuselage was too "draggy"—it created about 15 percent more wind resistance than Bell-Boeing's contract allowed. The Osprey was still about 3,000 pounds overweight, too, so to lift the required payload, it had to carry less fuel. Combined with its thirsty engines and draggy aerodynamics, that meant it couldn't meet its requirement to fly 2,100 nautical miles without refueling. Its estimated maximum range of 1,750 nautical miles was nearly 400 miles short. The extra weight also meant the engines and transmissions needed beefing up. Boeing had used gobs of metal rivets and fasteners to hold its composite fuselage together, though, in theory, one reason for using composites was to eliminate as many rivets and fasteners as possible. Excessive vibration in the prototypes had bothered pilots and caused rivets to fail. The flight control software needed a lot of revision. The "environmental control system"—air-conditioning and heat—sometimes roasted the pilots and sometimes spit little balls of ice at them. Test pilots found the computerized flight plan software a "horror show," as one put it in a report. Mechanics found it difficult to work on hydraulic lines and other parts inside the tightly packed nacelles, or even inspect them. The Osprey needed a makeover.

The only way to get the Osprey ready for production by 1996, Schaefer told Mundy, would be to build some new, improved prototypes and test them. For that to happen, though, Congress would have to provide enough money—and make Cheney spend it. Mundy told Schaefer to put together a plan. Schaefer did, then explained his plan to liaison officer Miller, who didn't have to ask what the commandant wanted done.

Miller drafted legislation embodying Schaefer's plan and got the draft into the right hands.

That May, Weldon got the revised Osprey program into the annual defense authorization bill; Pennsylvania Democrat John Murtha, chairman of the House Defense Appropriations Subcommittee and a Marine Corps veteran, put it into the defense appropriations bill. Most important, to make sure Cheney would have to carry it out, the details of the program were written into the appropriations bill itself, an unusual twist. By custom, Congress lumps appropriations for defense programs into large accounts—"Aircraft Procurement, Navy," in the Osprey's case. A conference report accompanying the bill specifies how much Congress intends the Pentagon to spend on each individual program. Earlier that year, Cheney had shown he wasn't going to be bound by custom when it came to the Osprey. In 1990, Congress had put $165 million for Osprey production into the defense appropriations bill. Cheney simply refused to spend it, treating the bill's conference report instructions as a mere suggestion. The Osprey camp wanted to prevent him from doing that again by writing the new plan into law.

As Miller and Howell sat in Weldon's office that autumn day, Weldon was trying to make sure his House colleagues in the appropriations bill conference with the Senate didn't agree to water down the House bill's firm instructions to Cheney on the Osprey. Cheney's point man on the issue, Pentagon comptroller Sean O'Keefe, was pressing the conference to do just that. By phone and in person, O'Keefe was negotiating with Murtha and other "appropriators," as members of the House and Senate appropriations committees are often called. Appropriators were calling Weldon that day to discuss O'Keefe's proposals. Weldon would ask Miller and Howell what they thought of O'Keefe's latest, then call the appropriators back with counterproposals. As Weldon talked on the phone, a secretary came in to tell Miller he had a call on another line. It was an officer at Headquarters Marine Corps.

"Get out," the officer told Miller. "Whatever you're doing over there, stop it. O'Keefe's got your name."

Miller never found out if O'Keefe really knew he was in Weldon's office helping the congressman negotiate legislation. To Miller's relief, he never heard anything more about it, either, and the House held its ground in the appropriations conference. The final bill included $790 million to start building three "production representative" Ospreys—

improved prototypes able to meet all speed, range, payload, and other requirements—by December 31, 1996. The bill said the new prototypes must be built "to the extent practicable" on tooling that could be used for production models. It also gave the Defense Department sixty days to send Congress a plan for carrying out the new program. Weldon and others in the Osprey camp couldn't wait to see what Cheney and O'Keefe would do next.

It didn't take long to find out. On January 26, 1992—the deadline in the law for submitting a plan—O'Keefe sent a letter to the House and Senate saying the Pentagon couldn't start the new program for several reasons. First, the Navy Department needed to study what work Bell-Boeing had left to do under their fixed-price FSD contract. Beyond that, O'Keefe said, "The Navy believes that the aircraft requires substantial redesign and test to meet the Joint Service Operational Requirements." Finally, he added, a second development phase might cost $2.5 billion, and Congress hadn't provided that much.

Weldon was steamed. He saw O'Keefe's letter as pure gamesmanship, a bunch of bureaucratic excuses to hide the fact that O'Keefe and Cheney were planning to defy the will of Congress yet again. Now, though, rather than fight head-on, they were trying to strangle the Osprey to death with the jungly tangle of rules, reviews, and regulations known as the "defense acquisition process." If that was the way they wanted to play, Weldon decided, he would, too. Confrontation got Weldon's adrenaline flowing.

★ ★ ★

On a hot afternoon in the summer of 1990, Dick Spivey was asked to go to the conference room at Bell Helicopter's Plant 6 in Arlington, Texas, to do a briefing on the Osprey and the tiltrotor's promise for a special guest. Ann Richards, silver-haired and sharp-tongued, had won the Democratic nomination for governor that spring after two terms as state treasurer. Spivey was excited to meet her. Richards had become a political celebrity two years earlier at the 1988 Democratic National Convention in Atlanta. In a prime-time speech, she poured a liberal dose of her acid wit on Republican presidential candidate George H. W. Bush, a Texan for decades but born into wealth in Connecticut. As vice president for the past eight years, Richards said, "George Bush hasn't displayed the slightest interest in anything we care about. And now that he's after a job that he can't get appointed to, he's like Columbus discovering America. He's found child care. He's found education. Poor George. He can't help it. He was born with a silver foot in his mouth." Richards gave the military-industrial complex a dose, too. "We Democrats are committed to a strong America, and, quite frankly, when our leaders say to us, 'We need a new weapons system,' our inclination is to say, 'Well, they must be right.' But when we pay billions for planes that won't fly, billions for tanks that won't fire, and billions for systems that won't work, 'that old dog won't hunt.'"

Spivey figured Richards might be a tough audience for a marketer like him selling a defense program like the Osprey. Instead, exhausted from campaigning, she proved a tired one. Spivey used slides to make his usual pitch: the tiltrotor could fly faster and farther than a helicopter; the disaster at Desert One might have been averted if the tiltrotor had been available; the Osprey was the Marine Corps' number-one aviation priority; the tiltrotor was a national asset; it could mean thousands of jobs and billions of dollars to the Texas economy. At first, Richards asked a lot of questions. Then she asked fewer. Then her eyelids began to droop. At times, Spivey was sure she was dozing. She would perk up and ask another question now and then, but when the two-hour briefing ended, Spivey wasn't sure how much she'd absorbed.

Richards won her election that fall, and a few months after she became governor, Spivey decided she must have taken in a lot of what he'd told her. In May 1991, Richards and several other top Texas officials Spivey had briefed at one time or another—the Democratic lieutenant governor, the Democratic Speaker of the Texas House, the new Republican state treasurer—publicly urged President Bush to build the Osprey. The tiltrotor, they said, was too important to sacrifice to post-Cold War pressure to cut defense spending. "It just seems to me so obvious that we need to build this airplane," Richards said.

A few months later, the 1992 presidential election campaign was well under way, and on March 5, ABC-TV hosted a debate in Dallas among the four remaining Democratic candidates. Spivey nearly jumped out of his chair when one them, Senator Tom Harkin of Iowa, criticized Bush and Cheney for trying to cancel the Osprey, which Harkin noted was built in Fort Worth. "We could build 12 vertical ports in our biggest cities on the East Coast, 12 of those, [and] buy 165 of these aircraft for the price of one-half a new large airport," Harkin said. "These are aircraft we

can build commercially, sell here, sell around the world, yet Bush is cut-
ting the funds for that, putting the money in the B-2 bomber. It makes
no sense." A moment later, Arkansas governor Bill Clinton chimed in.
"I support the V-22," Clinton said. Spivey went to bed happy that night.
Maybe that would get Bush's attention, he mused, even lead the White
House to put some pressure on Cheney to back down on the Osprey.

Spivey had been frustrated with the one shot he'd gotten at doing that.
A few months earlier, after a lot of phone calls, Textron's chief Washington lobbyist, Mary Howell, had gotten Spivey in to brief the White House
chief of staff, former New Hampshire governor John Sununu. Spivey
had flown up from Fort Worth, nervous but ready, and thrilled to get
his first-ever visit to the White House. Howell and Textron consultant
Charles R. Black, Jr., a prominent Washington lobbyist and Republican
political operative, went with him. Sununu had a Ph.D. in mechanical
engineering from MIT and a reputation for arrogance Spivey now experienced firsthand. Spivey had brought illustrations, charts, graphs, and
other material along in a big book. He wanted to sit next to Sununu and
show it to him. When the group reached an ornate room in the White
House, though, Spivey was ushered to a sofa while Sununu took a chair
across a coffee table from him. Spivey still tried to use his briefing book,
but it hardly mattered. Sununu barely glanced at the book, and showed
no interest when Spivey touted the tiltrotor's potential as a regional aircraft that could fly, say, from downtown Washington to Manhattan. "Got
it," Sununu would grunt occasionally. "Okay." Then he launched into a
monologue about how hard it was to arrange for the president of the
United States to land by helicopter in New York City. "How are you
going to get this thing to land there every hour?" Sununu scoffed. Spivey
left thinking Sununu was one of the most pompous men he'd ever met.
Getting the White House to overrule Cheney clearly wasn't in the cards.

Curt Weldon had reached the same conclusion, and it worried
the Republican congressman. Despite his fight with Cheney on the
Osprey, Weldon was loyal to the administration and wanted to see
Bush reelected. Weldon thought his home state of Pennsylvania, with
its twenty-three electoral votes, could be pivotal on election day, and
he was sure Cheney's opposition to the Osprey was going to cost Bush
there. Weldon had been trying to get that message to Bush for a long
time. The president, though, was clearly leaving the issue to Cheney, and
Cheney wasn't budging.

On April 2, 1992, Cheney sent Congress a letter saying that though the fiscal 1992 appropriations act required it, he didn't intend to build the new Osprey prototypes. The program Congress had approved "is not affordable within the overall constraints we face on defense resources," Cheney wrote.

Now, Weldon was sure, Cheney had overplayed his hand. Even members of Congress with no interest at all in the Osprey would get their backs up at the idea of the defense secretary simply refusing to carry out a *law*.

Weldon was right. Soon others in the Osprey camp were getting representatives and senators to sign a letter to Bush denouncing Cheney and calling his latest move the equivalent of a line-item veto by an "unelected political appointee." When the House Armed Services Committee marked up the new defense authorization bill a few weeks after Cheney sent his letter, Weldon had no trouble inserting an amendment aimed at sending him a message. Weldon's amendment provided that Pentagon comptroller Sean O'Keefe's office budget would be cut 5 percent for every month the Pentagon failed to implement the revised Osprey program. "When the check cutting office won't cut the check," Weldon crowed, "it's time to cut the check cutting office."

That was mainly for effect, a street fighter's punch in what had become a street fight. Weldon's serious move was a legal maneuver. The Congressional Budget and Impoundment Control Act of 1974 gave the General Accounting Office, a congressional agency later renamed the Government Accountability Office, authority to decide whether executive branch refusals to spend appropriated funds were illegal "impoundments." If the GAO ruled that a federal agency like the Pentagon had impounded money illegally, that agency had forty-five days to start spending it or else the matter would automatically go to court. Weldon asked the GAO to rule on Cheney's refusal to spend the money for new Osprey prototypes.

On June 3, 1992, Sean O'Keefe came to Cheney's office with bad news.

"The GAO has ruled against us," O'Keefe said. Cheney asked what their next move should be.

"There isn't one," O'Keefe replied. "This is it. Game, set, match." The strategy of using executive power to stall the Osprey had run its course. Two days after the GAO ruled, Cheney invited Weldon and other

Republicans in the Osprey camp to his office. Weldon told Cheney he was "playing into the Democrats' hands" with his opposition to the Osprey, "creating an embarrassment to the president and yourself." Cheney mostly listened, and made no promises. "He's like a sphinx," Senator Arlen Specter, the Pennsylvania Republican, told reporters afterward. "It's very hard to read him. But I think the pressure is building."

By now, Bill Clinton had the Democratic presidential nomination sewn up, and Democrats in the Osprey camp were urging him to use the issue against Bush. On June 23, Democrats in the Texas congressional delegation wrote Clinton a letter inviting him to visit Bell Helicopter, see the Osprey fly, maybe even ride in the XV-15. "Bell has assured us that such a visit can be arranged on fairly short notice," they said.

O'Keefe could see that Cheney didn't want to give in. Boxed in by the GAO ruling, though, he had to give ground. On July 2, Cheney sent Congress a letter offering a compromise. He would stop trying to kill the Osprey if Congress let him spend $10 million to study a new helicopter as an alternative. He also would "promptly" use the rest of $1.55 billion Congress had authorized for the revised Osprey program in the previous years' defense bills, though not for production, as the law required. The money would be used instead to work on the Osprey's weight problem, do more flight tests, and build some new prototypes, though how many would depend on "contract negotiations." Congress's plan for "production representative" Ospreys would be dropped, and a final decision on building the tiltrotor for the Marines would be "left for future years."

Weldon and other Republicans declared victory. Cheney's request to start work on a new helicopter was nothing more than a face-saving move, Weldon told reporters.

Democrats in the Osprey camp remained suspicious. On the House floor later that month, Democratic representative Martin Frost of Dallas explained their concern: "This whole process may just be a smoke screen by the administration to get past this election."

★ ★ ★

The Marine Corps base at Quantico, Virginia, is a major training facility and home to some of the service's most important commands. Located only thirty-three miles south of Washington, D.C., Quantico is also a handy showplace for the Marine Corps. The base is close enough that even senior generals and Pentagon officials, members of Congress, and top congressional aides can often squeeze a visit into their busy schedules. Legislative liaison officers frequently escort such VIPs to Quantico to see weaponry, watch field exercises, get a firsthand look at new equipment, maybe shoot a machine gun to see how it feels. Such field trips are one way the Marine Corps builds support for its programs in Congress, and in the spring of 1992, that's how Colonel Jim Schaefer wanted to use Quantico.

With Cheney and O'Keefe telling Congress the Osprey was far from ready for prime time, Schaefer decided it would be a good time to reassure Marine Corps leaders that their dream machine was becoming a reality. Early that year, the fourth prototype had been flown from Boeing's flight test center in Delaware to Eglin Air Force Base in Florida for a few months of special testing. On its way back, Schaefer thought, why not have Aircraft 4 stop at Quantico and invite some VIPs to see it? Schaefer got permission from Headquarters Marine Corps, and soon plans were in the works for the commandant and other top generals to be on hand when Aircraft 4 landed. To give the visit an official purpose, a unit of Marine Corps and Air Force pilots formed to help test the Osprey before it went into service were told they could use Aircraft 4 for a few days while it was at Quantico. That wasn't the point of the visit, though, Schaefer told me years later. "On paper, it was supposed to be familiarization," Schaefer said. "In fact, what we were trying to do was to show it off." Aircraft 4's scheduled stop at Quantico would prove fateful.

Aircraft 4 had been sent to Florida for some of the most grueling tests a prototype can undergo. Eglin Air Force Base, which covers 724 square miles of Florida panhandle near the Gulf of Mexico, is home to the McKinley Climatic Laboratory, a complex of test chambers worthy of a James Bond movie. Outside temperatures in the area vary from an average low of 48 degrees Fahrenheit in winter to a high of 88 degrees in summer. Inside the McKinley lab's vast Main Chamber, which covers more square yards than a football field and has a ceiling seven stories high, technicians control the climate. With powerful steam boilers and huge refrigeration coils, they can mimic the desert or the arctic, raise the temperature to a scorching 125 degrees Fahrenheit or plunge it to minus 65. Using big water pumps and machinery invented for ski resorts, they can re-create many of a flying machine's worst enemies: driving rain, sleet, snow, pea-soup fog, salt spray—the works. The lab's solar lamps can bake an aircraft with radiation worse than the Sahara's. Its special blowers can coat an aircraft in engine-choking dust. No matter what the weather is doing outside, the technicians at the McKinley lab can conjure up almost any climate to see how an aircraft will hold up in it. With the subject tethered like a torture victim to a "run stand"—each aircraft tested gets its own, specially designed—the lab's technicians can perform their meteorological magic even as an aircraft's engines roar, its propellers or rotors turn, if it has them, and pilots in the cockpit manipulate its controls to simulate flight. For pilots and any others who join them inside an aircraft tested this way, it's a you-wouldn't-believe-it experience, the kind you tell about to wow your grandchildren.

An aircraft being subjected to such controlled abuse needs mechanics to repair it after each session and engineers to monitor the tests and analyze the results. When word got around Boeing that Aircraft 4 was going to Eglin for several months, nearly everyone saw it as a plum assignment, though not for the often painful experience of working in the McKinley lab. Those on the small test team would be put up in beachfront condos on the Emerald Coast, aka "Redneck Riviera," and could take their families along. They were guaranteed plenty of overtime, which meant they'd get plenty of overtime pay. Four months at a Florida beach resort on the company with extra pay, or a dreary Northeast winter? There were plenty of volunteers.

One was Anthony Stecyk, a mechanic who in 1987–88 had spent most of a year in Texas with the Boeing crew sent there to finish the first Osprey fuselage. Stecyk's wife, Michelle, had come to Texas, too, and they'd enjoyed the western sojourn. Tony's passion was restoring and collecting old Harley-Davidson motorcycles, and he had added to his collection in Texas. Another fond memory was how he and Michelle won the Texan-look-alike contest at Billy Bob's nightclub. Michelle was glad to go along to Florida, too, especially since she and Tony now had a two-year-old son, Little Anthony, as she called him. Two good buddies of Tony's also would be there, Marines assigned to the Osprey flight test team in Wilmington. Master Gunnery Sergeant Gary Leader and Gunnery Sergeant Sean Joyce were the first Marines to be named Osprey crew chiefs, mechanics whose job is to tend the back cabin and help the pilots avoid hazards during flights. Leader and Joyce shared Stecyk's love of Harleys, and the Stecyks had entertained the two Marines at their home near Ridley Park, where Tony and Michelle liked to throw big par-

ties on holidays. Michelle had worked in airline catering and could whip
up a buffet for thirty or forty friends on special occasions with no sweat.
Tony sometimes went on short assignments to Patuxent River Naval Air
Station in Maryland, where Leader and Joyce were based, and the three
of them would ride Harleys together when he was there.

At forty, Leader was eight years older than Joyce and treated him
like a kid brother, though in fact they were brothers-in-law. Leader had
introduced Joyce to his sister, Yvonne, and the two had married. Leader
and Joyce, the Stecyks, and a couple of other Boeing mechanics and
their wives were a tight little circle. In Florida that winter, they convened
on Friday evenings at the Enclave, the condominium complex where
the Boeing crew was staying in Fort Walton Beach, just across two-lane
Scenic Highway 98 from the Gulf shore. They would play volleyball or
romp with the kids on the Enclave's private beach, then cook a seafood
feast back at the complex. They had a lot of fun in Florida that winter.

They also worked hard. The mechanics helped as a crane lifted the
sixteen-ton Osprey onto a run stand made of one tripod and one bipod
of tubular steel, with a metal platform and stairs for access to the aircraft.
The stand was tall enough for the Osprey's thirty-eight-foot-diameter
rotors to tilt all the way forward into airplane mode without hitting the
floor. An ingenious set of welded steel ducts shaped like crab claws sat
under the nacelles to suck the engine exhaust out of them at all angles
and blow it out of the building. Painted in gray and green camouflage,
Aircraft 4 looked bloated and spotted up there. One of the senior engineers on the test team, Bob Rayburn, nicknamed it "Piggy."

From late February through late May, Piggy was run through the
wringer. There were mechanical problems even at normal temperatures,
though mostly annoyances of the sort expected in a prototype aircraft.
The major pain was the Auxiliary Power Unit, an onboard engine akin to
a car motor, which was needed to gin up enough electricity and hydraulic pressure to start the Osprey's big 6,150-horsepower turbine engines.
The APU's clutch often disengaged, interrupting tests. There were other
nuisances. Dust filters in the engine inlets called Engine Air Particle
Separators tended to leak hydraulic fluid. Hydraulic lines in the nacelles
leaked frequently. The mechanics had plenty to do.

The hardest work came during extreme temperature tests, when a
crew would "fly" simulated missions featuring vertical "takeoffs" and
"landings" sandwiched around run time in airplane mode. With the

lab chilled to 40 below zero, and later minus 65, pilots, engineers, and mechanics had to wear arctic coveralls, arctic hoods, cold weather boots, and two layers of thermal underwear to fend off frostbite. When they waddled up the stairs in all that gear, Marine Major Paul Croisetiere, one of the test pilots, thought they looked like a gang of Pillsbury Dough-boys. The extreme cold and heat were hardest on the mechanics, who had to work longer hours in the lab than the pilots. They lined Air-craft 4's back cabin bulkheads and flooring with two layers of special blankets, but frigid rotor downwash bled in during tests anyway, and the cold lingered afterward. If you took off a glove to do a task, then absent-mindedly touched something metal, your skin usually stuck to it. Lead mechanic Marty LeCloux hated having to walk out on the wing to work inside a nacelle after a cold weather test. The cold would leave frost on the Osprey's skin, making it tricky to step on the slightly rounded, now slippery, wing. Like tightrope walkers in rehearsal, the mechanics would tie themselves to each other with ropes so that if one slipped, the other man's weight would save him from hitting the floor. You could still get hurt if you fell, though, so you had to move gingerly. Working in extreme heat, when the temperature in the Main Chamber could hit 125 degrees, was even worse. It was easier to get warm than to cool off, and if your bare skin touched the aircraft or run stand, you could count on a burn. The temperatures were hard on Aircraft 4, too. Hydraulic fluid wouldn't flow as it should, which meant swashplate actuators that changed the pitch of the rotor blades often didn't work right. Metal parts developed cracks in the cold. One day the APU caught fire, though the blaze flamed out quickly.

The beating the prototype took in the McKinley lab delayed its scheduled flight to Quantico, where Major Kevin Dodge, the leader of the team of Marine Corps and Air Force pilots formed to help test the Osprey before it was fielded, was eagerly awaiting Aircraft 4's arrival. Military aircraft go through two types of tests, "developmental" and "operational." Developmental tests, such as those in the McKinley lab, are conducted by specially trained test pilots and engineers to assess whether the aircraft is built right and flies as it should. Operational testing is done by special military units manned by regular military personnel—pilots and crew chiefs, for a transport like the Osprey—to see whether they have problems in using the aircraft. Dodge's Multi-service Operational Test Team—known as the "mot" from its acronym,

MOTT—had been organized at Quantico nearly two years earlier to do operational testing of the Osprey. With only four prototypes left after the loss of Aircraft 5, though, the MOTT's pilots and mechanics rarely got their hands on one. They were eager for the chance to have Aircraft 4 to themselves, even if only for a few days, and Dodge had drawn up a detailed plan for tests the MOTT would do with the prototype at Quantico.

Dodge initially was told to expect the prototype to arrive in late May, but the schedule kept slipping until the return date became July 20. After the last test in the climatic lab on May 23, Aircraft 4 was beat up. It needed a lot of work before it could attempt the 760-mile trip to Quantico. Its engines had to be removed for maintenance and reinstalled in the nacelles, which took two weeks. The clutch on the proprotor gearbox in the right nacelle had to be changed, another big job. Then Aircraft 4 had to be flown near Eglin a few times to make sure it was airworthy.

The work took long enough that, with tourist season beginning, the Boeing crew's families had to move from Fort Walton Beach to a complex in nearby Destin. The wives passed the time by taking the children to the beach most days. Sometimes they would see the Osprey flying out over the Gulf. "There's Dad!" the kids would shout. "There's the V-22!" That made Michelle Stecyk anxious. *Oh, my God, if anything ever happens with all our kids out there,* she would think. She also worried about how her husband, Tony, who loved to fly in the Osprey, was feeling during those flights over the Gulf. Tony was an avid boater and water skiier, but he never went on the water without a life preserver. Tony couldn't swim. And he had a morbid fear of drowning.

On July 12, Lieutenant Colonel Paul Martin, the top Marine pilot on the Osprey's developmental flight test team, arrived at Eglin with Major Brian James, who had just joined the unit. Martin and James needed more hours in the Osprey to beef up their qualifications, and they were scheduled to take turns copiloting Aircraft 4 to Quantico. Boeing's senior Osprey test pilot, Pat Sullivan, would be the pilot in command on the trip, but James would copilot to a refueling stop in Charlotte, North Carolina. Martin would arrive in a "chase plane" that would trail the Osprey and replace James as copilot during the stopover in Charlotte. As the test team's senior military pilot, Martin wanted to step off

Aircraft 4 when it landed at Quantico, be the officer who talked to the generals about the Osprey and the flight.

The last shakedown flights were July 13, but there was still a lot of maintenance and repair to do before leaving. The APU kept acting up, the fuel system wouldn't feed all its contents to the engines properly, and a long list of parts needed to be replaced. On Sunday, July 19, the day before the flight, a fuel pump had to be removed and replaced, which required putting Aircraft 4 in a special hangar to purge the fumes from one of its gas tanks. The mechanics could have used more time to get ready, but with the generals expected at Quantico when Aircraft 4 arrived on Monday, Boeing's test team managers wanted to avoid another delay that might disappoint The Customer. Boeing managers had been calling Sullivan frequently to be sure he was going to make it to Quantico on July 20, when the generals would be there.

Sunday afternoon, Sullivan went over his flight plan with the two Marines who would share copiloting duty, Martin and James, and Boeing test pilots Tom Macdonald and Grady Wilson. Macdonald and Wilson would fly "chase" behind Aircraft 4 in a twin-engine King Air turboprop plane, a standard practice with experimental aircraft such as the Osprey. With mechanics still working on Aircraft 4, Wilson could see that Sullivan was wound up tight. A former Army pilot and a U.S. Naval Test Pilot School graduate, Sullivan was forty-three. On Friday, he had given an engagement ring to his twenty-nine-year-old girlfriend, Sandy Knott, a flight operations assistant at Boeing in Ridley Park, who had come to Florida for the weekend. Once Sullivan got Aircraft 4 home, he and Sandy were planning to fly to Las Vegas, get married, and have a honeymoon. They had eaten lunch together that Sunday, then Sandy had driven to the airport to fly home while Pat went back to work. There was still a lot to do before Aircraft 4 could be cleared to fly to Quantico the next morning. One way or another, Sullivan had a lot on his mind.

Sullivan stayed at the hangar with the Boeing mechanics until nine that night. Wilson and Macdonald went to the bar in the Fort Walton Beach Sheraton to have a beer with Marine mechanics Leader and Joyce, who would be part of Aircraft 4's crew the next day. They spread maps on the table and talked about the flight plan. Joyce had been added to the crew just a couple of days earlier and was elated. Normal practice is to keep the crew flying an experimental aircraft to a minimum, putting as few people as possible at risk. Technically, Aircraft 4 needed only two

pilots, an engineer to handle its flight test instrumentation, and one crew
chief to operate the rear ramp and watch for problems to the sides and
rear as the Osprey flew. In early July, though, Boeing's test team leaders
had decided to send a crew of seven. In addition to two pilots, Aircraft
4 would fly with two engineers, Bob Rayburn and Jerry Mayan, and
two mechanics, Marty LeCloux and Tony Stecyk. To please the generals at Quantico, a Marine Corps crew chief, Master Gunnery Sergeant
Leader, would be on board as well. Gunnery Sergeant Joyce had been
left out originally, which had disappointed him. Joyce got his chance to
fly on Aircraft 4 when mechanic LeCloux, fifty-four, told his boss that
if he flew to Quantico, the company would need to fly him back to Destin so he could drive his wife home. Told that Boeing wouldn't do that,
LeCloux declined to go on Aircraft 4, and Boeing offered the Marines
the seat. Joyce jumped at the chance.

Engineer Jerry Mayan gladly would have given Joyce his seat. Tears
of joy had welled in Mayan's eyes a couple of years back when his boss
asked if he wanted to be Aircraft 4's lead instrumentation engineer, but
Mayan disliked flying. He suffered motion sickness so severe he had to
wear a medicated patch behind his ear to keep from getting nauseous
when he flew. If he refused the assignment, though, Mayan told his wife,
Kathi, he might have to look for another job. His bosses had made it
clear they wanted their best people on Aircraft 4's important flight to
Quantico.

★ ★ ★

That Monday morning, Michelle and Tony Stecyk rose at 3 A.M. to prepare for their departures. While Tony flew east on the Osprey, Michelle
would drive herself and Little Anthony back to Pennsylvania in her car.
Her mother, Doris Mahler, and a family friend, Joseph "Buddy" Connor, would drive Tony's pickup truck, pulling a trailer full of Harleys
he had bought in Florida. Tony had flown Doris and Buddy to Florida
for that purpose after he was chosen to fly back on the Osprey. Sunday
night they'd all gone out to dinner to celebrate Buddy's birthday. At the
restaurant, Tony kept explaining to Little Anthony that he wouldn't see
Daddy for a week, but next Friday, Mommy and Little Anthony would
pick Daddy up at the airport.

By 5 A.M. Monday, everything was ready to go, so Michelle drove
Tony to Eglin. At the gate, Tony said he felt guilty about leaving her and

her mother to make the eighteen-hour drive home without him. Maybe he should do like Marty LeCloux and just tell Boeing he couldn't fly today, he said. Michelle wouldn't hear of it. "This is something you've wanted to do," she said. "You're already set and ready to go." He'd worked as hard as anyone else, she reminded him. He deserved to step off the Osprey at Quantico and be applauded by all the big shots. Michelle watched Tony walk through the base gate, then drove back to Blue Water Bay to check out and start the trip home.

About four hours later, aboard Aircraft 4, Sullivan told Stecyk over the internal communication system: "Okay, Tony, get her buttoned up as soon as you can so we can get going." Stecyk was in the back cabin with engineer Mayan and crew chiefs Leader and Joyce. Mayan had a seat near a big pallet of test instruments toward the rear of the Osprey. Engineer Bob Rayburn would sit in a fold-down jump seat between and just behind the pilots in the cockpit, where Sullivan was in the left seat and Major Brian James in the right. It was 9:48 A.M., Aircraft 4's rotors were turning, and they were finally ready to go, but running late. Sullivan had expected to depart a couple of hours earlier than this when he'd assured his bosses Aircraft 4 would be at Quantico by 3 P.M. Eastern Daylight Time. Eglin Air Force Base was on Central Daylight Time, so their planned arrival time at Quantico was just over four hours away.

Mechanics had begun a final preflight inspection at 6:30 A.M. At 6:49, the crew synchronized the flight test and data monitoring instruments on board, including a tape recorder to preserve what the crew said throughout the trip. They had to postpone their takeoff when the inspection found a pop-up button protruding from an oil filter in the mid-wing gearbox, a sign the filter was so clogged it needed changing. Stecyk pulled the filter and replaced it, and by 8 A.M., they thought they were ready to go. On reinspection, though, Stecyk discovered the pop-up button triggered again and had to do more work on the gearbox. Then, when Sullivan tried to start the engines, the APU balked, shutting down before the turbines could power up. An advisory on a display screen told Sullivan the APU was overheating. Messages like that were often caused by faulty sensors instead of real problems in the prototype Ospreys, and pilots could override an APU shutdown by setting the device to "emergency start." The feature was meant to let combat pilots fly out of danger, and using it could damage the APU. If Sullivan overrode the shutdown, the APU might not restart after they turned off Aircraft 4's engines to refuel in Charlotte. With his window for getting to Quantico by 3 P.M. narrowing, Sullivan took the gamble.

The engines were roaring as Stecyk got the wheel chocks removed and closed the side door and rear ramp. Sullivan told James to taxi out to Eglin's runway 01.

* * *

At 9:53 A.M., Aircraft 4 begins rolling, nacelles pointed straight up, big rotors turning. James pauses the Osprey while an F-16 fighter plane takes off, then turns onto the runway.

"Okay, I'm just going to get a little more to center, if that's okay with you, Pat," James says. "I know we're in a hurry."

At 9:55 A.M., with Sullivan coaching him, James begins his fifth flight hour in an Osprey, tilting the nacelles forward gradually to make a rolling takeoff, which uses less fuel than taking off like a helicopter. For those in the back cabin, the takeoff feels like a ride in a dragster. As the engines start delivering full power, the acceleration presses their bodies rearward. The feeling is one reason the few pilots and crew chiefs who've had a chance to fly in the Osprey love it. The old joke is that helicopters don't fly, they beat the air into submission. The Osprey flies. Helicopters rattle and vibrate, shuddering under their rotors. The Osprey, with its rotors on its wingtips, doesn't quake like a helicopter. The ride is smooth, and as its big proprotors bite into the air, Aircraft 4 climbs hungrily. As it does, James brings the rotors and nose to the same angle. Less than three minutes after leaving the ground, Sullivan reports to the Eglin tower that Osprey Nine One Four is passing through 1,000 feet, on its way to 15,500, their cruising altitude today.

As they climb, Sullivan takes the controls. He also radios the tower to ask that someone call Boeing pilots Grady Wilson and Tom Macdonald in the King Air chase plane and tell them Aircraft 4 is on its way. The King Air, with Lieutenant Colonel Martin aboard as a passenger, has been orbiting miles to the south for half an hour, awaiting word to join up with Aircraft 4. The chase plane pilots were expecting Sullivan to wait for them, but he's in too big a hurry. At 10:10, Sullivan radios Wilson that the Osprey is at 14,500 feet and flying 180 knots on a course that will take them over Eufaula, Alabama. "Okay," Wilson says. "We'll try to catch up, Pard."

The weather is clear, and it's a perfect day to fly. Six minutes after talking to Wilson, though, Sullivan tells his crew they have a problem. "RTB Rotor," he reports, reading a display screen warning that means "Return to Base—Rotor." Aircraft 4's flight clearance, a list of do's and don'ts, requires Sullivan to land as soon as possible with such a caution. Sullivan tells James to take the controls while he, Rayburn, and Mayan discuss things. After four minutes, Rayburn tells Sullivan: "Okay, if we can't, ah, isolate that rotor, we're going to have to come down."

"Come down where, Bob?" Sullivan replies.

"That's urgent," Rayburn tells him. "That's a 'return to base.' You can't continue."

"Well, I know," Sullivan says. "We'll have to go back to Eglin."

"Right," Rayburn agrees.

"Any other troubleshooting we can do?" Sullivan asks hopefully.

"We're working on it," Rayburn assures him.

"Okay. We might as well push on and see what—you know, see what you can come up with," Sullivan says. "We've got plenty of fuel to turn around." Sullivan doesn't want to return to base. He wants to get to Quantico today, as he's promised his bosses.

Five minutes later, Rayburn tells Sullivan the problem appears to be a loose wire, judging by readings from an instrument in back. "Probably we don't have any kind of clearance to continue with that," Rayburn adds. "How do you call it?" Others can offer advice during a flight, but the pilot in command, like a ship's captain, holds the final authority.

"Well, you—you say you think it's a wire?" Sullivan replies. "Or not, do not think it's a wire?"

"We're pretty sure it is a wire."

"I say we continue, then," Sullivan decides. He asks copilot James if he has any objection.

"No," James says. "I can live with that."

A few seconds later, Sullivan asks Rayburn to calculate how much longer they can fly on the fuel remaining. "We'll have five sixty-seven miles to go," Sullivan says, citing the remaining distance to Quantico. Sullivan doesn't say so, but less than thirty minutes into the flight, he's thinking about skipping the refueling stop in Charlotte. If they land there, they might not make it to Quantico, for two reasons. First, the APU might not restart the engines. More important, after landing with a "Return to Base" warning, taking off again will be a major safety violation. Boeing and the Osprey program office at Navair want Aircraft 4 at Quantico today. Sullivan is determined to get it there.

As Rayburn works on the fuel calculation, Wilson radios from the chase plane to ask what Sullivan has decided.

"If things stay as they are, we're going to go ahead and continue," Sullivan tells him. "And also, we're going to have to make a call to push to Quantico, if fuel flow and distance allow it."

Wilson replies that he and Macdonald can't understand what Sullivan is saying because of static on the radio but assume he's decided to continue the flight.

"A little excitement in the beginning, huh?" James says to Sullivan.

At 10:32, Rayburn gives Sullivan their fuel status. "Two and a half hours to flame out," Rayburn tells him, adding that the Osprey is cruising at a ground speed of 240 knots, or 276 miles an hour. Two minutes later, Wilson radios to say the Osprey is leaving its chase plane behind. "We're pedaling as hard as we can," Wilson says. "We just can't catch up. You got too much on us."

"Understand," Sullivan replies.

Just then, Rayburn tells Sullivan they've lost all ability to monitor whether the left rotor is functioning properly. All sensor readings are "breaking up," he says. "They're all fluctuating, bouncing. Probably a slip ring wiring problem." A slip ring is a tube that conveys electricity to the Osprey's rotor heads through wire brushes. It powers sensors that measure vibration and other stresses on the rotor head and swashplate actuators and warn if they are exceeding their limits. A slip ring failure on the ground would keep an Osprey from flying until repaired.

Eight minutes after Rayburn gives Sullivan the slip ring diagnosis, a radio signal tells the pilots they are near Eufaula. "About five hundred miles to go," Sullivan says. It is 10:43 A.M.

Two minutes later, Rayburn reports a new fuel calculation. Boeing's rules require them to land with thirty minutes' worth of fuel, usually about a thousand pounds. "Unless we pick up some more headwind, I show us on the ground with seven hundred pounds, total," Rayburn says.

"That's at Charlotte? For Charlotte?" Sullivan asks.

"That would be Quantico."

"Wow," Sullivan says.

"We'd have the oodles to get to Charlotte," Rayburn says. "But you had asked me about Quantico, right?"

"Yes," Sullivan replies.

Two minutes later, Sullivan tells James, "Appreciate your hanging with us, Brian."

"What's that, now?" asks James, who has been navigating their course.

"This has not been an easy start up and go," Sullivan says. "I appreciate you hanging with us."

"Hey, man, this is my job," the young major tells him. "I'm loving it."

Within minutes, Aircraft 4 has crossed the Georgia state line and entered Eastern Daylight Time. At 11:53 A.M. EDT, Sullivan radios Wilson in the chase plane to tell him where the Osprey is. "We're going to look at pushing all the way to Quantico," Sullivan says. "Would you guys be able to make that?"

"Negative," Wilson replies. The King Air has burned too much fuel trying in vain to catch up to Aircraft 4.

"Okay," Sullivan says.

Shortly after noon, Sullivan and Rayburn talk again about fuel. At the speed they're flying, Rayburn reports, there's enough for two hours. Quantico is now about 470 miles distant, and Rayburn calculates they can get there in about an hour and forty minutes. The key question is whether they can arrive with a thousand pounds of fuel in reserve, as required.

"Well, it's doable," Sullivan says. "Let's keep an eye on things and make a decision outside of Charlotte. I think we ought to push it if it's feasible, because otherwise we're . . . you know, we'd never get out of Charlotte."

"Yeah," James agrees. "I personally don't have a problem with that, Pat." James says he's worried, though, about how Lieutenant Colonel Martin is going to react if they skip Charlotte, where Martin is supposed to replace James as copilot. "Hey, Pat," James says, "if you decide to go to Quantico, could you ask Grady to pass that to the colonel, and at least give him an opportunity to comment?"

"Yeah, okay," Sullivan says.

"I mean, I know you guys are the boss, but at least that makes it look like I tried," James says.

At 12:15, James perks up when he notices they're just six miles from Greenwood, South Carolina, about one hundred miles south of Charlotte. "Shee-dawgie!" the major exclaims.

"Yeah, beats a Phrog," Sullivan says, referring to the CH-46.

"We're humming," James adds a minute later.

A minute after that, Sullivan radios their position to Wilson and Macdonald. "We're going to make a decision here pretty quick, and perhaps proceed to Quantico," Sullivan tells them.

Three minutes later, Charlotte comes into view.

"How much time to Quantico, do you estimate?" James asks.

Rayburn replies: "About an hour and twenty-four minutes, twenty-five minutes, to Quantico." He and Sullivan discuss how much fuel they'll have left if they continue past Charlotte. Rayburn estimates they'll use 40 percent of their reserve, but Sullivan notes that they'll burn fuel less rapidly as they descend.

"Okay," Sullivan says at 12:23, "anybody have any problem with proceeding?"

"You just got to defend me when we get there," James says.

At 12:24, Sullivan radios the chase plane that the Osprey is going straight through to Quantico. He asks Wilson and Macdonald to call ahead when they land at Charlotte to alert the Marine base that the Osprey will arrive early.

"Could you ask them to pass that to Colonel Martin?" James says. "I know they will anyway, but I wanted to make it seem like I'm . . ."

"Oh, they will, Brian," Sullivan breaks in. "They got an overhead speaker."

"He's going to chew my ass, boy," James says. "Woooh! It'll be worth it, but I tell you what, I'm going to stay away from him."

"Yeah," Sullivan replies.

"He's going to be pissed, I'm telling you," James tells Sullivan a minute later. "Ooh, boy! He'll understand what you're trying to do, though, too."

"If we go into Charlotte, we—we were not getting out today," Sullivan offers. "And you know, I don't—I don't think there's any safety issues."

Neither Sullivan nor anyone else aboard has any way of knowing it, but as they fly, liquid from a leak somewhere has been pooling in the cowling of their right nacelle, a covering on the engine's mouth whose purpose is to improve aerodynamics. The liquid is flammable.

★ ★ ★

Two minutes later, James says everyone aboard will have to say they agreed with Sullivan's decision to skip Charlotte, "because I guarantee when we stop they're going to be asking us. I feel comfortable. I would not have flown, believe me—I've got four kids—I would not have done it."

"Yeah, I know," Sullivan says. "I hear you."

Martin is going to be angry in any case, James predicts. "And when I step out and if the commandant's there?"

★ ★ ★

The commandant, General Carl Mundy, had planned to be at Quantico when Aircraft 4 arrived. Banners advertising the arrival for 1430 hours, 2:30 P.M., this Monday have been hung at Headquarters Marine Corps. Following Cheney's decision less than three weeks ago to offer Congress a compromise on the Osprey, though, Mundy has decided not to risk agitating the defense secretary. Colonel Jim Schaefer, the Osprey program manager, has been told to host the event at Quantico instead.

As Aircraft 4 flies across North Carolina, Schaefer is driving to Quantico, expecting the Osprey between 2:30 and 3 P.M. With him are his wife, a neighbor, and a friend's daughter. They all want to see the exotic tiltrotor firsthand.

Major Kevin Dodge of the Multiservice Operational Test Team is at Quantico already. Dodge and the other Marines in the MOTT are also assigned to HMX-1, the eighty-pilot special squadron that flies the president and other government VIPs in helicopters and tests new rotorcraft for the Marines. Dodge is in his office at HMX-1 headquarters, getting ready for Aircraft 4's arrival. He's looking forward to using the Osprey this week, and to seeing Brian James, one of his best friends in the Marine Corps. Dodge and James went through flight school together, flew in the same CH-46 Sea Knight squadron, served in Beirut together. They've hit the bars in ports around the world. Dodge enjoys James, a tall, good-looking guy with wavy brown hair who's always cracking jokes in his inner-city Baltimore twang. They talked on the phone Sunday night and had a good laugh about how two knuckleheads like Brian James and Kevin Dodge might soon be running both types of flight testing, developmental and operational, for the Marine Corps' most prized aviation program. Dodge is eager to see James again.

★ ★ ★

At 1:05 P.M., over South Boston, Virginia, Sullivan begins a slow descent to 10,500 feet. "I have a big feeling the colonel is going to chew my ass," James says. "He's been planning on doing this for so long."

"I know. I know," Sullivan says.

"What can I tell him, Pat?"

"Tell him I whined so hard that they got sick of listening to me and . . ."

"I'm going to say, 'Pat overruled me,'" James interrupts. "I'm just going to take it like a man."

"Yeah."

"There's nothing I could have done anyway to convince you, would it have?" James ventures.

"No."

"That's why—"

"Yeah, you could have," Sullivan interrupts.

"I could have called it safety—called it safety of flight, but I couldn't—I couldn't do that, though," James says.

"No, I don't think so," Sullivan agrees.

Two minutes later, James asks Sullivan to let him take the controls again. "Might as well enjoy them now," James says. "Might be the last time I get them, after Colonel Martin gets a hold of me."

At 1:21 P.M., Sullivan is talking to the Quantico control tower on the radio. "Osprey Nine One Four will be requesting a high-speed flyby down runway two," he says.

Two minutes later, Sullivan takes the controls back from James. They discuss the best way to execute the flyby, a way to show off the Osprey's speed in airplane mode.

"Make it gentle on the flyby," Rayburn urges.

"Okay. Yeah, it will be," Sullivan replies. "I always fly this thing gentle."

"Yeah, I know," Rayburn says. "Extra gentle. Kid gloves."

"Extra gentle, okay," Sullivan promises. "I can do that."

Fifteen minutes later, Sullivan is descending to 1,500 feet with the Quantico Marine Base and the Potomac River in sight.

"Boy, is the colonel going to be pissed," James says.

"I'm going to tell him you didn't argue one bit, sir," Gunnery Sergeant Joyce teases from the back cabin.

"Aw, you can ruin my career if you do that, Gunny!" James replies in mock horror. "There's the runway, you can see it," he tells Sullivan.

As Sullivan brings the Osprey down through 1,000 feet, on the way to 500 for the flyby, James can hardly contain himself. "I'm sure the general will be here at the field," he says, meaning the commandant.

"If he's here yet," engineer Rayburn interjects. They're nearly an hour ahead of their most optimistic schedule.

A minute later, they see the Quantico runway. "All the people are going to be sitting about—you see where the cross runway is?" James says.

"Yeah," says Sullivan.

"They'll come up and should be sitting in stands just halfway between the runway and the hangars, if there are people there."

"Yeah," Sullivan says. "I don't see many."

"Well, good," James says. "I mean, that's good for me. Make sure you tell the colonel that."

As Sullivan executes his flyby at 500 feet, zooming past the airfield at 238 knots, he tells James: "See, nobody there."

"Good," James says.

"Yeah, there are," Rayburn interjects. "There's a few there." It is 1:40 P.M.

★ ★ ★

Rayburn is seeing Major Dodge, other members of his MOTT test team, a handful of Marines from HMX-1, and a few Boeing and Bell engineers and executives. Alerted by radio that Aircraft 4 is coming in early, they've gathered on the flight ramp to watch the Osprey do its flyby and land. After buzzing the field, Sullivan climbs back up to about 1,300 feet and makes a broad left turn across the Potomac. Now he is flying northward on the east side of the river, under scattered clouds. A Boeing employee standing next to Dodge is videotaping Aircraft 4's approach as Sullivan begins tilting the Osprey's nacelles upward, converting the rotors from airplane mode as he gets ready to fly like a helicopter and make a vertical landing on the Quantico runway. In the cockpit, on Sullivan's instruction, James has started lowering the Osprey's landing gear.

Watching from the ground as the Osprey flies past a cloud in the distance, nacelles angled upward at 44 degrees, Dodge is alarmed to see a puff of dark smoke come from the front of its right nacelle. A second or two later, a muffled "poomf!" wafts across the river from the Osprey.

"Ooooh," James says in the cockpit, then adds four seconds later: "Noise, a weird sound."

From the ground, Dodge now sees the Osprey give off a puff of white smoke, then hears another "poomf!" A couple of seconds later, he sees yet another puff of white and hears a third "poomf!" Then he sees flames licking out of Aircraft 4's right nacelle.

SURVIVABILITY 229

In the cockpit, James tells Sullivan the landing gear is down.

"Okay," Sullivan says, then adds five seconds later: "Looks like an engine fail."

"We just lost the right engine," James confirms.

On the ground, Dodge watches as Aircraft 4 turns left, banking slightly, and heads toward him across the river, nacelles still midway between airplane and helicopter mode. Then he sees the right rotor begin to turn more slowly than the left. What he sees next seems surreal, as if happening in slow motion. Aircraft 4 is dropping from the sky. *My God,* Dodge thinks, *they're coming down.*

In the cockpit, at 1:42 P.M., James shouts into the radio: "Mayday, Mayday, we're going in! We're going in!"

Over the next five seconds, as those on the ground watch in disbelief, Aircraft 4 leans slightly right, then yaws left, sliding through the air like a car skidding through a curve. Its bulbous nose dips downward and the big tiltrotor almost seems exhausted. Suddenly, like the bird whose name it bears, the Osprey plunges toward the river at terrifying speed. It does a ghastly belly flop onto the surface. A geyser of water sprays skyward. When the splash subsides, Aircraft 4 is simply gone.

* * *

A half hour or so later, the King Air chase plane neared the Marine base, having stopped in Charlotte to refuel. Grady Wilson was piloting, so Tom Macdonald radioed the Quantico tower to ask for landing instructions. The King Air couldn't land there today, the tower replied. Macdonald explained that they were part of the Osprey test team. "Stand by," the tower came back. "Orbit while we check that." As they waited, Macdonald and Wilson could hear the tower directing a search-and-rescue helicopter. Then the operator asked Macdonald and Wilson what color flight suits Boeing pilots wore.

"Oh, God, I know what that is," Wilson said.

About ten minutes later, after confirming there had been an accident at the field, the tower gave Wilson and Macdonald permission to land.

"You know what's happened," Wilson said as he began their approach. "This is not going to be pretty. Stay with me on the controls, because my knees are shaking so, I don't know whether I can get this thing down or not."

As they descended over the Potomac, they could see boats in the water and a helicopter hovering over the river. After taxiing to a stop, Wilson asked Macdonald to shut down the aircraft, then rushed to the back and opened the King Air's ramp. Ken Lunn, the head of Osprey flight-testing for Boeing, met him there. Lunn asked if they knew what had happened.

"You son of a bitches killed them, didn't you?" Wilson snarled. Then he walked away, over to the airfield fence, sat down on the ground, and wept.

When Macdonald got off the King Air, Lunn spoke to him, too. "I've got terrible news," Lunn said. "Ship Four has crashed out there in the Potomac. We're looking for survivors now."

★ ★ ★

Michelle Stecyk was driving up Interstate 85 near Greenville, South Carolina, that afternoon, listening to music on cassette tapes while two-year-old Little Anthony slept in his baby chair on the backseat. She was following her mother and their family friend, Buddy, who were driving Tony Stecyk's pickup truck and pulling his trailer full of Harleys. They had been on the road since an hour or so after Michelle dropped Tony at Eglin Air Force Base that morning, but they had stopped a few miles back for gas, so Michelle was surprised when her mother put on a turn signal to exit the interstate. *What the heck could they be stopping for?* Michelle wondered. When the pickup stopped on the roadside near a gas station, Michelle stepped out into the summer heat and started walking toward it. Her mother got out of the driver's side, walked to Michelle, and grabbed her arms. Michelle was surprised to see tears in her mother's eyes.

"Missy," her mother said. "We've been listening to the radio. They just said the V-22 'plummeted into the Potomac River and there are no survivors.'"

Michelle dropped to her knees.

★ ★ ★

Colonel Jim Schaefer had a mobile phone in his car. It rang that afternoon as he was driving through the gate at Quantico with his wife and the two civilian guests they'd invited to see the Osprey arrive. A member of Schaefer's team at Navair was on the line.

"It's down. It's down," he said.

"It's not going to get here for another hour and a half," Schaefer replied.

"You don't understand. It's down."

Schaefer thought he meant the Osprey was grounded in Charlotte for some mechanical reason. "Okay," Schaefer said, and hung up.

The phone rang again.

"You don't understand," the Navair employee said. "It's down in the river."

"What river?"

"The Potomac."

"It's not supposed to be here for another two hours or something."

"It got here early."

"Shit."

Schaefer drove to the Quantico air station gate, got out, and told his wife to take their guests home. Then he asked HMX-1's commander to temporarily take charge of the accident investigation. Major Dodge had started a rescue and recovery effort the moment Aircraft 4 went down. His first act was to seize the Boeing employee's videotape of the crash as evidence. The officers went to the air station headquarters to coordinate things. Soon, reporters and TV vans from various stations were crowding the chain link fence around the air station. Schaefer called the security detail and gave orders not to let the media inside: "Make sure that without proper military ID, no one gets through that gate. I don't care if it's goddamn Sam Donaldson."

Fishermen from the town of Quantico were on the river by now, looking for the Osprey's crew. Dodge was trying to contact Navy divers, find a salvage company to raise Aircraft 4 from the water, attend to dozens of details. He was keeping notes in the same green logbook he'd used to plan the tests the MOTT had hoped to do with Aircraft 4, only now, his handwriting was shaky.

The next day, Pentagon spokesman Pete Williams told reporters the crash raised "serious questions about the V-22 program." It was going to "significantly complicate our ability to proceed" with the compromise Cheney had offered Congress less than three weeks earlier, Williams said, "until we know more about what happened."

That evening, Curt Weldon and Pete Geren went to the floor of the House of Representatives to makes speeches about the tragedy. They expressed their condolences to the families of those killed. They also urged their colleagues in Congress not to "rush to judgment," as Geren put it. The Marines still "desperately" needed the Osprey, Geren said. "But we must look beyond that and show some vision in assessing the importance of this aircraft. The civilian applications are as broad as the imagination." Weldon noted that "in the last three years alone we have had nine accidents with the existing medium lift aircraft for the Marine Corps, most recently in March, where fourteen young Marines were killed when the CH-46 helicopter they were flying in went down."

As Geren had told the *Washington Post* earlier that day, Aircraft 4's crash came at an awkward time politically. "We're in the middle of trying to put together a compromise" with Cheney, Geren said, "and it's a fragile compromise."

Fellow Texas Democrat representative Charlie Wilson later offered Geren some solace. Crashes were nothing new in aviation, Wilson reminded him, especially military aviation. "If we canceled every program that crashed," Wilson told Geren, "Saddam Hussein would be drinking champagne in Riyadh today."

★ ★ ★

Navy scuba divers found Aircraft 4 lying twenty-seven feet below the surface of the river, mired in three feet of silt, the day after the crash. The left side windows of the cockpit were broken out, and the divers found Pat Sullivan still strapped into his seat. They released his harness and brought Sullivan's body to the surface. The other six crew members couldn't be found that day.

At 6:30 A.M. Wednesday, two days after the crash, two crabbers in a boat found Master Gunnery Sergeant Gary Leader's body floating on the Potomac two miles south of where Aircraft 4 went down. An hour and a half later, crabbers found flight test engineer Bob Rayburn's body floating nearby. Gunnery Sergeant Sean Joyce's body was found a mile farther upstream a couple of hours later. That afternoon, divers found the body of Major Brian James on the river bottom, still strapped into his seat but thrown fifteen feet forward of Aircraft 4's wreckage. An hour later, a search-and-rescue helicopter crew spotted Tony Stecyk's body floating a mile south of the crash site. On Thursday, as a salvage crew used a hoist line to raise part of Aircraft 4's wing out of the river, Jerry Mayan's body floated to the surface.

A Naval Court of Inquiry concluded that Aircraft 4 was falling at a rate of 6,300 feet per minute when it hit the water, impacting with seventy-nine times the force of gravity. The court said the impact was "well beyond the structural capabilities of the fuselage or human endurance." Jim Schaefer never forgot seeing coins found in the pockets of some of Aircraft 4's crew. They were bent.

* * *

On July 31, Boeing Helicopter Company held a memorial service for the crew of Aircraft 4 on the flight ramp at its Ridley Park plant. Several hundred Boeing Helicopter employees and officials from Boeing, Bell, Navair, and the Marine Corps attended. No media were allowed to cover the event.

By then, all seven of the crew had been buried. They left six widows and thirteen children. Yvonne Joyce lost both her husband, Sean Joyce, and her brother, Gary Leader. Sandy Knott, the Boeing secretary who had accepted Sullivan's marriage proposal two days before his last flight, had expected to be on her honeymoon that Friday evening.

Kathi Mayan, engineer Jerry Mayan's wife, didn't want to attend Boeing's memorial service. She was bitter. She couldn't get out of her mind how Jerry had told her he didn't want to make the flight but his bosses were pressuring him to go. Relatives talked Kathi into going to the service, but she was in a daze. She hardly noticed as eulogies were read, a Boeing employee sang "Amazing Grace," and a lone Marine Corps bugler at one end of the airfield played taps. Each of the children left by Aircraft 4's crew was given a $10,000 savings bond, bought with personal contributions from Boeing employees.

Michelle Stecyk buried her husband Tony at Edgewood Memorial Park in Delaware County under a bronze marker decorated with two etchings: the Harley-Davidson logo and a V-22 Osprey, shown with its nacelles pointing toward heaven. For about two years after the crash, Little Anthony often asked his mother whether it was Friday. "Daddy said we're picking him up on Friday," the little boy would remind her.

* * *

Eleven days before the 1992 presidential election, on October 23, 1992, Boeing held another ceremony on the flight ramp at Ridley Park. Shortly before noon that crisp autumn Friday, a motorcade pulled through one of the gates of the plant on Pennsylvania Highway 291, which runs through the facility. Outside the property, protesters waving anti-Republican placards lined the highway. They knew Vice President Dan Quayle was riding in one of the cars, accompanied by local congressman Curt Weldon, who had arranged for his fellow Republican's visit. Inside the fence waited a couple of thousand Boeing workers, mostly United Auto Workers members. Many, Weldon knew, were as resentful as the anti-Republican protesters outside toward an administration that for four years had tried to kill the Osprey, and with it a lot of jobs at Ridley Park. Reluctantly, local UAW leaders had agreed to sit on a stage with Quayle as he delivered a speech because Weldon had been their ally on the Osprey—and because Quayle was coming with good news.

The vice president's stop at Ridley Park was billed as "official business" but hardly could have been more political. Democratic presidential nominee Bill Clinton had led President Bush in the polls since July. Bush needed to win Pennsylvania to be reelected, Weldon kept telling the White House, and a show of support for the Osprey might get as many as ten thousand votes from Boeing workers and their relatives. Quayle was in Ridley Park to do that, though Cheney's position on the Osprey hadn't changed.

Cheney had offered only to fund some new Osprey prototypes while the Pentagon studied helicopter alternatives. Under his plan, the Air Force version of the Osprey would be dropped, and the Pentagon would decide later whether to build the tiltrotor for the Marines. Carrying that plan out fell to Sean O'Keefe, who as Pentagon comptroller for the past four years had been trying to kill the Osprey. O'Keefe was now acting Navy secretary, a post Cheney had gotten him named to after the incumbent resigned. Weldon and others in the Osprey camp were suspicious of O'Keefe, who had told a House Armed Services Committee hearing in August he wasn't sure the Marines really needed an aircraft that could fly 2,100 miles unrefueled and cruise at 250 knots. O'Keefe said the Navy Department still intended to give Bell and Boeing a contract to build new Osprey prototypes "as fast as we possibly can," but that would have to await the results of the investigation into the crash of Aircraft 4.

★ ★ ★

The Navy Department announced the preliminary results of the Aircraft 4 crash investigation in late September, laying the blame on "mechanical failure." Analyses of wreckage pulled from the Potomac and data from the aircraft's flight test instrumentation showed that the seed of the disaster was sown as Sullivan and James flew Aircraft 4 the two hours and forty-seven minutes it took to get from Eglin to Quantico. A Naval Court of Inquiry concluded that combustible fluid of some sort—exactly what fluid was later disputed—had been leaking inside the right nacelle as Aircraft 4 flew. Investigators said the fluid probably was oil from the right proprotor gearbox, leaking through a seal installed backward as mechanics were rushing to get Aircraft 4 ready to leave Eglin. As the prototype flew, the investigators concluded, the oil pooled in the bottom of the engine cowling. As long as the Osprey was flying like an airplane, nacelles horizontal, the oil just sat there. As Sullivan started tilting the nacelles upward to land like a helicopter at Quantico, though, the liquid poured into the engine's red-hot interior. The extra fluid choked the air flow into the engine, which set the fluid on fire and burped it back out its nose. The flash fire burned through a wall dividing the engine from the upper part of the nacelle, which houses rotor components. The gulp of what in effect was extra fuel also caused the engine to surge, creating the first puff of dark smoke seen by witnesses on the ground.

As in nearly every aircraft disaster, this first malfunction set off a deadly chain reaction. The surge triggered a governor designed to prevent the Osprey's engines from overspeeding. That disengaged the engines for a moment and flashed a flight control system caution light on the pilots' cockpit display screens. "Let's get a reset," Sullivan had said when he saw the light, then he or James reset the computerized flight control system. This standard practice—a way to make sure the problem was real, not a false alarm caused by a computer error—caused a rapid power increase to both engines, overspeeding both. In a matter of seconds, the already-damaged right engine failed.

Theoretically, Aircraft 4 could have survived even then. One of the Osprey's key survivability requirements was to be able to fly on one engine, a tricky task in a machine with two rotors driven by two engines separated by a wing nearly 46 feet long. As in Bell Helicopter's XV-15, the solution was to link the Osprey's rotors so one engine could turn both. This was accomplished by running an "interconnecting driveshaft" through the wing. Inside the nacelles, this connection had to turn a corner to reach the rotor, so there was another, shorter "pylon driveshaft" located above and parallel to each engine. To save weight, the pylon driveshaft had been made of composites, a tube of carbon wound with a skin of fiberglass and epoxy resin, materials that melt at 240 degrees Fahrenheit. The flash fire in Aircraft 4's right nacelle hit an estimated 900 degrees, melting the pylon driveshaft enough that its torque twisted it into useless deformity. At that point, its link to the still-healthy left engine gone, Aircraft 4's right rotor began to stop. The deformed pylon shaft, meanwhile, sliced through hydraulic and electric lines, causing the Osprey's flight control computer to fail and freezing the nacelles at their final 58-degree angle. Aircraft 4 and its seven-member crew were doomed.

Many who studied the accident said it might not have happened if Aircraft 4 had landed in Charlotte as planned. By then, too little fluid might have pooled in the right nacelle's cowling to start a fire when it drained into the engine. Many also said Pat Sullivan surely would have landed in Charlotte if he hadn't felt pressured to get Aircraft 4 to Quantico so the generals could see it. The Naval Court of Inquiry concluded, "There was tremendous pressure on Mr. Sullivan to get the aircraft to Quantico at the proper time on Monday, 20 July."

Boeing denied that management pressure was a factor. In a groundbreaking investigation of the crash published on November 14, 1993, however, reporter Nathan Gorenstein of the *Philadelphia Inquirer* cited contrary evidence in an "internal Boeing review of the company's test flight operations" he had obtained. The review, Gorenstein reported, "concluded that the V-22 and other Boeing Helicopters test flight programs had a 'high probability of safety being compromised due to budget and schedule pressures.'"

No one could ever know whether Aircraft 4's crew would have lived had they landed in Charlotte or earlier, as the Court of Inquiry said Sullivan should have done when he got the "Return to Base—Rotor" warning. No one could know if it was pressure from his bosses that led Sullivan to fly on despite the safety risk. No one could prove that after the abuse it had taken in the McKinley lab, the Osprey simply wasn't ready to fly that day, though the Naval Court of Inquiry found "various Boeing personnel made decisions which were not consistent with flight safety." Nor could anyone prove, at least not to a jury's satisfaction, that the fluid pooling in Aircraft 4's engine cowling as it flew was oil from the improperly installed seal. In a case that lasted nearly a decade,

Pat Sullivan's two children from his first marriage and three of the widows—Michelle Stecyk, Kathi Mayan, and Bob Rayburn's wife, Dorothy—sued Bell and the companies who made the Osprey's engines, the oil seal, and related parts. The families' lawyers argued that the companies were negligent in designing an oil seal that could be installed backward. Weary after years of pretrial motions and delays, Michelle Stecyk and the Sullivan children took a settlement from the companies. Kathi Mayan and Dorothy Rayburn persisted and lost the case after a six-week jury trial. An expert witness for the companies, an MIT materials engineering professor, testified that in his opinion, leaking hydraulic fluid had caused the fire. The trial judge barred from evidence the fact that, after the crash, the companies designed a new oil seal that couldn't be reversed. A federal appeals court upheld the verdict.

As the Court of Inquiry was taking testimony that summer and fall, Democrat Bill Clinton and his presidential running mate, Tennessee senator Al Gore, were using the Osprey as an issue against Bush and Quayle. Clinton and Gore said they would build the Osprey if elected because the tiltrotor was an example of "dual-use technology"—items that could be made for the military but converted to civilian use. Clinton endorsed the Osprey in an August speech in San Antonio. In September, Gore visited Bell Helicopter's Plant 6 and said the tiltrotor could "revolutionize the air transport infrastructure for this country." Clinton endorsed the Osprey again in a televised debate with Bush on October 11.

Eleven days after that debate, Navair gave Bell and Boeing a "letter contract"—precise terms to be settled later—to build four new Osprey prototypes and modify two of those built under the original Full Scale Development contract. The new Osprey program would be called Engineering and Manufacturing Development, newly adopted Pentagon jargon for what used to be called Full Scale Development.

In golf, a player who takes a second shot from the tee after flubbing the first is said to be "taking a mulligan." In essence, the Pentagon was giving Bell and Boeing a mulligan on the Osprey. During the new EMD phase of the Osprey program—called "E, M, D" by insiders—Bell and Boeing would get a chance to redesign the Osprey to solve the FSD version's major problems, starting with weight. Best of all for the companies, the EMD contract replaced the fixed-price FSD contract former Navy Secretary John Lehman had insisted on, which had cost Bell and Boeing—or saved the government, depending on your point of view— more than $300 million. Company executives were ecstatic.

The day after the EMD contract was awarded, Quayle paid his visit to Ridley Park to claim credit for a program the Bush administration had been trying to kill for four years. First he went to an indoor reception with Boeing executives and others. They gave him a gift the company's public relations staff had thought up, and gotten some laughs doing it: a white baseball warm-up jacket with "Dan Quayle" stitched in red over the left breast and on the back, in large red letters: "V-22 Osprey." The PR people loved the idea of the number-two man in an administration that had been trying to cancel the Osprey for years wearing a jacket advertising it. Quayle slipped the jacket on, smiling broadly, and went outside with Weldon and the executives to the flight ramp. They passed beneath a huge banner that read "V-22—America's Airplane" and walked onto a stage equipped with a lectern and a model of the Osprey. Boeing employees waved American flags and cheered as Weldon spoke, telling them, "I told you this day would come. And it's here!" Quayle followed, getting polite applause. "I am proud to announce a $1.4 billion contract to develop the V-22 aircraft, America's airplane," Quayle declared, beaming enthusiasm. A big replica of a check for $550 million—the first year's funding—was propped up on an easel nearby.

After Quayle left, the general manager of Boeing Helicopter, Ed Renouard, phoned Colonel Jim Schaefer to tell him about the visit. "You wouldn't believe it," Renouard said. "He put on our jacket and did a big old Rocky/Stallone 'yeahhhh' type thing."

After talking to Renouard, Schaefer convened a conference call with some of the Osprey program's top managers at Navair. "Guys," Schaefer said, "we're back in."

Dick Spivey, who was in Fort Worth that day, wasn't so sure. Spivey wanted to believe the struggle with Cheney was over, that the Osprey was now politically secure after the bitter four-year political battle he'd helped wage. When he saw a photo of Quayle in his V-22 Osprey jacket, though, acting as if "we just came up with a great idea," Spivey could only shake his head. How smoothly politicians could do U-turns. If it was that easy, what would keep Bush and Quayle from doing another U-turn if they were reelected?

Spivey had voted Republican all his life, partly because the Republicans spent more on defense. That was good for Bell Helicopter. This year, though, Spivey felt he had no choice. He voted for the Democrat, Clinton, who said he would build the Osprey. When Clinton won, Spivey felt like he was in hog heaven. His dream was alive.

CHAPTER NINE

ANOTHER PERIOD
OF DARKNESS

The sun was bright and the sky clear over Washington on Wednesday, September 8, 1999—perfect weather for watching a dream come true. Dick Spivey stood on a stone terrace outside the Pentagon's River Entrance that morning, looking over a grassy parade ground below and the Potomac River beyond. In less than three months, Spivey would turn fifty-nine; what remained of his once-red hair was now gray. Today, though, he felt like a kid on Christmas morning. Several hundred people were on the terrace, mostly U.S. military officers and Pentagon bureaucrats, but Spivey saw a sprinkling of foreign military uniforms as well. Lots of Marines were there, along with senior executives from Boeing Helicopter Company, Bell Helicopter, and Bell's corporate parent, Textron. Company public relations people were circulating among a gaggle of reporters and TV photographers. Spivey couldn't wait to see the looks on their faces when the show they were waiting for began.

More than a quarter century after he had started selling it, nearly eighteen years after the Marine Corps had caught his fever for it, a decade after former Defense Secretary Dick Cheney had started trying to kill it, and seven years after the terrible crash at Quantico, Dick Spivey was sure the dream he'd devoted his life to was finally becoming reality. Today people would see, as Spivey had believed for nearly forty years, that the Holy Grail of aviation—a machine offering full freedom of flight—had been found, and that it was the tiltrotor. The Marines were just as certain that, after years of waiting and fighting, they were finally getting their dream machine, the V-22 Osprey. That was why General James L. Jones, Jr., the commandant of the Marine Corps, had decided to hold today's event, Tiltrotor Technology Day at the Pentagon. It would begin with a little air show.

Spivey was going to enjoy the show, but he was there mainly to tell anyone who would listen about Bell's newest tiltrotor vision. Tents and booths were set up on the parade ground for contractors to display tiltrotor-related wares and other Marine Corps equipment. Spivey would be at Bell's display all day, talking up an idea called the Quad TiltRotor. He and three Bell engineers were applying for a patent on the concept: a tiltrotor more than twice the Osprey's size—so big it would need *two* wings and *four* rotors. The QTR, as Bell called it, would be large enough to carry ninety troops or 40,000 pounds of cargo—four times the advertised payload of the Osprey. It would be designed to fly as far as 2,000 miles and set down on a scrap of ground most anywhere in the world. It would be a dream machine most any military commander would want. Spivey had briefed General Jones on the QTR a couple of months before and the commandant was sold on the idea. It had been an easy sell. Jones had visited Fort Worth in 1997 and flown in the XV-15, the little tiltrotor demonstrator Bell had built for NASA in the 1970s and used as a potent marketing tool since the 1981 Paris Air Show. Jones loved it. He wasn't a pilot, but he was already talking about building a tiltrotor gunship the XV-15's size to go with the Osprey and the QTR. With a "family" of three different-sized tiltrotors, Jones figured, the Marines could replace *all* their helicopters. That was one reason Jones had arranged today's event.

The show formally kicked off at 9:15 A.M., when a military band on the terrace struck up a patriotic tune and Secretary of Defense William Cohen came out of the Pentagon to join the crowd. Soon a CH-46 Sea Knight, the tandem-rotor helicopter the Marines had wanted the Osprey to replace for years, came circling in and landed on the parade ground. Next came the XV-15. Then the star of the show arrived.

After flying past the Washington Monument, the first production model Osprey ever built came into view, rotors tilted up like a helicopter. The pilots were Marine Lieutenant Colonel Keith M. Sweaney and Air Force Lieutenant Colonel James Shaffer, the current leaders of the special unit formed in 1990 to test the Osprey, the Multiservice Operational Test Team, or MOTT. In the back cabin were Commandant Jones, Representative Curt Weldon of Pennsylvania, and a half dozen other members of Congress who had helped the Marines keep the Osprey alive. As a reward, the lawmakers had just gotten their first Osprey ride.

Shaffer and Sweaney exchanged grins and a thumbs-up as they brought the new Osprey in over a small stand of trees between the river and the parade ground and their rotor downwash only blew a few leaves and branches down. There was one less tree in the stand now than there had been before 8:20 A.M., when the pilots had flown in to pick up their VIP passengers. As Shaffer and Sweaney crossed over the trees that time, the hurricane-force downwash of the Osprey's massive proprotors knocked over a small oak, its roots probably loosened by torrential rains the night before. *This is going to be one of those days,* Shaffer thought as he saw the tree topple. Critics had always said the Osprey's downwash might make it unsuitable as a rescue aircraft at sea, maybe even unsafe for ground crews to hook cargo to as it hovered over them. Shaffer could only imagine what the critics would say when they heard he and Sweaney had felled an oak with their Osprey. To his relief and amazement, though, a crew of groundskeepers had swarmed out of the Pentagon within minutes, chopped up the tree, and thrown its remains into a van that appeared out of nowhere. By the time the commandant and his lawmaker guests had crossed the parade ground to board the Osprey, the evidence was gone. Even the hole the oak left in the earth was filled with fresh mulch. The reporters and guests hadn't gathered on the terrace by then, and the tree had stood on the opposite side of the grove from the parade ground. Even Spivey, who had been there at the time, hadn't noticed when the tree fell.

Jones and his guests didn't know it, but their Osprey flight hadn't been as smooth as it seemed, either. Shortly after taking off like a helicopter with the VIPs in back, Shaffer and Sweaney were chagrined to discover that one of the tiltrotor's two engines was delivering less than full power. The plan had been to fly the VIPs around Washington's approved helicopter routes with the nacelles tilted at 60 degrees, putting the rotors far enough forward to let the passengers feel the Osprey's power, but not far enough to exceed the capital's speed limit for helicopters. Now they were going to have to land as soon as possible, but trying to make a vertical landing back onto the parade ground without full power might be risky. Sweaney, forty-one, and Shaffer, thirty-nine, were Gulf War veterans, combat pilots who'd been in tighter spots than this. They quickly decided their best bet would be to convert the Osprey's nacelles all the way to zero degrees—airplane mode—to gain enough speed to get plenty of lift under the wing, then fly over to nearby Andrews Air Force Base.

They could convert the nacelles back to 60 degrees there and make a safe roll-on landing on a runway. As Shaffer began converting the nacelles, the Osprey leapt forward, sending bottles of water for the VIPs tumbling in the back cabin. Halfway to Andrews, though, Shaffer and Sweaney diagnosed the engine problem. Like many modern aircraft engines, the Osprey's were regulated by computer for maximum efficiency through devices called FADECs, pronounced "FAY-decks," an acronym for Full Authority Digital Engine Control. By switching the problem engine to a backup FADEC, the pilots were able to restore full power and complete the flight as originally planned. None of their VIP passengers was the wiser. When Shaffer set the Osprey down back at the Pentagon parade ground, Jones and his guests came walking down the back ramp with big smiles on their faces and joined Secretary Cohen at a lectern on the grass.

"Every few decades of this century, the world has witnessed the arrival of weapons platforms that have truly revolutionized national security," Cohen began, flanked by Jones and the lawmakers. "This technology is *the* revolution in military affairs," Cohen continued, using a popular phrase of the day. "These aircraft," he added, "through development and now into production, have stayed on time and within budget. And as the members of Congress will tell you today, that is no small accomplishment."

Cohen apparently was referring to the most recent batch of prototypes. As a program, the Osprey actually was eight years behind its original schedule and had cost nearly $3 billion more to develop than anticipated. No one asked Cohen to clarify what he meant, though, when he invited the reporters to pose questions.

"I'd like to ask you about Indonesia," the first journalist Cohen called on said. The Pentagon press corps was less interested in tiltrotors than in whether the United States might send troops to intervene in a crisis in East Timor.

"Does anybody here have a question about the V-22?" Cohen asked plaintively.

"Not really," another reporter replied.

Cohen started taking questions on East Timor.

The Osprey was no longer big news. As every cub reporter learns, "Man Bites Dog" is news; "Dog Bites Man" isn't much of a story, and certainly won't get you on the front page. In 1999, the Osprey was a dog-bites-man story.

★ ★ ★

If the media had largely lost interest in the Osprey, the Marines wanted it
more badly than ever. Over the past seven years, they had spent roughly
half a billion dollars to keep their Vietnam-era CH-46 helicopters flying
by upgrading engines and other parts to extend their service life from
10,000 to 15,000 flight hours. Over those years, seven Marine Corps
"Phrogs" had crashed, killing seventeen Marines and other passengers.
In 1998, General Charles Krulak, testifying to the Senate Armed Services Committee for one of the last times as commandant, said he was
looking for ways to speed up Osprey purchases. "I would tell you that
the greatest return on investment lies in procuring the V-22 tiltrotor
airplane as rapidly as possible," Krulak said. "There is no new capability
being procured by the DoD today which yields such a significant, such a
revolutionary difference, in our ability to fight the nation's battles, as the
V-22 Osprey." Krulak's enthusiasm for the Osprey got the better of him.
"Because it flies at speeds only achievable with a fixed-wing aircraft and
because it can refuel in flight, the Osprey can self-deploy," he told the
committee. "We can pick up combat-loaded Marines in CONUS [Con-
tinental United States] and move them to points of crisis quite literally
anywhere in the world." The Osprey never had been expected to carry
troops when it self-deployed, just aircrews, but no one contradicted the
commandant. His point was clear. The Osprey would give the Marine
Corps capabilities it had never before had. Now, a year after Krulak's
testimony, all that remained to be done before the Marines could field
the Osprey was for it to pass a final round of tests in realistic missions
and for the Pentagon to approve Full Rate Production. After that, once
enough were built and sufficient pilots and crews had been trained, the
Marines could start turning CH-46 squadrons into Osprey squadrons.
The target date for starting the transition was 2001.

The Marines and the Bell-Boeing partnership had been racing
toward that goal ever since President Bill Clinton's election in 1992,
which removed the Osprey's two biggest foes from the Pentagon. When
Bush administration Defense Secretary Dick Cheney departed, so did
David Chu, the Osprey skeptic who had run the powerful Office of Program Analysis & Evaluation for more than a decade. The Osprey had
been in the defense budget every year since their departure, though the
Marines and their allies on Capitol Hill had to work hard to keep it

there. With the Cold War over, sentiment for cutting defense spending ran high in the 1990s. Clinton shrank the size of all the armed forces, and in 1997, a top-level review decided a smaller Marine Corps needed fewer Ospreys. Instead of the 552 the Marines had long intended to buy, their future fleet now was to number only 360. The Air Force, cut out of the program in the Cheney years, now planned to buy 50 for its Special Operations Command. For the first time since the 1980s, the Navy was also back on record as wanting 48 Ospreys as search-and-rescue aircraft, though insiders said the admirals weren't really that interested. The total Osprey "buy," in Pentagon lingo, was now to be only 458, barely half the 913 that Bell and Boeing had hoped to sell all four armed services when the program began in 1983.

As with most major military purchases in those days, the Osprey buy also was going to be spread over more years to keep annual defense budgets down. The smaller buy, the stretched-out production schedule, and the cost of design changes, as well as inflation, were going to make the Osprey a lot more expensive than originally advertised. By the time mass production began, the cost of each Osprey was expected to average $55 million, though Bell and Boeing insisted they could get that sticker price down as they got better at producing them.

The companies said they could do that because now they had a cheaper design. Under the Engineering and Manufacturing Development contract announced at Ridley Park in 1992 by Dan Quayle when he was vice president, Bell and Boeing had made major changes in the aircraft. The redesigned Osprey was so different—about 80 percent of the engineering drawings were new—that it was designated the "B" model, with the Marine Corps version called the MV-22B and the Air Force version the CV-22B.

One of the biggest differences was using aluminum in key parts of the fuselage instead of composites, the carbon epoxy and other non-metal materials used in the first prototypes on the theory that would save weight. The theory had proven wrong. Using composites to make frames and formers—the skeleton of the fuselage—had turned out to be far more difficult and costly than anticipated. Boeing learned the hard way that arranging pliable strips of special fibers in layers thick enough to do that job, then baking them stiff in an autoclave, was a slow, labor-intensive, and inexact process. Two or three workers needed three to four weeks to make a frame, and no two frames ever came out of the autoclave with the same exact thickness and strength. In the 1980s, Boeing had been forced to throw out 30–40 percent of its composite frames, a huge loss in time and money. By 1991, though, a new high-speed machining process made it possible to make fuselage frames out of aluminum with greater precision and strength than previously. Aluminum frames for the Osprey weighed about six pounds less than the old composite frames, and making frames and bulkheads of aluminum eliminated 18,500 metal fasteners previously needed to hold composite structures in place. The new Osprey was no longer mostly composite, just 43 percent.

Bell had redesigned its composite wing, too, after "live fire testing"— shooting it with real bullets—showed that the seventeen composite spars used in the original design weren't strong enough to meet the Osprey's survivability requirement. Six of the spars, the ribs that hold a wing's shape, were replaced with titanium in the EMD prototypes.

There were other major changes. The companies corrected design inadequacies exposed by the crash of Aircraft 4 at Quantico in 1992 by putting a drain in the Osprey's engine cowlings and extending a titanium firewall in its nacelles to protect the composite pylon driveshaft from fire. The Allison engines were upgraded to get more power from them while burning less fuel, and the Osprey's transmissions and gearboxes were beefed up to accommodate the extra horsepower. The old "bed frame" wing stow mechanism was replaced with Boeing engineer Bill Rumberger's light and cheaper "flex ring," the design that got him dubbed "Lord of the Ring" around Ridley Park.

The companies cut another 800 pounds out of the B model Osprey by redesigning the electronic displays in the cockpit that took the place of the dials and gauges in older aircraft. The advent of liquid crystal displays made it possible to get rid of the original Osprey's bulky, balky cathode-ray tubes, which had driven test pilots to distraction with their overheating and frequent failures. Galloping advances in computer-assisted design software and in new machines used to fabricate composites, plus the experience Bell and Boeing engineers and workers had gained from developing the prototypes, were making it possible to improve the Osprey's design in other ways as well.

After lengthy study, the companies also replaced the Blottle. The new Thrust Control Lever was more ergonomic and no longer moved in an arc that made it feel like a helicopter collective. The TCL's top was shaped

Gerard Herrick (left) with his Convertaplane. The Princeton-educated lawyer and engineer spent most of his life and fortune trying to perfect his personal dream machine. (PHOTO COURTESY OF NATIONAL AIR AND SPACE MUSEUM.)

James G. Ray and Senator Hiram Bingham took off in a Pitcairn Autogiro from the parking lot on the East Front of the U.S. Capitol in July 1931. (PHOTO COURTESY OF PITCAIRN FOUNDATION.)

Arthur Young demonstrating the remote-control helicopter he obsessively spent nine years designing and building and rebuilding. After Young flew it in a hangar for Larry Bell and his engineers on September 3, 1941, the aviation entrepreneur agreed to spend $250,000 to build two full-size helicopters if Young would supervise the project. (PHOTO COURTESY BELL HELICOPTER TEXTRON INC.)

Dick Spivey with a version of the "Whisper Tip" rotor blade he patented as a young Bell Helicopter engineer. (PHOTO COURTESY BELL HELICOPTER TEXTRON INC.)

Dick Spivey caught his first glimpse of the XV-3 Convertiplane, Bell Helicopter's first tiltrotor, the day he started work at the company in 1959. From then on, the tiltrotor was Spivey's dream machine. (PHOTO COURTESY BELL HELICOPTER TEXTRON INC.)

Kenneth G. Wernicke, Bell's chief tiltrotor designer, was appalled when he saw what the military wanted the future V-22 Osprey to be able to do. Wernicke nearly resigned rather than try to design it. (PHOTO COURTESY BELL HELICOPTER TEXTRON INC.)

On May 23, 1988, Bell and Boeing staged a rollout of the first V-22 Osprey with the help of Hollywood producers. Painted camouflage, the Osprey looked ready for combat. It was far from it. (PHOTO COURTESY BELL HELI-COPTER TEXTRON INC.)

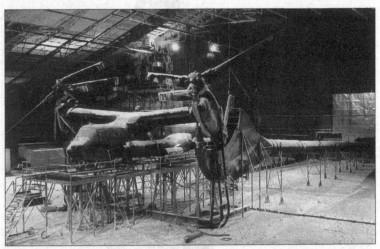

Aircraft 4 was sent to the McKinley Climatic Laboratory in Florida for some of the most grueling tests a prototype can undergo. Tethered like a torture victim to a "run stand," the Osprey prototype was subjected to temperatures ranging from a scorching 125 degrees Fahrenheit to a bone-chilling minus 65. The beating it took delayed its fateful flight to Quantico, Virginia. (PHOTO COURTESY OF KATHI MAYAN.)

The MOTT pilots, 1999. Front row, left to right: Major Ron "Curly" Culp, Major Mike "Pygmy" Westman, Lieutenant Colonel Keith "Mickey" Sweaney, Major Jim "Trigger" Schafer, Major Brooks "Chucky" Gruber, Air Force Major Jon D. "J.D." Edwards. Back row, left to right: Major Paul "Rocket" Rock, Air Force Lieutenant Colonel Jim "Dirtbag" Shaffer, Major Michael "Murf" Murphy, Major John T. "J.T." Torres, Major John "Boot" Brow. (PHOTO BY RONALD S. CULP.)

Brooks and Connie Gruber on their wedding day. After his Osprey crashed at Marana, Connie couldn't look at the moon without wondering if it was the last sight Brooks had seen before he died. (PHOTO COURTESY OF DR. CONNIE GRUBER.)

Cpl. Kelly Keith, a twenty-two-year-old crew chief from South Carolina, liked to sing "Let Her Cry" by Hootie and the Blowfish. Keith was killed in the crash at Marana. (PHOTO BY ERIC SAULSGIVER.)

Major Michael "Murf" Murphy (left), who died in the New River crash, with Major Jim Schafer. MOTT pilots called the gregarious Murphy "The Mayor" because he could enter a room full of strangers and leave with two new friends. (PHOTO BY RONALD S. CULP.)

Sergeant Jason Buyck (left) and Staff Sergeant Avely Runnels, the crew chiefs who died in the New River crash. (PHOTO BY MAUREEN MULLONEY.)

The Osprey returned to flight at Patuxent River Naval Air Station in Maryland on May 29, 2002, after being grounded for seventeen months. (PHOTO BY JAMES DARCY.)

Lieutenant Colonel Paul Rock and members of VMM-263 posed with an Osprey at Yuma, Arizona, in May 2007, as they trained to go to Iraq. (PHOTO BY FAYE K. ROSS.)

Everyone in VMM-263 loved the photo of a sign showing their reply to Mark Thompson's article in *Time* magazine predicting disaster for the Osprey in Iraq.

like a small bicycle seat, so that instead of gripping the lever like a base-ball bat, pilots could rest their left hand atop it, reducing arm fatigue and wrist strain. The TCL still moved forward to add power and backward to reduce it, but when it added power, it no longer moved downward. The change was expected to reduce the risk of "collective dyslexia," the chance that a pilot trained to fly helicopters would push the TCL the wrong way in an emergency, as Boeing test pilot Grady Wilson thought he might have done in the 1991 crash of Aircraft 5.

Navair approved the revamped designs in December 1994. Three years later, the Defense Acquisition Board, a top-level Pentagon committee, approved putting the Osprey into limited production, though flight-testing was still in its early stages. Only one of the four new "production representative" prototypes to be built under the EMD contract had made its maiden flight, and only two of the five prototypes built under the 1986 Full Scale Development contract were still flying. The boundaries of the Osprey's capabilities—what pilots and engineers call the "flight envelope"—had barely been explored. Even so, for the Pentagon to give Navair and the companies permission to start buying parts and tools for production at this stage was normal under a procurement practice known as "concurrent development." Critics derided it as "buy before you fly" and warned that it was risky.

The practice had evolved in the years after World War II, as military hardware grew more and more complex. In the old days, aircraft and other major equipment could be developed, tested, and cranked out of factories in volume with head-spinning speed, sometimes within months. By the 1960s, though, as technology grew more sophisticated, such items were taking years to develop. Given the sluggish pace of the procurement bureaucracy, military aircraft in particular often risked becoming obsolete before they entered mass production. To reduce that risk, the Defense Department started paying contractors to set up production lines and start making small numbers of production models of aircraft, tanks, and the like before they were fully tested. The idea was to allow manufacturers to work out kinks in their factory lines before mass production began and use the first production models for testing. Contractors liked it because they made money on such deals, and because setting up production lines early created jobs, giving members of Congress a bigger stake in a program. These early purchases were called Low Rate Initial Production, abbreviated LRIP and pronounced "ELL-rip."

On Tiltrotor Technology Day in September 1999, the commandant and his congressional guests were riding in the first LRIP Osprey.

To speed the Osprey along, during the 1990s the Marine Corps had gotten a Pentagon panel called the Joint Requirements Oversight Council to ease some of the Osprey's many requirements. Several "must" capabilities devised in 1983, when the goal was to build a tiltrotor able to do ten missions for four armed services, had been modified or discarded. Now the Osprey was being built only for the Marines and the Air Force, and to do fewer missions. As of 1995, the "self-deployment" requirement was to fly 2,100 nautical miles with one aerial refueling, rather than make it the whole way on a single tank of gas. The range requirement for Air Force special operations missions was now 500 nautical miles, rather than 700.

By Defense Department regulation, a new aircraft can move from LRIP into Full Rate Production—where contractors make their greatest profits—only after passing both developmental testing, conducted by special test pilots and engineers, and operational testing, conducted by military pilots and personnel. By Tiltrotor Technology Day, the Osprey was only a few months away from finishing both. The schedule had been compressed so the Marines could field their tiltrotor by 2001. Over the past seven years, the Marine Corps had pressed Bell-Boeing and Navair relentlessly to stick to that schedule, many involved in the program told me. "The push was all the way from the commandant right through the program office," said Webb Joiner, who was president of Bell Helicopter in those days. "They would have loved to move a lot faster."

Like the Osprey itself, its flight test program had been radically redesigned after Bell and Boeing got their EMD contract in 1992. The companies were reluctant, but Navair ordered them to consolidate developmental testing, the kind done by professional test pilots, at Patuxent River Naval Air Station in Maryland. Navair also rejected a Bell-Boeing proposal to build six new prototypes, saying it would cost too much. The EMD contract provided funding only to build four new prototypes and modify two of the old ones.

The Osprey wasn't the only program being treated that way. "Tremendous oversight pressures from governing bodies and funding sources are dictating shorter program schedules, less flying and avoidance of hazardous testing altogether," *Aviation Week* reported in its June 12, 1995, issue. "Flight test officials are adamant that skimping on development testing is much more expensive in the long term. They unanimously agree that, if there is any chance that a fighter, helicopter or transport aircraft can get into a particular flight condition, sooner or later it will. At that point, the man or woman flying the aircraft in line service becomes the test pilot, if that condition was skipped or deleted from the original evaluation." For the Osprey, that warning proved prophetic.

Developmental testing of the Osprey resumed in the summer of 1993, a year after the crash of Aircraft 4 at Quantico, Virginia. Bell and Boeing test pilots assigned to the project relocated to Pax River, as everyone called Maryland's Patuxent River Naval Air Station. They worked in a 350-person "Integrated Test Team" with company and Navair engineers, company and military test pilots and mechanics, and other specialists. For four years, all the pilots had to fly were two original Osprey prototypes, modified with what engineers and pilots call "scab-on" changes to remedy the design flaws blamed for the Aircraft 4 crash. The pace picked up in February 1997, when the new EMD prototypes started arriving. Even so, with only six aircraft to fly, getting every developmental test flown was problematic.

One problem was the weather at Pax River, located on the Chesapeake Bay about sixty miles southeast of Washington, D.C. In summer, heavy humidity often made the sky so hazy it was "like flying in a glass of milk," one former Osprey developmental test pilot remembered. In winter, flights might be scrubbed because of overcast skies, rain, or occasional snow. When they flew, test pilots often spent a lot of time circumnavigating clouds because the rotor blades on the Osprey prototypes were equipped with strain gauges, the tiny wire filaments used to measure stresses. Rain drops become tiny projectiles that can rip a strain gauge off when they hit a rotor blade whirling at hundreds of miles an hour, so rain clouds had to be avoided. In good weather the air around Pax River was congested with other traffic, and emergency landing sites were in short supply. The base was home to the U.S. Naval Test Pilot School, but a lot of pilots wondered why. The only advantage many saw to Pax River was its proximity to Washington. That made it easy for bigwigs to visit.

Even after all four EMD prototypes had been delivered in 1998, developmental test pilots had to share two with the Multiservice Operational Test Team. The MOTT's military pilots were on a tight schedule to get the Osprey's operational testing done so the Marines could field it in 2001. To compensate for the shortage of prototypes, Navair and the Marines overlapped developmental and operational testing as much as possible, with approval from the Pentagon's director of operational test and evaluation, Philip Coyle.

Theoretically, there was nothing wrong with doing both types of testing more or less simultaneously. An aircraft that works technically—the focus for developmental test pilots—still might prove unsuitable for those who have to use it. If changes are needed, better to find out as soon as possible. Trying to do developmental and operational tests with so few prototypes and so little time, though, wasn't very practical, former Osprey test pilots recalled. To make things worse, developmental test pilots not only had to share the four EMD prototypes with the MOTT, they had to train the first six MOTT pilots to fly them. That "really cut into completing developmental testing," one veteran Osprey test pilot told me.

The pilots' biggest complaint was how the schedule for getting the Osprey into service drove everything. Developmental test pilots were constantly pressured by Navair and Bell-Boeing managers to get their work done. Until enough developmental testing was done, operational testing couldn't be finished; until operational testing was finished, the Pentagon couldn't approve Full Rate Production; until Full Rate Production was approved, the Marine Corps couldn't put the Osprey into service. The flight test team worked six, sometimes seven days a week. A tight schedule, though, tended to defeat developmental testing's purpose: to find problems, fix them, and then retest. How long doing that might take was hard to predict, especially for a tiltrotor. A tiltrotor needed to be tested not only like a helicopter *and* like an airplane but also in three other distinct "conversion modes" it flies, when its rotors are tilted at angles between zero and 90 degrees. Logically, it should take extra time and money to test the Osprey to the edges of its envelope, but extra time and money were commodities Navair and the Marine Corps didn't think they had. The Pentagon and Congress were always breathing down their necks, wanting to know how much progress the Osprey was making before they spent more money on it. The solution was to hold developmental testing to as few "data points" as possible, just enough to get a rough outline of the Osprey's flight envelope and see if it could do what its latest Joint Operational Requirements Document said it must.

"You always felt like you were rushing," a military member of the Integrated Test Team in those days recalled. "You'd write a test plan to get fifty points and, because of delays, you might get thirty of them, and they'd say, 'Okay, that's good enough.' I guess decision makers at the time decided that was acceptable risk." A planned series of 103 flight control system and flying qualities tests, for example, was reduced to 49, and only 33 were flown in a real aircraft.

By August 1999, a month before Tiltrotor Technology Day at the Pentagon, the last major stage of the Osprey's developmental test plan had been completed. The first four phases of operational testing were done as well. Bell was weeks away from opening a new plant in Amarillo, Texas, where production model Ospreys would be assembled in the future. The next and final step before the Pentagon decided on Full Rate Production would be for the MOTT to do the Osprey's final phase of testing, Operational Evaluation, abbreviated OPEVAL, pronounced "OPP-ee-vall."

OPEVAL was going to be grueling, both for the Osprey and the roughly 210 members of the MOTT, whose fourteen pilots would fly the first four LRIP Ospreys continually for six months in mock missions aimed at proving the aircraft's suitability for war. The scenarios would cover every mission the Marines and the Air Force Special Operations Command had in their playbooks for the Osprey, from launching amphibious assaults off a windswept ship deck to infiltrating teams of commandos into hostile territory in terrain-hugging low-level flights, to rescuing embassy hostages under cloak of darkness. The MOTT would fly those missions in a variety of climates and at all hours of the day and night, from Pax River, from Marine Corps and Air Force bases in North Carolina, Florida, Arizona, and California, and from ships sailing off the east and west coasts.

For the Marines in the MOTT, the highlight, and most demanding part of OPEVAL, would be a series of exercises at the Marine Corps air station in Yuma, Arizona. Yuma was home to Marine Aviation Weapons and Tactics Squadron One, or MAWTS-1, the Marine Corps' toughest and most prestigious aviation school. Its instructors were the best and its coursework the most demanding, both mentally and physically. Graduating as a weapons and tactics instructor from MAWTS-1 was a feat Marine pilots bragged about for years. Holding a WTI certificate qualified a pilot to teach tactics to others in his or her squadron.

Two times a year, MAWTS-1 held special courses attended by entire squadrons of every aircraft the Marines fly, from transport and gunship helicopters and aerial refueling tankers to fighter jets. Supervised by MAWTS-1 instructors, those squadrons and Marine infantry units engaged in a series of exercises together, testing their ability to operate as an air-ground task force. To succeed, a squadron's mechanics had to be in top form, keep their unit's aircraft "mission capable." A squadron's pilots had to perform combat maneuvers while coordinating with other squadrons and ground units in complex missions. Those participating would be judged not only by MAWTS-1's instructors but by their peers in other squadrons. For Marine aviators, going through a MAWTS course was like playing in the Super Bowl. It was the toughest test they would face short of going to war.

The MOTT's leaders, Marine Lieutenant Colonel Keith Sweaney and Air Force Lieutenant Colonel Jim Shaffer, wrote the OPEVAL plan. The judge of whether the Osprey had passed, however, would be Philip Coyle, the assistant secretary of defense who ran the Pentagon's Office of Operational Test and Evaluation, so Coyle had to approve the OPEVAL plan in advance. So did the MOTT's higher-ups in the Marine Corps and the Air Force. OPEVAL was a big deal. Once it was over, if Coyle gave the Osprey passing grades, the Marines could expect the Pentagon to approve Full Rate Production. When that happened, the Corps would have its dream machine at last.

★ ★ ★

The MOTT's job was to test the Osprey, not promote it, but the unit's pilots were bubbling with enthusiasm long before OPEVAL began. MOTT leader Sweaney talked about the Osprey to his wife, Carol, a lot. Born in Charleston, West Virginia, Sweaney was a gifted athlete, named small college football player of the year when he played for Randolph-Macon College in Virginia. He joined the Marines after graduating from college in 1980 and flew CH-53 helicopters for close to a decade before being selected for the Osprey program. He had no doubt the tiltrotor was a dream machine, not just for the Marines but for civilian aviation, too.

Sweaney was hardly alone in his views. When Sweaney and Shaffer flew the first LRIP Osprey to Tiltrotor Technology Day in September 1999, they brought along Marine Major Paul Rock, Jr., to help with the

VIPs and sing the Osprey's praises to the media. Sweaney liked to use Rock as the MOTT's public face, partly because of Rock's own. Rock was thirty-three, married, and starting a family, but his smooth, lightly freckled cheeks gave him that sunny, All-American Boy look. He wasn't Hollywood handsome, but he was good-looking. He stood six feet tall, weighed 185 pounds, and had military bearing. He kept his bright, carrot-colored hair cropped in a good Marine Corps "high and tight" cut. He held his head erect. Thanks to his last name and flame-orange hair, plus the cheek and talent of an enlisted Marine who decorated the side of Rock's flight helmet when he was a lieutenant with a painting of a missile-shaped carrot blasting off, Rock's radio call sign was "Rocket." Rock was a "people person," Sweaney and Shaffer agreed. He seemed to light up in front of an audience, and though he'd flown the Osprey for the first time only three months before Tiltrotor Technology Day, Rock was sold. "The thing accelerates like a scalded dog," Rock said in one videotaped interview at the Pentagon event, the corners of his mouth turning up in a kid-in-a-candy-store grin. Rock had been in the MOTT since 1997, but he'd had to wait two years to fly the Osprey because there were so few of them. Rock's first flight, though, had made him a true believer. "It handles perfectly fine as a helicopter, but you can tell it wants to go fast," Rock told his interviewer. "It takes off, it gets going so fast, it's like the plane's trying to slip out from underneath you." Rock thought the Osprey really was a dream machine.

★ ★ ★

Strictly speaking, promoting the tiltrotor to the civilian world had never been Dick Spivey's job. By the mid-1990s, he was overseeing a military tiltrotor marketing staff big enough to field an after-work softball team, the "Pentagon Pedlars." Spivey was always ready, though, to do what he could to help Bell rekindle civilian interest, which had all but died when Cheney was trying to cancel the Osprey from 1989 to 1992. Back then, Curt Weldon and others in the Osprey camp had often warned that the Japanese or someone else overseas would build the dream machine if the United States didn't. No one did. Interest among potential civilian customers—commercial airlines, medical services, oil companies with offshore drilling platforms—evaporated when it appeared the U.S. military might drop the Osprey. Deals that Bell had made with British Aerospace, Dornier of Germany, and Aeritalia to test the tiltrotor market in Europe—announced at the 1989 Paris Air Show by Bell President Jack Horner—produced nothing. In 1990, two Japanese companies that had offered Bell and Boeing $250 million in "up-front" money for a joint venture to develop a civilian tiltrotor in their country withdrew the proposition. A third Japanese company, which had bought a building at an industrial airport near Fort Worth and hired some Bell tiltrotor engineers to build a civilian tilt-wing aircraft, abandoned the plan after a couple of years. Bell itself, preoccupied with trying to save the Osprey, shelved plans to develop a small tiltrotor for the civilian market while Cheney was secretary of defense. Webb Joiner, who succeeded Horner as Bell's president in 1991, told me that Spivey and a few other Bell marketers were "rabid" for the idea. They pestered him constantly to launch such a project. Joiner refused as long as the Osprey was in jeopardy. "I felt like we had to let the V-22 demonstrate to the world the capability," Joiner explained.

Bell's marketing department set out to revive civilian interest in the tiltrotor after Clinton took office in 1993, and Spivey was eager to pitch in. One day in 1995, he got a call from a Marine Corps recruiter in California who said a Hollywood film producer wanted to borrow a tiltrotor for a new movie. Could Bell help? When Spivey found out what the producer had in mind, he urged Joiner to offer the XV-15 for the project. The film's opening scene would show an elderly woman being flown out to a research vessel sailing off the coast of Newfoundland, where she was wanted to identify objects brought up from a shipwreck she had survived decades earlier. A tiltrotor would be ideal for the part, the producer thought, because it would look more futuristic than a helicopter, conveying to the audience how many years had passed since the ship had sunk.

Spivey was disappointed when Bell declined the request. The project would cost the company too much, the executives decided, and the filmmakers were insisting the XV-15 would have to fly off the coast of Nova Scotia. The XV-15 still belonged to NASA, and while the agency had let Bell use it to market the tiltrotor concept for years, every flight was technically a test. Flying the XV-15 in the humid and sometimes frigid air over the North Atlantic would risk running into rain or ice that might damage the strain gauges on its rotors. Besides, who knew if the movie would draw a big enough audience to make the whole exercise worth the trouble and expense?

When the film came out in December 1997, Spivey could only shake his head at what an opportunity Bell had missed. The movie won eleven Academy Awards and was one of the highest-grossing films in the history of Hollywood. It's title was *Titanic.*

Bell often used the XV-15 in promotional videos of its own, and Spivey enjoyed producing them. In 1995, he played a cameo role in a mini-drama he scripted himself with his counterpart in Bell's civilian marketing department. They spent $35,000 to have the XV-15 repainted metallic silver and black like an executive jet, then filmed it taking off from a new heliport the city of Dallas had built and landing on a helipad at a Bell office building near Fort Worth. They spliced in video of a man in airline pilot garb greeting Spivey and some other briefcase-toting marketers as they apparently boarded and deboarded the little tiltrotor. A viewer could get the impression tiltrotor service was already a reality. "None of us could get in because there wasn't any room for us," Spivey recalled with a laugh years later. The XV-15's cabin was crammed with test instruments and had no seats, he explained, "But they faked it pretty good, actually." Bell showed the video at trade shows all over the world, trying to encourage life to imitate marketing art.

With the Osprey apparently back on track, Bell was now going all-out once again to get people excited about the tiltrotor's civilian potential. In June 1995, the company took the XV-15 to the Paris Air Show for the first time since 1981. Navair and the Marines sent one of the scarce Osprey prototypes to Paris that year as well, where it and the XV-15 performed what *Aviation Week* called a "daily *pas de deux.*" With U.S. defense budgets tight, both Bell-Boeing and the Marines were hoping the militaries of America's allies abroad might decide they needed Ospreys, too. Foreign sales that increased the Osprey's production run would be one way to get its price down.

Spivey and his old Marine Corps briefing partner Bob Magnus, now a brigadier general, went to Paris again that November to try to interest the French military in the Osprey. As a young action officer in the Marine Corps aviation branch, Magnus had been a prime mover in getting the Osprey started in 1981–83. His career had taken him away from the issue after 1984, but by then he had "drunk the Kool-Aid" on the tiltrotor. Like Spivey, Magnus was still a true believer. While assigned to the Pentagon's Joint Staff from 1989 to 1993, Magnus had watched the Cheney fight from the sidelines. During his stint there, though, he had earned a master's degree in business administration from Strayer College in Washington with a thesis titled "An Assessment of Civil Tiltrotor Market Potential." In his thesis, Magnus cited University of Texas and NASA studies estimating that tiltrotor passenger fares would have to be 32 percent higher than those for equivalent turboprop planes and that civil tiltrotors would cost on average 50 percent more to build. Still, Magnus saw a bright future for commercial tiltrotors. "In the year 2000, tiltrotors could capture from one to two thirds of the U.S. short-haul market," he wrote. Magnus estimated the market in the United States, Europe, and Japan at 1,200 to 5,000 aircraft.

Bell and Boeing decided to go after part of that potential market in 1996. On November 18 that year, in a news conference at the National Air and Space Museum in Washington, the Osprey partners announced a joint venture to produce a nine-passenger tiltrotor for civilian use. Spivey had been urging Bell president Joiner to launch such a project for years, even suggested he might like to give up military marketing and sell a small civil tiltrotor instead. Joiner ignored that idea, so Spivey remained a military marketer, but he flew to Washington to be on hand for the civil tiltrotor announcement. The idea of bringing the masses such a versatile aircraft for everyday transport was what really fired Spivey's imagination. The Osprey intrigued him, and he was excited about it, but a civil tiltrotor was his *real* dream machine. Spivey wasn't the only one smitten with the tiltrotor as a commercial aircraft. "Timing Looks Right for Civil Tilt-Rotor," *Aviation Week* reported in that year's March 18 issue.

Joiner told the news conference that Bell and Boeing might sell as many as a thousand of the planned Bell-Boeing 609 civilian tiltrotors over the next twenty years for about $10 million each. That would be about twice the price of a helicopter the same size, but the 609 would fly 500 miles without refueling and cruise at 275 knots. That would give it 350 miles more range and more than twice the speed of a helicopter. It would be perfect for medical and rescue services, oil companies with offshore drilling platforms, maybe even the U.S. Coast Guard, Joiner said. If the Osprey succeeded, he added, the companies would pursue the "next logical step" and design a civilian tiltrotor big enough to carry forty to seventy passengers. Wiser by now about the problems inherent in a 50–50 partnership, the companies had agreed that Bell would take 51 percent of the 609 project and any other tiltrotors they designed for fewer than nineteen passengers; Boeing would take 51 percent of any future projects to build tiltrotors carrying twenty or more passengers. The 609 would make its first flight in 1999, Joiner predicted, be certified as safe by the FAA in 2001, and be delivered to the first customer in 2002.

By 1999, however, the 609 still hadn't flown, and Boeing Helicopters had dropped out of the project. Boeing Seattle had never been keen on the idea of civilian tiltrotors, and Boeing Helicopters had never succeeded with civilian products. Bell found a new partner for the 609 in Agusta S.p.A. of Italy, though, and the new BellAgusta Aerospace Company joint venture had taken several dozen advance orders for the renamed BA-609. Besides those in the United States, customers in Australia, Brazil, Britain, Canada, Dubai, Germany, Japan, Norway, Poland, and South Korea were eagerly awaiting their tiltrotors. Celebrity private pilots including professional golfer Greg Norman and Ross Perot, Jr., son of the famous billionaire, had placed orders for 609s, too.

The dream wasn't just alive, Spivey could see it coming true.

* * *

The dream turned into a nightmare the evening of April 8, 2000, at a dusty desert airfield near the southeastern Arizona town of Marana. The Marine and Air Force pilots and maintainers of the Multiservice Operational Test Team, the MOTT, had begun the Osprey's most important stage of testing yet, Operational Evaluation, five months earlier. The results of OPEVAL would determine whether the Osprey could go into Full Rate Production, so the aviation branch at Headquarters Marine Corps was paying close attention. The Marine Corps' deputy commandant for aviation, Lieutenant General Fred McCorkle, had visited Pax River on November 3, 1999, to kick the tests off. Legally, the MOTT reported to the Navy's Operational Test and Evaluation Force and to Pentagon test director Philip Coyle. As the head of Marine Corps aviation, though, McCorkle took a keen interest in what the MOTT was doing, and as a practical matter, the Marines in the unit answered to him as well. "Tell us what it does, tell us what it can't do," McCorkle told the pilots.

That was what the MOTT set out to do. OPEVAL was supposed to be a six-month road trip for the unit. Afterward, most of its Marine Corps pilots and mechanics were to transfer to a new Osprey training squadron at New River Marine Corps Air Station, so many sold homes near Pax River or Quantico and moved their families to North Carolina in advance. They didn't expect to see their wives and children much until OPEVAL was over. There was no time to lose. OPEVAL had to be done in time for the Pentagon to approve Full Rate Production before the end of 2000 if the Marines were going to field the Osprey in 2001. There wouldn't be much point in putting the Osprey into service if it wasn't going into Full Rate Production. By law, up to 10 percent of a major defense equipment purchase could be done as LRIP, but a delay in getting Full Rate Production approved would signal there were problems with the Osprey. Programs with problems often lost their funding. When the hungry lions within the Pentagon and on Capitol Hill hunt for defense dollars, the law of the jungle applies: To limp is to die.

The MOTT started OPEVAL in November at Pax River, did some tests at New River, then in December flew two Ospreys to an amphibious assault ship sailing in the Atlantic, the USS *Saipan*. There the schedule broke down. A few days after they arrived on the *Saipan*, they began running short of parts. Swashplate actuators, the hydraulic devices that change the pitch of rotor blades, were failing at unexpected rates. The new blade fold/wing stow mechanism wasn't working right. Problems with little things, like batteries for electronic navigation systems, forced the MOTT to cancel test flights. A company of Marines sent to the ship to fly mock missions in the Osprey was left idle. After nine days, the MOTT halted all tests and went back to Pax River to wait for Bell and Boeing to deliver the parts they needed. They stayed there through January.

By February, they were back to flying, and over the next three months the team spent a lot of time in the air. They flew the first four LRIP Ospreys to the West Coast to do shipboard tests aboard the USS *Essex* in the Pacific. They flew them empty and with troops in the back. They hovered over the ship while a dozen or more Marines fast-roped to the deck out of the back ramp of an Osprey to simulate boarding a hostile vessel. With a full load of twenty-four Marines in the back, they simulated an amphibious assault on Catalina Island off the Southern California coast. The MOTT's nearly two hundred enlisted mechanics, electronics technicians, and other maintainers kept busy. All aircraft require hours of work in the hangar for each hour flown, but the Osprey's "readiness rate," how often aircraft are mechanically fit to fly, was a disappointment.

The Osprey was a new aircraft with thousands of parts, and a lot of them were breaking or wearing out earlier than predicted. Still, by the time the MOTT got to the Marine Corps Air Station in Yuma, Arizona, in early March, its fourteen pilots had logged more than four hundred flight hours during OPEVAL. Things were starting to click.

Like most military pilots, the MOTT's were by and large "type A" personalities—driven, competitive, goal-oriented. They were all young men, mostly in their thirties, but several were veterans of the 1991 Gulf War. They were all confident, in some cases cocky. Most had applied for the MOTT, a cadre whose pilots and mechanics would teach and lead others in the Marine Corps and Air Force to fly and maintain the Osprey as it was fielded. Marine Major Mike Westman, who had flown CH-46s a dozen years before joining the MOTT in 1997, felt he was part of an elite group, some of the best and most professional military pilots around. All but one, Major John A. "Boot" Brow, were helicopter pilots with hundreds or even thousands of hours in the CH-53 Super Stallion or the CH-46 Sea Knight, which the Marines were still pumping money into and flying. Brow, at thirty-nine one of the oldest in the unit, was the only career fixed-wing pilot, a talented KC-130 driver—he had 3,400 hours in the aerial refueling tanker—and a former MAWTS-1 instructor. As preparation for the Osprey, Brow took helicopter training, logging about sixty hours in three types.

Over the three years most of them had been together, the pilots had grown close. Originally based at Quantico, the MOTT moved its headquarters to Patuxent River in 1998, when the unit started flying the Osprey more often. Most pilots moved their families there as well, but some left them at Quantico, commuting the eighty-eight miles home for weekends. One was Major James B. "Trigger" Schafer, sometimes confused by outsiders with the MOTT's Air Force leader, Lieutenant Colonel Jim Shaffer, or even former Desert One pilot and Osprey program manager Colonel Jim Schaefer, who had retired from Marine Corps seven years earlier. Trigger Schafer, who had begun his career as an enlisted metalsmith working on CH-46s, bunked during the workweek in a 40-foot boat he docked at Solomons Island, a waterfront village at the confluence of the Patuxent River and Chesapeake Bay. Major Michael L. "Murf" Murphy, a New York-born former CH-53 pilot who could enter a room full of strangers and leave with two new friends, shared the boat with Schafer. MOTT commander Sweaney slept weeknights on a boat a couple of slips down. Back home, their wives were friends and their children played together. Major Brooks S. Gruber, a Massachusetts native, gave Schafer's young son tips on playing ice hockey. Everybody liked Gruber, a former CH-53 pilot whose radio call sign was "Chucky," taken from the cult horror film *Child's Play*, whose lead character was a doll with a wicked grin. Gruber was a practical joker with an impish sense of humor. He dubbed Major Ronald S. "Curly" Culp's little Polynesian green Jeep Tracker "the Barbie Jeep," partly because Culp had two young daughters who played with Barbie dolls. One day when Culp and a couple of other pilots drove out to lunch in it, Gruber, Murphy, and a couple of others snuck into the restaurant parking lot and turned the Barbie Jeep sideways between two cars so Culp couldn't drive it out. Gruber cackled like his movie namesake over that one. Rock, the redhaired major Sweaney liked to use as the MOTT's public face, considered Gruber one of his best friends. They had been the two most junior officers when they joined the MOTT in 1997. They bonded in those days partly by commiserating about their inability to get Osprey flight time with the MOTT and Navair's developmental test pilots sharing the half-dozen aircraft available. During the January 2000 hiatus in OPEVAL, Rock and Gruber roomed together in enlisted barracks at Pax River and cemented their friendship.

Traveling for OPEVAL tightened the unit's bonds. Not long after they arrived at the Marine Corps air station in Yuma, Rock spotted an F-5 fighter plane on the ramp, a needle-nosed jet flown by an "aggressor squadron" to show Marine pilots enemy tactics. Brow, the former KC-130 pilot who had been a MAWTS-1 instructor, knew the squadron commander and got Rock a flight in the F-5. Rock thought that was really cool. Brow was six years older, and as his salt-and-pepper hair emphasized, one of the old hands in the unit. On the ground, Brow was the MOTT's director of safety and Rock was its safety officer, so Brow was also Rock's immediate supervisor. They were too far apart in age and seniority to be buddies, but Rock liked the way Brow looked out for him.

Interservice rivalry aside, Lieutenant Colonel Jim Shaffer thought his Air Force contingent of the MOTT enjoyed working with the Marines. At Yuma, the Air Force and Marine Corps groups quartered in separate motels for administrative reasons but crossed the street every day to eat breakfast and dinner together. The MOTT's officers and enlisted maintainers got along well, too. Military law and regulations bar "fraternization" between ranks—social relationships that erode discipline or the chain of command—but with the Osprey so new, pilots and maintainers had to put their heads together to solve problems no one had encountered before. They grew close. In the evening, it wasn't unusual to see officers and enlisted in civilian clothes cooking burgers together on a grill in the courtyard of the Best Western where the Marines were staying. Sometimes one of the guys would pull out a guitar and Corporal Kelly Keith, a cherub-cheeked twenty-two-year-old crew chief from South Carolina with a wrestler's build and a terrific voice, would sing with Sergeant Michael Moffitt, another crew chief the same age from the Philadelphia suburbs. At Pax River, Keith and Moffitt often went to karaoke bars together. Moffitt thought Keith sang "Let Her Cry," by Hootie and the Blowfish, just the way it sounded on the CD.

The best part of OPEVAL for the pilots was flying the Osprey often, something they had been anticipating for years. Until the LRIP Ospreys arrived and OPEVAL began, no one in the MOTT had been able to accumulate many hours in the aircraft. The more they got under their belts, the more comfortable they were getting in the tiltrotor, whose unique characteristics most had experienced largely in computerized simulators up until then. By the time they hit Yuma, Major Curly Culp thought the MOTT was clicking like never before. They were making nearly all their missions. Everyone was flying well. They were putting the Osprey through its paces.

The Osprey's flight manual was still a work in progress, so they flew according to a Navair "flight clearance placard," a thick document that set limits on altitudes, speeds, and maneuvers. Navair had issued this flight envelope based on flights by developmental test pilots, but given the tight schedule they had worked under, it was still loosely defined, a sort of connect-the-dots image rather than a complete picture. Within it, there were lots of ways to fly that had never been tested, lots of maneuvers a pilot might want to use in combat that no one had ever tried. As the MOTT pilots gained experience in the Osprey, they started trying some.

"Experimentation was encouraged within the limits of the flight clearance," Shaffer told me, and he offered an example. Shaffer was a special operations pilot, a combat veteran experienced in the treacherous task of dropping and retrieving commandos in hostile territory under cover of darkness. He wanted to find out whether an Osprey could get into a landing zone more quietly than a helicopter. The Osprey's rotors made just as much noise as a helicopter's when it flew like one, but when flying like an airplane, the tiltrotor was hard to hear until it got right on top of you. Could an Osprey sneak up on a landing zone by approaching it in airplane mode, then making a sharp turn into the zone as the pilot converted its rotors to helicopter mode, Shaffer wondered? A couple of weeks after the MOTT got to Yuma, Shaffer tried it. When he pushed his stick right to roll out of the turn while converting his Osprey's nacelles to helicopter mode, the aircraft didn't respond immediately. That made for an anxious moment. Shaffer had discovered a glitch in the Osprey's flight control software that needed fixing.

The Marines in the MOTT were trying other maneuvers. Some went up against the F-5 aggressor squadron, getting jumped by one of the speedy fighters while flying a normal mission, then juking and deking in airplane mode, firing off chaff and flares to fool missiles, and diving for the deck. For a young military pilot, it didn't get much more exciting than that. Sweaney and Shaffer never caught anyone violating the limits of their flight clearance, but in their enthusiasm, some skirted the edges. They were aggressive young men, and they were flying the Osprey hard. They were wringing it out, seeing what it could do.

By Yuma, the MOTT had flown dozens of mock missions with Marine infantry and Air Force special operations troops in the back cabins of their Ospreys. OPEVAL's purpose was to fly the Osprey as it would be flown in combat, and that meant carrying troops. Finding out how they felt about the ride was an important part of OPEVAL, the only way to learn if the aircraft would be effective in real missions, so the MOTT gave its passengers surveys to fill out. They asked fundamental questions: What was it like for you riding in the back? Was it cramped? Was it stuffy? When you ride in a V-22, are you combat-effective when you jump off it? The MOTT pilots would have to know the answers when they wrote their final OPEVAL report.

The mission to Marana on April 8 would be another carrying passengers, an exercise called a "Noncombatant Evacuation Operation," simulating the rescue of civilians from an embassy. Marines would play the role of evacuees; Marana Northwest Regional Airport, twenty-five miles northwest of Tucson, would play the embassy. The MOTT had done similar missions before. This time, though, they would fly at night, which would make it more challenging.

There was another challenge. The mission to Marana was part of a MAWTS-1 course in Assault Support Tactics. That meant the Ospreys would be in the air with twenty-six helicopters and jets from other Marine Corps squadrons—big CH-46s and CH-53s, little Huey transport and Cobra gunship helicopters, fast-moving F-18 Hornet fighter jets, KC-130 refueling tankers. The crews of the various aircraft would have to follow their parts of the choreography closely, fall into place like shards in a kaleidoscope, to make the complete picture come together. Still, for the Ospreys, the mission template was fairly straightforward.

At about 7:10 P.M., eight Marine pilots would take off from Yuma in the MOTT's four Ospreys, tilt their rotors to airplane mode, climb to 9,500 feet above sea level—about 7,500 feet over the ground, given Arizona's elevation—and fly east to Marana in two "sections," two flights of two aircraft. Cruising at about 240 miles per hour, they would cover the 212 miles in about fifty minutes. The first section of two Ospreys would carry Marine infantry—affectionately known as "grunts"—plus enlisted crew chiefs. There would be eighteen grunts in the lead Osprey and three crew chiefs, one of them a MAWTS-1 instructor, Gunnery Sergeant James Sharp, flying to evaluate the two crew chiefs from the MOTT in that aircraft. The second Osprey would carry fifteen troops and two crew chiefs. The two Ospreys in the second section would carry only two crew chiefs each, no troops. When they got to Marana, the first two Ospreys would land and unload their troops while the other two Ospreys circled five miles to the southwest at about 1,000 feet. As the infantry organized the role players at the airfield for "evacuation," the Ospreys that had brought them would take off and join the other two in their holding pattern. On getting a call from the ground that the "evacuees" were ready, the two Ospreys that had flown to Marana empty would land and pick up the Marines, then all four Ospreys would fly back to Yuma.

On its face, the mission for the Ospreys was routine: fly from one hard-surfaced runway to another, then back; no dusty landing zone to set down in, no heaving ship deck to land on in the dark. Night missions didn't get much simpler, and the crews would be wearing the newest generation of night-vision goggles, devices that amplify natural light invisible to the naked eye. Night-vision goggles had vastly improved since 1980, when the clumsy, eye-straining first generation of such devices had caused vertigo in pilots flying the ill-fated hostage rescue mission in Iran. These new goggles, AN/VIS-9s, were lightweight and compact, the size and shape of a small pair of binoculars. Attached to the front of the crews' helmets so their tubes hung 18 to 22 millimeters from the user's eyes, the goggles would let the crews see in the dark, turning the world outside their cockpits into a video-game monochrome of dark green and white. The goggles almost turned night into day, though that could be deceptive. Using them, the pilots would have to fly differently than in daylight, for the goggles would cut their field of view from 188 to 40 degrees. That would limit their depth perception, making it harder to judge distances and speeds. They would need to spend more time with their heads "inside the cockpit," relying on instruments to tell them how far and fast they were traveling, rather than flying by feel. The Osprey cockpit was equipped for this. Instrument readings would be projected on a glass Heads Up Display in front of each pilot, visible through the goggles. Each pilot could call up a moving digital map on a display in front of him by punching a button. To see other things inside the cockpit, the pilots would have to peer under or to the side of their goggles, but the eight MOTT pilots had used night-vision goggles often before. As usual, they also would navigate by instruments to checkpoints along the way, flying to specific altitudes over specific locations at specific times.

Each checkpoint would be easy to see on the digital map. From a cruising altitude of 9,500 feet, they would descend to a checkpoint at 5,000 feet as they neared Marana, then to one at 3,000 feet above sea level, putting them about 1,000 feet over the ground. As the second section of Ospreys took up their orbit there, the lead section would descend to another checkpoint 500 feet above the ground, then another at 300 feet. At that altitude, two miles from the airfield, they would tilt their rotors up into helicopter mode to land. Hitting every checkpoint would all but guarantee a safe landing. The flying should be simple.

Tonight, however, the pilots would have a lot of other things on their minds as well. Major Anthony J. "Buddy" Bianca, thirty-three, a former CH-53E helicopter pilot who was one of the MOTT's relative newcomers, had as much to think about as any. Bianca would copilot the lead Osprey but play two other roles as well. As assault flight leader, he would be mission commander for the four Ospreys. In that capacity, Bianca had planned the operation with his counterparts from the helicopter and fighter plane units taking part, and he would have to keep track of where all the aircraft in the exercise were at any given time. He also would be a student that night, working toward the coveted MAWTS-1 weapons and tactics instructor designation. In that capacity, Bianca would be evaluated during the flight by his Osprey's pilot, Major James M. "Lefty" Wright, a WTI graduate as a CH-53E pilot. Wright was scheduled to join MAWTS-1 as an Osprey expert after OPEVAL. The copilot of the lead section's "Dash Two," as Marines call the second aircraft in a section, also would be a student that night. Major Chucky Gruber would be evaluated for his WTI designation by his Osprey's pilot, Major Boot Brow, who had been a MAWTS-1 instructor when he flew KC-130 tankers. All eight pilots also would be required to write an evaluation the next day of how the Osprey had performed as a machine that night.

Bianca gave the Osprey pilots their mission briefing in a classroom inside the MAWTS-1 headquarters building at Yuma. As he finished, he reminded the pilots that in case of a mishap, the senior officer among them would be the "on-scene commander," responsible for coordinating the emergency response from the air. Tonight, Bianca noted, that would be Major Mike Westman, call sign "Pygmy," flying the second section's lead Osprey. When Bianca said that, Westman looked over at Brow, his oldest friend in the MOTT. At thirty-nine, Brow was often the most senior officer on a mission, but he had gotten his wings in 1986, two years after Westman. Brow flashed Westman a little grin, as if to say, "*You* get it tonight." Westman never forgot that grin.

The pilots were in their cockpits and the rotors were turning as the crew chiefs for the first two Ospreys waved toward the hangar for the Marine infantry to board. Carrying packs and weapons, the thirty-three Marines ran out to the rear ramps of the Ospreys at a 45-degree angle to avoid the powerful downwash. "Keep the barrel of your weapon down," Staff Sergeant Julius Banks, one of the crew chiefs in the lead Osprey, shouted into each Marine's ear as he boarded. There were eighteen Marines in his Osprey, less than capacity, but their packs filled the aisle, so the crew chiefs wouldn't be able to walk up and down the cabin during the flight. Banks stationed himself next to the clamshell rear ramp doors, leaving the top door open. Sergeant Michael Moffitt and MAWTS-1 instructor Sharp, the other crew chiefs on the lead Osprey, would ride up front by the crew cabin door on the right side of the aircraft. All three crew chiefs would wear night-vision goggles and spend most of their time looking outside the plane to help the pilots keep track of the other Ospreys and avoid any other aircraft they flew near.

The sun was just setting and the evening sky was pink when they took off, rolling down the runway a few yards, then leaping into the air and climbing fast. Some of the Marine passengers gave Moffitt a thumbs-up when they felt the Osprey's power, but soon it was dark inside the cabin and most of the infantry dozed off. Fifteen minutes after takeoff, the air crews put on their night-vision goggles. The sky was clear, the only clouds several thousand feet above, but around and below them it was dark. Only a sliver of a crescent moon and the lights of an occasional car, small town, or trailer park lit the barren desert below.

Both sections of Ospreys had begun their gradual descent toward Marana by 7:50 P.M., when the pilot of an F-18 fighter radioed that Landing Zone Swan, their designation for the airport, was "winter"—code for "cold," meaning "no enemy in sight." There would be no need to fly around simulated antiaircraft batteries or "hostile forces" that might "shoot" at the Ospreys. The first section would just need to hit their various checkpoints on time and land at the airfield. They were already down to 5,000 feet above sea level—3,000 feet above ground level, or "AGL"— when the F-18 radioed. The next checkpoint would be at 1,000 feet AGL, the one after that at 500. The last checkpoint, 300 feet above the ground, would come five miles from the airfield. This "Initial Point"—designated "IP Dodge"—was where Wright and Brow should start tilting the rotors of their lead-section Ospreys to helicopter mode to land. If their timing was right, the approach should be uncomplicated.

It wasn't.

★ ★ ★

"What the hell are those guys doing up there?" the lead pilot of the second section of Ospreys, Westman, asks his copilot, Major Jim Schafer, as they go into their holding pattern. Westman and Schafer, with Majors Murphy and Rock piloting the Osprey behind them, have been trailing the first section by two miles or so since they left Yuma. Now Westman's section is beginning to circle at 3,000 feet above sea level, 1,000 feet AGL. Wright and Brow should have been down to the same altitude some time ago, but there they are in the distance, still a couple of thousand feet higher. Westman is puzzled by this. By rights, he or one of the other pilots in his section could radio Wright and Bianca to ask why they're so high, but maybe they have a good reason, so no one does. Wright and Bianca are the mission leaders.

Wright and Bianca are also distracted. Midway through the flight, one of their two mission computers has gone out, prompting a discussion between them and the other pilots in their section, Brow and Gruber, on whether to reboot it. If they do, their cockpit displays will go blank for ten seconds or so as the two mission computers synchronize their data. During that time, Wright and Bianca will have to fly with a "black cockpit"—no primary instrument displays of their speed, altitude, fuel, engine performance, etc.—and no digital map. They decide to reboot the computer when they get on the ground.

Soon after this, less than a minute after the F-18 radios that LZ Swan is cold, there are more distractions. As Bianca and the leader of the troops in the back discuss how long their Osprey will need to stay on the ground at Marana, Bianca drops something in the darkened cockpit.

"Sergeant Moffitt, could you look underneath my chair for a paper that just fell off?" Bianca asks the crew chief, who is stationed just behind the cockpit.

"Yes, sir," Moffitt replies. As Moffitt leans into the cockpit and begins looking for the paper, Wright asks Bianca, "Whe—when do I come down to three thousand?"

"We should still be c—you should be coming down to three thousand," Bianca says. "I should have told you that earlier."

While Bianca has been talking with the F-18 pilot on the radio and over the intercom with the troop commander, Wright has flown past their 3,000-foot checkpoint. Now, to get to IP Dodge at 300 feet, where they should start converting their rotors to helicopter mode for landing, they are going to have to come down faster than planned. Otherwise, they might overshoot the airfield and have to "wave off"—fly around—to try their approach again, which will upset the mission timing. Wright puts their Osprey into a steep descent. Soon they are coming down at 1,860 feet per minute, though in airplane mode, the ride is smooth. The unannounced maneuver seems to catch Brow and Gruber in the Osprey behind them off guard, though neither says anything over the radio. Trying to follow, as a wingman should, Brow descends faster than Wright. Soon Brow's Osprey, Dash Two, is coming down at 1,965 feet a minute.

Twelve seconds into their descent, Moffitt is still looking for Bianca's dropped paper. "I don't see it," the sergeant says.

"Shit," Bianca mutters.

"Got a flashlight up there, sir?" Moffitt asks.

"I sure don't," Bianca replies. With a map in his lap, Bianca feels around and finds the paper himself. "Stand by, I got it," he tells Moffitt.

"All right," Moffitt says.

"Thanks, it didn't drop all the way down," Bianca tells him.

Bianca turns his attention back to their approach into Marana. "We want to be at IP Dodge at 1957 and we're just about there," he tells Wright. "We're looking pretty good." Over the radio, Bianca reminds Gruber to contact the Marana airport on the Common Traffic Advisory Frequency.

"I'm there now," Gruber replies.

A few seconds later, Bianca offers Wright more help. "You wanna cross the IP at, uh, 1957," Bianca says. "That's thirty seconds away and we're kinda at the IP already, so you can slow her down a bit, a hundred seventy, and turn towards the, uh, slow-down point."

Seventeen seconds later, Bianca talks to Wright again. "You wanna cross the slow-down point . . . ," he begins.

"Where's that?" Wright asks.

"Good to go, continue," Bianca replies, then adds: "Lefty, you okay, man?"

"Yup," Wright responds.

"You got it, you got it," Bianca tells him. "That's a good heading right there. You wanna take some airspeed out."

As Wright turns the Osprey in a sweeping descent toward the airfield, Staff Sergeant Julius Banks is looking out the open upper half of the rear ramp's clamshell doors. The ride feels normal to Banks. To Moffitt, the other crew chief, it doesn't feel dramatic at all compared to the quick turns and dives at low level he's experienced at Yuma riding in an Osprey evading an F-5 fighter jet. As Moffitt peers past the pilots out the windshield, though, he can see they are going to be coming in "high and hot," as aviators call it.

A minute into the descent, they cross IP Dodge, the point two miles short of the Marana runway where they're to convert to helicopter mode for landing. The flight plan said they should be at 300 feet by now. They are at 1,900, more than six times too high. Wright starts tilting his rotors upward. Eleven seconds later, Brow follows suit in the second Osprey. "Dash Two's looking good on the right side," crew chief Banks reports.

Brow's challenge now is to keep from passing Wright. As Brow's rotors tilt upward, his Osprey "balloons," rising like a skier hitting the end of a jump, and climbs back up to 1,350 feet. Now Brow needs to lose that much more altitude to land. As the rotors of both Ospreys angle upward, both lose forward airspeed. Their proprotors are becoming more rotor than propeller, no longer thrusting horizontally but at an angle. The Ospreys' wings are losing lift. Within seconds, Brow's Osprey drops more than 500 feet. With 820 feet remaining between his aircraft and the ground, Brow is coming down at 3,945 feet per minute, and though still traveling at 101 knots, about 115 miles an hour, it is losing forward speed rapidly. The crew chiefs of both Ospreys open their right-side cabin doors, preparing to land.

Bianca asks Wright if he can see the ground.

"Yup," Wright replies.

"Okay, you want me to turn on the searchlight?" Bianca asks.

Wright doesn't reply.

"You got your buildings in sight, you got your landing area in sight, here comes the gear," Bianca says as he lowers the landing gear. "Gear's coming . . . and you're gonna have to take some airspeed out . . . um . . . there's our buildings to the left, there's our landing area right underneath the nose."

By now, both Ospreys are fully converted to helicopter mode—and on the verge of overshooting the airfield. A tailwind blowing 8 knots or more has been pushing them toward the field even as they cut their speed. "We're kinda high at this point, we're at four hundred feet," Bianca warns Wright.

"I can't even get her to come down," Wright says. His Osprey has slowed to 60 knots and lost 600 feet of altitude in the past seventeen seconds, but with the tailwind, they still aren't coming down fast enough to hit their intended landing zone.

"Okay, if it's not sweet, we can go long if you need to, or you can wave off," Bianca tells Wright. "It's your call."

Wright tilts his Osprey's nacelles nearly as far aft as they will go, to 95 degrees, directing their thrust forward like air brakes. They are still at 300 feet. Behind them, still trying to keep from passing Wright, Brow has stopped his Osprey's rapid descent for a moment by adding power and ballooning again as his nacelles hit 90 degrees, full helicopter mode, 566 feet above the ground. Now Brow tilts his rotors all the way back, too. Crew chief Banks watches out the back of Wright's Osprey as Brow's crosses from left to right about 200 feet behind them and pulls up nearly even on their right side.

"We're hanging Dash Two out," Bianca cautions Wright.

Moffitt is looking toward the airfield out the door on the right side of the Osprey when crew chief instructor Sharp taps him on the shoulder and points a finger up. Moffitt sees Brow's Osprey, now even with Wright's but a hundred feet or more higher.

"Dash Two's three o'clock high," Moffitt reports to the pilots.

"Roger," Bianca acknowledges.

"He's getting back into position," Moffitt adds.

Now both Ospreys are slowing rapidly and coming down fast. At 250 feet, Wright's forward speed is 30 knots. His descent rate is 1,050 feet per minute and increasing. Brow is about 90 feet higher but flying faster, 48 knots, and losing altitude more than twice as fast as Wright, at 2,247 feet per minute.

No one will ever be able to ask Brow why, a few seconds later, he pushes his thrust control lever forward two and a half inches to add power, moves his control stick an inch and a half to the right, and depresses his right rudder pedal a touch, pulling his Osprey's nose to the right. At the time, he is flying forward at less than 40 knots and hurtling toward the ground at 2,050 feet per minute, rotors tilted as far back as they will go. Most likely, Brow is adding power to slow his descent and reposition his aircraft to avoid overtaking Wright. Maybe he is preparing to wave off and fly around. Neither Brow, nor his copilot, Gruber, says a word over the radio at the time. Whatever Brow's intention, his Osprey suddenly rolls hard to the right. Brow shoves the thrust control lever to full power and jerks the control stick all the way left, desperately trying to counter the roll. His Osprey snaps farther right instead.

Watching from the side door of Wright's Osprey, at first crew chief Moffitt thinks Brow is making a hard right-hand turn. A split second later, peering beneath his night-vision goggles, Moffitt watches, dumbfounded, as Brow's Osprey noses over, turns its belly skyward, and plummets into the sand next to the runway. As it hits, Moffitt hears a loud *crunch* and the sound of glass shattering. He sees the Osprey explode. He feels a wave of heat hit his face. A cloud of black smoke and fire mushroom into the night sky. The concussion blows Moffitt back from the cabin door.

Banks, watching out the open rear ramp door, is surprised when his night-vision goggles go black, their light sensors washed out by the flash of the explosion. He sees bursts of orange to the sides of his goggles.

Bianca catches a flash of orange out of the corner of his right eye. He looks out his right window, at first thinking the nacelle on that side has caught fire. That's when Bianca sees the fireball behind them.

"Oh, my God, they went down, they crashed!" Moffitt says over the intercom, a note of vacant awe in his voice. "Oh, my God, wave off left!" Moffitt then cries, coming to his senses as the Osprey he's in begins to drop abruptly. "Power! Wave off! Wave it off! POWER!" Moffitt screams.

Crew chief Banks joins Moffitt's cry. "Wave off, wave off, wave off," Banks repeats, his voice rising with each repetition.

"Wave off," Moffitt urges again.

"Wave off, WAVE OFF, WAVE OFF!" Banks choruses.

Screw this, I'm flying now! Bianca thinks, grabbing his set of controls. He and Wright both shove their thrust control levers forward to full power and tilt the Osprey's nacelles down to 65 degrees, trying to pick up speed and fly around. The maneuver doesn't work. They have slowed to less than 10 knots, and their Osprey's wings can't generate enough lift to keep them airborne. Two seconds later, the Osprey touches down on the runway, bounces back into the air a few dozen feet, then comes down again.

Banks falls out of a seat he had taken as he felt the aircraft dropping. Moffitt is knocked to his knees. He hears the Osprey's tires squeal.

"That's it, pull it back, you got it, Lefty!" Bianca shouts as they try to slow the Osprey. Bianca and Wright cut all power to the rotors. Still on his knees, Moffitt sticks his head out the door as they skid down the asphalt landing strip. He smells burning rubber. He sees a drainage ditch ahead.

"We're gonna hit hard!" Bianca warns amid a cacophony of shouts. Bianca sees the ditch, too. He fears the three-foot trench will shear the Osprey's nosewheels off.

"Shutdown!" Moffitt screams to the pilots as the Osprey slides toward the ditch.

"They're off, they're off," Bianca replies.

"Shutdown!" Moffitt repeats.

"They're off!" Bianca yells back as the Osprey keeps rolling.

Moffitt jerks his head back inside, sits on the floor with his back to the fuselage, and braces for the crack-up he is sure is coming. Instead they bounce across the ditch and screech to a halt on a taxiway beyond.

"Get the grunts off the plane!" Bianca yells as the Osprey shudders to a stop. "Get 'em off!"

Banks lowers the bottom door of the rear ramp. Black smoke wafts in. *We're on fire,* Banks thinks. He turns and starts grabbing Marines one by one, nearly ripping them out of their seats and throwing them toward the ramp. "Get the fuck out! Get the fuck out!" he shrieks. The troops start rushing out of the Osprey. Some wonder if the explosion was planned, a part of their mock mission.

"Get 'em off!" Bianca yells again as the grunts scramble down the rear ramp.

"Get 'em off," pilot Wright joins in.

"GET 'EM OFF!!!" Bianca screams again. "Get out, Lefty, we got it!"

Over the radio, the pilots of the two Ospreys still circling above hear the commotion on the ground. "Hey, Pyg, did you hear that?" Major Mike Murphy asks Major Mike Westman.

Bianca gets on the radio. "CRASH—CRASH, CRASH, CRASH!!!" he screams.

"Is that for real?" another pilot somewhere above asks.

"CRASH, CRASH, CRASH, IT'S REAL, THERE'S AN AIRPLANE ON THE GROUND!" Bianca screeches, then yells at Wright: "GET OUT, LEFTY, WE GOT IT!"

Wright jumps out of the cockpit and joins the troops on the runway behind his Osprey. At the other end of the airfield, a bright fire is burning, the source of the black smoke that made crew chief Banks think his Osprey was on fire. With the last of the infantry safely away, Banks runs out the rear ramp and stops. He takes a step toward the flames, then feels a hand grab his shoulder from behind. "Hey," crew chief instructor Sharp tells Banks somberly, "it's over."

With Wright out of the cockpit, Bianca takes a deep breath, then calmly reports over the radio: "This is Nighthawk Seven One. I am safe on deck and shut down. My Dash Two aircraft is on the ground." He shuts the Osprey down, exits the cockpit, and joins the others at the rear.

Wright borrows Banks's cell phone and starts making calls to Yuma. Bianca grabs a radioman from among the infantry. "You work for me now," Bianca tells him. Bianca has the Marine kneel so he can use the radio the grunt carries on his back. They feel the heat from the fire on their faces. A fire truck is already on the scene, but every now and then, oxygen bottles, antimissile flares, or some other volatile equipment on the crashed Osprey cooks off and explodes with a "pop!" The crew chiefs stand on the runway in shock, wondering how things could have gone so wrong so quickly.

From the moment they began their tardy descent to the moment Brow's aircraft hit the ground, exactly two minutes and twenty-six seconds had elapsed.

* * *

Westman, piloting the lead Osprey of the second section, and Rock, flying copilot in the Osprey behind, saw the explosion in their rearview mirrors, an orange flash that caught their eye under their night-vision goggles. They had just begun a second orbit in the holding pattern they had taken up five miles from the airport. For a few seconds, the radio fell eerily silent. No one wanted to be the first to acknowledge what all four pilots in their two Ospreys knew must be true. Westman looked in the mirror again. Orange and red flames were licking into the night sky from the Marana airfield. For a few seconds, the sight mesmerized him. Then Murphy radioed. Seconds later, the pilots heard Bianca shouting that there had been a crash.

"Holy shit, Pyg, you're the on-scene commander," said Westman's copilot, Schafer, jolting Westman out of his daze. "We need to go over there."

Schafer took the controls, peeled off toward the airport, and started circling at 1,500 feet as Westman got busy on the radio, directing air traffic. He couldn't believe this.

Five minutes or so later, Rock got Westman on the radio. "Hey, we probably ought to go back," Rock said, referring to himself and Murphy. Every pilot in a squadron has responsibilities on the ground. Rock was the MOTT's safety officer and Murphy its maintenance officer, he reminded Westman. "We need to get back and start making preparations for a mishap investigation." Westman told them to go.

Murphy banked into a tight turn and started flying back to Yuma—fast. He and Rock didn't say much on the flight back. From the size of the explosion, it was pretty clear there would be no survivors. They knew they had just lost some good friends.

There would be plenty of grieving to do later, grieving for Brow and Gruber, both of whom left wives and young children, and for the other seventeen Marines who had flown with them. Fifteen were infantry, the backbone of the Marine Corps, all but one serving in the 3rd Battalion/5th Marines at Camp Pendleton in California. The oldest was twenty-nine, the youngest eighteen. On average, they had lived twenty-two years. In the back cabin with them had been two crew chiefs, Staff Sergeant Bryan Nelson, thirty, a mild-tempered Virginian and a talented athlete, and Corporal Kelly Keith, the twenty-two-year-old who liked to sing "Let Her Cry," by Hootie and the Blowfish. Some MOTT mechanics would mourn later by getting forearm tattoos depicting dog tags with Nelson's and Keith's names and their dates of birth and death. One had an Osprey tattooed on his back, along with the title of a Kid Rock song the maintainers listened to a lot after the crash. It was called "Only God Knows Why."

★ ★ ★

By the time Rock and Murphy got back to Yuma, MOTT leaders Sweaney and Shaffer were at the hangar, organizing the thousand things that needed doing. By 10 P.M., Westman and Schafer had returned, after handing off air traffic control at Marana to the commander of MAWTS-1, who had arrived by helicopter. Not long afterward, Sweaney came into Westman's office and told him, sounding astonished, "It's already on CNN."

"If it's on CNN, we'd better start notifying family members," Westman said. Wives and other relatives would be burning up the phone lines, calling each other and anybody else they could reach to find out what had happened. Those who didn't get a call might assume the worst. No use putting anyone through that.

Sweaney hesitated. It was the middle of the night back home. Westman could see Sweaney was stinging inside. Sweaney had been through something like this before, at Quantico in 1992, when the fourth Osprey prototype crashed into the Potomac River. Sweaney, a captain back then, had helped pull bodies out of the river. Now he was a lieutenant colonel, and the MOTT's commander. His shoulders were broad, but the weight on them was crushing.

★ ★ ★

It was CNN's reporting that jolted Dick Spivey out of bed at the Thistle Victoria Hotel in London, where it was already Monday morning, and seared the moment into his memory. Spivey was to brief an aviation conference that day on the Quad TiltRotor, the bigger dream machine he was now promoting full-time. The news that an Osprey had crashed and killed nineteen Marines hit him like a punch in the gut. His stomach was grinding. He felt anguish for the Marines and their families. He felt angst for the Osprey. He wanted to crawl back into bed and go back to sleep, try to turn this nightmare back into the dream the tiltrotor had always been for him. *What could have caused such a thing?* he wondered. *A screw-up like the crossed wires that caused Aircraft 5 to crash at Wilmington in 1991? Design weaknesses like the ones that brought down Aircraft 4 at Quantico in 1992? Pilot error?* Spivey started to call Fort Worth to see what he could find out, then remembered what time it was in Texas. Way too early to call. All he could do for now was remind himself that bad things happened in aviation. Nearly every kind of helicopter or airplane crashed at some time or another for some reason or another. The old saying was true: "The history of aviation is written in blood."

As the MOTT's safety officer, the first thing Rock had to do when he and Mike Murphy landed back at Yuma was file various reports with MAWTS-1. When that was done, Rock and Murphy gathered up a "mishap kit" of crash investigating gear. Those sifting through the wreckage of Brow's Osprey at Marana would have to wear Tyvek suits, gloves, and respirators to protect them from the toxic fumes created by burning composites and fuel. Rock and Murphy gave teams of enlisted Marines orders and sent them to Marana in some pickup trucks the MOTT had rented for transportation in Yuma. Then the two pilots threw the mishap kit in the back of a rented Dodge Ram and started the 220-mile trip to Marana themselves. Before speeding out of Yuma on Interstate 8, they stopped at a convenience store and bought five boxes of PowerBars and some water for the Marines at the crash site. It was going to be a long night.

When they arrived, it was after midnight. The fire was out but the remains of the Osprey were smoldering next to the runway. The local fire department had gotten to the scene twelve minutes after the crash but the wreckage was still too hot to go near. There was nothing anyone could do for the nineteen Marines who had been on board. Their Osprey had hit the ground with what investigators later estimated was twenty-five times the force of gravity. The impact literally crushed the life out of the young men inside.

★ ★ ★

The morning after, some of the MOTT pilots gathered in Sweaney's office to listen on a speakerphone when Lieutenant General Fred McCorkle, the deputy commandant for aviation, called. McCorkle's call sign was "Assassin," and for many in Marine Corps aviation, the three-star general was a paragon, a walking icon of what an assault support pilot should be. Born in 1944 in San Francisco but raised in the Smoky Mountains town of Harriman, Tennessee, McCorkle never lost the hillbilly drawl and grammar that came with his roots, though he earned a degree in education from East Tennessee State University in 1966. He joined the Marine Corps out of college and two years later was in Vietnam, a jut-jawed, wiry little first lieutenant flying CH-46 helicopters with enough abandon to earn the radio call sign "Crazy Fred." McCorkle flew 1,500 combat missions and had several helicopters shot from under him in Vietnam. He won a raft of medals, earning the Distinguished Flying Cross twice, the Legion of Merit four times, and a Purple Heart, among others. Before his tour in Vietnam was up, his squadron mates changed his call sign to Assassin.

Over the next two decades, McCorkle attended all the right Marine Corps schools and held all the right commands, including two years as commander of MAWTS-1. As he rose through the ranks, McCorkle collected protégés, younger officers who had caught his eye for one reason or another. When he was commanding MAWTS-1, or Marine Aircraft Group 29 at New River, or later the 3rd Marine Aircraft Wing at El Toro, California, McCorkle often could be found at the officers club on Friday nights, having drinks with his "sons," as he called them. They listened and he talked, schooling them in aircraft and tactics, telling war stories, making wry comments in his folksy manner. They loved him. When something bad happened to one of his sons, McCorkle was there to help. McCorkle hadn't known Keith Sweaney very long, but since OPEVAL had begun, the general had come to count the lieutenant colonel as one of his sons. Now Sweaney needed a shoulder to lean on.

As a mentor, McCorkle was calling the day after the crash to buck Sweaney up. As the head of Marine Corps aviation, McCorkle was assessing how the crash might affect the Osprey. He wanted OPEVAL done so

the Osprey could pass its "Milestone III" review—the decision on Full
Rate Production—by the end of 2000. As a young major in the 1980s,
McCorkle hadn't been in favor of the Marine Corps building a tiltrotor
to replace the CH-46; he thought a new helicopter made more sense.
Once the decision to build the Osprey was made, though, McCorkle
saluted and supported it like a good Marine. As he rose in rank over the
years, McCorkle became impatient to see the Osprey get into service.
The Corps' CH-46 fleet was becoming more fragile all the time; Marines
died in CH-46s nearly every year, it seemed, but the Marines never got
the Osprey. Politics was the main reason, in McCorkle's view. In 1996,
when he was a two-star general, McCorkle grew more impatient with
the wait for the Osprey after he went to Fort Worth and flew the XV-15.
He was amazed at how stable the little tiltrotor demonstrator was in
flight. Later he flew the Osprey itself and became a tiltrotor convert.
McCorkle had been a true believer in the Osprey and its potential for
the Marines ever since, and he thought it was way overdue. McCorkle
wanted to field the Osprey as soon as possible. That meant getting it into
Full Rate Production, and that meant finishing OPEVAL.

Westman was leaning in the doorway as Sweaney and McCorkle
talked on the speakerphone. "Keith, I know this is tough, and we've got
everything down right now," McCorkle said. "We'll get this thing figured
out, but all you guys have to do is tell us when you're ready to go flying
and I'll get you back in the air."

"Who the fuck's he think's gonna fly 'em?" Westman blurted, loud
enough that he figured McCorkle might have heard him. Westman
didn't care. "I was convinced at that time that we needed to know why
that airplane crashed before we went and hopped back in it and started
again what we were doing," he told me.

★ ★ ★

Three days after the crash, McCorkle came to the Pentagon press briefing room to give the media the first of what he promised would be regular updates as the investigation into what had happened at Marana
progressed. In the three days since the crash, public affairs officers at
Headquarters Marine Corps had gotten more than a thousand calls
from reporters. "Right now we have no indication of what caused the
accident," McCorkle said. "I've heard on a number of news [reports] that
we were looking at pilot error. We are not. We're looking at anything that

caused the accident, whether it's material, whether it's mechanical, or whether it was human factors–related. And right now we have none of that information." McCorkle stiffened a touch when a reporter asked if he'd heard that the parents of some of the infantry killed were saying the Marines had used their sons as "guinea pigs" in a test aircraft, a machine that "was unsafe and their child had communicated that to them." The Ospreys at Marana were "in no way test aircraft," McCorkle said; they were production models the Marines would be flying in operational squadrons for years to come. He had flown the Osprey himself, and his confidence in it was unshaken. "I consider this to be the best aircraft that I've ever been in. This accident, to me, is not going to do anything to our MV-22 program," McCorkle said. No Ospreys, including the prototypes assigned to developmental test pilots at Pax River, would fly for now, but McCorkle was sure they would soon. "There's no doubt in my mind whatsoever, you know, that the full rate of production decision will be made with Milestone III and that it will go through."

For the first time since 1992, the Osprey was front-page news again, and the news was awful. Most coverage simply reported what was known so far about the crash, but some articles and commentaries took the Marines to task for putting troops in the back of an aircraft seen by out-siders as exotic and experimental. Three days after McCorkle briefed the press, the *New York Times* editorial page urged Defense Secretary Cohen to "appoint a panel of independent experts to review whether the Osprey is as mechanically sound and militarily advantageous as its champions assert." Others called for an end to it. "The V-22 Osprey is a misbegotten aircraft that tends to destroy itself," an editorial in the *Milwaukee Journal Sentinel* declared. "It is the result of a perverse deci-sion-making process that led to a wasteful and disastrous boondoggle." Denouncing the Osprey as "pork-barrel politics gone berserk," the com-mentary concluded that, "The V-22 program should be killed before it kills again."

The Marines, Bell-Boeing, and the Osprey's allies in Congress knew this was a crisis that could quickly get out of hand if they didn't handle it correctly. There always had been a lot of people who wanted to kill the Osprey, from those who coveted the billions being spent on it for their own pet Pentagon projects or domestic programs to those who thought the tiltrotor was just a crazy idea, a Rube Goldberg contraption foisted on the Marines by greedy defense contractors. The Osprey lobby, relatively quiet for years, rushed to circle the wagons. Representative Curt Weldon, the Pennsylvania Republican who had led the fight against Dick Cheney's attempt to cancel the Osprey a decade earlier, held his own news conference. "It's a terrible tragedy for those Marines and their families, but we've had seven years of unblemished success since the last accident," Weldon told reporters. "I have total confidence in the program."

Nine days after he first talked to reporters about the crash, McCorkle was back in the Pentagon briefing room. Since the last time he had been there, McCorkle had attended funerals for Brow and Gruber, two more of his "sons." He had also gone to Yuma to talk to engineers examining the wreckage of their aircraft and to give the MOTT a pep talk. McCorkle addressed the unit in Toad Hall, an auditorium in MAWTS-1's headquarters building named for former Navy Secretary John Lehman, who had set the Marine Corps off on its quest for the Osprey seventeen years earlier. "Toad" had been Lehman's call sign as a Naval Reserve helicopter pilot. As Navy secretary, Lehman had gotten MAWTS-1 the funding for its building.

Speaking from the Toad Hall stage, McCorkle told the MOTT's pilots and maintainers they needed to look beyond the crash, pick up the pieces, and go on. He told them about some of the times he'd been shot down flying CH-46s in Vietnam. He talked about how many buddies he had lost in crashes over the years. Theirs was a dangerous business, McCorkle told them. There would be other times when airplanes would go down, other times when friends and brother Marines would be lost. As he looked out over his audience, McCorkle could see a few faces that wore thousand-yard stares, guys who looked depressed. He tried to shake them out of it. "If you're not ready to get back in this aircraft tomorrow and fly," he told them, "you're probably in the wrong business."

The remark rankled more than a few of the pilots and maintainers. They were still mourning their fallen friends, and they still didn't know what had caused the crash, why those friends had died. Some knew McCorkle was only trying to motivate them, but his bravado left a sour taste in a lot of their mouths. "Okay, well, we must be in the wrong line of business," Staff Sergeant Julius Banks told a couple of his friends as they filed out of the meeting. Major John T. Torres, one of the pilots, felt the same way. "Well, I guess I shouldn't be part of this program, because

I'm not ready to get back into that plane and do the things I need to do," Torres told others in the MOTT that day.

Sweaney called a meeting of the MOTT after McCorkle left Yuma. Despite what the general had said, "Take as much time as you need," Sweaney told his unit. "If you're not comfortable getting back on the aircraft, that's your personal call."

At his Pentagon news briefing on April 20, McCorkle told reporters that in the days since he had last talked to them, the commandant, General Jones, had attended a memorial service at Camp Pendleton for the infantry killed at Marana, then joined him in Yuma to meet with engineers studying the debris for clues to the cause of the crash. The Osprey's flight data recorder had been recovered. Its information was being retrieved and it would be plugged into a flight simulator for study. The cause should be determined before too long. "We're still looking at maintenance, we're looking at mechanical, and we're looking at human factor," McCorkle said. Once the cause was identified, McCorkle said, test pilots at Pax River would start flying Osprey prototypes again. Once General Jones agreed it was safe, the Marines would start flying their Ospreys, too, at first without passengers. The commandant wanted to fly on the first one to carry passengers, as did McCorkle. In the meantime, the MOTT would do OPEVAL tasks on the ground, such as testing the Osprey's redesigned blade fold/wing stow mechanism. "If we don't have a major delay here, the OPEVAL will stay right on schedule," McCorkle said. "We have to be done with OPEVAL, as most of you-all know, by June the thirtieth."

★ ★ ★

McCorkle was in a good mood when he returned to the Pentagon press briefing room next, on May 9. As he took the podium, he bantered with reporters he knew. The deputy chief of staff for aviation had reason to be cheerful. He was there to confirm, as CNN had reported five days earlier, that the crash investigators had found nothing wrong with the Osprey. "The commandant is confident that our MV-22 Osprey aircraft are fully airworthy," McCorkle said. Flights by test pilots at Pax River would resume the next day. The MOTT would fly again soon. OPEVAL would be done in time for a Full Rate Production decision in the fall.

Using charts on an easel, McCorkle described how the accident had unfolded. He didn't name any of the pilots, but he explained that Wright and Bianca had missed their 3,000-foot checkpoint, forcing Brow and Gruber to follow in what none of the pilots seemed to sense was a pell-mell descent. McCorkle's third chart traced Brow's speed and altitude over the last seconds of the flight, as reconstructed from his Osprey's Crash Survivable Memory Unit, a device that records airspeed, altitude, and other data. Six seconds before impact, McCorkle noted, the Osprey was 350 feet high and traveling at 41 knots. One second before it hit the ground, it was at 210 feet and 30 knots. "In summary, the data shows that the mishap aircraft was in a high rate of descent at a relatively low forward airspeed," McCorkle said. "These characteristics can lead to a condition known as power settling, or vortex ring state."

With that, McCorkle introduced a new, and for many people occult-sounding term into the debate over the Osprey. "Vortex ring state" was esoteric not only to the general public but in the aviation world as well. McCorkle had never heard of it himself until he saw the report on the accident at Marana. It was a term from fluid mechanics, an expression even an aeronautical engineer could go a career without hearing very often. Vortex ring state described a condition a rotor could get into as a result of what Navy and Marine Corps pilots called "power settling" and Army and Air Force pilots knew as "settling with power." What it all amounted to was a way to describe a rotor that was no longer creating thrust and lifting as it should because it was descending into its own downwash too quickly.

A rotor creates thrust both by pushing air downward and by pulling air through the "rotor disk," the circle a rotor's blades describe as they rotate. At the tips of the blades, some downwash circles back over top of the rotor disk and is pulled back through. This disturbed air interferes with a rotor's ability to create thrust only minimally—unless the rotor descends into its own downwash at the same velocity the downwash is moving. In that case, most or all of the downwash recirculates through the rotor disk rather than racing downward faster than the rotor and creating thrust. The downwash is now churning in a "vortex ring," an air flow pattern seen in smoke rings, and the rotor has entered "vortex ring state." When a rotor goes into vortex ring state, it no longer creates the thrust it should, and the aircraft begins to descend faster than the pilot wants.

When an aircraft descends too quickly, a pilot's natural tendency is to add power to arrest the descent, but in vortex ring state, adding power produces the opposite of the desired effect. In a rotorcraft, adding power also adds pitch to the rotor blades, increasing the angle at which they hit the air. Adding power and pitch to a rotor in vortex ring state only creates more disturbed air and pulls it back through the rotor disk faster. Instead of flowing as it should and creating thrust, the air begins bouncing in and around the rotor disk chaotically and the aircraft loses lift even faster. Helicopter pilots are taught about the hazard and told that the best way to get out of it is to reduce power to slow the rotor while flying into "clean air" by tilting their helicopter's nose forward. That tilts the rotor forward and increases forward airspeed. Without sufficient altitude, though, there may be too little time to do that, so pilots are urged simply to steer well clear of vortex ring state by never descending too quickly at slow speeds. It's the rotary wing aviation equivalent of an ancient cartographer writing on a map "Here Be Dragons." Helicopter pilots learn the rule and avoid that edge of the flight envelope out of habit. They simply don't go there.

The combined rate of descent and speed at which any particular rotorcraft might go into vortex ring state depends on various factors—the size and shape of its rotors, its flying weight, wind conditions, etc. The rule of thumb for most helicopters, though, is to avoid descending faster than 800 feet per minute when flying forward at 40 knots or less. Where the actual line existed for the Osprey was something the program's developmental test pilots hadn't determined, though hundreds of test flights to explore that part of the Osprey's envelope had been planned. Nolan Schmidt, the Osprey program manager and a Marine Corps colonel at the time, told me years later that those tests were scrapped in 1998 to save time and money. The Navy Department was going to cut the Osprey program's budget for the coming fiscal year by $100 million, Schmidt said. After consulting with the Boeing engineer in charge of flight-testing, Philip Dunford, Schmidt said, the program managers decided they could save about $50 million and a lot of time if they didn't do all the tests planned for the Osprey at high rates of descent. A few tests already done had indicated that the Osprey could safely descend at 1,200 feet per minute below 40 knots airspeed anyway, so Navair and company managers decided to simply adopt the standard rule for helicopters. It was enough to know there were dragons lurking beyond a descent rate of 800 feet per minute at 40 knots or less, so why test? "There was no practical need for any rotorcraft that we knew of to have to exceed that boundary anyway," one of the Osprey's developmental test pilots in those days told me. The flight clearance placard setting the limits on how the MOTT could fly the Osprey simply adopted the standard from helicopter flight manuals. "Avoid descent rates of 800 fpm [feet per minute] or greater at airspeeds less than 40 KCAS," it said, "KCAS" being the abbreviation for "knots-calibrated air speed." Precisely what might happen if a pilot flew beyond that edge of the envelope wasn't spelled out in the MOTT's flight clearance placard, but there was no need to go into detail. The rule was labeled a "Warning," which meant failing to observe it risked loss of the aircraft and death. For pilots, "Warning" is the flight manual equivalent of a skull and crossbones.

At his May 9 news briefing, McCorkle was asked whether the Osprey that crashed had been "descending within the flight envelope."

"He was descending over a thousand feet per minute," McCorkle said, noting that the recommended limit was no more than 800 feet per minute at 40 knots or less. Why the pilot had descended so fast was still being studied, McCorkle said. The right rotor of the Osprey, he added, might have gone into vortex ring state only when the pilot moved his control stick to the right four seconds before the crash. "I think that that's probably what caused it," McCorkle said.

"Is it correct to say that pilot error is to blame for this accident?" a reporter asked.

"No, it's not correct to say that," McCorkle said. "I would really appreciate it if you wouldn't speculate on that until after the mishap board has reported out. We feel like we have enough information to say that it was not mechanical. There are a lot of things the board is looking at. And why was the pilot at this rate of descent? Why was he in this position at this time? And it would be very inappropriate at this time to say that it was pilot error."

The main thing McCorkle wanted people to understand was that the crash wasn't being blamed on a flaw in the Osprey. Developmental test pilots at Pax River were going to do a full range of tests to explore where the edge of the Osprey's envelope for going into vortex ring state lay, he said. Meanwhile, OPEVAL would go on. "We have waited really a heck of a long time to put the airplane back into the air," McCorkle said.

★ ★ ★

McCorkle was back in the Pentagon press briefing room on July 27, 2000, to announce the final results of the Marana investigation. This

time, cameras were barred. When CNN Pentagon correspondent Jamie
McIntyre protested that newspaper reporters would be allowed to quote
McCorkle by name but TV reporters wouldn't be able to use videotape of
him speaking, McCorkle told McIntyre the ban on cameras was "strictly
my decision." He really had nothing new to say about the crash beyond
the fact that the investigation was closed, McCorkle said. "In fact, I did
not desire to do this." McCorkle said others, whom he didn't name, had
told him making no comment on the final results might lead to suspicion the Marine Corps was trying to hide something, so he had agreed
to do a "roundtable" with reporters. "It won't break my heart if nobody
writes a word in the newspapers except to say, you know, the investigation is complete," McCorkle said.

Then McCorkle explained why he was so reluctant to go on camera.
He had spent more than two hours that morning with the widow of the
pilot whose Osprey had crashed. He had spent an hour on the phone
the night before with the copilot's widow. "I personally just feel like it's
just time to put it to bed, which I wanted to do off the record," McCorkle
said.

Beyond being distraught at the loss of their husbands, Trish Brow
and Connie Gruber had been upset for weeks about news coverage of
the crash. Much of it had implied, some had outright said, that the cause
of the crash was "pilot error." The widows resented the idea that their
husbands were to blame. McCorkle had always refused to use the term
pilot error, saying it would be illegal for him to declare a cause until the
mishap board had finished its investigation. Now Marine Corps public
affairs officers had given reporters a news release attributing the crash
to "human factors."

McCorkle began the briefing by reading a statement that said "an
unexpected tailwind and the pilot's extremely rapid rate of descent
into the landing zone created the conditions that led to the accident.
Although the report stops short of specifying pilot error as the cause,
it notes that the pilot of the ill-fated aircraft significantly exceeded the
rate of descent established by regulations for a safe flight." The statement
omitted all the pilots' names but described what had gone wrong in far
more detail than McCorkle had given in his earlier briefings: how the
lead aircraft, flown by Wright and Bianca, had begun the descent into
Marana too high; how Brow and Gruber had followed them; how none
of the pilots seemed to have realized they were descending dangerously

fast; how Brow's attempt to slide his Osprey to the right before landing probably had put the rotor on that side into vortex ring state, causing the aircraft to roll out of control.

When he started taking questions, McCorkle also revealed, again without using names, that he had suspended Wright's and Bianca's designations as "tiltrotor aircraft commander" for six months. To get the designation back, each would have to requalify by taking tests and check rides. McCorkle wasn't going to blame any of the pilots for the crash. The pilot of the lead aircraft—Wright—should have waved off and gone around, he said, if not earlier, then at the very latest when his copilot—Bianca—told him they were "a little high" and said it was Wright's call whether to try to land or wave off. "Now, did he cause Dash Two to crash?" McCorkle said. "No, because Dash Two could have said, 'I'm going around,' you know, 'whether you want to go around or not.'" There were "several links in the chain" that led to the accident, McCorkle noted. "And none of them—nothing—was ever done with intent." All four pilots involved had behaved professionally. This wasn't an accident "caused by cowboys," he said, though mistakes had been made.

When a reporter asked if anything in the accident report would prevent the Osprey going into Full Rate Production, McCorkle brightened. "I'm really happy that you asked that question," he said. The MOTT had started flying OPEVAL missions again in late May and finished in mid-July, using a revised flight clearance that forbade descending at more than 800 feet per minute anytime the Osprey's nacelles were tilted upward beyond 80 degrees. The Osprey had "met or exceeded all the key performance parameters," McCorkle said. "We're hoping for the Milestone III decision for full rate development to be sometime in October."

CHAPTER TEN

YOU WANT IT BAD, YOU GET IT BAD

O n the last day of his life, December 11, 2000, Lieutenant Colonel Keith Sweaney rose before the sun, had coffee with his wife, Carol, and was on his way to work by 5:30 A.M. Most days the MOTT leader drove a dozen miles from his Stafford, Virginia, home to his office at Quantico Marine Corps Base, where his headquarters had moved after OPEVAL ended in July. Today, though, Sweaney wheeled his spanking new silver Mitsubishi Eclipse sports coupe onto Interstate 95 and hotfooted it south to New River Marine Corps Air Station on the North Carolina coast. He covered the 305 miles in a brisk five and a half hours.

If Sweaney was in a hurry to get to New River, he had good reason. His orders were to spend a week there preparing for his next prestigious assignment. In a couple of months, Sweaney was scheduled to leave the MOTT and take command of the Marine Corps' first operational Osprey squadron at New River. The Pentagon hadn't approved Full Rate Production yet, but the Marines hoped it would soon, clearing the way for them to put the Osprey into service at last. "I'm confident it should be approved, and I've seen nothing to lead me to believe that it won't," General Jim Jones, the commandant, had told the Associated Press a few days earlier. Sweaney was the logical choice to head the new squadron, the most experienced Osprey pilot in the Marine Corps, but he needed refresher training. Over the past five months he had spent most of his time wrapping up OPEVAL and writing the MOTT's report on the testing. The report wasn't done until October, when Sweaney gave a briefing on it to Philip Coyle, the Pentagon's director of operational test and evaluation. The MOTT's Ospreys had been sent to New

River, so Sweaney hadn't had much opportunity to fly. This week, he was scheduled to catch up by making five flights in Ospreys assigned to the Marines' tiltrotor training squadron at New River.

Eager as he was to get back into the cockpit, Sweaney was looking forward even more to leaving behind the pressure-packed job of leading the MOTT through OPEVAL and the trauma of Marana. The unit's pilots and maintainers had needed time to recover from the shock of the Arizona crash, and their higher-ups hadn't given them much. The deadline for completing OPEVAL so the Pentagon could rule on Full Rate Production was tighter than ever after the mishap and the resulting delay in the schedule.

The month after the crash, when no one was flying Ospreys, had been hardest for the MOTT. First there were the funerals, then the crash investigation. The MOTT resumed flying in June at China Lake, a 1.1-million-acre naval air weapons station in the western Mojave Desert of California. Most of the pilots and crew chiefs didn't hesitate to fly again after vortex ring state was declared the cause of the Marana crash, but some did. Some crew chiefs agreed to go back up only after Staff Sergeant Julius Banks, who had manned the rear ramp in the lead Osprey at Marana, said he would fly again. Banks, thirty-six, was the noncommissioned officer in charge of the flight line for the MOTT. A lot of younger crew chiefs looked up to him.

Many Marine Corps ground troops were wary of the Osprey after Marana, a fact General Jones knew. Jones, a career infantry officer—not an aviator—who had fought in Vietnam, understood how the grunts felt. To try to ease their minds and show the rest of the world he still had confidence in the tiltrotor, Jones went to China Lake on June 17 and flew on the first Osprey to carry passengers since Marana. He even took his wife aboard with him. Top executives from Bell Helicopter and Boeing rode along, too. "If there was the slightest doubt—I mean the slightest doubt—we would not have done this today," Jones told reporters afterward.

After OPEVAL, the MOTT shrank. Its Air Force contingent moved to Edwards Air Force Base in California to continue testing that service's version of the Osprey. Bell and Boeing had delivered seven more Low Rate Initial Production Ospreys that year. During the summer, six of the nine remaining Marine pilots in the MOTT, and a number of its maintainers, transferred to the Osprey training squadron at New River,

VMMT-204. The Marines needed to train a lot of mechanics, pilots, and crew chiefs if they were going to have enough to field the Osprey in 2001.

With a presidential election campaign going on, the storm in the media and on Capitol Hill that had seemed to threaten the Osprey in the weeks after Marana died down almost as quickly as it had blown up. There were still rumblings of suspicion about how safe the tiltrotor really was, though. Some aeronautical engineers were beginning to study whether the side-by-side placement of the Osprey's rotors created some vulnerability to vortex ring state that didn't exist with helicopters. Developmental test pilots at Pax River were writing up plans to start testing that later in the year. Meanwhile, the Marines and their allies were taking steps to shore up the Osprey's political support. At Representative Curt Weldon's urging, Defense Secretary William Cohen let the Marines send an Osprey to the Republican National Convention in Philadelphia from July 31 to August 3, putting it on display along with other military equipment at the former Philadelphia Naval Shipyard. More than a hundred members of Congress were staying in housing on the shuttered base during the convention, something else Weldon had arranged. A few reporters wrote stories about whether it was proper for the Pentagon to inject itself into electoral politics that way, but Weldon knew it was a good way to get lawmakers interested in the Osprey again.

Other Osprey news that summer wasn't so good. In August, the Pentagon inspector general's office issued a report questioning whether the Osprey was ready for Full Rate Production. The report said the Navy Department had let the Osprey go into OPEVAL before it was ready, waiving twenty-two requirements that should be tested before the aircraft was fielded. Some waivers had to do with the Osprey's limited flight envelope, which banned pilots from doing "air combat maneuvers" during OPEVAL. Most involved what insiders called the "ilities"—reliability, availability, maintainability—measures of how hard it would be for the Marines to keep the Osprey ready to fly in the field. During OPEVAL, the Osprey had performed far below its goals for availability. Even with the waivers, and even excluding the maintenance and parts problems that forced the MOTT to stop flying from mid-December 1999 until February 22, 2000, the Osprey's availability rate during the tests had fallen well short of its targets. The goal for keeping all four of the LRIP Ospreys the MOTT used "mission capable," meaning they could fly even if some systems weren't working, had been a daily average of 82 percent. The actual mission-capable rate during OPEVAL was 57 percent. The goal for having all four Ospreys "full mission capable," meaning every system on them was functioning, had been 75 percent. The full-mission-capable rate during OPEVAL was a mere 11 percent. The MOTT's final report said the Osprey's availability rate was "unsatisfactory."

Even Navair's Osprey program office acknowledged it would take at least a year or more after Full Rate Production was approved to get the aircraft up to minimum standards on the ilities. Problems with spare parts, bugs in the Osprey's computerized maintenance system, and other deficiencies had kept the MOTT from meeting its OPEVAL goals. The inspector general's report suggested the tests should have been postponed until the Osprey was ready. "The desire to meet milestones resulted in demands being made to complete operational test and evaluation quickly . . . rather than delaying the program and risk losing the funding," the report concluded.

About the time that report was released, all eleven Ospreys in use were grounded for a week after one flown by VMMT-204 at New River made a precautionary landing at nearby Camp Lejeune. A coupling in its driveshaft had come loose, so the driveshafts of all Ospreys were inspected. The grounding didn't slow the Osprey's political momentum, though. On September 7, former Defense Secretary Dick Cheney, now Republican presidential nominee George W. Bush's vice presidential running mate, made a campaign stop in Wayne, Pennsylvania, eighteen miles from Boeing Helicopter Company in Ridley Park. Someone asked Cheney what he thought about the Osprey. "We're committed now, and we've made a significant upfront investment, and if I had to sit down today and decide what our needs are and given the status of the program, I'd probably go forward with it," Cheney said. Over the past eighteen years, the Pentagon had spent $10 billion designing, redesigning, and buying Ospreys. Navair's latest estimate was that it would cost $28 billion more to finish buying all 458 planned.

A few weeks later, despite the disappointing results in the MOTT's report, the Navy's Operational Test and Evaluation Force declared that the Osprey had passed OPEVAL and was "operationally effective" and "operationally suitable," two legal standards a major new piece of defense equipment must meet. All the Marines needed now was for the Pentagon's operational test and evaluation director, Coyle, to agree. If he did, the way would be clear for the assistant secretary of the Navy for research, development, and acquisition, the final authority on whether the Osprey was ready for Full Rate Production, to approve Milestone III. Coyle didn't. On November 17, he issued his own report on OPE-VAL. Coyle found the Osprey "operationally effective" but "not operationally suitable." By law, to be found "operationally effective," a piece of defense equipment had to be able to perform the missions it was designed to do. To be "operationally suitable," it had to be reliable and easy enough to maintain to meet minimum availability rates. Based on the Osprey's maintenance problems during OPEVAL, Coyle said the aircraft wasn't reliable yet and needed too many mechanics to keep it running. Coyle didn't say so in his report, but he couldn't understand why the Navy's Operational Test and Evaluation Force had declared the Osprey operationally suitable. During OPEVAL, the Ospreys flown by the MOTT had suffered twenty-seven failures of swashplate actuators, mechanical devices that raise and lower the pitch, or angle, of rotor blades, his report noted. "Failures related to the hydraulic system deserve special mention," Coyle's report said. To help hold down the Osprey's bulk and weight, its designers had been forced to use titanium hydraulic lines under 5,000 pounds per square inch of pressure, which were thinner and lighter than the 3,000-psi hydraulic lines customarily used in helicopters. The higher pressure "places great stress on hydraulic seals," Coyle's report said, noting that the four Ospreys flown by the MOTT had suffered 170 hydraulic failures during OPEVAL.

Coyle's report created a problem for the Marines. On December 5, six days before Sweaney headed to New River, the Navy Department held a meeting to decide whether to approve Milestone III and put the Osprey into Full Rate Production. Navair officials went into the meeting expecting H. Lee Buchanan III, the assistant secretary of the Navy authorized to make the decision, to give the Osprey a green light. Buchanan didn't. After listening to a briefing on where things stood, he wasn't persuaded the Osprey was ready, given its maintenance record. He asked for another briefing in two weeks and postponed a decision. Suddenly, whether the Marines were going to get the Osprey past Milestone III in time to field it in 2001 was looking iffy.

★ ★ ★

The Osprey that Keith Sweaney was supposed to use for his first flight at New River on December 11 had a maintenance problem, which delayed his schedule for a second time that day. Sweaney's plans had changed once already because another pilot called in sick. That wasn't unusual, but something else that happened that day was.

About 3 P.M., not long after Sweaney got out of a preflight briefing, his fifteen-year-old daughter, Katrina, called on his cell phone. Katrina had never done that before when her father was scheduled to fly. Today, though, she had a weird feeling. Nothing vivid, just a premonition. She hadn't had a bad dream the night before or anything. She just had a feeling something bad might happen to her dad.

"Hi, what are you doing?" her father said.

"I just got home from school. I wanted to make sure you got to work okay," Katrina told him.

"I did."

Katrina wanted to tell her father about her bad feeling, ask him not to fly today. Once she heard his voice, though, she couldn't bring herself to do it. *I'm just being weird*, she thought. Now she was unsure what to say, so after an awkward pause, she told her dad she'd taught a new trick to their year-old chocolate Labrador retriever, Koko.

"That's great," Sweaney said. Katrina could tell he was in a hurry.

"Do you want me to have Mom call you when she gets in?" she asked.

"No," her father said. "Tell Mom I'll call her when I get done flying. I love you. Talk to you later."

Those who love people who can lose their lives on the job, like the people who do such jobs, often suffer premonitions. Even if Katrina had told her father about hers, he surely would have flown. No Osprey pilot in the Marine Corps had more reason to shrug off such things. Sweaney had 271 flight hours in the Osprey, more than any other pilot in the Corps. He had made his last flight forty days earlier, though, and his last night flight way back on July 12, so today he was scheduled to make a daylight refresher flight. The pilot in command would be his former subordinate Major Michael L. "Murf" Murphy, a big, smiley Irish-American, a New York City cop's son so gregarious the guys in the MOTT called him "The Mayor." Murphy, thirty-eight, was now a VMMT-204 instructor. Under the original plan, Sweaney was supposed to do his day hop, then give his seat to a major. Murphy would coach the major as he practiced landing the Osprey in a confined area after dark using night-vision goggles. When the other major called in sick, Colonel Richard Dunnivan, who was slated to take command of VMMT-204 in January, was put on the schedule. Dunnivan, who had never flown an Osprey except in a simulator, was itching to get behind the controls. Murphy suggested Dunnivan take Sweaney's daylight flight and let Sweaney do the night hop instead. Regulations said a pilot had to have flown a day hop within fifteen days before piloting a night flight, but given Sweaney's experience, the rules could be bent, it was decided. Sweaney would "hot seat" with Dunnivan—take his place—when Dunnivan and Murphy landed.

Murphy and Dunnivan were scheduled to take off at 3:30 P.M., but when they walked out to the flight line to get into their aircraft, Staff Sergeant Julius Banks told them they'd have to get another Osprey. A preflight check on the one they were supposed to use had found a missing fastener on the wing, potential foreign object debris that could cause damage if the fastener were rattling around somewhere in the aircraft. Banks told the crew chiefs who would fly with Murphy that day, Staff Sergeant Avely Runnels and Sergeant Jason Buyck, to find the next aircraft scheduled. The next Osprey was already on the flight line, just refueled after a training flight. When Murphy started it up, though, a malfunction in the nose wheel steering mechanism posted on the cockpit display, and Murphy declared the aircraft "down," not flyable. By then, the first Osprey had passed an inspection for the missing fastener and been cleared to fly, so Murphy and Dunnivan got into that one. The aircraft was nearly new, the eighth LRIP Osprey, so it had "08" painted on its side. It would fly under the radio call sign "Crossbow 08."

By the time Murphy and Dunnivan took off in Crossbow 08, it was 4:41 P.M. The shortness of the late fall daylight hours meant there wouldn't be enough time for Dunnivan to complete an entire day familiarization flight, so Sweaney hung around the VMMT-204 ready room, waiting his turn. When Murphy and Dunnivan landed just over half an hour later, Sweaney met them on the tarmac. Dunnivan climbed out of the Osprey's right seat and stepped into the back cabin. He was elated. Murphy had let him do everything: taxi out, do a rolling takeoff, convert the nacelles a couple of times, come back in and land. Flying the Osprey for the first time had been a thrill. Dunnivan was all smiles as Sweaney came aboard and squeezed into the right pilot seat. Dunnivan leaned in and helped him straighten the straps of his shoulder harness, plugged in his radio and night-vision goggles for him, handed him a kneeboard for maps and notes, then tapped him on the helmet. "See ya," Dunnivan said. Murphy was in the left seat, his night-vision goggles perched on his head as he set up the cockpit for night flight.

Sergeant Michael Moffitt, who like Banks had been a crew chief on the lead Osprey at Marana, was standing a few yards from the VMMT-204 hangar, smoking a cigarette, as crew chiefs Runnels and Buyck rushed around the open back ramp of Crossbow 08 preparing it to fly. Runnels and Buyck, who pronounced his name "bike," were good friends with each other, and Moffitt considered them two of his best buddies in VMMT-204. Everybody liked Runnels, twenty-five, a Georgia boy who would do anything for a laugh. Buyck, twenty-four, was a tall, shy kid from Sodus, New York, a town on Lake Ontario. Other guys in the squadron liked to mess with Buyck just because he seemed bashful.

As Crossbow 08 started moving, Runnels and Buyck jumped up on the back ramp and looked in Moffitt's direction. Moffitt gave them the finger. They gave him the finger back. Moffitt was pumped up that afternoon. After the crash at Marana, he had refused to fly in an Osprey for months but started again after he transferred to VMMT-204. Tonight, after Crossbow 08 came back from this flight, Moffitt was scheduled to go up in it with Major Buddy Bianca, the copilot on the lead aircraft at Marana. It would be the first time Bianca and Moffitt had flown together since that awful night in Arizona.

* * *

At 5:39 P.M., Murphy and Sweaney take off on what will be their last flight ever. Slightly less than an hour later, with the Osprey's rotors in airplane mode, they contact the New River air traffic controller from eleven miles out and request permission to practice radar landing approaches to the field. The technique is to tilt the rotors upward gradually while approaching, as if preparing to land, then tilt them forward again and circle around. Sweaney does two practice approaches. Murphy takes the controls and does a third. Then, at 7:18 P.M., Murphy tilts Crossbow 08's rotors forward to airplane mode, accelerates to 160 knots—about 185 miles per hour—and climbs to 1,400 feet, heading north so they can approach New River's Runway 19 from that direction and land into the wind. A minute later, they're at 1,600 feet and 180 knots as the tower begins dictating a series of left turns to put them on their approach path. They tell the tower they're going to land this time. Four minutes pass as the tower guides them by radio, watching on radar as they turn over the southern edge of Hofmann Forest, an 80,000-acre tract of pine woods and swampland that starts a half a dozen miles north of New River and the nearby city of Jacksonville, North Carolina. As they bank slightly left and turn to 230 degrees, a southwest heading, Murphy reduces power and Crossbow 08's automatic flight control system begins raising the nacelles. Then a caution light posts on their cockpit display. HYD 1 FAIL, it says. In their Osprey's left nacelle, one of the pencil-thin titanium hydraulic lines, its fluid under 5,000 pounds per square inch of pressure, has just sprung a leak. Two seconds later, Hydraulic System One, one of three in the Osprey, shuts down.

★   ★   ★

Stevie Jarman and his wife, Sue, lived on five acres nestled against the southwest edge of Hofmann Forest. Afternoons and evenings, Sue liked to sit on a love seat next to the sliding glass doors of their modular home, a roomy double-wide, and crochet while she listened to police and fire calls on her CB radio. The glass doors looked out on a pretty, 25-acre field where their neighbor, Robert Smith, usually grew corn. Stevie Jarman was assistant fire chief in Jacksonville but nearing retirement. He spent a lot of time in Hofmann Forest, where a group of friends and relatives leased 2,500 acres from a paper company to hunt deer, quail, doves, wild turkey, whatever was in season. This evening, no one is in the forest. It's cold, drizzly, and past dark. Stevie is across the field at a neighbor's home for a men's dinner and Baptist prayer meeting, same as every Monday. Sue puts down her needlework as she hears a strange noise, an uneven whirring, something like an electric fan with a bad blade, only ten times louder. The sound grows louder and louder, rising in a crescendo that begins to rattle the sliding glass doors. Soon the whole mobile home is shaking. "That thing sounds like it's gonna crash," Sue says aloud. When she does, a shudder passes through her. One night just a week ago, Sue suddenly remembers, she dreamed about an aircraft crashing. Right there in Robert Smith's field.

★   ★   ★

By the time Sue Jarman hears that whirring sound, Keith Sweaney and Michael Murphy are no longer flying Crossbow 08 so much as fighting to keep it airborne. The flight control system has gone haywire. Three seconds after the HYD 1 FAIL caution posts in the cockpit, the New River controller radios Crossbow 08 and gets no response. A second after that, as their nacelles tilt up to nine degrees, another caution posts: HYD 1/3 FAIL.

The Osprey has three hydraulic systems, a redundancy created to meet its survivability requirements. If one system fails, the other two are supposed to keep the aircraft flying. Hydraulic System One and Hydraulic System Two work in tandem, powering the Osprey's flight control actuators, devices that resemble automobile shock absorbers. The actuators move the mechanical parts that raise and lower the pitch of the rotor blades and power other control surfaces, such as the tail rudders. Hydraulic System Three has a separate set of primary tasks. It powers the landing gear, the rear ramp, the blade fold/wing stow system and other moving parts that don't affect flight. Hydraulic System Three, though, also backs up Systems One and Two, taking over for either one if electronic sensors detect a failure in them. For the most part, the three hydraulic systems are independently routed. To back up Systems One and Two, though, System Three has to join them at certain points so it can take over their work. One such point is inside the nacelles, just before the hydraulic lines enter the actuators that power the swashplates, the leverlike mechanisms that change the angles of the rotor blades. Crossbow 08 has sprung a leak in that line, about two inches beyond where Hydraulic System One and System Three join. Within seconds, all hydraulic fluid in System One is lost. A fail-safe mechanism in System Three shuts off the flow of fluid before it gets to the leak point. This is why the cockpit display flashes HYD 1/3 FAIL. Now, in the left nacelle, only Hydraulic System Two is powering the swashplate actuators. A new caution posts: CRITICAL SWPL FAULT—"critical swashplate fault." With that, an automatic system for tilting the nacelles disengages and the rotors stop at 11 degrees. This all happens in six seconds.

The New River controller radios again, ending with "how do you hear?" The pilots are too busy to talk. Their aircraft has just told them its flight controls are failing and they're only 1,600 feet above ground. They have life-or-death decisions to make. In a hurry. In a darkened cockpit. Wearing night-vision goggles. With a shrill warning tone— "deedle-eedle-eedle-eedle-eedle"—sounding in their earphones. On the glare shield, a sort of dashboard in front of them, an inch-square button labeled PFCS FAIL/RESET—Primary Flight Control System Fail/Reset— blinks on red. The HYD 1/3 FAIL caution has illuminated it. Sweaney and Murphy know that the Osprey's display screens often post cautions and advisories that aren't real, just computer hiccups. Standard operating procedure is to reset the PFCS when certain faults deemed "critical" post to see if they clear or post again. If a critical fault posts again, the pilot is supposed to land as soon as possible. Eight seconds after the first hydraulic fault posts, one of the pilots pushes the PFCS reset button.

The effect is disastrous. The faults come back. Worse still, pushing the button doesn't just reset the displays. Against all logic, it takes the pitch of the rotor blades flat, reducing the angle at which they hit the air. That robs the blades of most of their thrust and slows the aircraft as if someone had jammed on the brakes. When that happens, Crossbow 08's nose pitches up, the pilots are thrown forward, and Murphy—probably involuntarily—pushes the control stick and thrust control lever forward. The engines overspeed with the rotor blades at flat pitch. A governor cued by the Osprey's rotor speed signals the swashplate actuators to restore the blades to their previous angle. With only one hydraulic system working in the left nacelle, though, the left nacelle's swashplate actuators are like a man trying to lift a barbell with one hand tied behind his back. The blades on the right rotor regain their pitch far faster than the blades on the left. With greater pitch, the blades on the right rotor create more thrust, so the Osprey's nose whips left and Crossbow 08 rolls in that direction. Murphy sticks the nose back right to level off. As he does, cautions and advisories light up the cockpit display like fireworks. In big, white, block letters, the panel virtually screams at Sweaney and Murphy in rapid succession: L & R TORQUE SENSOR FLT—LOAD LIMIT FLT—MULTI SWPL FAULT—R&L FADEC B TURBINE OVERSPEED—R&L ENG Np OVERSPEED. Nothing in their training has prepared the pilots for this. One of them pushes the PFCS reset button again. The rotor blades lose their pitch and regain it at different speeds again. The Osprey slows, speeds up, yaws left. The last three faults post again. One of the pilots pushes PFCS reset again. The blades lose their pitch and regain it at different speeds again. The Osprey slows, speeds up, yaws left. By now, Crossbow 08 is whipsawing through the air, slamming the pilots forward and backward, left and right, more and more violently, at as much as twice the force of gravity. As the Osprey bucks, it loses altitude and speed. For some reason—maybe wishful thinking, maybe by accident as they try to brace themselves—the pilots hit the PFCS reset button again and again, at least nine times within twenty-two seconds. Murphy pushes and pulls the thrust control lever back and forth from zero to full power and jerks the control stick from side to side, maybe trying to get the Osprey under control, more likely because he's being whipped back and forth and side-to-side. By now, Crossbow 08's gyrations are slinging him and Sweaney around like rag dolls. Only their lap belts and shoulder harnesses keep them in their seats.

"How do you hear?" the controller asks again.

"Yeah, stand by," Murphy says, sounding stressed.

Now the Osprey is at 1,375 feet and nosing over to the left. Murphy pulls his control stick back and right as far as it will go and holds it there. He tilts the nacelles down to zero degrees. Nothing helps. On the radio, the New River controller is saying "Seven miles from the runway . . ." when Murphy screams out Crossbow 08's last transmission: "Declare emergency, we're goin' down, we're goin' down!"

Thirty seconds after the first sign of trouble, Crossbow 08 screeches down into the darkness of Hofmann Forest and plows into the trees.

★ ★ ★

Sue Jarman heard the explosion. The men at the prayer meeting across Robert Smith's field heard it, too. When they went outside, they could see flames shooting up out of the trees about a half mile into the forest. Stevie Jarman ran home. By the time he got there, Sue had already heard talk on her police scanner of a possible crash. "Possible nothin'," Sue said. "It *has* crashed. I heard it." Stevie and some of the other men got into his four-wheel-drive pickup and headed into the forest. From the looks of the flames, the crash site was close, but there was no easy way to get there. The forest was dense and swampy; only a couple of roads ran through it. It was going to take a while to reach the crash.

Sue phoned her youngest son, Chris, a twenty-six-year-old lineman for a power company, who lived two miles away. "No, I'm not kiddin'," she said. "That thing has crashed up there on the huntin' club some-where." Chris ran to his truck and sped toward the forest.

★ ★ ★

Sergeant Michael Moffitt, who was looking forward to his scheduled flight that night with Major Bianca, had gone out to the flight line at New River about 7:30 to wait for Crossbow 08 to return. He'd been waiting outside for a while when it struck him that something was odd. Moffitt couldn't hear any rotors turning, not a single one. He'd never heard the flight line so quiet. That made him wonder where Crossbow 08 was. He headed to the operations office in VMMT-204's hangar to see what he could find out. When he got to the top of the stairs at one end of the hangar, Moffitt saw Major Paul Rock running down the hall the other way toward a stairwell at the other end of the building. Moffitt scurried back down the way he'd come, rushing into the hangar bay just in time to see Rock run into the maintenance control office. Rock looked pale. Moffitt followed him. By the time Moffitt got to the maintenance control office, Rock already had Crossbow 08's maintenance records under one arm. One of the first things a squadron has to do after a crash is secure the aircraft's maintenance records to make sure no one can tamper with them.

"Something's happened," Rock told Moffitt hurriedly. "I think the aircraft went down, and another helicopter reported flames." Rock rushed off.

From his office upstairs, Rock phoned his wife, Maria. "I'm okay," he said. "It's going to be a long night. I'll talk to you later." Then he hung up. Rock was rushing to get out to the crash site. He was the only officer on duty that night trained in how to handle the aftermath of an accident. He knew what needed to be done. He had been through this before. At Marana.

* * *

Telephone lineman Chris Jarman found the crash site at 7:35 P.M. He was the first person to get near enough to see the fire, but it was a hundred yards or so back in the trees. Jarman pulled to a stop on Swamp Road, a rutted dirt track that runs through Hofmann Forest, and called his father, Stevie, on his CB radio. Soon Stevie and his friends arrived, followed by a convoy of five trucks driven by civilians who'd heard what was happening on their CBs. A couple of paramedics from the Jacksonville Volunteer Fire Department arrived next. They walked toward the fire to look for survivors, slogging their way through the mud and underbrush. A few minutes later, a search-and-rescue helicopter from the Marine Corps air station at Cherry Point, about thirty miles northeast, arrived overhead and went into a hover. Thinking the paramedics were survivors, the helicopter crew hoisted a Navy corpsman and a rescue swimmer to the ground.

By now, civilian fire departments and rescue squads from all over the area were responding, along with the Camp Lejeune Fire Depart-

ment, a fire unit from New River air station, the Onslow County Sher-
iff's Department, and the North Carolina State Highway Patrol. At 8
P.M., Rock phoned the Onslow County Emergency Operations Command to warn the civilian responders to wear respirators if they got near
the Osprey's wreckage. The smoke from burning composites was toxic.
When Rock got to the scene, the remains of the Osprey were still on fire.
No vehicles would get near it until after 9 P.M. that night, when a forest service bulldozer cleared a path from Swamp Road to where Crossbow 08 had gone down. In the meantime, Marines and others, some in
Tyvek suits and respirators, some not, were combing through the trees
and underbrush, hoping to find survivors. Rock borrowed a respirator
from a local firefighter and joined the search. There was still hope, he
thought. The fire hadn't consumed Crossbow 08 the way the blaze at
Marana had engulfed the Osprey that went down there. Crossbow 08
was in pieces, but Rock could see its tail hung up in a tree off to the side
from where the fuselage lay. From what he could see, the tail was largely
intact. Who knew how hard they had hit? Maybe some of the crew had
been thrown free and were lying in the woods, injured but alive. It was
dark, it was smoky, it was hard to see through the mask of his respirator,
but Rock didn't want to give up. He knew Runnels and Buyck well, as
good Marines. Sweaney had been Rock's commander in the MOTT, and
a mentor. Murphy was a close friend. Murf and Rock had flown together
that awful night at Marana, driven back from Yuma, and worked the
crash scene there for days. Just a month and a day ago tonight, they and
some other VMMT-204 pilots, along with their wives, had adjourned to
a room in the Atlantic Beach Sheraton down the road from New River
after the Marine Corps Ball to continue the party. Murf and the others
laughed like crazy when Rock put a heavy-metal song on and started
playing air guitar, something he was prone to do after a few beers. Rock
wanted to find his friends. He wanted to find them alive.

After a couple of hours, it was clear that wasn't going to happen.

★ ★ ★

The next morning at about eleven o'clock, Lieutenant General Fred
McCorkle came to the Pentagon press briefing room. He'd been devas-
tated when he was called the night before and told about the crash and
who the pilots were. McCorkle considered Sweaney and Murphy both
among his sons, though he'd known Murphy far longer, ever since he

was a young lieutenant. Murphy had dropped by McCorkle's office just two weeks earlier to say hello when business brought him to the Pentagon. Murphy and his wife, Tricia, had a twelve-year-old son, Michael Jr., and a seven-year-old daughter, Grace. After expressing condolences to the families of all four Marines killed, McCorkle announced that all Osprey flights were being suspended until the cause of the crash was determined. A decision on Full Rate Production was on hold, too, he added. "I met with Dr. Buchanan this morning, and after talking with the commandant, we have requested a delay in the decision to proceed with Milestone III, pending the results of additional information," McCorkle said.

After McCorkle provided some basics on what was known so far about the crash, a reporter asked a larger question. "General, is this program in deep trouble?"

McCorkle wasn't ready to concede that. That morning a senior civilian in the Pentagon had told him how he hadn't had a car accident for seventeen years, then had two in quick succession, McCorkle said. Accidents happen, in other words. "We don't know what was the cause of this yet," McCorkle noted. "We plan on finding out what it was and fixing it." The investigation had barely begun, but McCorkle seemed certain the cause had been something mechanical, not vortex ring state or pilot error. "If I flew with anyone, I think, out of the entire Marine Corps, where I'd be in the back, I'd want to be with Lieutenant Colonel Sweaney," McCorkle said.

The questions turned to whether the Marine Corps was going to get the Full Rate Production decision it had wanted for so long. McCorkle had been pushing to get that decision as hard as anyone. Now he acted unconcerned. "Originally, when we looked at this earlier in the year, we were looking at not doing a Milestone III decision until March or April of '01," he said. "So there's a lot of time."

A reporter asked if this second crash, just eight months after Marana, combined with Pentagon test director Philip Coyle's finding that the Osprey was "not operationally suitable," might be "a showstopper."

"I don't think it'll be a showstopper," McCorkle said. Coyle was talking about tests done with the first four production aircraft, McCorkle said, "where at times we had a tough time getting parts for them and things like that. So it was reliability and maintainability. But nobody has ever questioned the safety of this aircraft."

Another reporter wanted to know what the Marines would do if Milestone III were delayed a long time. Would they have to spend more money on their CH-46 helicopters? McCorkle refused to even consider the idea. "I think that we're still going to have a Milestone III decision, it will just come at a later time," he said. "I just don't think that there's any other aircraft out there anywhere for the money that would do the mission for the Marine Corps."

"And so without it—" a reporter began.

McCorkle interrupted. "We don't plan on doing without it," he said.

★ ★ ★

For all the confidence McCorkle showed at his news briefing, he and everyone else at Headquarters Marine Corps knew that after the latest crash, the question might no longer be *when* the Osprey would pass Milestone III but *whether* it would get there at all. Two crashes within eight months made even General Jones, who was not only the commandant but a true believer in the tiltrotor, wonder if there was something inherently wrong with the technology. Whether there was or not, Jones knew the Marines had to satisfy the rest of the world that the Osprey wasn't fatally flawed. In politics, especially in Washington, perception is reality. If the Osprey became perceived as unsafe, its support in Congress could erode, possibly even collapse. Jones also knew the Marines needed to act fast. After the presidential election a few weeks earlier, the political lineup in the capital was changing. Jones had a special relationship with the current defense secretary, Bill Cohen. They'd been friends for two decades, ever since Jones had served five years on Capitol Hill as a legislative liaison officer while Cohen was a Republican senator from Maine. When Cohen became defense secretary in 1997, he tapped Jones as his top military assistant. Two years later, Cohen got President Bill Clinton to make Jones commandant. Jones knew he and Cohen saw eye-to-eye on the Osprey. Both had long believed the tiltrotor could revolutionize military and civilian aviation. In a few weeks, though, the president would be George W. Bush and the vice president would be Dick Cheney, the Osprey's old nemesis. A Supreme Court ruling on December 12, the day after the New River crash, had finally settled a dispute over Florida's electoral votes and decided the election in the Bush-Cheney ticket's favor. Soon a new set of civilian leaders would take over the Pentagon and a lot of new members of Congress would arrive on Capitol Hill. All many of them might know about the Osprey was what they had read in the newspapers or seen on TV. Who knew what their perceptions of the Osprey would be? Beyond that, Cheney would be back in power. During the campaign, Cheney had said he "probably would go forward with" the Osprey now, but that was before the New River crash.

Less than twenty-four hours after the crash, Jones called Cohen and asked him to name a panel of experts to pass judgment on the Osprey, a so-called "Blue Ribbon Commission." Cohen readily agreed. A commission was a time-honored way to deal with hot-potato issues in Washington. Rudy deLeon, the deputy secretary of defense, had suggested the idea to Jones. DeLeon said they should ask the director of the National Air and Space Museum, John Dailey, to head the commission. There was precedent for tapping the museum's director for such a task, deLeon pointed out. In 1996, the Clinton administration had gotten Dailey's predecessor at the museum, Donald Engen, to head a commission that studied the safety record of the White House military air fleet. Jones readily agreed to deLeon's idea. Dailey was a retired four-star Marine Corps general who, as assistant commandant, had helped turn back Dick Cheney's attempt to kill the Osprey a decade earlier.

Initially, McCorkle was concerned when he heard Jones wanted a commission to study the Osprey. At first, he didn't know who would be on the panel, and he knew that could make all the difference. Getting the Osprey through Milestone III had been one of McCorkle's goals since he'd taken over Marine Corps aviation in 1998. Though a skeptic in the Osprey's earliest days, McCorkle had been a believer in the tiltrotor for years now, as sure as anyone it was a dream machine for the Marine Corps. McCorkle had wanted the Osprey to go into service on his watch. A commission might take months to do its work, and who knew what it might decide? McCorkle was due to retire in the coming summer, and Milestone III was receding into the distance by the hour.

The next day, something happened that added to McCorkle's worries—and left him and Jones fuming. Mike Wallace, the star investigative reporter of CBS-TV's *60 Minutes*, called Keith Sweaney's home and tried to speak to his widow, Carol. A friend who answered the phone refused to put Carol on the line. Wallace persisted. *60 Minutes* was doing a story about the Osprey, he explained. He thought Carol might be interested in talking. The friend told Wallace it was outrageous for him to call at such a time. Then she hung up on him.

The next day, Wallace sent Carol Sweaney a handwritten apology. "I'm deeply sorry if my telephone call to your home yesterday was an unwelcome intrusion, and in retrospect I can see that you and your friends could well have perceived it as such," Wallace wrote. "Indeed, I suffered a similar intrusion myself when I lost a son, so I should have been more sensitive to what you're going through. Your husband was— and is—held in such high regard by his colleagues in the Corps that I'm afraid it triggered an inappropriate reporter's instinct. Sincerely, Mike Wallace."

McCorkle fired off his own letter to Wallace, denouncing his "predatory tactics." General Jones sent a similar letter to the president of *CBS News*. The call to Sweaney's widow before her husband's remains had even been recovered from the wreckage of his aircraft, Jones wrote, "went beyond the pale of common decency." A copy of Jones's letter found its way to Howard Kurtz, media writer of the *Washington Post*. Kurtz wrote a story that ran January 3 under the headline, "Marines Blast Mike Wallace for 'Insensitivity.'"

Besides being irate with Wallace for making that call, the generals were worried by the revelation that Wallace was working on a story about the Osprey. A story by one of the other reporters in the *60 Minutes* stable might be positive, maybe even a puff piece. Wallace didn't often do puff pieces. Wallace usually did investigative stories, exposés. When he did them, they often generated similar stories in newspapers and other TV broadcasts. They could establish the conventional wisdom on the topic Wallace had investigated.

Marine leaders had always put a high priority on dealing with the media. They had long understood that media coverage shapes public opinion, and if there is anything members of Congress pay attention to, it's public opinion. Favorable media coverage was one way the Marines had sustained their high standing in public opinion over the years, and that standing was one reason for the Corps' strong support in Congress. Strong support in Congress, in turn, had always been what saved the Corps when anyone started talking about disbanding or shrinking or folding it into the Army. Lawmakers with a vested interest in the Osprey—and there were plenty of them—could be relied on to defend the program almost no matter what. If public opinion turned against it, though, all bets might be off. The Marines, Bell-Boeing, and the Osprey's supporters on Capitol Hill had already known they had a problem. The fact that *60 Minutes* was preparing a story was a sign it might get worse.

They had no idea how bad it was about to get.

★ ★ ★

Even before this latest crash, enlisted mechanics and others at VMMT-204 in New River had been getting letters, phone calls, or e-mails from Paul Gallagher, a *60 Minutes* producer. Gallagher, who had started working on an Osprey story for Mike Wallace in mid-October, had gotten hold of a VMMT-204 roster that included home addresses and phone numbers. Some of those he contacted offered to help; some reported his calls to their supervisors. Squadron leaders cautioned enlisted maintainers against cooperating with *60 Minutes*. No one can stop you from talking to them, they were told, but if you appear on TV in uniform, you'll be in trouble.

One twenty-two-year-old flight line mechanic in the squadron, Corporal Clifford Carlson, never got a letter from *60 Minutes,* but Carlson was intrigued when he heard the show was working on a story about the Osprey. Carlson had disagreed with how maintenance statistics on the Osprey were handled during OPEVAL, when he was a member of the MOTT. Delays while parts were ordered from Bell and Boeing were sometimes excluded from the Osprey's test scores, written off as irrelevant to whether the Osprey was ready for service, Carlson told me. The Osprey didn't have a normal supply line yet, the logic went, so there was no need to figure such problems into OPEVAL test scores. Carlson thought that was wrong. After he got to VMMT-204, Carlson thought he saw similar things going on.

The squadron was under intense pressure from higher-ups to improve its readiness rate, a statistic showing how many of its Ospreys were ready to fly each day. After November, when Pentagon test director Coyle's report on OPEVAL declared the Osprey "not operationally suitable" because of poor reliability, the aviation branch of the Marine Corps was eager to show that the maintenance record was improving rapidly. Making that case might be important when Assistant Secretary of the Navy H. Lee Buchanan III decided whether to approve Milestone III and put the Osprey into Full Rate Production. On November 21, four days after Coyle issued his report, one of McCorkle's top assistants, Brigadier General James Amos, sent McCorkle an e-mail on the subject. Showing better maintenance and reliability figures was going to be difficult, Amos warned. His e-mail said the most recent figures from VMMT-204 were "a bad story," partly because the squadron was one of three in the Marine Corps using a new computerized maintenance reporting system.

The new system was stricter than the old one in recording when an aircraft was mechanically "down," meaning not flyable. Everybody in Marine Corps aviation knew that squadrons of all types had been gaming the old system for years to improve their readiness rates. Under the old system, there were ways to list an aircraft as "up"—flyable—even if it was "down" for maintenance or repair. The status of a down aircraft, for example, might be changed to up as soon as the parts it needed were in hand and were being installed, rather than waiting until the aircraft actually was ready to fly again. The new system couldn't be manipulated that way, so long as accurate data on what work and parts were needed for a particular aircraft was entered into the computer. Based on those entries, the computer automatically declared an aircraft's status, often in ways that made no sense to mechanics and maintenance officers. Under the new system, the numbers on how many Ospreys at VMMT-204 were rated "mission capable" or "full mission capable" on any given day were awful.

"Sir . . . this needs to be close-held," Amos wrote to McCorkle. Under the new reporting system, "which you can't cheat on," Amos noted, VMMT-204's mission-capable rate for the month of November had averaged 26.7 percent, far below the Osprey's published daily average goal of 75 percent. Its full-mission-capable rate was a mere 7.9 percent. "Had hoped to be able to use some recent numbers next month when you meet with Dr. Buchanan for his Milestone III/FRP decision in December . . . this isn't going to help," Amos concluded.

The disappointment with VMMT-204's readiness rate at headquarters grew in importance as it filtered down the ranks. Major General Dennis Krupp, commander of the 2nd Marine Aircraft Wing in North Carolina, had been firing off e-mails for months to subordinates at New River and managers at Bell-Boeing complaining about the poor readiness rates at VMMT-204. After Krupp saw Amos's Nov. 21 e-mail to McCorkle, Krupp e-mailed a subordinate, Colonel James Schleining, telling him to "see if we can put a positive spin on the month of Oct/Nov. Apparently they are in a sh.. sandwich in DC regarding FRP decision."

Two hours later, Schleining e-mailed the commander of VMMT-204, Lieutenant Colonel Odin "Fred" Leberman, telling him Krupp wanted to "see if we can put a positive spin on" the Osprey's readiness rates. Schleining explained that McCorkle "needs some help on the FRP decision."

The decision on Full Rate Production was a matter of high policy in Washington. Soon, though, even privates and corporals at VMMT-204 were talking about how important it was to get readiness rates up so the Osprey could pass Milestone III. "We clearly could feel the pressure from higher headquarters of pushing this thing to get it to Full Rate Production," recalled former Staff Sergeant Julius Banks, a senior noncommissioned officer in VMMT-204 at the time. "I think at that time everyone knew that the aircraft had a lot of deficiencies, but the thought was, we'll get the aircraft to Full Rate Production, we'll get the Congress to approve, and we'll fix the airplanes later."

After the crash on December 11, all Ospreys were grounded. To keep those at VMMT-204 in shape mechanically, though, crews were still running their engines, even taxiing around. The squadron's Ospreys still needed maintenance and repairs, and the pressure to show better readiness rates didn't let up. Flight line mechanic Corporal Cliff Carlson grew even more bitter than he had been before the crash. Staff Sergeant Avely Runnels and Sergeant Jason Buyck, the two crew chiefs killed in the accident, had been friends of his. While Carlson was on leave to attend Runnels' funeral, a friend at VMMT-204 called and told him the assistant maintenance officer, Captain Christopher Ramsey, had met with some of the mechanics and told them they needed to make the Osprey's readiness rate look better. Ramsey would later deny it, but Carlson's friend said the officer had told the mechanics they needed to be "smarter" in using the new system. Ramsey asked for suggestions, Carlson's friend said, and also made one. If an aircraft came in on a Friday with a "squawk"—a maintenance need—that would down it, the mechanics should wait until Monday to enter that information into the computerized reporting system. The work wouldn't get done over the weekend anyway, and the readiness rate would look that much better if the aircraft was listed as up those extra two days. Those in the meeting also decided they would start recording aircraft needing work that would down them as up in the computer, but add the symbol *D* in one of the information fields on the reporting form. "We literally had officers telling maintenance personnel that if the aircraft is—if there's a grounding write-up on the aircraft, we're not going to call it a grounding write-up, we'll call it an up write-up until we can get past Full Rate Production," Banks told me. "It was nasty back then."

Carlson was outraged when he heard about Ramsey's meeting. With no Ospreys flying, there was no risk that inaccurate maintenance reporting would cause a crash, but the officers were encouraging the maintainers to fudge the numbers, as Carlson saw it. Whose hide would it be if they got caught? During OPEVAL, Carlson had bought a microcassette tape recorder and surreptitiously taped meetings on maintenance data. He did it to protect himself if anyone ever accused him of falsifying results. When he got back from Runnels's funeral, Carlson took his tape recorder to work.

A couple of days later, VMMT-204's commander, Lieutenant Colonel Leberman, called a meeting of maintainers for December 29, the Friday before New Year's weekend. Carlson slipped his tape recorder into the pocket of his flight jacket and wore it into the meeting. When Leberman started talking, Carlson started taping.

The squadron needed to get its readiness rate up, Leberman said, and the new reporting system was a problem. With the old system, Leberman said, it was possible to "screw with the data a little bit," but the new system "does not let us lie. The problem is, we have it here and we need to lie. And the reason we need to lie—or, or manipulate the data, or however you want to call it—is that until Milestone III comes along, and Milestone III being a Full Rate Production decision, this program is in jeopardy."

Over the next twelve days, VMMT-204 reported to higher headquarters that the readiness rate of its Ospreys each day was 100 percent.

Carlson made five copies of his recording of Leberman's meeting. He took one each to Runnels's and Buyck's widows. He put the other three in brown manila envelopes, along with an anonymous letter describing himself as a mechanic with VMMT-204. "What we have been doing is reporting aircrafts that are down, as in they can't fly, as being up, as in full mission capable," Carlson wrote. "This type of deception has been going on for over 2 years, however this is the first time it will affect safety. During the test period maintenance records were accurate and the test report writers would just throw out the data they didn't like. Now, maintainers are being told they have to lie on maintenance records to make the numbers look good. This is not what caused the previous 2 mishaps this year, but if it continues it will cause many more." Carlson enclosed a copy of VMMT-204's Aircraft Daily Status Report for December 29– January 2 and photos of a whiteboard where the squadron's maintenance control department listed the actual status of each Osprey. The daily status report showed every Osprey up, he said. "The pictures show a different story though. Everything written in red is a downer, meaning the plane cannot fly. This is how we have been doing business, not documenting downers and just noting them on the board. This is illegal." Carlson mailed one package to the Naval Air Systems Command and another to the secretary of the Navy. He mailed the third to *60 Minutes*.

★ ★ ★

Besides trying to reach Carol Sweaney, CBS reporter Mike Wallace also called Connie Gruber, whose husband, Major Brooks "Chucky" Gruber, had been the copilot killed at Marana. A petite, pretty brunette whose stepfather was a retired Marine Corps sergeant major, Connie had met her husband in 1990, the day after Thanksgiving. At the time, Brooks was a first lieutenant flying CH-53 helicopters in a squadron at New River. Connie was a first-grade teacher in a school for dependents at Camp Lejeune. Mutual friends introduced them, and Connie fell in love with Brooks the moment she saw him. His big, warm smile put her at ease right away. Brooks later told Connie he liked her eyes. A year later, after Brooks came back from flying in the Gulf War, he gave Connie a sweetheart necklace, two hearts looped together, with small diamonds in the middle of each heart. On Valentine's Day 1992, they dressed up to drive to Raleigh, the state capital, for dinner. When they got to the restaurant, Brooks produced a dozen roses from somewhere, then dropped to one knee and asked Connie to marry him. "Yes!" she screamed. The rest of the evening, all Connie could do was look at the ring, then look at Brooks, her dream come true. They married on December 12 of that year at the First Baptist Church in Jacksonville, North Carolina, after Brooks returned from a six-month deployment to the Mediterranean. They moved to New Mexico, then to Florida after Brooks started flying as the Marine Corps' only exchange pilot with the Air Force's 20th Special Operations Squadron. When Brooks was selected to fly the Osprey with the MOTT, they moved near Patuxent River Naval Air Station in Maryland. On July 25, 1999, Connie gave birth to a daughter. They named her

Brooke, for her father. That fall, just before Operational Evaluation of the Osprey began, Brooks moved Connie and the baby to Jacksonville, North Carolina. After OPEVAL, Brooks was scheduled to join VMMT-204 at nearby New River. The last time Connie ever saw him was in Jacksonville on Valentine's Day 2000, the eighth anniversary of their engagement. It was the day Brooks left to go west with the MOTT. Connie hated to say good-bye. That weekend, she had walked into the baby's room as Brooks looked down lovingly at their six-month-old daughter.

"You know," Brooks said, looking up at Connie, "that baby is me and you."

"I know," Connie said. "She is the greatest gift you have ever given me, and the greatest gift God has ever given us."

Connie Gruber never forgot that precious moment. Nor could she get over losing Brooks. She couldn't look at the moon without wondering if that was the last thing he'd seen before his Osprey plunged into the ground at Marana. She often awoke with a start at 3 A.M., the hour her living nightmare had begun on April 9, 2000, when a Marine Corps casualty assistance officer had come to the door to tell her Brooks had been killed. She couldn't bear to hear or read that his Osprey had crashed because of "pilot error," as some news accounts had said or implied. She knew her husband and John Brow were two of the finest pilots in the Marine Corps. The blame for their crash had to lie with the aircraft, not the pilots. Connie Gruber didn't hesitate when Mike Wallace called and asked if she would appear on *60 Minutes*. It was a chance to set the record straight.

When *60 Minutes* producer Paul Gallagher received Corporal Cliff Carlson's anonymous package on January 5, 2001, he felt like a slot machine player who'd hit a jackpot. "Wow," Wallace said when Gallagher told him what he had. Wallace already had conducted a number of interviews for his story. Now they wanted to get it on the air as soon as possible, before some other news organization, or the Marines, went public with the anonymous mechanic's allegations. Wallace, Gallagher, and the show's executive producer, Don Hewitt, had a long discussion about when to call the Marine Corps for comment. They were worried that if they called too soon, the Marines might somehow undermine their scoop. They decided Wallace would make that call on the Wednesday before their Sunday evening *60 Minutes* broadcast, scheduled for January 21.

The evening of January 17, Wallace phoned Leberman and told him about the tape. Leberman declined to comment. Then Wallace called the general in charge of Marine Corps Public Affairs and told him what *60 Minutes* had. The general said the Marines would have no comment.

The next morning, the Marine Corps inspector general, Major General Timothy Ghormley, arrived at New River with a team of seven investigators. The investigators seized computer hard drives and documents at VMMT-204 and started interviewing the squadron's 241 members. Later that day, Leberman was relieved as the squadron's commander. Afterward, the Pentagon issued a news release announcing that General Jones had directed an investigation into allegations that the commanding officer of VMMT-204 had "asked Marines to falsify maintenance records on the squadron's MV-22 Osprey aircraft." The release said that "Marine Corps officials first became aware of these allegations Jan. 12, when they received a copy of an anonymous letter and audio tape that was mailed to the Office of the Secretary of the Navy." While the investigation had just begun, "at this point there appears to be no relation between these allegations and the causes of either the April 8 mishap in Marana, Ariz., or the Dec. 11 mishap in North Carolina."

Wallace appeared on the *CBS Evening News* that night, introduced by anchor Dan Rather. "A new shock tonight for one of the most controversial and troubled weapons programs ever undertaken by the military, the V-22 Osprey, a radical, innovative aircraft that takes off like a helicopter and flies like a plane," Rather began. "Under pressure, the Marine Corps ousted the commander of an Osprey training squadron and opened an investigation of accusations that he's told squadron members to falsify aircraft maintenance records. CBS News *60 Minutes* correspondent Mike Wallace is working this story, and he breaks tonight exclusive details. Mike."

"Dan," Wallace began, "the Marine Corps has been hiding the truth about the Osprey from the American public for months now." Wallace reported that "four Ospreys have crashed out of a fleet of fifteen," and that Leberman had "told his men they should continue to 'lie'—his word—about maintenance problems with the aircraft." Wallace said the Marines had refused to talk to him about the Osprey. "It seems apparent that the Marine Corps is deeply embarrassed by the cover-up of the failures of the Osprey's technology, especially since the Pentagon is asking for $30 billion to purchase 360 Ospreys for the Marine Corps. Their announcement late this afternoon of an investigation into the whole matter appears to be a pre-emptive strike to blunt the reaction to the report we'll air on *60 Minutes* this coming Sunday night."

Lieutenant General McCorkle came to the Pentagon press briefing room the next day. He told the roomful of reporters he'd intended to offer an update on the investigation into the New River crash, but now he also wanted to "share with you the Marine Corps' concerns on the recent allegations" that maintenance records at VMMT-204 had been falsified. "Although the MV-22 is very important to the future of the Marine Corps, nothing's more important than the safety of our Marines and the integrity of our Corps," McCorkle said. "Based on all of the information that we have," there was no evidence of a connection between the alleged falsification of maintenance records and the crashes at Marana and New River, he said. "In fact, the anonymous letter, which you'll be given a copy of, specifically states that this was not what caused the previous two mishaps." The preliminary results of the New River crash investigation indicated that Crossbow 08 had crashed because of "a hydraulic system failure followed by an error in software inputs to the flight control system." Using a diagram of Crossbow 08's final flight pattern laid over a map of the area where it crashed, McCorkle went through a rough outline of the last thirty seconds of the flight, from the failure of Hydraulic System One to Crossbow 08's final radio transmission. Then he took questions.

The first was whether the hydraulic failure in Crossbow 08 was related to maintenance.

"It's not possibly related to maintenance, and it's going to end up as a [hydraulic] line that was rubbed through, which we have on aircraft almost one a day in the Marine Corps and in other services," McCorkle said.

The next reporter asked a question on a lot of minds. Critics of the Osprey "have already started to say that this is more evidence that this is a bad program, it ought to be cancelled because of the cost, because of Mr. Coyle's report about the maintenance and reliability question. Do you—are you afraid that politically this program may be on its way down as well?"

"I'm not," McCorkle said, "and for the reason that I think that what's going to be shown in this hydraulics failure has zero to do with technology with the tiltrotor or with the MV-22."

When a reporter asked if the investigation of VMMT-204 wasn't politically damaging, though, McCorkle acknowledged the obvious. "Anything that's bad is politically damaging, and the accident itself is politically damaging," he said.

Just how politically damaging the events of the past five weeks had been soon became evident.

On Friday, the day after McCorkle's press briefing, Associated Press Pentagon correspondent Robert Burns, citing a "senior official," reported that Leberman had admitted asking subordinates to falsify maintenance records. The same day, the Council for a Livable World, a Washington think tank often opposed to major defense programs, issued a statement under the heading "Arrested Development: Troubled Osprey Should be Canceled." The group's president, John Isaacs, said the allegations of maintenance reporting fraud "illustrate the severity of the Osprey's many technical problems and the Pentagon's flawed procurement process." Isaacs predicted it would be "difficult for the Osprey to recover from this. The program has always been of questionable military value, but its strong congressional backing made it the Teflon weapon—no criticism could stick. But now that political cover is coming off."

On Saturday, George W. Bush was inaugurated as president of the United States. The next morning, an editorial in the *New York Times* said Bush's defense secretary, Donald Rumsfeld, should find out whether Leberman had acted on his own or with "the blessings of superior officers." As for the Osprey itself, the editorial said, "Dick Cheney rightly tried to cancel the Osprey program while he was defense secretary." It was rare for programs to be halted once they had gone into production, as the Osprey had, the *Times* noted, but "now it may be time to terminate the program altogether. The Bush administration's expensive plans to build 21st Century weapons leave no room for a 20-year-old idea with a poor safety record and maintenance data of questionable reliability."

That evening, CBS broadcast Wallace's *60 Minutes* story. It opened with Wallace seated in front of a large photo of the Osprey. "It's been a bad week for the United States Marine Corps: allegations of deception about flaws in the aircraft you see behind me, the V-22 Osprey, an ungainly bird that the Corps insists it simply must have to help fight this nation's battles in the 21st Century," Wallace began. "We'll hear from the families of Marines who died in two Osprey crashes in the past nine months, families disillusioned about what they see as the Corps' cynical use of

their husbands and sons, in effect, as test pilots on the flawed aircraft."
The first interview, however, was with former Osprey test pilot Grady
Wilson, who had resigned from Boeing five months after the 1992 crash
at Quantico. A year before that, Wilson had been lucky to walk away
from the fifth Osprey prototype after it went out of control and crashed
at Wilmington, Delaware, because its roll rate vyros were miswired. Wallace didn't mention the miswiring, but he showed video of Wilson's crash.
Talking over it as Aircraft 5 wobbled drunkenly just above the tarmac,
then flipped and ground its nose and left rotor into the runway with its
engines whining, Wallace said that "ever since its initial test flights, like
this one in 1991, the Osprey has been in trouble." Wilson told Wallace the
Osprey was "very complex," and "a hybrid. It's a crossbreed, if you will.
It's part helicopter, it's part fixed-wing. As such, it will never be an excellent helicopter or an excellent fixed-wing." The story went on to show file
footage of Cheney when he was defense secretary telling Congress the
Osprey was "a program I don't need." Next came Wallace in a confronta-
tional interview with Representative Curt Weldon. As Weldon defended
the Osprey, Wallace told him four of the first fifteen had crashed. "That's
25 percent of all the Ospreys at a cost, so far, of $12 billion," Wallace said.
The story cited the Pentagon inspector general's report the previous summer questioning whether the Osprey was ready for Full Rate Production
and noted that the Navy Department had let it go into Operational Evaluation with twenty-two waivers of requirements. Wallace cited Pentagon
test director Coyle's conclusion that the Osprey was "not operationally
suitable" because of its many maintenance issues. The interviews with
family members of Osprey crash victims came next. One was with Connie Gruber. She said her husband "would be on the schedule to fly and
come home early and say, 'We couldn't fly. Something was broken they
had to fix. We need to get a part.' Or on occasion, he would be flying, and
they would encounter some type of caution, some type of warning, and
they'd have to land early. And I'd say that—that was pretty much routine."

"You've said that your husband was doing a job that he was not supposed to be doing," Wallace said.

"It wasn't his job to get the bugs out of this aircraft," she said. "My
husband was not a test pilot. The remaining pilots are also not test pilots.
We feel that the aircraft is not ready. I think it's shown that it's unreli-
able, it's unpredictable, it's very high-maintenance, and the results have
been catastrophic."

Later in the broadcast, Wallace noted that the Pentagon had been on the verge of approving Full Rate Production in December when Sweaney and Murphy crashed at New River. "Apparently, the pressure to improve the Osprey's poor maintenance record led the Marine Corps to mislead the American public about the reliability of the aircraft," Wallace said. "As we were reporting this story, we got a letter from a Marine mechanic in the Osprey unit in New River, North Carolina. He explained what had been going on inside the unit." Corporal Cliff Carlson's anonymous letter and audio of his tape of VMMT-204 commander Leberman telling mechanics to "lie" to improve the squadron's readiness rate followed. Wallace ended his report by explaining how Leberman had flown to New York the night before the broadcast with his attorneys, planning to appear, but after a "lengthy discussion" with Wallace and others at *60 Minutes* had changed his mind. Wallace read a statement from Leberman saying his comments on the tape had been taken out of context and "in no way compromised the safety of any Marines or the integrity of the Osprey program."

For the integrity of the Osprey program, for Bell and Boeing, and especially for the Marine Corps, the broadcast was catastrophic. Wallace had portrayed the Osprey as a boondoggle. Worse than that, he had portrayed it as a boondoggle the Marines had lied about.

The night after the broadcast, Jones set out to defend the Corps, appearing on PBS's *NewsHour with Jim Lehrer*. Jones was on after former Pentagon test director Coyle and James Furman, a lawyer Connie Gruber had hired to sue Bell and Boeing. Furman questioned the Osprey's safety. Coyle questioned its reliability.

The allegation of maintenance reporting fraud was "particularly disturbing in an organization like the United States Marine Corps, which prides itself on integrity and truthfulness," Jones told host Ray Suarez. "There is no program I know of that would justify anyone to make false statements concerning the readiness of a program." Over its history, Jones said, the Osprey had "survived the critics because of its enormous potential, a potential that really transcends, Ray, the military community and extends, in my judgment, into the commercial sector as well. When you think of the potential benefits to our industrial base by being able to market this kind of technology, it's going to be, I think, a very big addition to reducing our crowded airways over our airports and the like. The military application, though, is beyond question: twice as fast, three times the payload, five times the range of any comparable helicopter." Getting an aircraft like that "is exactly what we should do—but not simply because it's a program that we have fallen in love with," Jones said. The Marines would "take a measured look" at the Osprey once the Blue Ribbon Commission appointed by Cohen in December had finished its work, Jones promised.

Frank Gaffney, a former Reagan administration Pentagon official and a longtime tiltrotor supporter, tried to help head off what he called "the emerging conventional wisdom" about the Osprey. Gaffney was now president of the Center for Security Policy, a conservative Washington think tank. The day after Jones's appearance on PBS, Gaffney published a commentary in the *Washington Times*. Despite "the powerful *60 Minutes* assault" on the program, he wrote, the Marines were right to want the Osprey. "Studies have shown that the V-22's significantly longer range and speed may contribute decisively to success on the battlefield," Gaffney argued. The tiltrotor could ease airport congestion in the United States and had huge potential as an export product. He concluded by saying the Osprey "might more appropriately be named for another creature—the Phoenix. Like that mythical beast, the V-22 can— and must be allowed to—rise again."

Whether the Osprey was going to rise again seemed doubtful. Within days, the themes of the *60 Minutes* broadcast were taken up by major newspapers around the country. The editorial in the *New York Times* calling for the Osprey to be canceled was followed by one in the *Chicago Tribune* saying the Osprey "should not fly again." The *Washington Post* and other newspapers, especially those published near Marine Corps bases, assigned reporters to investigate the Osprey. The crashes, the flap over Wallace calling Carol Sweaney, Jones's and McCorkle's reactions to that, plus the investigation of VMMT-204, followed by the *60 Minutes* story itself had created a perfect media storm.

Soon the storm threatened to sink the Osprey. Two days after Jones appeared on PBS, the Republican and Democratic leaders of the Senate Armed Services Committee sent Defense Secretary Donald Rumsfeld a letter saying the allegation that maintenance records at VMMT-204 had been falsified cast doubt on "the integrity of information" provided to Congress by the Marines. They asked Rumsfeld to shift the investigation to an independent agency. "This program will not be able to move forward unless and until the Defense Department has restored confidence in the integrity of the V-22 program and the people managing it," the letter said. Just before the Senate committee released the letter, Jones issued a statement announcing that he had asked Rumsfeld to have the Pentagon inspector general take over the New River investigation. Jones said he had "complete confidence" in the Marine Corps inspector general, who had launched the investigation six days earlier, but "I am concerned that the nature and gravity of the allegations may invite unwarranted perceptions of command influence or institutional bias."

Four days after that, Vice President Dick Cheney was asked his opinion of the Osprey during an appearance on ABC's Sunday talk show *This Week.* Cheney said he had tried to kill it for cost a decade earlier; the decision on whether to continue it now, however, would be made by Rumsfeld and Congress. At the same time, he added, "Given the track record and the loss of life so far, it would appear to me that there are very serious questions that can and should be and I hope will be raised about the Osprey."

Cheney's nonendorsement was followed by an article in *Aviation Week* reporting that the Air Force Special Operations Command was "reconsidering its commitment" to the Osprey. The same week, the Washington Bureau of Knight Ridder Newspapers, a big chain that owned the *Philadelphia Inquirer* and other important papers, published a story describing how support for the Osprey was flagging. Donald Trump, once a member of the Tilt-Rotor Technology Coalition formed by Representative Curt Weldon and Bell-Boeing in the 1990s, had changed his mind. "I believe you should fly in a helicopter or an airplane, but not both," Trump told Knight Ridder. "The Osprey has too many working parts to ever be a very safe plane." Within days, articles examining other criticisms of the Osprey appeared in *USA Today* and other newspapers around the country. The media storm was raging. The conventional wisdom had been established. The Osprey was no longer just another big defense program that was behind schedule, over cost, and targeted primarily by critics who coveted its funding for their pet projects. It was no longer just a weird aircraft with a question mark over it because of crashes. The Osprey was a national scandal.

CHAPTER ELEVEN

THE DARK AGES

D ick Spivey was horrified at what was happening to the Osprey. By the time of the New River crash, Spivey was working full-time marketing Bell Helicopter's new Quad TiltRotor concept, the giant Osprey follow-on he'd helped conceive and gotten Commandant Jones interested in the year before. The Osprey was no longer Spivey's responsibility, but he'd long believed it the key to his dream of a tiltrotor revolution. Spivey also still considered the Osprey his baby. He'd played a major role in selling the Marines on the Osprey. He'd helped nurse it through its near death at Dick Cheney's hands. Despite its horrible accidents, Spivey was absolutely convinced the Osprey would be safe if maintained and flown correctly. More than that, he believed it would save lives in the future by helping the military win battles and by flying casualties to medical care faster than any helicopter could. Beyond that, he had spent three decades promoting the tiltrotor as a dream machine that would reshape aviation. Now that dream was under attack. He desperately wanted to defend it.

In those early days of 2001, though, with twenty-three Marines dead in Osprey crashes over the past year and the scandal at VMMT-204 forcing the Marine Corps to defend not just the Osprey but its very integrity, Spivey and others at Bell and Boeing were keeping their heads down. There was no point in defending the Osprey too loudly until the New River crash investigation was over and the exact cause of the accident was known. There was no point in defending it too loudly until the Defense Department inspector general determined whether there was a link between the crashes at Marana and New River and the alleged falsification of maintenance records at VMMT-204. There was no point in defending the Osprey too much at all, really, until the Blue Ribbon Commission created by former Defense Secretary William Cohen issued its verdict on the program. The only good news was that President Bush and Vice President Cheney seemed content to leave the Osprey's fate to the Defense Department.

Spivey, like the Marine Corps and everyone else in the Osprey camp, was pinning his hopes on that commission, officially the "Panel to Review the V-22 Program." Spivey had known its chairman, retired four-star general and former Assistant Commandant Jack Dailey, since the early 1980s, when Dailey was an aide to a general who visited Fort Worth to see the XV-15. Dailey later flew the XV-15 himself, and Spivey considered him a friend. Spivey was also acquainted with another commission member, Norman R. Augustine, a big name in the defense industry. Augustine, sixty-five at the time, was a Princeton-educated aeronautical engineer who in the 1970s had held top civilian jobs in the Army Department, including acting secretary. Later in his career, he had run two big defense companies, Martin Marietta and Lockheed Martin. He also had published a popular book on business practices, *Augustine's Laws*, which included pithy maxims such as "It costs a lot to build bad products." Augustine's book famously predicted that, the way aviation industry costs were rising, "In the year 2054, the entire defense budget will purchase just one aircraft," which the Air Force, Navy, and Marines would have to share. Spivey didn't know the other two commission members, retired Air Force General James B. Davis and MIT aeronautics professor Eugene Covert, but clearly they weren't bomb throwers. Spivey was sure the Osprey would get a fair trial from a panel like that, just as surely as critics would dismiss its findings as a product of the military-industrial complex.

Commission chairman Dailey had worried about that from the moment Deputy Defense Secretary Rudy deLeon called and asked him to chair the panel. "Wouldn't I be seen as not objective?" Dailey had asked. Not only was Dailey a former assistant commandant, he had been a believer in the tiltrotor and the Osprey for years, at least since he'd met Dick Spivey in Fort Worth and seen the XV-15. "The commandant wants you to do this," deLeon had said, so Dailey went to see Jones. As Dailey recalled their conversation years later, he told Jones: "If you're looking for this to come out in favor of the Osprey, I'm not the right guy. I'm going to tell you the truth, whatever is it."

"That's what we want," Jones said. "That's why I want you to do it. I don't want to buy these things if we're going to kill Marines in them."

The commission, like the inspector general and the crash investigators, would need months to complete its work. Until the investigations were done, no Ospreys were going to fly, and no arguments in favor of the Osprey were going to fly, either. The whole program was in limbo. In the meantime, the Osprey was already being condemned in the court of public opinion. The media had begun routinely referring to it as "the troubled Osprey," as if "troubled" were part of its name, and by 2001, trials in the court of public opinion were being conducted in a new venue: the Internet. Spivey learned that the hard way.

One day in February 2001, someone at Bell Helicopter directed Spivey's attention to a website called G2mil.com, where he found a long article on the Osprey titled "The V-22 Fiasco." The text made Spivey's blood boil even more than the title. It was written by G2mil.com's creator, Carlton W. Meyer, who had served three years in the Marines as a combat engineer before deciding to become a military writer. Meyer, thirty-nine at the time, had created G2mil.com while managing his wife's dental practice in El Cerrito, California. His article declared that the Osprey "will soon become the largest fiasco in Marine Corps history unless changes are made. The V-22 can fill a role as a long-range transport, it cannot fill the assault helicopter role. The fundamental truth is: The V-22 is too expensive and too unstable for combat assaults, and requires modifications and at least two more years of development for non-combat roles. The V-22 can fly safely if it slowly comes to a hover over a landing zone, then carefully sets down. Obviously, this is not a good tactic in a combat zone, especially for something as large as a V-22. The V-22 can swoop down like an assault helicopter, but this is a risky maneuver. If the pilot does not perform the task flawlessly, the V-22 loses lift, flips over, and everyone dies." This was an allusion to vortex ring state, the phenomenon blamed for the Marana crash, in which a rotor that descends too quickly into its own downwash no longer creates thrust properly.

Meyer's article went on to say that the Marines had demonstrated "a lack of moral turpitude [sic] by claiming the V-22 costs $40 million each." Each Osprey would cost $76 million, Meyer contended. Citing Pentagon test director Philip Coyle's finding that the Osprey was "not operationally suitable" because of maintenance problems, Meyer called the existing Ospreys "hangar queens." Meyer said Sikorsky's UH-60L Black Hawk was a "better assault aircraft." Then he got nasty. "The Marines in

charge know the current V-22 is unsafe, but they plan to continue production until more crashes finally end the program," Meyer wrote.

Spivey was beside himself when he read the article, especially Meyer's argument that Sikorsky's Black Hawk would be a better troop transport for the Marines. That was the argument Pentagon budget analyst
David Chu had made a decade earlier. It was the argument Sikorsky
lobbyists had been making since the Osprey program began in 1982.
Sikorsky had been Bell's chief competitor ever since Igor Sikorsky and
Bell's Arthur Young had developed the companies' first helicopters in
the 1930s. The Osprey camp often suspected critics of being on Sikorsky's payroll, though no one had ever proven such a thing. Spivey fired
off a seething, insulting response to Meyer. To Spivey's horror, Meyer
quickly posted it on his website:

> V-22 Article was Trash
>
> You must be a Sikorsky employee or a United Technologies
> stockholder. There are more mistakes and misrepresenta-
> tions in this trash than I have seen in my 26 years with the
> Osprey program. You clearly don't know what you are talk-
> ing about. Good candidate for the Darwin Award.
>
> Dick Spivey

Spivey felt like a fool right after he hit the "send" button. When he saw
his e-mail posted on Meyer's website, along with an invitation to point
out the mistakes Spivey saw in the article, he felt even worse. Spivey
knew he'd been dumb to lash out, but he was seeing red at the time. He
wasn't going to make matters worse now by responding to Meyer's challenge. Meyer clearly had his mind made up. Besides, Spivey was already
afraid some Bell executive would see the exchange and be as embarrassed by it as he was. Spivey resolved never to do such a stupid thing
again.

★   ★   ★

The *60 Minutes* broadcast and the wave of stories about the "troubled
Osprey" in the traditional press worried everyone at Bell and Boeing,
but the fact that the Marines' integrity was being questioned because of
the maintenance scandal was what worried Spivey most. Spivey knew

Bell and Boeing would do everything they could to save the Osprey, and they had formidable resources. Bell and Boeing employed skilled lobbyists, and there were thousands of Osprey subcontractors around the country, giving many members of Congress a stake in it. Through their political action committees and other donations, the companies and their executives and employees made hundreds of thousands of dollars in campaign contributions each year to make sure lawmakers listened to their arguments. All that had helped in the past and would help in the future. The key, though, always had been the Marines' determination to have the Osprey, plus the Corps' high standing in the eyes of the public and Congress. The Marines had kept Cheney from killing the Osprey. The Marines had defended it in budget battles in the Pentagon and on the Hill. Now the Marines were under a cloud. The Osprey team's best player was on the disabled list.

General Jones and some of the Osprey's supporters in Congress, meanwhile, were wondering if Bell and Boeing had simply delivered a lemon, a shoddy aircraft. The Iron Triangle—the natural coalition of industry, the military, and politicians that had spawned the Osprey and shielded it for two decades—was in disarray. Even the Osprey's greatest supporter in Congress, Representative Curt Weldon, was distancing himself from the companies. In a February 1 conference call with reporters, Weldon said he still believed in the Osprey and still believed the Marines needed it. Word that a hydraulic leak had provoked the crash at New River, though, angered him, he said. "Boeing and Bell Helicopter Textron have to get their quality-control act together," Weldon declared. "We will hold them accountable. We will not continue with these types of incidents that should have been straightened out in the manufacturing process."

★ ★ ★

The New River crash investigation findings made it clear there was a lot to straighten out.

Major Navy and Marine Corps aircraft accidents are investigated separately and independently by two groups of investigators, an Aircraft Mishap Board and a Judge Advocate General Manual team, both composed of serving military officers. Aircraft Mishap Board investigation results are largely privileged, released only in redacted form. Witnesses and companies are given confidentiality so they can provide information that might improve safety without fear of legal liability. A Judge Advocate General Manual investigation, known as a JAGMAN report and pronounced the way it looks, describes an accident in detail, assesses responsibility, and makes recommendations. The JAGMAN report on the New River crash was completed in February and released in April 2001. It and the Aircraft Mishap Board report made clear that Boeing, Bell, and their overseers at the Naval Air Systems Command had made serious mistakes with the Osprey.

The investigations found that, as so often in such disasters, a complex series of events led Lieutenant Colonel Keith Sweaney and Major Michael Murphy to lose control of their Osprey. The root causes, though, were painfully simple. Bell had fallen short in designing the layout of the brittle titanium hydraulic lines and thick wire bundles that snaked around inside the Osprey's jam-packed nacelles. Boeing had failed to test the Osprey's flight control software adequately. Navair had failed to catch their mistakes.

Even more painful was another finding: Sweaney and Murphy might have been able to land their Osprey safely despite the hydraulic leak and the software error if they had pushed the Primary Flight Control System reset button only once or twice instead of eight or nine times. Pushing the button was what they were trained to do when cautions of the sort they saw on their cockpit display posted, but no one ever anticipated pilots pushing it repeatedly. Investigators were unable to determine whether both or only one of the pilots pushed the button. Nor could they tell whether it was pushed so many times on purpose or hit accidentally as Crossbow 08 bucked in the air and the pilots tried to brace themselves. Pushing it so much, though, threw the Osprey out of control by lowering and raising the pitch of its rotor blades over and over again with a hydraulic leak that restored the blade pitch at different rates on each rotor.

The investigations found that the hydraulic line that ruptured in Crossbow 08, one of ten such titanium tubes in each nacelle, sprang a leak because a bundle of wires had been chafing it. The wire bundle was supposed to be installed with slack so the wires could flex as the nacelle tilted up or forward, but the worker who installed this bundle left more slack than the blueprint called for, the investigators concluded. VMMT-204 mechanics couldn't detect the chafing during routine inspections because the lines were in a part of the nacelle that couldn't be seen without removing the entire outer skin.

Such chafing wasn't unique to Crossbow 08, the investigators found, and Navair had been aware of the problem for years. Mechanics had often found wire bundles chafing hydraulic lines. Navair had issued a bulletin even before the first Osprey came into the fleet directing mechanics to wrap Teflon around the lines to prevent chafing at thirty-one locations where they were held by clamps. Coyle, the Pentagon test director, had cited hydraulic failures as an item deserving "special mention" when he found the Osprey "not operationally suitable" a month before the New River crash. Despite all that, Navair never had addressed the problem in a comprehensive way. Inspections of VMMT-204's Ospreys after the crash found eight instances of hydraulic line chafing on seven aircraft.

The investigators concluded that the ultimate cause of the crash, however, was the way the flight control software reduced and then restored the pitch on Crossbow 08's rotor blades when Sweaney and Murphy pushed the Primary Flight Control System reset button. Pressing the reset button was standard operating procedure when faults such as HYD 1 FAIL posted on the Osprey's cockpit display. All that was supposed to do was clear the fault so the pilots could see whether it was real or just a nuisance, a computer error. Normally, the fault either would disappear, proving it was a computer glitch, or post again, indicating a genuine problem. When Murphy and Sweaney hit the button, however, the flight control software went through a series of steps that removed and then restored the pitch on the rotor blades. No one knew the software would do that.

Boeing had designed the flight control software years earlier and tested it in an unusual facility at Ridley Park called the Flight Control System Integrated Rig, known informally as the "Triple Lab." The lab was a Plexiglas-enclosed room roughly the size of a handball court. Inside, working parts of the Osprey's flight control machinery—the hydraulic actuators that move the aircraft's swashplates, rudders, ailerons, and other mechanisms—were installed in Plexiglas boxes of their own. Running between the boxes were wire bundles and titanium hydraulic lines the same size and in roughly the same layout as inside an Osprey. Just outside the lab was a series of computers that were loaded with the flight control software and connected to a mock cockpit with the Osprey's controls. This "in-the-loop" lab was how Boeing tested whether the software and machinery worked together as they should.

In the fall and winter of 1996, Boeing engineers ran fifteen tests in the

Triple Lab of how an Osprey would handle if it suffered a hydraulic leak, simulating leaks by cutting off hydraulic pumps. They never tested what would happen with simultaneous leaks in Systems One and Three— Crossbow 08's problem—because an actuator in the lab failed. Nor did they test what would happen if the PFCS reset button was pushed when a hydraulic leak occurred in flight.

* * *

By the time the JAGMAN report was released, the Blue Ribbon Commission had issued its own findings. The four-member panel, backed by a three-member professional staff consisting of a Marine Corps colonel, an Air Force colonel, and a former Marine Corps officer who had been a test pilot and an astronaut, examined the Osprey program from top to bottom. The panel members heard briefings and took testimony from officials in the Marine Corps aviation branch and Navair, from top officials down to Marine and company Osprey pilots. They flew the Osprey in a computerized simulator. They visited the Bell and Boeing factories, examined how key parts of the aircraft were built, interviewed executives, managers, engineers, and factory floor supervisors. They went to VMMT-204 at New River and had mechanics show them how hard it was to inspect and work on the Osprey's nacelles and to use its electronic maintenance manual, which the mechanics said was riddled with errors. Back in Washington, Pentagon test director Coyle briefed them on the maintenance issues that led him to find the Osprey "not operationally suitable." They interviewed a General Accounting Office investigator about her agency's concerns with the Osprey.

In March, they held a public hearing at a hotel in Crystal City, just over the Potomac River from Washington. The witnesses included Osprey supporters and critics, as well as Connie Gruber and Trish Brow, whose husbands had piloted the Osprey that crashed at Marana. Relatives of others who died in the accident, and their attorneys in lawsuits they had filed against Bell and Boeing, also testified. The widows and their attorneys didn't ask that the Osprey be canceled. They said they only wanted it made safe so other Marines wouldn't die in it. "This was an accident that could have been avoided if only Bell-Boeing had presented the Marine Corps with a safe aircraft," Connie Gruber told the commission.

The widows, some holding photos of their lost Marines in their laps, were seated in the front row of an audience of 150 or more on April 18, when the commission met in open session at the same Crystal City hotel to deliberate on its findings. The commission had found a lot of things wrong with the Osprey. The nacelles were "extremely poorly engineered," panel member Norm Augustine told me years later. "The pathways for the hydraulic lines inside the nacelles and the fuel lines were extraordinarily complex," he said. "The nacelle was just absolutely packed with many parts that were prone to need to be replaced not easily reachable from the outside. Just Engineering 101 failings." There had been far too little flight-testing before Marines were allowed to ride in the back, and despite the billions spent, the Osprey had been "funded on a shoestring," Augustine said, creating parts shortages that helped explain its poor maintenance and reliability record. As Augustine saw it, the easiest thing for the commission to do would be to recommend scrapping the Osprey. "The scuttlebutt was that the leadership of the Pentagon was very opposed to the program and wanted to cancel it," Augustine recalled. Instead, the panel said the Pentagon should fix it.

There was "no evidence that the V-22 concept is fundamentally flawed," the commission said in its report, and no other available aircraft would do the things for the Marine Corps and the Air Force Special Operations Command a tiltrotor could do. "As an example, the Desert One mission involved 2 days of hiding in the desert . . . a mission that could have been carried out by a V-22-like aircraft in a single period of darkness," the report said. After eighteen years of development and nearly $12 billion spent on it, however, the panel said the Osprey was still far from ready. The commission made seventy-one recommendations in all. It said the Osprey's nacelles should be redesigned to prevent hydraulic lines from chafing and to add access panels so mechanics could see and work in the nacelles more easily. It said the flight control software should be revised and thoroughly retested. The panel said the program should finish a series of flight tests begun after the Marana accident to determine how susceptible the Osprey was to vortex ring state. All Ospreys had been grounded after the New River crash, so the tests had been halted. The commission also said the Pentagon should reassess whether the Osprey should be required to be able to make an emergency landing the way a helicopter would, using a method called "autorotation." The panel emphasized that Navair needed to improve the way it, Bell, and Boeing worked together.

While the changes were being made, the commission said, the government should keep buying a few Ospreys each year to keep production lines open. Those and existing Ospreys could be modified with the prescribed design changes later. Until the changes were made, the panel warned, pushing the Osprey into service would "further discredit the basic concept of the tiltrotor" and risk more crashes.

"This aircraft can do the job and it can be made to work," Dailey said as the panel deliberated on its recommendations in the open session that April.

The Osprey camp was relieved, if not elated, by the commission's conclusions. The recommendations were just a reprieve, not a pardon, but the panel had found no fundamental flaw in the tiltrotor. If the Pentagon and Congress went along, the Osprey would live and Bell-Boeing would get another chance—a second mulligan.

The Osprey's critics were unimpressed. The Council for a Livable World think tank declared again that "the Osprey should be killed." Carlton Meyer began writing another Osprey article for his website. In it, he called the commission a "bogus review panel."

★ ★ ★

When Harry P. Dunn saw what the Blue Ribbon Commission had done, he was appalled. Dunn was seventy years old, a former career Air Force helicopter pilot who had spent fourteen years as director of congressional relations for Martin Marietta Corporation. Dunn was also just as sure the Osprey was a death trap as his old friend Dick Spivey was that the tiltrotor was the dream machine. By the spring of 2001, Dunn had been trying for months to get key people in government to see the Osprey as he did. Most recently, he had been e-mailing arguments against it to Blue Ribbon Commission member Augustine, Dunn's boss years earlier at Martin Marietta. Augustine read all of Dunn's e-mails and passed them on to the commission staff. He thought Dunn had some valid criticisms of the Osprey, such as his argument that its powerful rotor downwash would kick up a pilot-blinding "brownout" of dust and dirt in a desert landing zone. Augustine didn't share Dunn's view that the tiltrotor was inherently flawed and unsafe, however, and the commission clearly had rejected Dunn's advice, too. Dunn, however, as he liked to say himself, was a "bullheaded Irishman." He was determined to kill the Osprey, and the Blue Ribbon Commission's conclusions weren't going to stop him.

Dunn had credentials to go with his passion against the Osprey. An Iowa native, he had graduated from the U.S. Naval Academy in 1954 but joined the Air Force because at the time he could become a pilot more quickly in that service than in the Navy or Marine Corps. During his twenty-three-year Air Force career, Dunn flew all kinds of planes and helicopters and earned a master's degree in aeronautical engineering at the University of Colorado. In the early 1960s, he was flight test director for the HH-3, an upgraded version of a Sikorsky helicopter nicknamed the "Jolly Green Giant," which was used during the Vietnam War to rescue downed pilots. Dunn spent the last six years of his Air Force career as a legislative liaison officer in Washington, where he learned how the political game in the Pentagon and on Capitol Hill was played. After retiring from the Air Force in 1977, he went to work for Martin Marietta as the company's top staff lobbyist, though Dunn didn't like to think of himself that way. He retired from Martin Marietta in 1991, then moved to Florida and spent nine years doing genealogical research on his Irish roots. Dunn still kept track of what was going on in the aviation world, though, and when the Osprey crashed at Marana in April 2000, killing nineteen Marines, Dunn felt like a prophet. He had seen the XV-15 fly at the 1981 Paris Air Show, which he attended as Senator Barry Goldwater's legislative liaison escort. Dunn told me that after watching the XV-15, he told Goldwater and George Troutman, the Bell Helicopter lobbyist and one of Goldwater's great friends, that the tiltrotor was "an accident waiting to happen." Troutman never forgave him, Dunn said. Goldwater, however, later flew the XV-15 and became one of the Osprey's important advocates.

Dunn was sure the tiltrotor's side-by-side rotors and their wingtip placement made it unstable, apt to roll out of control if one rotor's thrust got out of balance with the other. He saw dozens of flaws in the Osprey, but the most important boiled down to the size and shape of its rotors. The Osprey's rotors had been sized to fit on an amphibious assault ship. Dunn was sure that made them too small to work well in helicopter flight. They also had far more twist than a helicopter rotor so they could function as propellers in airplane flight. Dunn was sure that meant the Osprey's rotor blades would stall—stop producing thrust—along at least part of their length if a pilot tried the kind of "yank and bank" maneuvers helicopter pilots did in the Vietnam War. The undersized rotors also meant the Osprey had high disk loading, the pounds-per-square-foot measurement of how much thrust a rotor needs to lift its machine at normal flying weight. At more than twenty pounds per square foot of rotor disk, the Osprey's disk loading was two to four times that of most military helicopters. This was why its rotor downwash was so strong. Dunn was sure the pronounced twist of its rotors, their light weight, and its high disk loading meant the Osprey would never be able to "autorotate" to a safe landing if it lost power in both engines, something helicopters always had been expected to do. In autorotation, a rotor's size and shape allow it to spin fast enough even unpowered to produce the lift a helicopter needs to descend to the ground under control—like a maple seed, in the classic example.

In the early 1980s, while he was at Martin Marietta, Dunn had written a paper on his arguments against the Osprey and given it to congressional aides, hoping to persuade key lawmakers that building the tiltrotor was a mistake. He'd failed. He hadn't paid a lot of attention to the Osprey in the years since, but when he read in November 2000 that Pentagon test director Phil Coyle had declared the Osprey "not operationally suitable" for fielding, Dunn sent Coyle a long e-mail on the subject. Dunn told Coyle the Osprey should be called the "Albatross" because it would never be safe or affordable. "If I can be of any assistance," he offered, "please don't hesitate to call me." Coyle sent Dunn a copy of his November 17, 2000, report on the Osprey's Operational Evaluation and thanked him for his interest.

Back when Dunn worked for Martin Marietta, he had known Representative John Murtha, a Pennsylvania Democrat and Marine Corps veteran who chaired the powerful Defense Subcommittee of the House Appropriations Committee. The day after the December 11, 2000, New River crash, Dunn sent Murtha an e-mail urging him to stop the Osprey. Dunn got no reply.

After the Blue Ribbon Commission issued its report the following spring, Dunn tried unsuccessfully to reach panel member Augustine by phone at his office and home, then e-mailed him a new set of arguments. "For your own integrity, you might want to consider finding a way to dis-associate [sic] yourself from what appears to be full support of the V-22 concept," Dunn wrote. Augustine, who had taken Dunn's criticisms of the Osprey into account previously but decided he was wrong, e-mailed back a couple of weeks later. He told Dunn the commission no longer existed and gave him the name and number of a Defense Department official to contact "if you have further inputs."

Next Dunn turned to a society of his fellow former HH-3 helicopter pilots, the Jolly Green Association, e-mailing its members and asking them to help him stop the Osprey. A few were interested and began trading information and opinions with him. Dunn was encouraged by that. Then he learned that the new Bush administration's undersecretary of defense for acquisition, its top weapons buyer, was going to be Edward C. "Pete" Aldridge. Dunn had known Aldridge for years.

Aldridge, a Texas-born aeronautical engineer, had been secretary of the Air Force and held other influential jobs in the Pentagon and the defense industry since the 1960s. Dunn had known him in the 1980s, when Dunn was promoting missile programs for Martin Marietta and Aldridge was undersecretary of the Air Force and in charge of its space programs. Even before Aldridge was sworn in to his new job as undersecretary of defense in May 2001, Dunn sent him some of his arguments against the Osprey. The day Aldridge took his oath of office, Dunn e-mailed him that he had "indisputable evidence" the Osprey should be canceled. He asked Aldridge to call him. Aldridge never did. Three days later, Dunn e-mailed Aldridge a report he'd written on the Osprey saying its rotors were "a major design flaw and safety issue." Dunn also sent the paper to other Pentagon officials and the General Accounting Office, the congressional auditing agency. Dunn told its recipients the report had been written by a group of veteran combat helicopter pilots, test pilots, and rotorcraft engineers.

Defense Secretary Donald Rumsfeld had told Aldridge the Osprey would be his to handle, and at first, Aldridge was inclined to kill it. The Osprey's speed compared to helicopters was a clear advantage, but Aldridge wasn't sure it was worth the extra money. When he added in the question of whether its side-by-side rotors made it more vulnerable than a helicopter to vortex ring state, the potential problems created by its powerful downwash, the Osprey's "very, very bad" maintenance record, the question of whether it would be agile enough in combat, plus what it would cost to fix all of its problems, its value seemed "marginal," Aldridge told me years later. "I was on the verge of canceling it," he said. The Marines, though, "desperately wanted the airplane," Aldridge said, and the only fair and logical way to decide whether they should have it was to fix it and then put it through the rigorous flight-testing that should have been done in the first place.

Aldridge thought some of Harry Dunn's arguments about the Osprey made sense, but he wasn't about to get into a dialogue with Dunn about it. Aldridge remembered Dunn mainly as the guy who had arranged meetings between Aldridge and Norm Augustine in the 1980s, when Aldridge was undersecretary of the Air Force and Augustine was a Martin Marietta executive. In June 2001, Aldridge sent Dunn an e-mail saying he had read all of his messages but hinting that there was no need to send more. "I have an action underway that will result in a decision on whether to proceed on this program or not. But it must be done in my way," Aldridge wrote. Aldridge said he had talked about the Osprey with the secretary of the Navy, Gordon England, "and he fully understands the situation. We will make a decision together. Regards, Pete."

A few days earlier, Aldridge had told the Navy Department to put together a plan to implement the Blue Ribbon Commission's recommendations. He told the Navy that, for now, it could ask Congress to provide enough money to continue building Ospreys at the lowest rate possible to keep the Bell-Boeing production lines open. He also rescinded the authority his predecessor had given the Navy to decide whether the Osprey could go into Full Rate Production. Aldridge personally would make that decision.

That spring, newspapers and magazines around the country published numerous articles on the Osprey. They examined the crashes, the Osprey's long and expensive history, the politics that had kept it alive. Some questioned whether the Marines needed such an expensive aircraft. Many questioned the Osprey's safety. Once the Blue Ribbon Commission issued its report, Representative Curt Weldon decided it was time to try to burnish the Osprey's increasingly tarnished image.

On May 9, Republican Weldon announced that he and Democratic representative James Oberstar of Minnesota, who as chairman of the House Aviation Subcommittee had arranged for the XV-15 to land at the Capitol in 1990, were reviving the Tilt-Rotor Technology Coalition. The alliance of congressional and business advocates had helped lobby Congress to reject Dick Cheney's attempts to kill the Osprey a decade earlier but fallen dormant in the intervening years. Weldon also announced that, as chairman of the Procurement Subcommittee of the House Armed Services Committee, he would hold a hearing on the Osprey at the Philadelphia Naval Shipyard on May 21. "The problem we've had is because of negative publicity," he told the *Philadelphia Inquirer*. The

Osprey had been damaged politically by "grandstanding done by the national media outlets," he said. Most members of Congress "don't pay attention to defense issues," he explained, "so they see headlines on accidents and think this program has a serious problem."

The media coverage was demoralizing many of those working on the Osprey. Even after the Blue Ribbon Commission urged the Pentagon and Congress to give the Osprey another chance, many engineers and test pilots on the project for Navair were still wondering whether it wasn't just a matter of time before the plug was pulled. Even if the Osprey survived, clearly it was going to be a long time before it flew again. More than a few looked for new jobs, or new assignments within Navair or their companies. Some left the Osprey behind that year.

Once the Blue Ribbon Commission issued its report, Spivey and other managers and executives at Bell and Boeing became less worried about media coverage than they were about whether Aldridge would go along with the commission's recommendations. This was why Spivey was alarmed when he heard from one of his contacts that Harry Dunn was sending e-mails knocking the Osprey to government officials. Spivey was afraid they might listen to someone like Dunn, whose e-mails to others often said he was speaking for a group of pilots and engineers who called themselves the "Red Ribbon Panel."

Spivey had known Dunn for years, ever since Dunn was in the Air Force and Spivey was a young Bell Helicopter marketer. They'd seen each other often at aviation trade shows after Dunn joined Martin Marietta, even gone out for dinner or drinks about once a year. Spivey had talked to Dunn a lot about the tiltrotor in those days, and he'd thought him intrigued by its potential for Air Force special operations. Now Spivey wanted to find out who Dunn was talking to and what he was telling them. On June 7, Spivey e-mailed his old friend:

Harry,

A voice from the past. Had lost touch with where you were.
I understand that you have written several things about the
V-22 lately. Would you be so kind as to share them with me.
I would greatly appreciate it.

Thanks,
Dick

Dunn was wary in his reply. "Ah Ha!!" he began. "I was beginning to wonder when you would surface." Dunn told Spivey he had been alerted by a friend "that some of our work was being passed on to you all." Dunn and his "little band of 40 to 50" pilots and engineers were digging up a lot of information on the Osprey and had done a lot of analysis, he said. "None of it would be new to you however, so I don't see any real purpose of going abck [sic] and sending you some of our work." Instead, Dunn suggested, maybe Spivey could send him some details on a nonstop flight an Osprey had made the previous year from California to Maryland with aerial refueling. "Great chatting with you—let's keep in touch!" he closed.

The two old friends circled each other again like wrestlers two weeks later, when Dunn sent Spivey a message asking if he was going to send any information and whether Spivey had known George Troutman very well.

Spivey replied without a salutation:

> Knew George very well. Would be glad to respond, but I
> have seen nothing of your work yet. Just that it exists . . .
> Thanks,
> Dick

Four days later, Dunn discovered Spivey's angry reply to Carlton Meyer's article on the G2mil.com website. Dunn copied it and e-mailed it to Spivey with a message that began, "My Dear Dick Spivey—My My—such tantrums!—trash???" Dunn told Spivey he should "get in a closed room with a couple of honest rotorcraft engineers for a review of what the red ribbon guys and others have discovered."

Spivey didn't reply, though he really wished he could find out what Dunn was saying about the Osprey, and whether any decision makers were listening. He also really wished he hadn't replied to that article on G2mil.com.

★ ★ ★

One thing was clear to everyone in the Osprey camp: this time they had to get it right. The Marine Corps, Navair, Bell-Boeing, and their allies all knew they had taken two swings at the ball already and missed both times. Pete Aldridge was giving them a third chance. They didn't want to blow it.

There were a lot of reasons things had gone so wrong over the years. The overly ambitious requirements of the original JVX program, the companies' blithe assurances on schedules and lowballing of bids, the attempt to cram so many new technologies into a new kind of aircraft, the 50–50 Bell-Boeing partnership and their culture clash, the design compromises dictated by the need to fly from amphibious assault ships, former Navy Secretary John Lehman's insistence on a fixed-price development contract, funding shortfalls during Cheney's attempt to cancel the Osprey, the push by the Marines to get the Osprey into service as fast as possible afterward—everyone had his list, and there was plenty of blame to go around. Most agreed, though, that the biggest mistake had been allowing time—schedules—to drive the program. Politically it would be difficult, but the Marine Corps leadership, those in charge at Navair, Bell and Boeing executives, and most everyone else involved all agreed that from now on, the Osprey had to be "event-driven," not "schedule-driven." Soon "event-driven" became the program's unofficial mantra, repeated in nearly every meeting, every congressional hearing, and every media interview. This time, they were going to do it right instead of in a hurry.

Navair's first step was to ask NASA's Ames Research Center in Mountain View, California, where research on the tiltrotor had begun more than thirty years earlier, to study two questions about the Osprey that the Blue Ribbon Commission said needed more work: vortex ring state and autorotation. The director of the Ames center, Dr. Henry McDonald, decided to chair the committee himself and recruited eleven other experts to do the study. They were mostly Ph.D.s and "graybeards" who had made their careers in rotorcraft research, but the panel also included a couple of test pilots, one of whom had directed the Osprey flight test team at Navair. McDonald also recruited twenty-seven other experts to advise the committee. Twelve were from NASA Ames but most of the rest, who included five test pilots, had worked on or had some connection to the Osprey. When McDonald invited Bell to send three of its best tiltrotor experts, the company sent two of its most senior engineers and Dick Spivey.

Serving as an adviser to the NASA committee was how Spivey learned that Harry Dunn wasn't the only one with credentials and contacts who thought the Osprey flawed, a discovery that triggered something in Spivey akin to parental protective instinct.

When the committee met in June 2001 to hear briefings by invited experts, one was Arthur "Rex" Rivolo of the Institute for Defense Analyses, one of a handful of federally funded think tanks paid to do independent research for the Pentagon. IDA had long been under contract to monitor the Osprey for the Pentagon's Office of Operational Test and Evaluation. Rivolo had been doing that work for IDA since the early 1990s, when he joined the think tank after an extraordinary early career.

Rivolo's dark hair and olive skin suggested his Italian birth, but his accent was all New York. His parents had moved from Genoa, Italy, to Queens, New York, in 1955, eleven years after he was born. Bitten by the aviation bug as a child, Rivolo earned a degree in aerospace engineering at Brooklyn Polytechnic University, then became an Air Force fighter pilot. He flew combat missions in F-4 Phantom jets in Vietnam, then came home and earned a Ph.D. in physics from the State University of New York at Stony Brook, on Long Island. To keep flying, he joined the Air National Guard on Long Island, where he switched to helicopters because the nearest unit with jets was too long a commute. Rivolo joined IDA in 1992 after six years of teaching astrophysics at the University of Pennsylvania and a failed attempt at an aviation-related business venture.

Rivolo spent a lot of time with the Multiservice Operational Test Team in the late 1990s. He even flew the Osprey with MOTT commander Lieutenant Colonel Keith Sweaney and others. As a pilot, Rivolo loved the Osprey. He thought its ability to take off and land like a helicopter and fly like an airplane was "sexy," and he believed the tiltrotor would be great for civilian air transport. Over time, though, Rivolo concluded that the Osprey was the wrong aircraft to fly troops into a landing zone under fire.

Rivolo saw two major flaws in the Osprey as a combat aircraft. First, like Harry Dunn, Rivolo was sure the Osprey couldn't autorotate to the ground safely if its engines were shot out or failed for any reason. Secondly, after the April 2000 crash at Marana, Rivolo became convinced the Osprey's side-by-side rotors made it unacceptably vulnerable to vortex ring state, the risk of a rotor failing to produce thrust as it should if it gets into its own downwash too quickly. By 2001, when he testified to the NASA committee, Rivolo also felt Navair officials had misled him in the past about how thoroughly the Osprey was being flight-tested. After that, he became one of the Osprey's most determined internal critics.

Like a lot of helicopter pilots, Rivolo thought the ability to autorotate was a vital safety feature for a rotorcraft going into combat. The U.S. armed forces lost thousands of helicopters during the Vietnam War, but Rivolo believed autorotation had saved many as well. The ability to autorotate had always been expected of helicopters, but from the time the Osprey was still called the JVX, whether the helicopter-airplane hybrid was required to be able to autorotate to a landing had been open to interpretation. The original Joint Services Operational Requirement for the JVX had said: "In the event that all engine power is lost while in flight, the aircraft must be capable of a power-off glide/autorotation to a survivable emergency landing." Unlike a helicopter, the tiltrotor had a wing and could fly like an airplane, so in theory, if an Osprey lost both engines, it might glide to a safe landing with its rotors pointed forward rather than autorotate to the ground with the rotors pointed up. The Osprey's rotors were too long to land like an airplane without them striking the ground, but if they hit anything, they were designed to "broomstraw"—shred into small pieces rather than large chunks that might fly into the aircraft. In 1995, as Navair and the Marines were preparing to ask a high-level Pentagon committee to approve Low Rate Initial Production, the implied requirement that the Osprey be able to autorotate was watered down even more. After that, the requirement simply said: "Power Off Glide/Auto-Rotation. The [Osprey] must be capable of a survivable emergency landing."

No matter what the official requirement said, Rivolo thought the Osprey needed to be able to autorotate to a landing like a helicopter, and in the late 1990s he checked with Navair to make sure autorotation landings were going to be done in flight tests. "I was told 'testing is progressing; it's going slower than expected, but it's progressing and everything is fine,'" Rivolo recalled. "That was an out-and-out lie."

Developmental test pilots had done some autorotation flight tests in the Osprey during that period, descending at high altitude with the engines idling and disconnected from the rotors. The rotors autorotated, but the pilots concluded it was too dangerous to try landing the Osprey that way. Even landing a helicopter by autorotation is tricky. To do it successfully, a pilot has to let the helicopter float toward the ground, then pull up at the last moment and flare to a landing. This requires milking the last bit of lift out of the rotor or rotors, whose inertia has kept them turning without engine power. The relatively small size and large twist of the Osprey's proprotors gave it a high rate of descent in autorotation and too little inertia to provide the necessary lift at the end of such a landing, the pilots found. Even so, recalled one former Osprey developmental test pilot, in the late 1990s there were "a number of people at Bell and Boeing who were making claims" that the Osprey could autorotate to a safe landing. "Us test pilots were going, 'No, you can't. It's a stunt in the simulator,'" this pilot said. "When you make a survivable one in a simulator, you make nine of them that aren't." The maneuver was so tricky, test pilots would bet beers on who could do it in the Osprey simulator without crashing.

Still, the test pilots agreed with those running the program that while the Osprey's inability to autorotate to a landing like a helicopter was a disadvantage, it wasn't a crippling one. Given the reliability of modern turbine engines, they calculated that the odds of losing both in ordinary flight were astronomical. There was certainly a chance an Osprey might have an engine shot out while coming into a "hot" landing zone. With the nacelles separated by about forty-five feet, though, having both engines shot out at once was unlikely, they concluded, and the interconnecting driveshaft would let one engine power both rotors so a pilot could land in helicopter mode safely even with one engine out.

Rivolo didn't buy such arguments. When he found out just before the Osprey's Operational Evaluation began in 1999 that Navair had long ago dropped the idea of doing autorotation landings in flight tests, he told me, "At that point is when I really got angry."

After the April 2000 crash at Marana, Rivolo also began to see vortex ring state as a reason the Marines shouldn't fly troops into combat in the Osprey. Like a lot of pilots and even aeronautical engineers, Rivolo didn't know much about vortex ring state then. The phenomenon had been recognized for decades, but little research had been done on it, for a couple of reasons. First, it was generally agreed that helicopter pilots could steer clear of vortex ring state by never descending too quickly at slow forward speed—no faster than 800 feet per minute at 40 knots or less was the standard limit. Secondly, if a helicopter *should* go into vortex ring state, the pilot usually recognized it right away—the machine would shudder and shake—and it was relatively easy to fly out of, unless the aircraft was too close to the ground. The pilot just had to tilt the helicopter's nose forward and fly into "clean air" so the rotor could stop churning in its own downwash. The way the Osprey at Marana had snap-rolled to the right when it went into vortex ring state, however, led Rivolo to suspect the phenomenon was more dangerous for a tiltrotor because of its side-by-side rotors.

After Marana, Rivolo looked around for an expert who could help him understand vortex ring state. He found J. Gordon Leishman, a forty-two-year-old professor of aerospace engineering at the University of Maryland, who had studied the intricacies of helicopter rotors and the air flows that affect them. Leishman was the author or co-author of dozens of scholarly papers on the topic and had written a book called *Principles of Helicopter Aerodynamics,* published in May 2000 by Cambridge University Press. Rivolo offered Leishman an IDA contract to run calculations on the wakes of the Osprey's rotors using a computer model Leishman and his graduate students had devised. The goal was to see how the air currents the rotors created might affect the Osprey's risk of going into vortex ring state. Leishman concluded that the downwash and other air flows around the Osprey's rotors collided with each other in ways that were different from a helicopter's and made the tiltrotor's aerodynamic behavior in descending flight hard to predict.

Armed with Leishman's findings, Rivolo tried but failed to persuade Pentagon test director Phil Coyle to declare in his November 2000 report on the Osprey's Operational Evaluation that the Osprey was "not operationally suitable"—a conclusion Rivolo knew might keep the Marines from getting the program through Milestone III anytime soon. Coyle's office also refused to let Rivolo present his views to the Blue Ribbon Commission. A few months later, however, Rivolo and Leishman were two of the experts the NASA committee on the Osprey invited to deliver presentations. Spivey didn't like what either one said.

Rivolo had come up with his own theory of vortex ring state by then, one that went well beyond Leishman's conclusions. Rivolo believed from his own experience that, despite rules against it, pilots were apt in combat to descend too quickly at slow airspeed. He also told the NASA panel there were other ways a rotorcraft could get into vortex ring state. It could happen if a rotor were hit by a gust of wind from underneath while hovering over a mountainside, he said. It could happen during the flare of an autorotation if the pilot's timing were off. It could happen anytime the flow of air from below a rotor equaled its downwash, which was most likely to occur close to the ground, he argued. A helicopter, with its rotor or rotors over the fuselage, could recover nine out of ten times in such circumstances but the Osprey would always crash, Rivolo asserted. This was so, he argued, because the side-by-side placement of its rotors would cause the Osprey to snap roll if one of them went into vortex ring state. Even though helicopters could get out of vortex ring state fairly easily, he added, his research suggested the phenomenon was the real reason for one out of three helicopter crashes.

Spivey was aghast. Rivolo was saying the Osprey was a death trap. His theory of vortex ring state causing one in three helicopter crashes was also novel, to say the least. "Rex, what kind of proof do you have of what you just said?" Spivey asked him at the NASA meeting. "I see every accident that happens to rotorcraft in the United States—that comes across my desk every day. I know what I've been told, I know what I see in the accident reports, and I've never seen anything like this. What is your authority to say that?"

Rivolo replied that while FAA statistics attributed only 8 percent of major helicopter accidents to vortex ring state, the figure really should include mishaps resulting from failed attempts to autorotate and other hard landings. "I am probably one of the few people in the world who understands vortex ring state," Rivolo told me. "How do you make a hard landing in a helicopter? A hard landing is because the pilot lost enough power to maintain altitude. That is a vortex ring state. So every single accident the FAA classifies as hard landing is a vortex ring state. And in autorotation, most autorotations end badly because the pilot, at the bottom, enters vortex ring state. And I showed them exactly how that mechanism works."

Spivey was relieved to see that the members of the NASA panel and others among its advisers found Rivolo's theory as far-out as he did. Several told Spivey they were glad he'd challenged Rivolo. Spivey was alarmed, though. Given Rivolo's position as the IDA expert assigned to the Pentagon Office of Operational Test and Evaluation, Spivey assumed Rivolo had influence in the Pentagon. *This is bad*, Spivey thought.

Spivey wasn't there when Leishman showed the NASA panel his studies of the Osprey's rotor wash, but he heard about the presentation later. Leishman's calculations were complex, but he essentially concluded that because the Osprey's rotors were side by side, they would necessarily fly through each other's disturbed air in descending flight.

The effects hadn't been adequately studied, Leishman said, and might mean the Osprey could go into vortex ring state for reasons other than an overly rapid descent at slow forward speed—by doing evasive maneuvers to avoid enemy fire when landing in a combat zone, for example.

When Spivey heard what Leishman had said, he was nearly as alarmed as he'd been about Rivolo's presentation. Spivey was sure Leishman was greatly exaggerating the strength and duration of the vortices created by a rotor. "He was talking about how dangerous it was to operate in all those vortices," Spivey recalled. "Well, heck, helicopters do that all the time." Spivey was also confident the tiltrotor was *less* vulnerable to vortex ring state than a helicopter. The few tests done by Osprey test pilots trying to put it into vortex ring state in the fall of 2000 already had suggested that.

One day while Spivey was still stewing over Leishman's briefing, he ran into one of the professor's University of Maryland colleagues and complained about Leishman to him. Leishman "wasn't being scientific," Spivey told the man. Leishman was outraged when he heard what Spivey had done. Leishman had made a few dollars doing his study for IDA, but his interest in the Osprey was scientific. He wondered why Bell didn't invite him down to Fort Worth to talk about his research if it bothered them, rather than snipe at him behind his back. At the same time, he knew billions of dollars were at stake for the company.

Spivey wasn't thinking about money. To him, the stakes were higher, and his faith in the Osprey had never been shaken. Spivey was sure the Osprey's crashes could have been avoided, and such accidents could be prevented in the future, with better training. He was certain the Osprey could be made safe, and that it would save lives once it got into service. Its speed would let Marines and special operations troops outmaneuver and defeat their enemies with fewer casualties. Its speed would get those wounded to medical treatment fast enough to save them. "The fact that we lost some along the way is excruciating, but that doesn't make you walk away from something you believe has the promise of saving more lives downstream," Spivey reasoned. "You're going to have mistakes along the way, unfortunately. All aircraft development has its price. Unfortunately, it comes with the territory."

Spivey had criticized Leishman to the professor's colleague because the dream Spivey had devoted his life to was in danger. If he had to bite and kick a little to save it, he would.

* * *

The NASA committee concluded that there were "no known aeromechanics phenomena that would stop the safe and orderly development and deployment of the V-22." The panel urged the Pentagon to resume flight-testing "without delay," especially tests to verify how vulnerable the Osprey was to vortex ring state. The committee said the available evidence suggested the Osprey was less apt to go into it than a helicopter, based on the tests conducted before the New River crash had grounded all Ospreys. "A tiltrotor aircraft, when deep within the vortex ring state region, can encounter uncommanded roll motions due to its side by side proprotor configuration," the panel acknowledged, but the tests suggested it was just as easy for an Osprey to get out of it. A pilot simply needed to tilt the Osprey's rotors forward and fly into "clean air."

As for autorotation, the NASA panel acknowledged that for an Osprey flying in helicopter mode, "a full power-off landing may not be practical." The preferred way for an Osprey to land with its engines out, it said, would be to tilt the rotors forward and glide to a landing airplane-style. The panel said the Osprey shouldn't be required to autorotate.

The NASA committee also urged the Pentagon to provide Navair more money, more people, and more Ospreys to test. "The panel believes that when fielded, the V-22 will truly revolutionize the role of transport aircraft in the defense of our country," the report said.

The committee's chairman, Henry McDonald, briefed Undersecretary of Defense Pete Aldridge on the panel's findings on August 14. The next day, Aldridge met with reporters at the Pentagon. "I'm going to reserve judgment," he told them when asked about the Osprey. "The plan, assuming we proceed, is to resume flying sometime early next year." The Osprey was "a very complicated airplane," Aldridge said. "There are lots of uncertainties regarding the flying qualities. There's still some uncertainties regarding reliability improvements. There's uncertainty regarding how long we actually will have to keep it in flight test before we continue back on production. It's just a very difficult problem to decide upon, and we are not going to decide quickly."

* * *

On September 11, 2001, less than a month after the NASA committee finished its work, Al Qaeda terrorists hijacked four civilian passenger jets and slammed two into the World Trade Center in New York and one into the Pentagon. The fourth plane crashed in rural Pennsylvania after passengers stormed the cockpit. On October 7, U.S. ships and planes launched missile and air strikes on the Islamic fundamentalist rulers of Afghanistan, the Taliban, for harboring Al Qaeda leader Osama bin Laden. U.S. special operations troops were already in Afghanistan, aiding the Taliban's enemies. The world was anticipating a full-fledged U.S. invasion. Four days after the U.S. air strikes in Afghanistan began, Representative Curt Weldon told the *Fort Worth Star-Telegram* that he was going to try to get Congress to approve extra funding for the Osprey. With its high speed and vertical takeoff and landing capability, he said, the Osprey would be perfect for ferrying U.S. troops around Afghanistan's vast and rugged terrain. "That bird is ready to go and we should get it up in the air," Weldon said. The causes of the Osprey crashes the year before already had been largely fixed, Weldon asserted. The Osprey could be ready to go to war in thirty to sixty days.

Those following the Osprey's travails could only roll their eyes. They knew Weldon couldn't be more wrong. Navair, Bell-Boeing, and the Marines were only beginning to sort out how to rehabilitate the Osprey as the Blue Ribbon Commission and the NASA panel had said they should. Blue Ribbon Commission member Norman Augustine told the *Star-Telegram* it would take at least two years.

Weldon's wildly optimistic description of the Osprey's status was part posturing. The annual defense bills were moving through Congress, and Weldon wanted to give his colleagues as many reasons as possible to keep building Ospreys. His remarks, though, reflected how much 9/11 had changed the defense debate in Washington. Earlier in the year, the key defense issue in Congress had been how to hold defense spending down. Now the nation was at war and Congress wanted U.S. troops to have whatever weapons could help them win. When the defense bills were finished that December, Congress had appropriated $1.3 billion to build eleven new Ospreys in the next fiscal year and fund the redesign and retesting Navair had told Aldridge it wanted to do. The legislation also required Aldridge to submit a report to Congress thirty days before the Osprey flew again describing what had been done to correct the flaws in its hydraulics and flight control software and what steps Navair had taken to implement the Blue Ribbon Commission's recommendations.

The defense bills cleared Congress and went to Bush for his signature on December 13. Four days later, Harry Dunn read in the trade newsletter *Inside the Navy* that Aldridge was expected within days to approve Navair's plans to redesign and retest the Osprey. In Aldridge's mind, the decision had been a close one. It was going to cost a lot to redo what Aldridge saw as Bell's "sloppy engineering" of the Osprey's nacelles, which had let its wire bundles rub its hydraulic lines. It was going to cost a lot to find out whether the Osprey was excessively vulnerable to vortex ring state and less agile than it needed to be for combat. He wasn't sure it would be money well spent. A few months back, though, the commandant, General Jim Jones, had come to Aldridge's office and urged him to keep the Osprey alive. The Marine Corps needed it, Jones said.

All that summer and fall, Harry Dunn e-mailed Aldridge regularly, often daily, passing on evidence to support what Dunn called the "findings" of the "Red Ribbon Panel." The Osprey's rotors were inherently flawed, Dunn kept telling Aldridge. The Osprey would never be able to do the maneuvers required in combat. If it did, its rotors would stall, or be damaged by the G's—gravitational forces—such flight would put on them, Dunn predicted. The Osprey's rotor downwash was so powerful it would be unable to land in dusty conditions because the pilot would be blinded by the cloud of dirt the rotors would kick up, Dunn argued. The fixes recommended by the Blue Ribbon Commission and NASA would be a waste of time and money. Dunn's e-mails, which often lapsed into diatribe, also accused Bell-Boeing and Navair of hiding engineering information from their Pentagon overseers. He urged Aldridge to have the Defense Department inspector general investigate them.

Aldridge had found some of Dunn's arguments persuasive at first, but he soon wearied of Dunn's constant barrage and stopped reading his e-mails. Now Dunn sent Aldridge another, which included the scoop by *Inside the Navy*'s Christopher Castelli reporting that Aldridge had approved a new program of flight tests. "It is hard and sad to conclude that all of my personal efforts (leave alone the dozens of others who did a lot of the work) have come to a total failure," Dunn wrote. If the report in *Inside the Navy* was accurate, Dunn said, the "140++" combat and test pilots he had been working with were going to "pull together a bunch of our findings and reports and facts and charts and dump them out onto the media." Dunn warned that Aldridge might soon "be reading about your inabilities to make solid, fact based decisions."

Aldridge confirmed his decision to let the Osprey program go forward in a December 21 Pentagon news conference. He also left the door open to canceling the Osprey later. The Blue Ribbon Commission and the NASA panel had found no fundamental flaws in the tiltrotor, but "I personally still have some doubts," he said. The flight test plan he was approving would last two years and be much more comprehensive than Navair originally had planned. Vortex ring state was only one thing to be tested. The Osprey's flight characteristics over a windy ship deck, while hovering, while landing in dust and debris also would be tested, along with its ability to do combat maneuvers, fly in formation, and refuel in midair. "The flight test effort will be event-driven, as opposed to schedule-driven," Aldridge said. "We will not be driven by trying to accomplish something within a certain period of time. The Secretary of the Navy and I will do periodic reviews of the flight test results to assess progress." In the meantime, production would be held to eleven Ospreys a year. His concerns, Aldridge said, were how stable an aircraft with rotors on its wingtips could be, and whether the Osprey's proprotors, with their relatively small diameter, could produce the thrust needed and handle the stresses that went along with flying in combat. He wasn't sure, he added, that the Osprey would pass its tests.

There were mornings that year when Major Paul Rock barely could summon the will to get out of bed and go to work at VMMT-204, the Osprey training squadron at New River. Rock loved the Marine Corps, he loved to fly, and he loved flying the Osprey. Now the Osprey was grounded and VMMT-204 was a miserable place to be. The crashes in 2000 had been devastating enough. Then had come the *60 Minutes* broadcast with its tape of VMMT-204's commander at the time, Lieutenant Colonel Fred Leberman, telling his Marines to "lie." Rock hadn't been in the meeting where Leberman said that, and when he heard it on television, he was stunned. Rock had never imagined he would hear such a thing coming from a Marine officer's mouth. Like the rest of the squadron, Rock was also demoralized by what followed.

The Marine Corps inspector general's investigators had swooped down on VMMT-204 that January 18, the day Leberman was relieved of command, like a SWAT team. They'd seized computers and set out to interview all of the nearly 250 Marines in the squadron. The same day, Colonel Richard Dunnivan, who had "hot seated" with Lieutenant Colonel Keith Sweaney before the crash of Crossbow 08, took command of the squadron. Just over a week later, the Defense Department inspector general took over the investigation of VMMT-204. The investigators stayed for weeks, their investigation lasted for months, and it threw the squadron into chaos. Every morning, they posted a list of twenty to thirty enlisted Marines required to report for interviews. Officers were called personally to report for theirs. Other pilots and maintainers were left standing around with little to do, except ask over and over whether the Osprey was going to be canceled. Morale plummeted.

The inspector general's report concluded that the squadron had filed some false maintenance reports, but only during a two-week period after Leberman held his December 29 meeting with maintainers. During those two weeks, VMMT-204 reported its readiness rate as 100 percent every day. The sudden improvement was clearly preposterous. The investigation found no connection between false maintenance reports and the Osprey crashes. It also found no evidence for the allegation by Corporal Clifford Carlson, who voluntarily left the Marine Corps a few months after taping Leberman, that "deception has been going on for over 2 years." After Article 15 hearings, a voluntary alternative to a court-martial, Leberman was found guilty of dereliction of duty and conduct unbecoming an officer and Colonel James E. Schleining was found guilty of dereliction of duty. They received letters of reprimand, a penalty that damages, and often kills, an officer's chances of promotion. Assistant maintenance officer Captain Christopher Ramsey, who had denied telling mechanics to write "down" aircraft as "up," was found guilty of dereliction of duty because he knew of false maintenance reports. He was cleared, however, on charges of making false statements and conduct unbecoming an officer. Ramsey received no punishment.

Uncertain when the Osprey might fly again, or whether it ever would beyond the tests Navair was planning, higher-ups at the 2nd Marine Aircraft Wing and some at Headquarters Marine Corps were eager to transfer many of VMMT-204's pilots and maintainers to other squadrons. Some wanted to go ahead and disband VMMT-204, whose purpose was to train pilots and mechanics for future Osprey squadrons. Headquarters decided to keep VMMT-204 in operation, but by early summer, it was clear its Ospreys weren't going to fly again for a long time. In mid-July, eight officers and thirty-three enlisted Marines were transferred out. By fall, the Marine Corps decided to move another thirty-two enlisted maintainers to Patuxent River to work on the redesign and testing of the Osprey that Navair was planning. Before long, VMMT-204's head count was down to about seventy, with just a handful of officers. Senior officers at the wing and headquarters were privately advising those pilots left to move on. Being assigned to the Osprey once had been a badge of distinction, an honor. Now people were being told it could damage their careers. Rock went down the list of officers left one day and came to a jolting realization. *I'm the last son of a bitch around here who's even flown this airplane,* he thought. *I'm going to be the last guy standing here turning off the lights.* By then, the only other member of the squadron who had ever flown the Osprey was Colonel Dunnivan, and he had logged all of one hour in it, the day Crossbow 08 crashed.

Rock began to worry about the Marine Corps career he had begun the day he graduated from the U.S. Naval Academy on May 25, 1988, two days after Bell and Boeing rolled out the first Osprey prototype in Fort Worth. Born in Baltimore and raised as an "Army brat," Rock was the son of a soldier who had enlisted out of high school, served in Vietnam, and retired as a lieutenant colonel. Paul Jr. decided he wanted to take his commission in the Marines after spending a week at Quantico Marine Base between his sophomore and junior years at Annapolis. He decided he wanted to be a pilot in the summer between his junior and senior years, when he was assigned to Marine Corps Base Hawaii at Kaneohe Bay, on the island of Oahu. He got a ride there in an F-4 Phantom fighter jet and a CH-46 helicopter and that settled it. Flying was the greatest. You strapped on a big machine and went up and defied the law of gravity. How cool was that? When he finished flight school at Pensacola, Florida, and got his wings, in December 1990, Rock chose helicopters and asked to be assigned to a CH-46 squadron on the East Coast. He got his wish, and early the next year joined up with Marine Medium Helicopter Squadron 263, known as HMM-263, as the unit was coming back from the 1991 Gulf War. Six years later, after he had become a CH-46 instructor, Rock put in a request to switch to the Osprey. He had heard ever since he joined the Corps that the Osprey was the future of Marine aviation, and he wanted to be part of that future. Rock was selected for the MOTT in 1997, one of six pilots chosen out of dozens who applied, but it was two years before he got his first chance to fly the Osprey. When he did, on June 11, 1999, he fell in love with it. Now the

Osprey was in trouble, and Rock feared his career was, too. He had to think about that and what it might mean not just for himself, but for his wife, Maria, and their three young children.

Rock decided to stay with the Osprey and VMMT-204 after a talk with Dunnivan. "Look, we're fighting a good fight here on a number of fronts," Dunnivan said. By then, Navair had begun its redesign of the Osprey and was preparing to start the flight-testing Aldridge had approved. Rock was now VMMT-204's maintenance officer. He and several of his mechanics were advising Navair and Bell on how to fix the nacelles. Dunnivan had decided the squadron also should take the Osprey's mistake-riddled electronic maintenance manual and perform each of its thousands of tasks one by one to validate or correct them. Dunnivan wanted Rock to supervise that tedious chore.

"You're the last guy I've got with any credibility piloting the airplane," Dunnivan told Rock. "I'm certainly not going to make you, but I'd like it if you stayed." Dunnivan also told Rock he should consider what staying might do to his career. Officers from higher headquarters had been telling Rock he should leave. Dunnivan couldn't tell Rock they weren't right.

Rock thought it over. He wasn't eager to stay, but he had a lot of respect for the enlisted Marines who worked for him. He knew he'd have a guilty conscience if, for the sake of his own career, he left those Marines behind, saddled with the humdrum work that lay ahead. He also still believed in the Osprey. Rock decided he couldn't leave.

Over the next two years, Rock sometimes wondered if he'd made the right decision. He later came to think of that time as The Dark Ages.

CHAPTER TWELVE

PHOENIX

B y December 2001, when Undersecretary of Defense Pete Aldridge first ignored his advice to kill it, the Osprey had become Harry Dunn's Moby Dick and Harry Dunn the Osprey's Captain Ahab. Dunn mulled and plotted day and night on how to slay the Osprey. Working by computer and phone from his home on Florida's Merritt Island, just north of Cape Canaveral, he scoured the Internet and filed Freedom of Information Act requests for government reports on the Osprey. He e-mailed attorneys who had filed lawsuits against Bell and Boeing on behalf of relatives of those killed in the Osprey's crashes, asking the lawyers to send him documents and offering to help with their research. He devoured engineering studies and other reports on rotorcraft that might bolster his case that the Osprey's side-by-side rotors were a fatal flaw. He sought out academic experts for help.

Dunn also contacted newspaper reporters who covered the Osprey, telling them about the "findings" of his "Red Ribbon Panel," which he described as an "organization" with more than one hundred members—a gross exaggeration. "Essentially there were about eight of us who did all this work," Dunn acknowledged when I met him years later.

"My impression is that Harry Dunn was the Red Ribbon Panel," I said.

"That was it," Dunn replied with a smile.

Newspapers and magazines all around the country were writing about the Osprey during what Paul Rock called the Dark Ages, and Harry Dunn wasn't the only critic quoted. Others with credentials were willing to comment, too, especially helicopter pilots, who sometimes thought the Osprey's advocates talked as if tiltrotors were going to replace all helicopters someday. The outside critic who worried Navair, Bell-Boeing, and the Marine Corps the most, though, was Dunn, for they thought they saw his arguments reflected in questions Undersecretary Aldridge was asking in quarterly meetings on the Osprey and his periodic briefings from Navair.

Many of those working on the Osprey wanted to reply to Dunn and other critics quoted in the media in 2001. Bell and Boeing, though, were lying low because of lawsuits filed by relatives of those killed in the crashes and the political risk of speaking out. Marine Corps leaders were wary of defending the Osprey too aggressively unless it proved itself. After all, twenty-three Marines had just died in it. Colonel Dick Dunnivan and his pilots at VMMT-204, though, were itching to fire back, and they got permission from the commandant to do that late in 2001. When Dunn published an article in the *Fort Worth Star-Telegram* that November saying the Osprey "would be a disaster in Afghanistan or anywhere else," Major Paul Rock wrote a reply, which the *Star-Telegram* published under the headline "Don't sell the V-22 short." Rock, Dunnivan, and Lieutenant Colonel Ronald S. "Curly" Culp, who like Rock had flown the Osprey in its Operational Evaluation, shared a triple byline.

"We like to think we've accumulated a little bit of experience in this arena ourselves and so feel qualified to respond to Dunn's familiar claims," the pilots wrote. Dunn was right in saying it would be "some time" before the Osprey was ready for service, they conceded, but he was wrong in writing that the Osprey's range was far less than advertised, that its cabin was too small to actually carry twenty-four Marines, and that it couldn't land on dirt or sand because its powerful rotor downwash would kick up pilot-blinding brownouts. The Osprey could "launch in the morning in California and land less than eight hours later within sight of the Atlantic Ocean (a non-stop trip made in the MV-22, by the way, by some of the authors of this essay)." The pilots had flown the Osprey with twenty-four troops in back and landed in the desert many times, they said.

Rock wasn't sure the response would do much good, but it felt good to fight back. Rock's co-author Culp wasn't done. Culp telephoned Dunn and invited him to visit New River. He could get inside an Osprey, fly the computerized simulator, ask any questions he wanted, Culp promised. Dunn turned him down.

Seven years later, Dunn still had never seen an Osprey firsthand. "Didn't need to," he told me.

★ ★ ★

Marine Corps Colonel Daniel Schultz saw the Osprey firsthand a lot, but he was especially eager to see it on May 29, 2002. That morning, Schultz was standing on the edge of a taxiway at Patuxent River Naval Air Station, waiting for the most important event yet in the eleven months since he'd taken over Navair's Osprey program. Out on the runway was Osprey Number 10, one of the prototypes built in the mid-1990s. Its nacelles were pointed skyward, its rotors whirling. Seventeen months after the New River crash, the Osprey was about to fly again for the first time.

Schultz had come in with a mandate from Navy Secretary Gordon England to make sure the Osprey succeeded in what everyone knew was its last chance. England, an engineer who had spent forty years working for defense contractors, flew to New River to examine the Osprey in June 2001, two weeks after he came into office. He found the design of its nacelles "extraordinarily poor." The Osprey's biggest problem, though, had been poor management, England later concluded. Bell-Boeing's 50–50 partnership, which left neither company in charge, had led to bad or tardy decisions when disputes couldn't be settled. England told the companies to give the head of their joint office authority to make commitments on behalf of both companies and funds to cover contingencies. With England's blessing, Schultz ordered Bell and Boeing to move their Osprey office to Pax River. From now on, company and Navair engineers would work in "Integrated Product Teams" with adjoining offices.

Their first task was to remake the Osprey as the Blue Ribbon Commission had recommended—revamp its nacelles, retest its flight control software, change hardware that had created problems. As the team redesigning the nacelles got started, Schultz had the engineers work with enlisted Marine mechanics from VMMT-204 to inject hands-on experience into the exercise. Rock, VMMT-204's maintenance officer by then, flew to Texas in the spring of 2001 with some Marine mechanics for the first big meeting on the issue, a gathering of about 150 engineers and others from Bell-Boeing and Navair. Rock had never seen so many smart people in one room. He figured the engineers all had master's or Ph.D. degrees. The enlisted maintainers, usually high school graduates at most, were intimidated at first, one mechanic who took part told me. Soon the maintainers spoke up, though, bluntly telling the engineers that parts of the Osprey's original nacelle design had been dumb. "Engineers are very smart people, but you give them a wrench and put them on the aircraft and say, 'Put that screw into that hole you were talking about,' and then they would start to see and appreciate that, 'Well, you know what? If I put that screw an arm's length into that cavity in the airplane, I'm not exactly going to be able to screw it in there, because you can't hold the screwdriver and the screw at the same time without dropping it,'" this mechanic said.

The engineers and mechanics came up with various ways to protect the Osprey's hydraulic lines, such as rerouting wire bundles through special trays. They also designed new access panels so mechanics could inspect and work inside the nacelles more easily. Schultz and his staff devised a plan to incorporate those and other changes into existing and future production model Ospreys. In the meantime, Navair would fly tests with the four remaining prototypes built in the 1990s to establish just how vulnerable the Osprey really was to vortex ring state, to study its handling qualities when landing on a heaving, windy ship deck, and to define its ability to maneuver at low airspeeds. First, though, the Osprey had to start flying again.

Tom Macdonald of Boeing, the program's chief test pilot, and Bell Helicopter test pilot Bill Leonard were at the controls as Schultz watched the Osprey's return to flight in May 2002. Macdonald and Leonard had flown about a thousand hours in Ospreys between them during their careers, but today they would take no chances. They would fly by the rules for the first flight of a brand-new aircraft—with utmost caution. First they just hovered about twenty feet over the runway for three minutes, then gently set the Osprey back down. Then they did another vertical takeoff, flew around the airfield in helicopter mode for an hour and a half, and landed. A little later, they did a rolling takeoff, tilted the rotors forward into airplane mode, and climbed to 2,000 feet. They took the Osprey up to about 285 miles per hour, flew twenty minutes, then landed for the day.

Ordinarily, such flights would have been regarded as routine. Schultz couldn't have been more excited. When Macdonald and Leonard first took off, Schultz let out a whoop. When the pilots landed for the final time, Schultz went over to Macdonald and shook his hand. Then he gave him a hug.

★ ★ ★

By the summer of 2002, Harry Dunn had discovered Rex Rivolo, the Institute for Defense Analyses expert assigned to monitor the Osprey for the Pentagon's Office of Operational Test and Evaluation. Dunn and Rivolo saw eye-to-eye on the Osprey's design. Both thought its side-by-side rotors and their size and twist made it unsuitable as a combat rotorcraft. Unlike Dunn, however, Rivolo wasn't trying to kill the Osprey; he just saw it as his job to make sure those who were going to decide its fate understood the shortcomings he saw. Even if he and Dunn had different goals, however, Rivolo was glad to find an ally. Rivolo had been frustrated by his inability to get his views on the Osprey accepted within the government over the past two years, and his efforts had made him more than unpopular at the Osprey program office. He was still tracking the Osprey for the Pentagon, though, and Navair was under orders to let Rivolo sit in as it planned flight tests to find the Osprey's vortex ring state boundary. Rivolo was "very, very vocal" in those meetings, recalled Donald Byrne, Bell-Boeing's flight test director at the time. "He would sit there and say, 'You're all wrong. You're not doing it right. You need to do this, you need to do that. You need to get into vortex ring state and demonstrate that it can roll at least ninety degrees and recover the aircraft successfully.'" The test pilots and engineers rejected a lot of Rivolo's suggestions as unnecessary and too dangerous, but they were under orders to address his concerns. Rivolo, Byrne volunteered, "was a nuisance."

For Harry Dunn, Rivolo was a source of information and advice. On July 2, 2002, Dunn e-mailed Rivolo asking if he could suggest expert witnesses to testify in an Osprey lawsuit filed by an attorney Dunn was trying to help. Rivolo replied that he would try to think of some. He also told Dunn that Aldridge had asked for a briefing from IDA on the Osprey's testing and Rivolo was going to deliver it. "I intend to get the maneuvering issue squarely on the table," Rivolo assured.

When he briefed Aldridge, Rivolo told me, the undersecretary seemed sincere and concerned about Rivolo's conclusion that the Osprey was unable to do the yank-and-bank maneuvers helicopters did in combat. Not long afterward, on August 8, 2002, Aldridge told the Defense Writers Group, a regular breakfast of military reporters in Washington, that he was "probably the most skeptical person in the Department of Defense" on the Osprey. "I've got some real problems with the airplane," Aldridge said. "It's a compromise between a helicopter, which wants very big [rotor] blades, and an airplane, which wants relatively small blades." Aldridge said vortex ring state was a real hazard for the Osprey. "When this happens on this airplane, you lose control," he said. "Once it starts to roll, you can't correct it." Those were Rex Rivolo's views. The Osprey could be flown to avoid vortex ring state, Aldridge said, but "is it operationally useful in that event? That's what the flight test program has to prove." He was going to visit Pax River on September 6 to see how things were shaping up, Aldridge told the reporters. In the meantime, the Pentagon was studying what aircraft the Marine Corps might buy instead if the Osprey failed its flight tests.

★ ★ ★

About noon on September 6, Aldridge was at the Patuxent River airfield, peering across a football-field-sized expanse of grass toward an Osprey at the distant end of a runway. Nearby was Colonel Dan Schultz, the program manager, feeling antsier than he had the day the Osprey returned to flight three months earlier. Aldridge, energetic and often cheerful, was poker-faced as he watched the Osprey prepare to take off. He was standing between chief test pilot Macdonald and another test pilot, who were telling the undersecretary of defense what the flight he was about to see was meant to demonstrate. Macdonald loved to talk, but he found it hard to get a conversation going with Aldridge, and that left Macdonald edgy.

Macdonald and Schultz weren't the only ones nervous about Aldridge's visit. The Osprey staff at Pax River had spent weeks getting ready, for they knew today could be a turning point for the Osprey—especially if it went badly. Politically, the Osprey was hanging by a thread. Aldridge had made that clear in private, and in his recent remarks to the Defense Writers Group. The goal today was to persuade him that Navair's flight test plans were going to address all his concerns.

Before coming out to the flight line, they had given Aldridge a two-hour briefing that already was making him reconsider what he had thought he knew about the Osprey.

Bell engineer Ronald Kisor told Aldridge the data collected so far indicated the Osprey actually was *less* vulnerable to vortex ring state than a helicopter. The reason was a feature the Osprey's critics saw as a weakness—the high disk loading of its rotors. Their literally hurricane-force downwash meant the Osprey would have to descend far faster at low forward speeds than a helicopter would for the flow of air from beneath its rotors to equal the flow of air the rotors created—the recipe for vortex ring state. The critics were right in saying the Osprey would roll sharply if one of its rotors went into vortex ring state, Kisor conceded, but a pilot could regain control quickly simply by tilting the Osprey's nacelles forward a few degrees and flying into clean air. The pilot who would fly for Aldridge today, Steve Grohsmeyer of Boeing, had been copiloting an Osprey that demonstrated the recovery method two years earlier, after vortex ring state was pinpointed as the cause of the crash at Marana. The test technique was to go up to 10,000 feet or so, ensuring plenty of altitude to recover, then slow the Osprey to a target speed in the danger area and descend rapidly. These High Rate of Descent tests, abbreviated HROD and pronounced "aitch-rod," had been interrupted by the Osprey's grounding since December 2000, but if Aldridge approved, they would resume soon.

Aldridge expressed no opinions, but Macdonald thought he seemed impressed with Kisor's explanations. Macdonald thought the next briefing went even better.

Tom Wood, Bell's chief aerodynamicist, had been assigned to talk about the Osprey's maneuverability at low airspeeds. Wood had a succinct way of talking that seemed to appeal to fellow engineer Aldridge. As Wood offered data to rebut the idea the Osprey was too clumsy to avoid hostile fire in a landing zone, Aldridge began asking questions. Soon the two were talking as if no one else were in the room. As they finished, Aldridge again offered no opinions, but Macdonald was sure Wood had knocked the ball out of the park.

Macdonald had assigned Grohsmeyer and Marine Major Paul Ryan to fly a fifteen-minute demonstration for Aldridge. All they needed to do, Macdonald told them, was show Aldridge that anyone who said the Osprey wasn't agile enough for combat was wrong.

Shortly after noon, their Osprey began rolling down the runway with its nacelles tilted at 60 degrees, then lifted off. Within seconds, Grohsmeyer took it to 150 feet, tilting the rotors all the way forward as he climbed, then came flying straight down the runway in airplane mode. *Boy, that airplane is quiet,* Aldridge thought as the Osprey zoomed toward him. Grohsmeyer banked and flew around the hangar, then returned, tilting the rotors up to 85 degrees as he and Ryan approached the grassy area in front of Aldridge. The Osprey slowed to 60 knots, apparently preparing to land helicopter-style. Instead, as if escaping ground fire, Grohsmeyer suddenly tilted the rotors forward and climbed away steeply, accelerating as he went. He brought the Osprey back around and landed on the grass about a hundred yards from Aldridge, then took off again straight up, hovered over the grass, turned the Osprey in a full circle, edged it sideways in each direction, then backward and forward. Finally, Grohsmeyer flew a series of figure eights in tight turns one hundred feet over the grass, flying at 40 to 80 knots with the rotors tilted between 70 and 80 degrees. Then he landed.

Macdonald asked Aldridge what he thought.

"I had no idea of the low airspeed agility," Aldridge said.

Aldridge's hosts took him to look inside a redesigned nacelle on another Osprey. He was impressed with how much cleaner the routing of the wire bundles and hydraulic lines was. He had been impressed with the briefings and the flight demonstration, too. He was no longer so worried about the Osprey's side-by-side rotors or its agility. He still wanted to see if what the engineers had told him could be proven in flight tests, and he still wasn't sure the Osprey was going to be worth its hefty price tag, but he was no longer inclined to cancel it. Aldridge told Schultz to proceed with the flight tests.

★ ★ ★

Once upon a time, test pilots like the famed Chuck Yeager tugged on a helmet and squeezed into a flight suit, strapped on an X-model aircraft, then bet their lives they could find the edge of its envelope without having to punch out or ride the experimental machine into the ground. Those days are long gone. Today's test pilots still fly to the edge of the envelope. They still need "the right stuff"—steady nerves, quick reflexes, maybe a little swagger in their walk. They still climb into new or modified aircraft and try things no one else has ever done with them. Today's test pilots, though, no longer routinely fly into the unknown. They don't even fly as often as they work on the ground. A test pilot today is more likely to be found manipulating a keyboard and mouse than a stick and throttle. He—they are still mostly men—is less likely to be sitting in a cockpit than in a meeting with engineers or at a desk, analyzing data and planning flight tests in meticulous detail.

Each step in a modern test flight is scripted on a "test card," which is carried on a clipboard strapped to the pilot's knee for easy reference while airborne. After a flight, the pilot writes a detailed report, which he and the engineers will go over in yet another meeting. The report may rely in part on tape recordings of observations the pilot spoke into a microphone as he flew. It will certainly rely on data gathered during the flight by onboard instruments that instantly and constantly record not only the machine's altitude, speed, pitch, yaw, roll, and other motions but its every moan and groan. The instruments radio the data in "real time" to a platoon of engineers on the ground whose job is to assess the results as they come in and watch for signs of danger. The engineers will warn the pilot to knock it off if they see him flirting with trouble. The era when the military was willing to risk a pilot's life or a multi-million-dollar aircraft in a test faded into history with the advent of computerized flight simulators. Today, pilots "fly" dangerous tests first in SUV-sized machines that mimic real flight with astounding fidelity, yet without ever leaving the ground. Equipped with the same cockpit as the aircraft to be flown, the best of such computerized simulators can project on a screen beyond a mock windshield a virtual-reality display of nearly any geographic location as seen from any altitude. Runways, buildings, mountains, rivers, and trees are depicted faithfully, in living color, the way they would appear from an aircraft in a climb, a bank, a dive. Some simulators ape the motions of flight faithfully enough to induce vertigo and airsickness. Based on calculations fed into their computers, simulators can be programmed to replicate how an aircraft will behave in almost any circumstance. Flying the aircraft itself is the only way to prove the calculations were correct, but as a rule, test pilots today aren't betting their lives when they go out and fly.

The Osprey's High Rate of Descent tests were an exception to that rule. The pilots who flew them would venture into that region on the map marked "Here Be Dragons." You could die there.

The HROD tests would be dangerous because vortex ring state was largely a mystery. The phenomenon was hard to describe, much less predict, partly because so little research had been done on it in the six-decade history of the helicopter. Beyond that, no one had ever devised an entirely reliable way to predict all the air flows created by rotors. Like the weather, there was a nearly infinite number of variables that could affect them—the configuration of the aircraft, the speed and direction of the wind, the aircraft's altitude, the rotor's angle of attack. The flows around an airplane wing, which moves into clean air constantly, can be predicted with great accuracy. The flows around a rotor, which moves in a circle but might be stationary or moving forward or backward or sideways as it rotates, are devilishly more complex. This makes engineering rotorcraft an art as well as a science. The pilots and engineers in the Osprey program were certain the aircraft's high disk loading made it far less likely to go into vortex ring state than critics assumed. The only way to prove it, though, was to take an Osprey aloft and go find its vortex ring state boundary. Based on calculations and the tests done in 2000, the engineers and pilots were confident an Osprey could get out of vortex ring state simply by tilting its rotors into clean air. If they were wrong, though, someone could die trying.

Tom Macdonald, as the Osprey program's chief test pilot, decided he should be the pilot in command for each of the dozens of flights planned in the second series of HROD tests. His copilot most often would be Steve Grohsmeyer of Boeing or Bill Leonard of Bell, though Macdonald always would have the controls. Only the two pilots would be aboard; there was no reason to risk more lives by having engineers or crew chiefs in the back.

Born and raised near Boston, Macdonald had become a test pilot during a twenty-one-year career in the Navy flying helicopters and jets. Since 1991, when he got out of the Navy, he had flown the Osprey for Boeing. He and Grady Wilson, the pilot who survived the first Osprey crash in 1991, were flying the chase plane in July 1992, when four Boeing employees and three Marines died in the second Osprey crash at Quantico. Macdonald had known all seven victims; some were close friends. He had lost other friends among the Marine Corps pilots and crew chiefs who died in the other Osprey crashes as well. Macdonald knew there were ways the Osprey could kill you—there were ways any aircraft could. He was equally sure the Osprey wasn't unsafe—and certainly not the death trap its harshest critics called it. Macdonald never looked at it that way, but he was betting his life on that when the HROD tests began on November 25, 2002.

The tests began only six months after the Osprey's return to flight partly because engineers had to come up with a piece of hardware to accurately measure the Osprey's forward speed at less than 40 knots. Then, from November 2002 to July 2003, Macdonald and his copilots did sixty-two HROD tests, flying a total of 104 hours over a restricted flight range between the towns of Cambridge and Salisbury on Maryland's eastern shore. Macdonald would climb to 10,000 feet, then tilt the rotors up into helicopter mode and slow to a target airspeed. As Macdonald held it there for a bit, a challenge in itself, the copilot would put his hands on his own set of controls, just in case. To duplicate the way the Osprey that crashed at Marana had been flying, Macdonald would lower the landing gear, tilt the nacelles back to 95 degrees, and start reducing power. The Osprey would begin to drop. Macdonald would let it fall until they hit a target rate of descent, then adjust the power to hold the Osprey at a steady sink rate. At that point, still descending, Macdonald and his copilot would talk into their microphones about the Osprey's stability and handling, the quality of the ride, and whether they heard anything unusual. They were looking for ways a pilot might detect the onset of vortex ring state before getting into it. They repeated the flight profile over and over during those months, taking their measurements at every 500-foot increment of sink rate at a series of ever slower airspeeds.

As predicted, they found it hard to put the Osprey into vortex ring state. The boundary for a helicopter was a sink rate somewhere around 800 feet per minute at 40 knots or less of forward speed. Macdonald had to let the Osprey sink at least 2,500 to 2,600 feet a minute at 40 knots before it would near vortex ring state. Even at slower forward speeds, the boundary was a sink rate of around 1,700 feet per minute. He and his copilots weren't actually trying to lose control of the Osprey, they were just trying to find the edge of the envelope, the point where they felt vortex ring state coming on. They got there a number of times without incident. "The thrust would begin to oscillate," Macdonald told me. "A little up-and-down motion would settle into the aircraft that we weren't commanding." The Osprey would rock a little bit in some cases, and at the lowest speeds they tested, as slow as 10 knots forward speed while plunging toward the ground, the pilots would hear "this eerie howling and audio sound of the air rush," Macdonald said. "We'd just get really silent and quiet." Eleven times during the tests Macdonald flew, one of the rotors went into vortex ring state and the Osprey did a sudden, uncommanded roll—seven times to the right, four times to the left. Each time, Macdonald was able to recover by pushing the thumbwheel switch to tilt the nacelles forward and put the rotors into undisturbed air. Two seconds was usually all it took. Those seconds, though, gave Macdonald and his copilots some hairy moments.

The hairiest was on July 17, 2003. The tests already had achieved their primary goal—charting the Osprey's envelope for vortex ring state—a couple of months earlier. Based on that envelope, the program had developed warning devices for the Osprey to alert pilots when they were flirting with vortex ring state. One was visual, a red light on the control panel in front of each pilot that would flash SINK, SINK if an Osprey exceeded a safe rate of descent. The other was a recording of a woman—a device that pilots call a "bitching Betty"—who would be heard in the pilot's headset saying "sink rate, sink rate" in an urgent monotone if the limit were exceeded. The HROD tests were continuing, though, because Navair was trying to satisfy Institute for Defense Analyses expert Rex Rivolo that the tests had been adequate. That July 17, Macdonald and Grohsmeyer were flying 7–10 knots and descending at more than 2,300 feet per minute, well beyond the vortex ring state envelope already established. They were dropping like a rock while a special test device alternated the lateral tilt of each rotor to see if that would prevent vortex ring state. Macdonald was on the radio with an engineer on the ground when the Osprey suddenly snap-rolled right more violently than Macdonald had ever seen it do. Instinctively, he pushed the stick left as the roll began but the Osprey didn't respond. By the time Macdonald recognized what was happening, the Osprey was flying on its side, left wing up and right wing down, and spiraling toward the ground ever faster. Macdonald pushed the thumbwheel to tilt the nacelles forward as fast as they would go, all the way to airplane mode. The seconds it took seemed like minutes, but finally he regained control and straightened the Osprey out. For a moment, there was silence in the cockpit and over the radio. Macdonald, Grohsmeyer, and the engineers on the ground knew the pilots had just had a close call. If the Osprey had rolled all the way upside down in helicopter mode, there was no telling what damage they might have done to the aircraft—or whether they could have regained control at all.

After Macdonald and Grohsmeyer landed, the program office and the pilots decided they had taken the HROD testing of the Osprey far enough. The Osprey's boundary for vortex ring state had been established beyond any doubt, and studied more than that of any rotorcraft in the world.

Three months later, at a dinner in Los Angeles, the Society of Experimental Test Pilots gave Macdonald its highest honor, the Iven C. Kincheloe Award for "outstanding professional accomplishment." The citation said Macdonald had flown "every flight in a test program where no test pilot has been before." Chuck Yeager was in the audience that evening. He shook Macdonald's hand.

★ ★ ★

Pete Aldridge was impressed by the Osprey's flight tests, but nothing was going to change Harry Dunn's mind. During the past two years, Dunn had never stopped trying to shoot the Osprey down. Nor had he given up on Aldridge, despite the scolding e-mail Dunn sent in 2001 after Aldridge ignored his advice to cancel the Osprey without further testing. Presumably encouraged by Aldridge's public comments in 2002 expressing doubts about the Osprey, Dunn resumed his one-way correspondence with him that year. By then, Dunn had plenty he wanted to share. While mining for data that might prove the Osprey was the Albatross he called it, Dunn had struck a rich vein. He had found a "mole" at Navair, a Marine with access to a senior officer's computer, who began feeding Dunn a steady diet of internal documents. They created special e-mail accounts to communicate with less risk of being detected, and there was seemingly no limit to what Dunn's mole could provide.

Flight test plans, PowerPoint slides shown by Navair and Bell-Boeing engineers at technical reviews, Navair messages reporting inspections of new Ospreys when the government accepted them from Bell-Boeing, biweekly status reports on every Osprey at Pax River and how much it was flying—it all landed in Harry Dunn's e-mail inbox. If a windshield on an Osprey at Pax River cracked, if an oil pump failed, if a fire extinguisher in the cabin discharged accidentally, Dunn knew about it nearly as soon as Colonel Dan Schultz did. Dunn passed some documents on to favorite reporters, but he largely used his trove of inside information in writing "Red Ribbon Panel" reports for Aldridge. Dunn seemed to think about how he might influence Aldridge around the clock. One day at 7:13 A.M. he sent Aldridge an e-mail saying he had been up since 4 A.M. "trying to find best approach to alert you and offer a suggestion or two."

Aldridge, however, had long since stopped reading Dunn's e-mails, and on May 20, 2003, Dunn learned that his efforts to sway the undersecretary had failed. Dunn got word that at a Defense Acquisition Board meeting that day, Aldridge had announced he was satisfied with the Osprey's flight tests and would sign an Acquisition Decision Memorandum recommending the Pentagon buy more Ospreys each year than the existing annual limit of eleven. Aldridge, who once had described himself as the Pentagon's greatest skeptic on the Osprey, was giving it his seal of approval. Dunn had stuck a few harpoons into his Moby Dick over the past two years, and left some scars, but his best chance to kill it—if such a chance ever existed—had passed.

Dunn e-mailed Aldridge a protest the next morning, telling him that "my 30 years of support to your career" had been a "gross mistake."

Aldridge didn't reply, but he explained his decision two days later at a Pentagon news conference—held the same day he retired, at age sixty-four. The Osprey hadn't fully proven itself, Aldridge told reporters, but the flight tests at Pax River, while still incomplete, had changed his mind about its vulnerability to vortex ring state and erased his doubts about its agility over a landing zone. "They have demonstrated very high rate of descent at slow forward speeds," Aldridge said. "They know the envelope in which the vortex ring state condition exists." Navair had put visual and verbal warning devices in the cockpit to alert pilots when they were verging on vortex ring state, he noted. The flight manual limit on the Osprey's descent rate still would be no more than 800 feet per minute at 40 knots or less, but "we know we can fly the airplane at twice that number, twice the sink rate, and much slower, and still not enter vortex ring state." Aldridge was equally enthusiastic about the Osprey's ability to maneuver over a landing zone while under fire. By tilting its rotors, he said, the Osprey "can accelerate out of the landing zone faster than any helicopter." The flight tests had shown that the Osprey could do sharp maneuvers too, he said. "That, to me, has demonstrated a certain amount of operational suitability that we had not appreciated in this airplane back when it started the flight test program," Aldridge said.

Reporters in the Pentagon briefing room were stunned by Aldridge's conversion. "A year of closely monitored flight testing has led to a reversal of fortune for the V-22," *Aviation Week* reported in a story on his decision. "Testing, including more than 460 flight hours, has won over at least those critics that matter." The headline on the story read MORE PHOENIX THAN OSPREY.

★ ★ ★

Major Paul Rock was a faithful Catholic, and by May 2003, he felt as if he had spent two and a half years in purgatory. Even after the test pilots at Patuxent River started flying their Ospreys again in May 2002, the Ospreys at VMMT-204 in New River were still grounded. Rock and the handful of others left in the squadron were reduced to trying to keep their eight Ospreys in good mechanical shape without flying them. Taxiing them near the hangar or sitting in the cockpit and running the engines was as close as they got to putting an Osprey to use. Rock's main project was even less thrilling: supervising mechanics as they found and corrected what turned out to be more than thirty thousand errors, inaccuracies, and other deficiencies in the electronic maintenance manual Bell-Boeing had provided with the Osprey. By temperament, Rock was well suited to the task. He was meticulous in everything he did, and a congenital record keeper. He kept a diary, akin to his detailed flight logbooks, in which he recorded every new beer he tasted. Sorting out the errors in the maintenance manual, though, was boring compared to flying. Rock had made his own bed when he decided to stick with the Osprey while most of his peers left VMMT-204 for other assignments, but it was hard to lie in it. When the alarm clock went off some mornings, Rock dreaded getting up. He dreaded reading about the Osprey in the newspapers, too. Nearly every article seemed to portray it as a multi-billion-dollar boondoggle the Marines were just too proud, too callous, or maybe too stupid to abandon. Rock seethed at that. The crashes in 2000 and the investigation of the maintenance scandal at VMMT-204 in 2001 were the lowest points, but another came in mid-2002, when the new deputy commandant for aviation came to visit.

Lieutenant General Michael A. Hough was fifty-seven and on the verge of retiring when General Jim Jones asked him to take over Marine Corps aviation instead. Jones thought Hough had the right stuff to make sure the Osprey got back on track and to defend the Corps in negotiations with the Navy on restructuring naval aviation. Hough—who pronounced his name "how"—wasn't the typical Marine general. He was a "mustang," slang for an officer whose career began in the enlisted ranks. A Wisconsin plumber's son, Hough had dropped out of the University of Wisconsin at La Crosse during his freshman year to work and help his family after his father was diagnosed with cancer, then went into the Navy. High scores on his entrance tests got him into the service's nuclear power program but Hough quickly concluded that enlisted life was "a slow boat to nowhere." He applied for a program that allowed sailors to get into the Naval Academy and graduated from Annapolis in 1969.

Hough took his commission in the Marines so he could fly and became an F-4 Phantom fighter pilot. After a dozen years of flying, he held jobs working on budget and procurement issues at Navair, at Headquarters Marine Corps, and elsewhere in the Pentagon. He also became a general, and by 2002, few of his Marine Corps peers knew as much as Hough did about weapons buying. For two years before he became deputy commandant, Hough ran a program to develop the Joint Strike Fighter, a new jet to be built in three variants, including a version that could take off and land vertically. The job required technological and political savvy. The Marine Corps, the Navy, the Air Force, and maybe a dozen foreign allies were to buy the JSF, making the project worth perhaps $300 billion. Hough owed his success in managing a hard-fought competition for the right to build the plane between defense giants Boeing and Lockheed Martin partly to experience, partly to intellect, and partly to political smarts. He also owed it to his personality.

Mike Hough was a red rubber ball of a man—colorful, bouncy, amusing, irreverent. Scarlet-cheeked, he had crafty eyes and an unpretentious manner that endeared him to officers and civilians who worked for him. He could be hard on defense contractors, and he could speak acronym-larded contracting jargon with the best engineers and bureaucrats. He more often spoke in the vernacular, though, and listening to him could be like watching fireworks, a dazzling display of metaphors and similes. After the Osprey crashes in 2000, Hough once told me, a lot of people in the Pentagon and even the Marine Corps "just wanted to get the booger off their finger." Praising a former subordinate's feel for the legislative process, Hough whispered that the man "knew how the sausage was made."

Hough saw the task of rehabilitating the Osprey not just as an engineering and management challenge but also a political and public relations problem. By July 2002, when he became deputy commandant, test pilots at Pax River were flying the Osprey again, but Aldridge, members of Congress, and the bulk of the news media seemed to be waiting for it to fail. Hough wanted to avoid any incident that might give the critics new ammunition. The Marine Corps' Ospreys already were grounded, but Hough went further. He barred VMMT-204's pilots from taxiing their Ospreys, or even cranking up their engines.

Hough's order was hard to swallow for Colonel Dick Dunnivan and his squadron. It smacked of paranoia, a distrust of the Osprey bordering on shame. It also created a practical problem for Rock, who was in charge of correcting the electronic maintenance manual. The best way to validate many maintenance tasks was to "ground run" an Osprey, but now VMMT-204 couldn't do that. Rock was finding it hard to keep his enlisted Marines motivated as it was. If they could only look at their Ospreys, not work on them, it was going to be even harder. Dunnivan asked Hough to reconsider. Hough wouldn't hear of it. The nacelles on the Ospreys at New River hadn't been modified yet with the new layout of hydraulic lines and wire bundles. Their wire bundles could still chafe their hydraulic lines, which might spring a leak and start a fire. There had been one such incident already. "I've got to think about the program," Hough told Dunnivan. "All we need is something else to happen."

Not long afterward, Hough came to New River to inspect VMMT-204. He met with Dunnivan and his pilots in the ready room for a couple of hours and found them as gloomy as the gray sky over the base that day. Hough explained why he had barred ground runs. He talked about the road ahead for the Osprey. He told the pilots it would be a long time before they flew one again. Rock asked Hough if he could say how long.

"You guys play golf?" Hough wisecracked. "You're going to have a hell of a golf game. You're going to have a lot of time on your hands."

Rock bristled. "Sir," he said, "respectfully, your Marines are working very hard here." Rock saw Dunnivan off to the side, waving his hand across his throat in the "cut" sign, but Rock couldn't stop himself. "We don't play golf," he added tersely.

"Hey, you know, I didn't mean anything," Hough said, apparently shrugging off the young major's petulance. Rock thought he had been tactful. He only realized he'd sounded insolent later, when he got phone calls and e-mails from friends in the Pentagon. "What in hell did you do to General Hough?" they wanted to know.

Hough made another decision a year later that changed Rock's attitude. By then, Aldridge had given the Osprey his blessing, but before the Marines could field it, the aircraft needed to pass another Operational Evaluation, the tests done in mock missions by military aircrews and known as "OPEVAL." Congress had written a law in 2001 that effectively required that. Hough decided he needed to "get the Marine Corps' fingerprints off" that testing by creating a special squadron to do it, a squadron that reported only to the Navy's Operational Test and Evaluation Force. That would be more credible, he thought, than a squadron whose Marine pilots also reported up through the Corps' chain of command. A call went out for Marine Corps, Air Force, and Navy pilots to man the new squadron, designated VMX-22. Rock applied and was quickly accepted.

VMX-22 "stood up" at New River Marine Corps Air Station on August 28 and Hough came down for a ceremony to mark the occasion. When he saw Rock, Hough smiled and said, "Hey, how you doin'? Still not golfing, I guess?" Rock smiled. He was relieved to see Hough had no hard feelings toward him. He was elated when he started flying the Osprey again that fall. Rock was out of purgatory. The Dark Ages were over.

★ ★ ★

Rock was one of the few experienced Osprey pilots still available when VMX-22 was formed. Even the test squadron's commander, Colonel Glenn Walters, had never flown the Osprey before. Walters was a U.S. Naval Test Pilot School graduate who had started out flying AH-1 Cobra gunships. Another Test Pilot School graduate, Lieutenant Colonel Christopher Seymour, an Osprey developmental test pilot since 1995, was VMX-22's test director, the officer primarily responsible for planning OPEVAL. Rock, Seymour, and former MOTT member Major Anthony Bianca spent much of their first year in VMX-22 just training its other pilots. By the spring of 2004, some still weren't fully trained, but they were proficient enough to do an "operational assessment," an initial set of tests to get ready for OPEVAL. The "Dirty Dozen," as Walters called the cadre who started the squadron, took six Ospreys to Nellis Air Force Base, near Las Vegas, from May 18 until July 9 that year. They flew tests in "austere landing zones," places where the Osprey's downwash would kick up a dust or sand storm as it landed.

A couple of months after they returned, Walters called Rock into his office one day and told him to close the door.

"Oh, shit, sir, you're closing the door," Rock said. "I must be in real big trouble."

When Rock left Walters's office, he was in a daze. He didn't dare tell any of his friends in the squadron what Walters had just confided because it wasn't official yet, but he called his wife, Maria, to share the news. Walters had told Rock he'd just received a message from Headquarters Marine Corps. If the Osprey passed OPEVAL the next spring, the Pentagon could be expected to approve Full Rate Production, the long-awaited Milestone III. When that happened, the Corps was going to form an operational Osprey squadron, the first that would field the tiltrotor and fly it in real missions. A selection board had chosen Rock as commanding officer of the unit, which would replace HMM-263, the CH-46 squadron Rock had flown with in the early 1990s. Rock's new squadron would be designated VMM-263, for Marine Medium Tiltrotor Squadron 263. He would take command when it "stood up" in early 2006. In the meantime, Walters told him, Rock would be transferred to Al Asad Air Base in Iraq to work on the staff of the 2nd Marine Aircraft Wing's forward headquarters there. Rock needed to learn the lay of the land at Al Asad and the intricacies of Marine air operations in Iraq, where the Corps was fighting insurgents in the vast western part of the country, Anbar Province. No final decisions had been made, Walters cautioned, but it was a good bet VMM-263 would be sent to Iraq on its first deployment.

Rock fairly floated out of Walters's office. Commanding a squadron had been his dream almost since the day he'd graduated from the Naval Academy. Leading a squadron into war would be the ultimate test for a commander.

In March 2005, a month after Rock went to Iraq for his staff assignment, VMX-22 began the Osprey's second Operational Evaluation, called "OPEVAL II" by some. The Navy's Operational Test and Evaluation Force and the Pentagon's Office of Operational Test and Evaluation were going to judge whether the Osprey passed. Walters and Headquarters Marine Corps were determined to do everything possible to make sure that happened, but without risking another disaster. By 2005, sentiment within the Pentagon for killing the Osprey had faded, and any inclination to scrap it on Capitol Hill had evaporated. The Osprey's public image, though, was much the same as it had been since the *60 Minutes* broadcast of January 2001. The Osprey was known as a strange, experimental aircraft that had cost too much and killed a lot of people in crashes. "The American public still didn't buy it," Hough recalled. "Everyone was still terrified of it." Those involved with the Osprey knew there was no chance the program would survive another crash in testing. The mood in the Pentagon and Congress would reverse overnight if that happened. By the nature of OPEVAL, Marines still needed to ride in the back for some of the Osprey's tests, but Walters decided to reduce the risk by keeping such flights to a minimum.

Over ten weeks that spring, Walters and his pilots flew eight Ospreys in 204 tests, eighty-nine of them realistic mock missions. They flew in the coastal humidity of New River, in the sands of desert ranges at Nellis Air Force Base, in the snow and high altitudes of the Marine Corps Mountain Warfare Training Center near Bridgeport, California, and off the USS *Bataan*, an amphibious assault ship. The flights included two reenactments of Operation Eagle Claw, the failed Iran hostage rescue mission of 1980, though trouble refueling in midair prevented all of the Ospreys flying from completing either attempt in "one period of darkness." Rex Rivolo and other critics deemed that a test failure, but Walters and his testers concluded the Osprey could do such a mission in a single night if need be, for a couple of reasons.

The ability to refuel in midair by hooking up to a tanker aircraft is a tricky feat but one that many U.S. military planes and even some helicopters perform routinely to extend their range and payload. Aerial refueling was one of the Osprey's original requirements, and a task it had been doing since 1998. Pilots of the MOTT flew their Ospreys coast to coast without landing during the original OPEVAL, as Rock and his co-authors had noted proudly in their reply to Harry Dunn published in the *Fort Worth Star-Telegram* in 2001. The Osprey was equipped for "probe and drogue" refueling, as opposed to the "boom and receptacle" system favored by the Air Force for its fixed-wing aircraft. In the probe and drogue system, a rigid tube—the "probe"—extending forward from the aircraft needing fuel mates in midair with the drogue, a device resembling a badminton shuttlecock and attached to a flexible fuel hose reeled out by the tanker. This "basket," as aviators call the drogue, holds the hose steady in flight and helps the pilot seeking fuel guide the refueling probe to its target. Once probe and drogue mate, valves in each open and fuel flows from the tanker to the aircraft needing fuel. During one of VMX-22's attempts to reenact Eagle Claw, FAA altitude restrictions required the Ospreys to fly between 7,000 and 9,000 feet, where turbulence that day whipped the tanker's basket around so wildly that only one of the four crews flying could guide their refueling probe into the drogue. A shortage of tankers made it impossible to refuel in midair at the right times in the second attempt. The testers reasoned that if the mission were real, FAA altitude restrictions wouldn't apply— the Osprey would be able to climb or descend into clean air—and commanders would make sure enough tankers were available.

In other OPEVAL II tests, two VMX-22 Ospreys each carried twenty-four Marines with packs and weapons in the back while making two round trip flights to an unimproved landing zone onshore from the deck of the *Bataan* as it sailed more than fifty miles off the Atlantic coast. The Marines were cramped, but they fit in the cabin. Two Ospreys also carried twenty-four Marines each on a flight of more than two hundred miles from California to an unprepared landing zone in Nevada. When VMX-22 flew night missions with their Ospreys, though, they carried sand bags in the back to simulate the weight of troops. The Marines weren't going to risk another Marana.

Walters briefed reporters on the results of OPEVAL II during a "media day" at New River on July 13, 2005, a steamy, at times stormy day on North Carolina's coast. In VMX-22's ready room, Walters showed video clips of various tests. There were shots of an Osprey refueling in-flight from a KC-130 tanker, shots of an Osprey hovering while Marines "fast-roped" to the ground from its back ramp, shots of an Osprey landing in the desert amid a cloud of dust and sand. Walters said the Osprey had passed all of its "key performance parameters." It had flown as fast and far as required. It had carried twenty-four Marines. It had exceeded all but one of its goals for the "ilities"—reliability, maintainability, availability.

To illustrate how much confidence they now had in the Osprey, the Marines invited the two dozen or so reporters who had come to New River for the briefing to ride in one. The pilot for the first flight was six-foot-five Lieutenant Colonel Seymour, whose radio call sign was "Mongo," after the hulking Alex Karras character in the comedy film *Blazing Saddles*. Seymour, the son of a Huey pilot who had flown in Vietnam and later piloted helicopters for Gulf Coast oil companies, had been flying the Osprey for ten years. He was eager to show the reporters that the "doctors of doom," as he called the critics, simply didn't know what they were talking about when they said the Osprey couldn't fly hard.

Once crew chiefs got the reporters strapped into passenger seats along each side of the fuselage, Seymour taxied his Osprey out to a runway and kept it rolling. A few seconds later, he lifted it half a dozen feet off the ground into a low hover. Suddenly the engines roared, the nacelles swiveled upward, and the Osprey began to climb—so fast the reporters were slung toward the back ramp, their bodies pushed hard into their seat belts and shoulder harnesses. Seymour put the Osprey's nacelles all the way down into airplane mode and climbed to 500 feet, then banked away from the airfield and began following the New River toward the North Carolina coast twenty miles away. Looking out the open back ramp, the reporters could see boats and a bridge whisk by below and a second Osprey with another group of journalists flying a few hundred feet behind them. When he reached the coast, Seymour banked his Osprey left, leveled off, then cruised over Onslow Beach, where Marines from Camp Lejeune practice amphibious landings. A few minutes later, he dipped the left wing down and whipped his Osprey into a tight turn, pushing the reporters on the right side of the fuselage against the bulkhead and those on the left against their harnesses with two times the force of gravity. The Osprey flew south a bit, turned inland over marshlands, then slowed abruptly, as if someone had slammed on the brakes, as Seymour tilted its nacelles upward. He came to a hover over a grassy field edged by pine trees, let the Osprey settle down to the ground, then took off again vertically and brought it into a hover. He turned it in a circle, then made it scuttle left and right with the fuselage level. Now the fuselage tilted up, the engines whined, and Seymour put the Osprey into another steep climb. As it rose, the reporters could feel their ears pop. Some looked at each other and grinned. The flight ended when Seymour brought the Osprey down in a "roll-on" landing at the air station with the nacelles angled up at about 60 degrees.

Several more flights of reporters went up that day, and the effect was exactly what the Marines had hoped to see. For the first time in years, there were positive stories about the Osprey in the media. The Osprey camp loved headlines such as the one that topped a Copley News Service account of the briefing: "After Decades of Tragedy, Osprey May Be Ready for Combat."

Media coverage of the Osprey since 2001, even after flight testing had laid the vortex ring state issue largely to rest, had often focused on problems with the aircraft. There were headlines when a leak drained the oil from an Osprey engine at Patuxent River, leading Navair to suspend flights until the cause had been investigated. There were headlines when Navair fired a company after it made hydraulic tubes for the Osprey that failed inspections. There were headlines when a nacelle access panel flew off a new Osprey and damaged its tail as it was being delivered to Pax River. There was seemingly no end to such incidents. Critics said they were evidence the Osprey still wasn't ready and might never be. The Osprey's advocates said failures had to be expected in a machine with tens of thousands of parts, and that mechanical problems weren't unusual in a military aircraft. The problems wouldn't have come to public attention if the Osprey weren't under such extraordinary scrutiny, they argued. There was truth in that. Given the Osprey's history, its problems were newsworthy. Detailed coverage of such problems, however, couldn't help but reinforce and solidify the conventional wisdom established by *60 Minutes* years earlier, before the Osprey had been redesigned and retested. In the public mind, the Osprey remained notorious.

After the HROD tests, Pete Aldridge's conversion, and OPEVAL II, however, the momentum was all on the Osprey's side within the Pentagon and on Capitol Hill. The Marines still wanted the Osprey as much as ever, and finally they were going to get it.

The Pentagon's Office of Operational Test and Evaluation issued a report on September 27, 2005, declaring the Osprey "operationally effective" in "low- and medium-threat" areas, meaning combat zones where it might come under sporadic fire from small arms, many large-caliber weapons, and older models of shoulder-fired missiles. The report also found the Osprey "operationally suitable," saying it had met all but one of its maintenance performance goals during OPEVAL II. The next day, the Defense Acquisition Board approved Full Rate Production, Milestone III. By 2012, the Pentagon was expected to be buying as many as 48 Ospreys a year. The Marines would get 360, the Air Force Special Operations Command 50, and the Navy had a long-range plan to purchase 48. They were going to be expensive. Until Navair and Bell-Boeing could make Ospreys more cheaply, as they vowed to do, the price for the Marine Corps version would be $71 million and for the Air Force version $89 million apiece. Adding in the more than $20 billion spent developing the Osprey, the cost per plane would average out to more than $100 million. The price tag was huge—similar to the cost of a modern jet fighter, far more expensive than a Black Hawk helicopter. The Marines were more than willing to pay it. With Milestone III at last behind them, the door was open to field the machine their leaders and aviators had fought relentlessly to have for twenty-three years. The time and money and lives spent getting it had been mind-boggling—far beyond what anyone could have imagined when the project began. Now the Marines wanted to prove the struggle had been worth it.

* * *

Six years after he decided to gamble his career on the Osprey, life looked
entirely different to Paul Rock. By 2007, Rock was a lieutenant colonel,
commanding officer of his own squadron. His career was back on the
rise. So was the Osprey.

Mid-morning on October 4 of that year, Rock and nineteen more
of the twenty-four pilots in his unit, Marine Medium Tiltrotor Squadron 263, climbed into ten MV-22B Ospreys on the flight deck of the
USS *Wasp*. The amphibious assault ship had been home to them and
roughly sixty other squadron members for seventeen days as it sailed
over the Atlantic Ocean, through the Mediterranean Sea, down the Suez
Canal, and into the Gulf of Aqaba, off the coast of Jordan. Now, four of
the Ospreys, lined up nose to tail on the *Wasp*'s deck, nacelles pointed
straight up, gave off a whine as their auxiliary power units awoke the big
turbine engines on their wingtips. Their rotors began spinning, grog-
gily at first, then in a blur. One after another, the first four Ospreys,
their back cabins stuffed with baggage and Marines, tilted their rotors
forward a few degrees and began rolling down the gray, gently swaying
deck. After a few dozen feet, they vaulted into the air and muscled into
the sky. Over the next two hours, the rest of the squadron, known as
VMM-263, boarded the remaining Ospreys and followed, executing a
departure they had practiced over and over prior to their cruise. Once
aloft, they tilted their rotors into airplane mode, climbed to 8,000 feet,
and winged toward Iraq, where U.S. troops had been at war for more
than four years. After a quarter century of struggle and sorrow, at a cost
of $22 billion and thirty lives, the Marines were sending the unortho-
dox flying machine they had staked their future on into a combat zone
for the first time.

The Marines in the back of the Ospreys were mechanics and other
members of VMM-263 who had accompanied the aircraft on the *Wasp*.
This wasn't an amphibious assault—on paper a key Osprey mission—
just a deployment from sea to shore, a way to get the Ospreys and the
Marines who would fly and fix them into Iraq. As always when a Marine
Corps Osprey flew, crew chiefs were riding in the back cabins. One, an
airframes mechanic with a puckish sense of humor, carried a digital
camera whose memory card held photos taken during the voyage. After
the squadron set up its computer network at Al Asad, the sprawling air

base one hundred miles northwest of Baghdad they would fly from for
the next seven months, the crew chief uploaded his photos to a shared
drive reserved for morale-boosting items. Everybody loved one image
in particular, and someone made a letter-sized print and tacked it to the
bulletin board in VMM-263's ready room. The photo showed a silvery
Osprey, captured in midair against an azure sky as it angled toward the
Wasp's flight deck to land, rotors upward. In the foreground stood a
member of the ship's crew, head and eyes hidden by a drab brown helmet
with a green-tinted visor, face and torso obscured by a large rectangle of
cardboard held toward the camera with both hands. The cardboard had
been cut from a box, judging by creases in it, and turned into a hand-
lettered sign. In large block letters, neatly printed in indelible marker,
the sign read:

FUCK-U

MARK THOMPSON

There was a story behind that message.

★ ★ ★

Two months before VMM-263 flew into Iraq, at a little before seven
o'clock on the evening of August 9, 2007, several dozen young men and
women, many carrying boxes of popcorn and soft drinks in cups, some
clutching babies or towing toddlers by the hand, filtered hesitantly into a
movie theater at New River Marine Corps Air Station. Most wore shorts
and T-shirts. Only the crisp, high-and-tight haircuts most of the men
wore identified them as Marines. Some took seats down near the stage.
The majority settled shyly into rows farther back. Small knots of single men were sprinkled among the couples. The mood was cheerful but
apprehensive. In a few short weeks, the roughly 180 Marines of VMM-
263 would take their MV-22B Ospreys to Iraq, where American troops
were dying and being maimed in combat and by insurgent bombs every
day. A good portion of the squadron was gathering tonight for a "Family
Readiness Meeting," called to tutor their spouses in what to expect during
the seven months their Marines would be away. For many of those left at
home, VMM-263's deployment would be a new, and scary, experience.

A little cheer went up as Lieutenant Colonel Paul Rock stood up in
the gap between the theater seats and the stage. Projected on the movie

screen above and behind the squadron commander was a caricature of a fierce-looking rooster with the muscular torso of a man, a thunderbolt gripped in each hand. A banner above the rooster's crown bore VMM-263's incongruous nickname: Thunder Chickens.

"This is a very important night leading up to a very important event—VMM-263's first combat deployment," Rock began in his timbrous voice. "There is a war going on. I'm sure everybody knows about that. This squadron is going over there to take part in that war." VMM-263 would go to Al Asad, Rock said, and replace an assault support helicopter squadron. "Assault support is what this squadron does," he said. "We provide assault transport of combat troops, supplies, and equipment, wherever they have to go." That could mean carrying riflemen, "the best weapon the Marine Corps has," into fights with "the bad guys," Rock said. One of VMM-263's main jobs, though, would be simply to carry Marine ground troops from base to base. "What does that do? It keeps them off the road," he said. There was no reason to add that the roads were where the infamous homemade bombs called Improvised Explosive Devices had taken many of the more than three thousand American lives lost in Iraq over the past four years.

"In one sense, it's been a long fifteen months," Rock said, referring to the time VMM-263 had spent preparing to deploy. Rock and a handful of officers and enlisted Marines had reconstituted the former helicopter unit as an Osprey squadron on March 3, 2006. Training began a couple of months later, after Ospreys and enough pilots to fly them began arriving. The squadron had flown their Ospreys at New River, flown them across the country and back with aerial refueling, flown them in mock combat exercises at MAWTS-1, the weapons and tactics school at the Marine Corps air station in Yuma, Arizona. To get ready for Iraq, they had sought out the sandiest, dustiest landing zones in the Mojave Desert and practiced landing their Ospreys in brownout conditions. To get ready for the voyage over, they had flown to an amphibious assault ship and practiced the departure they would make in the Gulf of Aqaba.

A squadron, like most groups of people brought together for a purpose, is an organization but also an organism, a living body that grows, matures, blossoms if nurtured correctly, and has a personality. By 2007, VMM-263's personality was an uneven mixture of experience and eagerness. The unit was top-heavy with seasoned officers and enlisted maintainers in their late thirties or early forties, a number of whom had spent more than a decade flying and fixing Ospreys. Rock and a few noncommissioned officers in the squadron were veterans of the MOTT, of VMMT-204, and of VMX-22. Half of VMM-263's pilots, however, were new to the Osprey. The years when VMMT-204's Ospreys were grounded had created a gap in the training pipeline. When VMM-263 was created, there were no captains available who had flown the Osprey. Six of VMM-263's pilots were captains in their early twenties who had joined the squadron as first lieutenants and never flown any other type of aircraft with any other squadron. Six were older captains who had joined the squadron after flying CH-46 helicopters. The six who had flown the CH-46, like a couple of the majors, had served in Iraq during the first years of the war. They had been shot at by insurgents, ferried wounded Marines from combat to medical care, in some cases had friends killed there.

Four months before the family meeting at New River, General James Conway, the commandant since January 2007, had announced that the Osprey was indeed going to Iraq and would be based at Al Asad Air Base. Al Asad was the nerve center of flight operations in Anbar Province, a territory spanning western Iraq whose 53,208 square miles made it almost precisely as large as North Carolina. The Army was in charge of combat operations in the rest of Iraq; the Marines were responsible for Anbar, where some of the bloodiest battles of the war had been fought. In early 2007, Anbar was still arguably the most dangerous place in Iraq for U.S. forces. It was the heartland of Iraq's Sunni Muslims, who had enforced and thrived under Saddam Hussein's rule, suppressing the country's Shiite Muslim majority for decades. Anbar was the hotbed of the Sunni insurgency that erupted after the U.S.-led invasion in 2003. Anbar was also the headquarters of Al Qaeda in Iraq, an offshoot of Osama bin Laden's terrorist organization that had infiltrated hundreds of foreign Islamic fundamentalist fighters into the province early in the war. Led by the notorious Jordanian terrorist Abu Musab al-Zarqawi, Al Qaeda in Iraq had used kidnappings and beheadings to take control of Fallujah, Anbar's largest city. For months, the group enforced its pitiless brand of Islam on the city's residents and dispatched hundreds of suicide bombers to attack U.S. troops and Shiites in other parts of Iraq. At a cost of 153 American and thousands of Iraqi lives, the Marines liberated Fallujah in late 2004 after a battle marked by the most difficult house-to-house fighting U.S. troops had seen since Vietnam. A U.S. air strike killed Zarqawi in July 2006, but Al Qaeda in Iraq and the Sunni insurgency were still active in Anbar when Conway announced the Osprey would go there.

Two months before the Commandant's announcement, on February 7, the Marines had lost their seventh helicopter of the war. Sunni insurgents used a surface-to-air missile to down a CH-46 piloted by Captain Jennifer Harris, killing her, four other Marines, and two Navy corpsmen. Captain Elizabeth Okoreeh-Baah, one of two women and the only African-American among VMM-263's pilots, had graduated with Harris from the Naval Academy in 2000. They were friends. Okoreeh-Baah had flown CH-46s around Fallujah and other hotspots in Iraq in 2004. She was glad to be flying the Osprey now. She felt guilty, though, that joining VMM-263 had kept her from serving a second or third tour in Iraq, as Harris and Okoreeh-Baah's other peers already had done. The pilots of VMM-263 were proud to be taking the Osprey to war, but the mission was their focus.

Rock wanted it that way. At the Family Readiness Meeting that August evening, he spoke for more than half an hour without ever mentioning the Osprey. For the generals and others at Headquarters Marine Corps, and for the media and the Osprey's numerous critics, VMM-263's deployment was seen as a test of the aircraft. Rock had spent months trying to crowd that idea out of his squadron's heads. Rock and his senior pilots were eager to "sell" the Osprey to other Marines by showing them that its speed and range could make a dramatic difference in how they did their missions. Rock stressed to his Marines, though, that their purpose in going to Iraq wasn't to prove the Osprey, it was to support their fellow Marines on the ground.

In his talk to family members, Rock assured them that, thanks to the Internet, communication with their Marines would be easy compared to the old days. He cautioned against putting specifics of the deployment into e-mails or on blogs or websites. Rock would send periodic reports to the families by e-mail as he could. If VMM-263 took casualties, though, the news would be brought to those affected at home in person.

At the talk of casualties, some of the young women in the audience exchanged worried glances. Tears welled in some eyes. Rock's wife, Maria, seated in the front row, whispered a reminder to him. "Thanks, m'love," he cooed. Other wives giggled. "Aw," some sighed sweetly. Rock urged the spouses not to make their Marines' departure too emotional. "We have got a great bunch of Marines here, and they are about to step off and do great things," Rock said. "It is a noble mission. It is a worthy thing that they are doing."

* * *

If the news from Iraq wasn't enough to worry the families, there were predictions of doom when the Osprey went there. In January, the Center for Defense Information, a Washington think tank critical of the Pentagon, published a report titled "V-22 Osprey: Wonder Weapon or Widow Maker? They warned us. But no one is listening." Produced by Lee Gaillard, a freelance military writer who had served in the Marine Corps Reserve, the report said the Osprey was "an aircraft waiting to increase its casualty list single-handedly if it is ever permitted to go to a combat theater." Gaillard's forty-seven-page study drew heavily on the writings of Harry Dunn. It also cited a memo Rex Rivolo had written four years earlier for the Pentagon's Office of Operational Test and Evaluation. Rivolo's memo set out his concerns about the Osprey's "lack of an autorotation capability," its "drastically different response" to vortex ring state compared to helicopters, and his belief that its proprotors gave it too little agility for combat. Dunn had obtained a copy of Rivolo's memo just after the IDA expert wrote it, and a draft had turned up on Osprey critic Carlton Meyer's G2mil.com website about the same time.

The memo contained arguments Rivolo had lost shortly after he made them in 2003. That year, he and chief Osprey test pilot Tom Macdonald argued the autorotation issue raucously in front of the chairman of the House Armed Services Committee, Representative Duncan Hunter, a California Republican with a son in the Marine Corps. Macdonald was among a group of Navair and Bell-Boeing officials Hunter called to his office to debate Rivolo after the congressman read Rivolo's "Lingering Safety Concerns" memo, which called it "unconscionable" to send the Osprey into combat when it couldn't autorotate to a safe landing. At Hunter's insistence, Rivolo later explained his views to the commandant at the time, General Michael Hagee, in a Pentagon meeting attended by Macdonald, others from the Osprey program, and a half-dozen Marine Corps generals. "I never felt more futile in my life," Rivolo told me. "Clearly they had been told to have this meeting, they did not want it, and basically they asked no questions, they raised no objections.

I went through my little pro forma and they said 'thank you very much' and showed me out."

Rivolo, like Harry Dunn, had lost the Osprey debate.

Four years later, the pilots of VMM-263 and others in the Osprey camp shrugged off Gaillard's report as a rehash of old issues. Some Osprey supporters were taken aback, though, when the current commandant, General Conway, told a Defense Writers Group breakfast in March 2007 that the Osprey might go to Iraq and would do well there, then added: "I'll tell you, there is going to be a crash. That's what airplanes do over time. We're going to have to accept that when it happens."

Conway was stating the obvious—virtually every aircraft crashes at some time—and apparently trying to prepare the public for the blow should an Osprey go down in Iraq. His comments, though, seemed to reflect another fact as well. The Osprey had produced so many unpleasant surprises over the years, Marine Corps leaders were more edgy about sending it to Iraq than the pilots who were going to fly it there.

"We were going to be very careful with the very first deployment of this aircraft, first operational deployment," the assistant commandant at the time, General Robert Magnus, told me. No one in the Marine Corps had a longer history with the Osprey than Magnus, who in the early 1980s, as a young major, had been the action officer perhaps most responsible for getting the program started. Magnus still believed the tiltrotor had been the right way for the Marine Corps to go, that its ability to fly fast and far were going to rewrite the service's tactics. Magnus and others at the top of the Marine Corps, though, didn't want the Osprey's past to prove prologue when it went to Iraq. "Our idea was to crawl, walk, run," he explained. Marine leaders didn't want critics to accuse them of being afraid to use the Osprey in combat, Magnus said, but they also didn't want Rock's squadron to feel they had to perform miracles "because the media was looking at them, which gets you back into the situation like at Marana, where you feel like you had to do something you might not be able to do." This was one reason the Marine Corps turned down dozens of media requests to spend time with VMM-263 before it left for Iraq, to accompany the squadron on its way, or to visit the unit at Al Asad. "We also didn't want to have a bunch of stuff on this airplane that was on the Web that Al Qaeda was looking at, because you can bet they would have loved to shoot down one of these airplanes," Magnus added.

That cautious attitude also was reflected in the decision to send VMM-263's Ospreys by ship rather than have them fly to Iraq from New River. The Marines had touted the Osprey's ability to "self-deploy" for years, but no emergency required rushing VMM-263 to Iraq. There were practical reasons to send their Ospreys by ship as well. Six to eight KC-130 tankers, an aircraft in short supply, would be needed to refuel them if they flew. The hours spent flying would require mechanics to spend extra hours working on the Ospreys once they arrived at Al Asad, delaying the date they could start flying missions. There was also the chance that one or more would break down on the way and have to make a precautionary landing. That had happened in each of two trans-continental deployments VMM-263 had flown in the United States during training. It had happened again to one of two Ospreys the Marines flew from New River to Farnborough, England, for the big international air show there in July 2006.

On September 17, 2007, Rock and most of VMM-263's other pilots flew their ten Ospreys, carrying baggage, tools, spare parts, and about sixty mechanics, to the USS *Wasp* as it sailed near the North Carolina coast. Twenty-six years to the month after Navy Secretary John Lehman had told the Marine Corps to buy a tiltrotor rather than another helicopter to replace its CH-46 Sea Knights, the Osprey was finally on its way to war.

★ ★ ★

The *Wasp* was roughly halfway to the Gulf of Aqaba when someone on the ship showed Rock something that turned his stomach: the most recent issue of *Time* magazine, dated October 8 but published earlier. Its cover boasted a "Special Investigation" of the Osprey titled "Flying Shame." The cover illustration depicted an Osprey in flight, nacelles in helicopter mode, casting a shadow in the shape of a graveyard cross. The art was accompanied by this text: "It's unsafe. It can't shoot straight. It's already cost 30 lives and $20 billion. And now it's headed for Iraq. The long, sad tale of the V-22 Osprey. By Mark Thompson."

Thompson, a veteran Pentagon correspondent and deputy Washington bureau chief for *Time*, described the Osprey's hybrid method of flight and its painful history, from Vice President Dick Cheney's failed attempt to cancel it for cost when he was defense secretary through the terrible crashes. The article focused most heavily on Rex Rivolo's argument that the Osprey's inability to autorotate was "unconscionable." Rivolo declined to give Thompson an interview but the article quoted Rivolo's "Lingering Safety Concerns" memo, written four years earlier and later leaked to Harry Dunn. Thompson also quoted VMM-263 pilot Captain Justin "Moon" McKinney, who said he and others who flew the Osprey would "turn it into a plane and glide it down" if they were to lose both engines. "I have absolutely no safety concerns with this aircraft, flying it here or in Iraq," McKinney told *Time*.

The article also raised an issue largely ignored in the past, emphasizing the Osprey's lack of a forward-firing gun for self-defense, an original requirement that had been waived for years to save money and weight. Retired General James Jones, the former commandant, was quoted saying he thought the Osprey needed such a weapon and was disappointed it lacked one. VMM-263's Ospreys were going to Iraq armed only with a 7.62-millimeter machine gun that could be fired out the rear ramp. Toward the end of his article, Thompson noted that the current commandant had predicted an Osprey would crash. The Osprey was "a radical aircraft crammed with compromises that may change combat forever," the article concluded, but "may also kill a lot of Marines while doing little of note on the battlefield."

Rock wasn't bothered by the text, which in his view contained no news. The cover art with its shadow of a cross, however, and the date of the publication enraged him and his pilots. The cover was sacrilegious, Rock felt, and the timing calculated to shock and sell magazines. Rock couldn't see any other purpose in predicting after the Osprey already was on its way to Iraq that it was going to kill Marines. "It was obviously aimed to inflame, not to educate, not to illuminate, not to help," Rock said. "The timing was downright malicious. The content of the article didn't shake my faith or the faith of any of my Marines. What it did is, it pissed me off, because I knew, correctly, the effect it would have on our families. Our families are back there reading all this." The article scared many of them.

Magnus sent *Time* a letter calling the article "a one-sided, sensationalistic view of the V-22 program, full of inaccuracies, and misleading to *Time's* readers." The magazine published his letter in its November 5, 2007, issue. Months later, Magnus was still angry about the cover story. "I've still got it sitting in my bathroom," he told me. "I just haven't used it for the purpose that I'd like to because it's slick paper."

Rock sent the families an e-mail to reassure them. Trust your Marines, he told them, they know what they're doing. Later, when he saw the photo on the ready room bulletin board of the handmade sign reading "Fuck-U Mark Thompson," Rock left it there. It was a good morale booster.

* * *

"I think we should do this again. It's still about selling the aircraft." Major Timothy Miller, thirty-four, was talking to Rock, Major Wesley Spaid, thirty-six, and Captain Sara Faibisoff, twenty-six. The four VMM-263 pilots were seated on wheeled office chairs at one end of the squadron's ready room at Al Asad on a Saturday afternoon in December 2007, two months into their deployment. They were discussing a mission they had attempted that morning but had to scrub after one of four generators on the Osprey that Rock and Faibisoff were flying failed. They had been carrying Marine infantry on a search for insurgents in the desert when Rock decided he shouldn't continue flying with the bad generator on a mission that could last hours. He wanted to fly back to base and get a different Osprey, but the infantry commander called off the mission instead. Rock was deeply disappointed. The flight had been the first time a ground commander had agreed to include Ospreys in a mission called "aeroscout," an armed reconnaissance patrol flown by a "package" of aircraft including Cobra helicopter gunships and a Huey transport helicopter to carry the officer in charge. Ground commanders were used to doing aeroscout with heavy-duty CH-53E Super Stallion helicopters to carry troops and extra fuel for the other helicopters. VMM-263 was awaiting a shipment of equipment that would let its Ospreys carry extra fuel as well. In the meantime, Rock and his pilots wanted to start familiarizing ground commanders with the Osprey so they would start including it in combat missions.

VMM-263 would fly other aeroscout missions successfully during its seven months in Iraq, but the breakdown on the first attempt was frustrating for the pilots. It also wasn't the first time one of their Ospreys had let them down. Two captains flying the sixth Osprey to depart the *Wasp* for the flight into Iraq on October 4 had made a precautionary landing at King Hussein International Airport in Aqaba, Jordan, after their cockpit display indicated faults in their flight control and hydraulic systems. A half-dozen VMM-263 mechanics were flown from the ship to Aqaba by helicopter as the rest of the Osprey squadron completed the hour-and-a-half flight to Al Asad. A damaged wire turned out to be the cause of the faults, but that wasn't obvious at first, and it took the mechanics nearly three days to figure it out and fix the problem.

Other mechanical problems, especially with electrical devices in the Osprey's rotor hubs called "slip rings," lowered the squadron's readiness rate, the number of aircraft available to fly every day, during its first couple of months at Al Asad. Like slip rings in helicopters, those in the Osprey proved sensitive to Iraq's sand, nicknamed "moon dust" by troops for its talcum powder consistency. The problem eased after VMM-263's mechanics devised a quick way to troubleshoot slip ring failures, but with that rough start, the squadron's average readiness rate for the entire seven months was 68 percent—well below its goal. Mechanical problems kept the squadron from flying only five of five hundred missions it was assigned over the seven months, though, and the five "dropped" missions were in the first two months.

Like much of the Osprey's history, the tiltrotor's first use in a war didn't turn out as a lot of people expected. The predictions of the critics who forecast disaster went unfulfilled. The closest call came when a piece of an absorbent pad inadvertently left in a fuel tank by a mechanic who had been working on it choked off the flow of fuel to one of an Osprey's engines in flight. The pilots made an emergency landing with one engine powering both rotors, as contemplated in the original design. None of VMM-263's Ospreys crashed or got shot up trying to land in hot zones. Only two were ever fired on, as far as the pilots could tell. One night some tracer rounds passed between two of the squadron's Ospreys as they flew at low level over a residential neighborhood in Ramadi. Another night, between Ramadi and Baghdad, someone launched a rocket that fell far short of some Ospreys as they sped past at several thousand feet.

By the time VMM-263 arrived at Al Asad, the fighting and terrorist attacks that had made Anbar so dangerous a few months earlier had fallen dormant for the most part. A "surge" of thirty thousand additional troops President George Bush sent to Iraq in the summer of 2007 was one reason. More important, Sunni leaders in Anbar had turned on Al Qaeda in Iraq and begun working with U.S. commanders against the terrorists, who fled to other parts of the country. By October, the Marines in Anbar were left without a lot of fighting to do. There were no hot zones for the

Osprey to take them into, no need for a forward-firing gun, no casualties for VMM-263 to evacuate, other than a Marine whose appendix ruptured on Christmas Eve. Captain Faibisoff and another pilot picked him up at an outlying base and rushed him to the hospital at Al Asad.

By December, Faibisoff and others among the pilots who had been excited by the prospect of flying in combat were actually bored. "I thought it was going to be a war," she grumbled when I ran into her outside VMM-263's headquarters at Al Asad that month. A quiet young woman with short hair and a wry grin, Faibisoff had graduated from the Naval Academy in 2003 with two of the twenty-two male pilots in VMM-263. She had opted for the Marine Corps and become a pilot to do something exciting. The war wasn't living up to her expectations.

I was one of fewer than half a dozen journalists the Marines permitted to visit VMM-263 in Iraq. Headquarters Marine Corps hesitantly granted my request because I was writing this book, and because a couple of senior active and retired generals felt I had written about the Osprey fairly in the past. As a Washington correspondent for the *Dallas Morning News*, I had covered the Osprey off and on for twenty-two years. I had written about the battle the Marines waged to defeat Dick Cheney's efforts to cancel it in the early 1990s. I had written about the crashes and redesign and retesting of the Osprey. I had been among the first reporters to ride in the Osprey at New River on July 13, 2005, and had written an enthusiastic first-person account. I had flown in a variety of U.S. military transport helicopters during my career. Flying in the Osprey was like nothing else. Its power and speed and novelty made the ride exhilarating.

By the time I got to Al Asad, I was a familiar face to most of the pilots and many of the maintainers in VMM-263. I had begun following the squadron in February 2007, when I went to New River twice to interview Rock and others. I visited when they trained at the Marine Corps air station in Yuma, Arizona, that spring, and spent a week with them at New River in August.

Rock was cordial when I first met him in February but initially seemed cautious toward me. By August, he clearly was more comfortable with what I was doing, but when I saw him at Al Asad in December, he was all business, zeroed in on his mission. Escorted by a public affairs officer, I was largely free to roam the squadron's rugged headquarters, a sand-colored, sandbag-surrounded one-story building that had been constructed when Al Asad was an Iraqi air base and whose plumbing had long ago fallen into disrepair. I could walk to maintenance offices in other buildings nearby or to the squadron's hangar on the flight line, interview anyone who wasn't too busy to talk, ask them whatever I liked. The mechanics were working in twelve-hour shifts around the clock seven days a week to keep their Ospreys flying. "When the kids go home, they're tired," observed Chief Warrant Officer 2 Carlos Rios, the maintenance material control officer.

"Home" was one of the portable, air-conditioned shelters with white metal sides, linoleum floors, and bunk beds where Marines and other service members and civilians lived at Al Asad, a major supply hub for U.S. forces in Iraq. Some called it "Camp Cupcake" because of its amenities, though nearly everything on the base was concrete or its basic ingredients, sand and rock. Al Asad had one of the largest and reputedly best dining halls in Iraq. It had a Burger King and several other fast-food restaurants, a gourmet coffee shop, and a post exchange selling everything from chewing gum to big-screen TVs. All of those conveniences, though, were located so far from VMM-263's location that many in the squadron bought bicycles to get back and forth to them, and few pilots bothered to make the trip very often. They ate near their hangar, where a small building had been converted into a rough-hewn mess hall, dubbed "Skinny's" for its limited fare. When the pilots were off duty, most simply went back to their "cans" and rested or slept.

Despite the lack of combat, they were flying their Ospreys a lot, carrying supplies and Marines and other passengers from Al Asad to remote "forward operating bases," to Baghdad, and to other parts of Iraq. The Osprey quickly became a favorite way to fly for generals and other VIPs. Like a lot of other passengers, they liked its speed and relative comfort compared to helicopters, whose ride is sluggish and tooth-jarring by comparison. VMM-263 ended up carrying 18,000 passengers and 1.4 million pounds of cargo during its seven months in Iraq—respectable numbers. For many of the pilots, though, the routine of "hauling ass and trash," as they called it, was a disappointment. They had come to Iraq expecting to fly in combat. Those who had done that already were happy not to repeat the experience, but those who hadn't had been looking forward to seeing how they would handle it.

The worst time for many of the pilots was December, when VMM-263 was assigned to keep three of its Ospreys on call around the clock to evacuate casualties should there be any. Pilots on "casevac" duty had to spend twelve hours at a time in or near the ready room, a rectangular space the size of a modest backyard swimming pool. Maps of Iraq showing geographic features and flight paths, as well as a dartboard, adorned three of the ready room's white walls. There was a table with a coffee pot near the door and a basket overflowing with cookies and candy sent constantly by concerned citizens back home. There was a refrigerator stocked with plastic bottles of water and nonalcoholic beer. In one corner was a plywood booth with a raised floor and a counter, painted black, where a miniature of the lady's-leg lamp seen in the movie *A Christmas Story* sat. One pilot serving as operations duty officer, or ODO, was posted in the booth at all times, keeping track of where the squadron's Ospreys were, monitoring radio traffic, answering calls from VMM-263 pilots wanting information. A whiteboard on the wall listed who was flying or would fly which Osprey on what mission and when. On a small shelf in the corner, above the ODO's head, sat the squadron's mascot, the "Ready Ape," a comical, dark wood statue of a gorilla about a foot and a half tall and, depending on the occasion, garbed in a variety of tiny Marine Corps uniforms. The bulletin board with the photo of VMM-263's message to Mark Thompson was on another wall nearby.

The center of the room was filled by two leather sofas, positioned in a V atop an oriental rug, with a coffee table in front of them. Beyond that were fifteen black office chairs where pilots and crew chiefs could sit for preflight and other briefings. Briefing slides could be shown on a big flat screen mounted on a pedestal situated in a corner in front of the chairs. Dressed in desert tan flight suits and carrying sidearms in brown leather holsters hanging from straps over their shoulders, the pilots sometimes passed the time while on alert for casualty evacuation by using the screen to watch movies on DVD. A favorite was *Superbad,* a comedy about three socially inept teenagers trying to get drunk and lose their virginity on the same night. The pilots on casevac alert, however, more often used the time to study their flight manuals and quiz each other on the steps to take if a particular fault or warning light posted on the Osprey's cockpit display during a flight.

When I visited Al Asad that December, none of the pilots had seen any evidence as yet of hostile fire aimed at their Ospreys. Rock observed that there was no way to be sure, but it was possible this was because of the way they were flying. In combat zones, helicopters generally fly low, which despite their noise improves their chances of flying past those who might shoot at them before being seen. VMM-263's pilots would execute a short or vertical takeoff, then quickly tilt the Osprey's rotors forward to fly like an airplane. They would climb fast and then cruise at 8,000 feet or more and about 275 miles per hour, roughly twice as fast as most military helicopters, and well out of the range of small arms. When landing, they would spiral down in airplane mode and tilt their rotors up late in their approach to land like a helicopter.

This is how Captain Newel Bartlett flies, with Rock in the left-hand copilot's seat and me in the jump seat between and just behind them, on a Sunday morning flight from Al Asad to a dusty and remote Marine forward operating base near the Syrian border called Korean Village. After taking off vertically at 10 A.M. from the flight line just outside VMM-263's hangar, Bartlett follows another Osprey, circling over a desert firing range in helicopter mode. Pushing a button on his Thrust Control Lever, Bartlett fires off some flares to test the Osprey's antimissile defenses. The flares crackle into the sky behind us, then one of the crew chiefs in back fires a few rounds from the machine gun mounted on the rear ramp. We circle back and land at the 2nd Marine Aircraft Wing's headquarters, a point called "LZ Ripper," so the lead Osprey can pick up passengers including a general on his way to inspect Korean Village. As we wait, Rock quizzes Bartlett on the rules of engagement for firing at suspected insurgents.

A few minutes later, Bartlett executes a short rolling takeoff, then tilts the rotors forward and climbs. The acceleration presses me back into my seat. Bartlett levels off at 8,200 feet. The cockpit display shows we are cruising at 243 knots, just shy of 280 mph. Rock starts quizzing Bartlett again, posing questions about tactics, "torque splits," the Osprey's generators, its gearboxes. This is Bartlett's final exam to earn the designation Tiltrotor Aircraft Commander, giving him authority to command Osprey flights. He must pass it while flying the Marine Corps' most expensive aircraft, and in a combat zone.

Half an hour after takeoff, we're ten minutes from our destination, 135 miles from Al Asad. We begin a wide, spiraling descent into the FOB. My ears pop. All I can see in any direction below, except the collection of concrete barriers and tents called Korean Village, is orangish sand. Dust swirls up as Bartlett gently eases us down on a metal mat inside the perimeter, a couple of hundred feet from where the Osprey carrying the general has landed. Bartlett and Rock keep the engines running.

Fifteen minutes later, after some civilian contractors with luggage and a couple of Marines have climbed into the back of our Osprey to catch a ride to Al Asad, Bartlett tells the crew chiefs over the intercom, "Okay, guys, we're going to come up into a fairly high hover." The Osprey zooms up into the promised hover, then Rock says, "Doors closed. Ready to go fast." On the cockpit display panel in front of me, in white block letters, I see a fault has posted: R EAPS FAIL. One of the right nacelle's two engine air particle separators, blowers at the mouth of the Osprey's engines to filter sand and dirt out of the air they suck in, has malfunctioned. The device is abbreviated EAPS and known as an "eeps."

"I've seen this happen before," Rock tells Bartlett. "Ever since we got that mod, that tightened up the parameters for declaring EAPS failed. If you come up very high power out of—on takeoff, that'll post. I can pretty much guarantee it won't reset just by shutting it off and turning it back on, but it probably will reset if you reset the circuit breakers." The entire Osprey fleet, Rock explains to me, has been having trouble with the EAPS, which operates through hydraulic pressure. Before VMM-263 left for Iraq, two engine fires at New River were blamed on hydraulic leaks in the device, and Bell-Boeing sent technicians to modify the EAPS on the squadron's Ospreys. They rerouted a drain to prevent leaking hydraulic fluid from flowing out of the EAPS into the engine. They also shortened the time required for an EAPS to shut itself down if an internal sensor detected a potential leak. Now the EAPS shuts down when the Osprey lifts off quickly, probably because the maneuver causes a quick rise in hydraulic pressure, Rock figures. Rock decides against trying to get the EAPS working again before we get back to Al Asad because resetting its circuit breaker might cause some other problem. There is no risk to safety involved; the purpose of the EAPS is to extend the long-term life of the Osprey's engines.

Despite such annoyances, VMM-263's Ospreys accomplished literally 99 percent of their missions in Iraq. Two additional Ospreys were sent to the squadron during its seven months there, and the dozen aircraft held up well enough that the Marines left them there to be flown by a second squadron, VMM-162, which replaced Rock's in April 2008.

After their return from Iraq, Rock, Faibisoff, and crew chief Sergeant Danny Herrman took questions at a Pentagon news conference with the deputy commandant for aviation, Lieutenant General George Trautman. The Osprey's critics were still taking shots at the aircraft, saying the Marines had only used it as "a truck" to haul cargo and passengers, and that it hadn't yet faced the true test of combat. Trautman said the Marine Corps was proud of what the squadron had achieved in Iraq, and pleased with the Osprey. As Rock had told him at Al Asad the previous Thanksgiving, Trautman recalled, the Osprey's first deployment had been a test, not a final exam. "We're on a journey to exploit a new and revolutionary technology," Trautman said. "And we're going to continue to learn lessons, and we're going to continue to improve and continue to work hard to exploit the capabilities this airplane brings." VMM-263, he added, "spent seven months deployed and came back safely and did every single mission that they were asked to do."

Accomplishing his mission and getting his Marines home safely were Rock's goals when he took his squadron to Iraq. He also wanted to demonstrate that the Osprey was a safe, useful transport whose unique tiltrotor capabilities were going to make the Marine Corps more effective, save lives, and help win battles. After devoting eleven years of his life to the Osprey, though, and after all he had lived through during those years, Rock's attitude toward the aircraft had been tempered by experience. "When I first started, it was absolutely the dream machine," Rock told me. "I didn't know any better, and I came in and it was just a tremendous opportunity to fly a tremendous airplane. I had no idea the cost, the trial that it would be to get it to that point. So some time— and no doubt slowly, gradually, over the course of my experience—it became less and less about 'I want this because I want the plane to succeed' and more about 'we have got great Marines working on this, they have dedicated themselves to it, it's a great capability and I'm proud to be among them.'" Rock still believed in the Osprey, but he no longer saw it as a dream machine. It had extraordinary capabilities, but it also had its "warts," as Rock put it. "The airplane is just an airplane," he said. "It's just a machine." He wanted the machine to succeed, but not for its own sake. He wanted it to succeed for the Marines who were going to fly in it, and for those who had died in it. "I never talked to anybody about it, because you can't explain that kind of thing," he told me, but it was something he thought about a lot in Iraq, usually when he was alone in his "can" at Al Asad. Rock only went there to sleep, and before he slept, he always prayed. He asked God to safeguard his family and friends. He asked for the wisdom and skill to accomplish his mission and get all his Marines back to their loved ones. He also prayed for all the brother Marines he had lost seven years earlier at Marana and New River. "I was just remembering friends of mine who died trying to get to this point," Rock said. "These were great Marines and good friends of mine. It was an honor to be able to realize—to be there at the realization of the purpose they had given their life for." He wouldn't have wanted it said they had died in vain.

★ ★ ★

In June 2008, after awarding Rock a Bronze Star for his success in leading the first squadron ever to deploy with the Osprey, the Marine Corps sent him to Fort Worth to speak at a conference of Marine aviators and representatives of the contractors who build their aircraft. Dick Spivey was there, and the two met, the salesman with a dream and the pilot of the machine the dream inspired. Now sixty-seven, Spivey had taken early retirement from Bell Helicopter in August 2002 but was rehired as a consultant almost immediately. He spent four more years with the company doing much the same job.

When his colleagues had thought Spivey was leaving Bell for good, 150 or so of them gathered one Friday night to mark his retirement, an event videotaped by his son, Brett. There was a lavish buffet dinner and an open bar. There were nostalgic speeches about Spivey's triumphs and trip-ups. There was praise for his ability to "make every customer feel like he's talking to *him*." One of his former bosses extolled Spivey's creativity and his unparalleled skill at delivering any of five briefings: the two-hour, the one-hour, the twenty-minute, the written, or the "elevator," when "you've got one floor to tell your whole story." Another Bell marketer harvested guffaws when he stood up with his elbows to his sides and his index fingers pointed toward the ceiling, then asked the group if it wasn't true that Spivey had "built his career by saying—correct me if I'm wrong—'takes off like a helicopter'"—the man rotated his forearms downward so his fingers pointed forward—"'flies like an airplane.'" Someone read aloud a congratulatory e-mail from General Jim Jones, the Marine Corps commandant at the time. Someone read a letter from Bell's president in those days, John Murphey, who couldn't attend. Without Spivey, Murphey said, "there wouldn't be a V-22 Osprey." Former XV-15 test pilot Dorman Cannon remembered the early years of Bell's efforts to market the tiltrotor. "Everywhere we turned, Dick Spivey was around," Cannon said. Selling the tiltrotor hadn't just been Spivey's job, it had been his passion.

Three weeks after his retirement party in 2002, Spivey was back marketing the tiltrotor, giving briefings on vortex ring state to help save the Osprey and promoting the Quad TiltRotor, the giant Osprey derivative Bell was trying to sell the Pentagon. The next year, two months after Undersecretary of Defense Pete Aldridge changed his mind and gave the Osprey a clean bill of health, Bell donated its XV-15 tiltrotor demonstrator to the Smithsonian Institution's National Air and Space Museum. In a story on the donation, reporter Katie Fairbank of the *Dallas Morning News* quoted Spivey saying he had never lost faith in the tiltrotor. "We never had any doubt. We thought the V-22 was tarred and feathered," Spivey said. "The future is so bright."

Spivey left Bell for good in February 2006, a month before Rock took command of VMM-263, but he followed the squadron's progress eagerly. Just before VMM-263 went to Iraq, in an e-mail to a list of people he knew were interested, Spivey said: "Cross your fingers folks, the time is near to find out if all our efforts will pay off."

After Rock's talk at Fort Worth's Worthington Hotel in June 2008, Spivey approached, introduced himself, and asked if they could talk a bit more. They sat on some folding chairs and Spivey asked Rock questions about how the Osprey had done in Iraq. Rock didn't remember Spivey's specific questions later, but he was struck by how intense he seemed in asking them, and how he drank in Rock's answers. As they talked, the older man seemed almost emotional.

Spivey was. He had marketed the tiltrotor to the Marines as a dream machine, but the Osprey had turned into a nightmare. The Osprey's cost in dollars and lives and its long, tortuous history had nearly discredited the tiltrotor, he knew, and indefinitely deferred the dream. Spivey was confident the nightmare was over now, and after talking to Rock, he was sure the Marines and the Air Force soon would be relying heavily on the

Osprey. The Army might even get interested again, he ventured. Spivey blamed the machinery of procurement—the way the Pentagon buys weapons—rather than the machine itself for the Osprey's troubles. The Pentagon had redeemed the Osprey in the end, he mused, but maybe Ken Wernicke had been right. Wernicke was the idealistic tiltrotor engineer who had nearly resigned from Bell in 1983 rather than try to design a tiltrotor to what he saw as the military's wildly ambitious specifications. "I probably didn't realize just how difficult it was," Spivey reflected. "The dreams were simplistic compared to the reality. The issues associated with a government procurement are so complicated. Name one that hasn't had its problems."

Now that the Osprey was fielded, Spivey was sure the dream was alive. Once the military proved tiltrotors safe, he predicted, civilians would want to fly in them, too. "You've got to figure out a way to build them less expensively," he conceded. "They don't need to be as complicated as they are." If that could be done, though, Spivey had no doubt the tiltrotor still would change the world as much as the jet engine had. He wasn't sure he would live to see it, but "I actually still do believe in it, despite what everybody thinks," he said. The tiltrotor was still his dream machine, and always would be.

EPILOGUE

A decade to the day after the disaster at Marana, tragedy revisited the Osprey for the first time since its Dark Ages. On a pitch-black night in southern Afghanistan, an Air Force Special Operations Command CV-22B Osprey, one of three carrying Army Rangers on a raid against an insurgent target, touched down at more than 90 miles an hour a quarter mile short of its intended landing zone, a desolate area five kilometers east/southeast of the village of Qalat. With its landing gear down and its nacelles tilted upward at more than 80 degrees—not quite in 90-degree helicopter mode—the Osprey sped across the flat, sandy earth in what some of the Rangers on board thought was just a fast roll-on landing. Then its front wheels bounced, smacked into the ground, and collapsed. The Osprey's bulbous nose began plowing into the soft soil, then hit a two-foot-deep gully, flipping the aircraft onto its back, tail over nose. The cockpit was crushed. The fuselage slammed into the ground upside down. The pilot and an enlisted flight engineer from the Air Force's 8th Special Operations Squadron, the latter sitting in the jump seat behind and between the pilots, were killed. So were a corporal from the Army's 3rd Battalion, 75th Ranger Regiment, and an Afghan woman interpreter, both riding in the middle of the cabin. The copilot, thrown from the aircraft still strapped into his seat, survived. So did another Air Force flight engineer, thirteen other Rangers, and a male Afghan interpreter, all of whom had been kneeling in the cabin, wearing safety harnesses attached to the floor. Many had serious injuries.

The Air Force took eight months to release its accident report, whose results were inconclusive and, for some, controversial. The president of the eight-member Aircraft Investigation Board, Brigadier General Donald Harvel of the Texas Air National Guard, ruled out enemy fire, vortex ring state or a "brownout" landing, in which dust kicked up by the rotors might have disoriented the pilot. Harvel concluded that as many as ten factors contributed to the accident, none of which could be singled out as the primary cause. Among them were a 17-knot tailwind and the crew being distracted while pressing to get to the target on time. Harvel included a loss of power in the Osprey's engines on the list of contributing causes. The vice commander of the Air Force Special Operations Command, Major General Kurt Cichowski, disagreed. Citing engineering studies by the maker of the engines and Navair, Cichowski officially declared that there was no evidence of power loss. The one piece of gear that could have settled the disagreement, the CV-22's Flight Incident Recorder, which records engine data and instrument readings, was never recovered, though troops who arrived to rescue the victims and sort through the debris removed many other items of classified gear. Four hours after the accident, on the recommendation of an Army commander, two Air Force A-10 "Warthog" planes dropped four 500-pound bombs on the wreckage to keep insurgents or others from getting their hands on anything that might be of value. Harvel retired from the Air Force as planned on Sept. 15, 2010, three months before the Air Force released his report, still troubled by the failure to recover the Flight Incident Recorder. He was sure the device would have shown that the CV-22 had lost at least some power in each of its engines that night, possibly from compressor stalls caused by the tailwind, possibly because of the thin air at the altitude where the accident occurred—5,226 feet above sea level—or perhaps because of mechanical failure. The pilot, Major Randell Voas, 43, had been one of the Air Force's best in the Osprey. Voas approached the landing zone that night too fast, but Harvel was certain that, rather than simply losing track of his altitude and flying his plane into the ground, Voas was trying to make an emergency roll-on landing, presumably because he lacked enough engine power to either maintain level flight or land like a helicopter.

In any event, the news media barely took notice. As in the late 1990s, by 2010 the Osprey was once again a dog-bites-man story. The frequency of helicopter and personnel losses in the wars in Iraq and Afghanistan was perhaps one explanation for media lack of interest. By the time the CV-22B went down, the U.S. military had suffered 546 deaths in 403 helicopter crashes in Afghanistan, Iraq, and elsewhere since the terrorist attacks of Sept. 11, 2001. Twenty of those killed died in five crashes of CH-46 Sea Knights, the Marine Corps helicopter the Osprey was primarily designed to replace. Over roughly the same period, the Marines had flown their MV-22B Ospreys more than 70,000 hours without a fatal accident, including more than 11,500 hours over Iraq and Afghanistan. VMM-263 and two other Marine Corps squadrons had flown the dozen Ospreys taken to Iraq in 2007 a total of 9,054 hours in that war zone. Poor reliability remained a problem. Marine Corps and Bell-Boeing mechanics in Iraq were hard-pressed to keep an average 70 percent of the Ospreys there "mission capable," a shortcoming largely laid to parts wearing out faster than engineers had predicted. At the same time, those dozen Ospreys safely delivered more than 44,000 passengers and 2.8 million pounds of cargo during their nineteen months in Iraq. Pleased with the Osprey's performance there, the Marines sent a dozen MV-22Bs to Afghanistan in November 2009, where the Corps was gearing up for a campaign against Al Qaeda and the Islamic fundamentalist terrorist group's Taliban allies in Helmand province. The Air Force Special Operations Command began flying its CV-22Bs in Afghanistan not long afterward.

Given its safety record over the previous decade, even after the CV-22B crash, the idea that the Osprey was a "death trap" and "widow-maker," as its harshest critics had charged, sounded like a hysterical echo from the past. In Afghanistan, reliability remained a stubborn issue for the MV-22B, but during its first year there, the Osprey defied the predictions of detractors who had warned that the tiltrotor would be an easy target for enemy fire in "hot" landing zones. In Afghanistan, the Osprey wasn't flying into ambushes of the sort helicopters faced in Vietnam, where enemy troops cloaked by jungle cover often met choppers with a hail of gunfire. The technology of war had changed greatly since the 1960s, and as a result, so had tactics. Enemy forces—especially in barren Afghanistan—rarely massed in the modern age, when unmanned surveillance drones and other airborne sensors could spot them as they gathered and aircraft carrying "smart" bombs could attack them with pinpoint accuracy—tools of war that didn't exist during Vietnam. Like helicopters flying in Afghanistan, the Osprey was more often a target for lone insurgents or small groups armed with AK-47 assault rifles or short-range rocket-propelled grenades. After a year in Afghanistan, the Osprey had so far proven equal to that challenge. During that year, Marine Corps Ospreys bringing troops into combat had been hit a confirmed five times by 7.62-millimeter bullets—standard ammunition for the AK-47. No one in those aircraft was killed or wounded. In each case, their pilots were able to fly them back to their base at Camp Bastion, where mechanics repaired the damage and put the aircraft back into service.

Even so, the Osprey's public image was little changed, and the debate was far from over. Those unfamiliar with the Osprey's rise from its own ashes since 2001 were often surprised to hear it still existed. Bloggers, think tank experts, and many journalists still described the Osprey as "troubled," ignoring its safety record and focusing on its low reliability rates and high cost. Critics derided the Marines for using the Osprey in Iraq as a "truck" and a "bus," or to ferry VIPs around combat zones. Some insisted the Osprey's inability to autorotate to a safe landing still constituted a major risk. A V-22 would be a dead duck, they said, if both engines were shot out or otherwise failed too close to the ground or with too little speed for its pilots to convert the rotors to airplane mode and glide on the wing to a safe landing. The most severe critics still contended the side-by-side placement of the Osprey's rotors would lead to an uncommanded and unrecoverable roll if one rotor went into vortex ring state at low altitude.

Marine and Air Force Osprey pilots were sanguine about their ability to handle such risks. They were also certain that the tiltrotor's ability to fly far faster and farther and higher than any helicopter, putting it well above the small-arms threat, was saving lives in Afghanistan by making the Osprey a far tougher target than the critics imagined. Still, the Marines clearly had much to prove before they could definitively claim the Osprey had been worth its hefty price. On March 28, 2008, two weeks before Lieutenant Colonel Paul Rock led VMM-263 home from Iraq, the Pentagon awarded the Bell-Boeing partnership a $10.4 billion contract to build 167 more Ospreys over the coming five years, 141 for the Marines and 26 for the Air Force. The Marines, the Air Force, and the Navy still planned to buy 458 in all. Calculating from the first contract in 1983 and including inflation, their total cost was projected at nearly $53 billion—$12 billion more than estimated in 1982 for what at the time was expected to be nearly three times as many aircraft. Bell-Boeing's multiyear contract was the kind of deal defense companies strive for, a near guarantee that neither President Barack Obama's administration nor Congress would cancel the Osprey before 2012. Cancellation charges would make writing off such an investment prohibitively expensive and politically difficult. Navair and Bell-Boeing were negotiating a second multiyear contract to begin in 2013 as well. In an era of trillion-dollar federal deficits, though, the Osprey remained a juicy target for defense spending critics and others searching for ways to cut the federal budget. In November 2010, the co-chairmen of the National Commission on Fiscal Responsibility and Reform, a panel created by Obama to find ways to close the budget deficit, recommended halting Osprey purchases at 288. Even so, there was little expectation the proposal would be adopted. Without commenting on the Osprey, Defense Secretary Robert Gates rejected the commission's proposed military spending cuts as "math, not strategy." Equally importantly, the Osprey's support in Congress remained strong, and Marine and Air Force leaders insisted their services needed all the V-22s planned.

As 2010 ended, the Marine Corps was well along in creating new operational squadrons to fly its expanding Osprey fleet. Six Osprey squadrons existed at New River Marine Corps Air Station and two more at Miramar Marine Corps Air Station in California. One of the busiest was VMMT-204, the training squadron at New River. Paul Rock, who had spent the Osprey's Dark Ages at the same squadron, was now its commander. After leading the Osprey's first deployment to Iraq, Rock had been promoted to full colonel in July 2009 and put in charge of preparing new Osprey pilots and mechanics for the Marines and Air Force both.

The Osprey's survival and initial success, meanwhile, was rekindling civilian interest in the tiltrotor. The aviation revolution predicted by the true believers was nowhere in sight, but the dream was alive. "I really do believe that tiltrotor aviation is going to revolutionize a lot of the things that we do," NASA Administrator Charles Bolden, a former Marine general and astronaut, told engineers in September 2010 at his agency's Ames Research Center in California—where tiltrotor true believer Dick Spivey was now running the co-located Army Aeroflightdynamics Directorate, that service's rotorcraft research arm. Spivey's agency was working on ideas for new rotorcraft, including tiltrotors, to replace military helicopters. NASA had built a computerized simulator of a 100-passenger civilian tiltrotor and was studying how such an aircraft might share the national airspace with other civilian traffic. Bell Helicopter and its Italian partner, AgustaWestland S.p.A., meanwhile, were flight-testing prototypes of a nine-passenger civilian tiltrotor roughly the size of the XV-15 called the BA609. Bell executives no longer saw an unlimited market for tiltrotors, just niches where its speed could make a big difference, such as emergency medical services and evacuating offshore oil platform crews in emergencies. AgustaWestland, though, remained committed as ever. Chief Executive Giuseppe Orsi forecast that the BA609 would be in production by 2013 or 2014, and with European partners, AgustaWestland was also working on another tiltrotor called the Erica. "We believe the future is in the tiltrotor," Orsi said.

Others were exploring tiltrotors with equal enthusiasm. California aircraft designer Abraham Karem, regarded as a genius by many in his field, hoped that by 2018, airlines would be buying his AeroTrain, a tilt-rotor designed to carry 120 passengers 200 to 1,000 miles per trip. "The obstacles to fielding a high-efficiency transport tiltrotor remain more political than technical," Karem told me. "I personally believe that there is no other effort in aeronautics today that can equal the transforma-tive potential of a civilian transport tiltrotor with efficiency rivaling our best fixed-wing transports." Others were studying technologies such as variable-length rotor blades to improve on those used in the Osprey and BA609. Who could say whether some technological breakthrough that would make the tiltrotor simpler and cheaper wasn't just around the corner? In 1936, Orville Wright had flatly declared the helicopter impractical. Three years later, Igor Sikorsky proved Wright wrong. The helicopter required two decades more to come into everyday use, but it did. Perhaps the tiltrotor just needed more time to change the world.

Or perhaps the true believers were dreaming. That might be so, but then progress often depends on dreamers, especially in aviation. Who-ever sets out to conquer the air just has to have a dream. It comes with the territory.

January 2011

AUTHOR'S NOTE AND ACKNOWLEDGMENTS

This book itself is the only repayment I can offer for the debt I owe many dozens of people who contributed their time, knowledge, insights, personal archives, research skills, advice, or simply encouragement to a project I began in the summer of 2006 with some trepidation. By then, as a Washington correspondent for the *Dallas Morning News*, I had written about the Osprey off and on for close to twenty-two years and found the experience akin to covering the debate over abortion. No matter what I wrote, I could usually count on being chastised by someone, for the Osprey was as close as a defense issue gets to being a religious question. There were believers and nonbelievers, and neither had much use for those who gave any credence to the other side. I was unsure how many would cooperate with a book whose goal was neither to praise nor to bury the Osprey but, as I frequently explained, simply to tell its story, good and bad, and let the facts speak for themselves. As it turned out, so many people opened their doors, their files, and their hearts to me that I truly can never hope to thank them all.

I am especially grateful to those relatives of men who perished in the Osprey who shared their memories with me, though that meant reopening old wounds and reliving pain they had spent years trying to put behind them. My heartfelt thanks to Connie Gruber, Anne and Buddy Murphy, Carol and Katrina Sweaney, Kathi Mayan, and Michelle Stecyk Kovtonuk for helping me tell this part of the story, without which this book would have been incomplete. I am also grateful to Lt. Col. (ret.) Jim Schafer for his trust, advice, and aid in reporting this saddest part of the Osprey saga. Jim's devotion to the memory of his fallen comrades, and to their survivors, is inspiring.

This book would have been impossible without the cooperation of the United States Marine Corps, which accorded me special access to VMM-263 and other forms of assistance based only on the promise that I would tell the truth as I found it. I thank all the Marines, active and retired, who helped, particularly Lt. Gen. (ret.) John Castellaw, who as deputy commandant for aviation agreed to support my project, and Col. David Lapan, who as acting director of Marine Corps Public Affairs put that support in writing. Lt. Col. (ret.) Scott Fazekas and, in turn, Maj. Eric Dent did the unenviable duty of serving as my primary point of contact at Public Affairs. I apologize to both for the heartburn I sometimes caused with my innumerable and sometimes impatient requests, and I thank them both for their professionalism. I also want to thank Gen. (ret.) Robert Magnus for finding time in his busy schedule while he was assistant commandant of the Marine Corps to do three lengthy, insightful, and refreshingly candid interviews.

Besides granting me several interviews apiece, Lt. Gen. (ret.) Fred McCorkle and Lt. Gen. (ret.) Michael Hough, each a former deputy commandant for aviation, were invaluable tutors on the inner workings of the Marine Corps, especially its aviation arm. They also helped me get to Iraq to spend time with VMM-263 when my desire to do so encountered obstacles. I thank Lt. Gen. George Trautman, deputy commandant for aviation at the time, for granting my request and I am grateful to Maj. Gen. Kenneth Glueck, Jr., for allowing me to accompany him and his staff on a memorable three-day C-130 flight from Cherry Point, North Carolina, to Al Asad. During my stay, 2nd Lt. Nick Mannweiler was an efficient escort and a cordial companion. Sincere thanks also to Lt. Col. Paul Rock, Jr., and the other Marines of VMM-263, who welcomed me into their midst and freely answered my many questions at New River, in Yuma, and at Al Asad. It was always a pleasure and a privilege to be among them. I especially thank Rock for sharing his personal feelings and memories.

I also received special cooperation from Bell Helicopter Textron Inc. and Boeing, which allowed me into their factories and arranged interviews with their executives, engineers, and other employees, both active and retired. Bell Helicopter spokesman Bob Leder and Boeing Rotorcraft Division spokesman Jack Satterfield, each of whom left his job in 2008, organized and facilitated my visits and interviews and were immeasurably helpful in other ways. Naval Air Systems Command V-22 spokesman James Darcy was equally diligent and helpful.

I owe thanks to a long list of people who provided or helped me find the many printed sources of fact that undergird this book. Eileen Dorschner of the Aeronautics and Astronautics Library at the Massachusetts Institute of Technology, Tom Koch of the McDermott Library at the University of Texas at Dallas, and David Schwartz of the National Air and Space Museum Archives led me to documents that told the story of Gerard Herrick and the convertiplane. Army Brig. Gen. (ret.) Dave Armstrong, chief historian for the Joint Chiefs of Staff, was a valued source of advice. Dr. Diane Putney of the Office of the Secretary of Defense Historian's Office tracked down obscure Defense Department documents for me. Zoe Davis cheerfully and efficiently helped by e-mail and during my several visits to the U.S. Senate Library. Constance Carter, science and technology reference director at the Library of Congress, was an indefatigable gumshoe in investigating the provenance of the obscure rhyme "One of Our Simple Problems." I thank them all.

When he heard I was writing this book, my old friend and valued colleague Otto Kreisher, Copley News Service's Pentagon correspondent for many years, immediately offered me a trove of clippings and documents he had hamstered away over a decade or more with a view toward writing an Osprey book of his own. Thank you, Otto, for your generosity. Richard Aboulafia, an aviation consultant many reporters rely on for incisive comments on a complex industry, put his Osprey files and photocopier at my disposal. Thank you, too, Richard. Dar Lundberg, Bob Balch, and Jim Magee, who as military officers were present at the creation of the Osprey and later worked on it during second careers at Bell or Boeing, loaned me personal archives containing documents I couldn't have hoped to find elsewhere. So did John Zugschwert, former vice president for government marketing at Textron Inc. Pete Rose, who as an aide to Rep. Pete Geren was a player in the battle with Dick Cheney over the Osprey, did me the favor of retrieving hundreds of documents and clippings from that period stored at the University of Texas library in Austin. Pete is among several people who went above and beyond the call of duty to help but whose names appear only in my list of interviews and chapter notes. I hope he and the others in this category will understand that the necessities of the narrative, not ingratitude, led me to omit them from the story itself.

Unrelenting Osprey foe Harry Dunn, whose name appears often in the narrative, was an unexpected and incomparably rich source of documents. When I interviewed Harry for the first time, he was clearly chagrined to hear that my aim was simply to tell the Osprey's story, not try to kill it. Even so, and at his own suggestion, Harry loaned me his entire Osprey archive: six banker's boxes and dozens of CDs containing hundreds of documents and his voluminous e-mail correspondence on the topic. The latter told a story previously unknown to me, and I thank Harry for granting me permission to make use of those e-mails.

Someone who deserves my special thanks is Dick Spivey. Some others who lived the Osprey story may wonder at the prominent role he plays in the narrative. Thousands of people worked on the Osprey over the years, and in many ways, Dick was far from the most important. As a marketer, he made no major business decisions, supervised no engineering, cast no deciding votes. Ironically, as of this writing Spivey had never flown in the Osprey. No one else, though, was more seized by the dream that the tiltrotor and the Osprey represented or worked harder to keep both alive. When I began this project in the fall of 2006, Dick and I had never met, though like many reporters I had interviewed him once by telephone. When we sat down to talk for the first time, I was struck by what a perfect prism his own story was for looking at the larger story I wanted to tell. Dick's forty-seven-year career at Bell Helicopter and his long love affair with the tiltrotor made him an ideal representative for the many others who shared his dreams. As I studied the role he played, I also came to agree with former Bell Helicopter test pilot Ron Erhart, who told me: "I don't think Dick Spivey was ever given enough credit for everything that happened. He may not have done a lot of these things himself but he sure put the idea in somebody else's mind that could do them." Over the nearly three years I worked on this book, I called on Dick frequently. He proved a candid witness to the Osprey's history as well as his own. He was also a walking encyclopedia on every technical aspect of the tiltrotor. Even better, his answers always checked out. I thank him for his ceaseless and cheerful cooperation through more than two dozen formal interviews and dozens of other phone calls and e-mails. I'm also grateful to Dick and his wife, Terry, for their hospitality when I was in Fort Worth.

For tutoring me in aeronautical and engineering concepts, and in some cases for checking the accuracy of what I wrote once I thought I understood them, I am grateful to a number of experts. I thank Troy Gaffey, Tom Macdonald, Don Byrne, Al Schoen, John Arvin, Michael Hirschberg, Kenneth Katz, J. Gordon Leishman, Alan Ewing, and Bill Rumberger for their patience. To help ensure accuracy on historical, political, and Marine Corps issues, I asked three experts in those areas to read the manuscript: Roger Connor, vertical flight curator of the National Air and Space Museum and chairman of the American Helicopter Society History Committee; Pat Towell, who for decades covered the annual defense battles on Capitol Hill for *Congressional Quarterly* and now puts his exacting research and analytical skills to work for the Congressional Research Service; and U.S. Naval Academy graduate Bob Timberg, whose service in the Marine Corps was followed by a distinguished career as White House Correspondent for the *Baltimore Sun*, authorship of the remarkable book *The Nightingale's Song* (Simon & Schuster, 1995), and editorship of the U.S. Naval Institute magazine *Proceedings*. I'm grateful to Roger, Pat, and Bob for their comments and corrections. Any mistakes, of course, are solely my responsibility.

Bob Timberg is also one of two authors who became mentors to me as I navigated the unfamiliar waters of the publishing world and learned how to write a book. The other is James Reston, Jr., author of fifteen enviable books, and one of the most decent human beings I know. Bob Timberg's enthusiasm and advice got me started and helped keep me going. Jim Reston's wise counsel, including a pivotal idea for how to structure the narrative, helped me finish the job. I look up to them both and thank them for their encouragement and guidance.

Another who read my draft proposal for this book and offered comments and encouragement is my steadfast friend Peter Schechter, whose website, www.peterschechter.com, accurately describes him as a Renaissance man—political adviser, farmer, winery owner, and author of two suspense novels.

I especially thank my literary agent, Richard Abate, who grasped the potential of the story I wanted to tell right away and helped me hone my concept for the book. No author could ask for a wiser adviser or a more astute advocate.

This book also bears the invisible but indelible imprint of my editor at Simon & Schuster, Colin Fox, a man of southern charm and a writer's editor if ever there was one. Colin's passion for the story and his support as I reported and wrote energized me. His deft touch streamlined the original manuscript and, to borrow a term from aerodynamics, much improved its lift-to-drag ratio. I also thank Colin's able assistant, Michele Bové, a woman of northern efficiency, for guiding me through the unfamiliar extraneous chores that go with completing a book such as this. I owe thanks as well to the inimitable Gypsy da Silva and to Tom Pitoniak, each a credit to their calling, for keen-eyed copyediting.

The deepest debt of thanks I owe is to my favorite photographer, and my dear wife, Faye Ross. As many authors' spouses do, Faye accepted the financial insecurity my taking on this project meant for our family. As many also do, she endured the fact that, for its author, a book rapidly evolves from a dream into an obsession—a word that often, and in my case correctly, connotes sometimes bizarre and annoying behavior. She not only put up with my increasing inability to talk or think about much of anything other than

"The Book" but also swallowed—usually—the temptation to tell me how sick she was of hearing about it. She consoled me when I ran into difficulties and gave me shrewd advice that helped solve many of them. She accompanied me to Yuma, where she took photographs of the Osprey and the members of VMM-263. Most important, she served as my first and most demanding reader. She helped me think through the story a chapter at a time. She read and reread as I wrote and rewrote. She repeatedly brought my focus back to the forest when my reporter's fascination with detail led me to zero in on the trees. In this way, she shaped the narrative as much as I did. Above all, she allowed me to live my dream. She has my everlasting thanks, and my undying love.

Richard Whittle
Chevy Chase, Maryland
May 2009

SOURCES

My goal in writing this book was not merely to recount the V-22 Osprey's history but to describe the dreams and drama behind the dry details of dates and dollars and Defense Department decisions. This is why *The Dream Machine* is a narrative rather than a conventional history, but a history it is. My sources for the historical facts include a number of books, hundreds of newspaper and magazine articles, and dozens of government and corporate documents. I have listed the most important sources publicly available in the Bibliography. Among them are government documents I obtained under the Freedom of Information Act, such as a previously unreported cockpit video and transcript of the crew conversations in the lead Osprey the night of the April 8, 2000, crash at Marana, Arizona. I also have benefited greatly from government documents that as a rule aren't released, such as test pilot reports, which were provided to me unofficially by sources who asked to remain unidentified. Former officials of Bell Helicopter Textron Inc. and Boeing Company provided me with copies of unclassified government and internal corporate documents never made public before. Dick Spivey loaned me the work diaries he intermittently kept in "MIT notebooks" between 1971 and 1996. I also reviewed forty-eight DVDs relevant to the story that were provided by Bell Helicopter, including video of the crash of the fifth Osprey prototype at Wilmington, Delaware, on June 11, 1991, and of the fourth prototype at Quantico, Virginia, on July 20, 1992.

As much as this book is a history, however, it is also a memoir—not my own, though I was present at various of the events described, but a memoir in the sense that much of the narrative is based on the recollections of those who lived the Osprey story. From the time I began my research in the summer of 2006 until I finished revising the manuscript in early 2009, I conducted more than four hundred interviews with more than two hundred people. As those numbers suggest, many of those I interviewed were kind enough to talk to me more than once, and in not a few cases, numerous times. With few exceptions, and always with the consent of the subject, I taped these interviews to ensure accuracy. A list of those I interviewed appears below.

Those interviews are the primary sources for many of the anecdotes and scenes in this book and the dialogue in them—with major exceptions worth noting. The crew conversations quoted in chapter eight as the fourth Osprey prototype flew from Eglin Air Force Base to Quantico on July 20, 1992, are taken from a forty-nine-page cockpit voice recorder transcript included as an exhibit in the Naval Court of Inquiry report on that crash. The pilot conversations in the lead Osprey at Marana quoted in chapter nine are taken from the cockpit video I obtained under the Freedom of Information Act. The pilot conversations quoted in chapter ten during the ill-fated flight of Crossbow 08 on December 11, 2000, appear in the Judge Advocate General Manual investigation report on that crash. Some other dialogue is taken from formal sources, such as transcripts of congressional hearings, Pentagon briefings, or television broadcasts. In the main, however, the dialogue is as it was recalled—usually many years later—by those who were present. Where possible, I have corroborated descriptions of scenes and events by reviewing relevant documents or contemporary accounts or by interviewing, often several times, others who were present. Where participants agreed on what happened but disagreed about precisely what was said, I have used the dialogue recalled by the person whose memory seemed strongest. Where others said to be present at an event couldn't recall it, I have reported what the person with the strongest recollection remembered but made clear that memories conflicted, either in the narrative or in the chapter notes below. The facts in this book are documented; the stories are told through the eyes of those who were there.

INTERVIEWS

Edward C. "Pete" Aldridge, undersecretary of defense for acquisition, technology, and logistics, 2001–2003; Brian Alexander, attorney for survivors of crash victims; James Ambrose, undersecretary of the Army 1981–88 (by e-mail); William A. Anders, former executive vice president, Textron Inc.; Capt. Charles Arnold, USMC, VMM-263 pilot; John Arvin, V-22 engine program manager 1985–88, Allison Gas Turbine Division, General Motors Corp.; James F. Atkins, former president, Bell Helicopter; Norman R. Augustine, member, Panel to Review the V-22 Program; Maj. Aisha Bakkar, USMC; Col. (ret.) Bob Balch, USMC; William L. Ball III, secretary of the Navy 1988–89; Staff Sgt. (ret.) Julius Banks, USMC, former MOTT member; Anthony R. Battista, former House Armed Services Committee aide; Brig. Gen. (ret.) Harry Bendorf, USAF, former Washington office director, Boeing Helicopter Co.; Lt. Col. Anthony Bianca, USMC, former MOTT pilot; Daniel R. Bilicki, former military marketer, Textron Inc.; Capt. Chris Bissette, USMC, VMM-263 pilot; Lt. Gen. (ret.) Harold W. Blot, USMC; Lt. Col. (ret.) Lance Bodine, USAF, Bell-Boeing CV-22 program manager; Capt. Jonathan Brandt, USMC, VMM-263 pilot; Robert C. Broadhurst, former contract manager, Boeing Co.; Staff Sgt. Andrew Bryant, USMC, VMM-263 maintainer; Lt. Col. (ret.) Roy Buckner, USA, former Bell Helicopter and Textron lobbyist; Donald Byrne, V-22 flight test director, Boeing Co.; Gerald Cann, principal deputy assistant secretary of the Navy for research and development 1978–85; Dorman Cannon, former Bell Helicopter tiltrotor test pilot; Cpl. (ret.) Clifford Carlson, USMC, former MOTT member; Ward Carroll, former V-22 spokesman, Naval Air Systems Command; Lt. Col. (ret.) Tom Carter, USMC, V-22 action officer, Pentagon Office of Operational Test and Evaluation; John Christie, husband of former David Chu aide Deborah Christie; Thomas Christie, former director, Pentagon Office of Operational Test and Evaluation; David Chu, former director, Pentagon Office of Program Analysis and Evaluation; Ross Clark, former deputy V-22 program manager, Boeing Helicopter Co.; Capt. Danny Cohlmeyer, USMC, VMM-263 pilot; Lionel Collins, former aide to Rep. Pete Geren, D-Texas; Virginia Copeland, former personal assistant to Dick Spivey; Matthew Cordner, manager, Bell Helicopter XworkS; Joseph Cosgrove, former Boeing Helicopter Co. marketer; Warrant Officer 1 Mike Costello, USMC, former V-22 maintainer; Gunnery Sgt. Joseph Cottle, USMC, former MOTT member, VMM-263 maintainer; Eugene Covert, member, Panel to Review the V-22 Program; Philip Coyle, former director, Pentagon Office of Operational Test and Evaluation; Charles Crawford, former technical director, U.S. Army Aviation Systems Command; Col. (ret.) Jimmie Creech, USMC, first JVX program manager; Col. (ret.) Paul Croisetiere, former V-22 developmental test pilot; Lt. Col. (ret.) Ron "Curly" Culp, USMC, former MOTT member; Jim Curren, senior manager for V-22 operations, integration, and functional test, Boeing Rotorcraft Division; Gen. (ret.) John R. Dailey, USMC, former assistant commandant of the Marine Corps, chairman, Panel to Review the V-22 Program; Brig. Gen. (ret.) Andrew Davis, former director, Marine Corps Public Affairs; Master Sgt. Maurice DeFino, USMC, VMM-263 maintainer; Rudy deLeon, deputy secretary of defense 2000–2001; Col. (ret.) Kevin Dodge, USMC, former MOTT member; Beverly F. Dolan, former chairman, Textron Inc.; Mike J. Dubberly, former branch head for structures, Naval Air Systems Command; Philip Dunford, V-22 program manager, Boeing Integrated Defense Systems; Harry P. Dunn; Col. (ret.) Richard Dunnivan, VMMT-204 commanding officer 2001–2003; Thomas Eager, MIT professor and expert witness in Aircraft 4 crash lawsuit; Gordon England, secretary of the Navy 2001–2003; Ron Erhart, former Bell Helicopter tiltrotor test pilot; Alan Ewing, manager, advanced concept development, Bell Helicopter; Capt. Sara Faibisoff, USMC, VMM-263 pilot; Lt. Gen. (ret.) William Fitch, USMC; Don Frederickson, former deputy undersecretary of defense for tactical warfare programs; Lynn Freisner, former flight test director, Boeing Helicopter Co.; Troy Gaffey, former vice president engineering, Bell Helicopter; Lee Gaillard, freelance military writer and V-22 critic; Paul Gallagher, former producer, CBS-TV's *60 Minutes*; Maj. Eric Garcia, USMC, VMM-263 pilot; Gerald Gard, former Bell Helicopter Washington representative; former Rep. Pete Geren, D-Texas; Maj. (ret.) Pat Gibbons, USMC; Lt. Col. (ret.) Mark Gibson, USMC, former vice president for advanced concept development, Bell Helicopter; Capt. John Gilbert, USMC, VMM-263 pilot; Lt. Gen. (ret.) Buster C. Glosson, USAF; Maj. Gen. Kenneth Glueck, USMC; Art Gravley, chief V-22 engineer, Bell Helicopter; David Gribbin, assistant secretary of defense for legislative affairs 1989–1993; Kenneth Grina, former vice president for engineering, Boeing Vertol; Lt. Col. (ret.) Steve Grohsmeyer, USMC, V-22 developmental test pilot; Connie Gruber; John Hamre, deputy secretary of defense 1997–2000; Carl Harris, former Bell Helicopter spokesman; Derek Hart, former structures engineer, Boeing Helicopter Co.; Michael Hirschberg, VSTOL historian and managing editor, *Vertiflite*; Lt. Col. (ret.) Bob Hodes, USA, military assistant to Undersecretary of the Army Jim Ambrose, 1983; Amoretta Hoeber, former deputy undersecretary of the Army; Roy Hopkins, Bell Helicopter tiltrotor test pilot; Leonard M. "Jack" Horner, former president, Bell Helicopter; Lt. Gen. (ret.) Michael Hough, USMC; Mary Howell, executive vice president, Textron Inc.; Col. (ret.) Tom Huckelbery, USMC; Stevie Jarman; Sue Jarman; Christopher Jehn, former Center for Naval Analyses researcher and assistant secretary of defense for manpower and personnel 1989–93; Webb Joiner, former president, Bell Helicopter; Gen. (ret.) James L. Jones, USMC; Dwayne Jose, former vice president for marketing, Bell Helicopter; Col. (ret.) Matthew Kambrod, USA, former deputy for aviation, office of the assistant secretary of the Army for research, development, and acquisition; Maj. Ken Karika, USMC, VMM-263 pilot; Gen. (ret.) P. X. Kelley, USMC; Frank Kendall, former director of tactical warfare programs, office of undersecretary of defense for acquisitions; Col. (ret.) Robert Kenney, USMCR, Bell-Boeing V-22 program manager; Capt. Brett Knickerbocker, USMC, VMM-263 pilot; Capt. Stewart Kotlinski, USMC, VMM-263 pilot; Maj. David Lane, USMC, VMM-263 pilot; Col. (ret.) Robert Lange, USMC, former Boeing Co. lobbyist; Maj. (ret.) Fred Lash, USMC; Thomas Laux, program executive officer, Naval Air Systems Command; Col. (ret.) William S. Lawrence, USMC, former V-22 deputy program manager, Naval Air Systems Command; Lt. Col. Evan LeBlanc, USMC, VMM-263 pilot; Martin LeCloux, former Boeing Co. V-22 mechanic; Bob Leder, former Bell-Boeing V-22 spokesman; J. Gordon Leishman, professor of aerospace engineering, University of Maryland; Bill Leonard, former Bell Helicopter V-22 developmental test pilot; Nancy Lifset, former aide to Rep. Curt Weldon, R-Pa.; Col. (ret.) Richard Linhart, USMC, Bell Helicopter marketer; Col. (ret.) Darwin Lundberg, USMC, former Boeing Helicopter marketer; Robert Lynn, former vice president for engineering, Bell Helicopter; Tom Macdonald, Boeing Co. test pilot; Capt. (ret.) Jim Magee, USN, former Bell Helicopter marketer; Gen. (ret.) Robert Magnus, USMC; Ron Magnuson, former Bell Helicopter engineer; Joseph Mallen, former president, Boeing Helicopter Co.; Ven Mantegna, Triple Lab engineer, Boeing Rotorcraft Division; Dr. Hans Mark; John O. Marsh, Jr., secretary of the Army 1981–89; Greg Marshall, composites engineer, Bell Helicopter; Stanley Martin, Jr., former vice president for engineering, Bell Helicopter; Kathi Mayan; Lt. Col. (ret.) Gregory McAdams, USMC, former Boeing Helicopter Co. business development manager; Lt. Gen. (ret.) Fred McCorkle, USMC; Dan McCrary, former vice president for contracts, Bell Helicopter; Thomas C. "Kit" McKeon, former Sikorsky Aircraft Corp. marketer and Bell Helicopter consultant; Capt. Justin McKinney, USMC, VMM-263 pilot; Maj. Gen. (ret.) Carl McNair, USA; Tony McVeigh, former Boeing Vertol engineer; Carlton Meyer; Col. (ret.) Parker Miller, USMC; Lt. Gen. (ret.) Thomas H. Miller, Jr., USMC; Maj. Timothy Miller, USMC, VMM-263 pilot; Sgt. (ret.) Michael Moffitt, USMC, former MOTT member; Lt. Col. (ret.) Mike Morgan, USMC, former V-22 operational test director; Gen. (ret.) Thomas Morgan, USMC; Douglas Necessary, former House Armed Services Committee aide; Capt. Andrew Norris, USMC, VMM-263 pilot; Philip Norwine, former Bell Helicopter marketer; Bob Oertel, Bell Helicopter military marketer; Sean O'Keefe, secretary of the Navy 1992–93; Capt. Elizabeth Okoreeh-Baah, USMC, VMM-263 pilot; Col. (ret.) Larry Outlaw, USMC, executive director government affairs, Textron Inc.; Capt. Mike Parrott, USMC, VMM-263 pilot; Bill Peck, former director of V-22 engineering, Boeing Helicopter Co.; Lt. Gen. (ret.) Chuck Pitman, USMC; Col. (ret.) Marvin Pixton, USMC, former aide to Lt. Gen. Thomas Miller; Staff Sgt. Jeffrey Poling, USMC, VMM-263 maintainer; Maj. Gen. (ret.) Arnold Punaro, USMCR, former Senate Armed Services Committee staff director; Chief Warrant Officer 2 Carlos Rios, USMC, VMM-263 maintenance chief; Arthur "Rex" Rivolo; Lt. Col. Paul Rock, Jr., USMC; Pete Rose, former aide to Rep. Pete Geren, D-Texas; Hal Rosenstein, chief engineer for advanced rotorcraft, Boeing Rotorcraft Division; Charles Rudning, former Bell Helicopter manager; Bill Rumberger, Boeing Rotorcraft Division engineer; Maj. Gen. (ret.) Mike Ryan, USMC; Lt. Col. Paul Ryan, USMC, VMM-263 executive officer; Jack Satterfield, former Boeing Rotorcraft Division spokesman; Col. (ret.) Jim Schaefer, USMC, former V-22 program manager; Lt. Col. (ret.) Jim Schafer, USMC, former MOTT pilot; Col. (ret.) William Scheuren, USMC, coordinator for rotary wing programs, office of the undersecretary of defense for research and engineering 1980–82; Maj. Todd Schiro, USMC, VMM-263 pilot; Col. (ret.) Nolan Schmidt, USMC, former V-22 program manager; Paul Schoellhamer, former House Transportation Committee aide; Allen Schoen, former V-22 technology manager, Boeing Helicopter Co.; Col. (ret.) Daniel Schultz, USMC, former V-22 program manager; Lt. Col. Christopher Seymour, USMC, former V-22 developmental and operational test pilot and Osprey squadron commander; Col (ret.) Jim Shaffer, USAF, former MOTT pilot; Sergei Sikorsky, former Sikorsky Aircraft Corp. executive; Clive Sloan, former Bell Helicopter V-22 program manager; Barbara Smith, former V-22 deputy program manager, Naval Air Systems Command; Larry Smith, former aide to Rep. Les Aspin, D-Wis.; Maj. Wes Spaid, USMC, VMM-263 pilot; Dick Spivey; Eric Spivey; Terry Spivey; Michelle Stecyk Kovtonuk; Maj. Gen. (ret.) Story C. Stevens, USA; Carol Sweaney; Katrina Sweaney; Tommy Thomason, former Bell Helicopter XV-15 program manager; Bob Torgerson, Boeing Rotorcraft Division marketer and former spokesman; Col. J. T. Torres, USMC, former MOTT pilot; David Traynham, House Transportation Committee aide; Sgt. Maj. Grant VanOostrom, USMC, VMM-263; Gail Walters; Brig. Gen. Glenn Walters, USMC, former commanding officer, VMX-22; former Rep. Curt Weldon, R-Pa.; Kenneth G. Wernicke, former Bell Helicopter chief tiltrotor engineer; Rodney Wernicke, former Bell Helicopter engineer; Maj. Gen. (ret.) Randy West, USMC; Lt. Col. (ret.) Mike Westman, USMC, former MOTT pilot; Robert Wichser, former Boeing Helicopter Co. executive; Gen. (ret.) John A. Wickham, Jr., USA; Vice Adm. (ret.) Joseph Wilkinson, USN; Pete Williams, assistant secretary of defense for public affairs 1989–93; Grady Wilson, former Boeing Co. test pilot; David Woodley, former Boeing Vertol engineer; former House Speaker Jim Wright, D-Fort Worth; John Zugschwert, former American Helicopter Society executive director, former vice president, Textron Inc.

NOTES

PROLOGUE

Page

3 *the "mishap aircraft"*: Judge Advocate General Manual Report 5830 B 0525 of 21 July 2000, Investigation into the circumstances surrounding the Class "A" aircraft mishap involving an MV-22B Osprey BUNO 165436 that occurred on 8 April 2000 at Marana Northwest Regional Airport near Tucson, Arizona (hereafter Marana JAGMAN Report).

CHAPTER ONE: THE DREAM

Page

9 *Dr. Alexander Klemin, the highly*: Hearings before the Committee on Military Affairs, House of Representatives, Seventy-fifth Congress, Third Session, on H.R. 8143, to authorize the appropriation of funds for the development of the Autogiro, April 26, 27, 1938, U.S. Government Printing Office, Washington, D.C., 1938 (hereafter 1938 House hearings), p. 9.

9 *Only two years earlier*: Orville Wright, Jr., letter to J. Franklin Wilkinson, Sept. 25, 1936. Copy provided to the author by Canadian Mountain Holidays CMH Heli-Hiking, Banff, Canada.

10 *"A vehicle that can take you"*: Proceedings of the Rotating Wing Aircraft Meeting, Philadelphia Chapter, Institute of the Aeronautical Sciences, 1938 (hereafter Rotating Wing Aircraft Meeting Proceedings), p. 63.

10 *One dreamer who shared that vision*: "G. P. Herrick Dies; Aircraft Expert," *New York Times*, Sept. 10, 1955.

10 *In a 1943 article*: Gerard Herrick, "Half Helicopter, Half Airplane," *Mechanix Illustrated*, June 1943.

10 *While serving as a captain*: Gerard P. Herrick, *A Request In The Form Of A Proposal With Regard To Obtaining Certain Data Concerning The Performance Of The Herrick Convertible Airplane Which For Convenience Is Styled "Vertoplane,"* Gerard Post Herrick Collection, National Air and Space Museum Archives (hereafter *Herrick Proposal*), preamble.

11 *Spanish engineer and inventor Juan de la Cierva*: Bruce H. Charnov, *From Autogiro to Gyroplane: The Amazing Survival of an Aviation Technology* (Westport, Conn.: Praeger, 2003), p. 19. For details of the Autogiro's history also see Jay P. Spenser,

Whirlybirds: A History of the U.S. Helicopter Pioneers (Seattle: University of Washington Press, 1998).

11 *Gerard Herrick's initial idea*: Herrick Proposal, p. 2.

12 *With the upper wing locked*: Herrick Proposal, p. 5, and Gerard P. Herrick, "The Herrick Vertoplane," *Aviation Engineering*, January 1932.

15 *America's armed forces numbered*: Allan R. Millett and Peter Maslowski, *For the Common Defense: A Military History of the United States of America* (New York: Free Press, 1984), p. 655.

15 *The first recorded sale*: Donald M. Pattillo, *Pushing the Envelope: The American Aircraft Industry* (Ann Arbor: University of Michigan Press, 1998), p. 6.

15 *The youngest son*: Charnov, *Autogiro to Gyroplane*, pp. 51–75.

16 *Dorsey didn't need much persuading*: 1938 House hearings, pp. 13–14, and Sergei Sikorsky, "Rotary-wing revolution," *Professional Pilot Magazine*, November 2003.

18 *Suddenly a pot of real gold*: Rotating Wing Aircraft Meeting Proceedings.

19 *The Nazis were using it for propaganda*: Hanna Reitsch, *The Sky My Kingdom: Memoirs of the Famous German World War II Test Pilot*, translated by Lawrence Wilson, (Drexel Hill, Pa.: Casemate, 2009). Originally published as *Fliegen—Mein Leben* (Stuttgart: Deutsches Verlags-Anstalt, 1951).

20 *One man in the audience who probably agreed*: Arthur M. Young, *The Bell Notes: A Journey from Physics to Metaphysics* (New York: Delacorte, 1979), pp. 9–15; also Spenser, *Whirlybirds*, and David A. Brown, *The Bell Helicopter Textron Story: Changing the Way the World Flies* (Arlington, Texas: Aerofax, 1995).

22 *Igor Ivanovich Sikorsky was no starry-eyed dreamer*: Spenser, *Whirlybirds*, and Sikorsky, "Rotary-wing revolution."

22 *Another was Lawrence D. Bell*: Brown, *Bell Helicopter Textron Story*, and Young, *Bell Notes*.

23 *The helicopter caught on slowly*: The AAF Helicopter Program, Study No. 222, compiled by Historical Division, Intelligence, T-2, Air Materiel Command, Wright Field, October 1946. Declassified 1950. U.S. Army Air Forces.

24 *"Engineers are devoting increasing attention"*: "Convertaplane: Key to Speed Range," *Aviation Week*, April 12, 1948.

25 *Herrick, now seventy-five years old*: Gerard P. Herrick, "Record of Invention," May 8, 1949, Gerard Post Herrick Collection, National Air and Space Museum Archives.

25 *Burke Wilford, the gyroplane developer*: First Convertible Aircraft Congress Proceedings, Institute of the Aeronautical Sciences, New York, 1949, p. 4.

CHAPTER TWO: THE SALESMAN

Page

27 *A specially modified blue and white*: Brown, *Bell Helicopter Textron Story*, pp. 95, 107.

28 *Tall, rail-thin, and cerebral*: Dick Spivey, Troy Gaffey, Kenneth G. Wernicke, James F. Atkins interviews; Young, *Bell Notes*; Brown, *Bell Helicopter Textron Story*, p. 29; Joe Simnacher, "Pioneer helicopter designer Bartram Kelley dies at age 89," *Dallas Morning News*, Dec. 24, 1998.

29 *Unlike Kelley, the Philadelphia-born Lichten*: Atkins, Gaffey, Spivey, Kenneth G. Wernicke interviews; "Robert Lichten Rites Scheduled for Tuesday," *Dallas Morning News*, Sept. 20, 1971.

30 *LePage came back from Germany with a film*: Rotating Wing Aircraft Meeting Proceedings, p. 124.

30 *Shortly afterward, LePage and Haviland H. Platt*: www.globalsecurity.org/military/systems/aircraft/tiltrotor.htm.

32 *Their frame of mind was illustrated by a cartoon*: American Helicopter, July 1948, p. 25.

33 *Against that backdrop, the U.S. military*: John P. Campbell, *Vertical Takeoff & Landing Aircraft* (New York: Macmillan, 1962).

34 *In the 1990s, aerospace engineer and VTOL*: Michael Hirschberg, interview; also www.vstol.org/wheel/wheel.htm.

36 *The first had been destroyed*: Martin D. Maisel, Demo J. Giulianetti, and Daniel C. Dugan, *The History of the XV-15 Tilt Rotor Research Aircraft From Concept to Flight*, Monographs in Aerospace History No. 17, NASA History Series, National Aeronautics and Space Administration, Washington, D.C., 2000; Robert R. Lynn, "The Rebirth of The Tiltrotor—The 1992 Alexander A. Nikolsky Lecture," *Journal of the American Helicopter Society* 38, no. 1 (January 1993).

41 *In 1962, a board of officers and civilian experts*: Lt. Gen. (ret.) Harold G. Moore and Joseph L. Galloway, *We Were Soldiers Once . . . And Young* (New York: Random House, 1992).

41 *Bell was pumping them out*: Brown, *Bell Helicopter Textron Story*, p. 117; Dorman Cannon, Spivey, Atkins interviews.

48 *Bob Lichten had been killed*: "Robert Lichten Rites Scheduled for Tuesday," *Dallas Morning News*, Sept. 20, 1971.

48 *NASA's interest had actually increased*: Maisel et al. *History of the XV-15*.

50 *Shortly after NASA and the Army*: Spivey interview; also, Spivey's work diaries.

CHAPTER THREE: THE CUSTOMER

Page

52 *The passing of the cake symbolizes*: www.marines.mil/usmc/Documents/CAKE_CUTTING_SCRIPT.pdf.

53 *"The mystique of the Corps transcends"*: Victor H. Krulak, *First to Fight: An Inside View of the U.S. Marine Corps* (Annapolis, Md.: U.S. Naval Institute, 1984), p. xvi.

54 *Barely eighteen months later*: J. Robert Moskin, *The U.S. Marine Corps Story*, 3rd revised edition (Old Saybrook, Conn.: Konecky & Konecky, 1992), p. 430.

54 *Geiger could see it would be suicide*: LTC Robert M. Flanagan, "The V-22 Is Slipping Away," *Proceedings*, August 1990.

55 *This revelation came at an awkward*: Krulak, *First to Fight*; Moskin, *Marine Corps Story*.

56 *Truman later cemented the Marines' victory*: "When I Make a Mistake," *Time*, Sept. 18, 1950, accessed at www.time.com/time/magazine/article/0,9171,813230,00.html.

56 *The helicopter wasn't advanced enough*: Lynn Montross, "U.S. Marine Combat Helicopter Applications," *Journal of the American Helicopter Society* 1, no.1 (January 1956).

57 *The CH-46 was a tandem-rotor*: www.globalsecurity.org/military/systems/aircraft/ch-46.htm.

59 *A military helicopter is a relatively slow*: The account of the Desert One incident is based on author interviews with Col. (ret.) Jim Schaefer, USMC; also Col. (ret.) Charlie A. Beckwith and Donald Knox, *Delta Force* (New York: Avon, 1983), and Mark Bowden, "The Desert One Debacle," *Atlantic Monthly*, May 2006.

68 *The June 30, 1980, cover story*: David C. Martin, "New Light on the Rescue Mission," *Newsweek*, June 30, 1980, pp. 18–20.

72 *Balch also helped Bell keep the XV-15 flying*: Col. (ret.) Bob Balch, Lt. Gen. (ret.) Thomas H. Miller, Jr., USMC, interviews.

73 *After the Navy started investing in the XV-15*: Col. (ret.) William S. Lawrence, USMC. Lawrence provided the author his written report and cockpit audiotapes of his XV-15 flights.

CHAPTER FOUR: THE SALE

Page

77 *James F. Atkins learned that*: Atkins, interview.

78 *The Iran contracts helped Bell remain profitable*: Atkins, Leonard M. "Jack" Horner, interviews.

78 *Jim Atkins saw the end coming*: Atkins, interview.

78 *One day Bell test pilot Dorman Cannon*: Atkins, Cannon, Ron Erhart, interviews.

79 *Not long afterward, a hundred or so Bell*: Atkins, Cannon, Gaffey, Spivey, interviews.

79 *Spivey had proved the previous summer*: Spivey, Cannon, Erhart, Tommy Thomason, interviews. The explanation for the XV-15's rotors hitting the trees is based on Maisel et al., *The History of the XV-15 Tilt Rotor Research Aircraft*. Erhart, copilot on the flight, disagreed with the book and with Cannon, who attributed the tree strike to a loss of altitude due to a failure to gain lift quickly enough. Cannon and Erhart also differed in their recollections of whether Cannon pulled the nose of the XV-15 up at the last moment. "We had sufficient airspeed," Erhart said. "They were making a dadgum movie, or actually they were shooting stills, largely. If we had not been doing that and trying to hotrod a little bit, we would have pulled the aircraft up a little bit. We did not feel that we were going to hit any trees. We just neglected to think—you do that sometimes, you don't think—neglected to think about how far those rotors actually came down below the airplane. All we had to do was pull the nose back a little bit and we would have cleared the trees. We were just trying to hold it straight and hold altitude. We did not lose altitude because we were not going fast enough." Spivey's recollection matched the book and Cannon's. The source for Cannon's statement to the engineers is Cannon.

81 *Bell's parent corporation, a Rhode Island*: Atkins, Horner, interviews.

82 *Cannon and Erhart flew a carefully*: Cannon, Erhart, interviews.

83 *Audiences just adored it*: Susan Heller Anderson, "The Paris Airshow: Wining Dining and Dealing for Military Might," *New York Times*, June 14, 1981.

83 *That same day, the secretary's military*: Lehman, Spivey, Cannon, Erhart, interviews.

84 *Once during his tenure, the deputy*: Hedrick Smith, *The Power Game: How Washington Works* (New York: Ballantine, 1989), p. 193; Lehman, Gen. (ret.) P. X. Kelley, USMC, interviews.

86 *One night toward the end of the air show*: Spivey, Atkins, Horner, interviews.

86 *The Navy Department had just done a study*: Magnus, Spivey et al., interviews.

87 *The Marines had been trying for more than a decade*: Balch, Lundberg, Magnus, Spivey, Kelley, interviews.

87 *seemed to be leaning toward the Model 360*: Lundberg, Magnus, Kelley, interviews.

87 *On September 24, Kelley was scheduled*: Kelley, Lehman, interviews. The dialogue was recalled by Kelley.

89 *his administration's first defense budget*: 1981 *Congressional Quarterly Almanac*, Washington, D.C. (hereafter *CQ Almanac*), p. 192.

89 *Reagan's new undersecretary*: Scheuren, interview.

90 *Joint programs had been in vogue*: Smith, *Power Game*, p. 199.

90 *literally turned into shouting matches*: Ingemar Dörfer, *Arms Deal: The Selling of the F-16* (New York: Praeger, 1983), p. 22.

91 *In August, Scheuren and Magnus wrote a memo*: Scheuren, Magnus, interviews. The quotation from the memo comes from LTC Robert M. Flanagan, "The V-22 Is Slipping Away," *U.S. Naval Institute Proceedings*, August 1990.

91 *who in turn sent a memo to Lehman*: Gen. P. X. Kelley, Memorandum for the Secretary of the Navy A/WJW/jpc 10 Sep 1981, Subj: Rotary Wing Aircraft Development, Ref: USDRE Memo of 27 Aug 81, Department of the Navy, Headquarters United States Marine Corps.

91 *Kelley didn't even mention the tiltrotor*: Gen. P. X. Kelley, Memorandum for the Record ACMC/CS:swb 28 September 1981, Subj: HXM Conversation with the SecNav, 24 September 1981, Department of the Navy, Headquarters United States Marine Corps.

93 *Troutman, who died of cancer in 2000, was smooth*: "Defense: How the weapons lobby works in Washington," *Business Week*, Feb. 12, 1979: Atkins, Horner, Norwine, Spivey, former House Speaker Jim Wright, D-Fort Worth, interviews.

94 *called this natural alliance*: Smith, *Power Game*, p. 736.

95 *The Paris Air Show was a first for NASA*: Maisel, *History of the XV-15*.

95 *Bell wasted no time putting its XV-15 to use*: Cannon, Erhart, Roy Hopkins, Spivey, interviews. Goldwater's comments in flight were recollected by Cannon. Goldwater's comment in the hangar was recalled by Hopkins.

97 *When Balch, Lundberg, and Creech finished their flights*: Atkins, Balch, Creech, Lundberg, interviews. The quotes were recollected by Balch.

97 *Two weeks after Atkins and the Marine colonels talked*: Creech, Col. (ret.) Jim, USMC. "The Tilt-Rotor MV-22 Osprey, Transport Vehicle of the Future," *Amphibious Warfare Review*, Fall/Winter 1986.

98 *Reports in the trade press*: "Washington Roundup," *Aviation Week & Space Technology*, Dec. 20, 1982. The $41 billion figure was used by Sen. Ted Stevens, R-Alaska, in a July 28, 1983, Senate Defense Appropriations Subcommittee hearing.

98 *The JVX program office also assembled*: Charles Crawford, Magnus, Lt. Col. (ret.)

Gregory McAdams, USMC, interviews. Crawford provided the author a copy of the report, titled *NASA Technology Assessment of Capability for Advanced Joint Vertical Lift Aircraft (JVX)*, Summary Report, Analysis and Preparation Chaired by AVRADCOM, May 1983.

99 *Spivey didn't know it at the time*: Boeing-Vertol Company Inter-Office Memorandum by R. F. Wischer, Dec. 21, 1981, Subject: Advanced Technology Program. Copy provided to the author by Wischer.

99 *who were antsy about the course*: Barrow testified that year at a Senate Armed Services Committee hearing: "My concern is that we may not be able to retain our capability [for amphibious assault] until the arrival of the new aircraft that has been proposed." Hearing on Department of Defense Authorization of Appropriations for Fiscal Year 1983, Senate Commmittee on Armed Services, Ninety-eighth Congress, First Session, Feb. 25, 1982, p. 1095. White told the House Armed Services Committee a couple of weeks later that the Marines were "planning to procure an off-the-shelf helicopter" as insurance "until this new program, the JVX, becomes a reality." Hearing on Department of Defense Authorizations of Appropriations for Fiscal Year 1983, House Committee on Armed Services, Procurement and Military Nuclear Systems Subcommittee, March 9, 1982, p. 402.

100 *For a fitness report, Balch once*: Magnus provided the author copies of his fitness reports from the period.

101 *After the program was announced*: Atkins, Lehman, interviews. Atkins recalled the dialogue.

102 *JVX program office invited representatives from twenty-five companies*: "Services Favor Tilt Rotor For Vertical Lift Aircraft," *Aviation Week & Space Technology*, July 5, 1982.

102 *The three service secretaries had finally signed an agreement*: 4 June 1982 Memorandum of Understanding on the Joint Service Advanced Vertical Lift Aircraft Development Program (JVX).

102 *Fitch would tell a Senate committee*: Senate Defense Appropriations Subcommittee hearings on Department of Defense Appropriations for Fiscal Year 1984, Ninety-eighth Congress, First Session, July 28, 1983, p. 283.

103 *The Army, though, which had started out*: Lt. Col (ret.) Bob Hodes, USA, Amoretta Hoeber, Col. (ret.) Matthew Kambrod, USA, James Ambrose (by e-mail), interviews.

105 *The XV-15 weighed about 10,000 pounds*: Maisel et al., *History of the XV-15*, p. 131, as well as Cannon, Erhart, interviews.

105 *The tiltrotor the services wanted*: Joint Advanced Vertical Lift Aircraft (JVX) Joint Services Operational Requirement (JSOR), Dec. 14, 1982 (hereafter 1982 JSOR).

CHAPTER FIVE: THE MACHINE

Page

107 *he quickly lived up to his introduction*: Rotating Wing Aircraft Meeting Proceedings, p. 11.

110 *A couple of years before the JVX came along*: Spivey, Rodney, Wernicke, interviews.

111 *Atkins had favored the bigger machine*: Atkins, interview.

111 *He was utterly absorbed*: Kenneth G. Wernicke, Gaffey, interviews.

111 *When he saw them, he hit the ceiling*: Kenneth G. Wernicke, interview.

113 *the tip of the closest rotor would have to clear*: 1982 JSOR, p. 6.

113 *envisioned a tiltrotor weighing about 20,000–25,000 pounds empty*: Magee, interview.

113 *requirements for "survivability" that far outstripped*: 1982 JSOR, Magnus, Magee, interviews.

113 *Navair set an upper limit of 31,886 pounds*: Ross Clark, interview. V-22 Osprey Specification Change Notice No. 280, provided to the author by Clark, cites the 31,866 pounds figure as a requirement in Naval Air Systems Command document SD-572-1, the engineering specifications for the Osprey.

114 *Most helicopters have disk loading*: "Outlook/Specification: Rotary-Wing Aircraft," *Aviation Week & Space Technology*, Jan. 16, 2006, p 89.

114 *Thanks to its small rotor diameter and heavy weight*: Descriptions of the design process and analysis of the relative advantages and disadvantages of the JVX design come from author interviews with Kenneth G. Wernicke, Bill Peck, Allen Schoen, Stanley Martin, Jr., Derek Hart, David Woodley, Robert Lynn, Troy Gaffey, and other engineers who took part in the project.

126 *observed a 1989 master's thesis*: Danny Roy Smith, "The Influence of Contract Type in Program Execution/V-22 Osprey: A Case Study," Naval Postgraduate School, Monterey, Calif., December 1989, p. 34.

128 *Grina didn't want "that junk on my airplane"*: William Rumberger, interview.

129 *The flex ring was 300 pounds lighter and cost*: Osprey Fax, A Bell-Boeing Team Publication, vol. 2, no. 10, Sept. 23, 1991.

129 *One of the most stinging arguments with Navair*: Schoen, Mike J. Dubberly, Martin, Hart, interviews. The quote from Grina was recollected by Hart.

130 *"Honeycomb with you guys is like a fungus"*: Dubberly, interview.

130 *refused to meet or talk with him anymore*: Hart, interview.

130 *One day Dubberly's boss came to him*: Dubberly, interview.

131 *"Get your ass down here"*: Hart, Dubberly, interviews. Hart recollected the quote. Dubberly didn't dispute it.

132 *structure cost about $1,000 a pound*: Ben R. Rich and Leo Janos, *Skunk Works* (Boston: Little, Brown, 1994), p. 64.

132 *Composites were supposed to make the JVX*: Schoen, Hart, Clark, Kenneth G. Wernicke, interviews.

132 *Three or four out of every ten frames and formers*: Hart, interview.

134 *'Screw those guys'*: Kenneth G. Wernicke, interview.

CHAPTER SIX: YOUNG WINSTON'S OSPREY

Page

136 *Bell's suggestions were*: Spivey work diaries.

138 *Ambrose announced he was pulling the Army out*: James R. Ambrose, Memorandum for Director of the Army Staff, Subject: Army Withdrawal from JVX Program, 13 May 1983, Department of the Army, Office of the Under Secretary.

139 *The July hearing was held*: Senate Defense Appropriations Subcommittee hearings on Department of Defense Appropriations for Fiscal Year 1984, Ninety-eighth Congress, First Session, July 28, 1983, p. 283.

139 *Chu's staff had done some back-of-the-envelope*: David S. C. Chu, interview.

140 *Magnus had armed the general*: Magnus, interview.

140 *Marsh preferred to deal with policy*: John O. Marsh, Jr., interview.

141 *The DRB met*: Defense Resources Board attendance record Sept. 19, 1983, and JVX briefing slides prepared by Magnus, provided to the author by the Office of the Secretary of Defense Historian's Office.

141 *Wickham began the discussion*: Kelley, Wickham, interviews. The quotes were recalled by Kelley. Wickham didn't recall Kelley's wisecrack but said he and Kelley were good friends and the quip would have been in character for Kelley.

144 *Spivey assured reporter Joe Simnacher*: Joe Simnacher, "Tilt-rotor aircraft utilizes copter, plane technologies," *Dallas Morning News*, May 16, 1983.

145 *One of the first projects that caught Mark's eye*: Hans Mark, interview.

146 *One of Lehman's big ideas for the Osprey*: Lehman, interview.

147 *Bell-Boeing's teaming agreement*: Bell Helicopter Textron Inc.–Boeing Vertol Company JVX Teaming Agreement, May 28, 1982, p. 2. Copy provided to the author by a former Boeing official.

147 *Bell and Boeing Vertol started negotiating*: Dan McCrary, interviews; also, Smith, "Influence of Contract Type," p. 8.

148 *hoping to reason with Lehman*: Horner, Mallen, Beverly Dolan, Lehman, Brig. Gen. (ret.) Harry Bendorf, USAF, interviews.

149 *it would probably cost at least $100 million more*: McCrary, Horner, interviews.

149 *The new deal set a target price*: Dean G. Sedivy, *Bureaucracies at War: The V-22 Osprey Program.* Executive Research Project, Industrial College of the Armed Forces, National Defense University, Fort McNair, Washington, D.C., 1992, p. 47.

150 *Lehman soon threw the companies another curve*: John Arvin, Lehman, Martin, Schaefer, Barbara Smith, Thomason, Woodley, interviews.

152 *Necessary finished his study*: Douglas Necessary, interview; "Unusual Rebuttal by Bell-Boeing Challenges House Panel's V-22 Osprey Report," *Defense News*, April 14, 1986, and "Programming a Revolutionary Aircraft: An Interview with Col. Harold W. Blot, USMC, Program Manager for the V-22 Osprey," *Amphibious Warfare Review,* Fall/Winter 1986, p. 50.

154 *That spring, the Corps asked the Center*: The paper was among eighty studies on the V-22 Osprey done by the Center for Naval Analyses between 1983 and 2006, according to a list provided to the author by a CNA official. A more senior CNA official declined by e-mail to release this and other studies to the author, explaining that they were "informal documents" and thus "not available for further dissemination outside of CNA."

157 *Blot showed them what he meant*: Blot, Cannon, Erhart, interviews.

159 *Blot went to Ridley Park one day*: Blot, Philip Dunford, interviews.

159 *In June 1986, Lehman announced*: Navy Secretary John Lehman, letter to Senator Barry Goldwater, chairman of the Senate Armed Services Committee, June 17, 1986.

159 *By November, Bell and Boeing had selected*: "V-22 Review Will Focus on Coast,

ASW Mission," *Aviation Week & Space Technology*, Nov. 17, 1986, p. 23.

159 *Bell got the Federal Aviation Administration*: "Civil Tiltrotor Missions and Applications: A Research Study," Summary Final Report, (NASA CR 177452), Contract NAS2–12393, July 1987.

160 *The FAA and the U.S. Department of Transportation*: "VTOL Intercity Feasibility Study, June 1987, for The Port Authority of NY & NJ," by Hoyle, Tanner & Associates, Inc., in association with J.A Nammack Associates, Inc., William E. Broadwater. John Zugschwert provided the author a copy of the executive summary of the report.

160 *On November 18, two House subcommittees*: Joint Hearing before the Subcommittee on Transportation, Aviation and Materials of the Committee on Science, Space and Technology, and the Subcommittee on Aviation of the Committee on Public Works and Transportation, U.S. House of Representatives, One Hundredth Congress, First Session, Nov. 18, 1987.

160 *the Osprey section of the shop floor at Ridley Park*: Jim Curren, interview.

160 *A few months later, the Army*: Naval Air Systems Command Chronology of V-22 Airframe Program (hereafter Navair Chronology).

161 *The fuselage wasn't really complete*: Curren, Hart et al., interviews.

162 *They hired Hollywood producers*: Bob Torgerson, Spivey, interviews; Bell Helicopter video of the event.

164 *In a September 1988 interview*: "U.S. Pursues Sales of V-22 to Foreign Military Services," *Aviation Week & Space Technology*, Sept. 12, 1988.

164 *overrun their $1.8 billion FSD contract badly*: McCrary, Horner, Spivey, Webb Joiner, William Anders, interviews.

166 *The aircraft's total weight was 39,450 pounds*: The weight was cited in the "Mondo Cucina Accords." Other details of the first flight come from author interviews with Cannon, Dunford, Spivey, and others who were present.

CHAPTER SEVEN: ONE PERIOD OF DARKNESS

Page

169 *he had been a $10,000-a-month consultant*: The figure comes from Tower's Jan. 19, 1989, Financial Disclosure Report to the Office of Government Ethics. A summary of his consulting work included in the record of his confirmation hearings listed, among other things he did for Textron, "Briefed senior management on defense and commercial future for V-22. Attended V-22 roll-out."

170 *Weyrich himself had seen Tower*: 1989 CQ Almanac, p. 404.

170 *Four days later, President Bush*: 1989 CQ Almanac, p. 410.

170 *Cheney thought the balance of power*: Christopher Jehn, interview. Other former Cheney aides agreed with Jehn's assessment.

171 *Bush agreed to take an additional $10 billion*: 1989 CQ Almanac, p. 427.

171 *When the budget deal was announced*: Spivey, interview. Bendorf was unable to recall the conversation.

172 *His parents had derived "S.C." from Chinese characters*: Chu, interview. The quotation from the *Analects* of Confucius can be found on the website of Brooklyn College at http://academic.brooklyn.cuny.edu/core9/phalsall/texts/analects.html

176 *Cheney had known he would face resistance*: Hearings on National Defense Authorization Act for Fiscal Year 1990—H.R. 2461, Committee on Armed Services, House of Representatives, One Hundred First Congress, First Session, April 25, 1989, p. 1.

177 *Three days after Cheney testified*: Letter to Commander, Naval Air Systems Command, from R.C. Broadhurst, Senior Manager, V-22 Contracts Bell-Boeing Team, April 28, 1989. Copy provided to the author by Curt Weldon.

177 *the companies didn't want to pour*: McCrary, Robert C. Broadhurst, interviews.

178 *Cheney signaled his first week in office*: Lee Ewing and Charlie Schill, "Cheney Criticizes Gen. Welch for contacts with Hill," *Air Force Times*, April 3, 1989.

179 *First Gray called the Osprey*: Hearings on Amended Defense Authorization Request for Fiscal Years 1990 and 1991, Committee on Armed Services, United States Senate, One Hundred First Congress, First Session, May 4, 1989, p. 173.

179 *A week after Gray's testimony*: "The Civil Tiltrotor: Is It Economically Viable?," *Rotor & Wing International*, August 1989, p. 34; Carl H. Lavin, "Copter-Plane Called a Cure for Crowded Airports," *New York Times*, May 15, 1989, p. A12.

179 *A few days later, Blot was confronted*: Blot, Glosson, interviews.

180 *Within days, Blot got orders*: Blot, Lt. Gen. (ret.) Chuck Pitman, interviews.

182 *"We are not going to build an airplane"*: "European Firms Agree to Joint Bell-Boeing in Marketing V-22," *Aviation Week & Space Technology*, June 19, 1989, p. 37.

183 *When the Armed Services Committee took up*: Weldon, Pete Rose, Parker Miller, Larry Smith, interviews; 1989 CQ *Almanac*, p. 433.

184 *If the next defense budget included*: "Bell, Boeing Push V-22 Flight Test Program," *Aviation Week & Space Technology*, Oct. 16, 1989, p. 38.

184 *Cheney and his aides recognized*: Sean O'Keefe, interview.

184 *A week later, Cheney showed them*: Kathryn Jones, "V-22 backers seek to restore funding," *Dallas Morning News*, Dec. 6, 1989.

185 *Weldon already had organized an Osprey team*: Weldon, Rose, Parker Miller, Nancy Lifset, interviews. Weldon provided the author a copy of his "V-22 Action Plan," which outlined the tasks assigned to members of his strategy group.

186 *A few months later, Bell delivered one*: Weldon, Maj. (ret.) Fred Lash, interviews. Weldon provided the author a copy of the "Dear Colleague" letter. Lash showed the author the poster.

188 *The XV-15 had been sitting on the parking lot*: Erhart, Spivey, Horner, Weldon, Lionel Collins, David Traynham, interviews. Erhart described the XV-15's flight.

189 *"This is the most significant contribution"*: Bell Helicopter Textron video.

189 *The Los Angeles Times described how*: Healy, Melissa. "Warplane Survives Attacks," *The Los Angeles Times*, Nov. 29, 1990.

190 *Even General Gray, the commandant*: "Washington Roundup," *Aviation Week & Space Technology*, May 8, 1989, p. 15.

191 *In his memo, IDA analyst L. Dean Simmons*: IDA System Evaluation Division, Interoffice Memorandum, 20 August 1989, from Dr. L. Dean Simmons to members of the V-22 study group. Curt Weldon provided the author a copy of the Simmons memo, including the Sikorsky white paper.

192 *The Osprey camp was ecstatic*: IDA Report R-371, Assessment of Alternatives for the

V-22 Assault Aircraft Program (U), Executive Overview, June 1990. Curt Weldon provided a declassified copy to the author.

192 *Chu told the subcommittee*: Hearing Before a Subcommittee of the Committee on Appropriations, United States Senate, One Hundred First Congress, Second Session, Special Hearing, July 19, 1990, p. 41.

193 *Commandant Gray had derided the idea*: Nicole Weisensee, *States News Service*, Subject: Osprey, Feb. 21, 1990.

193 *Schaefer had instructions from Cheney's office*: Schaefer, interview.

195 *On December 4, a Marine Corps test pilot*: "Shipboard Tests Confirm V-22's Operating Capability," *Aviation Week & Space Technology*, Jan. 14, 1991, p. 36; Schaefer, interview.

196 *Schaefer was ready*: Schaefer, interview.

196 *Five seconds into the flight*: Grady Wilson, Lynn Freisner, Schaefer, interviews; Bell Helicopter video; 2 March 1992 Judge Advocate General Manual Report, Aircraft Mishap Involving V-22 Osprey Aircraft Number Five That Occurred on 11 Jun 91 at Boeing Helicopter Flight Test Facility, Greater Wilmington DE Airport, (hereafter Aircraft Five Crash Report).

199 *"The point of the prototypes"*: Kelvyn Anderson and Lyn A. E. McCafferty, "V-22 just off grounding: Osprey tests were in 'safety stand down' last week due to problems," *Delaware County Daily Times*, June 12, 1991.

CHAPTER EIGHT: SURVIVABILITY

Page

200 *Bell Helicopter test pilot Ron Erhart*: Erhart, Wilson, interviews.

201 *The Navy Department's investigators didn't blame*: Aircraft Five Crash Report; Wilson, Freisner, Clark, Tom Macdonald, Donald Byrne, interviews.

203 *At Weldon's urging, the United Auto Workers*: Weldon, Geren, interviews.

203 *Two years later, now sure*: "Outgoing Marine Commandant Makes Strong Pitch for V-22," *Aerospace Daily*, May 20, 1991.

205 *pared the fleet to a mere 234*: "U.S. Marines Press for Decision on V-22 Tiltrotor," *Defense News*, Sept. 9, 1991.

205 *One day that autumn*: Col. (ret.) Parker Miller, Weldon, interviews.

205 *Shortly after General Carl E. Mundy, Jr., succeeded*: Schaefer, interview.

205 *In February, after Cheney*: Michael D. Towle, "The Osprey's fate is still up in the air," *Fort Worth Star-Telegram*, Feb. 17, 1991.

206 *The wing stow mechanism*: The description of the Osprey's shortcomings as of 1992 come from interviews with engineers and program officials at the time as well as the following documents: Naval Air Test Center Technical Report No. RW-21R-91, MV-22 Aircraft Navy Development Test DT-IIB, 16 July 1991; Memorandum for the Under Secretary of Defense (Acquisition), From: Gerald Cann, Assistant Secretary of the Navy (Research, Development and Acquisition), Subject: V-22 Osprey; "Review of the V-22 Aircraft Program," Feb. 28, 1992; and Audit Report, Office of the Inspector General, Department of Defense, June 14, 1994.

206 *The only way to get the Osprey ready*: Schaefer, interview.

207 *Miller drafted legislation*: Parker Miller, interview.

207 *As Miller and Howell sat*: Parker Miller, Weldon, interviews.

207 *The final bill included $790 million*: Letter from Defense Secretary Dick Cheney to Bob Michel, Republican Leader, House of Representatives, July 2, 1992.

208 *O'Keefe sent a letter to the House and Senate*: Letter from Sean O'Keefe, Comptroller, Department of Defense, to Thomas S. Foley, Speaker of the House of Representatives, Jan. 26, 1992.

209 *In May 1991, Richards and several*: "Richards joins effort to attract funding for new tiltrotor airplane," United Press International, May 13, 1991.

209 *on March 5, ABC-TV hosted a debate*: ABC News Transcript, March 5, 1992, Super Tuesday Debate.

210 *A few months earlier*: Spivey, Mary Howell, interviews.

211 *On April 2, 1992, Cheney sent Congress*: Letter from Defense Secretary Dick Cheney to Thomas S. Foley, Speaker of the House of Representatives, April 2, 1992.

211 *Soon others in the Osprey camp*: Rep. H. Martin Lancaster, D-N.C., At-Large Majority Whip, "Dear Colleague" letter to members of the House of Representatives, May 8, 1992.

211 *"When the check cutting office"*: "Tongue Twister," *Inside the Pentagon*, May 21, 1992.

211 *On June 3, 1992, Sean O'Keefe came*: O'Keefe, interviews; letter from the Comptroller General of the United States to the President of the Senate and the Speaker of the House of Representatives, GAO/OGC-92–11, June 3, 1992.

211 *Two days after the GAO ruled*: Tom Belden, "Backers of Osprey growing optimistic," *Philadelphia Inquirer*, June 14, 1992.

212 *wrote Clinton a letter inviting him*: Letter from Sen. Lloyd Bentsen, D-Texas, and Rep. Jack Brooks, D-Texas, to Gov. Bill Clinton, June 23, 1992.

212 *Cheney sent Congress a letter offering*: Letter from Defense Secretary Dick Cheney to Thomas S. Foley, Speaker of the House of Representatives, July 2, 1992.

212 *nothing more than a face-saving move*: 1992 *CQ Almanac*, p. 505.

212 *On the House floor later*: Congressional Record, July 29, 1992, p. E2294.

213 *Schaefer decided it would be a good time*: Schaefer, interview.

215 *There were mechanical problems*: Martin LeCloux, Tom Macdonald, Col. (ret.) Paul Croisetiere, interviews.

216 *Dodge's Multiservice Operational Test Team*: Col. (ret.) Kevin Dodge, interview.

217 *The wives passed the time*: Michelle Stecyk Kovtonuk, interview; Nathan Gorenstein, "Mission to Display Military Aircraft Was Fatally Flawed," *Philadelphia Inquirer*, Nov. 14, 1993.

217 *On July 12, Lieutenant Colonel Paul Martin*: V-22 Court of Inquiry Report, Investigation of the Circumstances Surrounding the Loss of V-22 UNO 163914 on 20 July 1992 Near Quantico, Va. (hereafter Court of Inquiry Report).

218 *Sunday afternoon, Sullivan went over*: Macdonald, Wilson, interviews.

218 *On Friday, he had given an engagement ring*: Joe Hart, "Crash took her love: Osprey tragedy claimed pilot who was to wed today," *Delaware County Daily Times*, July 30, 1992.

218 *Sullivan stayed at the hangar*: Court of Inquiry Report.

218 *Wilson and Macdonald went to the bar*: Macdonald, Wilson, interviews.

219 *Joyce got his chance to fly*: LeCloux, Macdonald, Wilson, interviews.

219 *Mayan gladly would have given Joyce his seat*: Kathi Mayan, interview.

219 *That Monday morning, Michelle*: Kovtonuk, interview.

220 *About four hours later*: Court of Inquiry Report: Cockpit Voice Transcript, V-22 BUNO 163914 Mishap 20 July 20, 1992. The account of the flight is based on the Cockpit Voice Transcript and interviews with Macdonald and Wilson.

226 *The commandant, General Carl Mundy*: Schaefer, interview; Gorenstein, "Mission to Display."

228 *Alerted by radio*: Dodge, interviews. The description of the crash is based on a video of the mishap provided to the author by Bell Helicopter.

229 *A half hour or so later*: Macdonald, Wilson, interviews. Wilson recalled the dialogue.

230 *It rang that afternoon*: Schaefer, interview.

231 *His first act was to seize*: Dodge, interview.

231 *The next day, Pentagon spokesman*: U.S. Defense Department Regular Briefing, Briefer: Pete Williams, July 21, 1992.

231 *That evening, Curt Weldon*: Congressional Record—House, July 21, 1992, p. H 6336.

232 *As Geren had told*: Barton Gellman, "Accident Is Latest Twist For Troubled Program," *Washington Post*, July 21, 1992.

232 *Crashes were nothing new in aviation*: Geren, interview.

232 *Navy scuba divers found Aircraft 4*: Court of Inquiry Report.

233 *Michelle Stecyk buried her husband*: Kovtonuk, interview.

233 *Eleven days before*: Bob Torgerson, Weldon, interviews.

234 *he wasn't sure the Marines really needed*: The Status of the V-22 Tiltrotor Aircraft Program, Hearing Before the Procurement and Military Nuclear Systems Subcommittee and the Research and Development Subcommittee of the Committee on Armed Services, House of Representatives, One Hundred Second Congress, Second Session, Aug. 5, 1992, p. 9.

234 *The Navy Department announced*: Memorandum for Correspondents No. 279-M, Navy Office of Information, Sept. 29, 1992.

235 *Analyses of wreckage*: Court of Inquiry Report.

236 *In a case that lasted nearly a decade*: United States District Court for the Eastern District of Pennsylvania, Civil Action Nos. 94-cv-01818/04343/04343; United States Court of Appeals for the Third Circuit, Nos. 99–2030/99–2051.

237 *Clinton endorsed the Osprey*: "CLINTON: WHAT? NO TRIP TO THE ALAMO?," *Hotline*, Aug. 28, 1992.

237 *In September, Gore visited*: Transcript provided to the author by Bell Helicopter.

237 *Eleven days after that debate*: U.S. General Accounting Office, Report to the Chairman, Committee on Armed Services, House of Representatives, Navy Aviation: V-22 Development—Schedule Extended, Performance Reduced, and Costs Increased, January 1994, p. 3.

238 *which had cost Bell and Boeing*: Tony Capaccio and Eric Rosenberg, "DCAA Audits Say Osprey Costs are Soaring As Technical Questions Persist," *Defense Week*, Dec. 9, 1991.

238 *After Quayle left*: Schaefer, interview.

CHAPTER NINE: ANOTHER PERIOD OF DARKNESS

Page

241 *He and three Bell engineers*: United States Design Patent US D453,317 S, filed Dec. 1, 2000, by John A. DeTore, Richard F. Spivey, Malcolm P. Foster, and Tom L. Wood. The Quad TiltRotor patent was assigned to Bell Helicopter Textron Inc. and granted Feb. 5, 2002.

241 *Spivey had briefed General Jones*: Spivey, Gen. (ret.) James L. Jones, interviews.

242 *Shaffer and Sweaney exchanged grins*: Col (ret.) Jim Shaffer, interview.

243 *"Every few decades"*: U.S. Department of Defense News Transcript, Tiltrotor Technology Presentation, Remarks As Delivered by Secretary of Defense William S. Cohen, The Pentagon, Washington, D.C., Wednesday, Sept. 8, 1999.

243 *No one asked Cohen to clarify*: U.S. Department of Defense News Transcript, Media Availability at Tilt-rotor Day with Secretary of Defense William S. Cohen, Sept. 8, 1999.

244 *Over the past seven years*: Statistics on CH-46E Class A mishaps in fiscal years 1993–1999 provided to the author by the Public Affairs Office of the Naval Safety Center, Norfolk, Va.

244 *In 1998, General Charles Krulak*: Hearings before the Committee on Armed Services, United States Senate, One Hundred Fifth Congress, Second Session, Feb. 5, 1998. Quoted in "Clippings: CMC Reports to Congress," Osprey Fax, Bell-Boeing Tiltrotor Team, vol. 9, no. 1, March 26, 1998.

245 *the cost of each Osprey*: Audit Report, Inspector General Department of Defense, V-22 Osprey Joint Advanced Vertical Aircraft, Report No. D-2000–174, Aug. 15, 2000, p. 2; hereafter Aug. 15, 2000, DOD IG Audit.

245 *80 percent of the engineering drawings were new*: Stanley W. Kandebo, "V-22 Team Lowering Osprey Production Costs," *Aviation Week & Space Technology*, Nov. 15, 1993, p. 58.

245 *One of the biggest differences*: Hart, Byrne, interviews.

246 *Aluminum frames for the Osprey*: Stanley W. Kandebo, "V-22 Modifications Focus on Cost, Producibility," *Aviation Week & Space Technology*, May 22, 1995, p. 35.

246 *no longer mostly composite, just 43 percent*: Bill Norton, *Bell Boeing V-22 Osprey Tiltrotor Tactical Transport* (Hinckley, U.K.: Midland, 2004), p. 52.

246 *The advent of liquid crystal displays*: "Situational Awareness Prompts Cockpit Redesign," *Aviation Week & Space Technology*, May 22, 1995, p. 38.

247 *Navair approved the revamped design*: John Boatman, "Osprey final design is frozen in latest review," *Jane's Defence Weekly*, Jan. 21, 1995, p. 6.

247 *Three years later*: Navair Chronology.

247 *Critics derided it*: Franklin C. Spinney and John J. Shanahan, "Great Idea! Buy First, Then Find Out If It Flies," *Washington Post*, Feb. 11, 2001, p. B1.

248 *As of 1995, the "self-deployment" requirement*: Operational Requirements Document (ORD) for the Joint Multi-Mission Vertical Lift Aircraft (JMVX), March 4, 1995, Serial Numbers: 384–88–94 (USN), AAS 48 (USMC), 021921 (SOC), p. 5.

248 *The Osprey wasn't the only program*: William B. Scott, "New Global Pressures Reshape Flight Testing," *Aviation Week & Space Technology*, June 12, 1995, p. 62.

252 *wrote the OPEVAL plan*: Shaffer, interview.

252 *MOTT leader Sweaney talked*: Carol Sweaney, interview.

253 *Sweaney liked to use Rock*: Shaffer, interview.

254 *In 1990, two Japanese companies*: "Costs of Developing Civil Tilt-Rotor Reduce Chances of Japanese Role," *Aviation Week & Space Technology*, May 7, 1990, p. 57; "Lack of partners forces Ishida to abandon TW-68 tiltwing aircraft," *Aerospace Daily*, June 25, 1993.

255 *Navair and the Marines sent one*: " 'Realites' From Le Bourget," *Aviation Week & Space Technology*, June 19, 1995, p. 86.

256 *In his thesis, Magnus*: Robert Magnus, "An Assessment of Civil Tiltrotor Market Potential," MBA thesis, Graduate School of Business, Strayer College, Washington, D.C., August 1992, p. 44.

257 *Besides those in the United States*: Bell Helicopter Textron Inc. press handout, April 2000.

257 *"Tell us what it does"*: Shaffer, Lt. Gen. (ret.) Fred McCorkle, interviews.

258 *The MOTT started OPEVAL in November*: Combined Operational Test & Evaluation and Live Fire Test & Evaluation Report on the V-22 Osprey, Director, Operational Test & Evaluation, Department of Defense, Nov. 17, 2000, and author interviews with MOTT members.

262 *They asked fundamental questions*: Shaffer, interview.

262 *The mission to Marana on April 8*: The account of the mission and crash at Marana is based on Judge Advocate General Manual Report of 21 July 2000, Investigation into the circumstances surrounding the Class "A" aircraft mishap involving an MV-22B Osprey BUNO 165436 that occurred on 8 April 2000 at Marana Northwest Regional Airport near Tucson, Arizona (hereafter Marana JAGMAN Report); "Nighthawk 71 Cockpit Video" and Transcript of Cockpit Voice Recording A/C 165433 8 April 00; and author interviews with Staff Sgt. (ret.) Julius Banks, Lt. Col. Anthony Bianca, Sgt. (ret.) Michael Moffitt, Rock, Lt. Col. (ret.) Jim Schafer, Shaffer, and Lt. Col. (ret.) Mike Westman.

274 *Sweaney had been through*: Paul Richter, "Osprey's Hopes and Heartbreak," *Los Angeles Times*, Feb. 19, 2001; Carol Sweaney, interview.

277 *Westman was leaning in the doorway*: Westman, interview. McCorkle confirmed the phone call and what he said to Sweaney but didn't recall hearing Westman's remark.

277 *Three days after the crash*: U.S. Department of Defense News Transcript, DOD News Briefing, April 11, 2000.

278 *Three days after McCorkle briefed the press*: "Doubts About the High-Risk Osprey," *New York Times*, April 14, 2000.

278 *Others called for an end*: "Aircraft a lemon with wings," *Milwaukee Journal Sentinel*, April 10, 2000.

279 *"It's a terrible tragedy"*: Dan Hardy, "Osprey craft has seen some other troubles," *Philadelphia Inquirer*, April 10, 2000.

279 *McCorkle was back in the Pentagon briefing room*: U.S. Department of Defense News Transcript, DOD News Briefing, April 20, 2000.

279 *McCorkle addressed the unit*: McCorkle, Banks, Col. J. T. Torres, interviews.

280 *Sweaney called a meeting*: Banks, Shaffer, Westman, interviews.

280 *McCorkle was in a good mood*: U.S. Department of Defense News Transcript, DOD News Briefing, May 9, 2000; McCorkle, interview.

283 *McCorkle was back in the Pentagon press briefing room on July 27*: U.S. Department of Defense News Transcript, DOD News Briefing, July 27, 2000.

284 *Beyond being distraught*: McCorkle, Connie Gruber, interviews.

CHAPTER TEN: YOU WANT IT BAD, YOU GET IT BAD

Page

286 *On the last day*: Judge Advocate General Manual Report of 23 Feb 2001, Command Investigation into the Circumstances Surrounding the Class "A" Aircraft Mishap Involving a MV-22B Osprey, BUNO 165440, That Occurred on 11 December 2000 Near Jacksonville, North Carolina (hereafter New River JAGMAN Report); Carol Sweaney, interview.

286 *"I'm confident it should be approved"*: Robert Burns, "Marines Expecting New Aircraft OK," Associated Press, Nov. 30, 2000.

286 *Over the past five months*: Shaffer, interview.

287 *Many Marine Corps ground troops*: Jones, interview.

287 *"If there was the slightest doubt"*: Ben Fox, "Marine Corps commandant takes first Osprey passenger flight since deadly crash," Associated Press, June 17, 2000.

288 *The report said the Navy Department*: Inspector General Department of Defense Audit Report No. D-2000-174, V-22 Osprey Joint Advanced Vertical Aircraft, Aug. 15, 2000, (hereafter August 2000 IG Audit).

288 *fallen well short of its targets*: OT&E OPEVAL Report. The statistics on the Osprey's mission-capable rates during the 1999–2000 OPEVAL and the characterization of its availability as "unsatisfactory" are taken from MV-22 OPEVAL (OT-IIE) Final Report Brief, Maj. A. J. Bianca, USMC, HMX-1 V-22 Operational Test Director, As given 11 Oct 2000 by Lt. Col. Keith Sweaney. The briefing was among documents provided to the author by Harry Dunn.

289 *all eleven Ospreys in use were grounded*: "Osprey aircraft to fly; CH-53 helicopters remain grounded," Associated Press, Sept. 5, 2000.

289 *Someone asked Cheney*: Dan Hardy and Ralph Vigoda, "Hybrid craft under heavy scrutiny, Osprey under fire for crash history, other testing issues," *Philadelphia Inquirer*, Dec. 24, 2000.

289 *Navair's latest estimate*: August 2000 IG Audit.

289 *the Navy's Operational Test and Evaluation Force declared*: U.S. Department of Defense News Release, MV-22 Declared Effective, Suitable for Land-Based Ops, Oct. 13, 2000.

290 *On November 17, he issued his own report*: OT&E OPEVAL Report.

290 *After listening to a briefing*: Navair Chronology.

290 *The Osprey that Keith Sweaney*: New River JAGMAN Report.

291 *About 3 P.M., not long after*: Katrina Sweaney, interview.

291 *Sweaney had 271 flight hours*: New River JAGMAN Report.

292 *Staff Sergeant Julius Banks told them*: Banks, interview.

292 *Dunnivan climbed out*: Col. (ret.) Richard Dunnivan, interview.

293 *At 5:39 P.M., Murphy and Sweaney*: The account of the New River crash is based on the New River JAGMAN Report and author interviews with Banks, Dunnivan, Stevie Jarman, Sue Jarman, Moffitt, Rock, and Westman.

299 *The next morning at about eleven o'clock*: U.S. Department of Defense News Transcript, Lt. Gen. McCorkle Briefing on the Recent MV-22 Osprey Crash, Dec. 12, 2000.

302 *A friend who answered the phone*: Carol Sweaney, interview.

303 *Wallace sent Carol Sweaney a handwritten apology*: Photocopy provided to the author by Carol Sweaney.

303 *McCorkle fired off his own letter*: Howard Kurtz, "Marines Blast Mike Wallace for 'Insensitivity,'" *Washington Post*, Jan. 3, 2001.

304 *Even before this latest crash*: Paul Gallagher, Cpl. (ret.) Clifford Carlson, interviews.

304 *On November 21, four days after Coyle*: Report on the Investigation Concerning the Falsification of MV-22 Osprey Maintenance and Readiness Records, Inspector General Department of Defense, Dec. 11, 2000 (hereafter DOD IG Records Falsification Report).

305 *Everybody in Marine Corps aviation knew*: Dunnivan, Gen. (ret.) John R. Dailey, interviews. Others disputed the assertion that units had been "gaming" their reports, a description offered by Dunnivan. Dailey agreed with Dunnivan.

305 *The disappointment with VMMT-204's readiness rate*: DOD IG Records Falsification Report.

307 *Carlson made five copies of his recording*: Carlson, interview.

309 *Now they wanted to get it on the air*: Gallagher, interview.

310 *Afterward, the Pentagon issued*: U.S. Department of Defense News Release, "Marine Corps to Investigate Osprey Squadron," Jan. 18, 2001.

310 *Wallace appeared on the*: CBS News Transcript, *CBS Evening News*, Jan. 18, 2001.

311 *He told the roomful of reporters*: U.S. Department of Defense News Transcript, Lt. Gen. Fred McCorkle Briefs on MV-22 Maintenance Allegation, Jan. 19, 2001.

312 *On Friday, the day after*: Robert Burns, "Officer admitted asking Marines to falsify Osprey records," Associated Press, Jan. 19, 2001.

312 *The next morning, an editorial*: "Dangerous Deceptions on the Osprey," *New York Times*, Jan. 21, 2001.

312 *That evening, CBS broadcast*: CBS News Transcripts, *60 Minutes*, Jan. 21, 2001.

314 *The night after the broadcast*: *NewsHour with Jim Lehrer* Transcript, "Commandant James Jones," Jan. 22, 2001.

315 *Frank Gaffney, a former Reagan*: Frank Gaffney, "Osprey as Phoenix," *The Washington Times*, Jan. 23, 2001.

315 *one in the* Chicago Tribune *saying*: "Kill the Osprey before it kills again," *Chicago Tribune*, Jan. 23, 2001.

315 *sent Defense Secretary Donald Rumsfeld*: Robert Burns, "Marines cede control of Osprey probe to Pentagon's top investigator," Associated Press, Jan. 24, 2001.

316 *Jones issued a statement*: United States Marine Corps News Release, "DoD IG asked to assume investigative lead," Jan. 24, 2001.

316 *Vice President Dick Cheney was asked*: ABC News Transcript, "Vice President Dick Cheney Discusses Washington Issues," *This Week*, Jan. 28, 2001.

316 *followed by an article in* Aviation Week: Robert Wall, "V-22 Support Fades Amid Accidents, Accusations, Probes," *Aviation Week & Space Technology*, Jan. 29. 2001, p. 28.

316 *Donald Trump, once a member:* Jonathan S. Landay and Peter Nicholas, "Congress wants review of Osprey; future funding could depend on findings," Knight Ridder Washington Bureau, Feb. 1, 2001.

CHAPTER ELEVEN: THE DARK AGES

Page

318 *He also had published a popular book:* Norman R. Augustine, *Augustine's Laws*, (Reston, Va.: American Institute of Aeronautics and Astronautics, 1997).

318 *Commission chairman Dailey had worried:* Dailey, deLeon, interviews.

319 *where he found a long article:* Carlton Meyer, "The V-22 Fiasco," www.g2mil.com/V-22.htm.

321 *In a February 1 conference call:* Jennifer Autrey, "Congressman blames makers for V-22 crashes," *Fort Worth Star-Telegram*, Feb. 2, 2001.

322 *The investigations found that, as so often:* New River JAGMAN Report; Naval Aircraft Mishap Report VMMT-204, Class A FM, 01-01, 11 Dec 00, MV-22B, 165440.

324 *the Blue Ribbon Commission had issued:* Report of the Panel to Review the V-22 Program, Department of Defense, April 30, 2001.

324 *"This was an accident that":* Transcript, Open Meeting, Panel to Review the V-22 Program, March 9, 2001.

326 *"This aircraft can do the job":* Otto Kreisher, "Osprey panel recommends continue program, but fix it first," Copley News Service, April 18, 2001.

326 *When Harry P. Dunn saw:* Harry P. Dunn, interview.

326 *Augustine read all of Dunn's e-mails:* Norman R. Augustine, interview.

328 *Dunn sent Coyle a long e-mail:* Harry P. Dunn e-mail to Philip Coyle, Subject: V-22 Osprey—a Political Program—Save the Crewmembers!, Nov. 29, 2000.

328 *"For your own integrity":* Harry P. Dunn e-mail to Norman R. Augustine, Subject: Facts Not provided to Blue Ribbon, May 6, 2001.

328 *He told Dunn the commission:* Norman R. Augustine e-mail to Harry P. Dunn, Subject: Note from Norm Augustine, May 22, 2001.

329 *Dunn e-mailed him that he had:* Harry P. Dunn e-mail to Pete Aldridge, Subject: Termination, May 11, 2001.

329 *Three days later, Dunn e-mailed:* Harry P. Dunn e-mail to Pete Aldridge et al., Subject: Critical & Fundamental Flight Safety FLAW in V-22 design Compromise, May 14, 2001.

329 *Defense Secretary Donald Rumsfeld had told Aldridge:* Edward C. "Pete" Aldridge, interview.

330 *In June 2001, Aldridge sent Dunn:* Pete Aldridge e-mail to Harry P. Dunn, Subject: RE: Personal for Mr Aldridge, June 11, 2001.

330 *On May 9, Republican Weldon announced:* Otto Kreisher, "Weldon reactivates tilt-rotor caucus to save Osprey," Copley News Service, May 10, 2001.

330 *"The problem we've had"*: Peter Nicholas, "Weldon battling for Osprey's future," *Philadelphia Inquirer*, May 14, 2001.

331 *On June 7, Spivey e-mailed his old friend*: Dick Spivey e-mail to Harry P. Dunn, Subject: V-22, June 7, 2001, and Dunn reply of same date.

332 *Dunn copied it and e-mailed it*: Harry P. Dunn e-mail to Dick Spivey, Subject: [no subject], July 3, 2001.

334 *He even flew the Osprey*: Arthur "Rex" Rivolo, interview.

338 *"Rex, what kind of proof"*: Spivey, Rivolo, interviews.

339 *complained about Leishman*: Spivey, Leishman, interviews.

340 *The NASA committee concluded*: Tiltrotor Aeromechanics Phenomena: Report of Independent Assessment Panel, November 2001, submitted to Naval Air Systems Command.

340 *The next day, Aldridge met*: U.S. Department of Defense News Transcript, Media Roundtable with Under Secretary Aldridge, Aug. 15, 2001.

341 *Four days after the U.S. air strikes*: Maria Recio, "Osprey helicopter may become phoenix of Afghan retaliation," *Fort Worth Star-Telegram*, Oct. 11, 2001.

341 *When the defense bills were finished*: 2001 CQ Almanac, p. 7–7.

342 *Harry Dunn read in the trade newsletter*: "Aldridge expected soon to approve V-22 Osprey flight test plan," *Inside the Navy*, Dec. 17, 2001.

342 *"It is hard and sad"*: Harry P. Dunn e-mail to Pete Aldridge, Subject: You and I both loose [sic]!, Dec. 17, 2001.

343 *Aldridge confirmed his decision*: U.S. Department of Defense News Transcript, Under Secretary Aldridge Briefing on DoD Acquisition Programs, Dec. 21, 2001.

343 *The Marine Corps inspector general's investigators*: Rock, Dunnivan, interviews; Mary Pat Flaherty and Thomas E. Ricks, "A Troubled Osprey Wounds the Corps," *Washington Post*, May 1, 2001.

344 *The inspector general's report*: DOD IG Records Falsification Report.

CHAPTER TWELVE: PHOENIX

Page

348 *When Dunn published an article*: Harry Dunn, "We shouldn't put all the eggs in Osprey basket," *Fort Worth Star-Telegram*, Nov. 12, 2001; Paul Rock, Ronald S. Culp, and Richard H. Dunnivan, "Don't sell the V-22 short," *Fort Worth Star-Telegram*, Dec. 3, 2001.

351 *On July 2, 2002, Dunn e-mailed Rivolo*: Harry P. Dunn e-mail to Arthur Rivolo, Subject: Re: V-22 Court of Inquiry—Report, July 2, 2002, and Rivolo reply of same date.

351 *Aldridge told the Defense Writers Group*: U.S. Department of Defense News Transcript, Secretary Aldridge Addresses The Defense Writers Group, Aug. 12, 2002.

353 *Shortly after noon, their Osprey began*: Lt. Col. (ret.) Steve Grohsmeyer, Macdonald, Aldridge, interviews.

359 *He had found*: Dunn, interview.

359 *One day at 7:13 A.M. he sent*: Harry P. Dunn e-mail to Pete Aldridge, Subject: PERSONAL Alert—IMMEDIATE Attention, April 17, 2002.

360 *Dunn e-mailed Aldridge a protest*: Harry P. Dunn e-mail to Pete Aldridge, Subject: Goodbye—Check out The Center for Public Integrity, May 21, 2003.

360 *explained his decision two days later*: U.S. Department of Defense News Transcript, Under Secretary Aldridge Briefing on the Results of the Tanker Lease Agreement, May 23, 2003.

360 *"A year of closely monitored"*: Robert Wall, "More Phoenix Than Osprey," *Aviation Week & Space Technology*, May 26, 2003, p. 26.

363 *Not long afterward, Hough*: Hough, Rock, Dunnivan, interviews.

364 *A couple of months after they returned*: Rock, Brig. Gen. Glenn Walters, interviews.

366 *Over ten weeks that spring*: V-22 Osprey Program Report on Operational and Live Fire Test and Evaluation, Office of the Director, Operational Test & Evaluation, The Pentagon, September 2005.

367 *Seymour taxied his Osprey out*: The author was among the passengers.

368 *The Osprey camp loved headlines*: Otto Kreisher, "After Decades of Tragedy, Osprey May Be Ready for Combat," Copley News Service, July 15, 2005.

373 *At a cost of 153 American*: Bing West, *No True Glory: A Frontline Account of the Battle for Fallujah* (New York: Bantam, 2005).

374 *Sunni insurgents used a surface-to-air missile*: Statement by Lt. Gen. George Trautman, Deputy Marine Corps Commandant for Aviation, during his V-22 Osprey news conference, 2008 Farnborough International Air Show, July 15, 2008.

375 *published a report titled*: Lee Gaillard, "V-22 Osprey: Wonder Weapon or Widow Maker?," Center for Defense Information, Washington, D.C., 2006.

375 *It also cited a memo*: Memorandum for: Mr. Thomas Carter, DOT&E, From: A. Rex Rivolo, Subject: Lingering Safety Concerns Over V-22, 17 November 2003.

376 *told a Defense Writers Group*: Defense Writers Group Transcript, General James Conway, U.S. Marine Corps Commandant, March 14, 2007.

377 *Its cover boasted*: Mark Thompson, "Flying Shame," *Time*, Oct. 8, 2007.

378 *The magazine published his letter*: "Letters to the Editor," *Time*, Nov. 5, 2007.

381 *Captain Faibisoff and another pilot*: U.S. Department of Defense News Transcript, U.S. Marine Corps, Deputy Commandant, Aviation Lt. Gen. George Trautman, May 2, 2008.

387 *There were nostalgic speeches*: Video provided to the author by Brett Spivey.

388 *In a story on the donation*: Katie Fairbank, "XV-15 flies into history," *Dallas Morning News*, July 12, 2003.

388 *Just before VMM-263 went to Iraq*: Dick Spivey e-mail to the author and others, June 15, 2007.

EPILOGUE

Page

391 *A decade to the day after the disaster*: Aircraft Accident Investigation, CV-22B, T/N 06-0031, Near Qalat, Afghanistan, 9 April 2010 (L), 8th Special Operations Squadron, 1st Special Operations Wing, Hurlburt Field, Florida, http://www.afsoc.af.mil/shared/media/document/AFD-101215-007.pdf, Dec. 16, 2010.

392 *Harvel retired from the Air Force:* Author interview with Brig. Gen. (Ret.) Don Harvel, Dec. 20, 2010.

392 *The frequency of helicopter and personnel losses:* 2009 Department of Defense Study on Rotorcraft Survivability.

392 *Over roughly the same period:* Naval Air Systems Command e-mail reply to questions from the author, Sept. 2, 2010.

393 *the Osprey wasn't flying into ambushes:* Author interview with Lieutenant Colonel Robert Freeland, Aviation Plans, Weapons 52, Medium Lift Requirements Officer, Headquarters Marine Corps, Sept. 24, 2010.

394 *the Pentagon awarded* : U.S. Department of Defense Contract Announcement, March 28, 2008.

394 *Calculating from the first contract:* U.S. Department of Defense Selected Acquisition Reports, Program Acquisition Cost Summary, Sept. 30, 2010.

395 *In November 2010:* Co-Chairs' Proposal, 11.10.10 Draft Document, National Commission on Fiscal Responsibility and Reform.

395 *Without commenting on the Osprey:* "Gates Warns Against Defense Cuts," *Wall Street Journal,* Nov. 16, 2010.

395 *"I really do believe that tiltrotor aviation":* Report of Bolden visit on NASA Aviation Division web site, www.aviationsystemsdivision.arc.nasa.gov/news/highlights/af_highlights_20100915.shtml#hilite1.

396 *"We believe the future":* AgustaWestland press briefing, Heli-Expo 2009, Anaheim, Calif., Feb. 21, 2009.

BIBLIOGRAPHY

The AAF Helicopter Program. Study No. 222, compiled by Historical Division, Intelligence, T-2, Air Materiel Command, Wright Field, October 1946. Declassified 1950, U.S. Army Air Force.

The Aircraft Year Book for 1919. Manufacturers Aircraft Association Inc. Reprint issued 1989 by the Aerospace Industries Association.

Ambrose, James R. 13 May 1983 Memorandum for Director of the Army Staff, Subject: Army Withdrawal from JVX Program.

——. "Convertaplane: Key to Speed Range." *Aviation Week,* April 12, 1948.

Beckwith, Col. Charlie A. (ret.) and Donald Knox. *Delta Force.* New York: Avon, 1983.

"Bell's XV-3." *Aerophile* 2, no. 1 (June 1979).

Binkin, Martin, and Jeffrey Record. *Where Does the Marine Corps Go from Here?* Washington, D.C.: Brookings Institution, 1976.

Blake, Bruce B. "Research and Development at Boeing Helicopters." *Vertiflite,* May/June 1988.

Bowden, Mark. "The Desert One Debacle." *Atlantic Monthly,* May 2006.

Brown, David A. *The Bell Helicopter Textron Story: Changing the Way the World Flies.* Arlington, Texas: Aerofax, 1995.

Campbell, John P. *Vertical Takeoff & Landing Aircraft.* New York: Macmillan, 1962.

Charnov, Bruce H. *From Autogiro to Gyroplane: The Amazing Survival of an Aviation Technology.* Westport, Conn.: Praeger, 2003.

Creech, Col. Jim, USMC (ret.) "The Tilt-Rotor MV-22 Osprey, Transport Vehicle of the Future," *Amphibious Warfare Review,* Fall/Winter 1986.

——. "Company representatives vie for funds in the 1980 defense budget." *Business Week,* Feb. 12, 1979.

Department of Defense Authorization Act, 1982, Conference Report 97–311, 97th Congress, 1st Session., Nov. 3, 1981.

Department of the Navy. Aircraft Mishap Involving V-22 Osprey Aircraft Number Five That Occurred on 11 Jun 91 at Boeing Helicopter Flight Test Facility, Greater Wilmington DE Airport. Naval Air Systems Command memorandum dated March 2, 1992.

Dörfer, Ingemar. *Arms Deal: The Selling of the F-16.* New York: Praeger, 1983.

Eisenstadt, Steven. "Unusual Rebuttal by Bell-Boeing Challenges House Panel's V-22 Osprey Report." *Defense News,* April 14, 1986.

First Convertible Aircraft Congress Proceedings. Institute of the Aeronautical Sciences, New York, 1949.

Flanagan, LTC Robert M. "The V-22 Is Slipping Away." *U.S. Naval Institute Proceedings*, August 1990.

Fleming, William A., and Richard A. Leyes. *The History of North American Small Gas Turbine Aircraft Engines*. Washington, D.C.: Smithsonian Institution, 1999.

Ganley, Michael. "Are Marines Heading to the 1990s with the Wrong Equipment Mix?" *Armed Forces Journal International*, April 1986.

———. "Hill Criticism of V-22 Osprey Program Prompts Sharp Response from USMC." *Armed Forces Journal International*, May 1986.

Gerard Post Herrick Collection, Historical Note, National Air and Space Museum Archives.

"G. P. Herrick Dies; Aircraft Expert." *New York Times*, Sept. 10, 1955.

"Groves Says Annihilation Threatens U.S." *Philadelphia Inquirer*, Dec. 10, 1949.

Healey, Melissa. "Warplane Survives Attacks." *Los Angeles Times*, Nov. 29, 1990.

Hearings before the Committee on Military Affairs, House of Representatives, Seventy-fifth Congress, Third Session, on H.R. 8143, to authorize the appropriation of funds for the development of the Autogiro, April 26, 27, 1938. Washington, D.C.: U.S. Government Printing Office, 1938.

"Helicopter Expert Tells Off Research." *Philadelphia Inquirer*, Oct. 30, 1938.

Herrick, Gerard P. "The Herrick Vertoplane." *Aviation Engineering*, January 1932.

———. "Half Helicopter, Half Airplane." *Mechanix Illustrated*, June 1943.

———. "Record of Invention." May 8, 1949. Gerard Post Herrick Collection, National Air and Space Museum Archives.

———. A Request In The Form Of A Proposal With Regard To Obtaining Certain Data Concerning The Performance Of The Herrick Convertible Airplane Which For Convenience Is Styled "Vertoplane." Gerard Post Herrick Collection, National Air and Space Museum Archives.

Hoffman, Jon T. *Chesty: The Story of Lieutenant General Lewis B. Puller, USMC*. New York: Random House, 2001.

Holley, Irving Brinton Jr. *Buying Aircraft: Matériel Procurement for the Army Air Forces*. Office of the Chief of Military History, United States Army, Washington, D.C., 1964.

Joint Advanced Vertical Lift Aircraft (JVX) Joint Services Operational Requirement (JSOR), Dec. 14, 1982.

Judge Advocate General Manual Report 5830 B 0525 of 21 July 2000, Investigation into the circumstances surrounding the Class "A" aircraft mishap involving an MV-22B Osprey BUNO 165436 that occurred on 8 April 2000 at Marana Northwest Regional Airport near Tucson, Arizona.

Kelley, Gen. P. X. 10 Sept. 1981 Memorandum for the Secretary of the Navy, Subject: Rotary Wing Aircraft Development.

———. 28 Sept. 1981 Memorandum for the Record, Subject: HXM Conversation with the SecNav, 24 September 1981.

Kimmel, Lewis H. *Federal Budget and Fiscal Policy 1789–1958*. Washington, D.C.: Brookings Institution, 1959.

Krulak, Victor H. *First to Fight: An Inside View of the U.S. Marine Corps*. Annapolis, Md.: U.S. Naval Institute, 1984.

Kurtz, Suzanne. "Semper Chai: General Robert Magnus." *Hillel Campus Report*, March 4, 2007.

Lynn, Robert R. "The Rebirth of The Tiltrotor—The 1992 Alexander A. Nikolsky Lecture." *Journal of the American Helicopter Society* 38, no. 1 (January 1993).

Maisel, Martin D., Demo J. Giulianetti, and Daniel C. Dugan. *The History of the XV-15 Tilt Rotor Research Aircraft From Concept to Flight*. Monographs in Aerospace History #17, The NASA History Series. Washington, D.C.: National Aeronautics and Space Administration, 2000.

Mark, Hans, and Robert R. Lynn. "Aircraft Without Airports—Changing the Way Men Fly." *Vertiflite*, May/June 1988.

Martin, David C. "New Light on the Rescue Mission." *Newsweek*, June 30, 1980, pp. 18–20.

McCutcheon, Lt. Gen. Keith B., USMC. "Marine Aviation in Vietnam, 1962–1970." *U.S. Naval Institute Proceedings*, Naval Review, 1971.

McLarren, Robert. "Convertaplane Interest Grows Fast." *Aviation Week*, Dec. 26, 1949.

Mayer, Allen J., et al. "Fiasco in Iran." *Newsweek*, May 5, 1980.

Millett, Allan R., and Peter Maslowski. *For the Common Defense: A Military History of the United States of America*. New York: Free Press, 1994.

Montross, Lynn. "U.S. Marine Combat Helicopter Applications." *Journal of the American Helicopter Society* 1, no.1 (January 1956).

Moore, Lt. Gen. Harold G. (ret.), and Joseph L. Galloway. *We Were Soldiers Once . . . And Young*. New York: Random House, 1992.

Moskin, J. Robert. *The U.S. Marine Corps Story*. 3rd revised edition. Old Saybrook, Conn.: Konecky & Konecky, 1992.

Nighthawk 71 Cockpit Video and Transcript of Cockpit Voice Recording A/C 165433 8 April 00.

Norton, Bill. *Bell Boeing V-22 Osprey Tiltrotor Tactical Transport*. Hinckley, U.K.: Midland, 2004.

Pattillo, Donald M. *Pushing the Envelope: The American Aircraft Industry*. Ann Arbor: University of Michigan Press, 1998.

Proceedings of the Rotating Wing Aircraft Meeting. Philadelphia Chapter, Institute of the Aeronautical Sciences, 1938.

Prouty, R. W. "From XV-1 to JVX—A Chronicle of the Coveted Convertiplane." *Rotor & Wing International*, February 1984.

———. *Helicopter Aerodynamics*. Mojave, Calif.: Helobooks, 2004.

Rich, Ben R., and Leo Janos. *Skunk Works*. Boston: Little, Brown, 1994.

Roman, Alfred I. "Designed for Conversion." *American Helicopter*, February 1949.

Rosenstein, Harold, and Ross Clark. "Aerodynamic Development of the V-22 Tilt Rotor." Paper No. 14, Twelfth European Rotorcraft Forum, Garmisch-Partenkirchen, Germany, Sept. 22–25, 1986.

"Rotary Wings Touted For Fool-Proof Plane." *Philadelphia Inquirer*, Oct. 28, 1938.

Second Convertible Aircraft Congress Proceedings. Institute of the Aeronautical Sciences, New York, 1952.

Sedivy, Dean G. *Bureaucracies at War: The V-22 Osprey Program*. Executive Research

Project, The Industrial College of the Armed Forces, National Defense University, Fort McNair, Washington, D.C., 1992.

Sikorsky, Sergei. "Rotary-wing revolution." *Professional Pilot*, November 2003.

Smith, Danny Roy. "The Influence of Contract Type in Program Execution/V-22 Osprey: A Case Study." Naval Postgraduate School, Monterey, Calif., December 1989.

Smith, Hedrick. *The Power Game: How Washington Works*. New York: Ballantine, 1989.

Smith, Maj. Gen. Perry M., USAF (ret.). *Assignment: Pentagon—How to Excel in a Bureaucracy*. 3rd ed. Washington, D.C.: Brassey's, 2002.

Spenser, Jay P. *Whirlybirds: A History of the U.S. Helicopter Pioneers*. Seattle: University of Washington Press, 1998.

Technology Assessment of Capability for Advanced Joint Vertical Lift Aircraft (JVX). Summary Report, Analysis and Preparation Chaired by AVRADCOM, May 1983.

Tyler, Patrick. *Running Critical: The Silent War, Rickover, and General Dynamics*. New York: Harper & Row, 1986.

West, Bing. *No True Glory: A Frontline Account of the Battle for Fallujah*. New York: Bantam Dell, 2005.

Wright, Orville Jr., letter to J. Franklin Wilkinson, September 25, 1936. Copy provided to the author by Canadian Mountain Holidays CMH Heli-Hiking, Banff, Canada.

Young, Arthur M. *The Bell Notes: A Journey from Physics to Metaphysics*. New York: Delacorte Press, 1979.

INDEX